332-2637

A LOVE STORY-

Bitter Sweet

THEIR JOURNEY

PAUL A. BLANKENBURG

TO MY PRECIOUS GUS

If I should leave this Earth before you, my Soul will enter your body and it will wrap around your Soul and my Spirit will soar into the Heavens, so I will not be physically with you, but my Soul and your Soul will be together just like we were, together always as Soul Mates and when you need the comfort of my Spirit, just whisper 332-2637 in your mind and I will come to you like I always did, then one day when your Soul and Spirit are released from this Earth, we will be reunited together again as one, just like I always told you that it would be, Gus and Lorrie Forever.

Love, Lorrie

CONTENTS

PREFACE

*L*orrie and I had always planned to write this book together. She could have done such of a great job on the part before I had any idea that she had her eye on me. So many of her thoughts are lost now on so much of this. When she was so sick with the cancer, she asked me to bring her a tablet and pin, so she could write notes for the book. I was so glad of this. When I would go and visit her, I would ask what she had written, and she would say that she just didn't have the heart to write. I would plead with her to write what-ever she could remember, and she finally told me that she couldn't and that I knew enough to write it, so now it would be my responsibility to write the book without her. I suddenly realized that I would have to go on memory from what she had told me of what she had thought and felt and did, during all of this long journey. I then became aware of how important all of those deep and long discussions that we had about those times had become. So now this book will have to come from my memory along with the notes I took, and I do have a lot of substance that is from Lorrie herself, because of all the information that I remember from many, many hours of our discussions. Lorrie felt that it was important to write this book and tell our story, because she felt that there was so much misery and unhappiness caused by people not matching up with their true love partner for one reason or another. She thought that our story was a perfect example that showed how some small mistakes can take your life, in a succession of disappointing relationships that are not based on true love with the partner you were supposed to be with in life. Lorrie told me, several times, that we were so lucky, because we had what everybody on earth was looking for, but few found. The Gus and Lorrie Story is written to target two specific age groups of people. The first group are the ones that are in their late teens to early twenties, that are trying to figure out if the feelings they are having about a special person are true lasting love or are they just lust that only lasts for a short period of time. Maybe reading Gus and Lorrie's story will help them to decide to take a chance and follow their heart or to back off before they make a mistake. The second group of people are those that are fifty years old and older that missed their chance with the person that they finally realized was their true love, and they thought about that person all of their lives like Gus and Lorrie did. Reading this book might inspire them to see if they can locate that person to see if they have the same feelings and maybe it won't be too late for them to get together like thy should have been when they were young. In writing this book Gus and Lorrie had no idea of the reader thinking that it would be a solution for their romantic love life, because that is not what it is. It was written with the idea that the reader might stop and think about their lives and ask themselves if they want their lives to be like Gus and Lorrie's or, do they want their lives to be happy with their true, romantic, lasting love.

THE EARLY YEARS

LORRIE—THE EARLY YEARS

*L*orrie was born on October the 26th, 1945. They belonged to the Methodist Church. She spent her childhood growing up with two siblings a younger brother and sister in El Campo, Texas. Her father was a U.S. Mail carrier and he also did part time work, that he was well known for, as an Official for high school basketball and football games and her mother was a housewife and worked part time for photographer in El Campo. Lorrie went to school in El Campo and was a very good student and started playing the French Horn in the Jr. High School band. Lorrie loved the band. She told me that she had very good grades in school, but that it came hard for her and that she had to study very hard. She loved music and dancing and started taking tap, ballet and ballroom dancing lessons at a dancing studio that ended being only one block from my parent's house. She became so good at the dancing that her dancing instructor would let her instruct the younger girls and the time that she spent doing this paid for Lorrie's younger sister's dancing lessons. Lorrie also worked for the Methodist church in their office doing odd jobs for them and she also did baby-sitting for .50 cents/ hour. Lorrie was very fond of her father's mom and dad, her Grand Parents. She called her my Granny and she loved her deeply. They were very close. Lorrie's Mom and Dad loved to go to dances, and they would take Lorrie with them some-times. Lorrie was good about trying to befriend girls in school that weren't popular, and she also was in the Girl Scouts. Lorrie grew tall for her age with long legs and when she was in Jr. High School, she was a head taller than most of the boys. With her baby-sitting money she liked to buy herself 45 records with the latest Rock-N-Roll music and she would learn all the words and all the dances to them. Her and girlfriends would ride around town in one of the girl's parent's car with the radio blaring and they would be singing at the top of their voices to the music. When Lorrie was in the 8th grade she was allowed to have dates with a nice boy named James that worked for a local laundry delivering cloths to homes and he also played in a local band that her parents liked to their dances. She said that James was a very sweet boy and that her Mom and Dad knew him and trusted him with her. Lorrie liked his old car. It was a 1939 Ford sedan and she said that James was a pretty good kisser. She said that they would ride around town and sometime go by an old shop to see what other boys were doing to their old cars. Lorrie said that in grade school that her Mom would pack her lunch and always had a little thermos of milk in it and Lorrie didn't like milk, so she would poor it out the classroom window and drink water. She said that she never got to like drinking milk even though she knew, it was good for her. Lorrie considered herself a tomboy when she was a kid. She loved to play cowboy and Indians with the neighbor boy's, and she had a stick horse that she loved, and she would ride it everywhere she went. She had it named, but I can't remember what it was. She had it for so long and it hung from a nail in the garage that she was teased that she wanted to ride it to high school. She loved horses and always dreamed of owning a real one. As a kid she had pictures of them and had all sorts of plastic toy ones that she would play with. Any movie that had horses in it she wanted to go see. Finally, she had a girlfriend in school that lived on a farm and they had horses and she would go there and ride. She said that she was in pure heaven on that horse. When Lorrie was a small girl, they lived in a garage apartment across the street from the Methodist church in El Campo. Later it was either 1955 or 1956 her parents built a new home on Avenue I in El Campo and that is where Lorrie and I have made a lot of memories. A couple of blocks behind Lorrie's parents new house there was a little muddy creek and she would sneak off with the boys to play there and catch crawdads and throw rocks at snakes and generally just get muddy. Lorrie would look at magazines and National Geographic and she decided she wanted to see Europe someday.

GUS—THE EARLY YEARS

I was born August 15th, 1942 at Edna Gladney's Home for Unwed Mothers in Dallas, Texas. I was the unwanted result of the bombing of Pearl Harbor, meaning that I had to have been conceived in December of 1941. I'm sure that I wasn't the only one that was conceived because of that sudden terrible event that struck such fear and uncertainty in people's lives. I was adopted from Buckner's Orphans Home in Dallas, Texas at just a couple months of age. I was adopted by the Brother and his wife of my birth Mother and they lived in El Campo, Texas. I grew up at 307 East Calhoun Street in a very old home that was one of the first to be built in El Campo and through the years it had been built on to several times in very odd ways. When I refer to my Mother or my Father I am talking about my adopted parents, not my natural parents. I went to El Campo Elementary, Jr. High and High School. As a child in the WW2 war years I seem to have a remarkable memory of events. I remember my Mom having black, black-out curtains on the windows, air raid warnings, tanks and war equipment going by on the train, sitting on the floor and listening to Winston Churchill and Franklin Roosevelt on my Dads radio, war posters on telephone poles and the side of buildings. One time my Mom and I were down at Palacious, Texas and I saw some soldiers take the tarp off of a big anti-aircraft gun on the seawall. I remember my Dad and I going to the German POW camp in El Campo and picking up some German POW's to work out at our rice farm. I remember German POW's marching down the street being escorted by Army Soldiers. I remember a lot of Army and Navy uniforms on men in down-town in El Campo. When I was 9 years old, I started my first business mowing three neighborhood yards and cleaning out flower beds. The lawnmower was a push type without a motor. I charged .50 cents to mow and .50cents to clean out the flower beds. I would put the money in my bank which was a cigar box. Mom never had to give me any money after this. When I got paid for my first yard, I did something I always wanted to do and that was to ride my bicycle up to the Drug Store and get me a banana split. My Mom never would get me one, because they were so expensive, they cost .25 cents. Also, now I had my own money to go to the Saturday afternoon movie shows. I would take .25 cents with me and it cost .09 cents to get in and I would buy a .05 cent candy bar, a .05 cent coke, a .05 cent bag of popcorn and a .01 cent bubble gum that would be a total of .25 cents. If I worked hard, I could make $3.00/week, but most of the time it was from $1.50 to $2.00 and that was big money for a kid. I would let that money build, because I didn't really have much to spend it on. One day a kid came riding by the house on a home-made motor bike made out of a regular bicycle and I stopped him to talk about his bike. I was very interested in it. This was the first time that something with a motor really caught my attention. After that I kept looking at my bicycle, but really didn't want tear it up to make a motor bike and also, I knew that my Dad wouldn't let me tear up a good bicycle. The idea of something to ride with a motor to power it seemed so exciting for a kid that I thought about it a lot and started trying to imagine what I could build. After scrounging around the place and scrap piles of different businesses in town I started putting together a flat wood framed vehicle from a 2X12 and wheels from my old wagon and I took the old gasoline motor from Mom's old washing machine to power it. This was my first experience working on a gasoline motor to get it running. You won't believe it, but it actually would run 35 MPH and I used my shoes on the ground for the brakes. The money I had in my cigar box came in handy when I had to buy a few things that I couldn't scrounge up for free. I wasn't big for my age, so in the third grade a school bully started harassing me and I was scared to death of him. He chased me all over the playground every day during recess. Finally one day he got me trapped in a corner and when he came at me I just leaped on him like a monkey and he fell down with me on top and then I just started hitting him and he crawled out from under me and went through some hedges and ran off. The next day at school I saw him with a black eye and I went up to him and we shook hands and became friends and I don't think that he ever bothered anyone any-more and it taught me a lesson too and that is always be prepared to defend yourself. I was a real good student till about the 8th grade then my grades started to suffer. I was in the Jr. High band and I also got a part time job in a service station and I discovered that girls were pretty. I saved my money and bought a 1929 Model-A Coupe. I was 13 and had no driver's license, but to me that didn't keep me from driving my car. I drove the Model A-Ford Coupe, my freshman year in High School and then decided that I wanted to make a street Hot-Rod out of it. I am now 15 years old and a sophomore and was working at a service station part time, working part time for my Dad and my Uncle going to school and playing in the High School band.

LORRIE—THE DISCOVERY AND FLIRTATION, MY SECRET.

Lorrie told me some things about when she first saw me and the things that she did to be around me. I didn't remember some of this. Lorrie said that she first saw me when she was 12 years old in the Girl Scouts with my sister. This was when I was 15 years old in High School and working on my Model A to make it into a Hot Rod. She said that she saw me pick my sister up from a Girl Scout meeting and that I talked to her and a couple of the other girls and that I imprinted myself on her and that she knew, from that point that I was the one that she was supposed to be with. She told me that she would always try to befriend girls at school that weren't very popular and that my sister was one of those girls. She said that she hated to admit that the main reason that she became friends with my sister was so she would be invited to my parent's house to maybe be able to see me. She said that when she saw me at home I would be leaving, and I would stop for a minute to say a few words to her and that she was always impressed that I was so friendly and that I always was a gentleman. Funny, but I don't remember any of this. She also told me that she would ride her bicycle from her house and ride around and around my parent's house to see if she could see me outside. I asked if she ever saw me like that and she said that some-time she did and that it would make her day. She said that she would go home and try to figure other ways to be able to see me, but she said that she didn't want me to know that she was watching me, because she was too shy, and it would be embarrassing. I don't remember this either, so maybe I never noticed her doing this. There is one thing that happened during this time though that I do remember. Several times when I was outside working on my Hot Rod I noticed this pretty young girl in a real tight black stretch dancing outfit, that fit tight from neck to foot, walking down the street and when she was a safe distance from me she would blow me a kiss and give a little wave of her fingers. She always walked on the far side of the street with her pony-tail swinging and a big smile on her round face and when she got to the corner where she would turn, she would look back and smile and blow me that kiss. I would step out and watch her as long as I could see her. I could see that she was young, but that dancing outfit really accented the shape of her body and you could see curves that normal cloths would never show. I was very curious as to who this pretty girl could be, but, came to the conclusion that she was too young for me. I ask Lorrie about this and she said yes that was her. She said that she would leave the dance class that was only 2 blocks from my parent's house and walk around the block in hopes of seeing me. I ask her what she would have done if I had walked out on the street to talk to her and she said that she probably would have run as fast as she could, because she was too shy to actually be close to me and talk by herself. I remembered that all those years, but never knew who it was. When I was working at the service station and her parents would pull in for gas, she said that she would slide way down the back seat so I wouldn't notice her, because she didn't want me to think that she was a little girl with her parents.

Lorrie said that from that first that she saw me that she fell in love with me and that from then on, she thought of me most of the time. She said that she would daydream about how it would be to be my girlfriend. She said that she didn't tell anyone about me, because it was too precious a dream for her and that it was her secret. As it turned out the owner of the service station, where I worked, had a daughter that was a good friend of Lorrie's.

GUS—TOTALLY UNAWARE AND OBLIVIOUS.

All this time I had no Idea that Lorrie was secretly flirting with me, because she was so private with it. I guess that it was more of a fantasy kind of flirting, because she was never obvious enough to alert me to it. I guess also that I always thought of her as being just a young girl that I wasn't thinking of having an interest in her as a girlfriend. Evidently this went on for several years without my knowledge.

LORRIE—TRYING TO GROW UP FASTER.

Lorrie told me that as the years went on that she saw me with older girls, and she thought that the only way she would ever get me was that some-how she was going to have to grow up faster. Her problem was how could she ever catch up with the older girls that she saw me with. It seemed to her that her parents wanted to hold her back from growing up. She wanted to start shaving her legs and wearing make-up, but her Mom said no. Then one day she decided to try to learn how to shave her legs when her parents were not at home. She found her Dads razor and proceeded to soap up her legs and shave them. Well she saw that she was making all sort of little cuts in the skin that were bleeding, but she said that she couldn't quit, because her Mom would notice that one leg would look different than the other if she didn't go through with shaving both legs. As it turned her Mom noticed anyway, because of all the cuts and she was grounded for a week. Not only that, but her Dad was mad because she used his razor and he gave her a spanking. Another time she sneaked some lipstick from her Mom with the idea of wearing it and walking up to the service station where I worked to see if I would notice it, but she heard her Mom come in the door, so she hurried up and wadded up some toilet paper to wipe it off, but her Mom went directly to the bath room and saw the red lipstick on the toilet paper before she could flush it. Well she was grounded for another week. Also, she said that she would practice flirting with her Dad to see what kind of effect it would have. She said that all Texas girls learn the art of flirting by practicing on their Dad. What you did was if your Mom would say no to something small then you go and sit on your Dads knee and flirt to see if he would go ahead and let you have your way. Then maybe you could use this on some boy. Lorrie said that she thought that if she could shave her legs, wear make-up and learn how to flirt good then it would help her to grow up faster to be in competition with the older girls that had my attention. She said that it was frustrating to be held up from doing what you thought you need to do to be able to get the attention of the boy that would make you happy for the rest of your life.

GUS—WHAT A CUTE YOUNG GIRL.

I had been working at this Humble service station for some time and the owner had two daughters. The oldest was a friend of Lorrie. By this time, I was a senior in High School. The oldest girl got her driver's license and she would get to drive her parent's car once in a while. Well she would come in the service station with Lorrie and some girl friends when I was working by myself and they would hit the candy and cheese cracker jar on the shelf and flirt with me. There are a couple of times that are funny that I especially remember. One time I was at the cash register trying to ring up a sale and Lorrie got behind me and pulled my shirt tail out of my pants trying to distract me and I remember swatting at her in fun and she was laughing and hopping around on those very straight long legs in a pair of shorts that really showed them off nicely. Another time I was at the stand-up desk making out a credit card sale, credit cards were just getting started and you had to write them out by hand, and Lorrie and the girls came in and she got beside me and turned around and leaned over backwards on the desk and leaned between me and my work and looked me in the face and started batting her eye lashes very fast. I couldn't help but laugh and she got the biggest kick out of that. I remember thinking, what a really cute young girl, it's a shame that she isn't a couple of years older. I am sure that were other times, but those two stand out in my mind.

LORRIE—I KEPT TRACK OF YOU.

Lorrie told me that through the years she kept track of me and what I was doing one way or another. From riding her bicycle or walking around my parent's house to visiting me at the service station to asking questions at the beauty salon where her Mom took her to get her hair cut, because she knew that my Mom went there. She said that she always had an ear listening to conversation to maybe pick up the word Gus, because it could lead to information about me or to some-one she could get information from about me. She also kept track of the girls that I dated to try and understand why I wanted to date them and to get ideas on how to get my attention. She knew that she might have to learn some tricks from the older girls, because those were the ones that I was interested in and if she ever got my attention then she would have to know what to do to keep my interest. When she was 14 her Mom and Dad let her date a real nice boy that was my age and had played in the band with me. She said that the main reason she wanted to date him was because he knew me and she thought that she would have a good chance of seeing me sometime and that if that happened it would show me that she was old enough for me to date, but also he had a nice car. She said that she saw me a couple of times when she was with him, but that she couldn't get the opportunity to be with me alone to flirt with me, because he was always close to her. She said that it was worth it though, because she at least got to see me and to see if I had a girl with me.

GUS—JOB, GIRLFRIENDS AND HOT ROD.

When I was in High School my mind was not on schoolwork. I had my service station job that was part time during the school term and full time in the summer vacation time, I had my Model A and I had discovered that I liked girls very much. I remember vividly the first day of school my freshman year, standing on the sidewalk at the school, just looking around and thinking damn 4 long years of this, 4 long years of this, how will be able to make it through 4 long years of this. By the time that I had finished the eighth grade and was set to go to High School I had started to develop my independence as a young man. As I look back actually, I guess that it started when I had my first yard mowing job and made my first money and then when I made that little go-cart type of vehicle when I was 9 against my parent's wishes.

Any-way I certainly had no interest in school, I was ready to move on to bigger things of independence and school just kept me under my parent's control. I had good parents and a good home, so it wasn't anything to do with that. I just wanted to me my own man and be on my own. During my freshman year there was a boy from Louise, a small town 10 miles west of El Campo, that I became friends with. He would hitch-hike to El Campo, because there was more to do in El Campo then in Louise and we would meet up and bum around. Well we decided that we were going to go together and rent a room in this old rooming house in El Campo and move in there together. That required that he would-have to find a job in El Campo, because my part time job wouldn't be enough and also it was only right that he pay his share. He went all over town looking for a job, but couldn't find one, so we never did it. This just shows how serious I was about wanting to be on my own. I drove my Model A my freshman year and then my sophomore year I decided to tear it down and make a street Hot Rod out of it. This was a big job for me, because I had limited money, limited tools and limited knowledge. My Dad had a fit, but true to form I had made up my mind and I was going to do it my way. I worked on it for months and finally had it running before my Junior year in High School. The transition from the eighth grade to High School brought about several big milestones in my life. I got a better job at another service station that paid me more than twice as much money as my old job had. This gave more money to use on my car and also for the first time I had money to use for girls. While my Model A was being converted into a Hot Rod, I had to borrow my Mom's car for dates. Usually I would suggest to the girl that we go to the Drive-in Movie, because I was interested in kissing and petting. On one of these dates this cute girl that I had a date with decided that we should get in the back seat. Well the kissing just got hotter and hotter until I had her blouse and bra off and then after a while her skirt came up and her panties came off. Wow that was really something, now I knew what I really loved about girls. We got lucky that she didn't get pregnant, but I had learned a lot in a short time, but I knew that I had a lot more to learn about having sex with a girl and the only way to learn was to listen to the older boys and also to take other girls out and practice on them and observe the results. The experience with that first encounter in the back seat taught me a lesson about girls and that was that you might never know when one would decide to have sex with you, so you needed to be prepared, meaning you need to have condoms with you all the time. Also, I started smoking and drank a beer every once in a while.

I had a fake ID made out of one of my Dad's old licenses. It wasn't hard to do in those days. There was no law against smoking and most places didn't mind selling beer to a minor, but some would ask for the ID just to say they checked you in case something came up. Because of all my other interests I was a poor student. Remember that till the eighth grade I made mostly A's and B's in school, but that was before a good job, a Hot Rod and the sweet smell of girls. How on earth was school going to compete with this!!! O.K. So I need to pass my classes some-how, so how will I do it. When classes were over for the school day I would walk to the parking lot with the girl that I was going to take home, throw my books in the trunk, where they would stay until the next day,, kiss her, light a cigarette, start up my Hot Rod, gun the loud exhaust pipes and spin out of the parking lot to go to the Dairy Queen and buy her a coke take her home and kiss her good-by, go home and change into my service station uniform and go to work till 10:00 pm at night. Then I would ride around town with a couple of friends and drink a quart of beer till about 12:00 am and go home take a bath, sleep till 7:00 am get up and drive to school, get my books out of the trunk, walk to class and find one of the girls I liked to go to class with. Sometimes if I had a book report that was due, I would have a girl write it for me quick before I went to class. I never read my books and I had to rely entirely on what I got out of the discussions in the classes. One thing that I didn't do was skip classes, because I knew that I had to at least attend class to learn something. When I was a freshman, I had an algebra class that was a disaster for me. I listened in class, but I really had trouble trying to understand the equations. I couldn't make them work, so I figured out my own way of doing algebra in long math and I would get the right answer every time. My algebra teacher couldn't figure out how I was getting the answers, so she decided that I was cheating. Every paper I got back had a big red zero circled across the page. I would compare my answers to a student's answers that sat next to me and mine would be just like his. I couldn't understand why I was getting zeros on all my papers. One day when the teacher returned the papers and I had another zero I held up my hand and asked why I got a zero and she had me come up in front of the class. She gave me a piece of chalk and told me to work the problem on the black board, so I did. When I was through, I underlined my answer and asked her if it was the right answer. She looked over my work with a kind of dazed expression and then she took the chalk from me and drew a big zero over my work. I was so embarrassed in front of the class, but I had the presence of mind enough to ask her if I had the right answer and she didn't want to tell me, so I asked her again and all she could say was, and she really YEALLED IT LOUD, yes it is the right answer, but it wasn't algebra. Well by that time I had had it with her and felt like I needed to take up for myself. It was very evident that she had no idea how I had arrived at the answer even though all my work was in front of her. She didn't want me to look smarter than her in front of the rest of the class, that is why she drew the circle on my work and didn't want to admit that I got the right answer. I said back to her. You know what, when I get out of school and go to get a job my boss won't care how I get the answer, all he will look for is the right answer and she hit the ceiling. She threw her hand out with a pointing finger and yelled, YOU GO TO THE PRINCIPALS OFFICE. That's what I did, and he just looked at me for a while after I told him what happened and then in a quiet voice said for me to sit there for a while till the bell rings and not to worry, but, go to my next class. Before it was over, he arranged it for me to take two algebra classes, but I still only made a grade of D in it. When I graduated from High School I was in the last quarter of my class, but that was O.K. with me, because I was finally out.

Lorrie—High School, Dances and Boy Friends.

Lorrie was 4 years behind me in High School because of when her birthday fell, and she was only 3 years and 2 months younger than me in age. Because of this I was not in High School with her. I graduated in 1960 and she was a Freshman in 1961. If she had been born before September first, 1945 then we would have been in High School at the same time, her a Freshman and me a Senior and then everything would have been different in our world, because we would have been in the same environment for making decisions. Lorrie would have so much to say here, but without her I can only relate what she told me about her High School years. Lorrie was a very good student and she studied hard and made very good grades. I believe that she was in the top 10 percent of her graduating class. She told me that she loved to read books and had since she was very young. She won some kind of award for reading the most books one year when she was young. She was very popular in High School and she was in the High School band and she played the French Horn and she just loved being in the band. Lorrie had looked to High School as a time when she could have more personal freedom from parental control. This happened to a certain extent, but with some very strict rules and controls.

Lorrie had always been a flirt and had, since she was about 10, been trying to perfect this natural part of her character. She was very out-going always wanting to get along with everyone and avoid conflicts. She dated a lot going to dances and the movies, which she loved to do, but she had to be in early and she was forbidden to go to the Drive-in Movie's. She was always being grounded for infractions to these rules and also her flirtatious character. She was accused often of sexual misconduct by her parents and there was a running battle about this with her Mom and Lorrie would be crying and telling her Mom that if she didn't believe her that she was still a Virgin then to take her to the doctor for an examination. Her Mom was so paranoid about Lorrie getting pregnant that she made life miserable for Lorrie. Lorrie's Mom would read her Diary to see if there was anything in it that would indicate sexual misconduct. Lorrie told me that she never did have sexual relations with any boy in High School. She was held on a really tight leash and it made her life miserable at home, because her parents didn't trust her. Lorrie liked to date boys that had nice cars. One time she was going steady with two boys at the same time from different towns. She said that she had senior rings from each and had to be careful which ring she wore when having a date with one of them. When she was a Freshman she went to the Senior Prom with a boy she knew and before the Prom Dance they went out to eat then when back in his car he proceeded to put his hand down her dress and she slapped him and asked him why he thought that he could do that, he said that he had bought her a big Mum corsage and dinner, so he should get something in return. Well she told him to take her home now and that was the end of the Prom night. Another Prom night she had turned out to be another disaster. She had a Prom date with this boy that was going to be a Preacher, so her Mom and Dad thought that he was going to be a really well-behaved young man. Well, not so much, because he proceeded to keep spiking her drink's un-till she was really drunk, and then she got sick. She was dressed in a really beautiful Prom dress and she had been to the beauty shop for a hair perm, which she seldom got, and she was wearing a pretty butterfly accent in her hair. After the dance they were leaving with another couple and he got her in the back seat of the car and proceeded to put his hand up her dress and tried to pull down her panties and she was struggling with him and she got real sick at her stomach and she vomited all over him and herself. They stopped at a service station and her girlfriend took her into the rest room and washed her up as good as she could, and she said that the perm was gone the dress was stained and the cute butterfly was all bent up. They took her home and she went straight to bed. She used to love to go to all the dances at the country dance halls, but she had to be home by 11:30 pm. That was pretty early, because the dances didn't end till 12:00 am on Friday and 1:00 am on Saturday. She had a hard time getting home on the dot of 11:30 because she would have to leave the dance around 11:00 to get home on time. These dances were out in country dance halls, so it took time to get home and she always pushed the limit, because she enjoyed dancing so much that she just hated to leave. If she was as much as 10 minutes late, she would be grounded for a week, which meant that she would miss the next weeks dances. She then would sit at her window in her room and look outside and watch for the boys that would drive by and honk their horns and gun their loud mufflers and she would cry herself to sleep. Another thing is when she would have a date to the show, she was allowed to only go to the walk-in movie, and not the Drive Inn movie. If the boy she had a date wanted to go to the Drive Inn, she didn't want to look like her parents treated her like a little girl, so she wouldn't say anything. The next day her parents would question her about the details of the movie and she would try to lie about it, but they knew that she had gone to the Drive In, because the people at the Drive Inn were friends with her Dad and had already told him. Here we go again with another week of being grounded. She had a boyfriend that her Dad let her date, but he didn't think too much of. Her Dad Refereed High School basketball and he told her that her boyfriend was a dirty player and he despised dirty players, but Lorrie liked his car, but he scared her the way he drove so fast and reckless. He ended up killing himself in a wreck later on several years after High School. There was another boy that her parents didn't like, and they forbid her to date him. He and his father had moved to El Campo to live with his father's brother. Evidently the boy's father was a known con man and had been in the pen and in and out of trouble for many years. His brother was a good man and always tried to help him. One of Lorrie's best girlfriends was this boy's cousin where they were staying, so Lorrie was over there all the time. She knew she couldn't date him, but they would sit on the couch and watch TV and kiss or they would play records and dance, but that was as far as it went. When they graduated from High School, he went to Blinn Jr. College and Lorrie went to WCJC. This boy will come back in her life after High School. Off and on during Lorrie's High School years she and her girlfriends would come into the service station where I worked to flirt.

GUS—SOMEONE IS WAVING AT US, LET'S PULL IN HERE.

This is where I see Lorrie in a much different light, and it changes both of our lives forever. I was still working in the service station and had dropped out of WCJC because of bad grades and poor attendance to classes and also, I was dating a girl from another town that I met at Jr. College. In short, I was on Attendance and Scholastic Probation if I ever returned to WCJC. So, I decided to drop out and work full time at the service station. Well one Saturday morning I and a guy that I worked with were off and we were driving around in my 1956 Dodge Texan and we drove in front of the High School and we noticed a couple of school buses with kids around them loading up. Out of this crowd of kids I spotted someone waving at us. From where we were, I couldn't tell who it was, so I said to my friend, let's pull in here and see who is waving and find out what they are going to do. So, we did and up trots Lorrie with her ponytail swinging and a big smile on her face just laughing and so bubbly. She comes to the window on my side and leans in looking me in the face real sweet. I ask what was going on and she said that it was a High School Band trip to Corpus Christi just to have a good time. We talked for a couple of minutes and they were calling for everybody to load up and she said that she had to go, but right before she went she said, why don't you follow us and we will have a good time, then she laughed and ran to the bus. I looked at my friend and said, what do you think. I would like to follow them we are off this weekend and it might turn out to be a blast. We were full of gas and had some money with us and he said O.K. Lets go, so we did follow them. On the way I stayed behind the bus most of the time and I could see Lorrie sitting in the very back of the bus waving at us every-once in a while and I would wave back. I asked Lorrie 50 years later after we got back together what she was thinking when she saw me following her, and she said that she thought, well I have been wanting this for years, so now I guess that I will have to make love to him, and I was a little nervous. When we got to Corpus their buses pulled up in front of the Hotel and we parked at a little park across the street from the hotel and Lorrie saw us there and came over. I told her to find a girlfriend and join us and we would ride around and see what there was to do. She left and we didn't have to wait more than 30 minutes and she came across the street with a cute girl for my friend. Before she came back, I got in my glove compartment and put a condom in my pocket, just in case I would need it and I told my friend that they were there if he needed one. This was in the middle of the afternoon and we drove around for a while, with my arm around Lorrie sitting very close to me, and found a place to get a coke, because Lorrie wanted something to drink, then we found the sea wall and drove down it till we found a place to park and it had steps down to the beach. I was hoping that my friend and Lorrie's friend would go walking on the beach and Lorrie and I would have the car, but it ended up that Lorrie and I went down on the beach and went walking. I didn't want to suggest that my friend go on the beach, because that would be to obvious. By this time, it was late afternoon and Lorrie and I just held hands and walked down the beach and talked. I don't have a clue any more what we talked about. It got to be sundown and Lorrie and I had found a quiet secluded spot that we stopped at. We had been walking and talking for several hours. We stood there for a while and I was looking at her and suddenly realized how beautiful she was. Her brown hair was in a nice ponytail, she had on a short sleeve pull over and a pair of nice shorts that showed off her beautiful long, straight legs. She had a little scarf tied around her slim smooth neck that was accented by a big smile and her sparkling hazel eyes. I turned her toward me, and she came to me as I put my arm around her. She molded her body to mine, and I could feel her small, hard breasts mashing into my chest and it seemed like her hard nipples were struggling to escape from her bra and pullover. She was breathing very hard and when our lips met, it was a perfect fit and we kissed passionately. I couldn't believe the feeling that I got, because it was like nothing I had ever experienced from a kiss before. I took my arms from around her and put them on her shoulders and looked at her real good, her face was flushed pink and she was breathing rapidly and I could see her nice breasts heaving up and down, and I thought Lorrie you are not a little girl any more. She was 16 now and I was 19. I didn't tell her that, but that is what I thought to my-self. I didn't know it, but that kiss was the defining moment that shaped the rest of our lives. We stayed there for hours kissing and talking and I was making preparations in my mind to make love to her on the beach, because it was dark now and there was no one around, the only sound was the surf washing in on the beach and there was enough moon light for us to see each other. It was a very romantic setting. We were like one person, kissing and molding our bodies together. I could feel her trembling and I knew that it was the time to lower her down on the sand and remove her cloths and I guess that she knew also that were getting to that. All of a sudden, she said I want to tell you something. I thought that she was going to tell me that she was on her period, but that wasn't it. She said I want to let you know that I am a virgin and I want you to take my virginity, I have always wanted you to be the one, because I have always loved you since I was 12 years old. I have waited 4 years for this opportunity. I want to give you the most precious thing that I have to give and that is my virginity, but I don't want to do it here. I want to do it in a regular bed, and I want to plan it so it won't seem to be vulgar, like in the back seat of a car. I want it to be lovely and sweet so we both will be able to remember it for the rest of our lives. She said that she knew that I had been with a lot of girls and that was O.K., because that would mean that I would know what I was doing, not like some high school boy experimenting. She said I don't expect you to stay with me, because I know that you have other girls that know what they are doing in bed and I don't have that experience, so after you have me you can go your own way if you choose to. This is the first time that I have got your attention and I have the chance to compete with the older girls and that is all that I ask, I won't try to make trouble for you, but I am yours and I have always been yours. This really shook me, and I had to rethink my original plan of making love to her there on the beach. All of a sudden I wanted it to be like she wanted it to be, and that is something that I couldn't imagine myself doing, because normally I would have resumed a little pressure on her until she gave in and I would have lowered her down on the beach and made love to her. This just wasn't like me to give in and not take advantage of the situation. I couldn't understand what had changed my normal way of dealing with girls that had been virgins. I had been with several such girls and knew that some of them had to be treated differently to get them to give up their virginity, but I always succeeded on that first occasion of opportunity. I had always believed that if you gave a girl the space of a day to think it over without the heat of passion, then she would back out, it had happened before and now I was doing exactly that. I was giving this very lovely, sweet girl the chance to back out, what was wrong with me anyway I didn't know. All I knew is I need to do it this way, because for some reason I wanted it to be special also, so I said O.K. what do you want to do. She said I will contact you when I have made the plans and it won't be very long and I agreed. All of this was just one week before school was out about the last week in May.

Lorrie—Well I got kicked out of band for the rest of the year, which was only a week, because school was out that next week and besides, I finally got the attention of Gus after waiting for four long years. It was certainly well worth it.

GUS—WAITING TO HEAR FROM LORRIE.

A few days later I was in town and I had parked my car, a 1956 Dodge Texan to go into a store, so when I came back, and I got in it I found a 45 RPM record and a note laying on my seat. The record was " In The Still Of The Night" by The Five Satins and it was one of the songs that we listened to when we were riding around in my car at Corpus that afternoon and I mentioned that it was my favorite song and Lorrie said that she loved it also. The note said that I should come to her Mom and Dad's house the next Saturday about 2:00 in the afternoon, because her Mom and Dad were going to be out of town all weekend and we would have time to make love and be together. She was right when she told me that it wouldn't be long before she had made her plans. She hadn't backed out after all like I thought she might do. Well it was all set now and I was excited to say the least. I couldn't wait to see what it was going to be like to make love to Lorrie the way she wanted it and I knew that we would have plenty of time to spend with each other, so I planned on taking my time to get her ready, so I could make love to her multiple times. I decided to take 4 condoms with me just in case that we would need them, because I really didn't know how it would go. All I knew was that I wanted Lorrie to have the most wonderful and memorable experience in her life. I felt that if I could do that for her, then I would also be the recipient of all the love she could give me.

Lorrie—I am so happy because this is the day, I have been waiting for all my life. I am all smiles and at the same time a little nervous, because I want everything to be so perfect for Gus when he comes over. I have made all the plans and I have been going over them for days now and now in just a few hours I will become a woman and not only that, but I will be his woman forever in my heart, no matter what happens after this. I have always loved him since the first time I saw him when I was 12 years old and I will always love him. I just hope that I don't mess up and act like a little girl. He has had so much experience with the older girls, so I hope that he will help me to know what to do to please him. Of course, Mom and Dad left me baby-sitting for the weekend with my little brother and sister, but I have all of that figured out. I know that one of their friends down the street is going to be setting up a lemonade stand to sell lemonade and they will be having fun there all afternoon with all the neighbor kids showing up. They seem to be excited about going over there. I made sure that I have clean sheets on the bed and also, I have heard that I might bleed a little, so I put a real nice towel on the bed and I also put some of my perfume on the pillow. I made a card out of construction paper and drew a nice red heart on it with a cupid arrow going through it and Lorrie and Gus on it and inside I wrote I will love you forever and I put it on the pillow. I am not going to wear any jewelry, because I feel that I will be too nervous to take it off. I am going to wear my hair down, put my best lipstick on along with my best perfume. I am going to wear my best bra and panties, some nice shorts, a blouse that buttons down the front and put nail polish on my toenails and fingernails. So much to think about and do to get ready, but it will be worth it. I have been waiting four years for this day and it is hard for me to believe that it is actually going to happen. I get a warmth of happiness that washes over my whole body ever time that I think, in just a short time we will be in each other's arms in my bed naked and become one forever. I am giddy with excitement. It's getting close to the time for him to come, so I take my little brother and sister down the block to the neighbors and I tell them to stay there and help sell the lemonade till I come and get them for supper. Then I go back home to wait for him and make a last-minute check on things to make sure everything is perfect. It's almost time for him to be here and I have to go pee again. It seems like I have gone to the bathroom fifty times today. I hope that he doesn't come while I am in the bathroom. Now I am waiting and looking out the door, because I don't even want to miss getting the first glimpse of his car driving up. Oh my gosh there he is. I can hardly breathe, and I can feel my-self shaking with excitement, because it is actually going to happen. He is walking up to the door and I am so ready for him. I open the door and he walks-in the house with a big smile and a Hi Baby. Can you imagine that now he is even calling me sweet names like "Baby".

Gus—She kisses me and takes me by the hand and leads me into her bedroom. Once in her bedroom we moved close to the bed and she pulled the covers back and I saw the towel she had placed there and immediately knew the purpose for it. She then smiled that big beautiful smile of her's and came to me and molded her body to mine just like she had done on the beach in Corpus and we, while standing, began very passionate kissing and moving our bodies together in a mutual rhythm of love so hot that all reality of time and place are swept into one small capsule of extreme deep inner feeling so strong of two people blending together and becoming one person in mind, body and soul. I then started to unbutton her blouse and unsnap her bra and she moved her shoulders to let them fall to the floor. Before me were the most beautiful shaped breasts and nipples that I had ever seen. I then kissed her again and kissed her neck and started licking her nipples and she exhaled, through her head back and became weak in my arms. Then she took the belt from her shorts and let them slip to the floor and I couldn't believe that I was seeing the most, lovely body I had ever seen in my life. I mean her naked body was, well, it was so beautiful that it would be hard for me to explain!. Her breasts were small, perfectly shaped and very firm with her nipples pink and extended. Her hips nicely rounded, small waist and long straight legs. Everything was just of the right size and shape that made the most beautiful work of art that the mind of God could fashion. I took off my shirt and boots and unbuckled my pants and then she came next to me again and we started kissing. Suddenly she stopped kissing me and listened for a second and in a hushed voice said oh no, my little brother and sister have come into the house. We came apart instantly and began getting dressed. I finished first and walked into their kitchen and in an instant her little brother and sister also came into the kitchen. They just looked at me, not knowing what to do or say, because they had never seen me before and I had never seen them either. Actually, I didn't even know that she had a little brother and sister. Then her little sister asked where Lorrie was and I said that she had walked to the other room, but she would be right back. Lorrie then walked in like nothing had happened and took me by the hand and walked me to the door and whispered to me that she was sorry, but that we would make other plans and that she didn't even care anymore if we did it in the back seat of my car. She said for me to call her and we would get together.

Gus—I have every intention of calling her, I mean, my goodness, what a beautiful girl and she wants me to take her virginity!! What a fabulous opportunity, why not?? I decide to wait a couple of days, before I call her, to let things cool down at her house to see if her little brother or sister get her into trouble. During this time, I am thinking about her all the time. I start turning it around different ways in my mind, to try and see all sides of it. This experience with Lorrie is so different from any that I have had, that I have a deep feeling about it. I'm not sure what it is that I am feeling. I know what lust is and I know what sex is, but what is love?? Aw hell, why am I thinking like this anyway?? I just need to call her, and she will tell me what she is planning and then we will do it and it will be over with and she and I will go on doing what we always were doing. I don't know, something seems different here. She is sixteen, but that isn't a real problem, because I have had sex with other sixteen-year-old girls before, so what is the problem here?? Why am I worried about this all of a sudden and hesitating?? You know, seeing her naked again would probably make me lose my mind and I think I would forget everything else. I imagine that making love to her has to be just absolutely out of this world. Let's see, she has two more years of High School and if I want to keep on seeing her then that means that I will have to keep hanging around El Campo for two more years. Wait a minute, the more I think about it, the more it scares me, because I now realize that if I make love to her, then I know that I won't want to stop. I will want more and more of her. Why do I feel this way?? I have never felt like this before about a girl, why now?? I need to go back to College and then I will be going off away from here to another College to finish. I won't be able to do that, because I won't want to be away from her, and she won't want to be away from me. I know what is going to happen if I make love to her. We will want more and more of it and she will end up getting pregnant and not finishing High School. We would have to run off to Mexico to get married and all of her girlfriends will be prohibited from seeing her, because she will be considered a bad influence on them. Her parents would be disgraced, and we would have bad problems. I don't know about this idea of taking her virginity. The more I think about it the more it seems like I will end up ruining her life by doing it. If I don't do it, she will finish High School, go to College, or get a job, meet a nice guy and get married and have a normal life. I feel so bad now. Something that sounded so wonderful might turn out to be terrible. I don't think that I want to ruin Lorrie's life, but I really want to make love to her very bad. I feel like I am supposed to make love to her, but what about the bad things if she would get pregnant and I can guarantee that she will if we would keep seeing each other. Of course, we would keep seeing each other, how could I ever stay away from her?? I think that there is only one mature way to look at this, I am sad to say.

THE START OF THE LOST FIFTY YEARS

*G*us—The big decision to leave Lorrie alone was a super hard one for me to do. I would need to call her and meet her to explain why I was doing it. No that won't work, because the minute that I see her I will want to take her into my arms and have the experience of those wonderful Corpus kisses once again. How in the hell will I ever do without those? Well then, I will just have to call her and tell her over the phone. I don't think that it will work either, because I will picture her naked in my mind and the first thing you know I will be making arrangements to meet her to make love to her. No nothing will work if it has to do with contact with her. I simply can't understand why I am like this. It has never happened to me before. Why should I be so concerned about Lorrie's future life? I mean, maybe she wouldn't even get pregnant. I know that's not right, because I can tell that she will be just as crazy about making love to me as I will be about making love to her and then things will get out of hand and we will be experimenting with all sorts of sexual fulfillment and we will get careless about using condoms and that will be dangerous. No, she will be pregnant within six months, I bet, because I know me and by that time, I wouldn't be able to resist her anything that she would want to do. I can just hear her saying, oh please let's do it without a condom one time, because I want to see what it feels like and that would do it. What do I do, oh what do I do!! This is driving me crazy. I have to make a decision here and stick to it no matter what. Alright here is what I am going to do. I won't call her, I won't talk to her, I won't see her. I am not in the High School circle any-more, so I will be able to do that. I will just do my work as usual and I will stay away from any place that I might run into Lorrie. I also need to get ready to go back to College, and that means I need to get engaged to that girl that I have been dating from out of town. She goes to College also and that will put an anchor on my butt, so I won't be running around. That's what I need to do to settle down and get to business with my studies and this is also what Lorrie needs, so she can have a good future and a normal life. I think that this is the best thing I can do, but I will surly miss her. She is young and will have a lot of boyfriends and it won't be long till she forgets all about me.

Lorrie—I waited for two weeks for you to call or contact me some way and you didn't. I was afraid to leave the house because I didn't want to miss your call. Every time the phone would ring, I would run for it expecting it to be you and I didn't want anyone else to talk to you. In those days the phone was in the kitchen on the wall and the only place to talk with some privacy was in the little pantry next to it. I would have to sit on the trash can to talk and Mom would open the door every now and then and frown at me to get off the phone. Mom and Dad thought that something was wrong with me, because I was hanging around the house all the time. School was out for the summer and we were going to go on a family vacation to the Seattle World Fair in another couple of weeks and usually I would want to go to dances, movies and be with my friends talking about our vacation and I was doing none of this. They would ask me if I was going to do this or that and I would just shrug my shoulders. I would even turn down dates that normally I would jump at. One day all of a sudden it hit me square in the face. He isn't going to call. He isn't going to contact me. What has happened. Everything was going good, and I know that he liked me, because he kissed me so wonderful and he came to take my virginity and I was going to happen if my brother and sister hadn't broken it up. He didn't seem upset when he left. He even said that he would call. I kept running everything back and forth in my mind as to what could have made you mad at me and nothing made any since at all. Then it came to me. I finally figured out what happened. It had to be what happened, because everything else was so good. The only thing that was different was that I had taken my cloth's off and I was naked in front of him. That had to be it. He didn't like what he saw when I was naked. Oh my gosh I was so mortified. He has been with the older girls and they have such good bodies and I know that I have small breasts and my legs are too long and my feet are too big. That is what went wrong. Well that has taught me a good lesson. From now on I am not going to risk losing a boyfriend by letting him see me without cloths, never. After that I never saw you. I never saw your car and I never heard your name spoken. You simply vanished from my life and I cried myself to sleep every time I thought of us on the beach in Corpus and how wonderful it was. Maybe if I hadn't been such of a hurry to give you my virginity and we could have been together more things would have been different. But now all of that was gone and the chance that I had taken in Corpus that worked out good had ended in disaster and it was all my fault. I had waited for four years for this chance and I had blown it, typical Lorrie. I guess that he is gone forever. Well I will always have those wonderful kisses in Corpus to remember and his and my song "In The Still Of The Night" by The Five Satins.

Lorrie—A week later we left to go on our family vacation to the Seattle World Fair and I didn't care where we went or what we were going to do. While at the World Fair everyone except me seemed like they were having a lot of fun, but not me. I was so depressed and bored that I just couldn't get into it. Mom and Dad had also planned to go to Wyoming to visit my Aunt there and she had a daughter that was a teenager also. She was fourteen, a couple of years younger than me. Actually her and I had always got along good and she had a sweet nature, but I found out after we got there that she had a nice boyfriend that was my age and that really aggravated me, because I had just messed things up with Gus and I had nobody. Well my cousin introduced me to her boyfriend and that was her big mistake. I made her miserable after that and even made her cry. I was a real little bitch. I flirted real-heavy with him and actually took him away from her while I was there. I did it out of meanness, because she had him and I didn't have Gus. He was a real sweet boy and he had no idea what I was doing. I wanted to prove to myself that I could get any boy to pay attention to me if I flirted with him. I wanted to feel that I was attractive to boys and that they couldn't resist me. I just could never ever take my cloth's off for another boy, because it would ruin everything. I tried and tried to get Gus out of my mind, but even with all of this flirting and turmoil that I was causing with my cousin, it didn't wash away the disgrace I felt, knowing that my body wasn't acceptable to Gus. I was a very unhappy person and we were on this vacation for two weeks and all I wanted to think about was what was Gus doing and what girl was he with now. Even though I knew that I could never face Gus again, I still wanted him terribly and was jealous when I thought of him with another girl. After all he was my Gus and would never belong to another girl no matter what happened. I decided that I would just have to try to get on with my life some-how, because what else could I do when Gus wouldn't cooperate. I knew that I would always love him, because I had fallen in love with him the very first time that I saw him. I had loved him when he never even knew that I loved him. I loved him when he just thought that I was a little girl, so how could I ever stop loving him. I knew that I never could and that it would be my cross to carry, for the rest of my life.

Gus—That summer, after I decided to leave Lorrie alone, I tried to concentrate on what I had to do to get back in College at WCJC and how to approach my girlfriend from out of town about getting married. I was still feeling guilty about the way I treated Lorrie in not talking to her about my decision. I felt kind of like a coward, but I couldn't see another way to do it. I knew my desire for her was strong and I had to fight myself every day for several weeks before I finally could push myself forward and get in a semi-routine that would keep me busy enough, so I didn't think about it all the time. I knew that if I got married and went back to College that I would be out of her world, so to speak, and then after that I would be transferring to Sam Houston in Huntsville and I would really be away where everything would be different and there would be a lot of space between both of us. That is what I did. I married my girlfriend that fall right before College started and after that I never saw Lorrie or heard her name again, but I still thought about her. That summer of 1962 I took my Mom out to the Big Bend National Park of Texas and I fell in love with the high rugged, dry climate of the mountains in the Chihuahua Desert and I decided that some-day I wanted to live out there.

THE 50 LOST YEARS

I think that you will see that during these 50 years that Lorrie and I made very similar mistakes in the decisions that we used to direct our lives. It is actually a very sad tale, because our decisions devised nothing but pitfalls for both of us to fall into. This tragic accumulation of bad decisions, for both of us, started immediately after I decided not to see her again and it lasted for the whole 50 years. From this story you will see how one little decision will influence a whole lifetime of decisions. It's just a wonder that it didn't take us down to the bottom of disparity sometime. I guess that it would have if we hadn't both been strong people.

Gus—I and my new wife are back in College now at WCJC. My plan to marry her and go back to school seems to be working, because my grades are improving. She is a pretty girl and she is trying to learn how to be a wife to me and also go to school. We agreed that she shouldn't get pregnant, so we used birth control. We rented a tiny apartment and set up housekeeping, on a shoestring. We both went to school full time and I worked for my Dad and my Uncle on the weekends and holidays to pay for school. I was in a completely different environment now then I had been when Lorrie and I were planning to get together. I no longer was working at the service station and I was no longer living at home. My entire life now was concentrated between College, which was in a town 15 miles away, the little apartment and working at the farm, so I was in a whole different circle of life that would make it hard for me and Lorrie to accidentally run to each other. I was extremely busy, which is what I needed to occupy my mind and body, so as not to give me time to think so much about Lorrie.

Lorrie—After my family came back from our vacation there was still some summer-time vacation from High School left. I continued my flirty ways with boys and got some satisfaction with their attention, but in the back of my mind I really just wanted to see if I could get them and then go on to another one. I was never serious about any of them. I was a Junior in High School now and I tried to stay busy studying, dating, going to dances, playing in the High School Band, baby-sitting, but secretly I was miserable and felt sick inside. I had to stay busy so it would distract me from thinking about Gus. I would pick a boy that had a nice looking, fast car and flirt with him till he wanted to go steady and I would date him for a while and then I flirt with another and go with him. One time I was going steady with two boys at the same time and had both of their senior rings. Boy I had to be careful to put on the right ring with the right boy on a date. One time one of the boys I had a date with got sick at the last minute and called to cancel, so I called the other boy to see if he could take me to the dance and he said yes, but I forgot that I had already put the first boys ring on my chain and when I got into his car is when I remembered it, so I stuck it in my blouse and told him I had to go to the restroom and we pulled into a service station and I put it my purse. He asked me where his ring was, and I told him that I had it sitting in some cleaner and it wasn't ready yet. Boy that was a close one. Any-way this will give you an idea how I was operating.

Gus—I have now finished a year and one half at WCJC, because I dropped out for one semester when I was doing so bad and running around. My wife and I are going to transfer to Sam Houston College in Huntsville, Tx. This school year will be my Sophomore and my Junior year, and my grades have been steadily improving. After this first semester at Sam Houston I was asked to join an Agricultural Honor Society named Delta Tau Alpha, because I had maintained a B average. In order to join you had to have a B average and if your grade average ever went below that you were kicked out, so maintaining a B or above became important to me. I was an Agriculture Major and a Biology Minor, so belonging to this Honor Society was something that would stand out in my field of study. I actually started competition with myself to beat my own grades each semester and it worked. They just got better and better. Also, since we were going to school on a shoestring, I got three part time jobs. One at the College farm, one at a Texaco Service Station and one at a Shipley Doughnut Shop, all at .50 cents per hour. My wife got a part time job in the office in our apartments that paid for our apartment rent. I also would go hunting, in the local National Forrest, for game that would furnish meat for our table, because it would help on our grocery bill. I was pretty successful at hunting and would bring home deer, squirrel, dove and armadillo. I thought of Lorrie less often now, but when I would get a little slow time she would come back into my thoughts and I would wonder how she was doing and who her boyfriend was and think how lucky he was. I would then go back to whatever I was doing, and she would be out of my mind again.

Lorrie— When I was a Junior in High School, 1963, this boy that was a Senior invited me to his Senior Prom and I was excited about that. He and I had been flirting with each other for a few months, but I had never dated him. He seemed nice and Mom and Dad thought it was alright, so I told him I would go. Me and my girlfriends would do all kinds of talking making plans for what we would wear and what kind of hair-do we would wear for the Prom. Pretty exciting time to be in High School. I was studying hard and my grades were real good and I didn't think about Gus all the time like I once did, but especially when the song "In The Still Of The Night" would play on the radio, I would remember that time on the beach in Corpus with Gus and I would think, what happened, it was so good. Well the school year went on and it came time for the Junior and Senior Prom, and I had my dress and Mom had taken me to the Beauty Shop that we had gone to since I was in Junior High. The nice lady that owned it was so full of jokes and humor that she kept me laughing. She was only about 5 or 6 years older than me, but she seemed much older, because she was married, and she had her own business. All the schoolgirls went to her when there was something special like a Prom to get your hair dome in a real Beauty Shop, so there were all kinds of gossip about what girl was going with who. I had my ears pricked up to see if I heard the name of Gus, because sometime a Senior girl would invite a boyfriend that was already out of High School, but his name didn't come up. All of a sudden it was the day of the Prom. It seemed like it would never get here, then it just kind of zoomed in on me and I was excited to say the least. My date and I had planned to meet another couple for dinner at a local Mexican Cafe before the Prom. We were all dressed up in our Prom finest. Us girls had taken special care to make sure that our hair and make-up was perfect and had chosen the cologne that we had been saving for only special occasions. We were nervous and giddy and ready to enjoy ourselves. My gosh to go to the Prom meant that you were really growing up to be an actual adult. My date came to the door and he had brought me a nice corsage to wear and it was the first corsage I had ever had. I was so pleased to have him pin it on me. Then we went to the Mexican Cafe to meet the other couple and we had a good time there and I was especially careful not to spill anything on my pretty dress. It came time for us to leave there to go to the Prom, so we said good-by and that we would see them there. We got into my dates car and he looked to me and said for me to sit close to him, so I slid over as much as I could, because my dress took up a lot of room, and then to my surprise he leaned over and pushed his hand down the front of my dress to feel my breasts and I freaked out. I jerked his hand out and I slapped him, and he seemed so surprised. I said what do you think you are doing, and he said well I got you a corsage and I bought you dinner, so I should get something for it. I couldn't believe what I was hearing. We were having such a good time and now he just ruined it. I screamed at him to take me home and he didn't want to do it, but I started crying, because I was afraid of him and I couldn't be with him all night anymore. He finally took me home and that was my first Prom. I didn't go out with him any-more and in a couple of weeks school was out and I was on my way to becoming a Senior, yea!!!

Gus—Well it's the end of class in the spring of 1963 and I was going back to El Campo to work all summer for my Dad and Uncle then go back to school in the fall of 1963 to finish the last half of my junior year, then I would be a senior at the end of December 1963. I was very busy, but I was enjoying my classes and my grades were so good that even I couldn't believe it. The only class that I had trouble with was Genetics. Here we go again with all the formulas kind of like Algebra, but I actually passed College Algebra with a strong C at WCJC before transferring to Sam Houston. Everyone in the class was having trouble. I will never forget the grades. There were 112 students in the class and even after the Professor averaged the grades out, there were 3 A's, 5 B's, 7 C's and 10 D's and the rest were F's. I was so glad that I got a D, because the class was needed for my Major. During the summer months when I was in El Campo, I would drive by the Service Station that I had worked at two years before and I would think about Lorrie and her friends coming up there to flirt with me, oh well those days are over. Me and my wife are living in a little house for the summer that my Grandma was living in before she was moved to the Nursing Home. I worked that summer in the rice field and working cattle and breaking horses. Soon it was September again and we were off to Sam Houston for the last half of my junior year in College. I was glad to get back to college. I had made some friends there that also enjoyed going hunting with me in the National Forrest. We made several interesting discoveries while on hunting adventures. We discovered an old graveyard that had an iron fence around it and it had some Civil War graves in it. We also discovered an old log cabin sitting on a little hill in a beautiful clearing that had shoot windows in the cellar and had bullet holes poked in the logs of the cabin. My grades continued to be very good mostly A's and B's. Nothing spectacular happened that semester just the same old thing of classes, part time jobs and back to the apartment to study. First thing that you know the fall semester of 1963 was over and the spring semester of 1964 would be starting, and I would be a Senior.

Lorrie—Wow I can't believe that in a couple of weeks the fall semester of 1963 will start and I will be a Senior graduating in the spring of 1964 and that means that just one more year and I will graduate and I will be either going to College or maybe going to Houston to get a job and be out from under Mom's and Dad's thumb. It will be so good to finally get to the point where I can make my own decisions about my life. My Senior year should be a lot of fun, with new boys to date, senior parties and of course the Prom. I can't wait to complete this year and maybe get out of El Campo and have some new experiences. If I can just leave El Campo, then the things that remind me of Gus will be behind me. I don't think of him so much, just when I go by places that I used to see him at and when that song of ours "In The Still Of The Night" plays on the radio. I wish that they wouldn't play it any-more, because it brings back that same memory of us on the beach and how wonderful it was. Oh, why can't it be that way now?? I must never think of that again. I will just try to think of my Senior year. I have a new girlfriend and she has a boy cousin that has come to live with them that is my same age and he is kind of cute. Maybe I will get to know him better, because he will be a Senior too. Lorrie's Senior year was going good with her playing in the High School band and going to dances. One problem was that her Mom and Dad had her grounded a lot. They were concerned about her getting to involved with some boy and having sex. It seemed that like they were obsessed with it to the point that it made Lorrie miserable. Any infraction of coming home, just maybe 10 or 15 minutes late, or going to the Drive-in Movie instead of the Walk-in Movie would get Lorrie grounded for a week. It wasn't like her grades were slipping, because they were very good. It was just their fear that she might get pregnant. They would have such terrible confrontations on this subject that Lorrie would just break down in a crying jag and tell her Mom to just take her to the Doctor for a check-up if she didn't believe her. Her Mom would even read Lorrie's diary when she wasn't home to see if she could get evidence of any sexual misconduct by Lorrie with some boy. This caused a lot of trouble at home and all Lorrie wanted to do at this point was to get out of High School and away from home the control of her parents. Lorrie was absolutely miserable at home during her High School years. Her parents thought that they were protecting her and the family, because there was such a bad stigma placed on a family that had a daughter that got pregnant unmarried in those days. Lorrie was popular with the boys, because she liked to dance and flirt with them, but she never had any sexual relations with them. The cousin of her girlfriend was a good-looking boy and Lorrie and he got to know each other at school and also when Lorrie would go over to her girlfriend's house to visit. She would have liked to date him, but her parents forbade it, because his father was a known criminal that had even spent time in prison. She saw him a lot at her girlfriend's house and they would play records and dance, kiss a little and sit on the couch hold hands and watch TV. That went off and on, with him, all through Lorrie's Senior year. The school year was coming to a close and it was time for the Prom. A friend of Lorries Mom and Dad from out of town had a son that was going to TLC College to be a Preacher and they thought that he would be the perfect Prom date for Lorrie, so they picked out her date for her. After all he was going to be a Preacher, so they knew that he would be a perfect gentleman. That decision was a bad start right there and it got worse. Lorrie said OK. He was nice looking and at least she would be going to the Prom with a good-looking boy. It was the day of the Prom, so the girls spent all day getting ready to go and Lorrie was no exception to this. She had a really pretty Prom dress that had an overlay of lace on it. It wasn't to low cut, but just enough to show some cleavage if Lorrie would be able to stuff enough Kleenex in it to push her breast's up. It had thin shoulder straps to hold it up and that is what Lorrie wanted, because her worst fear was that it would slip down and show the Kleenex. Her Mom took her to the Beauty Shop for a permanent and a new hair style. This is the same Beauty Shop that was owned by my friend that I grew up with and went to school with. But Lorrie didn't know this. After the Beauty Shop her mom took her to the Drug Store, so she could choose a color of lipstick and nail polish that would go good with her dress. While at the Drug Store Lorrie also found a little delicate butterfly that was on a thin wire that you could twine in your hair to hold it and it was the crowning touch that would make her beauty stand out. She was so excited. This would be her last Prom and she was determined to have a blast, not like that other one that was a dud. This one was going to be spectacular and it was going to be the launching of her new life out of High School and into the world that she had been longing to reach for so long. It was the world of adulthood where she could make most of her own decisions, finally, and it was only two weeks away till graduation. It was time to leave for the Prom and she had herself just perfect and for once she even thought that she looked pretty. They were going to ride with another couple that she was friends with. He came right on time and brought her a very nice corsage and told her how lovely she looked. He looked really handsome also, she thought. They said good-by to her parents and got in the back seat of her friend's car to go to a Cafe to eat before the Prom. Everything was going good and she was careful not to spill anything on her beautiful dress. They finally got to the Prom and Lorrie was introducing her date to all her friends and they all agreed that he was one of the most handsome boys there and also, he was older and going to College. She had never danced with him and she was a little worried about that, because she loved to dance so much, and it would be really awful if he couldn't dance good. The music started and when they danced, she was very happy that he was a real good dancer. When she went to the restroom, she didn't know it, but he had brought a bottle of Vodka and he spiked her drink. Lorrie had never done any drinking, but it tasted pretty good, so she didn't protest, and he just kept spiking her drinks all through the dance. By the time the Prom was over she was so drunk that she had to hold on to him to walk to the car. They got in the back seat of the car and were supposed to go to an after the Prom Party, but on the way there her date kissed her and then put his hand under her dress and was rubbing her crotch and she was trying to fight him off when she got sick at her stomach and started throwing-up all over her date and her Prom dress. Well they went to a Service Station and her girlfriend took her in to the restroom there and washed her up and her dress up as good as she could, but the dress had stains on it, her hair was a mess and the pretty little butterfly accent in her hair was all bent up and hanging sideways. They took her home and her date walked her to the door, but she wouldn't kiss him. She unlocked the door and walked past her parents and went in and undressed and went straight to bed. She never saw that Preacher boy again. She would have never dreamed that the Prom night would have been like this. Two Proms and both had been a disaster. Life after High School certainly should be better than this.

Gus—The spring Semester of 1964 is in full swing now and my grades continue to just get better and better. I am actually having fun studying, because I know that my ultimate goal is to make a straight A in all my grades for at least one semester. After I got married and decided to buckle down and study at WCJC I had to figure out how to study, because I had never really done any studying. I finally figured out a plan that worked for me. Since I was married that kept me from running around, so I got to bed at a decent time at night. That gave me a good start in the morning from being rested for class. I decided that I would attend every class on time, be alert, and take extensive notes. Since I wasn't really into doing that much reading, I knew that if I took down almost everything that the Professor said then I could go back to my notes to study for a test. This worked really well, because I was really getting subjected to the information four different ways. I was listening to it, writing it, seeing it and reviewing it. This way it stuck to me really good. Using this formula at Sam Houston served me well and that is why my grades continued to improve every semester. I had carried a heavy class load all through College so far, from eighteen to twenty-one hours per semester, because most of my classes had labs. Between classes and part time jobs there wasn't much time left. What time I had left I would still go and do some hunting and that helped on the grocery bill. I was really busy, so the only time that I thought about Lorrie was when that song "In The Still Of The Night" would play on the radio, then my mind would wander back to the beach in Corpus for a few minutes and I would wonder what she was doing. Time went so quick and all of a sudden, the 1964 spring semester was over, and I was going back to El Campo for the summer to work for my Dad and my Uncle. When the summer is over, I will start the fall semester of 1964 and it will be my last semester and I will have my BS Degree. I am not sure what I will do then. I guess that I have never really had a long-term plan for my life after College. I must start thinking about that.

Lorrie—Her grades had been really good all through High School, so she graduated in the top ten in the Class of 1964 and she had received a Band scholarship that would pay for tuition at WCJC, so that had to be the plan for her immediate future. Her Mom and Dad had already told her that they couldn't afford to send her to a major University, because it was to expensive. Well to Lorrie going to WCJC was better than nothing. A draw back was that she would have to ride the bus to the next town to WCJC and that would entail walking every morning, real early, for seven blocks to catch the bus. At least it was in another town and there would be new boys to meet. She had no idea what to study for, so she would just take the required classes for a Freshman till she figured it out. She planned to do as much babysitting as she could to save money to buy some new school cloths. She was over at her girlfriend's house visiting and that cousin of hers was there and Lorrie asked him if he was going to go to WCJC and he said no that he was going to go to Blinn Junior College. They decided that they would see each other every chance that they could, because now they would have excuses to be out of town and also out of-sight, of Lorrie's parents. He had his own car, so he could meet Lorrie when the WCJC Band went to the football games. Lorrie thought that things were looking up a lot with this new development. Now she could make her own plans as to seeing him without being grounded. Lorrie started College at WCJC in the fall of 1964 and everything was going good with school and also seeing the boy that she had been forbidden to see. Lorrie was feeling like an adult with some freedom at last, but her Parents still treated her like a kid when she was home wanting to make all her decisions for her. Lorrie resented this more and more. She wanted to run her own life. Lorrie had completed the fall semester of 1964 at WCJC and had completed the spring semester of 1965 there also. She had kept on seeing the cousin without being found out and also she had started running around with some girlfriends that taught her to smoke and drink a beer. Now her grades were suffering, because of her interest in running around with them and meeting the forbidden cousin. She started WCJC College again in the fall semester of 1965. Everything was going along pretty much as it had been before. This didn't last too long though. Toward the end of September, the WCJC Band was playing at a home football game and the forbidden cousin had come to the game to see Lorrie. Lorrie's parents were also at the game to watch Lorrie march in the band at the half time program. After the marching at half time Lorrie met the cousin behind the stands to plan how he was to meet her to go out after the game. They were kissing and discussing the plan when Lorrie's parents were looking for her and they discovered her kissing him behind the stands. They were caught red handed and no getting out of it. There was a big argument that ensued, and the cousin was sent packing and told by Lorrie's Dad that he never wanted to see him around Lorrie again. After the game Lorrie's parents made sure that Lorrie rode home with them. On the way home to El Campo Lorrie was crying and told them that she was miserable and that she didn't want to go to school anymore and that she wanted to get out of El Campo and go to work some place and that she was tired of being treated like a little kid because she would be 20 years old at the end of October and that was only a month away. Well that was the end of her WCJC College. She had only completed one full year and about a month on her fall semester in 1965.

Gus—I graduated from Sam Houston at the end of the fall semester of 1964 with a BS Degree in Agriculture Science and a Minor in Biology. I almost had a straight A for that last semester but didn't quite make it. I needed three points on my Engineering final to make an A on it, which would have given me an A instead of a B, but I still had done very good in my College career. Who would ever believe that me, who had graduated in the last quarter of my High School class would almost have a straight A for my last semester in College? During this last semester I had a job interview with Aetna Life Insurance Company in Houston, working in their land loan department, but I really didn't have my heart in it, because I really couldn't see myself wearing a white shirt and tie every-day with a suit and fighting the city traffic. I was used to the outdoors and a lot of manual man type of work, not sitting at a desk shuffling paperwork. One afternoon after my marketing class the Professor asked me to come into his office. I wondered what was up. He seated me and told me that he had received a call from North Carolina, and they were looking for someone to hire as their Assistant County Agent there and he thought of me and wanted to know if I might be interested. The salary was actually a little better than the Aetna job and it would permit me to get out of doors into the countryside from time to time. Seemed to be better to me. I asked how long I would have to consider it and he told me that he would have to know by the next day after lunch. I was curious as to why they would call to Texas for that job when they had Colleges in North Carolina and mu Professor told me that Sam Houston and Texas A & M were known for turning out good quality agriculture graduates, so this is the first place that they think of when needing good agriculture men. I told him that I would sleep on it and let him know the next day. After sleeping on it over-night and thinking about it the next morning I decided to turn the job down. I didn't know if I was making the right decision, but I was feeling like maybe I should go back to El Campo and try to help my Dad, because his health was going down pretty fast and I knew that he couldn't afford to hire the kind of help that I could provide. I knew that the pay was small, but I would have the chance to build my own farm and ranch business. A couple of days later my engineering Professor talked to me about coming back to College to study for my Masters Degree. He even said that he could get me some grants, because of my grades. I thanked him and told him that I had decided to help my Dad and also, I was tired of going to school and just needed to get out in the world and work toward something. Again, I had no idea if I was making the right decision, but I had made it, so I was headed back to El Campo and a job of hard physical work, long hours and poor pay. It was December 1964 and after Graduation I was packed up and driving back to El Campo.

Lorrie—Lorrie road home with her Mom and Dad after the football game and it was a very tense time with them. The next morning, they all got together and discussed the previous evenings happenings. Lorrie said again that she didn't want to go back to WCJC. She said that she had decided that she wanted to go to Houston and find a job there. Her parents were against her going to Houston, they figured that she would get back with that cousin of her friends again if she went to Houston. Her Dad came up with the idea that maybe she could go to Florida to live with his sister and her husband. Her Uncle worked for NASA there and maybe he could find a job for her and she could stay with them. He called his sister and her husband, and they said that would be fine with them and that her Uncle would see about a job for Lorrie at NASA. He said that it might take a little time to get lined up with a job, but it was very possible, and he would let them know when to send Lorrie to Florida. A couple of weeks later her Uncle called and said that he had found her a job at NASA and her room was ready and she would be able to ride to work with him. So now it was all set and Lorries Mom and Dad thought that it would be a good deal, because Lorrie would be far away from the boy that they disliked, and Lorrie would be taken care of by her Uncle and Aunt and have a decent job. This was the perfect solution for everyone concerned. Lorrie's Mom and Dad didn't know it at the time, but this was probably the worst thing they could have done for Lorrie. Lorrie was packed up and put on a Gray Hound bus to Florida a couple of weeks before her twentieth birthday in 1965. Remember now that this is just a couple of weeks before her twentieth birthday in 1965 and there will be a very fast series of events take place, in just a few months-time, that will change the whole direction of Lorrie's life forever. From this time on Lorrie kept most of the things she did in her life secret from her family, because she had experienced so much tight control from her Mom and Dad that she didn't want to give them a chance to try to run her life anymore. From now on she was going to do what she wanted to do, in her own way.

Gus—At the end of December 1964 I and my wife were settled back in El Campo. This time we were living my Grandma's small two bed-room house, because she had been moved to the Nursing Home. My Dad let me live there rent free as part of my work benefit, because I was only going to be paid $50.00/week. I was still driving my old 1956 Dodge Texan that I had bought when I was in High School. I needed something to drive to the farm and ranch, so I found an old 1951 Chevrolet pick-up for $250.00 that someone had painted orange with a paint brush, and I bought it. That would leave the 1956 Dodge Texan for my wife to drive. The year turned to January 1965 and I was really working as a ranch and farm hand doing anything and everything from can, to can't. I was so busy getting myself readjusted to my new life that I didn't really have time to think about anything else, so it was a long time before Lorrie entered my thoughts again. I remember that I was on the way to Mom and Dad's house and I drove by the old Service Station that I had worked at and I looked over there and suddenly remembered when Lorrie and her girlfriends would come in and flirt with me and then the time in Corpus came to me and those Corpus kisses and I thought, I wonder what happened to that sweet, pretty girl. Then my thoughts went back to what I had to do, and I didn't think about her any more at that time. I had a little bit of a stake in the ranch. After the Carla hurricane in 1961 I had bought three young heifers to try and start my own cow herd. My Dad had let me run those with his cattle. These heifers had now born two sets of calves, some were bull-calves and some were heifer calves. I saved the heifer calves and when they got big enough, I branded them, and I now had seven cows in the pasture. It didn't take me but a few months to figure out that my wife need to find a job, because $50.00/week was paying just the bare necessities with very little left over. We didn't plan on having children for a long time so there wouldn't be a problem with her working. She finally found a job at Mustang Caterpillar working as the secretary to the manager there and it paid $220.00/ month, which was $20.00 dollars more per month then I was making. Wow this was great, because it really took some of the pressure off us about money. I was working anywhere from ninety to one hundred hours a week, in the rice field, training and breaking horses, working cattle, riding pasture, bailing hay, fixing fence and everything else that goes on working on a farm and ranch. Home life was going pretty-good, but we really only saw each other on nights and Sundays. I didn't have much time for entertainment. Every now and then we would go to a movie or to a dance. Finally, 1965 turned into 1966 and I wanted to start farming, but I had no rice allotment from the Government, so I decided to try farming Milo Maize, because I could farm it without any allotment.

Lorrie—In January 1966 Lorrie had been Florida and working for NASA in their office doing all kinds of starter position tasks like making copies, filing, delivering documents to different offices, typing and general office work. The job payed pretty good, so she was saving money, because her expenses were almost nothing while living with her Uncle and Aunt. Also, she got to meet some cute young guys working there. She had a couple of dates with two different guys, but when they came to her Uncles house to pick her up her Aunt was drunk, and she made an ass out of herself by flirting with them and wanted them to dance with her. Lorrie was so embarrassed about this and finally realized that her Aunt was an alcoholic. Her Uncle and Aunt didn't hold a tight string on Lorrie like her parents were hoping, so she did pretty much what she wanted to do. She found out though that they were screening her mail and any letters that came from that cousin that she was prohibited from seeing were kept from her. Her parents told her Uncle and Aunt that he was not to have any contact with Lorrie. Lorrie's Uncle and Aunt lived very close to the beach and Lorrie loved to go there when she was off work. With the money she was saving she bought herself some nice work cloths, a couple bikini swim suites, and a surfboard. There were a few surfers down on the beach and there was a place there that had a place to change, shower and to store your surfboard when you weren't using it. When she was trying to learn to surf, she met three guy's and two girls that hung out there all the time. Two of the guys, in their middle twenties, were Trust Fund baby's that had a steady income from wealthy families and the other one was much older. The two girls were just along for the ride with two younger boys. They had traveled with them from California. The older guy was thirty-six and was called the Surf Duke and all the rest of them looked up to him, because he made surf boards and seemed to know everything about surfing. He had surfed all over the world. He had been in the Navy and had been married before and had a couple of kids someplace, so he was a man of the world for sure, but no one seemed to know his real name, and no one seemed to care about that. Lorrie enjoyed being around them, because they were so free and could do whatever they wanted to do. Lorrie loved the beach life and would go there and spend time with her new friends every chance she got, and her Uncle and Aunt never told her not to go. The only thing that she didn't like about the two younger boys was that they would tease her about being a Virgin. The girls had told them about it from a conversation that they had with Lorrie. The young boys were always telling Lorrie that they could cure that virgin problem that she had, and it would be over with, but Surf Duke would take up for her and tell them to lay off of her and they would stop for a while. Lorrie was learning to surf pretty good and she found out that her friends were going to Porto Rico for a surfing tournament and the girls were going to be in it also. Lorrie thought that it would a fun thing to do, so she took a long weekend of three days and paid her airfare with them to Porto Rico. Surf Duke had a little place there to stay in and a small shop that he made surf boards and an old Volks Wagon hippie bus that they used to get around the island in. She found out after they got there that the girls were not allowed to surf in the tournament that it was just for the men. The girls just watched the men surf and drank a lot of Rum, because it was cheap there and smoked pot. It was the first time Lorrie smoked pot. They could get a lot of it there and Surf Duke knew where to get it. When the tournament was over, and it was time to go back to Florida she was the only one to go back. The rest of them stayed in Porto Rico. The only disturbing thing that happened on the trip was that at the beach they played the song "In The Still Of The Night" a lot and she thought, damn that song again, I can't seem to get away from it. It made her think of Corpus and Gus again and being on a beach made it even worse. It was four years ago now and she still thought about it. This was in January of 1966 and Lorrie's life was starting to change quickly. She just didn't realize how much and how fast and what the impact would be.

Gus—I really started to make plans to farm some Milo Maize in January 1966. There was so much to do, because I didn't even have my own tractor or equipment to do it. I thought that it would take me all of 1966 to get everything ready and maybe I could get a crop planted in 1967. What I didn't know was that events were about to happen to me in 1966 that were going to change my life just as fast and the impact would last forever. I talked the idea of farming Milo Maize over with my Dad and he could see that I really needed to start planning for my future. He was sick with a disease that was incurable and knew that he would be unable to do very much before too long. He asked me if I was still going to work. for him while I was trying to build my cow herd and farm and I told him that I had planned on doing that. I said that I would do as much of my own work at night as I could. He said that if I would do that then he would let me farm one hundred acres of land that he had that nothing had been done with for several years. He said that he knew that it wasn't very good land, so he would let me farm it rent free. We went to look at it and I agreed to the deal. I was just so happy to have some land to farm that I really didn't care how good it was. I figured that I was young and strong and not afraid to work hard and some-how I could make it work. It was really pretty sorry land. It had a lot of alkali in it and it was very uneven and would need leveling and drainage. It had been in rice several years before and all the old levies would have to be knocked down and it was grown up in tall weeds. A lot of work to do there, but I was up to it. First, I would have to look for some equipment to do the heavy work of getting the dirt work on the land done. I didn't have much money to invest, so I knew I would have to find equipment that was obsolete that no farmer would want to use anymore. There was a lot of that kind parked around farmers barns that had been sitting in the weeds for years. I found a 1946 International tractor and an eight-foot Case disc at one place that I bought for one hundred dollars. I would have to work on the tractor there to get it running. That didn't bother me, because I was a pretty good mechanic from all the work, I had done on my Hot Rod I had built back in the 1950's. The tractor had steel wheels and would be hard to move and the disc didn't have any wheels, but I had an older friend that had a hauling truck with a wench on it that would haul it for me, if I traded some work to him. I found another old tractor that one of my Uncles had left standing in a pond for several years and it had rubber tires, which was good, but I had to also get it running before it would be able to move. He said that I could use it for free if I got it running. Then I found a five-foot Case disc that I bought for twenty-five dollars and it had no wheels either. An old farmer that I knew gave me two old flat three bottom John Deer moldboard plows. None of this equipment, including the tractors, had any hydraulic pumps or controls. This is why they were obsolete. All this equipment was from the 1930's and 1940's. Now I had something to work with to get the hard dirt work done with. I would be like a farmer back in the old days with this old equipment. I got it all repaired and started working on the land on my Sundays if I was off and at night with the lights on the tractor. Some time I would work till 1:00 am the next morning. Go home, take a bath, eat a little something, sleep for a few hours, get up at 6 am and get ready to go to work for my Dad at 7am. When this was going on, I thought that I needed to have a real serious talk with my wife about what it was going to take to get the farming and ranching operation off the ground and running. We did have that talk and she seemed to understand that there wouldn't be much time or money for us to do things that other couples were doing. That stuff would just have to wait for who knows how long, but hopefully some-day all the things that we were doing without now would pay off for the future. The next thing I would have to think about was some row crop equipment to put up rows, plant the crop and cultivate it to keep it clean from weeds and grass. I decided that I would go to the Bank and try to borrow the money for this equipment and to discuss with the Banker my plans to farm one hundred acres of Milo Maize. I had to borrow $3000.00 for the equipment and for crop expenses and this was a lot of money, at the time for me to borrow. I had to put up my small cow herd and the equipment as collateral for the loan, which made me very nervous, because all I owned was at stake on one crop. This was all going on in the spring of 1966.

Lorrie—She flew back to Florida by herself and went back to work at NASA. After a couple of weeks, she got a letter and a romantic poem from Surf Duke in Porto Rico saying that he wanted her to come back to Porto Rico, because he missed her, and he wanted her to be a part of his surfboard making business. To Lorrie this was very exciting, because everyone looked up to Surf Duke and for him to say he missed her must mean that he liked her a lot. It all sounded very romantic, so she quit her job at NASA and flew back to Porto Rico to be with Surf Duke. This is in the spring of 1966 and Lorrie is twenty years old. Lorrie and Surf Duke had never had a romantic relationship. Their relationship had been more like a middle-aged man, that she looked up to, protecting a young girl. Now to Lorrie there seemed like a possibility of a romantic relationship with a man, not a boy, that the other people in the group looked up to. When she landed in Porto Rico, he met her at the Airport and had a reservation at the very nice cafe there where they could watch the planes take off and land and they had time to talk and have some wine and a candle-light dinner. It was very romantic to say the least and Lorrie was very pleased. They left there and went to his small apartment by his little shop and they sat on his couch and played music and drank rum and smoked pot and kissed. Lorrie decided that the time had finally come to lose her virginity and Surf Duke was the one to do it. She knew that he had plenty of experience, he was a grown man not a fumbling boy, he was good looking and he had seen her almost naked many times when she was wearing her bikini swim suit, so he shouldn't be turned off by her body like Gus was four years ago and the pot and rum was giving her some courage to go through with it. She started dancing to the music as sexy as she could, and she danced her way into his bedroom and motioned for him to follow. She stood on the bed and started undressing and he kept asking her if she was sure she wanted to do this. She laid on the bed and he came to her and they had sex and he was gentle and easy with her and all of a sudden she wondered if she was in love with him and not Gus, no she knew that she wasn't in love with him, because she didn't even feel the same thing that she felt when Gus kissed her on the beach in Corpus, not even after having sex with Surf Duke, which she liked very much, but it just wasn't the same thing as the feeling that she had always had for Gus. She still wished it had been Gus, but that couldn't happen now, because it was done and done forever. Now she had to look forward to a life with Surf Duke in the islands helping him make surf boards, going surfing whenever they wanted to and of course making love. She thought wow, I waited for four years and that didn't take long. It was a funny feeling now to think that she wasn't a virgin anymore and couldn't ever be again and now the other surfers couldn't call her the virgin, as a remark against her, anymore. Lorrie felt like now she had transitioned from being a girl virgin to being, a grown woman at last, and because of this she could forget about that silly young girl crush she had for Gus. Time for her to move on to other things.

Gus—I was very busy in the spring of 1966 working most days for my Dad and my Uncle and at nights and weekends for myself. At the same time, I was getting financing together and working on old machinery to get it ready for service to work the land. I finally got it all together and was working the land. It was a slow process because this old obsolete machinery was small compared to the more modern machinery, so it covered less acres a day. It seemed like I would work all day and get very little ground plowed up. Also, there were the break downs and the rainy weather to deal with. I would come home late at night too tired to take a bath, to dirty to go to bed, so I would set my coffee thermos and lunch kit and water container on the kitchen table and lay down on the kitchen floor, in my filthy cloths, to sleep for a couple of hours. This would give me enough energy to get undressed and get in the bathtub. Even then I would go back asleep in the tub and when I would wake up the water would be cold, and I would still have to bathe. I would sleep a couple of more hours, wake up, drink two cups of coffee and put the rest in my thermos, make my lunch and leave for work. Day after day of this. I would get a couple of days off if it rained a lot, but then after it quit raining, I would have to go to the field and drain water. One evening that spring my tractor broke down and I came home early, before dark, because I needed to get parts to fix it. When I got home my wife was gone, but she left me a note that she had gone to church, and supper was in the oven. I opened the oven and there was a nice casserole there and I liked casseroles, so I was looking forward to having supper. It felt good to be home early for a change. I needed to take a bath and get all cleaned up before I would eat. I picked up the note and read it again. For some reason something just didn't seem right, and I couldn't put my finger on it. All of a sudden, I thought, she isn't at church, she is with another man. I can tell you that I had no reason to suspect that my wife was running around on me and why that came into my mind I can't explain. I only knew that I was sure of it. I thought that I must go ahead and eat while supper is still good and hot or it will be ruined, then I thought, no, I don't have time for that I have to find out what is happening. I sat down at the table to think it out. If it was true, then who could she be with. I could come up with only one answer. It must be someone from her work. I got in my pick-up and thought I need to go through the parking lot at the church first to see if my car is there. If my car is there, then I must be going crazy for some reason to think like this. I drove to the church and I drove around in the parking lot there twice to make sure that I hadn't missed my car, but it wasn't there. I knew then that my hunch was right, and it gave me a sick feeling in my stomach. I then drove out where she worked. It was way on the north side of town and there were, no business around it. There was only one car in the parking lot, a station wagon. I didn't see anyone around, so I thought that whoever owned that car would be back to get it sooner or later. I left the parking lot and there was a dark gravel road across the street from it, so I backed down it and parked with my lights out, so I could see when someone was driving toward the business. It didn't take but about twenty minutes and I saw a car coming from a blacktop country road that comes into the highway that the business is on and I thought, I bet that it is my car. Sure enough, my car pulls into the parking lot next to the station wagon and I start my pick-up and I pull behind both cars and block them in. A man and my wife get out of my car and I motion for them to come over and I tell them to each get in their own cars and that I am going to follow them to my house, because we needed to have a good talk. All three of us drove to my house and went inside and I told both of them to sit side by side on the couch. I sat in a chair facing them. I wasn't quite sure what I was going to say, but on the way home I decided to keep the conversation on a mature level and try to find out a few facts and then decide what to do about the whole situation, depending on how things went. The man that my wife was having this affair with was the head of the parts department where she was working. They admitted to having this affair for nine months before they were caught. I asked if they were in love with each other and they said no that it was just a sexual relationship. The man had a wife and two small children that I had met on one occasion when me and my wife had been invited to their house for dinner. I thought about that as I was making up my mind on how to handle this. My wife said that she was going to quit her job, because she was afraid there would be talk at work. I told her that if there would be talk at work then it would because either she or her lover would be the ones to start it, because no one but us three knows what has happened and if talk started then it would be their fault and she could face it on her own. I told her that she was going to work like she always did that I wouldn't let her run from this problem. I told both of them that if I found out that they were associating at work more than their work requirements permitted then I would find more drastic measures to cure the problem. I told him that he had a wife and two small kids at home and that I would not say anything of this to his wife or anyone else, so he should not be afraid that she would find out. I told him that I was not in the business to cause him or his family any trouble. I told him that causing him trouble and maybe breaking up his family wouldn't solve the problem that me and my wife now had and that we would just have to try and work that out between ourselves and that would be hard enough in itself. I told him to go on home and not worry about it, because it all stopped right here. He left and I just sat there looking at my wife. The first thing that I said was, this is Wednesday and we had sex on Monday, so I don't think that you are suffering from not getting enough sex, you just went one night without sex, so what is it. She just sat there and looked at me for a while then started crying. I told her that I had the feeling that she wasn't crying because she was ashamed of what she had done, but because she had been caught and she was stressed out expecting to be beaten or a big fight or shooting between me and her lover. I told her that if she would have had any loyalty or self-regret or shame then she had nine months to adjust her behavior and she would have never been found out. I told her that I would not tell her family what has happened. I told her that I wasn't sure what I was going to do about our situation that I would just have to approach it on a day by day basis. Then I told her that I thought she need to go take a real hot bath to get all of that extra sex washed off of her. I then went into the kitchen and re-heated up my casserole supper and ate, then bathed and went to bed. Two days later my wife's lover's wife called me on the phone and wanted to meet with me. I told her that I would meet her at the Dairy Queen that evening and we did so. We got a cold drink and sat down in a booth. She was all dressed up and looked like a million dollars. She was a good-looking redhead and her figure was very good for a woman that had two children. We talked about what had happened and she wanted to know how I had discovered them and how I had caught them. I told her that I had no reason to suspect them, that it was just a hunch that came to me out of the blue and that I had no idea who my wife could be seeing, but the only thing I could think of was that it had to be someone at work. That is when I went out to the business and waited there for them. I asked her what excuse her husband had given her to be at work at night. She told me that he said he had to go in and inventory new parts that were coming in, because they didn't have enough help to do in during work hours. She said that he had been doing this once a week for months. I told her that they had been seeing each other for nine months and she said that made since on the time frame. I told her that I had told her husband that I wouldn't tell her about what happened, so why did he tell her, and she said that she didn't know, but he just did. I said that I thought that we had covered about everything and if she didn't have any-more questions, I thought that our meeting was over. She said that there was one more thing and I said what is that. She said that she thought that we should do what they had done and that she was ready to go to a Motel or even in the back seat of my car to have sex. I was shocked for a minute and I am sure that I must have had a stupid look on my face before I finally was able to think. I told her that if we did that then we would be no better than they were. I told her that under different circumstances I would love to go to bed with her, because she was beautiful and very tempting, and I thought that we should leave now before I changed my mind. That was the last that time that I saw or talked to her. One thing was clear to me and that was that I had decided to get married to the wrong person, now what will I do. This was the spring of 1966 and I had to get mind off of this so I could continue to execute my plans to build my farm and ranch business and this stuff with my wife had nothing to do with that. My original idea of her being a part of those plans was now over.

Lorrie—Ever since Surf Duke had taken Lorrie's virginity she had felt like a different person. She felt completely liberated from all the restraints that her parents had put on her. She knew that as long as she stayed away from El Campo and her parents she could do as she wished, but she also knew that she would have to keep her present life secret from them. Everything was going like she thought it would after she had made love to Surf Duke. They had become much closer. She was living with him in his little apartment. He would go to his shop and work on a surfboard sometime, but he really wasn't very busy making surf boards, so they had a lot of time to go surfing. Her and Surf Duke and the same other four, that had come to Porto Rico, would go to a beach that Surf Duke knew about. There were local people that lived in little houses along this beach and they liked to watch them surf. The drawback about this place was that the locals would throw all their garbage in the water off the beach and it would draw the sharks there. Surf Duke would have to watch out for sharks and when he would see them, he would yell, SHARKS GET ON YOUR SURF BOARDS, so they wouldn't get attacked by them. They would go there in his old Volk's Wagon hippie bus that had an air mattress in the back and when they would get tired of surfing he and Lorrie would crawl in the back and make love, smoke pot and drink rum. It seemed like they lived on pizza, tacos and rum. Lorrie had even bleached out her hair blond to go with her new identity of being a surfer. Wow this was a great life! She was getting very tanned and Surf Duke didn't seem to care that she had small breasts, long legs and big feet. One day when they were in the back of the hippie bus Surf Duke told her that he thought that she needed to get a job to make some money and he had found the perfect job for her and he knew the owner. It was a bar in town just a few blocks from his apartment and he would take her there to show it to her after they got back in town that night. Lorrie didn't know what to think about this, but if Surf Duke thought that this would be a good idea then she would do it, after all he was the one that always took charge, and everyone depended on him to make the decisions. That evening, when they got back to the apartment Surf Duke had her shower, put on some good shorts, blouse, fix her hair and put on some make-up, then they drove down to the Bar. It was farther than Lorrie thought it would be from the apartment in a kind of bad part of town. They went inside and most people in there seemed to know Surf Duke. The owner walked up and shook hands with Surf Duke and said well so this is the pretty little lady that you have told me about, so I guess that Surf Duke had already told the owner about me. Really it was just a formality for me to meet the owner and say yes to getting the job. Surf Duke told me that he would take me to work at 6:00pm each day and pick me up at 2:00am each morning and I would work five days each week from Tuesday through Friday. The owner said that he would pay me minimum wage plus I could keep all of my tips. I had never done any waitress or bar maid work before, so it sounded kind of exciting. It was a couple of days before I started work, so Surf Duke took me to a shop in town and bought me some new shorts, crop tops, high heal shoes and bright ribbons to put in my hair. He said that this would get me more tips from the customers. The owner wanted me to dance with the customers when I wasn't delivering drink's, but I wasn't so sure about that and Surf Duke told him that if I didn't want to do that, then don't make me do it and the owner agreed to it. I started work and it was kind of fun and I did make some pretty good tips and Surf Duke would take me to work and pick me up like he said. It all went good for a while, but then Surf Duke started to make excuses why he couldn't come and get me from work and I would have to walk back to the apartment after 2:00am in the bad part of town and I was afraid, because it was a long dark walk. After a couple of more weeks our friends that come over to Porto Rico with us decided to go back to Florida. We took them to the airport and say them fly out. Before they left the two girls told me that they would write to me to let me know what they were doing and for me to write them back to let them know the news here. So now it was just me and Surf Duke to make our lives together here on this beautiful island together, how romantic. I kept trying to find out why he stopped picking me up after work and I told him that I was afraid to walk back in the dark. He just kissed me and laughed and said that I was being silly. Everything went on like that for a-while. We would surf after lunch for a couple of hours or I would sit around in his shop while he would work on a surfboard and we would smoke and drink rum until it was time for me to go to work. When I would get home from work at night I would shower, and we would smoke some pot and drink rum and make love and then sleep most of the morning. I had been with Surf Duke in Porto Rico for a couple of months living the good life, but it seemed that something was changing about it that Lorrie couldn't quite figure out. For one thing, at work in the Bar, they had that damn song "In The Still Of The Night" on the juke box and it seemed like every night someone would play it. I just couldn't get away from it and it always made my memories come back of Gus and me back on the beach in Corpus and the way that he held me and kissed me. I couldn't understand why I couldn't just forget about that and I would wonder what girl he was with and what he was doing, but I never told Surf Duke any of this. Another thing was that there were always a new bunch of young girls coming to Porto Rico from the States to spend some time here and Surf Duke would have them out there surfing and telling them how much better his surf boards were then the ones they were buying. I got to noticing that he spent some time looking them over. I was getting letters from the girls that went back to Florida and they told me that they had got jobs in this big club on what we called the strip. It was the Rocket Club and it was a place that a lot of the men that worked at NASA came to after they got off of work and that the tips were very good. One of them was a waitress and the other one was a Go-Go dancer. They had rented an apartment not to far down the beach from the Rocket Club, so they could walk to work. It wrote them back and told them about my job at the Bar in town and that all was great with me and Surf Duke. I kept working and Surf Duke kept trying to sell his surf boards to the young girls. He still was not picking me up from work at night and it got so that when I got back to the apartment and showered and we would sit up and smoke pot and drink rum and it would be time to go to bed and make love he started saying that we couldn't, because it was my fertile time and I would get pregnant. I thought OK, because we had never used any type of birth control, not pills or condoms, but I couldn't understand why he was all of a sudden concerned about it. To tell the truth I had never even considered getting pregnant, because he had never even mentioned the possibility of it. That started to worry me some, because what little I knew about girls fertile times were that you had to have very steady period schedule that came the same time every month and mine always came at unusual times and you couldn't depend on a certain time for it to start or stop. It got so that we only made love when he wanted, and he always used that same excuse. I couldn't figure how he knew when my fertile time was. I would ask him, and he would laugh and say, just let me worry about that and you will be fine. I got to suspecting that he was making love to some of the young girls while I was at work and that is why he didn't want to make love to me as much anymore. In fact, I get to thinking that is the reason that he got me that job in the first place so I would be away from the apartment and also that is why he didn't pick me up from work anymore, because he was busy with these girls. It all started to make since to me now. I started deciding that I didn't think that I wanted to live a life of a surf bum anymore living off of rum, pot, pizza and tacos. Also, I was having a lot of trouble with a kidney infection and I started thinking about leaving Porto Rico and going back to Florida. Maybe I could live with the girls there and find a job. I wrote to them and in a week, I got a letter from them saying that they had a spare bedroom and that the Rocket Club had a job open for another Go-Go dancer. I was glad, because I was really burned out on this kind of life. Well Surf Duke had done me a big favor though. He had taken my virginity and had been real sweet, in the way he did it and I had got to see and live in Porto Rico for a few months. This had all been a new and crazy experience and I would never forget it, but I knew it was over now. I told Surf Duke that I was going back to Florida and he took me to the airport to see me off. We kissed good-by and there was no romance in it for me like it once was. I was glad to go and knew that I would never go back. I had picked the wrong man to plan a life with. It was now going into late April of 1966.

Gus—Well the situation between me and my wife were, I guess that you could say sort of distant from each other. We didn't argue or fight. We just existed in the same house together. She went to work and took care of all the necessary things that needed to be done around the house and I continued to my planning and work on the farm and ranch. At home we were mostly quiet, and we didn't talk about what happened to us each day like normal couples do. I was to the point that I didn't really care what she did, and I certainly wasn't going to tell her what I was doing. There was just a minimum of conversation and no sex, kissing or hugging. The affection was gone in the marriage. We were just like two roommates sharing a house together. I thought that maybe in time we could overcome it. When I had some time off, I couldn't stand to stay at the house and spend time with her. I would look at her and try to make up my mind if I could have sex with her. I was not yet twenty-four and I had been used to a very active sex life since I was fourteen years old, so I missed that a lot. I started going out some at night when I wasn't to tired and I told her that I was going to continue going out and that she wasn't invited, and I didn't want to hear anything about it. She simply said OK. I tried to go to a local Bar, but there wasn't anyone there my age to visit with, so I started to go to a popular Drive-In named Lands Drive-Inn. There were a lot of younger people that hung out there, some younger than me and some my age and older, so it was a better place to socialize and it wasn't a Bar. I started to see friends there that I hadn't seen in several years and it was a nice relief to get away from the stress at home. We would sit in each-others cars and talk, drink beer and listen to music and every-once-in a while the song "In The Still Of The Night" would play and I would think of Lorrie and those wonderful kisses on the beach in Corpus and wonder how she was doing, then the conversation would go to a subject that I would have to comment on and that memory would disappear for the time being. One night when I was at Lands Drive-In a car pulled in beside me that had some younger guys in it that I knew. They were all going to WCJC in Wharton. We got to talking between the cars and finally they came and sat with me in my car and we talked and drank some beer. One of the guys I knew pretty good because, I had dated his cousin in High School, so we started to catch up on all the things that had happened from that time till the present. They were all excited about graduating from Junior College at the end of May 1966 and that was only two weeks away. The guy I knew said that his Mom had been transferred to Corpus Christi and that someone was buying their house and he was going to have to find a place to live for two weeks till he graduated, then he was going to move to Corpus with his Mom and go to College there. We drank a few more beers and I told him that I had an extra bedroom that he could use if he wanted to stay with me for two weeks. He said that it would sure solve his problem and he asked what I would charge him. I told him that it would cost him nothing if he was only going to stay for a short time. He knew where I lived. He said that he would let me know when his Mom had signed the papers on the sale because he would have to leave then. I told him that would be fine to just let me know. There was a real pretty Car Hop that was working at Lands Drive-In at that time and she would bring us beer and burgers and fries and flirt with all of us. She was tall and slim with brown hair, brown eyes, a long ponytail and big breasts that bounced when she would deliver orders to the cars and we had a lot of fun watching her and of course making comments about how good she looked. This was a favorite pass time for us at the Drive-In. The next week the guy called me and said that his Mom had signed the papers on the sale of their house, so he needed to get out in three days. I told him that it would be OK, and I would be waiting for him. He said that he was going to have a last party before he left on Saturday night and that it wouldn't start till late, about 11:00 pm that night and if I wanted to come, I was invited. He said that we would meet at Lands Drive-In and go from there. I was looking forward to going to the party, because I hadn't done anything like that since I had been married and that was almost five years ago. Saturday finally came around and I made sure that I had come in from work early enough to get cleaned up and go to Lands Drive-In to eat a burger and fries, because I knew that we more than likely would be drinking a lot of beer that night and I didn't want to do it on an empty stomach. I got to the Drive-In about 10:00 pm and got my supper and started drinking beer and the guys started showing up. Some had girls with them and then some girls showed up in their own cars to go to the party. You know how it is with young people. When there is word out of a big party with beer and a record player going, then it gets around and there is no telling how many people will show up. The boys had gone together and bought a sixteen-gallon keg of beer and all kinds of chips and some girls had made a bunch of different kinds of dip and also someone brought several pizzas wine and whiskey. There were a lot of people already there partying by the time I got there and before long the whole house was packed. I could see that this was going to be one great big party. It was a good thing that the house was at the end of a dead-end street and the neighbors were not right next door, because there was going to be a lot of noise. The sound system was going full blast and people were dancing, talking, kissing and bullshitting each other. Most of them I didn't know, because they were so much younger then me and I had been away at College and then out of circulation being married and also keeping myself out in the country farming and ranching, so I hadn't really kept up with anyone or what was happening in town. There were a few people there that I knew though and then about 12:30 in the morning the pretty carhop, from Lands Drive-In walks in and everybody sees her and starts yelling for her to get a drink. You had to yell, because there was so much noise with the music going full blast and everyone talking that it was the only way to communicate. I was standing around visiting with a few of the guys that I knew and they would call someone over ever-so-often and introduce them to me and we would get to know each other like you do at a party and then someone called over the pretty Car Hop and she said that she knew who I was, because she had asked the owners of Lands Drive-In and they knew me, so they filled her in on me. I did know them but hadn't visited with them in a long time. She and I started talking and then she asked me to dance and we danced good together, so we danced several times and then ended up in a back, empty bedroom on the carpet making love. That was real-nice, because I hadn't had sex in a very long time and her body was much better than I had even imagined when I was watching her carry out orders at the Drive-In. I told her that I was married, and she said that she knew that, because her boss had told her. I asked if it bothered her and she said that it didn't and to prove it she wanted to see me again and wanted to know when we could meet, then she said that if I wanted to take her again that she would love it, so I did and it was even better that time. Well I knew that I was going to keep seeing her as long as she wanted to. This was just to good, because I was twenty-three and she was eighteen or nineteen, I wasn't sure, but you had to be at least eighteen to sell beer in Texas, so I knew she was eighteen or over. She gave me her phone number and I promised to call, and we would make plans. I didn't feel any guilt about this, because I didn't feel like I was cheating on my wife. In fact, I didn't feel like I even had a wife anymore, just a roommate. I still didn't want my wife to know about this though, because it might cause trouble in a divorce, so I would have to make sure that the girl knew that we would have to see each other on the sly. I talked to her about it and she was OK with it. She said that it was exciting and that she was all for it. This was about a little over a week before the end of May 1966. WCJC had about a week and a half to go before the graduation, so the guy had moved into my spare bedroom and all was going fine. He would leave the house the same time I did every morning to drive to Wharton to WCJC. That next Sunday I got up and made coffee and got ready to go to the ranch and everyone else was still sleeping. I left in my old pick-up and got about six blocks from my house and it quit running on me. I pulled over to the side of the road and opened the hood to see if I could determine what the trouble was. It had never just quit running like that for me. It was usually quite dependable. I had tools with me, so I started trouble shooting. First, I unscrewed the fuel line and cranked the motor over, and fuel shot out of the line, so it wasn't fuel. Next, I pulled a spark wire off and turned the motor over and it had no spark. Then I pulled the coil wire out and turned the motor over and there was no spark there. Well there was nothing to do but walk home and see if I could get someone on the phone to open the parts house for me to buy a new coil. I could get the College boy to take me to the parts house if I could get them to open up, or he could pull my pick-up home for me if I couldn't find anybody to open up. I walked home and cut through the back alley, so I wouldn't have to walk all the way around the block, and I went through the back yard and the back door into the kitchen. Then I got a surprise. I could see from the kitchen door into the living room and on the couch was my wife and the College boy naked having sex. I couldn't believe what is was seeing. I mean I had only been gone maybe an hour. Well I just leaned against the kitchen door frame and watched for maybe five minutes and they were so busy that they didn't notice me. Then I just backed up and went out the back door and walked to a convenience store about three blocks from the house and used the pay phone there to call a parts man I knew and he answered and he came over to the convenience and picked me up and we went to the parts house and I bought a coil and then he took me to my pick-up and waited for me to install the coil to make sure the pick-up would start and when it did, he left and I want on to the ranch. My wife and the College boy never knew that I had seen them having sex on the couch. I never said anything to him about it. It was only a few days before he was to leave for Corpus Christi and that would be over, but I was going to keep this to myself till I needed it. This was now the end of May 1966 and we were starting into summer. The College boy left for Corpus and I had second thoughts about seeing the young Car Hop that worked at Lands Drive-In. I was very busy at the farm helping with the rice crop and also working cattle. I had been working on all of my old machinery off and on as I had the time and it was now in good enough repair to work the land and get it ready for next year's planting. When I had time I would drop by Lands Drive-In and drink a couple of beers and the Car Hop would bring them to me, and ask me when we were going to get together, that she had decided to not date anyone else, because she only wanted to see me. I told her that I had been very busy working, but that I would start seeing her and we made a date to go out and have sex. I told her that it would have to be in my car, and she said that was fine and that it would be exciting. That summer I started seeing her about once a week and it was always in my car on a lonely country road. That summer I also tried to have sex with my wife a couple of times, and we completed the act, but the intimate feeling just wasn't there anymore, so I stopped trying. From then on all of my sexual activity was with the young Car Hop. I came home from work one evening in August and the College boy's car was parked in the front of my house. I walked in the house and he and my wife were sitting in the kitchen talking. I asked what he was doing in El Campo and he said that he had decided not to go to College in Corpus. He said that he had got a job in Houston and he was going to share an apartment with a friend there and he was just on his way through and wanted to stop to say hello and to thank me again for helping him out. We talked for a little while and then he left for Houston. I wondered if they had sex before I got home. Well what did it matter now.

Lorrie—It was almost May 1966 now and the girls met me at the airport when I flew in from Porto Rico. They asked how things were over there and how Surf Duke was, and I told them that everything was about the same there except there were some new young girls there for Surf Duke to pay attention to. They laughed and said that was the way it was with him. I told them that the first thing I had to do was find a doctor to get some medicine for this kidney infection and they said that they knew one that wasn't expensive. Lorrie got settled in with the two older girls in their apartment. A couple of days later she met them at the Rocket Club where they worked, one was a waitress and the other one was a Go-Go dancer, to see about the Go-Go dancer job there. She met the manager of the Club and he interviewed her to find out her age and other information for the job. He then put on some music and told her that she needed to show him how she could dance to it. There was a small round little stage about two feet high that was next to the band stand. This was where the Go-Go dancers performed. Lorrie was wearing shorts and a crop top, the same ones that she wore for her Bar Maid job in Porto Rico. She mounted the stage and danced to three different songs that the Manager had played, and he told her that she had the job. She was only twenty, but she had to have an ID that showed her to be twenty-one and she would have to make her own Go-Go outfit to wear while dancing. The manager said not to worry about the ID that he would have her one made, and she would have to come back the next day to show him what she came up with for a dancing outfit. He said that it needed to be sexy and also her and the other girl were to take turns on the dance stage and when she wasn't Go-Go dancing she was required to dance with the customers, also she would be paid minimum wage and she could keep all her own tips. She was so happy to find a job so quick and one that she could dance at all the time, because she had loved dancing from very young. Her and the girls went to a strip mall and did some shopping and she bought a pink stretch body suit, some white boots with tassels on them and a lot of white fringe to pin all over the body suite so it would shake all around while she was dancing she also bought a cheap overcoat to wear over the Go-Go outfit when she was walking to and from work, because she had to suit up at the apartment. Lorrie thought she looked very sexy dancing in it and when she went back to the Club the next day and performed in it for the Manager he was impressed and said that it should turn the men on watching that. So with this her Go-Go dancing career took off and it was now May 1966. Everything was great with her dancing job and she was making great tips, so she had some money to spend and pay her share of the rent. One of the girls moved out with her boyfriend and that left Lorrie and the other Go-Go dancer girl with each their own bedroom. Lorrie was really enjoying all the attention that she was getting from the men at the Club. When she was dancing with them, they all would ask her out after the Club closed and she told everyone of them that she would meet them in front of the Club after it closed. There would be five or six men waiting for her in the front and she would slip out the back door after closing and walk home. None of them ever got wise and checked the back door. She had a couple of real scares though. She excepted with one real handsome guy and got in his car and he drove her down on the beach and proceeded to tell her that if he wanted to he could kill her and no one would ever find her. She made the excuse that she had to go to the bathroom, so he let her out of the car and she ran off in the dark and when she got to the road a couple of Cops saw her walking and picked her up and took her home. She was sure glad to see them, because she was scared the guy would see her and follow her home and then he would know where she lived. Another time she excepted an after-hours date with this guy that seemed real-sweet. They were supposed to go to this real good place to eat and when they left the Club, he said that he had to go by his apartment to get some more money. When they got there, he invited her in while he got what he needed and he unlocked the door and let her go in first then when he was behind her he closed the door and locked both locks on it and Lorrie was scared to death. He immediately started grabbing her and trying to get her overcoat off. She fought him off and told him that she was going to scream and keep screaming and he settled down and then they got back in the car and she had him take her to some apartments that weren't hers and drop her off there. She waited in the dark for a-while, then she walked home. It was now June 1966 and she was still having a blast Go-Go dancing. The small band that always played there became great friends with her and they always tried to protect her from over aggressive men. They would let her know who to dance with and who to avoid, also they are the ones that let her out the back door and would check to see if the coast was clear there before she left. In June things changer at the Club. The owners decided to make it a Topless Club in June 1966 and Lorrie knew that would never work for her, because she had those small breasts. Her roommate though had the body to dance topless. The Manager of the Club gave her roommate a big raise in pay. So, she decided to dance topless. The Manager then gave Lorrie a waitress job there, so at least she had a job, but she missed the Go-Go Dancing. Lorrie had always had trouble with math and with so many people sitting around the tables she would get mixed up on the amount that each owed and also what drink went to who, but they were all patient with her and would help her out so she wouldn't get into trouble with the money and also the bartenders did all that they could to help her keep things straight. She said that she never got good at it.

Gus—It was now the middle of June 1966 and everything was going good at the farm and ranch and I was seeing the young Car Hop from Lands Drive-In and still living with my wife and she was still working at Caterpillar. At the farm we were still irrigating the rice, working cattle, fixing fences, bailing hay and I was training a couple of horses to make cow ponies out of them. I knew that the college boy was still coming to El Campo from Houston, because I would see some of his friends at Lands Drive-In and they would ask me if I had seen him when he was in town. I wondered if he was coming to town to see my wife, but I really didn't care anymore, so it didn't bother me, but what did bother me was that when I was sitting there in my car playing the radio and drinking beer that song "In The Still Of The Night" would play and I would think of Lorrie and be right back on that beech in Corpus kissing her and for a minute I would just wonder what she was doing, but that was a long time ago now. My Dad's health was getting worse and I was having to take over more of his responsibilities all the time, but I was up to it and I did it to the best of my ability. It was July 1966 now and we were starting to get the machinery ready for rice harvest that would start in a couple of weeks and that would be a very busy and exciting time. I had plowed the one hundred acres, that Dad had let me farm, a couple of times and it was just sitting there till the fall and I would have to re-work it and level it and put up rows so I could farm Milo Maze on it. My little cow herd was doing good and I was branding all the heifer calves to keep them for cows to add to my herd and it was growing year by year. Well we finally started harvesting rice and that went on till the end of August 1966. While harvest was going on, I didn't have much time to take out the young Car Hop or do anything else, because all my time and energy went into the harvest. I didn't know it at the time, but August 1966 would be another event that would bring big change in my life.

Lorrie—The waitress job at the Rocket Club in June 1966 was good for Lorrie, because the Club was extra busy since it became a Topless Club and the tips were real-good. Lorrie was still having the same trouble with getting mixed up on the drinks and the money, but it was all working out because everyone knew how she was, and they all helped her get it straight. She and the girl friend that now was the main stripper at the Club still shared the up-stairs apartment together, so her life had taken on a little bit of stability in a fashion. Ever since Lorrie had been back in Florida from Porto Rico, she hadn't had the time to get back to the surf boarding. Well, all of that had sort of disappeared because the friends had split up. First, she had left Surf Duke in Porto Rico and then one of the girl friends had left with her boyfriend and Lorrie and the other girl friend had been busy with their Bar jobs and a date ever now and then. She did get down to the beach ever once in a while to swim though, when she could wake-up early enough to get things done so she could go. June 1966 was now gone, and July 1966 was just as busy for Lorrie as it had ever been. The only time that she ever thought about Gus now was when that damn song "In The Still Of The Night" would play and she would drift back in time to when she was so happy on the beach with him and then she would think of that embarrassing time in her room and he didn't come back to take her virginity. Well that's OK, because Surf Duke did it and that was over with now. She got a surprise letter from the boyfriend of her cousin in Wyoming, that she had flirted with and stolen from her. He said that he got her address from her Mom and he was now working for the FBI in Washington DC. He said that some time, if Lorrie had the time, maybe she could fly to Washington DC and he would show her around. This sort of intrigued Lorrie, because she always thought of him as just a nice country boy and had never thought of him moving to a big city like Washington DC and working for the FBI. She wrote him back and told him that she would come and see him sometime, but she didn't make a date of it. Lorrie didn't know it now, but at the end of July 1966 something would happen that would take over her life and steer it in a direction that she didn't want and one that she was unprepared for.

Gus—1966 August 1966 we were still harvesting rice and we wouldn't get through till the first of September. August is also my birthday month and I will be twenty-four years old. August 1966 you might say was another milestone in my life. My wife informed me that she was pregnant. This was not the happy moment that it would have been for most married couples. All this did was to further complicate an already complicated situation. I didn't say too much at her announcement. I just listened and decided that this was something that I was going to have to put a lot of thought into, so as to come up with a decision. I was so busy at the time with the rice harvest that I knew that it would take me some time to be able to devote time and energy to work this out in my mind. There were a lot of different things and people to consider. In September, I finally found the time to be able to seriously contemplate the circumstances that we found ourselves in. I would work out a time that I could get off by myself in a quiet place and think things over. I went all the way back to that first time I caught my wife with that parts man where she worked. Then the things that happened after that I thought back on them, trying to look at each one to try to determine why things kept deteriorating in our relationship. I went step by step and even made a notation of each step to get the real picture in my mind, so I could read the landscape, to see where our marriage stood. I came to the conclusion that there was too much damage done to be able to save the marriage. I had tried to remember when the last time my wife and I had sex and concluded that it was too long ago for this baby to be mine. The most likely daddy was the College boy. I had a sit- down discussion with my wife about this and she admitted that she and the College boy had sex. She never said that she thought that I was the daddy. I told her that I thought that it was time that we thought about divorce and she cried and said she didn't want a divorce. I said that we needed to do something to make a new start on life and I didn't know what else to do, because in my opinion there had been to much damage done to our relationship for us to be able to trust each other again. I told her that I was going to go see a lawyer about it and that she needed to start thinking about moving out ant she needed to tell her family about it. I told her that I would never tell her family that she had cheated. She thanked me and said that it was going to be hard enough to tell her family and that if they knew that she had cheated it would go hard on her. I didn't tell her about the young Car Hop that I had been seeing and she didn't know about her. I went to see a lawyer as soon as I had enough time during the day for an appointment. I told him the truth about everything that had happened, even about me seeing the young Car Hop. I told him that I didn't think that I was the daddy of my wife's pregnancy. He told me that it might not be my bear, but that it was caught in my trap and that the State of Texas would not make an illegitimate child, so I could file for divorce, but the divorce wouldn't final till after the child was born and that the child would have my name. I decided to go ahead and file for the divorce, but it would be eight months before it would be final. In the meantime, my wife would move to her parent's house in another town and we would just wait the time out. I found out that the College boy was driving over to her parent's house to see her and that didn't surprise me. All that did was to convince me that my thoughts about the pregnancy were true. I went on with my work on the farm and ranch and I also kept seeing the young Car Hop.

Lorrie—1966 It was at the end of July 1966 Lorrie was upstairs in her apartment taking a bath getting ready to go to work at the Club and her landlady knocked on her door and told her that a Soldier was there to see her. Lorrie couldn't imagine who that Soldier could be, so she hurried up and got dressed to go down and see who it was. When she got downstairs and saw him, she was shocked to see that it was the cousin she was forbidden to see by her parents. She hadn't heard from him since she left El Campo. He said that after Blinn Junior College he had decided to join the Air Force and they stationed him there in Florida. He had gotten her address from his cousin, who was Lorrie's friend, the one that he had stayed with when they were in High School and Lorrie would go over there and they would watch TV, listen to music, dance and kiss around. Lorrie was really happy to see him and now there was no one to say that she couldn't see him. He said that he had written her letters and sent them to her Uncle and Aunt's house. He had gotten their address also from his cousin. Lorrie told him she had never received them and that they probably had thrown they away, because her parents had warned her Uncle and Aunt that Lorry wasn't to communicate or see him. He only had a twelve hour leave, so he wouldn't be able to stay very long, so he went to the Club where Lorrie worked and visited with her there and they made plans to be together the next weekend when he could get his next pass off base. He had to leave early to make it back so he wouldn't be AWOL. He told her that the next weekend was his birthday and he would try to get a twenty-four leave and they could celebrate his birthday together. Lorrie was tickled to death about this. Here was one more thing that her parents couldn't control anymore. Now she could do as she pleased and that is exactly what she was going to do. A week would give her time to ask her boss for some time off and also to think of something special to plan for his birthday. As the week went by, they stayed in touch by phone. He was granted his twenty-four leave and Lorrie got two nights off from work. Everything was set for their first date together by themselves ever. Lorrie was so excited, and she had high hopes for a very romantic night with him. She had thought and thought about what to get him for his birthday. This would be a very special day not just because it was his birthday, but also it was the first time they were to be together romantically since that terrible night of the football game at WCJC where they were caught behind the stands by her Dad and Mom and there was that big blow up and ultimately she was sent to Florida to live with her Uncle and Aunt. It was kind of funny now that the very place that her Dad and Mom had sent her to be away from him that he was stationed to by the Air Force. She bought some nice scented candles and some wine and made sure that the apartment was clean, and everything was in order. She picked out some of the forty-five records that they used to like to dance to when they were in El Campo and made sure that they were on top of the stack that they had in the apartment. Her girlfriend roommate was to stay with her other friend that had moved in with her boy- friend and that would leave the apartment just for them alone. Everything would just perfect and Lorrie had come up with the perfect gift for him. She was going to give him herself, meaning that she was going to make love to him. She had known him for a long time, and she didn't think that he would be turned off by her small breasts and he had seen her big feet and long legs a long time ago. She had some experience with sex now because of the time she had spent in Porto Rico with Surf Duke and now that experience would come in handy. She knew a small Cafe close enough to the apartment, to walk to, where they could eat dinner when he got there. She was really going to go all for his birthday, and it would be a day to remember for all time. The day finally came, and he showed up right on time late in the afternoon. He looked really nice in his uniform and Lorrie had on her best mini-skirt with a sleeveless, low-cut pull-over, a nice ribbon on her ponytail, her best flat shoes and some of her favorite cologne. She had also sprayed some of the cologne around the apartment and on the bed. Everything was perfect and when he came in the apartment, he kissed her, and he handed her a little wrapped up gift. She was surprised and she could tell that it must be a record and she bet that it was one that they always like to dance to, and that would be good, because she didn't have that one. They sat down close to each other on the couch and he was anxious for her to unwrap the record, so she tore into it and then she couldn't believe what she saw. She just froze and didn't know what to do. He waited a minute and said don't you like that song, it's one of the good old ones. She was quiet and barely heard him, because she was looking at "In The Still Of The Night" by The Five Satins. Oh My God she thought, Gus is going to ruin everything that I have planned. Then she thought that it was an omen, that he was going to not like her body like Gus and he would run out of the apartment when he saw her naked. She shook herself out of the trance she was in and told him how sweet it was to bring her a gift, but it was his birthday not hers and that she was going to give him his birthday present after they went to eat dinner and came back to the apartment. Now she was nervous about having sex with him and she had been so confident before that damn record showed up. Well she was going to go through with it anyway and hope for the best. Lorrie put the record on the bottom of the stack of the forty-five records and they went out to the Cafe to have a nice dinner. The small Cafe she had chosen had a nice table in a corner that would provide some privacy and they would be able to talk without anyone over hearing. The time they were there it wasn't too crowded ant he table had a nice white long table cloth and napkins. Lorrie asked for a lit candle to be put on the table. They ate baked chicken with vegetables and drank two glasses of wine each and the wine was starting to have a nice warmth in her stomach and it also was loosening her up and wiping out the shock of seeing that damn record. She took off one shoe and started to rub his leg under the table to his shock. She had never had the chance to do that and her girl friend told her that it was a good trick to get a man in the mood for a romantic evening. She smiled as sexy as she could while she rubbed his leg and he didn't quite know what to think. At first, he looked a little embarrassed, but soon seemed to enjoy it. Lorrie thought that he must never had that done to him before. She wondered what else he didn't know about a sexual experience with a woman. Well she would find out. The dinner went really nice, and they walked arm in arm and kissed a little going back to the apartment. By the time they reached the apartment and got inside the timing was perfect, because it was getting dark and she could light the scented candles in the bedroom and the small sitting room with the couch. Then she put on some of the music that they used to like and she helped him off with his uniform jacket and his tie and she unbuttoned his shirt four buttons so she could slide her in there to his bare chest and rub his nipple when the time came. She opened the bottle of wine that she had put in the ice box and poured two glasses and set them om the table by the couch. They sat on the couch and kissed and then they would get up and dance and Lorrie would dance closer then she had ever done when they had been in El Campo and she had learned another trick and that was to put her leg between his and use it to rub on his penis to get it hard and it worked at once. She could tell that he was nervous, and she liked the power she seemed to have on him, because all of a sudden, she for the first time was in complete charge of what would happen. He seemed not to know what to do next, but he would do whatever she led him to do. While the music was playing she took him by the hand and led him into the bedroom where she unbuttoned his shirt and unbuckled his belt, then she took his hands in hers and together they lifted her pull-over off and then she took the ribbon from her pony tail and let her hair fall to her shoulders. She then took his shirt off him and unbuttoned his pants and let them slip to the floor and then she stepped out of her mini-skirt and got under the bed covers before she removed her bra and her panties. She was still cautious about him seeing her completely naked and she was glad that there was only dim candlelight in the room. He removed his cloths and got under the bed covers with her and she wrapped herself around him and started passionately kissing him. He had always been good at kissing, so this was a very good start to their love making. While they kissed Lorrie took his hand and moved it to her breast and he squeezed it to hard and it made her flinch, but he seemed not to notice, so she moved it down on her thigh and then she put her hand on his hard penis and he finally got the message that he was to massage her crotch, but he instead immediately just poked his finger in her and began moving it back forth at a rapid speed. This was unsettling for Lorrie, so she removed his hand and then she opened her legs and pulled him over on top of her. Finally he was in her, but he was sweating and pumping fast and breathing like he had run a mile and then it was over with and he laid on her stomach and was shaking, sweating and breathing hard and Lorrie just laid there holding him and wondering what had gone wrong. She had planned everything so well, so romantic for this first time of love making between them and this was all there was to it. Well she had got all her ideas from what had happened when Surf Duke had made love to her for the first time and she had tried to follow those same plans, but this was over rather fast. Lorrie had thought that their love making might go on for a long time. Well maybe he would start kissing on her again and they would start all over again. She told him that she had to go to the bathroom, so he moved off of her and she went to the bathroom and peed and washed up a little to get his sweat off her and by the time she got back into bed he was asleep. She was shocked and didn't know what to do except let him sleep. She got up out of bed and went to the sitting room and blew out the candles and then blew the candles out in the bedroom, she put on her panties and bra and got into the bed under the covers and just laid there and thought about their first sexual experience together. She woke up first the next morning about the same time she always woke up on days she had to work at the Club. Since she always worked late, she woke up about 10:00 am in the morning. She went to the bathroom, brushed her teeth, hair put on some cologne and her robe and then she woke him up and told him that she was going to make some coffee and he needed to go get cleaned up, so they could drink coffee and talk and then she would make them something to eat. He went to the bathroom to take a bath, shave and get ready. While he was getting bathed and dressed Lorrie busied herself making the coffee and picking up the wine glasses and washing them up and straitening the couch pillows and the covering throw. He came in and she served the coffee in the sitting room. They sat on the couch together and he kissed her a sweet little kiss and he told her that he loved her. She knew that she didn't love him, because there wasn't even the electricity between them as there was when Gus had kissed her and when their bodies were together she didn't feel the magnetism that she had felt when her body and Gus's were together in her room in El Campo. That is how she knew that she hadn't loved Surf Duke. So, all she did was to put her finger on his lips, and she told him that they still had a lot to learn about each other and it was much too early to talk about love. In the apartment small kitchen, she fixed a very late breakfast of scrambled eggs, bacon, toast, orange slices and coffee. It was now about 12:00 noon and he would have to be leaving very soon to get back to the Air Force Base. She called a cab for him and he walked around looking to make sure that he had everything back in his grip bag. They sat on the couch talking, avoiding discussion on the sex of the night before, like it was an embarrassing subject, and instead talked about what had happened since he had joined the Air Force and what future that he thought it might hold for him. She was impressed with his attitude toward making a career out of the military. He said that he needed to finish his College education so he could become an officer. She knew that he could do it, because he had always been very smart in High School. It came time for him to leave, so she went down with him to catch the cab and kissed him good-by, and he told her that he would call her when he got back to the base. She watched the cab drive away and then slowly made her way back up to the apartment deep in thought. She went in and washed up the breakfast dishes, cleaned up the kitchen and sat down on the couch with a glass of wine that was left over from the night before. All of a sudden, she realized that she was relieved that he was gone. She thought, why was this, she should be sad that he had to leave, but she wasn't sad at all. She needed this time alone to think about what had transpired since the day before and the reason for how she was feeling now. Everything had been nice, but her expectations of the big romantic love making encounter were not fulfilled. On the contrary it was a big disappointment. What had gone wrong. She thought that this morning that they would feel even closer together then they had before, because sharing sex between them should have welded a closer and stronger bond, but the opposite was the case. They didn't talk about it, they didn't kiss passionately this morning or try to have sex again. It was almost like it had pushed them apart. She would have to think about all of this. She sipped her wine and then she remembered that damn record that he had brought her. God it could have messed up the whole thing, but thankfully she had put it away and had forgot about it. Lorrie thought, where did I put it. Then she remembered and she went to the stack of 45 RPM records and retrieved it from the bottom of the stack with the idea of breaking it in half and throwing it into the trash, but she just stood there looking at it and all of a sudden she found herself turning on the record player and putting on the record and pushing play. Then she picked up her wine glass and took a sip and the song started playing and she wrapped her arms around herself and started dancing slowly to the music "In The Still Of The Night", and she was transported back to 1962 on the beach with Gus and she was dancing slowly with him and it was as beautiful as it was then and then the song was over and she was all by herself standing in the middle of her sitting room in the little apartment and she fell on the couch and started sobbing and babbling, oh Gus, oh Gus, why couldn't this have been us, why couldn't this have been us. The next thing that she knew was that the telephone was ringing and it was him on the phone telling her that he had made it back on base on time and he was sorry that he had been a little slow in calling, because when he got back he had a message that he needed to go see the Duty Officer and he found out from that on Tuesday he was being sent to another Air Force Base for a month of training, so he wouldn't be seeing her for at least a month and maybe more. She wished him luck and told him that she would be thinking about him and then said good-by. She thought that she sure would be thinking about him, but not in a romantic way, but just to try to figure out if there could be a future between them. Well if nothing else she had scratched off one more thing that she was prohibited from doing by her parents when she was living in El Campo, by being with him. She had slept several hours on the couch and she went to the record player and removed the record and just looked at it for a minute and ran her fingers over it, like you would rub a bottle to make a Genie come out to give you your wish. She got lump in her throat and all of a sudden she bent it and broke it in half and threw it in the trash and she said oh Gus you won't let me live my life, somehow you always show up to let me know how miserable I am, it's not May 1962, it's the end of July 1966 and I'm not 16 years old, I'm 20 years old and I wonder who you are with and if you are happy, because I am not, but I can put up a good front, I can be a good actress.

Gus—1966 August 1966 had been a very stressful month with all the harvest going on and also the announcement by my wife that she was pregnant We had been married four years and had always used some type of birth control and she hadn't managed to get pregnant all that time and now that she had been having sex with that young College boy she was suddenly pregnant. Well that is what happens. I guess it is like the old saying that he was poking fun at her, and she took it serious. The start of September wasn't any better with having to go through the business of getting a Lawyer, filing for Divorce and moving my wife to her parent's house in another town. At least now when I had the time, I could see the young Car Hop and not hide out about it. I had also started getting my one hundred acres of land ready for next year's planting. This was to be the first year that I would actually have my own crop to plant, care for and harvest. I was betting everything that I had on that crop that would be harvested in 1967, because the Bank had required everything that I owned for collateral on the loan, so there was a lot of stress building on me to get the land in as good of shape as I could, put it in rows, apply the pre-plant fertilizer and keep the winter weeds from taking over the land before the planting season would start which would be the first of March 1967. Between working and spending time with the Car Hop it was about all I could do. I was having serious misgivings about my relationship with her. The more time I spent with her the more I just wanted to find how to get out of the relationship. She was young and seemed not to have a serious thought in her head. When we were at my house, she didn't have any desire to pick up anything, cook anything, wash anything, take any interest in what I was doing or talk about real life. All she wanted to do was have sex, which was fine, but there are other things to consider also. I have to say that she was good at the sex part, but that is about all that I can say about the relationship between us. Oh well I guess that this is about all that I could expect from someone just barely eighteen years old. I can take care of myself on all of the basics of life, so I don't really need a wife type person. I guess that sex is the only thing that I can't furnish for myself, so I guess that she is furnishes something. I am still trying to get reorganized after my wife moved to her parent's house. All the things that you have to replace after she had stripped the house of almost everything. I was left one bed, one living room chair, my Grand Mothers pots and pans and dishes and cook stove, one spoon, one fork, one knife, one drinking glass and one coffee cup. I didn't have much money, so replacing things would be slow and some of it would come from garage sales and things that I found on the side of the road that had blown off of someone's truck when they were moving. For an example I was going to the farm one morning and I saw a wooden kitchen chair in the ditch, so I pulled over and got it. It was broken up pretty bad, but I used glue, nails and wire and I fixed it enough to use at the old little kitchen table I had found at a garage sale for five dollars. It was nice to be able to sit down to eat now. Well this was how September of 1966 was going. I didn't know it yet, but October was going to blow my mind and change everything in my life for the worst.

Lorrie—1966 It's August 1966 now and I haven't heard much from my Air Force guy. I get a phone call every weekend when I'm not working, and in the apartment to get it, because he is so busy with his new training. I'm starting to really wonder about this relationship. I am starting to think about trying to get in touch with the boy from Wyoming that I took away from my cousin that summer when Gus didn't come back. He works now for the FBI in Washington DC and maybe I can go see him and see if there is any chemistry between us, because he was such a nice boy and he was real taken with me at the time. After all he has contacted me, so maybe I should go and see what it's all about. My Air Force guy is going to be gone a month on training, so that will give me enough time to go see the FBI Agent and get everything sorted out to see which way I am going to direct my energy. Lorrie waited about a week to build up her courage to call the FBI Agent. He was very glad to hear from her and they made a date for the following weekend. She was to fly into DC, and he was to pick her up at the airport. She took some of her nicer cloths, because they were supposed to go to dinner and dancing after he was going to show her around Washington DC, and she was to spend the night at his apartment. She took some sexy sleep wear with her just in case things got to that point and she hoped that they wood, so she could compare the difference between the two guys at their approach to having sex. She hadn't been impressed with the Air Force guy at all. I mean with him he was fumbling around, and it was all over in maybe two minutes. Even Surf Duke did a lot better than that, but of course he had a lot of experience and Lorrie came to the conclusion that The Air Force guy must have been a virgin himself, because he certainly didn't know the first thing about sex with a girl. Lorrie thought that even she knew more, and she had only one lover in Surf Duke, but also her girlfriends had told her a lot of things that a man should do, if he was any lover at all. The weekend finally came around and Lorrie flew to Washington DC with the hopes that the spark from two years ago would burn bright again. She knew that she hadn't wanted him at the time when she stole him from her cousin, in 1962, she had done it only because she was being a bitch, because Gus had turned his back on her and she was trying to see if boys would go for her, to rebuild her self-confidence about her desirability to attract them. Well Lorrie was going to see how this was going to turn out. He met her at the airport and presented her with flowers and gave her a kiss on the cheek. Things were off to a good start. They went to his apartment to leave Lorrie's luggage and then they went to a small cafe and ate a lite lunch. He had planned a lot of sight-seeing for them to do, so they spent all afternoon doing that and that was fine, but it wasn't Lorrie's main objective. She was hoping to spend more time at his apartment that afternoon to be able to feel him out more about his feelings and to see if he liked to have a little private party there with some wine or beer and music and personal conversation. She wanted to try to figure how his mind ticked and sight-seeing wasn't going to do it. He was just like she had remembered him being thoughtful and with a sweet nature, but also, he had matured more, and he was more handsome. While they were sight-seeing, he never tried to hold her hand or rub against her or kiss her. He was the perfect gentleman. Well Lorrie thought this evening when we go to dinner and dance, I will see the difference and he is going to get romantic and things will proceed from there, because I will help it along. They went to a very nice restaurant that also had live music and it was a little high class from what Lorrie had been used to and also, she felt like she didn't have the right cloths or hairdo for the occasion. He was very polite and would pull the chair out for her and wait for her to decide what she wanted to order and he would get up and pull out her chair when she went to the restroom and just everything that a gentleman should do, but Lorrie wasn't used to this and it left her a little off balance. The meal was great, and the band was very good, except they didn't play rock-n-roll or country and western, it was more ball room music. Lorrie thought OK I can do that, so finally he asked her to dance. He was a long way from the best dance partner she had ever had, but at least he was trying and that was more than Surf Duke did. He never danced with her. She ordered wine with her dinner and he had water and she had several glasses of wine before they left at 11:00 pm to go to his apartment. Lorrie had to have the wine to loosen her up, because the evening was great, but it was also very dull to her. She was wanting romance in the way that she imagined romance to be and not this old-folks type of building up to who knows what. They went to his apartment and they changed their cloths and she put on some very short shorts and a crop top that was also pretty small, touched up her make-up and refreshed her favorite cologne, Schalamar. When she came into his living room, he was sitting on the couch wearing slacks, a long sleeve pull-over and tie shoes. He was looking through some 78 RPM long play records, not the usual 45 RPM that Lorrie was used to. Again, the music was orchestra. Lorrie asked him if he had changed his taste for music, because she had remembered that when she was in Wyoming Lorrie, her cousin and he were playing the latest rock-n-roll. He said that yes, he had grown out of that ever since he had moved to DC, because everyone there preferred this kind of music and he had developed a liking for it. Well OK Lorrie would still try to light the fire under him. She sat close to him and propped her left arm on the back of the couch and pulled one leg under her so she could sit sideways, but still be touching him and this way she could look him right in the face and maybe he would kiss her with her lips that close to him. They talked about their lives after High School, but there was a hell of a lot that Lorrie wasn't about to tell him. It was 2:00 am in the morning when he suggested that they needed to go to bed and he hadn't tried to kiss her yet. Time was running out real fast. He got up and waited for her to get up then he led the way to his spare bedroom that he had made ready for her and he grasp one of her hands and kissed her on the cheek and told her good night and that he had set his alarm so they would get up in time have coffee there and visit some more and go down to that nice little cafe for breakfast before it was time to take her to the airport. Lorrie lay awake for a long time just trying to put everything in perspective. She was certain that there wasn't any chemistry between them. He was the same sweet boy that she remembered, but that was all, and she could see that they could never be anything but friends. Lorrie thought what a stupid idea she had in flying all the way to Washington DC to check out a possible romance that could stem from the terrible way that she had treated her girl cousin by stealing her boyfriend four years ago. At least he hadn't wanted to play "In The Still Of The Night". Why was she thinking of that damn song again at a time like this? He came into her room early in the morning and she woke easily, because she had slept fitfully. She went to the bathroom and showered and got herself dressed and packed up to leave, because they would leave for the airport directly from the cafe that they were going to for breakfast. He had made coffee and orange juice and they sat and enjoyed their coffee and juice and he gave her his business card and told her that if she ever needed him for anything that she could reach him at work during the week. They left for the cafe and Lorrie didn't feel like anything heavy, so she just sipped on her coffee and ate a pastry. They left for the airport and he walked her to her departure area and waited to send her off when the flight was called and he hugged her and gave her a little kiss on the cheek and told her that he really enjoyed seeing her after all those years. He said for her to keep in touch that she had his numbers and she entered the plane for the flight back to Florida. The flight was smooth but all of a sudden Lorrie started feeling a little dizzy and then sick at her stomach, so she made her way to the restroom and vomited her breakfast up. She washed her face and thought what could be making me sick, I only had coffee, orange juice and a pastry to eat, then she went back to her seat and a few minutes later she felt sick at her stomach again and went into the restroom and vomited again. She washed her face with cold water and went back to seat and thought that she must have air sickness from flying, but she had never had it before, and she had flown several times. The lady Flight Attendant came buy and Lorrie stopped her and ask her if she had anything for air sickness and she questioned Lorrie about her symptoms. Lorrie told her what had been happening and the Flight Attendant ask her if she was pregnant. This shocked Lorrie, because she had never even thought about getting pregnant. The Flight Attendant told her that maybe she shouldn't take an air sickness pill if she was pregnant, so Lorrie didn't take it. Now Lorrie was worried, because she sure didn't want to be pregnant. Well she would just let this go, because it probably wasn't anything to worry about. Just look at all the times that her and Surf Duke had sex and she hadn't got pregnant, so it couldn't happen from just one quick time with her Air Force guy. No, this must be something else, maybe she was catching a stomach flu of some sort. She would deal with it when she got back to the apartment in Florida. The plane landed and her girlfriend roommate and her boyfriend picked her up from the airport and took her to her apartment. She unpacked and what the Flight Attendant told her was still ringing in her ears, but she refused to believe something like that. In fact, she refused to believe a word of it, it just wasn't possible. It had to be the stomach flu and she would take something to settle her stomach down. She took her temperature and had none. Well maybe it was all over with anyway. She was in such a dither now that she was glad that she didn't have to work till the next day. She usually slept late in the mornings, but decided to get up early to see how she was going to feel, in the mean time she was going to eat some soft food like cream of wheat to pamper her stomach and take something to line her stomach and settle it down. The rest of the day she basically just took it easy and then went to bed early. The next morning, she got up early, her roommate was still sleeping, and she put the coffee on and then went to the bathroom to pee and wash her face and get dressed. She walked into the little kitchen and the nausea hit her hard, so she ran back to the bathroom and hugged the toilet and vomited and vomited till she thought her guts would come out. She took her temperature and it showed that she didn't have any. This was very confusing to Lorrie. How could she be feeling so sick and not have at least some temperature? All of a sudden, she was afraid to drink any coffee and her throat was burning from all the acid she threw up, so she just sat down to a big glass of water to cool her throat and to see if it would stay down. She wanted to ask her roommate some questions, because she was older and more experienced about these things, but she was still sleeping, so Lorrie just went back to bed till her roommate woke up. Lorrie's roommate finally woke up and Lorrie was waiting to leap like a cat on a mouse. Lorrie started telling her what was going on and her roommate told her to wait till she got some coffee down so she could make since out of what Lorrie was saying. After about thirty minutes her roommate told Lorrie to calm down and start from the beginning. Lorrie told her about having sex with her Air Force boyfriend, which she hadn't told her before, then she told her about what happened on the flight back to Florida with the Flight Attendant. Lorrie told her that she couldn't see how she could be pregnant, because she and Surf Duke had a lot of sex when she was in Porto Rico and she hadn't gotten pregnant, so how could she get pregnant with that one time, two or three minutes, of sex with the Air Force guy get her pregnant.

Her roommate just laughed and told her that she was sorry for laughing, but it was entirely possible, because Surf Duke had a Vasectomy. Lorrie just looked at her perplexed and said what is that, so her roommate explained it to her. Lorrie said that Surf Duke never told her that he had one. She told her that he would say that they couldn't have sex in her fertile period and he always knew when it was. Lorrie's room-mate just laughed and laughed till tears came in her eyes and she told Lorrie that Surf Duke was always like that with the young girls because they didn't know the difference and how could he ever know when her fertile period was, that it would be hard for her to figure it out itself and that it wasn't an exact science anyway. Her roommate told her to just look at the Catholic women that used that method of birth control and see how many kids that have. Lorrie was all down-in-the-dumps now. Her roommate told her that they would go to the local Drug Store and buy one of the do-it-yourself Home Pregnancy Test kits. That they weren't expensive and that they were supposed to be pretty accurate. That was what they did and when they got back to the apartment Lorrie just sat down and looked at as if it was going to bite her. Her roommate asked her when she was going to go into the bathroom and use it and Lorrie said she was afraid of the results. Her roommate told her that not using it wouldn't change whether she was pregnant or not, so Lorrie went into the bathroom and used it. In about five minutes her roommate heard Lorrie crying, so she went in the bathroom and Lorrie was sitting on the toilet with her head in her hands just crying her eyes out. She said that it showed positive, so now what was she supposed to do!! Lorrie's roommate told her that the first thing that she needed to do was to tell her Air Force guy that he got her pregnant and see what his response would be. Lorrie told her that she wouldn't hear from for another week. Lorrie said that she couldn't call him, because of his training and that he only could call her on the weekends, so she would have to wait. Lorrie told her roommate that getting pregnant never seemed like a real possibility to her. She said that facing the reality of it was hard for her to do, because this was going to change her whole life and that it would mean that she was going to miss the whole exciting time that she should have had in her twenties before deciding on who to marry and settle down after her twenties. She didn't want to get married now and she wasn't in love with anyone and didn't think that she could ever be in love with anyone except, Gus. Lorrie continued to go to work as usual, but every morning she was deathly sick at her stomach. She was just glad that it wasn't at night and she could still go to work. That weekend her Air Force guy called her, and she couldn't wait to talk small talk, so she went right to the subject that had dominated her mind for a whole week. She told him that she had something that was very important to tell him and that he need to listen carefully to what she had to say. She didn't tell him that she had first found out about the pregnancy when flying back from Washington DC after going to see another boy. Oh, he didn't need to hear that, so she just said that she had been feeling sick in the mornings and she had done the Home Pregnancy Test and it was positive, now what were they going to do. He was quiet for a minute and then he told her that they would just have to get married. They discussed this for a few minutes, and he said that he wasn't twenty-one yet, so he would have to call his Mom and get her to sign the License Application so he could marry her. Lorrie was twenty and the legal age in Florida for a girl was eighteen, so she was OK, but for a boy it was twenty-one. Lorrie was nervous about calling his Mom, because she wasn't to sure what his Mom thought about her, but it had to be done. He told her that he was going to finish this training class in one more week and then he would be back at the Air Force Base in Florida and they would get together then and call his Mom together and then they would start trying to figure what they had to do to get organized. Lorrie hung up and cried, not from happiness, but in sorrow. Lorrie thought to herself, Oh My God, I'm not even twenty-one yet and I haven't even been on my own for a year and look how I have screwed things up for myself, forever. If only Gus would have come back this wouldn't have happened.

Gus—1966 September 1966 had been a constant drain on my physical and emotional strength, because of filing for my divorce and working almost night and day for myself and my Dad as his physical strength was becoming less and less due to his poor health. His mind was still good, thank goodness, because I still had a lot to learn and all the years of his experience and I needed to be able to pick his brain for information from time to time. He was never very good with explaining things to me as I grew up and it was no different now. His old way of teaching me something was to give me a certain job to do and give me very little instructions on how he wanted it done. In his mind he always had a certain way he wanted things done, but he wouldn't go into detail on that. The way I learned was to go ahead and do the job that he had given me to do and when he came to look at what I did if he didn't like it, he would jump all over me and make me do it again. If he came up and looked it over and left without saying anything, then I knew that he couldn't find anything wrong with it. He never bragged on the job I did or gave me credit for a good job. I longed for him to do that. Now things had changed in our relationship some. He couldn't get around to see everything, so he had to depend on me for a change. This gave me the latitude to be semi in charge enough to make decisions and then be able to discuss problems with him without him actually nit-picking everything apart, because something wasn't done exactly his way. September had gone into October 1966 and I was busy working cattle, gathering the last of the big calves to sell and the old cows to sell before winter and vaccinating the young calves. There was constant field work either for my Dad or for my own work. Late one evening when I came home from work, the young Car Hop was sitting on my front steps looking sort of glum. I was tired and I really didn't want to see her that evening. She was supposed to be working at the Drive-Inn and I thought, well I guess that she got fired for something. She got up and I gave her a little kiss and unlocked the door and we went in the house. She was kind of quiet. Usually she would have some chatter about a girlfriend or her dis-functional family that I wasn't interested in hearing to tell me. I was stripping off my dirty cloths, washing my hands and face and looking forward to just sitting down for a minute with a big glass of tea to unwind. When I finally succeeded in doing this, she sat down at the kitchen table with me and told me that she had something important to talk over with me. I said OK tell me. She said that she had missed her period this month and it was almost time for it again and she was afraid that she might be pregnant. I just looked at her a minute and then I told her, how can you be pregnant, I use condoms every time e have sex. She said yes, but don't you remember that one broke while we were doing it and we didn't know it till we were through. I thought for a minute and then remembered it, but I couldn't remember when it had happened. I told her that she needed to wait and see if she would have her period and if she didn't, then we would see what we were going to do. She said that if she was pregnant that her Dad would beat her and kick her out of the house. She said that she would run away and go to live with her older sister in Louisiana. I thought that she might be right about her Dad, because of all the things I had heard about him, I could easily see that he might be a brutal SOB. I ask her if she was going to work and she said that she had taken the evening off, because she was so upset about this. I told her to try not to think about it and go on home, that I was too tired to have her here tonight and that time would tell us what we were to do. She left and I thought damn, this is just what I need with all the other troubles I have to deal with right now. I might have two women in my life pregnant. My wife pregnant with College boy's baby and the Car Hop with my baby, what a mess that will be. I started counting up the months and realized that even if everything went good with my Divorce it wouldn't be final till at least April or May depending when my wife's baby was born. Damn, if my Car Hop girlfriend was really pregnant there was a chance that I wouldn't even be divorced in time to marry her to have my child be born legitimate. What a mess all this could be. Well nothing that I could do about it now but wait and see what was going to happen and to try and not let it affect my work or my sleep which I need really bad right now. The next morning, I woke up as usual at 5:00am and the first thing that I thought of, as I was drinking my coffee, was the Car Hop girlfriend being pregnant. Wow, my life was getting more and more complicated all the time. It seemed like I was getting boxed in with all of these woman troubles. It looked like a very long time before I could get things straightened out to just lead a normal life. I wonder if all of life is this completed. I guess that I have no-one to blame except myself. I shouldn't have chosen my wife just to settle me down so I would study for College. I should have waited and found some sweet girl that I really loved. How in the hell do you really know if you love a girl? I am sitting there at my little kitchen table drinking my coffee thinking all these things, then out of the blue I think of that sweet, cute Lorrie. I think of her and me on the beach at Corpus and those wonderful kisses and the record that she put in my car with our song "In The Still Of The Night" and it gives me pleasure to think of it, because it was so sweet and there wasn't any trouble with her. So different then what was happening now. I wondered if she was married to some lucky boy now and I hoped that she was happy where-ever she was. Well that was May 1962, and this is October 1966, what a difference four years can make in my miserable life. October went by and in November the Car Hop told me that she had missed her second period. Now things are getting serious, so I told her that I would marry her when my Divorce was final and that seemed to settle her down, so she wasn't so afraid. I really, really didn't want to marry this girl. I wished that I hadn't ever seen her before. I was so tormented that I seemed to be afraid to have sex with her, like that would keep her from being pregnant. I thought, Gus you idiot what are you doing, you had just as well go ahead and have sex with her, because you can't get her any more pregnant. So, I started to settle down to the realization that

I was probably stuck with this girl whether I wanted to be or not and I had better make my mind up to make the best of it. Maybe I would be able to train her to be a wife and mother with time. A couple of days later she came to me and told me that she had told her Mom and her Mom had told her Dad and he wanted to talk to me tomorrow night at 7:00pm. I told her that I would be there. She told me to watch him, because they ever knew what he would about things. I came home a little early from work and got cleaned up to go to the meeting with the Car Hop's Dad. I drove over to their dilapidated house and the minute I walked into the house her sister said what's up slick dick. I just looked at her and then The Car Hop came up to me and pointed to a doorway that was covered with a curtain and told me that her Dad was waiting in there to talk to me. I pushed the curtain aside and walked in and introduced myself and neither of us offered a hand for a handshake. He was a big man with iron gray hair that was cut close in a flat top. He motioned for me to sit down and I did so. He opened the conversation, if you could call it that, with a demand. He said that since she was a minor and I had gotten her pregnant he would overlook it and not go to the Police to report me, if I would pay him fifteen thousand dollars. I could not believe what I was hearing from him. This should have been a time for me to be afraid and I am sure that he had planned it that way to scare me into paying him, but he had misjudged me. The opposite happened. This for some reason struck me as being funny and it was all I could do not to break out laughing. I told him that I wasn't going to pay him anything and I didn't take kindly to black mail and that she was eighteen years old. He told me that she was only seventeen and not eighteen and that made her a minor. I said then why was she serving beer at the Lands Drive Inn when the Law required her to be eighteen to serve alcoholic beverages and he said that she had told them that she was eighteen and since she looked like she was they didn't check her out. I told him that she was over the age of sixteen and that was the age of consent in Texas and he could do whatever he wanted to do about it, but I planned on marrying her, but I absolutely was not going to pay him fifteen thousand dollars. Then I got up and walked out of that little room and out of the house without saying good-by to anybody. The Car Hop came running after me and asked me what happened, and I told her not to worry about it and I would tell her about it the next time we were together. I kissed her good night and drove home and didn't let his black mail attempt bother me anymore. October 1966 was coming to an end and November 1966 was upon us and that would be the beginning of the Holiday Season and I didn't feel like I could get in the mood to celebrate anything.

Lorrie—1966 October 1966 was a time of transition for Lorrie. She was having to plan to leave behind the life of the free, single girl for the life of a wife and mother. This seemed like two lives that were at the other ends of the earth from each other. When they had called his Mom and he told her that he was going to marry Lorrie, the first thing that his Mom asked was if Lorrie was pregnant and he told her that she was. His Mom said that she was against him getting married so young, but in that case, she would sign his application to get married. She said that she wouldn't be down there for the wedding, but that she wished him the best. Lorrie thought, well she didn't ask to talk to me, or even say HI to me and she didn't wish us the best, she only wished her son the best. When Lorrie called her parents and told them she was marrying that boy that she was never supposed to see again they were astonished, because they had no idea that he was even in the picture anymore. She told them that they were going to have just a very small civil ceremony and that they would try to come back to El Campo for Thanksgiving if he could get a few days leave. Her parents were not excited about it, but they did not openly voice their objections. There was a lot to do to get ready for the wedding, not that it was going to be a big one, but there were things for him to take care of with the Air Force about paper work on everything that involves a married couple and that would take time to run through the proper channels. It looked like it was going to almost be November 1966 before they could get married. There were still a lot of days when Lorrie was sick and vomiting. Lorrie went to work as usual as a waitress at the Club and when her now fiance came to see her on his days of leave they would stay at her apartment and try to plan their future. He was interested in making the Air Force his career and Lorrie didn't have any problem with that. He said that for him to make officer grade he would have to get a College Degree and that would mean he had to spend a lot of time studying and writing papers. Lorrie told him that she would be glad to help him any way that she could. At lease they were off to a good start on agreement about his career. They finally got married and rented a small trailer house off Base to live in and Lorrie quit her waitress job at the Club. Lorrie was now twenty-one years old. Her birthday had been on October 26, 1966, but she was feeling much older, because she was sick a lot and also sort of depressed about going back to El Campo to her parents with a husband that she knew that they wouldn't like and she also was worried about hiding the fact that she was several months pregnant, when they had only been married a short time. He did get his Thanksgiving leave and they traveled to El Campo to have Thanksgiving with Lorrie's parents. This was a very tense time for Lorrie, because of several different reasons. First her parents had disliked her husband ever since she was in High School and getting her away from him, was the main reason they sent her to live with her Uncle and Aunt in Florida. That had all backfired on them and she knew that they were very unhappy with her marriage to him, but also for her to be pregnant with a grand baby that was of his blood would not be a happy moment for her to share with them. Lorrie chose to hide this from them. She was worried about being sick around them and thought of ways to avoid them knowing it if it occurred, she was starting to gain a little in her stomach, so she chose clothing that had some room there to hide that. She knew that they had to find out about her pregnancy sooner or later, but she preferred for it to happen when she was back in Florida and she didn't have to face them in person with it. They stayed three days and there weren't many bright spots in the visit. Her husband and her Dad mixed like oil and water and her husband tried to go visiting by himself as much as possible and Lorrie was glad of that because when he was gone there was less tension. If her parents suspected that she was pregnant they didn't mention it, to Lorries relief, because if her Mom would have asked that question, she knew that she would have broken down and cried. Lorrie saw a couple of her High School friends for short visits and she wanted to ask them if they had seen Gus, but she refrained from asking them. Using an excuse to go to the store for something, she did drive by Gus's Mom and Dad's house to see if she could see him standing outside there for Thanksgiving Holiday, but no one was outside and she didn't know what kind of car Gus would be driving, but as she got closer to that house a lot of memories came back to her like times when she would ride her bicycle around there or walk around there just to get a glimpse of Gus and she was getting the same excited feeling with the anticipation that she might see him. If she did see Gus would she have stopped to talk to him, she thought, but then she started crying softly and knew that she would never be able to have Gus now, no not now. She dried her eyes and went back to her parents and acted like nothing had happened. It was going on five years since she had seen or heard anything about Gus, but she couldn't forget him. She thought about him less and less, but he was still there in her heart and he always would be, but she just had to push him down deep now.

Gus—1966 November 1966 found my life in the continued mess that it seemed it had been in for a long time. I came to the conclusion that I would just have to deal with it and out last it. The mental stress was real-bad, but I knew that it was all my own fault because of the decisions that I had made. They were all coming back to haunt me. So much now was out of my control like the Car Hop being pregnant, my wife being pregnant with the College boy's baby causing the divorce to be delayed, my Dad's health in decline. It seemed like my responsibilities kept increasing, but some-how I had to deal with them without getting depressed. I needed to think positive and look at the good things that were happening. For one, I had my land in good shape to put out fertilizer in January to get ready to plant my first crop of Milo Maize, my health was good and I was strong as an ox which I needed to be able to do all the hard physical work of farming and ranching, my little cow heard was slowly increasing in size which would give me a little more cash flow. All I really need to do was to take care of first things first, which was my business and let the rest work itself out over time, because I couldn't rush time and all the other problems were time related, so I would deal with them as they came due, similar to what you do with debts. I hadn't heard anything from my wife in a while except for bills that were sent to me from her Doctor for her pregnancy check-ups and I assumed that she was still living with her parents. I was still seeing the Car Hop of course, because I was committed to that now with regret. Thanksgiving came and it was without any true Holiday feeling from either myself or my parents, I guess because of my pending divorce and my Dad's declining health. Anyway, it was a rather solemn affair. December 1966 was upon me and the months were dragging by with what I thought seemed like the slowest speed ever, because I was anxious for time to go by, so I could confront my personal problems and get them behind me and go on to other things. December 1966 finally got here and I wasn't really looking forward to Christmas, but I was looking forward to December 1966 coming to a close and January 1967 getting here, because 1967 was the year that a lot of my personal problems would mature in and I would be able to finally be able to confront each and come up with a solution for each. Waiting was hard, but it was just something that I had to do, because I had no way of knowing what each problem was going to require for a solution to solve, so I could get on with my life. Christmas came and went much as Thanksgiving had done and it was finally the New Year of 1967, yea!

Lorrie—1966 Thanksgiving 1966 was over now, and Lorrie and her husband were back in Florida. Lorrie was glad to be back, even though she did enjoy seeing her family, her Mom, Dad, little brother and sister and also a few girlfriends The girlfriends were single and they had been full of questions about married life and what she had been doing in Florida before she got married. She couldn't tell them the truth, because it would end up getting back to her parents, so she acted like she was the happiest girl in the world with her new husband and that she had been a secretary at NASA and done surfing before she married. No way could she tell them the truth about Surf Duke or working in the Club or about getting pregnant. She had to make her life in Florida seem like the regular average life a girl her age would be living. She thought that if they really knew what she had been up to they would probably pass out on the floor. Christmas 1966 was almost here, and Lorrie was trying to get a few decorations up with her limited money, because her husband didn't make very much in the Air Force, and Lorrie had always enjoyed decorating for the Holidays. Maybe the decorations and the Christmas music would make her feel better, because she was still sick a lot and had lost a lot of weight, which she didn't need to lose, because she was always thin anyway. She wasn't eating very good for two reasons, Some food made her sick just to smell it and her husband had got an evening job at the Base Snack-bar, so instead of them cooking at their trailer they ate left overs that he brought home from the Base Snack-bar and that saved them money on food. This food was mostly the fast food stuff like nacho's, cold hot-dogs, pizza cheese sandwiches and stuff like that. Her husband wanted a big stereo-console record player for Christmas, so instead of saving the money to buy things the baby would need he bought himself the stereo-console. Well, Lorrie thought, at least it will play some beautiful Christmas music and some-how we will get what we need for the baby. Christmas went by for them and New Year 1967 arrived, and Lorrie and her husband went to a small gathering of his friends at the base for the New Year celebration. There was a record player going full blast and some wine and beer and snacks available. Lorrie was talking to some of the other wives of the Air Force men there and trying to get to know them some. Her and her husband would dance now and then, and he would also ask some of the other wives to dance and there were single girls there with their boyfriends that he would dance with also. He was always a good dancer and had been ever since she had known him when they had been in High School. Lorrie noticed that he was dancing often with the girlfriend of this other guy that he knew, but that was OK, because Lorrie was being asked to dance every-once-in-a-while even though she was pregnant and her tummy was pretty big and she had always loved to dance every-since she had been very young. Her husband was dancing with the girlfriend of the other guy when twelve o'clock came and the New Year and Lorrie saw him kiss her a long kiss and this embarrassed Lorrie. She had just been sitting there and wasn't dancing. After that they all sang Auld Lang Syne and her husband came back to sit with her and she didn't say anything about him kissing the girl like he did, because she didn't like confrontation. She had plenty of that when she was living at home in El Campo with her parents, but immediately when he sat down the music started playing again and the song was, of all things "In The Still Of The Night' by The Five Satins and Lorrie jumped up and grabbed the first guy close to her and asked him to dance and he did. She held him close and buried her head in his shoulder and softly wept and he ask her what was wrong, and she told him don't worry Gus I'm OK and he said my name is Stanley not Gus and Lorrie told him she was sorry. So, 1967 had arrived and she would see what the New Year would bring besides the baby she was carrying.

Gus—1967 January 1967 was a very welcome year and month for me. That sounds like I am happy that my life is slipping by, but the reason I was glad to see it was that I knew some of the timetable for the events that would affect my life were getting closer to happening. That meant that the sooner they happened the sooner I could deal with them and find solutions and then move on with my life. I knew that I would plant my crop of Milo Maize the first of March, that my wife should have her and the College boy's baby in March or April and that my girlfriend should have our baby in June or July, so there were at least three major things that I knew the approximate timing of. I also knew that each event had its own problems that would accompany it, and each would have to have its own solution, even the planting of the crop, which I and the weather would have to deal with. In the field I was working, even at night, to finish putting out the fertilizer to get ready for the planting season. During the daytime I was working on the land that my Dad wanted to plant in rice, which would be in the middle of March. I was also trying to stay on the look-out for some more cheap furniture, dishes, kitchen cooking utensils, a used washer and dryer and some baby things to start out with. I had plenty of time to amass all of this stuff, but I didn't want to wait till the last minute, because I wanted to be able to take advantage of bargain prices when I had the opportunity. I wasn't seeing much of my Car Hop girlfriend and that suited me just fine. She had quit her job and her last year of High School, because she was beginning to show that she was pregnant. I wasn't really sure what she was doing, and I didn't really care. I just felt better when she was out of my hair, because she was absolutely no help to me and right now, I didn't have the time to try to teach her anything. My only hope was that when the time came that she would be willing to learn how to be a wife and mother. Well that's another thing I will have to deal with when the time comes. With these women that I have been involved with I never seem to get one that wants to become a big part of what I am trying to build. They don't seem to get the picture that we should be in this together, each doing our part to support the other one to try and make a success out of our business. With them I feel like a lone soldier fighting the battles by myself. They all seem to have their own private, selfish ideas secretly plotting against me for something that they desire right now and not looking down the road to the future. I usually don't have much time to just sit quietly and think everything over, but now was one of those times and I would usually get a clearer picture of the whole mess when I took the time like this to go over it all. Now thoughts of sweet Lorrie drift back into my mind and I am wondering how her life is going. I sure hope that she has done a lot better than I have. Surely, she hasn't screwed her life up like I have. I am glad that I stayed away from her and didn't mess up her life, like it surely would have. Lorrie, in my heart I wish you the very best, but I really miss those kisses you gave me on the beach in Corpus. OK I have to quit thinking about Lorrie and get back to reality. February 1967 is here, and I have to clean up my land and get it ready to plant the first of March.

Lorrie—1967 In January 1967 Lorrie was still struggling with her pregnancy. She was sick at her stomach a lot and she seemed to be getting weaker. She made up her mind that when she had the baby, she was going to get on birth control pills, because she didn't think that she could survive another pregnancy like this. Looking back now she couldn't believe that she had been such a fool to be so unconcerned about getting pregnant when she was having sex. After all, it had always been just sex and not love. With love you are really making love with the one that you love and there was only one person that she could ever really love and that was Gus and she knew it all the way into her bones. No, she just couldn't ever get pregnant ever again. Having sex with a husband is simply taking care of an obligation as a wife to him, some-time you might enjoy it and some-time you might not. They were still living in Florida in that little trailer and he still had his extra job in the evenings at the snack-bar on Base. Lorrie suspected that her husband had himself a girl there, because he was coming home later then he did when he first went to work there. There were other clues also, because when she would wash his cloths, she would find make-up on his shirt and it would have the smell of girl's cologne. She had also found a stray long blond hair wrapped around the button on his shirt sleeve cuff and of all things, lipstick on the fly of his underwear. What else could it be but a girlfriend at work. Oh well she wasn't going to fight with him about it, because she didn't like confrontation and fighting, and he always talked down to her like she was just a stupid kid. He was still bringing left over snacks from the snack-bar for her to eat and she guessed that he was eating the same thing when he was working, but he wasn't sick like she was. Lorrie went to the Doctor in February 1967 for a check-up to see what he could do for her about her sickness all the time and he said that her being this sick this far along was very unusual. He was an Air Force Doctor on the Base, because medical treatment there was free to the wives of all enlisted men. He told her that he thought that her baby would be born in April 1967 and that from now on she should get plenty of rest, try to eat food that wouldn't upset her stomach. He told her to be sure to tell her husband that she needed to eat healthy and to quit eating the snacks that he was bring home from the Base snack-bar. That night when her husband got home from work, she made sure that she was awake to talk to him about what the doctor had told her. She told him what the doctor had said and he said that if that doctor wanted her to eat expensive food then the doctor needed to buy it for her and not him and another thing is that he was going to continue to bring home what he could and if she didn't eat it then it was her business. This is the way things were in February 1967 and Lorrie was looking forward to April when this would all be over.

Gus—1967 In February 1967 I was working in the field when the weather was good and feeding cattle when the weather was cold and raining. It was all miserable work, because you were cold and wet most of the time walking around in the mud and rain or sitting on the tractor with the cold wind blowing you in the face. It was so good to get back home to a warm house in the evenings and warm up something to eat and take a hot bath and get ready for bed, just to be able to get up the next morning to do the same thing. My Car Hop girlfriend would come over a couple of times a week and we would sleep together, and she was starting to look very pregnant. She didn't seem to be having any trouble with her pregnancy and that was good. I would give her money to pay the doctor, because I didn't want to have any records with my name on them, because of my divorce. I guessed that everything was going OK with my wife, because I hadn't heard anything from her in months. I guess that the College boy was keeping her occupied and that was good too. I was starting to think about what to do about her baby having my last name when it should be the College boys last name and also was hoping that my divorce would be over in time to marry the Car Hop so our baby would have the right last name. I needed to try to find out when my wife's baby was supposed to be born, so I could start to make some plans.

Lorrie—1967 By the middle of March 1967 Lorrie was struggling to get things done in the little trailer they lived in. She hated to let her housework go, but she just didn't have the strength to get it all done the way she liked it to be. She thought, well I will catch up after I have the baby, it's not that far away now. She had slowly been trying to get all organized with the necessary baby supplies they would need, but they still needed some big things like a baby bed and a baby stroller just to name a couple things. She sure wished that her husband would have saved the money for these things instead of buying himself that big console record player. This whole pregnancy nightmare seemed like it had gone on for ten years. She had been so sick with this pregnancy ever since she got married that she hadn't been able to get to know any of the other wives that had husbands at the Base, and she wished that she had a girlfriend to visit with. Her other friends that she had made while surfing and working at the Club had other lives that wouldn't fit with hers now, so they had disappeared from her life. All of that old life of thinking of herself and doing just what she wanted to do was gone now and very soon she was going to be saddled with even more responsibility. My gosh, it seemed like it had been twenty years since she had left El Campo and rode that bus to Florida to live with her Uncle and Aunt, but it had been only one year and five months. Then Lorrie started thinking about all she had done during that short time and she started counting the months from the time she left El Campo and the time she got pregnant and she was shocked that it was only ten months. Could it be true that it was only ten months? She came to the conclusion that she had been a very busy girl, because during that time she had worked at NASA, lived in Porto Rico, been a Go-Go dancer at the Club on the strip and a waitress and then she got pregnant by the boy that she had been sent to Florida to get away from. Oh my, what a fast life and now I am a wife and soon to be a mother. March 1967 was almost finished, and April was just around the corner and then it would be time for her baby to be born.

Gus—1967 It's the first week in March 1967 and thank goodness the weather has been good enough for me to start planting my one hundred acres of Milo Maize. This time of year, you can never tell what the weather might do, it can be so unpredictable. I have been able to do a good job with my field work, so I am off to a good start with my crop, but there is a long way to go before the harvest and anything can happen, that is why farming is such a gamble. It's like you are rolling the dice to see if you will make any money and it takes one hundred and twenty days of growing season till the dice stop rolling to see what you end up with. Now I have to go immediately to working on the rice land to finish getting it ready to plant and that will be a big job, because it will be three hundred and fifty acres to get ready to plant. After that I will be gathering the cattle and working them to vaccinate, drench, spray, castrate the new calves and separate the big calves and sell them. At the same time there is all the things to take care of with growing the Milo Maize and the rice crop. It seems like my personal life has settled down some into just a wait and see holding pattern until my wife and the College boys baby is born, so the divorce can proceed from there and thank goodness I have not heard anymore from my Car Hop's Dad on the threat he gave me about paying him fifteen thousand dollars or he was going to report me to the law. I think that threat is all dead now. She is staying at my house more and more now, but I don't see much that she accomplishes when here. I don't know what she does, really. Seems like I do most of the cooking and cleaning like I did before. She will wash dishes and wash clothes though, so that is something. I am to busy working to pay much attention to her. She is back and forth between her Mom's house and my house and I am trying to encourage her to learn some wife and mother skills from her Mom, but I am not to sure how excited she is about that. I am not sure when my got pregnant and I haven't thought about it much, but her baby should be due next month in April maybe. Any way April 1967 is right around the corner now and I will find out.

Lorrie—1967 The start of April 1967 was bad for Lorrie, because of the months of her sickness with her pregnancy had left her weak and feeling very ill health. She started having labor pains and she called her husband at the Air Force Base and he came home to take her back to the Base Hospital for the delivery of their baby. Her labor was terrible, because she was so weak that when the doctor would tell her to push, but she was so weak that she didn't have enough strength to push like she should be able to do. They finally had to use metal tongs to help her deliver the baby and a big baby boy it was. She was so exhausted that she passed out and didn't see the baby until several hours later after they had cleaned her and the baby up and the next thing that she knew she was in a room and the doctor and nurse was there with her. The doctor asked her if she felt well enough to see the baby and she said that she was, so they brought the baby in the room and then the doctor called in her husband into the room with them. Lorrie took the baby in her arms and kissed it and had to see for sure that it was a boy, then the doctor told her all about her labor and how concerned he was about it, because her health was so bad. Immediately the doctor glared at her husband and told him in no uncertain words how he had put the life of his wife and baby at risk by being so uncaring of her health, as to let her get in such a weak state. The doctor lectured him on the responsibilities of a husband and father and told him that from now on he had better shape up for the good of his family. The doctor told her and her husband that normally that he would keep her and the baby in the hospital for three days, but because she was in such bad health that he was going to keep her and the baby there until he felt that she was strong enough and her health had improved enough to let her go home. He said that no way would she be able to take care of the baby and herself now. He would have to evaluate her day by day till he felt sure she was healthy enough before could release her. Her husband just hung his head and didn't say anything, because he knew that everything that the doctor said was true. Lorrie was glad that the doctor gave her husband that lecture, because Lorrie had never been able to talk to him like that, because she hated confrontation, and would do almost anything to avoid it. Lorrie now wondered how it would be with him when she and the baby came home from the hospital. Lorrie's health was so bad that she was in the hospital on the Air Force Base for three weeks before the doctor felt like she had improved enough to release her to go home. Lorrie had stayed so long in the hospital that it was now May 1967.

Gus—1967 April 1967 was going along pretty good with the Milo Maize and Rice crops up good and growing and the cattle were having new calves and with the new green grass they were fattening fast. I was glad that winter was over, and I was watching a new crop and new calves that would give new hope for a more stable financial future. I was feeling pretty good even though all the personal problems were still hanging over my head. I knew that it would just take time to work those out. How much time I didn't know, but I had survived it so far and I planned to do what it would take to get my personal life back on a straight line. One night I got a call from one of my wife's sisters that her and the College boy's baby, a baby boy, had been born in a hospital in Wharton, a town close to El Campo. I thought, well that is good, because I will be able to talk to my lawyer to find out more about when my divorce will be final. I struggled with the decision whether to go to the hospital to see her and the baby. I finally decided to go to the hospital and see the baby, but not see her, so that is what I did. I went there and looked in to the window of the nursery and saw a baby bed with my last name on it and I looked at their baby and a nurse came to the window and pointed to me and with hand signs wanted to know which baby I wanted to look at, I guess so she could pick it up and bring it closer to the window for me to see, but I acted like I was just looking at all the new born baby's and I just smiled at her and waved her off. I couldn't tell much about the baby. I was never able to tell much about a new born baby, so then I just turned around walked down the hall and I noticed my wife's name on a room and I was glad that the door was shut and she wouldn't accidentally see me and I left the hospital and drove back to my house in El Campo and I didn't see that baby boy again till he was sixteen years old. The next day I contacted my lawyer to tell him the news and asked him about the timeline on the divorce and he said that it all depended on what her demands were and what the Judge would do. Well I was still in limbo on it, but at least it might move forward now.

Lorrie—1967 Lorrie and the baby came home from the hospital in May 1967 and she was feeling almost as good as her old self again. She had the usual things that women have to do to completely get over childbirth, but otherwise all was going pretty well. Her husband was much more agreeable to her eating good healthy food and following the doctor's instructions since the doctor had jumped all over him that day at the hospital and Lorrie was getting good reports from the doctor on the baby and herself. Her husband had also been coming home at night earlier then he had been before the baby was born. Lorrie ask him how he was managing to do that, and he said that the snack-bar had hired an extra employee to help clean up after closing. Lorrie wondered about that, because she noticed that he no longer had make-up on his shirts. She thought that he had broken up with his girlfriend because of the baby and that is why he was coming home earlier, but she just kept that thought to herself. Maybe he would turn out to be a good husband and father after all. He told her that he had decided that it was time for him to start working on his College degree again, so he could go up for promotion to be a Commissioned Officer after he completed his degree. If he would get promoted that would give them more pay and also the chance to have housing on Base that would save them money. Lorrie agreed to help him all that she could, so she started helping him do research that his subjects required and also, she typed all of his papers for him. Lorrie's life was very busy with the baby, housework, helping her husband with his College work and trying to improve her cooking abilities. Cooking became one of her favorite things to do. Finding new recipes that would fit with her budget was a fun thing to try out. Like the cookbook on two hundred ways to cook hamburger meat. The baby was growing, and Lorrie was putting on a little weight and she felt like she looked better in her cloths. Her and her husband were getting along pretty good most of the time except when he would tell her that she was to skinny to wear shorts and crop tops and he would talk down to her a lot like she was stupid. This would depress her, because she was trying to be a good wife and Mom. It seemed to Lorrie like she never could never come up to his standards.

Gus—1967 It was May 1967 now and my lawyer and I were still waiting for my wife and her lawyer to come up with what she wanted, so we could proceed with the divorce. I was continuing to take care of the Milo Maize and Rice crops and I was working cattle again to sell the calves that were big enough for market and vaccinate the young calves that had been born in the spring. There was always plenty of work to do and you never really caught up with it. My Car Hop girlfriend went for a check-up at the doctor and he told her that he thought that our baby would be born in July. Wow, that means that I need to get my lawyer and my wife's lawyer busy to get my divorce finished as fast as possible because if it goes past July, then my baby might be born illegitimate. That would make me have to adopt my own child at a later date. I got notified by my lawyer that my wife's lawyer got a thirty-day delay from a judge to be able to have a medical evaluation on my wife and the baby. Thirty days runs the divorce in to June at least. Well nothing can do about that. Whatever happens, happens and I will have to deal with it.

Lorrie—1967 Lorrie has her hands full in June 1967 taking care of the new baby and all of the other things wives do to keep everything running smooth for the family and on top of this she was typing and editing pages and pages of College research for her husband's College degree. Home life for Lorrie has been better since the baby was born and her husband started his College studies. He evidently had broken it off with the girl that he was having an affair with at the Base snack-bar, because he was coming home on time and studying. This was a big relief for Lorrie, because it took a lot of worry away about where the marriage was going. If she hadn't been pregnant, she wouldn't have married him in the first place, but then to suffer the humility of him having an affair while she was pregnant with his baby was almost more then she could stand. She was never able to confront him with the affair because he was not the kind of man that she could reason with. He would overpower her with his importance and superiority. Lorrie never did like confrontations, because she had so many when she had lived at home in El Campo with her Mom and Dad. They planned a trip back to El Campo to visit the family and show off the new baby. When they got to El Campo and Lorrie's parent's house everyone was very glad to see them and they unloaded all of their luggage and unpacked, then had to pass the new baby around for everyone to hold and kiss and make over. There was a lot of chatter going on, but she noticed that her Dad was quiet, so she turned around and caught him and her husband glaring at each other. She turned back around and thought that there was no love lost between them. She so had hoped that her Dad had gotten over the dislike that he had for her husband, but it was evident that he hadn't and it looked like her husband felt the same way, because he wasn't making any move to be friendly to her Dad. Lorrie had purposely kept the troubles that her and her husband had gone through away from her family, just for that reason, hoping that they could all be a family together and all the bad feelings would be behind them, but she guessed that it would be too much to ask for. Not long after that her husband said that he was going to go visit his Aunt and Uncle, so he left and didn't come back till late that night. He didn't even eat dinner with her family but said that he had eaten dinner at his Aunts. The next day he said that they needed to go to his Aunt and Uncles to show them the baby and visit, so they got everything in the car and Lorrie noticed that her husband had an extra bag he brought out to the car. She asked him what it was, and he said that he was going to stay at his Aunts and Uncles, and he wasn't going back to her parent's house till it was time to leave. Lorrie and the baby want back to her parent's house, without her husband, after the visit to his Aunt and Uncle and everything at her parent's house seemed to brighten up after that and no one even mentioned her husband's name till it was time to leave and go back to Florida. While in El Campo Lorrie couldn't help herself. She just had to drive by Gus's parent's house to see if she could see him outside. She didn't see Gus, but she did notice that his old Hot Rod wasn't there any-more. She thought this is just like High School when I was trying to keep track of him, when will I ever change and get over him. I am married and now have a baby and I am still thinking about Gus. Why can't I think of my husband like I think about Gus. I sometime think that, in a way, my life has been ruined forever. They stayed in El Campo for four days and it was time for them to leave, so Lorrie and the baby said good-by to her parents and siblings and she went to her husband's Aunt and Uncles and picked him up and they left for the trip back to Florida. He didn't even ask her what she had done all the time that she was visiting with her parents. It was like they didn't even exist, so she didn't say anything either and they drove back to Florida. It was the first of July 1967 now and there was to be a big celebration on the Base for July fourth and Lorrie was looking forward to that, because she had always been patriotic, because her Dad was a WWII and Korean War veteran.

Gus—1967 June 1967 found Gus in a dither, because he found out that the divorce wouldn't be over till August 1967. The Judge had decided to delay the divorce till the first of August to give him and his wife time to get used to the idea of being parents in hopes that they would decide to cancel the divorce. Well Gus couldn't do anything about that, but just wait it out. He had plenty of work to do repairing the harvesting machinery to harvest first the Milo Maize and then the Rice. Also, something very interesting came up that Gus had to deal with for the first time and it became the beginning of a learning process that would grow over time and become a source for income in the future. A small Oil Company wanted to make an Oil Least on a small piece of his Dad's land and Gus had to do the negotiations for it. He had no idea what he was doing whether it was good or bad, but he did at least get to pick the Oil Company's representative brain and learn what some of the terms and wording meant, because it was written in Lawyer oil language that looked like Latin. This was very stimulating for Gus and he enjoyed it very much and hoped that in the future he could learn more of how it all worked together. The Oil business seemed to have a lot of interesting facets to it and Gus vowed to learn more when he could. Right now though the most important thing happening that Gus had to do was to finish up getting the harvesting equipment repaired up, take care of the last minute field work that leads to a smooth harvest environment and line up the truckers that will be hauling the crops to the grain elevators. There are a multitude of small details to take care of for the harvest operation to run as smooth as it can and that includes trying to anticipate problems that might arise because of foul weather, unhappy truckers, break downs of equipment and even problems that occur because of break down delays at the grain elevators. There are numerous small things that can put a kink in the momentum of harvest and if one happens and it ultimately will, then Gus has to be ready to have a plan that will offset the problem so the harvest can continue in the field to be ahead of the constant threat of bad weather that can destroy the crop and a whole years work and also his livelihood. July 1967 was here already, and Gus had moved the harvest machinery to the Milo Maize field which was the first to be harvested. It was an exciting time for Gus, because this was the very first-time that he would harvest his very own crop. Gus would always remember that first harvest, for more than just one reason, because his girlfriend went into the hospital in labor during the first few days of that harvest and Gus needed the money to pay for the hospital bill before they would dismiss her when that time came. Yes, July 1967 was a very busy and stressful time for Gus.

Lorrie—1967 In July 1967 Lorrie found out that her husband was going to be transferred to an Air Force Base in Nebraska. Lorrie thought, we are going from warm to frigid weather in the winter and none of them had enough cold weather clothes or enough warm bedding. These things are some of the first things that a wife and Mother will think of to take care of her family. He had been at the Base in Florida more than a year and he told her that the Air Force usually transfers you at least every two years. They were sending him there for some more training. They got their official orders and drove to Nebraska to her husband's new Post on the Air Force Base there. Lorrie thought, as they drove through Nebraska to the Base, that she had never seen a more-bleak flat landscape. She saw nothing interesting to look at. The arrived and got unpacked and settled in to make a new home there for as long as the Air Force kept them in Nebraska. August 1967 would soon be approaching, and Lorrie would have to get used to this new place.

Gus—1967 Milo Maize harvest in July 1967 was completed without difficulty in time for Gus to be able to pay the hospital bill to have his girlfriend and new baby released on time. Her Mom and Dad and siblings had moved back to Louisiana while she was in the hospital. This brought about a big problem, of now where was she, and the baby going to go to recuperate after the childbirth. She and the baby couldn't go to Gus's house yet, because the divorce wasn't final. Gus's Mom finally suggested that his girlfriend and the baby come over there till the divorce was final and then they could move to Gus's house and that is what happened and what a blessing that was. Gus got them settled in at his Mom's house then he had to get ready to start the Rice harvest that would last till the middle of September 1967. In August of 1967 Gus's Lawyer called and told him to be at the Court House in Wharton, because the Judge was going to make a ruling on the divorce, so Gus went and heard the ruling that his divorce had been granted. Well finally that was over and now he could move on and start to straighten out his personal life after harvest was over, because he wouldn't have the time till then. In the meantime, his girlfriend and his new baby moved in his house with him and it was like a family, except that his girlfriend hadn't learned very much about taking care of a baby or of a house. Gus would drive out to the farm and find a quiet place and just think about all of this for a while. He had serious thoughts about not marrying her. He thought that he ought to just buy her and the baby a bus ticket to Louisiana and be done with it. Gus could see that if he married her that it would probably turn out to being one big mess and he had already had one divorce and he didn't want to go through another one, so what was he going to do. He was torn between doing the right thing by marrying her and getting rid of her the easier way by sending her to Louisiana. After all the baby didn't even have his last name, so there wouldn't be anything to keep his girlfriend from meeting someone in Louisiana and marrying him. All of a sudden Lorrie slipped into his mind. Sweet, pretty Lorrie, the girl with the big smile, the wonderful kisses. He should have not turned his back on her. Neither his first wife or his girlfriend had even come close to showing him that they wanted him like she had done, and she was only sixteen years old. How odd that he had talked himself out of going back to her. Well that was a long time ago, but he was still thinking about Lorrie from time to time, I mean how could he ever forget such a wonderful young girl. That was in the past now and Gus knew that he had messed that up and there was no going back. Well Gus thought that he would go ahead and marry his girlfriend and then he would have to adopt his own son. Things were still a mess and he could see that it would be one step at a time to straighten them out, so better just get at it, because it wasn't going to fix itself. It was now the end of August and Gus could see the end of Rice harvest would be about the middle of September 1967. He told his girlfriend to call her Mom and tell her that they would be in Louisiana in a couple of weeks and if she wanted to be at their wedding Gus was going to plan it to be a simple Civil Service in Beaumont, Texas and also to tell her Mom that we will need her to sign an age wavier to get a Marriage License because she was only seventeen now and the age in Texas to get married for a girl was eighteen. Soon it will be September 1967 and the Rice harvest will be over.

Lorrie—1967 August 1967 had arrived, and Lorrie was still busy getting everything organized to make living in Nebraska as smooth as she could. She was busy trying to discover the location of the different stores and places of business that she would need to use while they were stationed at the Base in Nebraska. Her husband was getting settled in to doing his new job on the Base. They had been there for several weeks and her husband had got a part time job at the library in town in the evening after his day was over at the Base. This was a big benefit for him, because it brought in a little extra money and allowed him the opportunity to do research for his College degree. It made things a little harder for Lorrie, because she had to have a separate dinner for him. Because he didn't get home till 10:30 or 11:00 pm from work and she had to feed the baby early and get him to bed, so she was in the kitchen till late at night getting him dinner and then cleaning up the kitchen. Lorrie could never stand to see dirty dishes in the morning in the kitchen, so she always cleaned everything up at night no matter how tired or how late it might be. When Lorrie had caught up with her work at home she would write and type her husband's papers of research that he was preparing for his College degree. As time went on, she was getting used to the schedule that she had set up for herself so that she could be efficient in what she did, because the baby took up more and more time as he was growing and getting into things. It seemed to Lorrie that the closer that her husband got to finishing his College degree the more he talked down to her as if she didn't have any common sense at all. It was depressing to her that he treated her that way when she was doing the best that she could and everything seemed to be running smooth enough and she was even doing a lot to help him with his degree, but she couldn't confront him with this and risk a big argument with him. August went into September 1967 and the weather was getting cooler as a hint to the winters that Lorrie had heard could be brutal in Nebraska.

Gus—1967 It was the last week in September of 1967 and Gus and his girlfriend and baby had gone to Louisiana and picked up his girlfriend's Mom and her two sisters and then gone back to Beaumont to the Court House there to get a marriage license and find a Judge to marry them. They went to the Clerk's office and her Mom signed the age wavier, her two sisters were witnesses and then they got the District Judge there to marry them with some Court House staff as attendees to the service. Then they all went to a restaurant for a late lunch and drove back to Louisiana. It was all very simple, but it got the job done. They stayed in Louisiana for two more days and then drove back to El Campo. Gus thought that now he was going to have to, somehow, try to have the patience to slowly motivate his new wife to try to learn how to be a wife and mother. Gus had no illusions about how tedious this might be. It was going to take a lot of watching and waiting to find the right moments to initiate conversation on how to do this or that, so as not to raise the ire of his new wife. Gus knew that if he made her mad then she would close her ears to any suggestion that he might have. For an example he would start cleaning something, like he was helping her, and he would ask her to come and watch him to make sure that he was doing it right. In other words, he acted like he didn't know exactly how to do it, but at the same time showing her how to do it hoping that some of the information would stick with her, so she could learn. He did this with taking care of the baby also. It was mind numbing, because she didn't seem interested in anything that had to do with the house or the baby. September went into October and then to November 1967 and she wasn't any better than the first day of their marriage. Finally, she said that the grocery store was hiring some extra help for the holidays and she was going to work there for a while. When Gus put a pencil to what she was going to get paid against the cost of the baby sitter, he showed her that she would have maybe only seven or eight dollars a week left out of her pay check and all that she said was that maybe she would get a raise. Gus knew that she only wanted to get away from the house and the baby and she didn't care if she made any money or not. Well what could he do. If he threw a fit and they had a big fight what would it accomplish. He was trying to do things in a quiet and understanding way, but he was very unhappy. Also, he needed to go to the lawyer to start proceedings to adopt his own son. At this same time Gus was still running the farm and ranch operation for himself and his Dad and Mom. November 1967 was supposed to be the beginning of the holiday season, a happy time, but there wasn't much happiness at Gus's house.

Lorrie—1967 The weather in November 1967 in Nebraska was terrible. Lorrie's husband was getting home from the library even later than usual. He said that the weather slowed down, but Lorrie was always suspicious of him now because of his affair with the girl when he was working that part time gob at the Base snack bar. She didn't want to look to close to what he was doing though, because she was afraid at what she might find. Lorrie was not to happy living in Nebraska with the weather so bad and the dismal landscape thing only thing to look at. She was invited to a Thanksgiving dinner at the Base. Because all the wives were supposed to attend with their husbands and Lorrie was looking forward to getting out mixing with some new people, because she had mostly been confined to the house except for the needed shopping to keep the house running. She had got the OK from her husband to go to the beauty shop to have her hair done and that would be a special treat, because she hadn't had it done in a beauty shop for maybe a year. She picked a day when the wind wasn't blowing hard and snowing and she went to a beauty shop not far from where they lived. She went in and the shop had some real nice older Rock-N-Roll music playing and the ladies there were real-nice, and all introduced themselves. She picked up a magazine and was thumbing through it and she was called to get into the chair. She was chatting with the beautician and telling her what she wanted done and the lady went to work on her and every-once-in-a-while she would turn Lorrie around to get approval on what she was doing since it was the first time that she was doing Lorries hair. The beautician was working on the back of Lorrie's hair and " The Still Of The Night " started playing and the beautician said oh, it's my favorite song, I love to dance with my husband when it plays, it reminds me when we were sweet hearts in High School. She saw Lorrie's shoulders shaking and she turned Lorrie around and looked at her and saw that Lorrie had big tears running down her cheeks and she thought that somehow that she had hurt her while cutting the back of her hair and she told Lorrie, I'm so sorry if I hurt you, what did I do to hurt you and Lorrie couldn't answer her for a minute she just shook her head and used the towel that was on her shoulder to wipe her eyes and cheeks and Lorrie told the beautician not to worry that she hadn't hurt her, that she always cried when that song played, because Lorrie said that it had been her favorite song since she had been sixteen years old. Then Lorrie sat there in that chair and made believe that she was getting all prettied up for her and Gus to go out together. She stayed in her little dream world till the beautician finished and asked her if she approved and Lorrie said yes, and I have had an out of this world experience here this afternoon. They had no idea what the real meaning of what she said was, but they were glad that she was satisfied. Lorrie drove all the way back home with that song going on in her head. For once she wanted to hear it and not close it from her mind. She had been mostly unhappy with her marriage and the only bright spot in it was the baby. Lorrie knew that she was stuck in this marriage and that she would just have to make the best of it, she only hoped that it would get better over time. If only Gus had come back things wouldn't be like this. November passed and December 1967 arrived with cold and wind and snow. Christmas 1967 was disappointing for Lorrie, because instead of her husband saving money from his part time job at the Library to get things for the baby and the house he spent it on a new motorcycle for himself, with the excuse that in good weather he could ride it to the Base and the library and that would leave the car for her use. It seemed to Lorrie that he always had money for himself, but non for her and the baby. It was going to be a new year soon, yes January 1968 and Lorrie had made her mind up to try to be more upbeat about her marriage. If she could only love her husband like she loved Gus.

Gus—1967 November 1967 Gus's wife went to work at the grocery store, and she seemed in a better mood. She had found a babysitter for the baby and she was off to work every morning looking forward to the day at work. Truth was that there wasn't too much difference at the house in what got done around there. The babysitter folded some cloths and did the dishes and that was about it. Gus did the rest when he found the time. He knew that he would never be able to teach his wife to be a housewife and Mom, because he could see that she was going to pull against it every way she could. She had no desire to learn anything domestic or about motherhood. Gus thought that if he could hold the marriage together long enough that maybe by the-time she got to the age of twenty that she might decide to grow up enough to start excepting the responsibilities of a wife and Mother. He could see that it was going to be a long pull. Thanksgiving dinner was at his Mom's house and she wanted his wife to help her prepare the thanksgiving dinner. Gus sent her over there, but it was embarrassing for him, because he knew that his wife didn't know the first thing to do to help with a big meal like thanksgiving. He wondered what his Mom was going to think about it all. When he went over for the dinner his Mom tried to make his wife look like she had cooked some of the side dishes. His Mom kept saying that your wife did this, and she did that, but Gus knew that his wife couldn't have done any of that. His Mom was just trying to give his wife credit for part of the dinner to make his wife feel better. Gus would just smile in approval, but in his heart, he knew that it was all for show and his wife never disputed his Mom, but she took credit for some of the cooking like it was true. Well November ran into December and Christmas came and went with the only pleasure for Gus being the gifts for the baby. All these fall and winter months, in between the holidays, Gus was busy feeding cattle and working land for the 1968 crop year. The work never ends in farming and ranching. January 1968 blew in with a new norther and it was very cold which meant that more time would be spent taking care of the cattle. One evening when Gus was home, he got a phone call from someone that his wife worked with that told him that she had been caught having sex with the manager in the storeroom, but would not tell her name, just thought that Gus should know. This is the way that the new year January 1968 started out.

Lorrie—1968 January 1968 was very cold and nasty in Nebraska and Lorrie was very tired of the bad winter weather. She had been raised on the Gulf Coast of Texas and then moved to the warm weather of Florida, so she had no background for the bad, long winter storms of Nebraska. Having to stay inside the house so much at least gave her more time to work on her husband's papers for his College degree. He was doing real good with it and was ahead of where he should have been for the time that he had applied and that would look real good on his record when he finished his degree, so he could be commissioned an officer. Lorrie was proud of her husband's intelligence in learning and had always thought that he would accomplish something great someday. She just wished that he didn't think himself so far above her in intelligence that he constantly talked down to her on a daily basis, because it was depressing not to be able to take up for herself. She wondered why he thought that he had to down grade her in the first place. January went into February with the weather being pretty much the same and Lorrie sometimes felt like she was getting cabin fever from having to stay in the house so much, but she couldn't chance taking the baby out in bad weather. She used part of this time to go through magazines and clip out recipes to experiment with. She found out that some of the recipes sounded good, but when she went to the grocery store to buy the ingredients that the seasoning was too expensive for her to experiment with. She would put those recipes in a folder for another time when she might have more money to spend. She had to concentrate on recipes that used pasta, rice, potatoes, hamburger and chicken. She started getting pretty good at making a Mexican style dinner with tacos, re-fried beans, salsa, hot peppers and fresh sliced onion on the side. This was starting to be their every Friday special dinner and they looked forward to it. She was so glad to be able to pick up the needed skills of running a household and taking care of a husband and baby. This made her proud of herself even though her husband thought that it was trivial compared with what he was doing. She didn't really have anyone to teach her these things, because ever-since she had been married she had been away from her Mom and her Granny which is who she should have been learning the fine art of being a wife and Mother from. Instead she had to figure ways to get the knowledge herself and she felt pride it that, as she should. February went into March 1968 and the weather started getting a little better, with the winter storms not being as bad or lasting as long. Now Lorrie could start thinking about spring cleaning, airing out their little rent house and hanging out bedding on the close line to freshen-up. The baby was healthy and doing fine and so was Lorrie after that bad time with her pregnancy and recovery. She was glad that it was behind her and she was hoping to never get pregnant again. Lorrie was so thankful for birth control pills and kept her fingers crossed every time that her husband wanted to have sex hoping that they would keep her from getting pregnant, because she sure didn't want any more of his baby's. Sometime Lorrie would have a quiet time to let her mind go back to the sweet times that she had hopes of being with Gus forever and she would say to herself that she would have loved to have had his baby's. She would giggle to herself and think that she would have been pregnant every year and loved each of them as she loved Gus. Oh well, that will never be now, but how nice to have a little fantasy of how sweet it would have been. March was now going into April 1968 and Lorrie got a card in the mail addressed to her with no return address, but it had been mailed in town. She opened it and it said that this girl had been having an affair with her husband and that she was in love with him. It said that if Lorrie wanted to know more, to call the phone number below. Lorrie wasn't sure that she wanted to know more. She had hoped that when they had left the Base in Florida and been transferred to Nebraska that it would end this stuff. Lorrie never turned her husband down on sex and they had practiced different sex acts from some books that they had bought, because neither of them knew much when they married, so why was this happening all over again. April 1968 becomes decision time again for Lorrie.

Gus—1968 January 1968 found Gus contemplating what to do about that disturbing phone call he had received from some woman telling him that his wife was caught having sex with the manager of the grocery store in the storeroom. Gus thought, damn and women were portrayed to be these angel-like humans that have morals that are way above those of dirty minded men. Well this certainly hadn't been his experience with women so far. In fact, out of two wives both had cheated on him, so that was one hundred percent backwards from what women were supposed to be. Didn't you always hear that some couple were getting a divorce, because the husband had been caught having sex with some other woman. Gus was starting to make up his own mind about the morals of women. He started naming off all the things, to himself, that women were involved in that were considered to be unacceptable by the, so called upstanding society crowd. Let's see whore houses are run by women, sex magazines have nothing but naked women in them, X rated moves star naked women doing all sort of things, beauty contests have women wearing sexy cloths and skimpy bikinis, so what is supposed to be so pure about women. To Gus it looked the other way around, because women were dominating all of the things that men were not supposed get involved in. Could it be that women were the root of all evil and not money like everyone had always been told? Well Gus thought that from now on he would not bother to fall in love with a woman, in fact he would do everything to protect himself from doing so. He decided that he would just keep his heart to himself and use women for what the circumstances called for at the time. He hated this way of thinking, because he had always liked to be around women and had always believed that they had much more to them then just their sexual side, but that didn't look like it was the case. Gus was getting a very scarred version of relationships with women. He decided to just let it go about his wife being caught having sex in the storage room, what the hell anyway. January went into February and Gus was preparing to start planting his second Milo Maize crop the first of March 1968. While Gus was in the field planting his crop, his wife got fired from her job at the grocery store. The wife of the manager forced him to fire her, so she mopped around the house for the rest of the month and one day in April 1968 she told Gus that she had a bus ticket to go to Louisiana to see her Mom and sisters. The next day she left for Louisiana and Gus kept the baby while she was having a good time in Louisiana. Gus wondered who she was going to have sex with, in Louisiana, but really didn't really care at this point. He had a baby and a business to attend to and that was more important then what ever she was up to. Gus was wondering what all was going to happen in 1968, because it wasn't going so good with his personal life. Taking care of the baby twenty-four hours a day did put some extra stress on Gus, but as he got things organized it was working pretty well. He had his Mom make a little pillow for the baby to take his naps with, in the seat of Gus's pick-up and Gus had already been doing a lot of things like sterilizing the bottles and nipples and mixing the baby's cereal and feeding him. Gus would take the baby on the tractor by holding him with one arm and driving the tractor with the other. Gus did the same thing when he had to be horseback riding pasture checking the cattle. After lunch Gus would let the baby take his nap in the seat of the pick-up while Gus worked close by and this slowed things down some, but Gus thought that in years to come these memories would be precious ones. Gus had to keep the baby this way, because he couldn't afford to hire a babysitter every-day, and besides he didn't know one that he could trust. Gus's wife was gone for a whole month and during that time Gus had finished planting the Milo Maize and Rice crops and had begun rounding up the cattle for the spring working. She finally showed up back home in the middle of May 1968 expecting Gus to be on his knees begging her to stay, because having to take care of the baby by himself, but instead she found a clean house with all the laundry and dishes organized and a baby that was afraid to go to her, because he had been used to a different schedule and she had been absent for too long. She also found a husband that was in total control of the situation and found out that she was going to have to adjust herself to new circumstances in the way that the house was organized and the schedule that the baby was used to. She felt totally out of place and decided to pout for several days until she saw that no one cared if she pouted or not. Gus didn't even ask her what she had been doing all of the time that she had been gone, so all the things that she had prepared to tell him were useless to her now. She came home to find nothing wrong and it seemed like she hadn't even been missed and this made her angry, so she thought that what she needed to do was just to get another job and she would start looking for one in a couple of days when she rested up from her trip. By now it was June 1968 and Gus, was doing what he needed to do to keep everything running as smooth as possible, regardless of what his wife was doing. It was time to get all the harvesting machinery ready to harvest the Milo Maize and Rice crops.

Lorrie—1968 That card that Lorrie received in April 1968 from her husbands supposed lover posed a problem that would require a decision from Lorrie. Lorrie decided to keep the card and phone number secret from her husband until she had the opportunity to try to find out more somehow. She decided that she would call up to the Library every-once-in-a-while to see if he was really there and then to document it if he wasn't there to see if there was a pattern to his absence from the Library. She could use any number of excuses to call there for him. Lorrie waited about a week and then decided that she would call on the weekends when he said he was going to work at the Library. She called that next Saturday and sure enough he wasn't scheduled to work that weekend. This went on through the rest of April and May and sometime, he was there and sometime, he wasn't. Lorrie finally decided that this had gone on long enough and she needed to know more about it, so she got out the card and just looked at it for a while trying to decide if she had the courage to call the number. She had just called him at the Library, so she knew he was there and thought that it might be a good time to call the phone number on the card, because if he was at the Library then he wouldn't be with his lover and also it would give her time to talk without worrying about her husband coming home while she was on the phone, so that is what she did. She called the number and a girl answered and Lorrie identified herself and the girl ask her why it took her so long to call. Lorrie told her that she had more important things to do besides getting involved in a discussion with the supposed mistress of her husband. Lorrie didn't want the girl to know how truly upset she really was, so she tried as hard as she could to keep up the appearance of being in total control of her emotions. They talked for a few minutes and the girl admitted that she and Lorrie's husband had been having an affair for some time. Lorrie invited her to come over to the house so they could talk and then when her husband came home, he could decide what he wanted to do. The girl accepted and they made a time for the meeting that would allow Lorrie to have the baby fed, bathed, and in bed before the girl arrived. When the girl arrived, she brought this big strong girl with her, Lorrie guessed for a body- guard, in case that Lorrie wanted to fight. They all sat down, and Lorrie asked them if they would like some wine and they said yes that they would, so Lorrie opened a bottle of wine and cut up some cheese with some crackers and they sat around discussing the problem at hand. The girl did most of the talking and she told Lorrie that she was in love with Lorrie's husband and that he had told her that he was in love with her and that he was going to get a divorce from Lorrie and marry her. She told Lorrie that she just got tired of waiting for him to tell his wife, so she thought that if he didn't have the courage to tell Lorrie then she would do it herself. They heard Lorrie's husband come in and he walked in the room with them and just stood there for a minute not knowing what to say. Lorrie finally told him to sit down that his girlfriend had been telling her all about their plans to get married and that Lorrie was glad that he had finally found the girl that could make him happy and that she wished them all the best. Lorrie looked at him and asked him when he was moving out and when he planned on filing for the divorce. His girlfriend and the big girl were in a very good mood and they were just smiling and looking at him for his response. He looked back and forth at them and then at Lorrie and then in a voice so soft that no one could understand him muttered something. Everyone got a puzzled look on their face and Lorrie said for him to speak up that they didn't understand him, so he stiffened himself and said that he had changed his mind. The girlfriend suddenly lost her composure and her smile and said what do you mean by that and Lorrie also said yes, what do you mean, because I have already told her that she is welcome to you with my blessings and we had everything already worked out. Lorrie's husband then got up and told them that there wasn't going to be any divorce and that he and his girlfriend were through for good and he walked out of the room and went into the bedroom and closed the door. The girlfriend got up and told the big girl that it looked like they needed to go. They left and didn't even thank Lorrie for the wine, cheese and crackers. Lorrie had held her cool and it looked like this problem might be over, but Lorrie could already see that there was a pattern to her husband's infidelity. Transfer to a new Base and leave the old girlfriend behind and get a new girlfriend at the new Base and start all over again. Lorrie decided that she needed to hang on to her marriage for two reasons. She needed a husband to help raise their baby and she didn't want to hear her parents say that they had warned her about him and had tried their best to keep them apart, she just simply wouldn't be able to stand their gloating on I told you so. Well the year was half over with June 1968 over and July 1968 next on the calendar.

Gus—1968 July 1968 found Gus harvesting his Milo Maize. This harvest season had problems with a lot of rain that caused delays in the field and machinery break downs along with a poorer quality of grain which meant it sold for less money. These problems followed into the Rice harvest also. The entire harvest season was a struggle all the way that produced disappointing results. Cattle prices were still good though, so that helped to make up for the dismal profits from the farming operation. Gus had been adding to his cattle herd every year and it was now to the point that it added a great deal to the overall stability of his agriculture operation. He had also bought his own used harvesting combine and two old hauling trucks to deliver the grain to the grain elevators in town. This saved him thousands of dollars in expenses that would have been paid out to custom operators. His wife had found her another job at a local dry-cleaner, but Gus didn't bother himself with that much, because he knew it was just something to get her away from housework and taking care of the baby. That was OK, because Gus already had everything organized to cover for the undependable behavior of his wife. He was to the point with her that he operated like she wasn't there. When there were things large or small that she wouldn't do or didn't do he just found a way to get them done without her. August had ended the harvest season and in September Gus was busy again working the fields up getting them ready for the next year's crops. He had another chance to deal with an oil company out of Houston for a neighbor that had been contacted by them. The neighbor wanted Gus to negotiate the oil lease for him, so Gus did for a small fee and this gave Gus some more experience dealing with oil companies. Gus also started to get interested in the geology of the oil business and figured that knowing more about it would give him another tool to use when negotiating a lease, if he knew something of the geology that they were going to drill and the language of the geology. He started to go to drilling locations and talking to the Drillers, Tool Pushers and Geologists on the drilling rigs. This was an improvised education on the oil business that started to build him a reputation in the local area as someone to contact for information and advice. November 1968 brought cold winter weather and that meant spending more time taking of the cattle. His wife got fired from the job at the dry cleaners and Gus didn't even inquire why, but he heard a rumor later that it was because the wife of her boss was jealous and forced him to fire her. She said that she was so upset that she needed to get away for a while, so she left on the bus for Louisiana to stay with her sister for a while. Well it was just Gus and the baby again and except for the uncertainty of what his wife was up to in Louisiana things were proceeding with a planned daily schedule. Gus would try to give his baby all the love that he could to try and make up for what he was missing from his mother. Gus would rock the baby to sleep sometime after dinner was over and just hold him tight and wonder how things would have been if he had gone back to that sweet Lorrie. He would think again about that time on the beach in Corpus and those wonderful kisses that he missed so much. He would think that surly as sweet and thoughtful as Lorrie was that she would have been a great mother. Oh well, that was then, and this is now and he just needed to make the best of things as they were. The winter was pretty hard for the Gulf Coast and his Dad's health kept getting worse. He was in and out of the hospital a lot and also his Mom was failing in health too. It seemed like there was more and more responsibility personal and business that he was responsible for. There was just no end to it, so he would just have to buck-up and take care of it. His wife didn't come back for the Thanksgiving or Christmas Holidays and all of a sudden it was the New Year of January 1969. She had now been gone for two months.

Lorrie—1968 July 1968 Lorrie's husband was acting more like a husband and father lately since she had caught him with another woman. He continued to work the extra job at the Library and study for his degree and he was making excellent grades. If his progress kept pace and his grades held up he would finish the requirements for his degree in just a few months and then he could be promoted to officer grade and they would be in line to get Base housing, and more money on his pay check. Things were looking up for Lorrie, but she was only cautiously optimistic wondering when he might decide to stray again. The baby had been growing and developing fine and he was walking getting into everything and saying a few words that you could understand, but most was just a jabber. The weather was good now in Nebraska, but Lorrie still didn't like it there and she actually looked forward to the time when the Ai9r Force would transfer her husband to another Base. Hopefully it would be in a better part of the United States. Lorrie was anxious for the baby to advance to the point where she could get a job to help out with the expenses and maybe with his upcoming promotion, Base housing and her getting a job they could be more comfortable financially, but that was a long way away yet. She was still helping him with all the typing of his papers and doing some of the research that he was required to do and she had always been the one to have to take care of paying all the bills and making sure that the rent was paid and that their little bank account was balanced. That was really hard most of the time, because there really was no extra money, because her husband was still paying on that motorcycle he bought, and Lorrie would have to decided what they would have to do without on a day to day basis. Some time she could get really exasperated with him for his selfishness. The year was speeding by and all of a sudden it was cold weather again in Nebraska and the holiday season was upon them. Lorrie wanted them to spend some of the holidays in El Campo with her parents and siblings, because she hadn't been with her family for any of the major holidays for two years and she was lonesome to be with them and show off all the new tricks that the baby could do. She talked it over with her husband and he said that the weather was to bad there in the winter to try to drive all the way to Texas and they couldn't afford to fly. Lorrie called to El Campo and talked to her Dad about the problem they had coming to El Campo for the holidays and he said that he would send her the money to fly and rent a car if she could convince her husband to come. Lorrie told him to go ahead and send the money and if she couldn't talk her husband into going then she would send the money back. Lorrie knew that her husband wouldn't go if he knew that the money had come from her Dad, so she thought that she would tell him that she had been saving money slowly for quite some time with this in mind. This way he would think that her family didn't have anything to do with it. She discussed it this way with her husband and he then agreed to go back to El Campo for Christmas. Lorrie was thrilled with this and she called back to her parents and told them, but she also told them that her husband could never know that they had payed, for the trip. Lorrie also took extra pains to do everything just right to please her husband so he wouldn't have any single excuse to back out of the trip. She knew that she could hide the ruse of saving the money herself, because he never did anything with the paying the bills or the bank account, or shopping, so it would be very easy to have rat holed a little money a little at a time over several months. After Thanksgiving Lorrie was full steam ahead making plans and getting everything ready for the trip back to El Campo for Christmas. She even went ahead and purchased the airplane tickets and made arrangements for the rental car when they arrived at the Houston airport. She thought that with all of this done it would give her husband less chance to find another use for the money and Lorrie couldn't let that happen. Also, she found out that if everything went good with her husband's College work that he might get his College degree in January 1969 and that would mean he would get a promotion. Lorrie typed all of her husband's final papers to complete his required work for his degree plan and it would be wait and see what his final grade would be, but she knew he would pass with flying colors, because his grades were exceptional all along, so it was just a matter of waiting for the final results. Her husband was in a real good mood, because he had been tired of studying all the time and now that was over. A week before they were to leave on their trip, he received notice that he had passed and that his degree would be presented to him in January 1969.

Gus—1968 Christmas 1968 had actually gone real good for Gus, the baby and his Mom and Dad except that his Dad was having more and more problems with his health and that meant that he could take less of a part in all the activity and he had to rest more often. It was the end of January 1969 now and Gus's wife had been gone for three months and he was real used to her not being around. Things were certainly a lot quieter and running more smoother without her. He almost hoped that she wouldn't come back. After all, what good was she to his family. Their son didn't really know her, because she was so seldom around to take care of him and Gus did most of the cleaning, washing and cooking but still she was his Mom and Gus's wife and Gus didn't want another divorce. All he hoped for was to let the marriage run and see if after a few more years his wife would settle down and accept her proper role as Mother and wife. Gus had been doing some extra work during the winter months for a small Oil Company out of San Antonio that was trying to lease small acreages around El Campo and Gus became the Land Man that put together the leases and talked to the landowners. It went good and Gus had made several thousand dollars extra during that time, but Gus had told the Oil Company that he would have to quit at the end of February, so he could get back to the full-time business of farming and ranching. He started planting the first week in March 1969 and made good progress, finished the Milo Maize and got prepared to start planting the Rice. One evening when he and his son came home, he noticed that the front door on his house was open, so he got his gun out of his pick-up just in case there was a intruder in the house. He put the gun in his belt behind his back and slowly approached the house and went up the steps quietly and into the small living room. Once in the house he drew his gun and looked in the kitchen then slipped slowly through the short hall to the bedroom and what did he find, but his wife sleeping on his bed with her luggage thrown on the floor. She hadn't heard him and for a minute he just looked at her, then he tip-toed out to the truck and put up his gun and got his son and the bag of baby stuff he always carried with him and went back into the house making as much noise as he could to wake her up. She had been gone now almost four months. He didn't go back to the bedroom, but instead busied himself in the kitchen putting the things from the baby bag into the sink and talking to the baby. She heard him and came into the kitchen and tried to act like she was so glad to see him and the baby, but the baby ran away from her to his room and hid. She said I wonder what is wrong with him and Gus told her that the baby was probably just playing hide-in-seek with her. Gus was nervous with her home and really didn't know how to respond to her. She looked around and said that she was glad to see that the house looked so nice, because she was tired and since it was so nice, she wouldn't have so much to do. Gus thought to himself, and when did you do so much anyway. Gus told his wife that he had to go ahead and get the baby bathed so he could get dinner, and everything squared away for the night, because tomorrow was another work- day. His wife looked at him for a minute and finally said that she would bath the baby if he wanted to do other things and Gus told her to go ahead and do it. When she got the baby undressed and in the bathtub Gus had to get everything she needed to bath and clean the baby, because she didn't remember where anything was located. Gus then went to the kitchen and started to wash up everything from the baby bag and get out some leftovers for their dinner. The baby wasn't used to her and Gus didn't leave him with a babysitter, so the baby was afraid of someone new, so to speak, since he hadn't been around her for so long. Gus had the baby with him twenty-four hours a day and he wasn't used to anybody except his own Daddy and a few other men that Gus would be around while working cattle or farming. When everything finally calmed down and they went to bed his wife rolled over next to him and tried to initiate some sex, Gus told her that he was simply to tired and that he was also not used to having a woman in bed next to him and that he needed time to get used to her being home again, so she rolled over on her side and went to sleep. Gus was terribly tired, but he couldn't sleep, and he laid there for hours wondering what he was going to do, because he, at that moment, had no sexual desire for his wife. Gus woke up in the morning and put on the coffee as usual, but he didn't follow his usual schedule. Instead he waited for his wife to wake up by herself. The baby got up early, because he was used to that schedule and Gus had trouble keeping him quiet so his wife could sleep. Gus had decided to take off the morning so he and his wife could talk to see what she had on her mind about their life together. He didn't need to lose this time in the field, but they needed to talk. Gus's wife finally got up and strolled into the kitchen, poured herself some coffee, sat down at the table and started to try to start some small talk with Gus. Gus listened to her for a few minutes and he interrupted her and told her that he had taken off the morning so they could have an adult conversation about their married life, so he wanted to get to it. He told her that he wanted to know when she was going to start accepting her responsibilities as a Mother and wife and that was basically the heart of what he wanted to talk about, because her running off to Louisiana all the time wasn't working for the family. He said that he had basically been father and mother to their son ever since he had been born and she needed to step up and learn how to be a Mom. She listened quietly until Gus quit talking, then she said that she needed to discuss something important with him also and she didn't quite know how to start. Gus thought that she was going to say that she wanted a divorce, but that isn't what it was about. He told her that whatever it was that she just needed to say it and get it over with. She told him OK, I'm pregnant. For a minute Gus was stunned. Then he said OK, now I can see why you were putting the announcement off. Gus told her that she had been gone too long for it to be his, but that he didn't want to hear any of the dirty little details of how it happened. He said that she had been on birth control pills when she left, so was she too lazy to take them, or was her lover to cheap to pay to have them refilled. Then he told her to just forget it. He said that now they were going to have to decide what to do about this latest development. He asked her if she wanted a divorce so she could marry the father of her baby. She told him no and that she guessed that a divorce was up to him. Gus asked her how far along she thought she was, and she told him that she thought that she was three months pregnant. Gus told her that he was going to have to think about all of this to try to decide what would best for the family. He told her that he had to go to work and that he was taking the baby, because the baby wasn't used to being around her yet and that they would talk more when Gus got in from work. He told her that he hoped to have it all worked out in his mind by then. He got the things he needed, dressed the baby, told her to try and make herself useful while he was gone, then he and the baby left for work. Gus didn't get a lot of work done that day, but he just needed to get away from his wife, so he could think this thing out and come to a conclusion before he got home that evening. He knew that it was time to lay the law down and stick to whatever decision he came up with. That evening when he got home from work, he told his wife that they would talk after dinner, baths and the baby was asleep that he had decided on what they would do and that it was non-negotiable on her part. After dinner, baths and the baby went to sleep, Gus told his wife to sit across the kitchen table and he would tell her the decision that he had made. He told her that she wasn't to talk until he had finished and then after he had finished, if she had any questions that she could ask them. Gus told her that from now on there would be no more trips to Louisiana, no more part time jobs, that she would have to stay home and learn the things that a wife and a Mother needed to do and if she didn't know then she needed to ask and learn how to do things. He told her that she would have to keep the house reasonably clean, keep up with the laundry, do the grocery shopping, plan good meals, make sure that the baby was clean, fed and in good health and basically concentrate on making a good home for the family. He said that he would provide for the family and support her in every way that a husband should support his wife and that he would see to it that she had the right medical care during her pregnancy and that when the baby was born that he would raise it as his own. He told her that they both would have to work hard to overcome a lot that had happened in the past, but if they worked together that there was still a chance that they could have a successful marriage and a happy family and that if she excepted these simple rules, then they would start over and go forward, but if not then she could leave the next morning to go back to Louisiana. His wife looked at him a minute and then said that she would do her best and then she asked him if she could hug and kiss him. Gus told her yes and from now on she could whenever she wanted to. Gus had his doubts, but at least this was a chance to see if it could work. It was April 1969 and time would tell.

Lorrie—1968 Christmas 1968 found Lorrie, her husband and the baby in El Campo and Lorrie was having a wonderful time. She had even seen several of her old High School classmates that had come home for Christmas also.

The four days that they stayed with her parents her husband actually stayed there every night, but he went his own way during the day, which Lorrie didn't mind, because it gave her time to be herself with her parents and siblings. Her Dad got her off by herself and asked her how things were in the marriage and she told him that she thought that maybe a little better and she expected that things might improve more, because her husband had finished his degree, so soon he would be promoted to officer grade and that would make him happy. One day when she visited one of her High School classmates and they were talking about events that had taken place in school the girl started talking about what had happened on their Corpus band trip and asked Lorrie what had really happened to get her in trouble and get kicked out of band that last week of school. Lorrie put her head down and then looked up and bit her bottom lip and she told her that a boy she had a crush on had followed them to Corpus and that they had gone walking on the beach and when he kissed her she realized that it wasn't a crush, that it was and always had been true love and that it was still the most wonderful day of her life. She told her friend that it was something that she would never forget and that it was worth it to get kicked out of band and she would do it again if she had the chance. Her friend asked her if it was the older boy Gus that had that red Hot-Rod and Lorrie said yes, and he will always be the love of my life. Her friend ask her if she knew what ever happened to Gus and Lorrie said she didn't know, but she only knew what had happened to herself and she started crying and her girlfriend held her close and Lorrie told her that if she ever found true love to never let it go, because it was precious and may never happen again. Lorrie wiped her tears and drove back to her parents and they packed up to go back to Nebraska. Back in Nebraska they decided not to go out for New Years, because they didn't need to spend any more money and they needed to just rest up from their Christmas trip to El Campo. January 1969 brought some real changes to Lorrie and her husband's life. He received his degree and a month later he was promoted to an officer and put in charge a Company Supply Depot on the Base. Lorrie thought well, now he can boss some people around, so maybe he won't boss me around so much. He got a small raise and the big thing was that he got Base housing that saved them some real money. Soon after Lorrie got a shock that she hadn't expected. She found out that she was expected to have get-to-gathers with the other officer's wives and she had no idea what to do about that. This really worried her, because it would be a reflection on her husband if she didn't do things right. The Company

Commander's wife got things started with a get acquainted lunch at her house with all the Officer's wives in the Company in attendance. Lorrie was kind of bashful and quickly discovered that she was very under dressed and she had worn the very best dress she owned. She observed everything, because she knew that she would have to emulate everything that they did and from what she observed she didn't have anything that could compare to the dishes, glasses, napkins, snack trays, flat ware and decorations that were displayed and all the other women seemed perfectly at home and comfortable with it all. They were all very nice, but the gossip was astounding, everything from who was homosexual to who was having an affair, to who had the most money and who was the biggest flirt. Lorrie thought, well girl, you just need to listen and learn. When she got home, she sat down and wrote a list of everything she would need to put on a get-to-gather similar to that. She even put dollar prices by everything, and this even included bathroom towels and matching hand towels. She knew her husband was going to hit the ceiling, but what could she do, he was an Officer now and this all came with the rank. When her husband got home and asked her how the gathering went, and she laid the list that she had compiled in front of him and he wanted to know what it was. Lorrie explained that these were the things that they would need when it came her turn to give a ladies lunch or tea and that she also needed some better cloths now if he expected her to go to any more of those affairs, because she was embarrassed how she was dressed. He said that he didn't know how they would be able to afford all of that and Lorrie told him fine that maybe he needed to get demoted and then they wouldn't need any of it. She told him that she was going to have to start to shop for these things slowly as they had the money, but she had to have some better cloths now because there were going to be some more gatherings coming up soon. He marched around and muttered for a while and then exclaimed that she would just have to work it out and that if anyone was to give up anything for this it would have to be her and the baby. Then he asked what was for supper and went to clean up. Lorrie thought well, I guess that me and the baby are the only ones in the family. Several months went by and Lorrie was slowly acquiring the things she would need to be a hostess for the Officer wive's gatherings, but everyone that she attended she felt out of place. The year went by and Lorrie put had put on a couple of these gatherings and they seemed successful, but she never felt comfortable around all these women acting like they were so much better than the wives of the enlisted men. Lorrie thought that she just didn't belong to this type of society and it made her unhappy to have to put on airs when she knew who she really was. She thought if only she could have married Gus then she could have just been herself. The year 1969 went fast for Lorrie and the Baby was growing and talking up a storm and into everything. New Year 1970 came with an Officers dance and for once her husband acted the gentleman. Lorrie wondered what 1970 would bring.

Gus—1969 With the talk and agreement that Gus had in April 1969 with his wife, he could tell that she was trying to do better, but she had so much to learn. He tried to help her without making her feel bad about herself. They had begun having sex again, but for Gus it was mostly just a way of relieving pressure and relaxing before sleep. It was July now and he was into the Milo Maize harvest and soon into the Rice harvest. His wife was trying to cook for him and the baby. He had bought her a good cookbook hoping that she would improve with its guidance and it helped some, but there were still a lot failures that he ate anyway and bragged on her so she would not get discouraged. She was trying her best to be keeping up with the laundry and the baby was clean and fat. Gus got a shock in July 1969 when he opened a Certified Mail envelope from a lawyer in Houston and there were adoption papers and a letter in it. The letter said that his ex-wife had married the College boy and they wanted to adopt the baby that his ex-wife had birthed. Gus was surprised, but he thought, well this is good, because it straightens out that part of his and the baby's life to what it should be, so he signed the adoption papers and sent them back. Now the baby boy could have the right last name. Gus thought that it looked like time was going to help him iron out some of the mistakes that had been made along the way. In September 1969 harvest time was over for Gus and he was busy gathering and working cattle to vaccinate the calves that had been born since the spring working and also to sell all the big calves and some old cows before winter. He came home one evening and his wife told him that she was having small pains that she thought might be labor pains, so they started timing them and sure enough they got stronger and stronger. About two in the morning his wife woke him up and told him that her water had broken, so he called the Doctor and took her to the hospital. About four hours his wife had a baby girl. Gus had hoped that the baby would not look to different then their little boy, just to keep down the usual gossip when a woman had a baby, especially since his wife had a known reputation of being a loose woman. When Gus looked at the little girl baby, he knew what the gossip would be, because this baby looked so different that no one in their right mind could ever accuse him of being the father. His little boy baby had been very fair skinned with blue eyes and thin, wispy blond hair. This little girl baby had an olive complexion, dark brown eyes and very thick black hair and eyebrows. Oh well, what will be will be he thought. He would raise her as his own just the same. His wife and the baby were doing just fine. So, she and the baby came home after three days in the hospital and Gus hires the wife of one of his workers to help out for a couple of weeks till his wife could take over on her own. This worked out fine and the other woman even taught his wife to cook a few simple recipes that helped with the meals. As the months went by Gus noticed his wife started to lose interest again in trying to keep up the house. She did learn to make a pot roast that was just perfect with carrots, potatoes and onions seasoned very good and with great gravy. He was astonished when he came home one night, and the house was very clean, and this pot roast was ready for dinner. He thought that he must have been mistaken about her losing interest. Then she would lap's back into losing interest in what things were like. Then she would have a clean house and the pot roast dinner again. Thanksgiving and Christmas holidays came and went, and they were celebrated as a family should. New Year day January 1970 found Gus, his wife and the two kids over at his Mom and Dad's house eating black eyed pies ham and cabbage and corn bread for a New Year lunch. They then went home put the kids to bed for a nap and got in bed themselves had sex and took a long nap. It looked to Gus like 1970 was starting out on the right foot and maybe it would be a good year.

Lorrie—1970 In March 1970 Lorrie's husband got another promotion and orders to transfer to San Antonio, Texas and Lorrie couldn't have been happier. What a relief to get away from all the bad weather in Nebraska and also San Antonio was only three hours from her family in El Campo and that meant that they could visit more often. Lorrie was twenty-four years old in March of 1970, and her son was, almost three years old. This Air Force Base close to El Campo would give her parents a chance to know their grandson better, because they could visit more often. Lorrie was a Texas girl all the way and San Antonio was the heart of the Texas revolution with the famous siege and massacre there of so many Texas patriots. She thought that as soon as she could she was going to take her son to the Alamo, because every Texas kid should go to the Alamo as soon as he could. They got moved and settled into the Base housing and her husband took over his position there. He was in charge of a much larger supply compound and he had a larger staff to supervise. The Base officer's wives had a welcome party for her and by now she was familiar with their social event's, although she had never really felt that she fit in. In April her son turned four years old and the officer's wives had a big birthday party for him with their children in attendance. It was nice to see her son have so much fun with the other children and the facility it was held in on Base had a very nice playground for them. As time went on Lorrie made some casual friends with some of the officer wives, but she was never totally close to them enough to be confiding personal feelings. She just was never in the same mindset as they were. Many times, she had wished that her husband wasn't an officer. After several months at the Base her husband started talking about his assistant, how dependable and competent he was and that he wanted to invite him over for dinner one Friday. Lorrie told him to just let her know in time and she would make them a Mexican dinner with tacos, re-fried beans, cream cheese stuffed hot peppers and avocados with lime juice on them and some beer. Sure, the next Friday her husband called and told her that they would be home about 6:00 pm after work. Lorrie made sure that their home was straightened up nice and she had done the shopping to get everything that she needed to make their Mexican dinner. About 6:00 pm her husband walked into the house and following him was this very handsome man with a smile on his face and when her husband introduced him he put out his hand to shake hers and he said that he loved her hair that he thought it was real pretty. This caught Lorrie's attention real fast, because her husband never complimented her looks, ever. Her dinner turned out really good and while the men talked and had a couple of beers after dinner, Lorrie did the dishes and the thought of that compliment kept her smiling to herself. It was so good to think that a handsome man would find something about her attractive. After she cleaned up everything, she joined them at the table with her own beer and listened carefully to their conversation. This handsome assistant of her husband's was very interesting. He was full of jokes and had a country sort of way to him. Lorrie finally asked him where he was from and he told her that he was born and raised in East Texas on a ranch there. The very next question that Lorrie asked him was if they had horses, because she had loved horses since she was a little girl and she had always hoped someday that she could have one that was her very own. He laughed and said that yes, they did and that he had grown up riding and training them. Lorrie was all ears now and she couldn't get enough of this conversation. He told her that actually he had his horse out on a place just south of San Antonio that he had rented and that he liked to ride every chance he got when he was off. He told her that the place came with a little house, so he didn't live on the Base. She just couldn't help herself, but to ask him if they could come out sometime and if she could ride his horse. She then looked at her husband and he looked at his assistant and his assistant told them sure any time that they all could meet, so it was all set and Lorrie couldn't believe that she might be able to ride a horse again. She hadn't ridden since High School, so this was really something to look forward to. The middle of the next week her husband asked her if she wanted to go out to his assistant's place that next Saturday to see his horse and they would also B-B-Q something out there for dinner. Of course Lorrie jumped at the chance and told her husband that it was a silly question, because he had known how much she liked horses and he laughed and told her that he thought that she would want to go, but he didn't know if she had something else planned and she told him that it wouldn't matter, because she would have canceled it for this chance. He laughed again and she thought that she hadn't heard him laugh like that in an awful long time. She wondered why this had him in such a good mood. That next Saturday Lorrie her husband and their boy went out to his assistant's place to ride his horse. When they got out there her husband's assistant was waiting for them and led them over to the corral where he had his horse and he had the horse all brushed down and saddled. Lorrie was thrilled when he took her into the corral and let her stroke the horse's mane and talk to him. She got on and the saddle was just right, because she had those long legs and she went riding around the corral in her height of glory. Her husband was a little afraid of the horse and stood a to the side close to the corral fence. She asked his assistant if she could go out of the corral with the horse and he told her that he really didn't want her to, because the horse wasn't used to her and he didn't trust his horse in the open pasture with anyone else on him, so Lorrie had to settle for just riding him around the corral, which was alright, because this was the first time she had the opportunity to get the smell of horse on her in a lot of years and she had always loved the smell of a horse. After about an hour of riding in the corral her husband's assistant told them that they needed to go over to his house where he had prepared everything for them to start a fire for the B-B-Q and he had some beer and they could play some country music outside while they talked and cooked. While they were doing the B-B-Q Lorrie was telling her husband's assistant how she had always wanted to have her own horse and that he was so lucky to-be able to have grown up on a ranch with horses. He told her that if she wanted to buy a horse that he would take them to some horse sales and help them to pick out one that would be good for her and that they could rent one of the houses out where he lived and the stall would go with the house rent and then she could ride whenever she wanted to. She looked at her husband and he said that he didn't think that they could afford it on his salary and if she could find a pretty good job, then maybe they could talk about it. Lorrie thought that at least he didn't say no, so maybe there was a chance she could do it. They went home that night and Lorrie's mind was buzzing with ideas about how she could make this work. Wow, this would give her something wonderful to dream about and work toward. This move to the Base in 1970 was turning out to be even better then Lorrie could have ever hoped for.

. Gus—1970 Gus had hopes that 1970 would be a real turn around for his wife to becoming a good wife and mother to their two kids. There were signs that she was starting to make some improvement in that direction. After all she was now almost twenty-one years old and she should be maturing enough to realize what the responsibilities she had consisted of and how important they were. She was still irresponsible about how she would cook and take care of the house, but she didn't talk about running off to Louisiana or getting part time jobs anymore and that was an improvement. She would do things like tell Gus that he didn't have to take his lunch to the field, because she would cook him something and that would really please Gus, because it looked like she was making a special effort to do something nice for him. Well that never worked out, because Gus would wait and wait for lunch to arrive and finally at 2:30 pm his wife would pull up to the field with a cheeseburger and a milkshake from the Dairy Queen. What a let-down that was and it happened every time that she offered to do that until Gus finally told her that he couldn't wait to eat that late in the day and he was going to take his lunch from now on. Gus didn't know it at the time, but the only reason that she wanted to bring him lunch is so she would be sure of where he was to be, because she was having sex with other men and she didn't want to take the chance that he would discover her accidentally. She was pretty sneaky, and he never caught on to it till several years later when he was told by one of her old friends. One evening when Gus came home, he noticed that his car was gone, but didn't think anything about it. He went in the house and he found a note on the table and it said I thought that I could do it, but I can't. Your son is at your Mom's and I have taken the girl, your car is at the bus station and I have gone to Louisiana ". Gus thought well, I wonder how long it will be before she comes back pregnant again. He thought that at least she hadn't taken the boy. He went over to his Mom's house and she didn't know anything about his wife leaving for Louisiana, His Mom said that his wife said that she had to take the little girl to the doctor and then do some shopping and could his Mom please keep the boy for a few hours. Gus thought that his wife's whole life with him had been nothing more than lies and excuses and he was glad that she was gone and hoped that he never saw her again. He and his son would simply go back to their old way of doing things. He and his son went home, and he cooked dinner for them and cleaned up the kitchen and gave his son a bath and put him to bed. Gus opened her closet and drawers and found a few things that she hadn't taken, and he put them in a sack and dumped them in the trash. He made up his mind that he was through trying with her and he would just let time go by to see what was going to happen, but he was not going to bend over backwards to make his marriage work. As far as he was concerned his marriage to her was already over. He was just going to let it play out to see how it was finally going to end. He had already planted the Milo Maize and the Rice, and both crops were doing good and now he was gathering cattle for the spring working. His Dad's health had become really bad and they had to hire some extra help, because his Mom wasn't able to take care of him herself, so the expense of this was laid on Gus's shoulders also. Gus had to laugh at himself when he thought of the beginning of 1970 and the hopes that he had that his wife would straighten up and how he could have been so stupid as to think that, because it was now the end of June 1970 and that was only six months ago. One day when he came home there was an old Black lady waiting for him and she introduced herself and told him that his wife owed her some money and that she had been by several times but could never catch her at home. Gus asked her what she had done to earn the money. The Black woman told him that she would come over sometime and clean house, do the laundry and cook a pot roast with carrots, potatoes and onions and make a real good gravy to go with it. Gus invited her in and paid her but didn't tell her that his wife had left. After she left Gus just shook his head and remembered how he had believed that his wife had cooked the pot roast and how he had bragged on her and how good it was and his wife had taken all the credit for the cooking and cleaning the house. How stupid he had been. He wondered what else he would find out in time. It wouldn't be long till harvest time now and the 1970 crop would be over.

Lorrie—1970 In June of 1970 Lorrie started to look through all the San Antonio papers for jobs that she might be able to get. She was determined to find a job that she could make enough money at so she could afford to buy and keep a horse. She knew that just buying a horse was the first step, because she would need other things like a saddle, bridle, saddle blanket, brushes and combs to groom the horse and how about boots, jeans, hat and belt for herself. Then there was grain and hay and someone to shoe the horse and maybe some vet-medicine, so there was a lot to owning a horse. Oh, and then they would have to move over to the same place as her husband's assistant to have a place to keep the horse and have a place to ride him. That would cost a lot of extra money, because they would have to give up their Base housing. Yes, she would have to find a decent paying job. After a couple of months, she found one at the Sears Roebuck store downtown. Lorrie was so glad to have found that job. She was making almost as much money as her husband and it wouldn't be to long for her to save the money that she would need to buy the horse and move to that country place at the edge of San Antonio. In the meantime, they kept going out to her husband's assistants place to ride and for him to teach her how to care for a horse of her own. She watched and listened to everything that he said and did, and she would practice on his horse. Lorrie was so glad that she had someone that knew so much about horses, because her husband didn't know anything about them and all she ever really knew was how to ride them. He was real patient with her, and she learned everything pretty quickly. He finally would let her go into the horse stall and catch his horse and brush him down and saddle him all by herself and she was so proud of herself. She was never afraid of the horse and her husband's assistant showed her how to walk around a horse and watch the horse, so he wouldn't kick, bite or step on you. They went to several horse sales, but all the horses they saw, her husband's assistant said, were either too expensive or they were not gentle enough for her to ride. Lorrie was getting discouraged till one day they were out at her husband's assistants place and he told her that he did have an older mare back in East Texas at his parents ranch that had been put out to pasture for several years and hadn't been ridden and he would go there to see her and if everything was OK, then he would bring her back in his trailer and Lorrie could have her to take care of and ride. Lorrie was thrilled beyond belief. Her husband told her that he had one more rule that she would have to do if he was to let her have the horse and that was that she would have to quit smoking. She had been smoking steady ever since she left home at nineteen, but she said that she would do it so she could have the horse. That evening when they got home Lorrie threw her cigarettes away. The next weekend her husband's assistant met them at his place with the horse in the trailer and Lorrie was just about jumping off the ground waiting for him to unload the horse so she could get on her. The mare was just as he had got her from the pasture. She had a real long mane and tail that were tangled with briars and weeds and her hoofs were split and overgrown, but to Lorrie she was the most beautiful horse she had ever seen. As soon as she was out of the trailer, Lorrie went up to her and hugged her neck and then, to the assistant's shock, Lorrie grabbed her mane and jumped on her back without a saddle. The assistant was afraid that the horse would buck and kick, because she had been loose for so long and hadn't been ridden, but the horse took to Lorrie at once. It was love at first sight for Lorrie and the mare. After Lorrie had ridden the horse around the corral bare-back for a while her husband's assistant told her that they needed to put the horse in a stall and feed and water her, because she needed to settle down from the trip and just get used to her stall and the surroundings. He told her that they needed to get away from the horse and let her be quiet and also it was getting late and if they were going to B-B-Q and drink beer and listen to music they should finish the chores there and go to his house and they could talk about the horse there. They finished up at the horse stalls and went to his house and started the fire and he put on some music and they all got a beer and sat around and talked about the horse and listened to old country and rock-n-roll music. Lorrie had all kinds of questions about her new mare, and her husband's assistant answered all of them. Lorrie was so impressed by him and he seemed to be very interested in what she had to say, which was a new experience for her, because her husband never seemed to be interested in anything she had to say. Their conversation was just flowing along so good until the song "In The Still Of The Night" was playing, and Lorrie stopped talking in midsentence and got quiet. The men just looked at her and her husband's assistant asked her if something was wrong and she said that no, she just liked that song and wanted to listen to it, so they all got quiet till the song was over. Her husband's assistant told Lorrie that he would feed her horse every-day, until they could get moved out there, but then she would be responsible for all responsibility of her own horse. Lorrie couldn't thank him enough and she gave him a big hug and shook his hand. She thought that it felt good to give that handsome man a hug. After they got back home and Lorrie was in the bathroom getting ready for bed she thought about everything that had happened that afternoon at her husband's assistants place and she thought that this move to the Air Force Base in San Antonio and being able to have her own horse was the answer to her dream and what more could she ask for, then she remembered the song " In The Still Of The Night " playing and she thought that if only Gus would be here with me then it truly wood be the answer to her life-long dream. It was August 1970 now and soon they would move out to the place next to her husband's assistant so she could ride her horse.

Gus—1970 Despite all the turmoil that had gone on so far in 1970 Gus was plugging along doing his farming and ranching and taking care of his son and the extra responsibility brought on by his Dad's continued failing health. Since Gus had never witnessed watching someone physically decline with an incurable ailment, he didn't realize just how precarious a situation his Dad's health was in. He knew that his Dad was very sick, but he couldn't relate it to nearness of death. He simply assumed that his Dad would slowly get weaker over a long period of time, maybe years. Gus kept up visits to his Mom and Dad's house every couple of days to see how things were going and to relate what he had been doing at the ranch and the farm that would interest his Dad. By the end of August 1970 Gus had finished the Milo Maize and the Rice harvest and started preparing for the fall cattle round-up. The fall cattle round-up took a little more time than usual, because Gus now had expanded his cattle herd to where he had cattle in six big pastures and his calf crop had increased dramatically compared to the small herd, he had started out with in 1961. He started to have an after-harvest appreciation B-B-Q when all the crops and the cattle round-up in the fall were over. He would have his farm and ranch hands and anyone that had helped with them invited and he would furnish all the meat and food and a sixteen gallon keg of beer and they would all pitch in with the wood chopping, building the fire, B-B-Q cooking and someone would play a guitar and while all of this was going on they would sing Country and Western and Mexican songs till late at night and everyone really looked forward to this end of harvest get together, so they could do something together besides work. It was time now to start getting the land prepared for the 1971 crop year. Gus thought that even though there had been a lot of unexpected reverses in his personal life and his Dads health, that there was still a lot to be thankful for. The harvest and calf sales had been very good and his and his son's health was good and even his wife leaving for Louisiana had made him finally make a decision on the finality of their marriage. While contemplating these things Gus's mind drifted to remembering Lorrie and for a minute wondering if they could have been happy together. He thought oh well, that was a long time ago and no use dreaming about that now. After all January 1971 wasn't that far away and it would be a new year.

Lorrie—1970 Lorrie and her husband moved out to the ranch by his assistant in October 1970 and Lorrie was up very early every morning feeding, watering, brushing and loving her mare. She would brush her and talk to her about everything. She would tell her mare things that she would never tell a human. While she was taking care of her mare her husband's assistant would also be at the same stalls taking care of his horse, so they were in contact together a lot now and she thought it nice, because they had a lot in common. Then she would run back to the house and get their son ready to go into town to the babysitter and Lorrie would go to the Sears building to work. Her husband and his assistant would ride together to the Base to their jobs. Since San Antonio and El Campo were so close together Lorrie wanted to spend these special holidays with her family, but her husband didn't want to go there. He finally told her that she could go there but he wouldn't. This was OK with Lorrie, because it would be a much happier time for family with the tension of having him around. Thanksgiving holiday found Lorrie and her son in El Campo with her family and she had all of the pictures of her horse and of her riding her horse with and with the saddle. She had pictures of her feeding her horse carrots, apples and her hugging her horse, you name it and she had a picture of it with the horse. She and her son had a wonderful time with her family and her Dad was getting to know his grandson better. Her son was three and one-half years old now and he was everywhere all at once and you had a real job keeping up with him. Her little brother and sister were a big help keeping track of him and figuring out things that would keep him bust and out of trouble. This gave Lorrie a chance to go visit one of her old High School girlfriends. Her girlfriend had come back to El Campo after graduating from University of Houston and married her High School sweetheart. She had given up a job at an accounting firm in Houston to marry him. He had his own truck and was hauling from coast to coast and her his wife, her girlfriend, was doing their books and all the paperwork that they needed for his trucking business. Lorrie asked her how it felt to come back and live in El Campo after living in Houston for four years. Her girlfriend told her that it didn't matter to her where she lived as long as she was with the man she loved. Her girlfriend asked Lorrie why she was so against living in El Campo and Lorrie told her that her Mom and Dad had control of her life so much when she lived here that all she could think of was to get away so she could run her own life. Her girlfriend asked her if she thought that she could ever move back to El Campo in the future and be happy here. Lorrie looked at her for a minute with her eyes tearing up and said that if she would have had the right man to love that she might never had left El Campo. Her friend asked her who that would have been, and Lorrie said it would always be Gus. Her friend said wasn't he the boy that worked for my Dad in the service station and Lorrie told her that it was him. Her friend said that she remembered when they used to go to the station and flirt with him, but that she didn't know that Lorrie had been love with him. Lorrie told her that the word wasn't, had been in love, because she would always been love with Gus. Her friend asked her what had happened, and Lorrie told her that she didn't want to talk about it, because it hurt too much. So, they hugged, and Lorrie went back to her parent's house and her and her son finished the Thanksgiving holidays and then went back to San Antonio. While she was gone her husband, with his assistants help, was supposed to take care of her horse. When she went into the house, she found her husband in an easy chair with his foot propped up on a stool with a big bandage on it. She asked what in the world happened to him and he told her that damn horse of hers didn't like him and that she had stepped on top of his foot on purpose and then wouldn't get off and leaned her weight on it and he couldn't move her and had to yell to his assistant, who was feeding his own horse, to hurry and help him. She said well who is feeding my horse and he told her that his assistant was doing it, because he couldn't go out there with his foot all swollen up. Lorrie acted real-sorry for him and tried to do everything she could to make him feel better, but secretly she had to grin, because she thought what a smart horse to be able to make the right judgment of her husband. When Christmas came around Lorrie couldn't go to El Campo, because she was sick with a bad virus. For New Year they and her husband's assistant and his girl date went to a famous old country dance hall, not too far away and brought the New Year of 1971 in there. They would exchange partners dancing with each other and Lorrie noticed that when she danced with her husband's assistant that he held her very close and rubbed his hand on her back while dancing and she liked it and got the idea of seeing what might happen when feeding the horses together if she sort of gave him a little encouragement. After all it is a New Year of 1971 and a chance to start something new and that means maybe a new romance might put the memory of Gus way back in her mind and bring some excitement into 1971.

Gus—1970 The Thanksgiving and Christmas holidays were a little subdued, because of Gus's Dad's continued declining health, even though the farming and ranching operation in 1970 had been very profitable, which helped. Gus hadn't heard anything from his wife since she had left for Louisiana in June and that had been about six months and he thought, that he hoped that he never would hear from her again. Gus was looking ahead to the 1971 farming and ranching year and taking care of his son, who would be starting four-year-old preschool. That would mean that Gus would have to look for a real good babysitter that could take care of his son after he got out of school till the time that Gus got home from the farm and ranch. There was still time to do that because his son wouldn't have to start till September 1971. Gus bought a new tractor and some new equipment for his Milo Maize farming and another used combine for harvest operations. This will help speed up the planting and harvest which are the most critical times during the farming year. He had also saved back the largest number of his biggest and best heifers to save for the cow heard that he had ever done, so the farming and ranching operations were growing faster now. Yes, Gus was looking ahead into !971 and he didn't need a wife to help him do it, in fact he felt that the wife he had was just a draw-back instead of an asset to his family and business. Gus had also borrowed money and bought some of his Dad's land during the year. An independent oil company had contacted him about an oil lease and from his past experience negotiating leases for others he was ready to negotiate his own. The negotiations were on going and Gus didn't expect them to be over till the New Year 1971, because of all the holidays it was hard to get anything done. If 1971 would be a good farming and ranching year Gus was set to expand his business once again. New Year morning 1971 found Gus and his son eating breakfast together with party hats on and his son blowing a New Year whistle.

Lorrie—1971 Living off-Base on that ranch suited Lorrie just fine. She had to drive farther to work, but the advantages of living away from town more than made up for it. She had her horse right there and she could ride most anytime even sometime when she got off from work and now she also had her husband's assistant right there also, she just had to figure out what she was going to do to tempt him into letting her know what his real feelings were. She didn't want to be to forward if he wasn't serious in wanting to have an affair, because then he could go to her husband and she would be in trouble. She had made up her mind though about him. She had liked him from the first time her husband had brought him over to dinner and he complimented her on how nice her hair looked and then when she saw how much he knew about horses and she had watched him now for a while around the place, well to put it plain, she was ready to have an affair with him, if they could keep it a secret. She just had to be sure that it happened in a natural way that wouldn't make her look like the aggressor. She decided that in the feed barn with the horse stalls would be the best place for an accidental close contact, because they had been there together before and it could be pretty close quarters working at the same time in there, so she had the place, but now she would have to wait for the right time when no one else was around and he would be there doing the same thing that she was doing. Lorrie's husband had been cheating on her ever since they had married, and she decided that this New Year 1971 in January that she was going to enjoy her horse and hopefully an affair with a handsome rugged horseman. They both went to the feed barn every-day in the mornings, but had to be in a rush because of going to work and in the evenings they weren't always there at the same time because of getting back from work and running errands, so it would have to happen on a weekend when things slowed down. The very next Saturday morning Lorrie got up early, as usual, and went to the corral and feed barn to feed her horse and left her son and her husband sleeping. She messed around there till she saw her husband's assistant drive up and then she pretended that she was having a hard time getting a feed sack open, because she knew that he would offer to help her. She had it sitting up on the edge of the feed bin in a precarious fashion when he walked in and she was muttering to herself and he came over to see what she was doing and she told him that the sack didn't want to open, so he grabbed it and they were very close together so it gave Lorrie a chance to rub against him and lean on him for a minute to keep the sack from falling on the floor. She just giggled when she did this and he looked at her with a big smile and told her that he loved the way that she smiled and then he leaned over just a little and kissed her on the lips while they were both just standing there holding that feed sack. He then put the sack down and took her in his arms and kissed her and she kissed him back and then there was no stopping it, because the passion exploded and before she knew it they were laying on the hay bales having sex, and it was good too. It lasted longer then, when her husband had sex with her, but this is what she needed, for different reasons. Finally, it happened and now Lorrie knew that they would have to make plans, because she knew that it wasn't going to be just a onetime thing, she felt that her and her lover would really enjoy 1971.

Gus—1971 It was pretty cold New Year day 1971, so Gus dressed his son warm and they drove out to the ranch to feed the horses and ride around some of the pastures just to check on things to make sure that no cows were out on the roads. Gus had let the farm and ranch workers off for the holiday, so there wasn't any hurry and he could enjoy this time with his son. They went by the last pasture and they were on their way home driving down the gravel country road when his son took off his new stocking hat and held it out the window. Gus told him not to do it, but he just looked at Gus and smiled and kept it out the window. Gus told him that it would blow out of his hand and then he wouldn't have a cap, because Gus wasn't going to stop to pick it up and sure enough no more than Gus said that, it blew out of his son's hand. His son looked at Gus with astonishment in his eyes and Gus just kept driving and his boy looked out the back window of the truck and Gus told him that he needed to listen to his Dad from now on, because now he wouldn't have a warm hat to wear in cold weather. Gus really hated to leave that good stocking hat laying on that gravel road, but he was trying to teach his son a lesson. Later in the day he took his son over to Gus's Mom's and told her what had happened and asked if she could keep his son for about an hour that he wanted to go back to see if the hat was still on the road. He thought that it might still be there since it was a holiday and there might not be anybody driving on that country road. His Mom told him that he should have stopped and picked it up, but Gus told her that how else was his son to learn things unless he understood that he made mistakes it would might cost him something that he liked and needed. Gus drove back out there, but someone had already picked up the stocking hat, so that was the end of that. Gus was right about the lesson for his son, because he never held another cap or hat out of window when they were driving. In February Gus located a babysitter that was only two blocks down from his house. She was a real nice young married woman with no children and Gus had known some of her relatives. She was perfect and Gus told her that when he started planting in March, he would bring his son over so he could get used to her before his preschool classes started in September 1971. March and planting season started, and Gus took his son to the babysitters. Hus son was a little reluctant at first, but in no time, he adjusted, and he and the babysitter bonded. When Gus could take his son with him he would, because Gus was used to having him all day every-day and he missed him, but Gus knew that it would have to be like this and he was just glad that he had found this wonderful loving young woman to keep his son. Gus's Dad's health really started to go down-hill fast and on April the ninth 1971 his Dad died. Thank goodness Gus had been used to pretty much running the farming business, making most of the decisions and even arranging for bank financing. Gus's Mom didn't know anything about the business, so Gus knew that making all the arrangements for the funeral, paying for it and then assuming responsibility for his Mom was going to be up to him. Gus's Mom's health was not so good either, because she had always had several health problems, but for Gus this was just one more responsibility that he would have to carry on his shoulders. After all, didn't his Dad and Mom adopt him and raise him, so now it was his turn to take care of them. Gus was twenty-eight now and wouldn't be twenty-nine till August of 1971. Gus had planted most of the crops by the time his Dad had died, and he went right back to the work at hand after everything had been settled with the new paperwork that had to be done after his Dad died. Gus even borrowed more money to buy the rest of his Dad's land, so now the old era was gone and the new era of Gus's Open Pitchfork Land and Cattle Company, which is what Gus named the farm and ranch, had begun. Gus kept his same schedule, with the babysitter, all through the growing season and the harvest season and in September had made arrangements with the babysitter that Gus would take his son to preschool in the morning before he went to the farm and ranch and she would pick his son up at noon, because it was only half of a day and then Gus would get him from her house when he came in from work. It couldn't have worked any better. Gus thought that this was much better than having a sorry wife that he couldn't depend on. This is the way the rest of the farming and ranching year went and now the Thanksgiving and Christmas holidays of 1971 were upon him.

Lorrie—1971 January 1971 was the start of a torrid romance between Lorrie and her husband's assistant and he was a thoughtful and affectionate lover. They usually were able to be together at least once and sometimes twice a week. This was pure relief for Lorrie, because it was such an easy affair that just flowed along with both of them having a lot of the same interests. They rode horses together and had sex and her lover had made good friends with her son, so there wasn't any friction there. Her and her husband and her lover and this girl, that he would always bring when times required couples, would go to that country dance hall often and dance, drink beer and just have a great time. They would switch partners a lot and Lorrie would have to remind her lover to watch how he danced with her, because they were sometimes getting too carried away around each other and Lorrie didn't want her husband to get suspicious and start asking questions. After several months of seeing each other Lorrie and her lover's relationship, in their affair was becoming more and more comfortable and at times they took big chances, which even made their sexual desires stronger. Lorrie and relaxed her caution so much to be with her husband's assistant, her lover, that she would actually go over to his house to have sex, which was close to her own house and also to several other houses that were on the premises. One time when she was at her lovers house and they had finished having sex, her lover had even fixed a bubble bath for both of then to wash up in before she went back to her house and this was in broad daylight when her husband could have simply walked over there at any time. After that she realized what a chance they had taken, and she had a talk with her lover to try to get back to being more careful. They met out at the corral in the feed barn, because Lorrie started feeling uneasy about being at his house even though she had been doing it for several months. He wanted to know what was so secret that they couldn't see each other at his house like they usually did and she told him that she had been thinking about that and that she was sure that almost everyone that lived out there had seen them many times and that she was sure that they assumed that they were having an affair. She told him that if she had seen those things that she certainly would have thought that, and she didn't want one of them to go to her husband. Her lover took both of her hands and kissed her, and he told her that he had something to tell her that he wasn't supposed to tell her. He told her that they needed to sit down on a couple of stools that were in the feed barn. They sat down and he smiled and told her that what he was going to tell her couldn't get back to her husband and that he hoped that it wouldn't make her mad. He told her that first of all he wanted her to know that he had fallen in love with her and that it wasn't supposed to be that way. He told her that her husband had come to him before he had even met her with the idea that he could keep Lorrie busy without any fear of reprisal from her husband. Her husband told his assistant that if he would do that it would distract Lorrie and keep her from discovering that he was having his own affair with a girl on the Base. He told his assistant that Lorrie had always found out about his cheating and that he figured that if she was involved with her own affair then she wouldn't be looking so close at what he was doing. He told her that her husband then invited him to dinner, that first time, so he could get a better look at Lorrie to make a judgment if he thought that she was pretty enough for him to get involved with. He told her that is why he was never afraid of getting caught, because her husband didn't want to catch them. He told her that the first time that he saw her at dinner that evening that he thought that she was very pretty and sexy and that he couldn't believe how lucky he would be to have the chance to seduce her without fear of his boss, her husband. He told her that he could never have had the nerve to do it, because to be caught with your bosses wife in the Air Force would have been a sure demotion and a transfer to a shit-hole assignment and he wouldn't have wanted that on his personal record. He said so see we don't really have anything to worry about if we keep what I am telling you from your husband and keep making it look like we are sneaking around. Lorrie couldn't hardly believe what he was telling her, and she wasn't too sure what she was thinking right then. He said again that he just thought that he was going to have a great time with her if she wanted to have an affair and he didn't know that he was going to get serious and fall in love, but he did and he couldn't help it, that it just happened. The only question that Lorrie could think of right then was who was the girl that her husband was having an affair on the Base and her lover told her that it was the girl that he had always brought with him as his date when they went dancing. Lorrie was beside herself and she was quiet for a few minutes thinking. Finally, she told her lover not to worry that she wouldn't say anything to her husband and that everything was OK between them, but she still wanted to be a little more careful, because of all the other people that lived close out there. She told him that some of them had children and if those kids picked up some gossip about their affair from home then it might back to her son and he was getting older and he might understand that something wasn't right and she didn't need any questions from her son that would be hard to answer. He agreed and they kissed passionately and had sex on the hay before they left. The two couples kept going to dances and B-B-Q together and that's when Lorrie really started seeing the interaction between her husband and the girl. She noticed that every time that the girl had to go to the bathroom that her husband would disappear at the same time, and she had to giggle to herself that her husband had been right about her being distracted with her own affair. Her and her husband's assistant's affair went on as usual for several more months and soon the Thanksgiving and Christmas would be upon them. One Saturday right after lunch Lorrie had laid down with her son, so he would take a nap and her husband was at a meeting on the Base her telephone rang, and it was her lover. He told her that he had some very important to discuss with her face to face and could he come over. Lorrie thought that maybe he had decided to break off the affair, but she told him to come over. He came in with a big smile on his face and told her that it wasn't anything bad, but that it was much too important to do over the phone. He sat down by her on the couch and took her hand and looked her in the eyes and said that at the end of November his tour of duty in the Air Force would be over and he had decided not to re-enlist. He said that he was going back to East Texas to his family's ranch there and raise horses. He said that he wanted to take her and her son with him, because he loved her, and he loved her son and they got along great. He told her that he had been thinking about this for a long time and that she would be the perfect mate for him, because she loved horses so much that he knew she would make a wonderful Show Woman that could show their horses at the big horse shows all over Texas and be able to add that special quality that he believed only she could do. He told her that she needed to make her decision right then and when her husband got home from his meeting on the Base, they could tell him their plans. He took Lorrie's breath away, because this is not what she expected at all. Her mind was whirling around in circles and she knew that her face was getting red and hot and she just stared at him. He said well don't you want to go with me and still she just stared and was stiff and couldn't move. Then all of a sudden he got a strange look on his face and frowned and he said oh, I see and he got up and went out the door and she didn't see him again till his going away party and he didn't even talk to her or say good-by to her when he left. The next day she saw him drive off with her horse in his trailer going back to the pasture in East Texas where she had come from. Well 1971 had been a hell of a good year and she had been able to have her own horse to enjoy for almost a year and a real good affair with a very sweet man. She hoped that she hadn't made a mistake by not going with him to East Texas and divorcing her husband. She thought that now she could start back smoking again. She had kept her promise to quit smoking, so she could have the horse, but now the horse was gone, so she was free from the promise. The next holiday was Christmas 1971 and then it would be New Year 1972.

Gus—1971 Thanksgiving and Christmas holidays 1971 were the happiest that Gus experienced in several years. The only down side was that these were the first Thanksgiving and Christmas holidays to celebrate since his Dad had died in April of 1971 and the family didn't quite know how to treat these holidays now with his Dad not present for them, so there were a lot of discussions about past holidays and things that had happened on them when his Dad was there. Other than that it was a happy time. After Gus and his son left his Mom's house on Christmas day they drove to the grave yard where his Dad was buried and Gus stood there and talked to his Dad about the farming and ranching operations and his personal life and plans for the future and also to tell him that he missed him and loved him and to thank him for adopting Gus and raising him. While standing at his Dad's grave, with Gus's son just playing around it, Gus started thinking back through the years of different happenings and talked to his Dad about them, telling him things that he had never told his Dad before and in a sort of a sad way he brought up the times he had been with Lorrie. He told his Dad that he wished he could have had the courage to have told him about Lorrie and maybe his Dad could have given him some good advice on what to do. While talking to his Dad at the grave site Gus told him that he might have made a mistake by not going back to Lorrie and claiming her for his own. Gus bowed his and said a little prayer and he and his son left the grave-yard and went home to their own Christmas, so his son could open the presents that Santa had left for him under their own Christmas tree at home. Gus really had no social life of his own, because all of his time was dedicated to his farming and ranching and raising his son. With his wife being gone so long Gus didn't even feel married to her anymore and he felt no obligation of faithfulness to her. As far as Gus was concerned, he was a single man, but he had no time to get acquainted with any young ladies. His natural feelings and attraction to good looking women were all there and he would notice them from time to time when he was in town, but he simply just didn't have the time to spend to develop a relationship with one. That would have to wait for now, but he yearned to have the sweet feeling of a woman next to him. New Year 1972 came, and Gus celebrated it quietly by himself at home. He had put his son to bed and decided to go ahead and sit up till the New Year came in. He had some whiskey and some eggnog, and he was going to sit up and play some old records that was going to be his New Year celebration. Gus had a lot of 45 RPM records left over from his High School days and he went through them and would put four or five on his record player at a time then he would sit and listen to them and sip on his eggnog and whiskey and as each would play Gus would think back at times that now seemed like they were one hundred years ago. He would pick out a few more as the other record's finished playing and he saw the one that Lorrie had put in his car that day " In The Still Of The Night " by the Five Satins, with the note giving him the instructions of when to come to her house to take her virginity and it all came back to him. He sat down with the record in his hand and just looked at it and drifted back to 1962 on the beach in Corpus Christi with that sweet, beautiful girl Lorrie and he could almost taste those hot lips of hers against his with the sweetest kisses he had ever had, with her body molded against his. He decided that he wasn't going to play it until right after midnight on the New Year of 1972 and then it occurred to him 1962 and now 1972 that was ten years, oh-my-god that would make her twenty-six now and not sixteen. Gus thought, yes he would play that record right at New Years 1972 and he would get up and go into the kitchen on the tile floor and he would dance the first dance on New Year with sweet Lorrie and then he would kiss her when the dance was over. He decided that would be a sweet memory to start 1972 with. Little did Gus know that it would actually be forty more years before he could have those same Corpus kisses from Lorrie. So, Gus brought in the New Year of 1972 and he was determined to try to make the most of it.

Lorrie—1972 After Lorrie's husband's assistant, her lover, left for good and went to East Texas, Lorrie sort of breathed a sigh of relief. That was all over now, but she would still have to put up with her husband's girlfriend on the Base and he wanted to move back on Base now that she didn't have a horse to take care of anymore. Lorrie sold her saddle and bridle and all the things that she used to take care of her horse and in a way, it was a sad day. She missed her horse more than her lover, because her horse had unconditional love for her and that was the only time in her life that Lorrie had experienced that kind of love. She thought, to herself, that she loved Gus that way and always would, so her and her horse had that in common, to love someone unconditionally. They moved back on Base between Thanksgiving and Christmas and Lorrie was planning to go to El Campo to spend Christmas with her family and she knew that her husband would make up some excuse so he could spend Christmas with his girlfriend, which didn't make Lorrie any difference. Lorrie loaded up the car with her son and everything would need for a four-day visit. She would get to El Campo on Christmas Eve and stay two days after Christmas and get back to San Antonio on the twenty-eighth of December in time to get things ready for a small New Year celebration at their house on the Air Force Base. Christmas with her family was real-good for Lorrie. She really got a chance to get away from all the memories of the past year and anytime she could get away from her husband was a feeling of freedom and enjoyment. Even her son acted different when she got him away from his Dad, because her husband was so negative and critical of their son. While Lorrie was gone to El Campo, she didn't know that her husband had put in for a transfer to another Air Force Base in Albuquerque, New Mexico. He had been told that if he transferred there and took over the big Base Supply Depot, that he would be up for a big promotion immediately and that he was a shoe in to get it. While Lorrie was in El Campo for Christmas, she had to drive by Gus's parent's house, just for old time sake, she just couldn't help herself. She thought how long ago that it was now that she had planned for Gus to take her virginity and now she had had sex with three different men and she really hadn't wanted any of them like she had wanted Gus and if she had a clue that Gus would still want her that she would run to him in a second. She thought that she would have too much baggage now with a son for Gus to even look at her. After Lorrie got back to the Air Force Base in San Antonio and got settled back into their home there her husband told her that they might be moving to Albuquerque, New Mexico after the New Year. Lorrie was beside herself, because she didn't want to move that far away from her parents. It had been so nice to be able to drive to El Campo in just three hours and now she would either have to make a fifteen-hour drive or fly to Houston and then rent a car, but what could she do about it. They had a nice low key 1972 New Year celebration at their house on the Base with just a couple of friends there and Lorrie was wondering what the New Year would bring and what to expect if they had to move to New Mexico. Well her husband got the word of his acceptance to take the position in New Mexico the first week in January 1973 and they were on the road to his new Base in Albuquerque.

Gus—1972 The 1972 crop year was going better than before, and his cow heard was growing also. He was now farming over six hundred acres of Rice and Milo Maize and his cow herd was now over five hundred head. He had two men working full time and it was all they could do to try to keep up with it all. Gus knew that he would have to keep expanding, because he had borrowed a lot of money to buy out his parent's land and it would take a lot of acres of grain and a lot of calves to be sold to make the payments on it. He was hoping for the opportunity to make some more money doing some oil deals, but that was something that you couldn't depend on. Gus was also determined to somehow get the time to have a social life. The spring planting season was a good one and all the crops had been planted at the right time, because timing was critical with everything associated with production agriculture If the weather held you up and you got late with planting or grass chemical control or insect control your crop would suffer and your yields and profits would diminish. Everything was dependent on timing and that was a constant battle. The crops were looking very good, and Gus had been able to round up cattle for his spring working and sold a good number of spring calves to put money on his debt to the bank. It was now June 1972 and it wouldn't be a month before the Milo Maize harvest began and Gus was already working on all the harvesting machinery to get it ready. One Sunday afternoon Gus was sitting in his front steps watching his son splash around in a plastic pool, that Gus had bought for his son to enjoy, when he all of a sudden he realized that his wife had been gone for a whole year and Gus got to thinking that he had no idea what she was into. I mean what had she been doing and who had she been with. She might do something crazy and she was still classified as his wife, so that would make him responsible for her and maybe for whatever crazy thing that she would do. All of a sudden Gus was in a dither to get to his lawyer, but it was Sunday, and nothing could be started until Monday. Now Gus couldn't think about anything else except getting to see his lawyer to file for divorce and trying to get it over with before his wife pulled something that would create huge problems, because he knew how unstable she could be. That night he couldn't sleep because he was so worried about what might happen. He was wondering why he had waited so long to decide to file for divorce. Monday morning Gus called his lawyer's office as soon as it was open and got an appointment first thing and told his lawyer the whole story. Gus's lawyer told him that he would have the paperwork done that day and he would file it with the court on Tuesday morning, so if there weren't any delays the divorce should be finished in sixty days. Gus knew that was all he could do, and he would just have to wait on pins and needles till it was over. July and August 1972 was the harvest season for Gus and it all went reasonably well. September was the time he rounded up cattle for the year to sell calves and old cows that would have trouble going through the winter. The yields on the crops were good and he sold some really big calves and held back more good heifers for his cow herd. He made enough money to pay off some of the land he had bought, and he bought more machinery, because he was going to expand his Rice and Milo Maize acreage once more and also try a new crop of Soybeans. This would bring his farming operation up to one thousand acres of crop land and Gus was planning to expand his cow herd to seven hundred-fifty head. By the second week in September Gus was a single man again, because his second wife didn't even show up for the divorce proceedings in court and Gus had full custody of his son. It was a happy day for Gus, because it looked like his personal life was straightening out except for the little girl that his second wife took with her. That little girl had Gus's last name, but she had been the product of an affair his wife had when she had gone to Louisiana. Gus thought that time would solve that problem someday. A couple of months later Gus met a nice girl that was sweet to his son and he started dating her. He knew that he would never get serious about her, because he had been to her apartment and it was terrible. He could see that she wasn't a good housekeeper and she kept her car the same way. Both were dirty and cluttered, and Gus knew that he would never be able to live like that, so she would be a sweet person to be with, but never be considered for marriage even though she was very good to his son. Thanksgiving and Christmas holidays of 1972 went very good and Gus was looking forward to the New Year of 1973 and the challenge of running his ever growing farming and ranching operations. Gus had made an oil lease on some of his land a while back and 1973 would be the last year on that lease, so Gus hoped that the oil company would drill a well in the New Year.

Lorrie—1973 When Lorrie and her husband got to Albuquerque and started driving through the town all that Lorrie saw was old run-down adobe houses with old junk cars and all kinds of trash laying around and the typical landscape around was desert brush and cactus. She thought that it was terrible. When they got on Base and found their housing and got unloaded Lorrie told her husband that she didn't want to be there that it was worse looking then Nebraska. She told him that she wanted him to go see his commanding officer and to ask for a transfer to some other Base. He just looked at her and told her that he would see what could be done about it. Lorrie thought that if this was where she would have to live for maybe two years that it would drive her crazy and that 1973 was going to be hell on her, if they couldn't move. After a couple of days her husband told her that nothing could be done about a transfer. Lorrie thought to herself that he probably didn't even talk to his commanding officer. She went outside and looked around and she did see some mountains finally and that seemed to be the only interesting quality on the landscape. She thought that now her husband had her stuck out in this God forsaken desert country and how long could she take it. After a few days her lips started to crack and her skin around her fingernails cracked and were bleeding from the dry weather. Then one morning her nose started to bleed when she blew it. She decided that before long that her whole body would just dry up and she would look like an Egyptian Mummy. Finally she met some of the officers wives and they told her that it wasn't as bad as she thought it was. They agreed to get together and to show her around the town and show her were to shop. Lorrie and two of the officers wives made plans to leave the Base giant yucca plant one morning and spend the day in Albuquerque just looking around and visiting different small shops and stores that she would need to shop at and to go to the Old Town to eat lunch and look at the art galleries and the curio shops with all the local hand made art works by the local Mexicans and the Navaho, Zuni and Apache Indians. This was right up Lorrie's alley. She did love to look at art work and she had always had an interest in the Native American Indian culture, so she was excited about this girl day out on the town to make new discoveries. The officer's wives told her not to worry about her skin cracking that they would show her what to get to cure that and that after a few months out there in the desert climate, that her body would adjust to it and she wouldn't have that much trouble with it. They told her that one of the main things was that she needed to make sure that she and her son would drink a little water during the day, because their bodies would lose moisture with sweating and she wouldn't notice it until she and her son were dehydrated. Lorrie actually had a wonderful time with the two officers wives on their outing in Albuquerque. She enjoyed the hand made art work in the little old shops in Old Town Albuquerque the most. She even bought a few things there. The most important one was a woven Navaho Dream Catcher that was guaranteed to bring back beautiful memories to you in your dreams. You could hang it from your rear view mirror in your car or you could hang it in your house and look at it before you went to sleep and it would bring back the memories of good times with your loved ones in your dreams, whether they be of humans or of your favorite pet. Lorrie just loved the Dream Catcher and the way it was made. It was made entirely of desert plants. It had a round hoop that was made out of a small green desert willow branch and inside the circle formed by the hoop there were airy designs that were woven with the thin cordage made from the giant yucca plant. These designs would catch the dreams that were floating through the air and keep them for you when you went to sleep, so you could enjoy them. She had never seen anything like it before and she was determined to try it out to see if there was any truth in this Native American Indian curio. She had two dreams that she wanted it to re-capture. The one of her and Gus on the beach in Corpus Christi and the one of her sweet horse. She thought that these would be super nice dreams to have since it would be all that she would ever get of her horse and Gus ever again.

Gus—1973 New Year 1973 Gus and his son spent at home, with the new girl that he had met just before Thanksgiving. He had been invited to a New Years party at a local bar that was owned by a friend of his, but he wasn't used to going to bars. Gus put his son to bed at ten pm and he and the girl stayed up to watch the New Year come in and have a couple of beers. After that she wanted to spend the night and Gus told her OK, but that she would have to leave before his son woke up in the morning and she agreed. Gus asked her if she was on birth control pills and she told him that she wasn't, because she was a virgin and hadn't had any use for them before. Gus knew then that he would have to use condoms. Gus was surprised that she was a virgin, because she was twenty-four years old. At six am the next morning Gus woke her up and told her that it was time for her to go home. She didn't argue, but she told him that she loved every minute of her first time having sex and that she hoped that there would many more times. Gus told her that if that was what she wanted then she needed to get a doctors appointment as soon as she could and get some birth control pills and she said that she would. He kissed her good by. After she left Gus made coffee and sat in the kitchen thinking about the night sleeping with her. It had been almost a year and a half since he had sex with a woman and it did feel really good. He could tell that she didn't really know what she was doing, but he could teach her and maybe that was better then having to break her from some bad habits that some other mad had taught her. It was quiet now and his son was still sleeping and the thoughts of having sex drifted to thoughts of sweet Lorrie. He thought of them on the

colors after a few months and got a job at a local Hospital in the emergency room. She liked it a lot and got along good with the rest of the staff there. With this Nursing job and the possibility of her husband going over seas, living in Albuquerque in 1973 was looking better and better. In April of 1973 Lorrie's son turned six years old and that meant that he would be going to the first grade in the Public School in Albuquerque in September. All of a sudden thinking about her son going to the first grade, it hit Lorrie that she had been married to her husband almost seven years and she was going to be twenty-eight years old next October. She just shook her head and thought that her twenties were almost gone and those were the years that she should have been single finishing up her wild younger days before deciding to settle down with some nice man. Heck if she had stayed single she might even have run into Gus again and renewed their relationship. If she had only known then what she knew now she wouldn't have pulled that stunt of having sex with her husband without some birth control. Getting pregnant by him was a huge mistake. She hated to admit it, but her parents were right in trying to keep them apart. She had made her bed, so to speak, and now she had to lay in it as miserable as it was. Her husband came home one evening and told her that he had received his orders for over seas duty and that he would be going to Thailand in about two weeks. Lorrie smiled and told him that if that is what he wanted it would be OK with her. She acted like she would be lonesome with him gone, but secretly she could jump for joy at his announcement. Oh yes, 1973 was looking up for Lorrie. She had her Nurses Degree and a good job and she really liked living in this desert climate since she adjusted to it and her husband was leaving for, Lorrie hoped at least, a year. Yea!!!

Gus—1973 Gus was so delighted with the way things were going in 1973. He had always heard that you had to be standing in the right place at the right time to be really successful in life and he felt like things were shaping up to make 1973 that time in his life. Cattle prices were skyrocketing and he had already sold a big crop of spring calves and he had made several thousand dollars on an oil deal and all the crops that he was farming were looking good with their prices going up every day well beyond anything anybody had seen since World War Two. It was the first week in July and he had already harvested his first field of Rice and the price was still going up and now he was harvesting his Milo Maize and the price was three times what it had been in past years. His son turned six years old and that meant that he would be starting in the first grade in Public School in September. Gus still had the same girlfriend that he had met in 1972 after his second divorce. She had been a sweet girl and he enjoyed the female company, but he had never told her that he loved her, because he didn't and he had no plans to get serious about her. She hadn't changed her ways on how she kept her own apartment and her car, so Gus knew that she would be a terrible housekeeper and he had had enough of that with his second wife, the Car Hop and never wanted that again. In fact when he got his divorce from the Car Hop he had the divorce framed like a picture and he had put it on his living room wall so he would see it and it would constantly remind him of how bad a decision he had made getting involved with her. It took him years and a lot of grief and money to get out of that one. He now was harvesting the rest of his Rice crop and the money that he had already made had payed off all of his crop expenses and he still had the rest of his Rice to sell, his Soybeans to harvest and sell and his fall calf crop, which was always the biggest to sell. His Soybeans were the last to harvest, because they didn't get ripe till October. By the time that November arrived and all of the money had come in Gus realized that he was going to have to pay a huge Income Tax bill to the government. He went to his accountant to get an estimate of what it might be and was shocked to hear that it could be as much as five hundred thousand dollars. That was more money then he usually made in a year. His accountant told him that he needed to start spending money on things that he could deduct from his taxes. Gus made a list of what he was going to buy before the end of 1973. He paid off all of his land notes and now it was free and clear. He bought himself a new pick-up and a new car. He paid ahead for the 1974 crop all of his seed fertilizer and chemical and he bought a full truck load of cedar posts for building fences. Still when everything had been calculated up for the year Gus had netted a little more then one million dollars and he ended up paying over two hundred thousand in taxes even with all the money he had spent on deductions before the end of 1973. Christmas and he bought his Mom a new car and a micro-wave oven for her present. His son was now in the first grade and Gus was getting organized to get his farm land ready for the 1974 crop. He was going to raise more rice and he had expanded his cow herd also. Gus's operations were now going to be 600 acres of Rice, 350 acres of Milo Maize, 300 acres of Soybeans and 1,000 cows. The total of 1,250 acres of farming and the 1,000 head of cows would put his land at the maximum and it would make it the most efficient agricultural unit that it could be. Gus was at the maximum of what his operation could be with the land that he had. Gus was going into the New Year 1974 with high hopes for the future, it was just a shame that he didn't have some super girl like sweet Lorrie to share all of this with him. Gus hoped that her life had been happy.

Lorrie—1973 Lorrie's husband left for Thailand in the late spring of 1973 before Lorrie had even completed her Nurses training, so he had no idea how good she was doing. Her and her son were having the time of their lives with all the sudden freedom that they had with out him around. Life without her husband was much more enjoyable because he wasn't talking down to her and he wasn't constantly berating her son for something that was minor. Even her son's mood had changed and he was happier. She would get a letter form her husband every couple of weeks, but he never called on the phone and that was just fine to Lorrie. Time began to slip by and she discovered that she had been working the emergency room at the Hospital for a couple of months and it was the first of September of 1973 and her son was starting in the first grade. He was excited to be in the big school and to make some new friends. On her days her and her son would make little trips to some Native Indian Reservations and eat some of their fried pan bread, that they were famous for, and a soda for their lunch. They would shop for Indian curios in their little shops and Lorrie would buy her son an Indian head-dress, a bow and arrow or a tomahawk for him to play with and she would get some hand made silver and turquoise Indian jewelry. She decided that turquoise was her favorite stone and she loved it with silver. She thought it much more beautiful then diamonds, rubies or emeralds. Lorrie decided that she liked the New Mexico weather being dryer and clearer then she was used to and she saw beauty in the rough dessert terrain, but best of all was when there was a little shower of rain the wind brought the wonderful sweet smell of desert herbs to her nose and it made her appreciate what God had done when he designed and made the desert. He had hidden many things of beauty that you had to look for and discover and it was a wonderful experience for her and her son. She found out that she was going to be able to take off for Thanksgiving for four days, so she decided to fly to Houston and rent a car and drive to El Campo. It would be much more pleasant now that her husband was over seas. She had been in Albuquerque now for almost a year and she had changed her mind completely on what she thought of it. She remembered that she was totally against staying there at first, but now she just loved it and thought that maybe some day she would like to live and make a home here permanent. Going to El Campo for Thanksgiving was a happy experience for Lorrie and her son. She no longer had to worry about the tension between her Dad, Mom and her husband, because he was far away and out of everyone's mind including Lorries. Lorrie only had four days of holiday time to spend and that included two days traveling. The day after Thanksgiving she went over to see her old High School friend, the girlfriend that her Dad had owned the Service Station that they used to go to and flirt with Gus. Her girlfriend told Lorrie that she had seen Gus one time in the grocery store and that he had a little boy with him. Lorrie asked if she knew what kind of work that Gus was doing and she said that she didn't ask, but that Gus was wearing a cowboy hat and cowboy boots. Lorrie told her that she always thought that Gus would have an auto repair shop, because all she knew was that he had built a Hot-Rod and that had always stuck with her. Her girlfriend asked if she was going to try and look Gus up and Lorrie told her no, that it would be impossible now, because she was married with a son and evidently Gus was married with kids also, so there was too much water under the bridge. Lorrie told her girlfriend that she still had sweet memories about Gus and they would have to be a lovely secret that she would always keep in her heart. After Lorrie left her girlfriends house she did what she had done since she was just a girl and that was to drive by Gus's parents house to see if she could get a glimpse of Gus, she didn't see him. She thought that it would be something if Gus had a horse. When she and her son got back to Albuquerque she had to finish up her Christmas shopping and decorations, because she would have to work during the Christmas holidays at the Hospital emergency room. Lorrie thought my goodness the New Year 1974 is almost here and it seemed like it came so fast. She chuckled to herself that since her husband had gone over seas that things had gone so smooth that time seemed to just fly by. She new that she shouldn't feel this way, but she and her son were much happier with him gone. Lorrie was looking forward to the New Year 1974 as being a happy one without him around.

Gus—1974 New Year 1974 Gus went to a New Year party at his friends Bar and had a great time having drinks and dancing with some of the girls that attended it. He even kissed a pretty girl when the clock struck twelve and she told him that she wanted to go home with him, but he had a baby sitter there with his son, so he turned her down. When the party was over about two in the morning and Gus went to his truck he saw the girlfriend's car parked by his, so he went over and looked in and she was sitting in it asleep. He knocked on the window and woke her up and asked her what she was doing and she told him that this was her way of spending New Years with him. Gus told her to go to her apartment and they would talk later in the day after they got some sleep. After lunch Gus called her and told her that there was no need for her to wait for him like she had done and that he would do what he wanted, when he wanted and she wasn't going to change that. She said that she knew it, but that she couldn't help herself, because she wanted to be near him. Gus just said OK if that is the way you want to be, but you might see me leave some place with another girl. She got quiet for a minute and she told him that she knew that he had not ever made her any promises, so he had always been free to do what ever he wanted to do and they ended the conversation. It bothered Gus some that she was clinging so tightly to him, but there was no way that he could get his mind in the position to accept her as being anything more then a girlfriend that he couldn't get serious about. Yes, she was good to him and yes, she was sweet to his son and he didn't think that she was seeing anyone else, but that didn't change a thing and he was not about to make promises to her just because of that. If she wanted to hang in with him under those circumstances then that was her decision. They could enjoy times together and have sex, but when he wanted to be with someone else he would and that was just the way it was going to be. Gus thought that sooner or later she would get tired of it and go her own way. During January and February !974 Gus was feeding and taking of his expanded cow herd along with finish field work when the weather permitted. He also met a really beautiful young woman that was a telephone operator in the Wharton office. He and his friend that owned the bar in El Campo were on their way to Houston to party and they stopped into a restaurant in Wharton to eat lunch and the telephone operator was in there eating a salad for lunch. Gus went over to her and introduced himself and they began talking and she invited him to sit with her. He got her telephone number and told her that he would call her for a date and she agreed to go with him. The next day Gus called her and set up a date for the next weekend to take her to a really nice restaurant and bar out of town, because he didn't want to put up with his girlfriend following them around town. During their date Gus learned that she was divorced and that she had been working for the telephone company for five years and that she had two young children, a boy two and a girl three years old. They got along really well on their date and when Gus took her home to Wharton she invited him in for a night-cap. Her kids were with their Dad for the weekend, so she was by herself. He noticed that her apartment was clean and in order even though she had two small kids and Gus knew how small kids could trash up a small apartment. They talked and started kissing and ended up in her bed for the night. In the morning she fixed Gus breakfast and he kissed her good-by and drove home to get his son and spend Sunday with him. Gus decided that he wanted to see more of the telephone operator. He thought that she might be someone that had possibilities to look at that would be a good step mother for his son. He would have to find out more about her though and spend more time with her. That was going to be hard with planting season about to start and her kids being with her every other weekend. Oh well, somehow he would see her when ever he could make it work. In the mean time he would have to keep it from his girlfriend or she would be following him around and also he didn't want to hurt her if he didn't need to. Right now though planting season was the most important and everything else could wait till Gus had the time.

Lorrie—1974 In 1974 Lorrie got the chance to go into private Nursing and started taking of an elderly lady on a full time basis. The money was better and it gave her a more flexible schedule to spend more time with her son. She was very happy with this new job and her patient and her family were very appreciative of the way that Lorrie was taking care of the elderly lady. In February 1974 Lorrie got a letter from her husband telling her that a Thai girl had a little girl baby and she couldn't take care of it. He told Lorrie that they had talked about adopting a little girl in the past and maybe they should think about adopting this baby from the Thai girl. Lorrie read the letter several times and remembered that conversation she had with her husband. Lorrie had been so sick during her pregnancy and after the birth that she had to stay in the hospital for weeks to regain her strength, actually the Doctor was so concerned about her that he really talked rough to her husband for letting her get in such of a weak physical condition. The Doctor was afraid that Lorrie might take a turn for the worse and be close to death. After that Lorrie told him that if he wanted more baby's they would have to adopt and if they did adopt then Lorrie wanted it to be a girl baby. Lorrie wrote her husband back asking questions about the mother of the baby. Two weeks later she got a letter back from him telling her that the mother had worked in the Air Force PX there and a soldier had made her pregnant, but he had been transferred out of country. Lorrie wrote him back and told him that she didn't think that she wanted to adopt a baby from overseas, because there wasn't enough information on the parents. She got a letter back from him telling her that he was going to be transferred back to the Air Force Base in Albuquerque in another month. This letter put Lorrie in a bad mood, because she was hoping that he would be overseas for another year. Her and her son had been doing so good and were so happy without him that she knew that they were in for a big adjustment when he got back home. Lorrie's husband arrived back from Thailand in March 1974 and after a couple of days told her that they needed to talk about getting a divorce. He told her that while he was in Thailand he had fallen in love with the Thai girl that had the baby. Lorrie asked him if the baby was his and he told her that it was. She wasn't surprised at this. She told him that she wouldn't protest the divorce,but she wanted custody of their son, the car and furniture and the appliances in the house. He agreed to the terms that she proposed and she also got some child support. She called her parents and told them about getting a divorce and her Dad was very happy. He told her that he had always disliked her husband and that he wanted her to come home and they would work everything out together. Her Dad told her to come as soon as she could after her divorce was final. Lorrie told her private duty patient and her family that she was going quit when her divorce was final and they begged her to stay. They asked her how much money it would take for her to reconsider quitting. Lorrie told them that money had nothing to do with it and that she was sad to leave them, but it was time that she left and went back home to start new on her life. By June 1974 Lorrie was back in El Campo living with her parents. Her husband actually drove her back with a U-Haul trailer behind her car and was so nice about everything. He was so happy to get the divorce and be able to marry the girl from Thailand that he was ready to do anything. Her husband didn't know it, but two years later his Thailand wife would hire a hit man to kill him for his Life Insurance that she was going to split with the hit man. She didn't know that the hit man that she made the deal with was a under cover policeman. She went to prison and never got to kill Lorrie's X-husband. By early summer 1974 Lorrie was looking for a job in her old home town El Campo. Lorrie thought to herself that her life had already moved with a lot of twists and turns and she was just twenty-eight years old. Lorrie was glad to be out of the depressing marriage that she had been in for eight years. Lorrie knew that for the rest of 1974 she would have to concentrate on re-building her life.

Gus—1974 Planting season 1974 went good for Gus and he was able to see the telephone operator a few times. The crops were growing good and Gus was in the middle of his spring cow working. Gus had bought a horse for his boy and had taken the time to make sure that it was broken well and trained for his son to ride. His son could ride good, drive a small tractor and even drive Gus's pick-up when needed. The boy was seven years old now and he had been raised primarily around men and the things that men do and talk about. Gus started to think about the telephone operator in a different way then just a girlfriend. When he looked at his boy he could see a man-child that had not been subjected to much of the softness of a woman's touch in his raising and the boy had no experience of having grown up with any siblings. Until now Gus was proud of the way he had raised his son by himself since the boy was just a baby, but at seven years old he was now in the second grade in school and had been several little fights. Gus didn't want his son to grow up to be a tough, spoiled kid and he knew that a good woman's touch in raising him would be the solution to that problem. Gus had taught his son the importance of good manners and had brought him up with saying his prayers at bed time and saying the blessing at mealtime and had even enrolled him in Sunday School at a local church, but there was still something missing and that was a woman that could be a mother to him, so Gus started to look at the telephone operator and her two children and tried to imagine them with Gus and his son as a family. The more Gus thought about it the more it made since, because her children also needed a daddy. Their daddy was not spending much time with them and he wasn't paying the small amount of child support the Court had ordered him to pay. Gus was making enough money now to support a nice family, so if he got remarried his wife wouldn't have to work. She could be a full time wife and mother to the children. He decided that he was going to ask the telephone operator to get married. Gus didn't really want to get married again, but he knew that it would be the best thing for his son to have a regular home life with a mom and dad and some siblings to grow up with. When Gus was contemplating this decision his thoughts drifted to that sweet young girl Lorrie and her wonderful kisses that she gave him on the beach in Corpus Christi way back in 1962. He felt that maybe his life would have been a lot different if he had gone back to her and ended up marrying and having a family with her. She sure was a sweet girl, but that was long past and he had to think of now. Gus asked the telephone operator to marry him and she accepted, so they started making plans to put their children together as a family. Harvest season for the Milo Maize was good except that the price was way down from the very high price of 1973 and the cattle price was down also. Rice harvest was in full swing and the high price of Rice in 1973 was also way down, and on top of that when Gus was harvesting his last field of Rice a hurricane blew in to the west of him and knocked down a lot of the Rice and flooded the field so the yield on that field was way down. The farm and ranch profits for 1974 were going to be way off from 1973. Well, that was farming and ranching, you could never tell what was going to happen. Gus would always say that farming and ranching was the only business that you bought what you needed at retail prices, sold your products at wholesale prices and had no control of the market. That along with the dangers of the weather created a very risky situation in production agriculture as a primary business. Gus thought that it had been a good thing that he had paid off so much of his debt and had expanded his cow herd and farming operations and bought land when he had made big profits. Gus still made money in 1974, but not what he was hoping for after being spoiled in 1973.

Lorrie—1974 Her move back to her home town of El Campo in 1974 was at first a relief to get away from everything that reminded her of her failed marriage to the Air Force Officer, but then she soon learned that her Dad and Mom started treating her like she was in High School again. She tried reminding them that she was almost twenty-nine years old and had been married and she had a seven year old son, but they just couldn't help themselves. They had something to say about everything that she wanted to do, from what her son was going to wear to school to who she would have for friends. Her nursing training came in handy, because she landed a job at the Nightingale Hospital in El Campo. She worked the Emergency Room and the Maternity Ward. On the weekends that she worked the Emergency Room when people were brought in with knife and bullet wounds the Doctor in charge would tell her to go through their pockets and get their money, because it would be all the payment that he would get. He said that once they left the hospital he never got paid and that if they had ten dollars in their pocket then that would be all he would get. There was a Black Nurse in the Maternity Room that had been there a long time and she new everything there was to know about birthing baby's and their care. Lorrie was very glad to be able to work with her and they became good friends. The Black Maternity Room Nurse told Lorrie that many times when a baby was delivered late at night that she was the one that delivered the baby and that the Doctor would show up at the Hospital late and drunk, but he still got the credit for the delivery. When Lorrie would be on her break at work she would go down to see who had been admitted and if she might know them. One day she was going through the list of new admitted patients when she saw a name that almost took her breath away. It was the name of Gus's Mom. Lorrie thought that now she would maybe have a chance to accidentally bump into Gus when he was visiting his Mom. Lorrie wanted to rush down to see his Mom right then and ask her a lot of questions about Gus, but she decided to wait till the next day to see her. Until then Lorrie could find out what his Mom was in the Hospital for. When Lorrie got off of work all she could think about was that maybe it would be her chance to see Gus and be able to talk to hem. She felt desperate to find out why he hadn't come back to her in 1962. She knew that she still loved him and that he would be the only man that she would ever love, but she just couldn't brazenly make an advance toward him, because of how he had left her and hurt her so bad. She had really never gotten over it and was still embarrassed to let a man, even her husband when she had been married, see her completely naked. Even after having a baby her breasts were, in her opinion, to small and she was sort of skinny and it made her legs look even longer and her feet bigger then when she was sixteen. She wondered if Gus would even look at her or remember her. She decided that she would visit his Mom several times and maybe she would run into him there, but if not then she didn't have the courage to seek him out, but she sure wanted too. She went to see his Mom and visited her on her break three different times, but never saw Gus and she didn't have the courage to ask his Mom about him. Lorrie would ask about Gus's sister that she had been friends with in school hoping that his Mom would say something about Gus, but she never did. Lorrie thought that maybe his Mom would mention her to Gus when he came to visit, but she would never know that if Gus didn't look her up at the Hospital. She thought that if she just had the courage to take the initiative and look Gus up then she could find out what had happened and maybe even her dream of being with him could be reality, but she just couldn't muster up the courage to do it, it would have to happen by accident and even then, she didn't know if she could face him without crying. How could she ever be with Gus if she acted like this and this seemed like the most perfect time in years, but where was her backbone.

Gus—1974 In 1974 Gus had a lot going on besides his regular business activities. He had proposed to the telephone operator girlfriend, so she was now his fiance and he was trying to keep this from his old girlfriend until a little time passed and he could figure the best way to let her down easy. His Mom was in the Hospital and every night after he came in from the farm he would go and visit her for a couple of hours. She would be in the Hospital for a week or ten days so they could put her on a strict diet of twelve hundred calories and limit her intake of fluid. This would happen once or twice a year, because she would collect a lot of fluid in her body and also she would gain weight that together would worsen heart trouble, high blood pressure, gout and sugar diabetes and all the fluid and extra weight caused her a lot of trouble. Gus had no idea that Lorrie was working at the Hospital. His Mom never said anything to him, and why should she, because Lorrie had been his sisters friend and his Mom had never known about he and Lorrie's time together, so Gus went to see his Mom never knowing that the woman that he truly really loved was just down the hall from him working at the Hospital, what a disaster this was. Having no idea that Lorrie was in El Campo and working at the local Hospital Gus continued to make plans to marry the telephone operator. He was having a hard time trying to figure out a way to let his old girlfriend down easy and not hurt her to bad. Gus knew that she was really fond of his son and she had been good to him, even taking him to see her Mom and Dad. Gus had never told her that he loved her on purpose so she wouldn't get the idea that they were going to get married, but he knew that secretly she wanted to marry him. He just could never consider marrying her, because of the way she kept house. Gus felt that she saw the way that he kept his house and it didn't seem to make any difference in her improving the way she kept her own apartment, so he felt that if he married her that she would keep his house the same way and he couldn't live that way and he wasn't going to be fussing at her all the time to clean house. He had enough of that with the young Car-Hop he had married. Gus decided to let her see him and the telephone operator together and that would put her on notice that her days as his girlfriend were numbered. Later in 1974 Gus and the telephone operator got married. On his way to the church for the wedding service his old girlfriend saw him and Gus and his best man had to drive fast and dodge around to loose her and he was almost late for his own wedding. When it was over he and his new wife went to Gus's house to change and pick up their luggage for their honey moon trip to San Antonio on the river and when they walked in to the house the phone was ringing and it continued to ring when they left and locked the door. When they got back from their honey moon Gus had the house moved to the ranch head-quarters to be built on to and re-modeled for the new big family. There was a lot of re-organization to be done and he and his new wife worked together and slowly got it done. In the mean time he still had his responsibilities for the farm and ranch. Gus's boy was much older then his new wife's kids. They were to young to go to school, but his boy was starting in the third grade and Gus had no idea that Lorrie's boy was also in the third grade and they were going to the same elementary school and in the same class. One day when Gus got home from work his wife told him that the school had called and that his boy was in trouble and that Gus was to go to the school the next day and have a talk with the Principal. Gus knew the Principal good, because he was a teacher when Gus was in High School, so when he went to the Principals office they were on good terms. The Principal greeted Gus with a smile, and Gus just shook his head and told the Principal that he was sorry that his son had caused trouble at school and that the Principal had his permission to spank his son anytime that he caused trouble. The Principal described what Gus's son had done and told Gus that his son and another boy together had tried to catch the fish in a small aquarium,in the class room, during class and they had disrupted the class and had made a big mess. He told Gus that the other boys Mom had come up the same day and had a conference and had told the Principal to spank her son also. Gus asked the Principal if he would have his son brought to the Principals office, so he could hear his Dad tell the Principal to spank him when he got into trouble and that is what they did. Gus left there to go back to work and never thought to ask who the other boy was and who his Mom was. If Gus had done this he would have found out that Lorrie was living and working in El Campo and then what would have he done since Gus had just remarried. This was just another close encounter that could have changed his and Lorrie's lives if Gus had only known it. Just think about it. Both of their sons the same age in the same school in the same class and getting in trouble together and neither Gus or Lorrie has the knowledge that their boys know each other. How close can it get, but yet be so far. Gus and Lorrie wouldn't know this until fifty years later when they were having one of their many talks about their separate lives. When they discussed it they almost broke down in tears to think that they were this close to finding each other again when they were still young enough to get married and have their own children together. This was another disaster.

Lorrie—1974 In September of 1974 Lorrie's son started the third grade at an elementary school in El Campo and she was working at the Nightingale Hospital there. He was a smart boy that would finish his work quickly and then get bored and end up causing trouble. Lorrie had been called up to the school more then once for a conference with the teacher or the Principle. She had known the Principle when he was a teacher in high school when she was going there. Usually Lorrie's son got into trouble by himself, but this time he and another boy in his class proceeded to try to catch the fish in a small aquarium in the class room and both were sent to the Principals office and their parents were called. Lorrie was off of work at the time, so she went up to the school right away. When she went to the Principals office the two boys were sitting there at opposite ends of a long table with the Principal between them. He told the other boy that his Dad wouldn't be able to come to the school till the next day, so he could go back to class, then he greeted Lorrie and they began discussing what her son had done to be in trouble. She never asked the Principle or her son who the blond headed boy was that also was in trouble. Lorrie was always so upset when her son got into trouble at school, because when her Mom and Dad found out they would bring up her ex-husband and that her son had his blood in him, so he would always be trouble. Lorrie was having a lot of trouble living with her parents, because they were treating her as if she was a teenager in high school. She would move to her own place, but she wasn't making enough money to be able to afford it yet and wouldn't be for a couple of more years, if she could stand it that long. Lorrie worked the night shift a lot and this kept her from having much of a social life. When she got off of work early in the mornings she would go over to her Grandma's house and drink coffee with her for a while, then she would go to her Dad and Mom's house to get her son ready for school. They only lived three blocks from the school, so he could walk to school if the weather was good. After that she would take a shower and go to bed till her son was home from school and she would have to let him play for a while, fix his dinner, make sure that he did his homework, run a few errands in town, then get ready for work again. Her nights were his days and her days were his nights. This was not a very happy arrangement to live with for her or her son. Basically her and her son had minimal time together and she had no social life. It was simply a disconnected type of life that provided a basic existence for survival with little hope for improvement in the future. The year 1974 ended and 1975 dawned with the same schedule that had dominated 1974. Lorrie found herself becoming increasingly pessimistic about her future working the night shift at the Hospital and living with her parents. She wanted a place of her own, so she could organize her life and not be under her parents thumb, but she just wasn't making enough money to do it. One day in the late summer she was driving to work she pulled up to the stop sign where she turned, her lights shone on a huge sign that was across the road from her and it said "Join The Navy As A Career And See The World". She just stopped there and read it over several times and it resonated with her, because her Dad had been in the Navy in World War Two and he always said that the Navy was a good place to build a future. She wrote the telephone number of the Navy Recruiter down and decided to talk to her Dad about it. She thought that this might be a solution and 1975 could be the turning point for her life that she wanted.

Gus—1975 In 1975 Gus was still making improvements to the house that he had moved to his ranch Head-Quarters for his new family, after his marriage to the telephone operator. Inside the house was finished, but there was a lot to do outside like pouring cement for the front porch, a cement slab for a big carport and a connected storage room and the construction of them. He would have to make the outside improvements as the time and money would allow it to happen. He was still very busy with his farm and ranch operations and now he was trying to get his new wife and family organized and settled into the rural farm and ranch life. The kids were all riding the school bus to town and that was a new experience for them. To get into the full swing of rural life they were planting some peach and pear trees and digging up a plot for a garden. Gus got the chance to buy a good Jersey milk cow and his new wife said that she would milk, if he could teach her, so he bought it. The cow had been trained very well and was gentle and it didn't take to long for his wife to learn how to milk her. Gus taught his wife everything that went along with the milking, from pinning the calf away from the cow at night, so he didn't suck all the milk before milking in the morning, to how to wash the cow's utter clean before milking and when through, to apply a salve to her tits to keep them soft so they wouldn't crack and get sore. He taught her to strain the milk and separate the cream they would need and how to make butter. She only milked once a day, because the cow gave plenty of milk for the family and her calf got the rest of it. Gus was so busy with his farm and ranch operations and teaching his new family the in's and out's of living on a farm that it seemed that there wasn't enough time in the day. On top of all of this he had a call from the President of the Youth Fair Association that he had been selected to be a Director of the Youth Fair if he would serve. This was an honor to be selected, so Gus decided to serve as a Director. The Youth Fair Association was new and had only been organized a year before, so there was a lot for the Directors to do to put on the first Youth Fair and Livestock Show and Rodeo. He also signed a Bank Note, with five other Directors, to help the Fair Association build facilities for the upcoming events. During this time Gus got word of a new Texas State Livestock Association that was being organized and he went to their meeting in Houston, Texas and was chosen to be the County Chairman. That meant that he would have to organize the livestock men in the County and plan monthly meetings and the election of the officers. It was really hard for Gus to squeeze all of this into his already crowded schedule, but somehow he did it successfully. 1975 was a really busy year from morning to night and even at night with the meetings of the Youth Fair Association and the Livestock Growers Association. The prices for farm and ranch products were slowly dropping and inflation and interest rates were rising, which was making it harder to make decent profits on crops and livestock. One thing that was helping was that Gus was able to make a couple of decent oil deals to help bolster his operations. Time and again the oil end of his business would step in and help him out. His wife was planning a birthday party at their home with some of their friends for Gus and she was going through his records to select some for the music for the party when she came across the record "In The Still Of The Night" by the Five Satins and on the label was written from Lorrie to Gus with love forever and a heart drawn on it with Gus and Lorrie in it. She brought it to him and asked him about it and he said that it had been given to him by a very sweet young girl a long time ago. His wife became jealous and told him that she was going to throw it away and Gus grabbed it from her and told her that he wanted to keep it that it had a special meaning for him and that she was never to destroy it. She became very irritated and wanted to argue about it. Gus tried to explain that it was from a sweet young girl that he had known many years ago and that it had nothing to do with his wife, but she went on and on about it and seemed like she wasn't going to let it go. Gus finally got tired of this and told her that she could argue with herself, because he had better things to do then to listen to her foolishness about the record, so Gus left to go back to work. After he was away from the house he thought that this was a side of his wife that he hadn't seen before. He couldn't understand why she would want to argue about something as trivial as a record and wouldn't accept his explanation about it. He hoped that maybe she was having a bad day and that this wouldn't be the start of some pattern of behavior that she couldn't control, because if it was then it was going to create a lot of trouble for their relationship. Gus hated to admit it, but if it came to a decision of destroying the record "In The Still Of The Night" or loosing his wife, he would keep the record and let his wife go, because that record was the only thing, other then his memory of Lorrie, that he had to hold on to about her sweetness and those wonderful Corpus kisses that he thought about once in a while. No he wouldn't get rid of that record because it was he and Lorrie's song and it always would be. Gus stopped his pick-up in the pasture and thought back to that time thirteen years ago in Corpus Christi when he and Lorrie were kissing on the beach and about when he and her were in her room in El Campo and how beautiful she was naked. He knew that he couldn't think about her very long, because it would create a problem for him wondering about what happened to her and he couldn't afford to start going down that line of thinking. Thirteen years was much to long ago to be second guessing himself on his decisions. It was 1975 now and he was married and was starting a new life with a new family, but he still wondered how it would have been if he had married Lorrie in the first place. Why was he still thinking about her after all these years anyway, it was crazy, what could it mean. She had just been a young, sweet pretty girl. Why couldn't he just forget about it, he never thought about any of the other girls that he had been with, but Lorrie would keep coming back to him every once in a while through the years and why!

Lorrie—1975 Lorrie worked her shift at the Hospital that night and knew that she wouldn't be able to talk to her Dad about the Navy till he got home from delivering mail late in the evening after she woke up. She had never considered the military as a career even though she had lived the military life when she had been married to her Air Force husband. She sort of liked the idea of being moved around to different Military Posts because of being able to experience different places and people that she would never have the opportunity to do so otherwise. After all that is how she found out that she liked Albuquerque and the desert environment so much. She would have never discovered it on her own in a million years. Yes, the more that she thought about the Navy the more excited she became about the idea. She just hoped that her Dad wouldn't come up with something bad that she had no idea of. Oh well, it was good that he had the Navy experience to talk about anyway. Late that evening when Lorrie woke up her Dad was at home and she sat down with him and discussed her idea of joining the Navy as a career. He listened carefully and told her that it might be a solution for her if she could get it to fit with her present situation of being a Mother with a small child. He told her that the Navy had a cut-off date on the age that a person could sign up and he couldn't remember what that age limit was. He encouraged her to call the Recruiter and talk to him. Lorrie had to admit to herself that in her excitement over possibly being able to actually have a chance at a career that would have a future in it, she had not thought about how her son would fit in the overall picture. Maybe the Navy wouldn't even consider her if she was a Mother. That was a possibility she hadn't thought about. She called the Recruiter and he made arrangements to meet her for lunch in El Campo, so he could discuss her situation with her and he could get her idea of what she wanted her job to be after she completed her initial inductee training. The Recruiter told her that she was still within the age limit for Navy recruitment, but that her age of being almost thirty years old was older then most of the female recruits. At their lunch meeting a few days later the Recruiter was going through a lot of recruiting folders and information on what to expect when joining the Navy and he approached the problem of how she had planned to handle the care of her son, because he would not be able to accompany her until she was well established in the Navy with a career path in her chosen job that would allow for a Post that could include a family member. He told her that it could take her some time to get to that point in her Navy career and she need to consider giving temporary custody, of her son, to some family member she could trust until she could resume being her sons only Legal Guardian. At the end of their lunch meeting Lorrie took all the information that he presented to her and thanked him and told him that she would get back to him as soon as she had the situation worked out with her son's situation and that she would be thinking about what job she intended to apply for. Lorrie told the Recruiter that she was not in the least disappointed with their meeting and that she was very excited about what she had learned from it and that he could be sure that she would back in contact with him. They shook hands and she went home with a better idea on what she needed to do. She knew that she had a lot to think about and she would have to put a reasonable plan in place that would insure the welfare of her son till she could resume the role of being his Mother. The only avenue of temporary Guardianship that she knew she could trust would be her parents and if they wouldn't agree to that then she would have to talk to her ex-husband about it and she would rather not have to do that. Because of her work schedule Lorrie had to wait till the next day to talk to her parents about her meeting with the Navy Recruiter. Lorrie had already read over all the job descriptions that the Navy had to offer, from the information that the Recruiter had given her and she had decided on Cryptology which dealt with Navy codes. In the job description and requirements it stated that she would have to go through a serious and detailed background check along with intense testing to qualify for training. All of this caught Lorrie's interest and it all sounded like secret warfare. She had always been interested in the code breakers of World War 2 and she had read several books on them. She knew that this would be her primary objective for her job and she was determined to try her hardest to get accepted. The meeting with her parents went reasonably well and they thought that they could accept the responsibility of temporary custody. The only point of contention was between her and her Dad when, as usual he was trying to tell her what job she needed to do in the Navy. He stressed that she needed to stay with the Medical Nursing career route, because he felt that because of all her civilian Nursing experience it would give her a chance for fast Navy Rank advancement. Lorrie tried to tell him that she wanted to try something different and exciting, but he wouldn't listen, so she acted like she would take his advice just to calm things down and put an end to the tense discussion and it worked. The next day she called the Navy Recruiter to schedule a meeting. This time the meeting as in Bay City at his office, because she was going to have to fill out all the forms required and be tested and also she was to be given a physical examination. Lorrie had to take one of her sick days off from work at the Hospital for this meeting, because it was to be an all day thing. When she filled out the required forms she chose Cryptology as her Navy job or in Navy terms her (MOS). In the mean time her parents called on a friend that was a Lawyer to fill out all the legal forms to file for them to obtain Temporary Custody for Lorrie's son. Lorrie passed all her tests with flying colors and her physical examination was excellent, so it was just a matter of time till the Navy notified her when her induction date would be and she would be sworn in to the United States Navy. Lorrie was very excited about this new opportunity to change the direction of her life and actually have a Career to work toward and to look forward too. It was the fall of 1975 now and Lorrie was glad that she had seen that Navy Recruitment sign. To her it was a sign from God that saved her from the despair of the situation that she had felt trapped in. Now she was free to be her own person and maybe be able to roam the whole Planet while making her Career in the Navy, how exciting. She looked back at when she had first left home to go to Florida to live with her Uncle and Aunt and work at NASA when she was nineteen years old and that was exactly ten years ago. She just smiled and shook her head thinking about how much she had learned about life since then. She had missed her twenties when most people do all their partying and wild things, because of all the stupid mistakes that she had made. She had left home a Virgin, but now ten years later she had had sex with three different men and become a Mother with a son and a failed Marriage. Lorrie considered this not a great record of accomplishment for ten years of life, in fact she considered it mostly a failure. Lorrie thought that only if Gus had come back to her when she was sixteen her life would have been what God would have wanted it to be, but now she was going to have to do what she could with it on her own. Well she knew now that she wouldn't be sworn into the Navy till she was thirty years old, because it was now October 1975 and her birthday was coming up quick.

Gus—1975 It was the fall of 1975 now and Gus was thirty-three years old. The harvest of the Rice and Milo Maize crops was complete and the fall cattle round-up was over. The only crop left to harvest was the Soybeans. This crop could always be difficult to harvest, because of the chance for rainy weather that time of year. When that happened the Soybeans just had to sit in the field, sometimes for a couple of months, till the land dried out enough to get a combine in the field. When this happened fire ants would build up their mounds till they were tall enough to be scooped up in the combine header and cause problems with choke ups and the quality of the Soybeans would go down along with the price. Things like this didn't help with all that was going on with production agriculture in the United States. The prices of agriculture products were falling and interest rates on production loans were going up at a steady rate. Every time Gus would go to the Bank for another loan the interest rates had gone up and the Bank would also require more collateral to cover the loan. Also inflation had been increasing and all of this together was taking a real big toll on his profits. The only bright points to this was that his land value was going up and the oil business was seeing an increase in drilling and prices, but in order for Gus to profit in the oil business he had to make oil deals on oil Prospects or do work for some oil company and this was not a stable part of his normal business operations. He thought that he was OK for now, but it was still a worry as to how long this would go on and what could happen in the mean time that could make things worse. Gus knew that his Mom's health was getting a little worse all the time and taking care of her was getting more expensive, so that was just another part of the total picture that was adding to the strain of the times he was living in. Gus had purchased another tract of farm land next to him in 1974 and now he was wondering if he had made the right decision to buy it at that time. He did it, because the price on it had gone from two hundred twenty-five dollars per acre in 1971 to seven hundred-fifty dollars per acre in 1974, so he decided that he had better buy it then. That was all well and good, but now everything seemed to be getting very unstable and it was kind of scarey to think about how he was going to make all of his payments on his Bank Notes if things got worse. At least the value of the land kept climbing, so it looked good on his balance sheet. Gus had another problem and that was with his farm and ranch help. Since the oil field drilling had been expanding all the oil companies and their service companies were hiring a lot of help and they were paying a lot more and offering benefits that Gus just couldn't afford to do, so he couldn't compete with them and he was constantly loosing help to the oil field and that meant that he had to be training help all the time. A lot of these people had never been on a tractor or a horse and had no idea what to do with them. This was time consuming and expensive and also dangerous for everyone involved, because farm and ranch work is dangerous in itself even for hands that have been around it all their lives. That is why you see so many cowboys and farm hands with permanent physical disabilities. Gus had been lucky so far in this regard himself that he hadn't had a bad accident to give him a permanent disability even though he had some real close calls on those types of accidents. The bottom line here though was that it was extremely hard for Gus to run a large farm and ranch operation using new green help all of the time that would have to work on thousands of acres they had never seen before. Some time now he felt like a training school for farm and ranch help, but if he was going to stay in business this was what he was going to have to do. Gus thought if only his boy and step son were old enough to be trained then they would be dependable and accomplished at their tasks and some day they would be the ones to own his land and farm and ranching operations. With this thought his memory went back to Lorrie when she was sixteen and he nineteen and if they had been married then and started their family together. They would probably would have at least two children old enough to be good help by now and some smaller that would be right behind them to be good helpers in a short time. How nice that would have been, but these thoughts were just make believe and they wouldn't help in the world that Gus was living in now. Soon it would be 1976 and Gus hoped that things would settle down in the United States, so he could once again plan his business on something that resembled stability.

Lorrie—1976 Lorrie was finally sworn in to the United States Navy and received orders to report to the Navy Co-ed Training Base at Orlando, Florida. When Lorrie got there and got settled in enough to be able to have some of her own thoughts instead of what her Drill Instructor was telling her she thought that here she was in Florida where she had first come to after leaving home. What a difference this time was compared to that first time when she was nineteen years old. Instead of her wearing a tight pink body suite with fringe and white boots with tassels doing Go-Go dancing and surfing for a living, she was wearing fatigues, dungarees, boots and doing physical training and going to the Firing Range to qualify with the Navy's automatic pistol. It was 1976 now and at thirty years old Lorrie was finding a lot of muscles in her body that she had forgotten she had, because they were aching and cramping every night while she was trying to sleep. She found that she was the oldest recruit there by a long shot. Most of the other girls were from seventeen to nineteen years old, but Lorrie was excelling in her Boot Camp training, because she was determined to be the best in her Company to show her Instructors and the young girls what she could do. Lorrie was looking forward to finishing Boot Camp so she could see if she had been accepted for her (MOS), job in Cryptology. When her Boot Camp training was over she wasn't assigned immediately like the rest of her Company was and it worried her that she had been left out of this transition into the regular Navy. She soon found out why this happened. She had caught the eye of the Officer in Command of the Recruit Training for Women and she was called in to a meeting with one of her Staff Officers. They were ready to make her a special offer for her consideration. They told her that because of her excelling in her Basic Training and her very good test scores along with her age that the Navy wanted to offer her an opportunity to advance in Rank to a Grade Five which was a Sargent Grade, all she had to do was to except the position that the Navy offered her. Lorrie couldn't believe what she was hearing and she was on pins and needles to find out what the new assignment was. She wished that the Staff Officer would hurry and get to the point, because all of this was making Lorrie nervous. Finally the Staff Officer told her that the United States Navy was prepared to offer her the (MOS) of Drill Instructor for a Company of new Recruits and that if she accepted her Rank would be immediately be upgraded to Drill Sargent (DI) status and she would have her own private Quarters which included a bath and shower with a Staff Assistant that would be at her Command to assist her with any duties that she would assign to her. The Staff Officer told her that the only catch to it was that she had to sign on to this (MOS) DI job for a year then after she had completed the year of her assignment she would be immediately sent to a Cryptology Training Facility so she could train for her chosen MOS. The Staff Officer told Lorrie that she would retain her rank after her assignment of DI was completed and that she had excelled in all her exams for the acceptance into the Cryptology program which was a very prestigious position and that she had twenty-four hours think it over, before the offer would be withdrawn. The Staff Officer then told her that she wouldn't be assigned any duty to perform that day to give her time to make her decision and for her to meet back at the same office at the same time the next day and not to discuss this offer with anyone else. With this, the meeting was over and Lorrie stood and saluted did an about face and went back to her Barracks to digest all that she had heard. While everything was still fresh in her mind from the meeting with the Staff Officer Lorrie wrote the entire conversation that had taken place at that meeting down on paper, so she could read it back to herself a little at a time to be sure of the meaning and also to see if she would have any additional questions to ask when she met again the next day. She then went to the Mess Hall for her lunch. While Lorrie was trying to eat her lunch she became so nervous from the excitement of thinking about it that she became sick at her stomach and two girls that she was sharing a table with rushed her to a restroom so she could throw up. They thought that she should report to Sickbay for an examination and she couldn't tell them what was causing it, so she just told them that she had made the mistake of trying to drink some milk and milk had always made her sick ever since she was a kid. After her lunch Lorrie went back to her Barracks and went over her written text of the meeting and she could only think of one question she had and that was if all the information that was covered in the meeting would be included in a report that would be put in her personal file and if so would she be able to review it before it was an official document. The next day when she went for the meeting to the Staff Officers office she was called in and she went in stood at attention and saluted and the Officer told her to be at ease and for her to sit in the chair across the desk, then the Officer produced a two page official document that outlined the entire conversation of their meeting the previous day that was signed by the Commanding Officer and the Staff Officer and he asked her to review it. Lorrie was surprised, because this was her only question and it had been anticipated before hand by them. She reviewed it carefully while the Officer sat quietly behind the desk and then she noticed that there also was a place for her to sign the document and it had her rank as a pay grade five, Sargent. The Officer asked her if she had made her decision and Lorrie said that she would accept the Promotion and the new MOS of DI and the Officer then told her to sign the document using her new rank, because it would be active immediately and that is exactly what she did. The officer then congratulated her and smiled and shook her hand and handed her her new rank patches for her uniforms along with an order for new uniforms from Supply, to go with her MOS, a new identification card and also a twenty-four hour Pass to celebrate her promotion. Lorrie couldn't believe her good fortune and she went immediately to Supply to get her new uniforms then she went back to her old Barracks for the last time to attach the new rank patches to her new uniforms and she carefully ironed all of the wrinkles out and made sure that all the creases were in the right places and straight. Then her Staff Assistant that she had chosen arrived to help her pack up and get moved into her new Quarters. Her Staff Assistant had been busy getting Lorries new Quarters ready for her, so it was nice and clean and in order when she got there and unpacked and organized her belongings. When they finished Lorrie dismissed her new Staff Assistant, but told her that she might need her later in the evening, because she was going use her Pass to test out the NCO Club and have a few drinks to celebrate. Her Staff Assistant came to attention and saluted Lorrie and said that she would be at Lorrie's service on command. So Lorrie became a Drill Instructor in the Navy and her mature age along with her excellent achievements in her physical training and her excellent test scores promoted her at this fast pace. Lorrie was starting to feel pretty good about herself and she thought that the Navy was starting to build up her confidence for the first time in her life. She was determined to give the Navy her best in all that she did. Lorrie thought that at the age of thirty-one this was the best decision that she had ever made toward a real career and that 1976 was a real turning point on her life for the better.

Gus—1976 The situation in the United States was still unsettled with the economy and the markets in 1976 and it was all beginning to take a toll on Gus's Farm and Ranch operations. The United States Department of Agriculture was implementing all sorts of Government Programs to try and bolster farm prices. All ready Lawyers, Accounts and large farmers were trying to figure ways to exploit the loop-holes in the Programs. This seemed to always happen when the Government got involved in anything and Government money was involved and this aggravated Gus. He didn't believe in a lot of Government involvement in private business. There were payment limitations of fifty thousand dollars per individual person that owned a farm. The Bankers got quickly involved and required the farm owners to be signed up in these Government Programs to be considered for their crop loans. During Gus's time in farming this had never happened. Along with this Government money there were many rules and regulations to abide by that basically gave the Government and the Banks the ability to actually run your farming business. It got to the point that you simply became the day to day manager and they became the decision makers of your long term agriculture plan. The payment limitation of fifty thousand dollars was avoided by farmers by setting up Corporations, because a Corporation was considered as an individual under the law, that would divide up their operations into units that would be controlled by these separate Corporations and have as their President another family member or trusted friend. This would allow them to receive multiple payments of fifty thousand dollars. To Gus this was not honest and he just couldn't make himself do it. This would handicap him, because his whole operation was limited to the fifty thousand dollar limitation. During 1976 Gus's wife informed him that she was pregnant. Gus hadn't really thought about having any more children, because between them they already had three to raise. His wife had been on birth control pills and Gus had heard that they weren't always perfect in preventing pregnancy, but they were supposed to work like ninety-nine percent of the time. Gus presented the outward appearance of being happy about the announcement, but privately he wondered if his wife had planned her pregnancy in secret. He was happy about the idea of having a baby, but hoped that she hadn't done this behind his back. His idea about it was that something this important should be discussed and planned by both of them. He would always wonder, because he wasn't about to bring up that subject to her. They had arguments enough as it was and what could bringing up a subject like that do except start another long argument. As Gus was finishing harvesting his crops and started receiving the checks for their sale he noticed that on the PAY TO THE ORDER OF line of the check was not only his name, but also that of the Bank. Not only that, but the Bank's name was first. This had never happened before and he was angry that the Bank would demand that their name be first on his check like he was going to somehow cheat them. As far as Gus knew he had never cheated anyone in his life let alone his Bank. He compared his check with other farmers and some that used other Banks and they were the same. Evidently the Banks had partnered with the Government and had some rules passed to do this. To Gus this was just another way that the Government and the Banks were in conspiring to control the farmers. He felt trapped, because he was borrowing very large amounts of money to keep his operations running. Gus thought that maybe the Banks knew something that was coming in the financial sector that the regular person didn't know. Well if he was going to keep operating he was locked into doing it their way, but it sure didn't set well with him. His farming and ranching operations were holding their own, but the margin of profit was declining all the time. Gus felt that something would have to change if he was going to be in production agriculture in years to come. There were starting to be to many things that he couldn't control and they were all taking a toll on his operation. The new year of 1977 was right around the corner and everyone was hoping for some good news for production agriculture, because it looked like Gus was to have one more mouths to feed and raise with the new baby coming.

Lorrie—1976 The big responsibility of Drill Instructor that the Navy had intrusted to Lorrie suited her just fine and she was doing a great job of it. She had trained several Companies of new women Recruits and all of them had excelled in their training which was a very good reflection on Lorrie's Navy Record. She was getting to the end of her assigned duty agreement with the Commander of the New Women Inductees Training Corps. And she was looking forward to 1977 when she could transfer to her chosen MOS in Cryptology for her training. Lorrie had made several friends with some of the other women Drill Instructors and they would eat lunch together in the Mess Hall and talk about their individual Companies that they were training at the time and compare notes about the trainees that were excelling and the ones that they were having trouble with and what to do with them to bring them along to where they should be to graduate training. They also talked about all of the interesting new men that came on Base for training and Lorrie would listen to their conversation about them. The women seemed to always have their eyes out for some good looking man there and would discuss how to get their attention. Lorrie kept hearing them talk about this young Navy Seal that looked so good and that they were keeping tabs on him and were trying to get him interested in them, but he seemed to be so involved with his training that he didn't have any time for dating. Lorrie had been involved in several romantic relationships since she had been a DI there on Base in Orlando, but they hadn't lasted very long and they had been on her terms. She wasn't interested in anything permanent, because she wanted to be able to party and romance who she wanted to without any ties. She got a kick listening to the other women DI's talk about this Navy Seal. One day at lunch with them one of the DI's told Lorrie to look at the lunch counter and she would see the Navy Seal that they were talking about, he was getting his lunch tray. Lorrie turned and looked at him and she was impressed to see that he was very handsome and she could see that he was well endowed with a lot of muscles that showed through his fatigues, but he looked very young. One of the girls waved him over to their table so Lorrie could get a good look at him and he stood there holding his lunch tray and they told him that this was Sargent Roy. Lorrie just sat there and looked at him and he held his hand out and told her that he had heard a lot about her on Base since he had been there and he was finally glad to meet her. Lorrie didn't take his hand and he asked if he could sit down and join them and Lorrie smiled and told him to sit in her place, because she was leaving. He looked shocked and Lorrie got up and left and didn't look back. She had already decided that she was going to make him want her, so she could brag to those younger women DI"s that they couldn't get him, but an older woman like her could. Lorrie was thirty-one now and most of the other DI's were in their early twenty's about ten years younger then her. She knew that the way she played this first encounter would hurt his ego as a Navy Seal when all women should lay down in front of a Navy Seal and it would make him try harder to get her attention. Lorrie knew how to play the game with these types of men, especially these Navy

Seal types. 1977 was approaching fast and Lorrie had been right about the young Navy Seal. He had contacted her at every opportunity and Lorrie had turned him down till he was begging her for a date. She finally excepted and they had been dating for a couple of months when he asked her to marry him. She told him that she would think about it. To herself Lorrie was trying to imagine being married to this young kid. She had suspected the first time that she had seen him that he was young, but he was ten years younger then her. He was twenty-one and Lorrie was thirty-one. Lorrie had to admit that he was a very active lover, because of his youth and his physical condition was always at its peak, because he worked out all the time. In fact there were times that she had to slow him down, because he was exhausting her. He thought that marathon sex was the way to impress her and she tried to explain to him that it wasn't what counted that what happened before and after was more important, but he was to young to listen. She sat him down and told him that she would marry him if he would never complain about her ambition of making her Career in Cryptology in the Navy, because it would mean that they would be separated much of the time especially when he also was going to be away at training. She knew that they would be passing each other back and forth most of the time because both of them would be in training all of the time and she also told him that when she finished her training that she had no idea where the Navy was going to station her, but she was going to go there no matter where it was. He was agreeing to everything and told her that he didn't care that all he wanted was for her to marry him, so Lorrie relented and they considered themselves engaged. When it was official that Lorrie was to leave the Training Base in Orlando her last Company that she trained gave her a going away party and at the party when the music was playing the song "In The Still Of The Night" came on and Lorrie stood up and saluted and started crying, of course this was after a few drinks. All of her Company of trainees wanted to know what was wrong and she told them that she was saluting a lost love that she would never have and that she hoped that he was happy. They couldn't understand, because she had just got engaged to that handsome Navy Seal that every girl on the Base was after. In 1977 Lorrie does marry the young Navy Seal and she then goes to Cryptology training at an Air Force Base in San Angelo, Texas. When their training schedules had days off that match up they meet somewhere for a couple of days and it is exciting because they have been apart for sometime several months so they party, go out to eat and lay in bed together and then it's time to say goodby till the next time. They never really get the chance to know each other, but it's a lot of fun. In 1978 Lorrie finished her Cryptology and she received her orders to be stationed in Virginia at the Navy's high security coded tracking facility there. She called her husband and told him and he said that he would try to put in for a transfer to be close to her.

Gus—1977 came in for Gus with disappointment on all the points that had to do with his farming business. He had hoped for some positive changes to what had been happening in 1976, but there wasn't anything that looked like it was going to improve. The markets for all of his agriculture products were still weak and interest rates on his loans were still creeping up. When he went to his Bankers with all of his projections of his expenses and income they all were trying to convince him that he should divide up his operation into several Corporations to take advantage of the extra Government payments that he would receive which would add up to being a lot of money to his bottom line. Gus just told them that he didn't consider that business honest and that he felt that if the Government decided to have it stopped then all the farmers that had used that method to receive those payments might have to pay back the money and where would they get it when they had already used it to pay back their Bank Loans. He asked if the Banks were going to forward that money to the Government if that happened and the Bankers got mad at Gus for laying the blame on them for forcing the farmers to take the extra Government Payment money before they would loan them any money for their farm loans. It made the Bankers look like they were greedy and they were, but they didn't want anybody telling them that they were greedy. Gus was lucky that he had built up so much equity in his farming and ranching operations by paying off all of his land except the last tract that he had bought and he didn't owe any money at all on his cattle or farming machinery. He was still OK, but he wondered how long it would be till he would have to re-mortgage some of his land to keep operating. Surely something positive would happen before he would have to result to that. Gus's baby was born in March of 1977 and it was another boy. Gus still wondered how his wife had gotten pregnant when she was on the birth control pill. He had even consulted with a Doctor about it and the Doctor told Gus that there were cases of pregnancy while on the pill, but they were rare. This left Gus with the belief that his wife did go behind his back to get pregnant, so he decided to have a vasectomy in a couple of months to give time to see if his new son was going to be OK before he had it done. He thought that if he couldn't trust his wife to consult him before she planned to get pregnant then he would stop it this way and that is what he did. His son was a healthy boy and that made four kids for them to raise and Gus thought that was enough, period. The 1977 harvest was just a normal crop and nothing to brag about, but the increasing cost of production expenses continued to depress the profits Gus was expecting to have and his margins of profit were razor thin. He was under constant pressure from all sides and it was starting to show with some gray hair and him being unable to sleep good waking up in the middle of the night and finding himself at the table with his calculator trying to come up with ideas that would put some profit in the operation. One time when he was up in the middle of the night with his calculator sipping on a glass of tea and trying to figure out what he should do, he stopped and thought when was the last time he had been truly happy. The last time he could remember being really happy was the time in 1962 when he was on the beach with Lorrie and they were so close and those wonderful Corpus kisses. He just sat there for a few minutes and daydreamed about that before he shook himself back into reality and continued his troubled thoughts about his farming operations. He thought that surely this couldn't last much longer till farm prices would start rising. Gus was now looking forward to 1978 in hopes for some good times again.

Lorrie—1978 The Navy's Cryptology tracking center Virginia was a sweet post for Lorrie in 1978 and she lived in the Navy's dorm there. She was so into her work and enjoyed it so much that she couldn't imagine doing anything else. There was no doubt about it that the Navy had rebuilt Lorrie's confidence in herself after that terrible mistake she had made by getting pregnant by her first husband and having to marry him. He had done all he could to take her self confidence away from her. The only bright part of their marriage was her horse and the affair she had had with his sweet assistant and even that was something that her first husband had secretly planned so he could be with his girlfriend. Now everything was different and she was in control of her own life even with her new young husband she was wearing the pants and calling the shots and it felt really good for a change. The Officer in charge of her shift was an old Chief and she got along with him real good. They would even meet after their shift sometime on the sly, because the Officers weren't supposed to be associating with their NCO's like that, so they would meet at out of the way Bars that none of their team would visit. He was a blast and he had so many stories about the Navy. He knew she was married and he had been married several times and he had been busted down in rank several times for getting in fights when drunk, but they got along good, because Lorrie liked to party also and she liked to hear all his stories about the Navy. Her Seal husband finally got a transfer to a Base close by her, so Lorrie rented an apartment and they set up house keeping there. He was still doing a lot of training, so he was gone a lot and that was just fine for Lorrie, because it was always exciting to see each other when they had been apart for a month or so. Lorrie started to learn some disturbing things about her new husband though since they were living together. His mail was now coming to their apartment and Lorrie learned that his credit had been charged to the limit for a long time and that he was just paying the minimum on it and even that was sometime a late payment. Also when he came home and he was payed instead of paying on his credit card debt he would go out and buy the most expensive steaks and get her a dozen of the most expensive roses and she didn't like this. It showed her that he was very irresponsible with his money. When the rent came due she would sent the money with him to pay the rent and then that night he would plan a night out on the town and then a few days later the landlord would be knocking on Lorrie's door wondering when they were going to pay the rent. This was all very unsettling for Lorrie, because she had always believed in being very responsible about paying your rent and debts on time. She had big sit down meeting with him and told him that they had to stick by their budget that she had made and he just shook his head yes, but to no avail and it kept happening, so Lorrie told him that he was going to have to get himself a part time job some where so they could catch up on his credit card bills and all the training equipment that the had bought and put in their spare bedroom. There wasn't even anyplace for her to have someone spend the night. Then he had starting ordering all of these additives for bodybuilding and they made his breath smell like something had died in his mouth and they were expensive also. It was time again for another sit down meeting with him. He did get a part time job as a bartender at a local Bar, but he spent more then he was making at it, so the sit down meetings came more often now and Lorrie was getting to the end of the line with it. All he would do at these meetings was agree with her and say that he would do better, but he never would. Then one night when he was working at the Bar and it was his birthday, Lorrie had baked his favorite cake for him and she surprised him at the Bar with it and there was a young blond girl sitting at the bar across from him and Lorrie didn't say anything. She just set the cake down on the bar and the girl started telling Lorrie that she thought that Lorrie's husband was so sexy and that she wanted to go to bed with him and that she had plans for him, not knowing that Lorrie was his wife. Well this was all that it took for Lorrie to decide that she had had it with her husband. The girl went to the restroom and Lorrie took the cake and pushed it into her husbands face and left and went back to the apartment. When he got home she was up waiting for him and told him that she was divorcing him and he agreed to it, so they got a simple divorce and went their separate ways with no yelling or fighting. Lorrie moved back into the Navy's dorm and she was single again. When she started thinking about it she couldn't believe that she had out smarted herself by trying to out do those young women DI's and get that young Navy Seal, boy did that backfire on her. No more young guys for her, they didn't have a brain in their head as to what real life was all about. From now on she wouldn't get involved with any man unless he was her age or older. They hadn't even been married two years and with all the separation for training the total time that they had spent together probably wasn't more then six months. Oh well she hadn't been in love with him anyway and the truth was that she hadn't been in love with any man since Gus and she knew that she could never love another man, because she still loved Gus and she always would. 1979 was coming up quick and so would be her enlistment of four years toward the end of 1979 and she had every intention of re-enlisting to see where this Navy Career was going.

Gus—1978 The new year of 1978 was starting to look a little better for Gus with the farm prices holding their own, but inflation was still driving up production costs. He had finally gotten all his farming loans done for the 1978 year. Trying to make out production cost estimates for his loans was getting harder, because prices of goods and services were changing almost on a daily bases, so how could be very accurate with them. Years ago when Gus first started in business the costs of raising a crop changed very little from year to year. In fact if you went to the Bank to make a farming loan the Bank's Loan Officer could tell you how much money you would need to farm that particular crop for the year, but no more of that. Now everything was complicated. The prices of oil and gas were climbing and this presented an opportunity for Gus to make a little extra money from an oil deal. Also inflation was still driving the value of his land up and this made his Balance

Sheet look better then it really was. What Gus really needed was a big increase in the prices of his farm products and cattle to be sold. He was thankful that at least they were holding their own and not going down. As the 1978 crop season went along his crops were looking pretty good and Gus was pleased with how the year was progressing. At home things were changing. His wife decided that she didn't want to milk the cow anymore or deal with a garden, so he sold the cow and forgot about working up the garden plot. She wanted to get the kids involved kids sports in El Campo and also she wanted to join some different clubs that were for bowling, jewelry, etc. that women liked to associate with. So now the family car was running to town almost every day and nothing was being accomplished at home. Just something else that disgusted Gus. Gus had harvested all of his Milo Maize and all but two fields of Rice and out of the blue a Hurricane pops up in the Gulf of Mexico and heads straight for the Gulf Coast of Texas and makes land fall just fifty miles West of where Gus is farming and the wind blows and it rains about twelve inches and it ruins the two fields of Rice and destroys most of his Soybeans. Now Gus has a big problem. He needed all of his crops to pay back his Bank Loans and provide living expenses for the next year. On top of this his Mom was spending more time in and out of the Hospital and this was extra expense also. If it wasn't one thing it was another and it seemed that just when there might be a turn around in his fortune unexpected disaster stepped in to take the profits away. The rest of 1978 Gus spent trying to finish harvesting what was left of his Soybeans and gathering his Cattle to sell. He had planned on saving some heifers to replace some of his older breeding cows, but now all would have to be sold to bring in extra income because of the big losses caused by the Hurricane. There was so much water standing around on the farm land that Gus could see that he was going to be later then usual getting his plowing done and that could even affect the timing of planting of the 1979 crop. These kinds of things is why farming was always considered as a gamble. He hoped that 1979 would better and he was going to keep going at it come hell or high water, as the old saying goes.

Lorrie—1979 Lorrie had divorced her young Navy Seal husband in 1978 and she was glad to be free from him. She had decided that he needed to grow up, because he was so immature about almost everything. Lorrie came to the conclusion that what he really needed was a Mama that he could sleep with. The new year of 1979 Lorrie is right where she wants to be. She has proved herself as being very dependable and competent in her work. She has been noticed by her peers as having leadership qualities and they are constantly upgrading her work performance standing. Now though there has been huge problem that Lorrie has to deal with and that concerns her son, who has been living with her parents as temporary Guardians. Lorrie had always kept up with what was happening with her son and the situation with her parents, but not being there she wasn't seeing the whole picture. She wrote her son a letter at least every week and would call home to talk to her parents and to her son every week and there were always conversations about some trouble he had been in school or problems that her parents were having with him obeying them. They would discuss it and Lorrie would talk to her son about it and he would promise her that he would do better and he would for a while, but then he would repeat his disobedience and be in trouble again. He was almost eleven years old now and this problem had been growing for several years as he got older. Lorrie's Dad told her that it had become way to much for him and her Mom to handle and that they just couldn't control her son any more. It had become a big worry and they were exhausted with taking care of all the problems concerned with her sons behavior. Her Dad suggested that she find another responsible adult to take over the temporary Guardianship of her son. He told her that he hated to let her down, but they were getting older and they just couldn't do it anymore. He told her that maybe her first husband, the boy's Father would take temporary Guardianship. Lorrie told her Dad that she would talk to the boy's Father and see what she could do. Lorrie would have rather had her finger nails pulled out then to call her first husband with this problem, because she despised him so much and she thought that she didn't think that she could even be in the same room with him, but she couldn't think of anything else to do. Lorrie worked up her courage and got hold of her son's Father and told him what the problem was and he agreed to take temporary Guardianship of their son till Lorrie was in the position to take care of him. So that is what they did and her son went to live with his Father and a Stepmother. When Lorrie had first had the idea to join the Navy she didn't really take the time to consider all the problems that her son would bring to bare as he grew older, because he was still at the age, when she joined the Navy, that he could be controlled pretty easy. His Father was still in the Air Force with a wife and he was strict on behavior, so maybe his Father would be a strong hand on him. Well it was done now and her parents could rest easy knowing that their grandson was with his Father, even though they also despised him as a man. Lorrie continued her steady progress in her position at the Navy's high security code tracking facility in Virginia. She had a very good relationship with her boss who was in charge of several teams of Cryptology trackers that kept track of the locations of every Navy ship and submarine on the planet, minute by minute. In fact she and he had hit it off right from the start of her assignment to that top secret Cryptology facility and they had met at bars after their shifts and had drinks and enjoyed each others company. This was prohibited by the Navy, because he was her boss and also he was an officer and she was a non-com. and they were well aware of this regulation. There were ways to get around this regulation by being cautious and not leaving work together, riding in the same car or going to the Bars that were close to their work facility. Lorrie really enjoyed his company and they would meet, have drinks and dance and talk about their lives. This became an accepted pattern of meeting two or three times a week after work for relaxation before they would separate to go to their separate apartments. Lorrie found out that he was a Louisiana man and his Mom and Dad still lived in a small town there. This was just another thing that pleased Lorrie, because her Dad had relatives in Louisiana also plus her boss loved to fish and crab and Lorrie had grown up with that on the Texas Gulf Coast with her Dad and her Grandparents so they were finding out that they had several things in common. He told her that when he got out of the Navy he planned to have a Bait and Fishing business in Louisiana and this idea appealed to Lorrie. She started thinking of her boss as a possible romantic partner in life. She knew that she would never love him, but he seemed like he was easy to be with and they had a lot in common, plus she had respect for him as an older man that had built himself up in rank and position in the Navy at this top security post. After a few weeks they started ending their Bar meetings by renting a Motel room and finishing off the night with a little sex, before going to their separate apartments. This progressed to planning to rent an apartment together that would be rather tricky, because they would have to ride to work in separate cars and he wouldn't be able to get his mail there, he would have to rent a Post Office box. There was no way that the Navy would condone their relationship together, because of the very strict regulations against it. They did it anyway and would enjoy fishing and going crabbing together on their days off. He was a very good cook of all kinds of sea food and they enjoyed all of these outings and also sitting outside and grilling seafood over the open coals and drinking beer and listening to good old country music. He and Lorrie would go over to his Parents home in Louisiana and one time Lorrie even took him to El Campo to meet her Parents. Everything seemed to be working out real good. Lorrie knew that his Parents were expecting them to get married and she really liked them. His Mom even gave Lorrie some dishes that she had hand painted herself, that is how close they were getting and Lorrie started thinking that maybe she could marry him. He had never asked her though and the only thing that Lorrie could see that might have given her pause on the matter was that sometime he would just get falling-down-drunk and Lorrie didn't like it, but he wasn't violent at all to her. He had told her that he had had trouble with his drinking in the Navy before and he had been busted in rank several times and sent to alcohol rehab, but he had always regained his rank, because he was very competent in his work. 1979 was slipping away and Lorrie was trying to search her heart to decide what she was going to do with her Chief, Boss that she was living with. She liked him, but didn't love him, not surprising to her, because she knew that it would always be this way with a man. There was only one man that she could ever love, so she would have to settle for a man that she thought that she could live with if she ever married again, she new that she could never have it all. She wasn't for sure what she would do if he asked her to marry him, she might say yes if he caught her at the right time. All she really knew for sure was that she was going to re-enlist when her time came up and it was fast approaching. Lorrie was thirty-four years old now and she was already submitting her re-enlistment papers to see what the Navy would offer her as advancement in her Cryptology Career.

Gus—1979 found Gus deeper in debt then he had been in many years, because of the Hurricane damage to his crops and the out of control inflation in the United States kept driving up production costs, so that he had to borrow more money to keep his farm and ranch operations moving forward. The only bright spots in all of this was that farm prices were rising a little and the value of his land was steadily increasing which gave him more borrowing power. Gus still thought that things looked out of control, but the question was what could he do about it! Gus was thirty-seven years old now and with all the pressure he was under he was feeling even older then his years. He had an interesting phone call one night from an Real Estate Agent in Wharton Texas that was looking for a farm and ranch to buy for a client. Gus went over to his office in Wharton to discuss it with him. The Real Estate Agent told Gus that his client wanted a place that was about the size of his place and that in the agreement Gus could keep all of his mineral rights on the land and he could keep all of his cattle. All that his client wanted was the land, irrigation wells and the farm machinery and that his client was ready to pay Gus one thousand eight hundred dollars per acre for it. Gus thought that it was a really high price to pay for it especially without the minerals included. He was tempted to agree to the deal right there, but he told the Real Estate Agent that it was a huge decision and that he wanted to sleep on it and he would let him know in a couple of days, so they left it right there and Gus drove home almost dizzy headed from this offer right out of the blue. On the way home Gus did some rough calculations and the price would give Gus approximately two million one hundred sixty thousand dollars gross. Wow that was a lot of money and on top of that to keep and sell his cattle would bring him another five hundred thousand dollars. Gus had no intention in ever selling his mineral rights, because he new that they could be extremely valuable if there was ever oil discovered, but with them on his balance sheet with all that money that would bring his gross worth to around three million dollars less taxes and debt payback. Gus almost had to laugh when he thought back that he had been nothing but a struggling farm hand and cowboy starting with three fifty dollar heifers. All of this sudden realization that he was worth a lot of money made Gus began to think about all of the possibilities it might bring about. He had never really thought hard about how much money that he was worth, because ever since he had first started farming and ranching he had been strapped for cash money. He had never thought in the terms of wealth, because he had never felt that he was wealthy. To Gus wealth was the ability have plenty of cash on hand to do most anything that you wanted to do without going to a Bank and borrowing money to do it. Gus had never been able to build up this kind of cash surplus. All the money he earned went to pay back loans and invest directly in his business, so Gus was always asset rich and cash poor. Now when thinking about selling his land with his home and farm equipment it started to bring up some interesting questions in his mind. He was only thirty-seven years old and that meant that he had a lot of productive working years left unless something terrible happened, so what would he do with all of this money if he sold out? Gus wasn't the kind to buy big fancy, expensive homes or expensive automobiles and go on expensive holiday vacations all the time. He also knew that he wasn't the type to be a Stock Market investor. He had spent most of his life around agriculture, so this was the heart of his thinking now. He started to think about his boys.

He had three of them now and if just one of them would want to go into the farming and ranching business then they would need his land as stepping stone to build on for the future of their own family. In a way this realization was a sort of a let down for Gus and he suddenly felt obligated to hold on to the land for the future if his boys needed it. The next day he called the Real Estate Agent and told him that he didn't want to sell. The Agent tried to talk Gus into selling, but Gus told him no. The Agent told Gus that he would call his client to see if he could get Gus even more money for his land, but Gus told him not to do it, because he had made up his mind and that was final. So Gus went through his crop year of 1979 the same way that he always did, except that now his oldest boy was twelve years old and Gus had started to train him on the big farm machinery and working cattle in a serious manner. To Gus this was the kind of thing that he had turned down the sale of his land and all of the millions of dollars for, but would it be worth it. The only way to find out was to keep working hard and planning and hope that he could hold it all together till the day his boys could take over. 1980 would soon be here and that meant that a new crop year with its own challenges would start. Hopefully everything would level out so he could see better how to plan for the future.

Lorrie—1980 This year Lorrie would be thirty-five and it is 1980. She has been approved for re-enlistment and she had her Uncle that lives in Florida, who she first lived with when she came to Florida when she was nineteen in 1965, do the swearing in ceremony for her. He had been in the Army and had stayed in the Army Reserve, so he could do that. Lorrie hadn't received her orders yet as to her new Post, but she knew where it was to be and also she had received another stripe which upped her pay grade to a six, which would be a Staff Sargent. She hadn't told her live-in boyfriend where her new Post was going to be yet, because she knew that it might hurt him and even though he had always been good to Lorrie and she had enjoyed being with him, this new Post was the most exciting chance of her lifetime and she wasn't going to let it slip by for anybody, well she would have, if it would have been a choice between it and Gus. Her new Post was to be in London, England and it was the answer to a life long dream ever since she was just a girl, when she would read about Europe and look at all the pictures of the works of art and the historical architecture, the ancient battles, as a girl, she would pretend that she was there and now she would be there. With all this excitement it was hard not to tell her boyfriend about it, but she knew that it would be much better to wait till almost the last minute to tell him. He had become very close to her this last year and been living in secret almost like husband and wife. He had come to look at their relationship like that, but he had never asked her to marry him and she sure wasn't going to do it now, so she was trying to dodge any chance that he might ask her if he found out to early and he had a chance to think about it. She was to leave for England in about a week and she was putting things together a little at a time so he never discovered it. Then all of a sudden out of the blue Lorrie got some real disturbing news. In compliance with the Temporary Guardianship Agreement that she had with her ex-husband, her son's Father, she was notified of a change of address that her son would be at. It was in the Philippines. Lorrie gasp, because this didn't sound good to her. Her son was now out of the United States. She knew that she had to find out more about it, so she called her husbands wife and talked to her. His wife told Lorrie that they were getting a divorce and he had applied for a transfer to the Philippines to make it harder and more expensive for her to get any kind of a divorce settlement from him and that he had been right that she was just going to let him off with a simple divorce, because of the expense of hiring two Lawyers, one here in the United States and another in the Philippines. Lorrie thanked her and saw this as maybe an omen that she might also have a lot of trouble with this. Two days before she was to leave Virginia for England she told her boyfriend and he was shocked. He told her that he was going to try to get a transfer some where close enough to her so they could be together. Lorrie sat there and listened to him, but gave him no encouragement, because she was through with him and she was on her own new adventure in exactly the place that she had always wanted to be, but never thought in her wildest dreams that it was going to happen. After their discussion on the subject he asked her if she wanted to go out to the Bar and she told him that she had to much to do to get ready, so he went by himself and came back stumbling drunk. This was just fine with Lorrie, because it gave her a chance to pack up things that she hadn't had the chance to do while he was at the apartment. Lorrie can't wait to get to England and start learning the culture over there and also she would like to meet and get to know the British people. She just knew that 1980 was going to be the year that would open up a whole new and exciting life for her.

Gus—1980 All of Gus's hopes for 1980 were dashed when Banks were starting to close their doors and rumors of a wide spread collapse of the economy were spreading. Gus could remember listening to the stories his parents told about the hard times in the 1930's in the Great Depression when the farmers went broke and everyone that had money in the Stock Market lost everything they had. Gus's own Grandparents had gone broke during the Great Depression and they had never recovered from it. This is the main reason that Gus had never ventured off into investing in the Stock Market. He had always felt that it was manipulated by big money and the Government and that things that you could actually stand on and feel with your hands were the best investments. Things like land, cattle and machinery and hard money, silver and gold. Already some of his friends were being denied loans for their farming operations and they were having to go to the FHA and apply there. The FHA was a Government Agency that would finance farmers and ranchers and it was the considered the last resort for financing on agricultural loans that the Banks had turned down. These friends of Gus had been farming for years and were considered to be reasonably good farmers, but they just didn't have enough assets built up in their business to keep supporting loans. The reason for this is that during the years of inflation their assets were gaining in value and they were being loaned money according to that value. Now though because of this panic the Banks were automatically lowering the value of their assets and the new value wouldn't support their loans, so they were suddenly caught in a trap, not of their doing, that they hadn't imagined could happen. Farmers are usually asset rich and cash poor and Gus was no exception on this. His only salvation right now was that he had invested heavily in land and he had most of it payed off and that gave him the strength in his operation to borrow for his farming loans. His assets were also devalued automatically, but he had built up so much equity in them that he was still solvent. His Bankers required that he put up more of his land as collateral on his loans though and they wanted his cattle, but Gus said no, because cattle were an immediate source of income that had a ready market and you could sell them fast for cash to take care of expenses that maybe a Bank would take weeks to decide if they would loan you money to use for those expenses. To Gus the cattle were an ace in the hole in case of an emergency for money. Also to make things worse interest rates on loans were still going higher which meant there would be a shrinking margin of profit even if he made a good crop. Gus went ahead and did his farming and ranching as he had always done except now he was thinking of ways to shrink his operation so he wouldn't have to borrow as much money to keep it going. The trouble with this thinking was that it was set up to operate as a unit and if he changed one part of it, it would affect another part. Almost any change that Gus would do would have to be a major one. As the crop year went on things were happening that would almost make Gus dizzy. Interest rates were rising, prices of farm products were going down and production costs were going up, so the farm plan that you started with didn't mean anything, because there was no way Gus could stick to his budget. All of this was moving fast. Every time Gus would go to the Bank for another loan the interest rates would be higher and this would on a monthly basis. It was crazy and the Banker would just shake his head and tell Gus to either take it or leave it, but the Banker knew that once a farmer started a crop there was no way that he could just stop, because crops required constant care that were cash intensive on a daily basis right up to the finish of harvest. On top of this his family life was growing more complex. His children were getting older and requiring more expensive cloths and his wife seemed to think up all sort of activities for them that required an outlay of money that Gus thought unneeded. She seemed to think that he was some sort of endless supply of money. When Gus and his wife first got married in 1974 they got along pretty good. They had a few arguments, but it seemed as time went on she went to extreme lengths to press for an argument. An example of this was when Gus would be explaining why he was not in favor of something that she thought should happen, she would tell him no what you really mean is this and it would completely twist what he has said into something else. Gus wasn't about to have his words twisted into something that he didn't say so the argument would go on for hours with Gus talking in a controlled manner and his wife yelling all of these completely twisted arguments. They would simply call it off out of exhaustion without coming to an agreement. Gus was getting tired of this, because he had much more important things to take care of then to argue with her. Sometime he felt like he was the enemy when he was out there every day fighting the world for his family. He thought of Lorrie and how sweet she had been and couldn't imagine her acting like that, well he had married this woman, so he was going to try to stick to it. The situation in 1980 for his farming and ranching operations continued to deteriorate all through the year and his operation only broke even when the crop year of 1980 was over. This was the first time that his operations hadn't at least made a little money. He thought that things were getting a little scarey and decided to go back and re-think shrinking his business. He was determined to try something new for 1981, just what it would be he wasn't sure just yet and 1981 was just around the corner. Gus was going to be thirty-nine years old in 1981 and he was feeling uneasy about his financial situation. He sure didn't want to go broke and have to start over. Well he would see what he would come up with in the new year of 1981.

Lorrie—1980 was a marvelous time for Lorrie. She was very pleased with her decision to go to England. Her career was advancing even better then she had expected. She had been put in charge of a team of Cryptology trackers in a super sensitive high security Navy installation in London. Lorrie was positioned in the middle of her Cryptology team on a high island platform, so she could see their computer screens at the same time she could see a huge electronic map on the wall that would show the positions of all the Navy ships and submarines as their positions changed every minute of the shift that she was on. It was so sensitive that the Navy personnel working there weren't even allowed to wear their uniforms out of the building. They had to look like they were just regular civilian employees. At the end of their shift they had to do their own clean up with collecting all of the unnecessary paper and bagging it and taking it to the incinerator and burning it, then sweeping, mopping and dusting the room to make sure that nothing was left that could be picked up and given to the enemy for information. The Navy was also giving her extra money for a clothing allowance since she had to wear civilian clothing to work, also she was given money for an apartment (flat in England) allowance for rent, because she was required to rent this flat where other Navy employees lived. Lorrie was a little disappointed that she hadn't got to meet any real English people that she could get to know and hang out with. Everyone that she had got to know in England so far were Americans what worked for the American Government in one capacity or another. During this time Lorrie had been writing letters to her son every week at the address that was furnished to her in the Philippines, but she had not received an answer from him and she began to get the feeling that her letters were being with held from him. She tried to call him without result. It was like she had run into a dead end on communication. This was worrying, so she stared making copies of her letters before she sent them to him, in case she would need them as evidence at a later date. Lorrie got a phone call from her former boyfriend Boss in Virginia that he wanted to come to England to see her and she told him that it would be OK and they made plans for his visit. Lorrie really wasn't looking forward to his visit, because she was way beyond having any romantic relationship with him, but she would let him know that, some way, when he came to see her. Lorrie had a small spare bedroom in her flat that she had been ignoring, but now she was fixing it up for her ex-boyfriend. She thought that this should send a message that they were not going to share a bed together. She also made plans for some day trips to places and sights that she knew that he would like to see. This would occupy him, so they wouldn't have a lot of time to be alone together. She sent him a letter as to the planned places and sights that she had picked out for him to see and he seemed delighted with her choices. He arrived at the airport and Lorrie met him there and told him that she had taken off for three days to show him around and that also she had planned a party for him on his last night at her flat with some of the people that she worked with that lived there. He tried to kiss her, but she turned her cheek to him to kiss instead of her lips. He looked a little surprised, but said nothing. They went to a Pub not far from Lorrie's flat for lunch and were joined there by two of Lorrie's work mates that she had invited, so as not to be alone with him right at the start. This she thought would set the tone for his visit. After their lunch she took him to her flat and showed him to his room so he could unpack. After that they sat down in Lorrie's little kitchen and she went over the plans that she had for his visit. It was then that he produced a ring box and Lorrie was scared to death that he had bought her an engagement ring, but instead it was a promise ring with a tiny diamond in it. Lorrie was at first hesitant in accepting it and she asked him what it meant. He told her that after all that they had meant to each other that he wanted her to have it to remember him by and that he promised to always love her. He didn't ask for her love and she didn't offer it, so she accepted it. She thought that he might be interested in seeing some of the old castles, Buckingham Palace and the museums, but what he really wanted to see was the sights from World War 2. She took him to the the bunker that Winston Churchill used when he was Prime Minister during the war and it was where he ran the war when the Battle for Britain and the bombing of London was going on. Then she took him to the nondescript cottage that was turned into the top secret code breaking instillation for the British intelligence service that broke the famous German code machine Enigma' secrets. She took him to some of the British Military Grave Yards and to the World War 2 RAF Museum with the real Spit Fire and Hurricane fighter planes. He really enjoyed all of this. Lorrie made sure that she kept his visit strictly friendly, no kissing or sex. She treated him like an old friend, which is how she looked at him know. She knew that he wanted more, but she just couldn't do it. She wasn't dating anyone else, so it wasn't that, it was just that she was through with their romantic relationship and she was moving on. She did hope to find a good man to date though and she hoped it would be an Englishman, because she really wanted to get into the culture there and so far she hadn't had the chance to meet any British men other then men that worked in the shops close to her flat that she shopped at for her daily necessities. When her ex-boyfriend left for the United States he told her that he had a lot of time built up and that he wanted to come back to see her soon. Lorrie told him that it would be OK, but it would be on the same basis and that she just wanted to be friends. He agreed and they parted that way. Lorrie was so glad that things had worked out the way they had. Now that part of her life was behind her she could concentrate on her job and just maybe catch a nice British man to enjoy her off days with. She no longer wanted to live with anyone on a permanent basis. If she found some man to have a romantic relationship with he would have to leave her flat after they had sex and go to his own place. Lorrie made that promise to herself to never let a man sleep in her bed all night. Lorrie was really enjoying her job and living in London. She and a girl that worked with her on her team became good friends and they liked the same off work activities, so they spent a lot of time together sight seeing. They were both interested in European history, architecture, archeology, art works and the Roman era in England. This girl was a great friend, because they had so many interests that were alike and she had a sweet nature, easy to get along with, but there were a couple of things that bothered Lorrie about her. The first was that she would sleep with almost any man that was nice looking at first meeting without knowing him at all. The second thing was that her vocabulary was terrible. She would use the F-word three or four times in a single sentence. Lorrie never did like that word and she finally told her friend that if she didn't stop using it Lorrie would quit hanging out with her. Lorrie's friend struggled with that, because she had been using it as part of her language for so long that she didn't know when it was going to pop out of her mouth. It took her some time, but she finally got to where she seldom said it, but once in a while it would pop out and she would apologize for it. Lorrie and her friend were in Lorrie's flat one evening enjoying a bottle of wine, talking and listening to music on the radio, after their dinner, and all of a sudden Lorrie held up her hand for her friend to stop talking and be quiet when this song started playing. Lorrie put her wine glass down and just stared off into space not really looking at anything and then she started to tear up and the tears were running down her cheeks and she was breathing in real deep and slow. Her friend just watched her not knowing what was happening, but she was quiet and reached over and touched Lorrie's shoulder to comfort her. Lorrie shook her head no and her friend withdrew her hand and waited till the song was over, It was "In The Still OF The Night" by The Five Satins. Lorrie got up and turned off the radio and for a few minutes they both just sat there in silence. Lorrie was drying her eyes and her friend, in a soft voice, asked Lorrie if she liked that song so much, was that the reason that she reacted to it like that every time it played. Lorrie looked at her for a minute and then told her that there was something that she had never told her or anyone else after she had left home. Lorrie told her that it was a precious, sweet secret that she would never be able to overcome. Lorrie told her about Gus and how perfect everything had been and that she had known since she had been a little girl that he was the man she was supposed to be in love with and she couldn't even think about ever being in love with any man but him. She told her friend that she had tried every thing to forget Gus, but never could and that she had known for a long time that she never would. Her friend told Lorrie that some man would come along some day and seal her heart. Lorrie told her friend that she didn't understand, that her heart and soul had already been stolen when she first saw Gus when she was just twelve years and that a day hadn't gone by since then that she hadn't loved him. She told her friend that song was her and Gus's song and that it had played every place she had ever been and that when it played she was right back on that beach kissing Gus and it was so real as long as it was playing. Lorrie told her friend that every man that she had been with or had been married to was just a need and a distraction for her so she could go on with her life and that even now at night she would bury her head in her pillow and cry for Gus and that was 1962 and now it was 1980, so it was a long time ago. Her friend ask her why she didn't try to find Gus that maybe he felt the same way. Lorrie just looked at her and told her that Gus didn't want her, then she started crying again. Lorrie's friend vowed to herself never to bring up anything that would that would lead Lorrie to think of Gus, she hadn't ever been in love with a man and she thought that if this was how it effected you she didn't want to ever be in love. Several months went by and Lorrie's old ex-boyfriend called her to see if he could make another visit. Lorrie told him OK and this time she took him to France. She wanted to show him all the museums in Paris, but he wasn't interested. Instead he wanted to see Napoleon's beautiful grave vault that was in a special designed crypt deep in the ground that was lighted twenty-four hours a day and you could look down on it, it was beautiful. Then he wanted to go to Normandy and see the beach that the US troops landed on D-Day and visit the Military Grave Yard there. They visited several more World War 1 and World 2 memorial sites then went back to England.. There wasn't anything that came up during his visit that was improper, not even him trying to hold her hand. They parted at the air port with him telling her that he would write, but she never heard from him again. It was finished for good and 1980 was also finished for good and Lorrie was thrilled to be looking forward to an exciting 1981.

Gus—1981 The United States seemed like it was starting to come apart at the seams financially in 1981. 1980 had seen a few Banks close their doors, but in 1981 Banks closing became an everyday news item. For years inflation had run unchecked and the Federal Reserve Bank had steadily increased interest rates so it was extremely expensive to borrow money and hard to pay it back with interest. This was supposed to get inflation under control, but it was bringing everything in business to a breaking point. Gus did get his 1981 crop loan and he wondered how he was going to pay it back the way everything was going. The stress on him was mounting all the time with his business and his personal life. His Mothers health continued to fail and she had fallen and broken her hip. She had gone through a major hip operation and come out of it alive, which was a miracle in itself, but two days after the operation the hip came apart again and she hadn't even been released from ICU when it happened. She laid there in ICU for several weeks with the Bone Specialist from a Houston Hospital trying to figure out how he was going to redo the operation to reconnect the broken parts of her hip. It was broken so short on one side that there wasn't much to work with. Then his Mom's health took a turn for the worse and she was on the verge of death. Her health benefits ran out, so there were no more insurance payments to the Hospital. The Hospital Administrator called Gus and told him to come in so they could have a meeting to see if they could solve the problem. Gus met with the Administrator and in this meeting he learned a lot. What Gus learned appalled him. He learned that the Hospital had been milking the Insurance Company for all that could. The Administrator proceeded to show Gus how many things that the Hospital was billing the Insurance Company for that his Mom would suddenly not need. She didn't even need to be in ICU which was a very expensive intensive care unit. The Hospital Administrator kept striking off the things that his Mom suddenly didn't need till they got down to what she actually needed in order to stay in the Hospital and have care till her health improved so the Specialist could do the new operation. The cost of his Mom's Hospital care went from eighteen thousand dollars a week, that had been charged to the Insurance Company, down to two thousand five hundred a week, that Gus would have to pay out of his own pocket. The Hospital Administrator told Gus that if he would bring a check for two thousand five hundred dollars every Monday that would pay for a weeks stay for his Mom in advance and if Gus couldn't do that then the Hospital had no choice but to notify him that they were going to dismiss her and he could come and pick her up and take her where ever he decided. Gus saw right away that he had no choice in the matter. If he didn't pay the money then his Mom would die. Of course he agreed to do it and he knew that he was going to have to raid his crop money to accomplish this, because he simply didn't have that kind of cash reserves to draw on. This would cause other problems later on he knew, but you have to confront major problems when they occur and solve them then. This was the only way he could save his Mom and he was going to do it. They moved his Mom to a private room and her health continued to fail till she didn't even want to eat and she was on deaths bed. Gus had been going in to see her twice a day, during lunch and at her dinner period trying to get some food down her. He was succeeding to get her to eat very small bits and slowly she was improving. During this time Gus also hired two women to go on shifts to sit with his Mom, when he wasn't able to be with her and to try to help her anyway they could. This was also extra money that was being diverted out of his crop expense loan. This went on for three months until his Mom had regained enough health and strength so that the Specialist decided that he could take a chance to do the new operation. The Specialist and Gus had a private meeting and the Specialist showed his Mom's x-rays to him and described the problem involved with the operation. Gus could see it at once. The Specialist asked Gus where he wanted him to do the operation there in the local Hospital like before or to take his Mom to Houston where the Specialist had better equipment to work with. The Specialist told Gus that it would be quite a bit more expensive to take her to Houston in an ambulance and operate there. For Gus this was an easy decision, of coarse taking her to

Houston was the best option, because his Mom's health was barely good enough to even consider an operation, so Gus knew that this was the last chance to make it work and if it didn't, then his Mom was doomed to die, because of this mess of a failed first operation and he would worry about the money later, so he told the Specialist that he could do the operation in Houston. Because of all the health problems his Mom was suffering through Gus was spending valuable time away from his farming and ranching operations. 1981 was getting extremely difficult to navigate in for the business world and agriculture was taking a huge hit in it. Gus was only getting his crop loans because of all the equity he had built up in his land and now he was spending a lot of money on his Mom's medical expenses that he knew he was going to need later. His only option for obtaining the money later in the crop year would be to make another loan and then he would have to put some more of his land up for collateral to back it up. Also with all the time away from his business he wasn't able to have his thumb on everything like he usually did and he was worried about a lot of the little things that ending up making a lot of difference at the end of the year. Another worry at this time was that his second wife, the young Carhop had been calling wanting to buy his son a motorcycle. He hadn't heard from her in years and now it seemed she had a boyfriend that had a little money and she was trying to bribe his son with a new motorcycle. Gus's son was almost fourteen now, but Gus had a fear of him having a motorcycle, because Gus had a friend get killed on one when he was in High School. This turned Gus against motorcycles. Gus had even wanted one himself at one time, but talked himself out of it knowing how he always had the propensity to push the limits for speed and handling with the Hot Rod he had built in High School and he didn't want to put his son in the position to want to do the same thing with a motorcycle that only had two wheels. He told her no, then she called back and wanted to get his son a dirt bike and Gus told her no, then she called back and wanted to get his son a Honda three wheeler and Gus told her that he would think about it. Just another problem on an already stressed out Gus. With all of this going on there were Banks and Savings and Loans going bankrupt and closing their doors on a daily basis now and the US Government passed a law that established an Agency they called the RTC to take over these failed lending institutions and try to do something with their assets and the RTC was also sending out Bank Examiners to all lending institutions to go over their books to see if they were at risk of defaulting and closing their doors and this was causing fear in these institutions to the point of extreme fear of being taken over by the RTC. This all filtered down to the people wanting to do business with the Banks and you could see the fear in the eyes of the Bankers every time you went to talk to them about a loan. It was getting ridiculous to try and do business with them. Gus thought and thought about the three wheeler that his second wife wanted to get his son. He thought that probably his son would think that Gus didn't want him to have it just because his Mom was the one to get it for him and Gus didn't want his son to think that, because that wasn't the reason. Well it did have three wheels on it and that made it a little safer, so Gus called his second wife and told her to go ahead and get it for his son. That was one thing out of the way now that Gus didn't have to think about. Gus's Mom survived the operation and it was successful and he moved her to her home in El Campo and then had to find people to be of help for her. This ended up being a big undertaking to be able to find the kind of responsible people to do this. His Mom's care ended up as a business in itself, because Gus had to hire a staff to take care of her twenty-four hours a day along with a cook- housekeeper and two extras to relieve those that wanted time off. He hired six women to do this job of taking care of his Mom and that was more help then he had working on his farm and ranch operation. With this extra help taking care of Gus's Mom he could concentrate on his business. He now only went to town to check on his Mom once a day and that was at night after he was finished at the farm. Gus remembered from some Preachers Sermon that God only put on you the weight of responsibility on you that God knew you could carry. He thought that God surely knew more then he did, because the weight was damn sure getting heavier then he had ever experienced and he hoped that no more would pile on, because all he could think about was how could he unload some of it. The money thing was getting serious and Gus kept trying to figure ways to generate more income. The idea he came up with he had seen when he was traveling and it was developing Country Subdivisions way out of town for residential housing. He had done a lot of research on it for the County that he lived in and he came up with a plan. Gus bought twenty-five acres next to some of his farm land and used his farm land working and leveling machinery to put it in shape, then hired a Surveying Company to survey it out in lots. Gus then developed a pricing and financing system that would permit the buyer to put ten percent down and have a five year payout. He then started advertising it and within one week he had sold two lots and was getting calls on it almost daily. Gus was financing these lots himself, so he was gaining the interest also. For once he was on the other end of this borrowing thing and it felt good. Gus was almost through with harvest and he had already had to go back to the Bank for two more loans and he had to put up more land to secure them. The value of his land was now dropping, because a lot of land was going on the market. The failing Banks and the reluctance of the others to make loans was creating a snow ball effect that was forcing Banks to call in loans that would otherwise be deemed good loans and that was forcing a lot of land to go on the market which was depressing prices. All of this made Gus have to put up more land on his loans then he would normally have to do. It was very depressing to say the least. Gus wondered when all of this would straighten out or was it going into another Great Depression. There already had been a few of the farmers that he knew that had committed suicide and it was scarey to think who might be next. After Gus's 1981 harvest and the last sale of his calves Gus was putting all the numbers together to figure what he should do. He thought that he sure made the wrong decision about selling his land when he could have got one thousand eight hundred dollars per acre for it and now he would be lucky to get one thousand dollars per acre for it. Well the numbers were telling a dismal story about the shape he was in as far as being profitable. His farming business was loosing money, but his cattle business was still making a little money and his Residential Subdivision was booming. The trouble with this was that farming was the main source of income if it made money, but it was also the main source of big loss. Gus pushed back the paper work that held the story of his businesses and just sat there exhausted from all of the stress of reviewing it. He thought what a long way it was from High School and working at that filling station for seventy-five dollars a week. How stress free that was he remembered. Then his mind drifted to those girls that came into the station and flirted with him and how enjoyable that was and that pretty girl Lorrie who he was with on the beach in Corpus was one of them. He would never forget her how sweet she was and my goodness how she could kiss him. Why he had never been able to experience any kisses even close to hers since then and that was a hell of a long time ago. He felt that he really could use a bunch of those kisses now, maybe they would help relieve the stress that he felt. The kisses he was getting from his wife weren't helping especially with all the fighting that went with them. Oh goodness what a mess everything was and he hoped that sweet, pretty Lorrie didn't have the stress he was having, some how he felt that if they would be together then she could help him through all of this. Surely 1982 wouldn't be worse. He looked to 1982 with trepidation and also hope. Gus would be forty years old in 1982 and it was right around the corner.

Lorrie—1981 was starting out real good for Lorrie. Her career in the Navy was solid and she and her Cryptology team were doing outstanding work. Lorrie had always been a reader and she was now reading everything she could find on England's history and also the art works and of the artist's that produced them. She was visiting all the museums that she could find and she was simply overwhelmed with all the wonderful knowledge that she was obtaining. As a young girl she had always been drawn to the wonderful pictures and articles of England and Europe that she saw in the National Geographic magazine and others and she checked out books to read about them. Now her dream had come true and she was becoming a part of this culture, but she had not yet met any English man that she was interested in that she could date and enjoy her days off with, but she was looking. To Lorrie it was important to try and become as much a part of the British culture as possible since she was going to be living in England and dating an American was pretty much out of the question. Her objective was to find this perfect English gentleman that would introduce her to other English people that she wouldn't be able to do herself and then she would be invited to different gatherings that only the British were attending and through that she could learn the true nature and the culture of the British and she wouldn't feel so like an American tourist which is what she felt like now. Lorrie was trying to get used to the British food and discovered that it was much to bland. She was used to food that had more seasoning in it to spice it up and she found out that so many food products that she was used to buying in the United States just didn't exist in England. Another thing was that Lorrie liked to drink Kentucky Bourbon Whiskey and it was like very scarce and if you found it you couldn't afford it, so she started drinking Vodka, Brandy and Wine they were relative in-expensive to buy. It's like the British never heard of Mexican food and you couldn't find anything to make it in the Food Markets, they didn't even have pinto beans for heavens sake. She found out that if you wanted beans or rice you would have to go the part of London that people of the Middle East occupied and browse their shops to find these and also hot peppers. Another thing that would puzzle Lorrie when shopping for food products was that there was no brands that she knew, so she would have to ask some lady that was close to her in the shopping isle what she was buying and if it was some what similar to something that she would buy in the United States and then the sometime way that a British woman would talk to describe something was like a foreign language to Lorrie. She just hadn't been in England long enough to pick up their way of using their everyday language with a heavy accent. Lorrie and her best girlfriend would pal around together trying to experience as much as they could and that took up much of their off of work time. Together they even took off their shoes, rolled up their pants and waded in the huge fountain in the middle of Trafalgar Square and had a passer by take their picture to remember the occasion. Of coarse there were always parties at the flat they lived in, but that was always mostly Americans with on occasion a British man or woman as a guest of someone. Lorrie and her friend would take trips to Paris to all the famous museums and Lorrie fell in love with Paris and all of the sidewalk Cafes there and especially their coffee, wine and pastry. Lorrie and her friend went to a concert there and the song "In The Still Of The Night" was played by one band and Lorrie thought of Gus. Lorrie could see why everyone thought of love when in Paris. She thought that Paris was the perfect place to have a honeymoon and then she thought of Gus again. She thought that it would fun run into him in Paris if he was a tourist and they could get married there and spend their honeymoon in the City Of Love. Well she thought it was nice once-in-a while to have those sweet thoughts of Gus. 1981 turned into 1982 and it was snowing hard when Lorrie was riding the Bus to work. She thought that she was going to be thirty-seven years old and only had two more years left on her tour of duty in England, then what??

Gus—1982 The Subdivision Gus had developed in 1981 was filling up with residential homes and he was considering buying another tract of land across the road from it that was the same size and developing it also. He was running short of different size lots in the first Subdivision and he wanted an inventory of different size lots to show his buyers to choose from. It was 1982 now and Gus had been studying his farm and ranch operation to see how he could start shrinking it down slowly so he didn't have to borrow so much money to operate. He still had his Mom to take care of and it looked like she would always have to have the twenty-four hour care at her home, so he couldn't depend on cutting any expenses there. It came down to shrinking his farm and ranch business. The first thing he did was notify the land owners of his leased land that he wasn't going to re-new the leases. This was a considerable amount of land and it would shrink his operation down about one third which meant that he could release two of his farm hands and that would add to his savings in expenses. Gus was now going to move his operation back entirely on land that he owned. So he would not have to give up any of the crop as rent to the Landlords, all profits would be his. He could sell some of his equipment since his farm acres would be one third less and that would go to paying on his loan. Gus's Bankers had wanted him to expand and get bigger, but Gus was finished with all of this high pressure and his idea was just the opposite. He was going to get smaller and try to build a operation unit that would work with less money and be easier to manage. Gus was hoping that the Banking crisis and inflation and low farm prices that had been slowly destroying his business for several years would start to subside and pulling back on his own land would help to buy time for something like that to happen. Gus also knew that if these terrible times went on much longer that he would have to start selling his land at deflated prices just to pay off all the loans he had. All of this was a big gamble, but wasn't life just that, a gamble. Gus thought back when he was offered so much money for his land and he decided not to sell, wasn't that a gamble. And how about the different women he had married through the years, that hadn't worked out so good, wasn't that a gamble. This brought up thoughts of that pretty, sweet girl Lorrie. What he had decided there wasn't a gamble, it was simply just wanting to do what he thought was right, but he already knew in his heart that it had been a terrible mistake. He should have just thrown caution to the wind and went for it. Well enough of that thinking. Now Gus was into his 1982 crop year hoping that all the changes he made would show some improvement in the way his operation worked and also of coarse he was hoping for positive results in his profit margin to help pay off some of his debt. Gus was turning forty years old in 1982 and he was carrying a huge burden that he was trying lighten up some.

Lorrie—1982 was the start of the third year of Lorrie's tour of duty in London, England with the Navy's Cryptology Installation there. To Lorrie the choice she had made to join the Navy and join their Cryptology branch was the best decisions that she had ever made. The Navy had rebuilt her confidence in herself after the demoralizing first marriage to the Air Force Officer. She wouldn't have married him if she hadn't been pregnant and that was still causing Lorrie problems. Lorrie would write her son at least once a week, but she hadn't received a single letter from him since his Dad, her first husband, had taken him to the Philippines when he transferred there with the Air Force and Lorrie had tried every option that she could to think of to get information on her son to no avail. She knew that her ex-husband was just doing this to punish her for divorcing him, because that was how he thought. He would try to get revenge against her not even thinking of the boy. As long as she had known her ex-husband and that went all the way back to their High School days, everything had always been about just him. He always thought himself superior to everyone else, because he was smarter then the average person and that he had always talked down to Lorrie and made her feel inferior to him. Lorrie thought that now her only option was to keep doing like she was doing in writing her son letters and making copies of them to prove that she had always been trying to be in touch with him. Maybe one day he would get the chance to get in touch with her and she could let him read the copies of the many letters that she had sent him, so he would know that she hadn't abandoned him that it was his Dad that had isolated him from her. Lorrie realized that she had almost two more years left on her time in England before she would have to re-enlist and she knew from talking to other Navy personnel that her next Navy post wouldn't be the kind of wonderful place that London was. More then likely the Navy would send her to some out of the way listening station out in the middle of nowhere like off the coast of Alaska or Midway. They told her that the Navy always rotated their Cryptology personnel like that so everyone would get the chance of a good post and also share the isolation of their out of the way Installations. Lorrie was already trying to think about what she might do when that time came up. All she knew was that she was loving her time in England and the opportunity that she was having to visit Europe. Lorrie and her friend would book little vacations to some of the least expensive places in Spain, Italy or Greece to small villages and they would enjoy all the local food, wine bread and music of that little village. Each village would have different food and wine that they were proud of and the girls would have the best time flirting with the local men and trying to do the local dances which more then often then not they would just stumble through and laugh till they were hoarse. They really enjoyed these little vacations, because each one would show them a different side of Europe and the people that lived there. Lorrie was also into the history of the Roman period in England and she had signed on to an archeology dig that was going on in England and she was almost overwhelmed when she was brushing a section of earth from one of the square grids and uncovered a

Roman mosaic on the floor of a room. She thought that it was very beautiful and wondered about the artists that had designed it and built it and all of the long gone people that had enjoyed that room and wondered what intrigue might have been planned there against the British and Scottish tribes. A Roman General in England had so much trouble with the warring tribes of Scotland that he had a wall built that would help to reduce their raiding. It was built at the narrowest part of England and it was eighty miles long with guard towers often and a lot of it was still standing. It was named Hadrians Wall after the Roman General that ordered it built. Lorrie and her friend walked the entire length of the wall, eighty miles. They didn't do it all at one time, but they did it in segments and Lorrie loved that experience. Lorrie and her friend were always on the look out for new and inexpensive little vacation trips to learn more about Europe and they ran across one that they considered very interesting. It was one for a week in Yugoslavia and it included a room with access to a beautiful beach. It was priced extremely cheap, because Yugoslavia was such of a depressed Communist country. They were excited about it, so they booked it and while they were waiting for their vacation time Lorrie started to have some pains in her abdomen. At first she tried to doctor herself and she kept having them, but she hated to go to the doctor. Then one day at work the pain hit her so hard that she doubled over and fell to the floor. Her workmates immediately called for help and she was taken to the Navy Clinic and the doctors examined her there and decided that she would need an operation. They didn't tell her at the time, but they suspected it was some type of cancer. There was no US Military Hospital there so they had to admit her to a British Military Hospital and there is where she underwent exploratory surgery. The British doctors cut her abdomen from one side to the other all the way across her stomach in search of the problem and what they found was a very infected ovary that they had to remove. When Lorrie came out from under the sedative and was moved to the recovery room the British doctor came in to talk to her. He told her not to worry that she didn't have cancer and Lorrie almost fell out of bed, because she had never thought of cancer and none of the doctors either American or British had mentioned it. He tole her that she would have a long recovery, because of the extensive surgery and she would have to stay in the British Hospital till she recovered. He told her that it was mainly a British Military male facility, so they had fixed up a private room for her so as to separate her from the male patients. They moved Lorrie to her private room and she started on her way to being well again. She was so sorry to have missed the vacation in Yugoslavia, but maybe she could do it next year. The British doctor was right her recovery was painful and slow. She had a lot of visitors though from her coworkers and also Americans that were living at the same building of Flats that she had rented. Her strength was improving and her pain was much better after a couple of weeks. The hospital staff had installed a radio in Lorrie's room so she could keep up with the news and also hear programs and music. Lorrie thought that when she had the music turned on that the radio played "In The Still Of The Night" everyday and she would use the song to pretend that Gus was visiting her and encouraging her and telling her that he loved her. Some time she would cry and sometime she would smile. She thought that if Gus didn't like what he saw when she was naked with him in 1962 that he sure wouldn't like what he would see now with a big, ugly scar all across her stomach. She would never be able to wear a Bikini swimsuit again that was for sure. One day when she was looking out her room window she saw a red headed handsome young man with a red mustache, in a British Military uniform motioning for her to open her window. She was curious to say the least, so she complied and to her astonishment he was much more handsome without that window between them. He had red hair that was somewhat wavy and blue eyes with a big smile that made his British Soldier mustache turn upwards. Lorrie was quite pleased. He told her that he had heard that there was a beautiful American Navy lady in this room and that he didn't believe it, because this was an all male hospital, so he took it on himself to find out and he could see that it was true. Lorrie loved his flattery and she started asking him questions. She asked him if he was a patient at the hospital and he replied that he was. She told him that he didn't look sick and he said that he would discuss that with her later, but that he had to get back now,because he wasn't supposed to be having contact with her and he didn't want to get caught, but he asked if he could come and visit her again outside the window and she told him yes. After he left the window Lorrie had to laugh out loud, because for a couple of years she had been wanting to meet a real British man that she could get to know and she had to almost die to do it. She sure hoped that he would come back to her window the next day. Lorrie was so excited and curious about the British Soldier's window visit that she had a hard time going to sleep that night. The next morning the first thing that Lorrie did was to look at the window to see if he was there and she was a little disappointed to see that he wasn't. All of a sudden she realized that now she was going to have to close the window blinds when she was being examined with her gown off because she would be naked then and although she might get naked with the British Soldier sometime in the future, now was not the time for him to get a preview. Lorrie was still self-conscious about being naked in front of a man ever since she had been naked for Gus and evidently he didn't like what he saw about her body, because he didn't come back to take her virginity, so from then on when she decided to have sex with a man she would wear her bra and panties to bed and disrobe under the covers and she still did that even though that had been twenty years ago. The British Soldier did come back the next day and he was flirting heavy with her. Lorrie loved it and flirted right back with him like she hadn't in a very long time. It felt good to Lorrie for him to seem to want to spend so much time with her outside her window. When the Doctor or one of his assistants would come in to check on her the British Soldier would drop down below the window so as not to be discovered. Lorrie found out that he was an SAS Solder and that impressed Lorrie. She knew that the SAS were the British Military elite Soldiers that were sent in to all sorts of hazardous missions all over the world. She asked him what he was doing in the Hospital, because he looked perfectly healthy to Lorrie and all he would tell her was that all of a sudden he had hit a brick wall and a medical team was trying to figure out why. Lorrie left his explanation at that and didn't press him anymore, because she was having too much fun with his clandestine visits. He came to see her everyday after that and it lifted her spirits so much that she credited him with speeding up her recovery time. Lorrie was getting around in the Hospital pretty good after several weeks and one day when her SAS Soldier was visiting her she kissed him through the window and he wanted to crawl through the window and get in bed with her, but she told him that he would just have to wait till she was discharged from the Hospital and she was home in her Flat and then she would see what she felt about that. Lorrie already knew what she was going to do, because for one thing it had been over two years since she had been to bed with a man and this SAS Soldier had all the right qualifications to attract her. First he was a British SAS Soldier and he was handsome and looked just like you would think that a British Soldier would, with his red hair and his red turned up mustache. He seemed to have a wonderful, happy way of flirting with her that was so sexy and manly, so Lorrie made up her mind that as soon as she had completely recovered she was going to have sex with him. He was going to be the very first Englishman that she would have sex with and she wondered if British men had any different techniques in bed then American men. She knew that she was going to find out. Just before she was discharged from the Hospital she gave him her address and phone number, so now the rest was going to be up to him and Lorrie crossed her fingers and hoped that he would call her. For Lorrie even though she had a terrible setback because of the operation and the long painful recovery 1982 was looking up with the discovery of the SAS Solder as a possible exciting lover and companion and he was very British which was what she had been looking for ever since she had landed in England. Lorrie thought that the rest of 1982 on her days off from work would be spent really learning how to be British.

Gus—1982 As 1982 was progressing Gus could tell that the drastic changes that he had made in the size of his Farming and Ranching operations was starting to show some positive results. Because of his downsizing Gus was able to lay-off several farm hands which saved considerable money that he would have had to borrow and he was able to sell some extra machinery that he wouldn't need and the money he received from this he payed on his loans. He also had to sell some of his cattle, because when he didn't re-lease several sections of land (a section=640ac.) it cut down the pasture he would have to graze them and he put this money into another bank for emergency funds. Also since he was farming less, his planting time went faster and he had a chance to get his crops planted during the most favorable window of opportunity that each crop would have for their best production results. His crops were coming along nicely and also Gus had sold two million pounds of Milo Maize that he had stored in some big grain elevators in Houston, waiting for the price to increase enough to make a profit. This sale helped bring down some of his loan debt and it made Gus feel a little better. Gus's home life was still a mess, but he was dealing with it trying to avoid arguments with his wife when possible. Gus started thinking about taking his family on a trip out to the Big Bend of Texas. It was the trip that he and his Mom had taken in 1962 when he had fallen in love with the high Chihuahua Desert of the Trans Pecos in Texas. He thought that if his crop season finished early enough without difficulties then he was going to try to do it. For the first time in many years he had money tucked away to do something like this. His family had never had a family vacation together and this time might be the last time that he might be able to do it. Gus wanted his family to have the same experience that he had and he wanted to see what they thought about the Mountains and Desert. The only way was for them to see it themselves. The way things were going Gus never knew from year to year what to expect. There was absolutely no way to have any security in his business any more. To Gus this might be the last time he had the money for them to take a week to go on a big vacation like this. His Banker told him that if things worked out for him that Gus might be able to pay off his big debt in two more years, but Gus didn't think that to be possible. Gus was still paying for six women to take care of his Mom seven days a week and he also had all of the other expenses concerning her, so the burden of that was still creating problems with debt. The United States was still in a hell of a mess with the failing Banks and the devaluation of business assets, so there was nothing really pointing to a fast recovery of the economy and that meant to Gus that it was going to be a long hard time ahead for his business. The crop year for Gus went reasonably well and his harvest was complete earlier then usual because he was farming less land and also he got to finish planting his crops earlier then he would have before. Gus put the final touches to his plans for his families vacation to the Big Bend National Park of Texas and also to expand it to several West Texas towns that are in the Chihuahua Desert so he could see the difference between them in 1982 and when he and his Mom saw them in 1962. He was excited to take his family on this trip and hoped that they would develop the passion for the area as he had done. His oldest son was fifteen years old now and Gus had secret hopes that he would be the one to especially fall in love with this high Mountain Desert country known as the Chihuahua Desert. It was a unforgiving rugged landscape, but Gus thought it was simply beautiful. From the first time that Gus had seen it in 1962 he had secret hopes to one day live out there. Gus and his son were a lot alike and Gus had raised him virtually by himself till he was eight years old, until Gus had married his present wife with her two kids, a boy and a girl. It was the middle of August 1982 now and all of Gus's crops had been harvested and the only thing that would be left to do when they got back was to start rounding up the cattle for the fall working and selling the big calves and old cows that Gus didn't want to carry through the coming winter. School would start in September so this was the perfect time to take the family on this week long vacation into a place in Texas that was like being in another county in itself. Not only was it completely different then anyplace they had ever been, but the Chihuahua Desert covered a huge area of Far West Texas. Gus felt excited to be able to show his family the Desert that he loved and that 1982 would be a very special year that he could always remember. Since Gus had already made the trip in 1962 he knew what to expect and what to prepare for. They had the family Custom Van that had plenty of seating and two tables, an icebox, sink, and a seat in the back that pulled out to make a full size bed. This would come in handy when the younger kids got sleepy and need a nap. Gus made a list of everything that need to be taken along to make the trip as comfortable as possible and he made a list of things that he needed to take for emergency break downs and for first aid. Everything was ready and packed and they were to get up at 5:00 AM the next morning and be ready to drive off at 7:00 AM. Well Gus was up at 4:00 AM to go over the list to make sure that he didn't leave anything out, because he knew that they would be going into some of the most rugged and unpopulated areas of Texas. He knew that if you weren't prepared a trip like this could be very dangerous. Gus had gone through all of his inventory and found it complete and he herded all of them including his around and into the Custom Van like they were a flock of sheep and they were off. They drove through San Antonio and on to Brackettville where they spent the night and then visited the Movie location that John Wayne used for the Movie of the Battle of The Alamo. From there they drove to Del Rio and on to Langtry to see where Judge Joy Bean had his Law West Of The Pecos office and saloon. They drove on and went through Sanderson to Marathon and got a room for the night in the same Tourist Cabins that Gus and his Mom and stayed in twenty years before. The next morning they ate breakfast at the Gage Hotel. It was a famous old Hotel that was built in the 1920's by a wealthy Rancher from San Antonio that had bought a large amount of land there and established a huge ranching operation. After their breakfast and browsing around the nice grounds of the Gage Hotel they drove to Big Bend National Park. The drive up into the Basin is beautiful and so different then the Desert below it. It is a steep winding road with many sharp curves that have beautiful views at every turn and it is always climbing. All of a sudden you realize that the road is going down and you end up at the bottom of the Basin at the Head Quarters of the Big Bend National Park. The Basin is actually inside an extinct Volcano and is the location of not only the HQ of the Park, but also a very nice Cafe and Shop, some Cabins for rent and a camp ground There several hiking trails and a Corral that you can rent horses to ride the longer trails to explore. Gus and his family did some hiking on one of the easier trails so the kids would be able to walk along with any difficulty. As they were hiking Gus would point out different rock formations, Desert plants, birds and small animals that his family weren't used to seeing, because they were unique to the Desert. Gus was really enjoying this outing and his oldest son seemed to be as excited, with his first real introduction into what the Chihuahua Desert was all about, as Gus hoped he would be. Gus's wife and the other kids didn't seem to be to impressed. They went to the Cafe in the Park and ate a nice lunch and then Gus and his oldest son saw a cave far up on the mountain side that they decided to climb to, hoping that it might be an Indian Cave that they had lived in. As their progress brought them farther up the mountain the slope became steeper and there was a lot of loose rock that became harder and harder to climb. Gus finally realized that he wouldn't be able to climb all the way to the cave, because he had on his cowboy boots and they just weren't what he should have worn to do the climbing. His son had worn some hiking boots and he wanted to proceed by himself, but Gus told him that he didn't want him to, because there could be almost any kind of animal in the Cave and Gus wouldn't be able to help him if he got into trouble with a Mountain Lion, Bear or Javelina. Going back down the way they went up was dangerous because of the loose rock and not much to hold on to so you didn't slide, so Gus decided to go side ways holding to small shrubs as they went until they found a place that water had washed all the loose rock away and they could make their way down safely. Gus and his son made it down safely and they rested for a while in the Van. It was getting later in the afternoon now, so they drove out of Big Bend National Park on the West side through Study Butte and on to the Ghost Town of Terlingua where they were going to spend the night. Terlingua was a mining town that was established around a quick silver (Mercury) mine and it had been abandoned except for a few really unusual characters. This is why it was called a Ghost Town. It had a very colorful past and was basically a Mining Company Town, where everything had been owned by the mine owner who had lived in New York. When the price of Mercury went down the mine closed and the town was abandoned. There were a lot of very small old falling down stacked rock dwellings that had been occupied by the Mexican miners that worked the mine. It also had an old Grave Yard that had the graves of the miners that had died there and the graves were constructed in the old way of the Spanish with rocks stacked on top and little Grotto's to place candles with Spanish style Crosses. The Grave Yard was very dilapidated standing out in the middle of a rugged, windswept Desert with the Crosses leaning at angles and tumble weeds clinging to anything that would hold them. It was certainly ghostly looking. Gus went to the little Cafe-office there and paid for one night in a trailer house that was parked close to the Grave Yard and his wife was afraid of the Ghostly Grave Yard and wanted to leave. Gus told her that there wasn't anywhere else to stay between there and Presidio. Gus and his oldest son loved it, but his wife was so afraid that she made Gus push the full sized bed against the door and sleep with his pistol all night. Gus slept great and his wife said that she had stayed awake all night hearing strange sounds. Gus and his son just laughed at her, which made her mad at them, so she started the day off with a chip on her shoulder. Gus and his oldest son walked to the Cafe for coffee and breakfast and waited for his wife and the younger kids to join them. They then drove to Lajitas, another almost Ghost Town along the Rio Grand River to Presidio and the scenery was just beautiful along the river with it's deep canyons and it's twists and turns. The road was twisting up and down, sometime sharp and sometime steep, but beautiful. They stayed the night in a small Motel there and left the next day for the beautiful drive to the old Silver Mining town of Shafter and then to Marfa to look around and get a Motel with a swimming pool so the kids could swim and his wife could feel less afraid. Gus found a store where he could buy him some cold beer and he sat by the pool and watched the kids swim as he enjoyed his beer and he even shared one with his oldest son who had been having the time of his life on this trip to the Chihuahua Desert. The next day they drove to Alpine and visited Sul Ross University so his son could get the feel of the campus of a University and talk to some people there. They also visited a nice museum there that had a lot of Indian artifacts, fossils and mineral samples found in the area. From there they drove to Fort Davis to go through the old historic fort built there to protect pioneers from the Apache Indians that were attacking them at that time. The McDonald Observatory was just a short distance, so they visited it and then set out for Fort Stockton which was to be their last night on their trip in West Texas. Gus woke everyone up very early the next morning and they packed up, ate breakfast and left Fort Stockton for the long drive back to their Ranch. It was time for them to get back, because the kids would start school in a few days and Gus needed to find out what had been happening with his business. Gus was so glad to have spent that much time back in the part of Texas that he had grown to love and his oldest son seemed to share his enthusiasm for the beautiful rugged high Mountain terrain of the Chihuahua Desert with it's history and its secrets that were yet to be discovered by them. This trip in 1982 was the high-light of the year for Gus.

Lorrie—1982 For Lorrie 1982 had been a year of disappointment and expectations. First her job was going wonderful and Lorrie and her friend had been excited about their vacation in Yugoslavia, but then her health problems popped up with the terrible pain and the ultimate operation that removed an infected ovary and she was confined to a British Military Hospital for a very long recovery, so her vacation plans were canceled. This disappointment had an unexpected bright side to it though. In this Hospital Lorrie met this very interesting SAS British Soldier that seemed taken with her and Lorrie saw in him a avenue to finally get more introduced into the mainstream of real English culture. She had given him her phone number and address before she had discharged from the Hospital and he had been calling her on a regular basis. He hadn't been discharged but he had been given freedom to phone and also to sign out of the Hospital for a few hours each day but he had to return to the Hospital as long as he was under going evaluation. When Lorrie was off duty her SAS Soldier would call her and they would talk for long periods and he would always use his British humor to suggest romantic situations that Lorrie loved to fantasize about. Before long Lorrie was doing the same thing to him, so the relationship between them became one of anticipation of exploring a sexual encounter together. At first he would sign out for a lunch hour and they would meet on her days off for lunch at a Cafe and have lunch and flirt with each other. Then their lunch time extended to another hour at her Flat in bed and Lorrie thought that he was a lover that was not exceptional but he was a lot of fun to be with. He certainly was not what Gus would have been, because he couldn't even get close to the kisses that Gus gave her. She wasn't surprised about that though, because no man she had ever been with had kissed her and aroused her like Gus had. She knew that she would never, ever have that again, so she would just have to take what ever man she was with had to offer in that department. He was finally discharged from the British Military Hospital and He and Lorrie were able to see each other when they both were off duty. Lorrie was invited to several of the parties that he and his friends had and Lorrie discovered that his only friends were also SAS Soldiers and they stayed to themselves with their girlfriends for almost all of their social gatherings. Lorrie was the center of attention at these gatherings and his friends drank toast after toast to her until everyone was very drunk. At one of these Lorrie asked one of his friends what exactly did her SAS Soldier do and he just looked at her and with a smile he told her that his friend was a small arms expert and that was all that he would say, so there were secrets there somewhere and Lorrie dropped it at that. Lorrie would also invite him to some of the parties that were given by the people that lived in the same complex as she did and he was the subject of a lot of interest at these parties. Lorrie was curious as to why everyone whether British or American would have such an unusual interest in their relationship. Lorrie was enjoying her relationship with the SAS Soldier, but it hadn't produced the results that Lorrie had hoped for, because he only associated with his Military buddies and not the regular English citizens. She was wondering if she would ever be able to really get to know the in's and out's of the English culture while she was stationed in England, because at this rate her time was going to run out on her enlistment. After all 1982 was almost over and she would have only one more full year there in London before she would have to re-enlist and she knew from the experience of others she had known that the Navy assigned them to Posts that would be in some out of the way place, so she could expect the same thing to happen to her and she had to admit that she was already spoiled to England and Europe. Lorrie thought that she had to figure out some way to stay in England, but she had no idea how to do it without discharging from the Navy, then what would she do to make a living for herself. This was starting to worry Lorrie. It was the end of 1982 now and she took her SAS Soldier to a New Years Party and they had a great time. Lorrie could see that there wasn't going to be a future with him though as far as her staying in England. Their relationship was just one of having a good time together and he never broached the subject of anything else, which disappointed her some. Well 1982 was over now and Lorrie was looking forward to the New Year of 1983 and maybe other possibilities, because she new from experience that she never knew what might be right around the corner for her to take advantage of for her benefit.

Gus— 1982 was going by fast and he was now back at his farming and ranching operations. His trip to the Chihuahua Desert of Far West Texas had been very good for him. It had relived his mind of the troubles that had been weighing him down for several years and now he had a more positive view of what he need to do to accomplish the process of slowly shrinking the size of his farming and ranching operations. When Gus and his family got back from their trip school was about to start and Gus had to make the rounds and check on all of his fields and his pastures to determine what his next decisions would be for moving forward to finish out the year. His wife was busy getting the kids organized with cloths and school supplies. After several days of catching up, Gus was putting together a plan for his 1983 crop year and this included some advance estimates of crop acreage for each crop and the expenses for each, because he knew that it would soon be time to present a budget for 1983 to his Bankers and the sooner he started to plan for it the better. Gus also had looked at all of his cattle to determine how many calves that he would be able to sell from his fall round-up. While there was good weather Gus had all of his tractors working land for the next crop year. Gus's kids were back in school now and it was the fall of 1982. His oldest son, the one that he had raised by himself, was now fifteen years old and he had been good help on the farm and ranch since he had been twelve and Gus really missed him when he started school. He knew that when he had his son working on something that he would do it right and that kind of help was hard to find. Gus's son still worked for him on weekends and Gus would save some of the important jobs for him, so he would be able to learn how to accomplish them. It was time for Gus to round up his cattle for the last time in 1982 to vaccinate all the calves that had been born since the last round-up and to sell all of the big calves and old cows that Gus didn't want to hold over through the winter. He had been working cattle for about a week and was on the last two pastures where he had left several big trailer loads of calves to be hauled to the sale. In the last pasture his son had three big calves that were going to be sold and they were the first calves from his son's young cows that he would sell. It was a big thing, you might call it a milestone in his son's life to be able to sell his own calves for the first time. It showed the beginning of another rancher in the family and Gus was very proud of this day. Gus and his cowboys had worked all day separating and hauling calves to the auction sale and he was going back for the last load to be hauled. As Gus drove back from the auction sale in El Campo and he was passing the road that went to his Ranch House, Gus started to drive by there and pick up his boy, so he could help load the calves and he could check them in himself at the auction sale, but Gus looked at his watch and saw that it was getting very late and he didn't want to be caught in the dark finishing up, so Gus passed the road by and drove the next ten miles to the pasture. Once there he and his cowboys loaded his trailer and another trailer and they turned the rest of the cattle out of the pen to the pasture and Gus went in the lead with his truck and trailer to the sale in El Campo. When Gus got close to the road that cut off to his Ranch House he could see something in the road, but he couldn't tell what it was, so he slowed down and kept looking then he could see that it appeared to be something red in color scattered on the road. All of a sudden Gus's whole body tensed up when he realized that his son's three wheeler, that his Mom had bought him, was red and then he saw his son laying in the middle of the road. Gus pulled over and his cowboys pulled over behind him and Gus ran over to see about his boy and Gus saw that his son was dead. Gus was in such shock at first that he had a hard time trying to think, but he knew that he had to pull himself together and fast to try and piece together what had happened and also to get some Law Enforcement out to the accident site to protect it from other traffic going down the highway. A car passing by asked if they could help and Gus told them to go to the nearest phone and call for Law Enforcement and an Ambulance. Gus then told his cowboys to drive his truck and trailer and their own to the Auction Sale and he was going to stay with the body of his son's and protect it from someone running over it. They all left and Gus was there with his dead son waving off traffic, because his dead son was laying cross ways in the road. By now it was almost 7:00 pm on October the eighteenth and it was starting to get dark. The Sheriffs Department showed up first and then the Ambulance, but his son couldn't be moved until a Justice Of The Peace pronounced his son officially dead. Gus was furious that his son had to just lay out there when anyone with an ounce of brains could tell his son was dead. The Sheriff Deputy had to physically restrain Gus from picking up his son and carrying him in his arms down the road one half of a mile to Gus's Ranch House. Once it was known that it was Gus's son that had been killed the word got around El Campo fast and a lot of people showed up to console Gus, but the Justice Of The Peace didn't show up until 10:30 pm that night. Gus kept looking at his son laying there and saw that he was in his sock feet without his shoes and Gus looked all around the accident site but couldn't find his son's shoes and then he thought could someone come by before he had arrived on the accident site and stolen his boys shoes. Gus's wife and the other three kids finally drove up at 8:00 pm, because they had been in El Campo and on the way back home they had seen all the lights flashing and wanted to see what was going on. Gus told her that his son was dead and for her and the kids to go on home and he would be there when he could. Gus still didn't know what had happened. All he had discovered was that their was a car involved that had hit his son's three wheeler when his son was crossing the road and that the car had then veered off of the road and gone through a fence and was sitting out on a pasture. The occupants of the car had been taken to El Campo to be checked out by a Doctor, so Gus hadn't even seen them. After his son had been pronounced dead and taken into El Campo to the Funeral Home, Gus went home to tell what he knew to his wife. He heard a knock on the door and their Pastor from their church in Danevang came in to pray with them and wondered if he could do something for them and Gus told him that he was going to go to El Campo and tell his Mom and it might be good for the Pastor to accompany him for his Mom, so they went to tell Gus's Mom. It was 12:30 am by the time Gus and the Pastor got to his Mom's house and he told her ll that he knew. She almost collapsed when he told he what had happened and she kept saying that she just couldn't believe ti over and over. Having the Pastor there seemed to help when he said some sweet prayers so Gus's Mom finally calmed down and they went out of the house. Gus told the Pastor that he was going over to the Funeral Home, because he wanted to see all of the wounds that his son received in the accident and find out the one that actually killed him. They went to the Funeral Home and knocked on the locked door and two of the Morticians there answered the door and Gus introduced him self and the Pastor. They went in and Gus told them what he wanted to do and at first they told him that it was very irregular for someone to do that. They told him that no one ever wanted to see their loved ones before they were fixed up and ready for viewing. Gus told them that he wasn't the average person and that he was the boy's Dad and that he demanded to see him and that he would see him right then and wouldn't take no for an answer. They looked at the fire in Gus's eyes and knew that he meant what he said and wouldn't be put off, so they escorted Gus into the preparation room and his son was laying on the stainless steel table where the Morticians perform their embalming technique. He had only been whipped clean of the blood and Gus looked him over real good and asked how many bones were broken. Gus found out that his son's neck had been broken and there was a deep gash in his forehead that had gone through his skull and into his brain. His son had also had several broken bones. Gus was satisfied and thanked the Morticians and left to go home. He said goodby to the Pastor when they got to Gus's house and he went in and sat in his chair at the kitchen table and drank coffee for the rest of the night. It was no use for him to go to bed, for he knew there was no way that he could rest. He didn't know how long it would be before he could sleep. All Gus knew right then was that his oldest son was dead. The son he had raised by himself when the boy's Mom had run off and the boy was just a baby in diapers. Gus and his son had been very close and they loved each other and the boy had been so much like Gus in so many ways and now it was all gone, just that quick. Gus knew that now when things settled down and he had the time that he would have to re- think about his idea of life and how to proceed with it in the future, because deep down Gus knew that this was a turning point, but he just didn't know yet which way it would turn. The Funeral was held at the Lutheran Church in the small community of Danevang and the church overflowed out into the front lawn. Someone told Gus that there were over eight hundred people that attended to pay their respects. This was the second Funeral that Gus had to take care of and he knew that the business of burying people was all about paper work and money, so he had been busy ever since his son got killed taking care of all of that and he hadn't had anytime to himself to try to sort things out. A few days after the Funeral Gus got another depressing blow. He received a Registered Letter from a Lawyer in Houston that informed him that he was being Sued by the passenger of the car that was involved in the accident that killed his son. Gus was furious and this was just rubbing salt into his already big wounds. Gus wanted to get his hands on that Lawyer really bad, because he felt that this Lawyer was what were referred to as Ambulance Chasers and these were considered to be the scum of the Legal Profession. Gus knew however that he had to calm down and think it out, before acting. Gus knew the lady that had driven the car, so he contacted her and told her that he was being Sued by a Lawyer hired by her passenger. The lady told Gus that the passenger in the car was a friend of hers and that she didn't know the girl had a Lawyer. She told Gus that there wasn't anything wrong with the girl and that the girl had gone to a dance the next night after the accident and she had left with her boyfriend to go back to Phoenix, Arizona. Gus took the Registered Letter to his Lawyer and told him what the driver of the car had told him about her passenger friend. His Lawyer told him that if that Lawyer got a Court date then Gus would have to fight it in Court. Gus just looked at him and told his Lawyer that he would see about that and then he left and he knew what he had to do. Gus went straight home and sat down and composed a letter, hand written to the Houston Lawyer and told him that he had lost all that he was going to loose when he lost his son and that he knew that the passenger in the car wasn't hurt and that if the

Lawyer persisted in pushing Gus's back in a corner that Gus knew how to find him and that Gus would be the one to settle the case to his satisfaction. Gus told the Lawyer that he hand written the letter on purpose instead of typing it, so he would know that Gus was serious and he could judge his hand writing and read what he wanted in it. Gus then made a copy of the letter and mailed it Certified Mail to the Houston Lawyer. Gus then took the copy to his Lawyer and his Lawyer told him that he couldn't send it to the Houston Lawyer, because there was an implied threat in it and Gus just laughed and told him that the letter was already in the mail and that he meant every word in it and would carry it through with pleasure. Gus kept looking for a reply from the Houston Lawyer, bu none came, and neither did he get Sued. To Gus these final few month in 1982 had become a living Hell. Gus knew that he had to concentrate on his business and he forced himself to do it during the working day, but in the evening after work Gus would drive to the Grave Yard and talk to his dead son. Some time he would take a bottle of whiskey with him and then find himself there in the morning laying across his son's grave. Gus had lost family and friends, but nothing had come close to the pain of having his son killed and Gus finding him laying in the middle of the road dead. Gus started to going to a local Mexican Cafe in El Campo that one of his friends owned and he would sit in the bar there after work and drink whiskey till they closed then he would drive out to the Grave Yard and sleep by his son's grave. One time Gus was stopped by the Police on the way out there and they saw that Gus was very drunk, so they locked him up in a jail cell for the night and turned him loose the next morning. The police asked him who Lorrie was and Gus asked them how they knew about Lorrie and the Police told Gus that they didn't know Lorrie that he kept calling her name in his drunken sleep and begging her to help him. Gus just told them that Lorrie was someone special that he hadn't seen in many years and he left it at that. Gus thought and thought, but he had no memory of calling Lorrie's name. Now this brought up other thoughts of sweet Lorrie. Gus thought, how many years has it been since he was on the beach in Corpus with Lorrie and he realized that it had been over twenty years. The memory of Lorrie was always with him hidden deep and sometime evidently he thought of her even when he was sleeping. Gus was forty years old and it was the end of 1982 now and Gus was ready to get it behind him. Surely in 1983 he could start to fight back against this terrible pain of loss and push on with his life. He knew that he would have to take 1983 day by day and make the best of it.

Lorrie—1983 It was1983 now and Lorrie still had her SAS Soldier as her boyfriend and they were still going to parties and having sex at her Flat when they could. They had been dating now for a couple of months and Lorrie was starting to loose interest in him as a novelty. He was a lot of fun, but she really had her eye out for a man that could give her the opportunity to stay in England after the end of her Duty and her Enlistment in the Navy was over, because she simply couldn't think of any other way to be able to stay in England. Her job at the Navy's Cryptology Installation in London was going fine and for the first two months of 1983 Lorrie's team had earned exceptional ratings. Lorrie was really into her work and always had been, but she really wanted to stay in England. One morning she was notified to report to the office of the Commander. Lorrie had never been called to report to that office and she wondered if her Team was going to get a Special Award for outstanding work, because she knew that her Team had come to the attention of her Superiors several times for receiving glowing evaluations. She could think of nothing else that it could be and she was excited about this meeting and to have the chance to be complemented by the Commander himself. Lorrie was shown in to the Commanders office and she stood at attention and saluted. He returned her salute and told her to be at ease and to have a seat. Lorrie noticed that the Commander didn't have a smile on his face like she had pictured he would. Instead he was stern faced and looked very business like and he had a file open on his desk that Lorrie presumed must be hers. The Commander got right to the point and told Lorrie that a very disturbing report on her had been presented to him and he wanted to discuss it with her and that he wanted there to be no doubt in her mind as to how the Navy stood on the subject he was presenting to her. Now Lorrie was so nervous that she was shaking and her previous mood of excitement turned to dread. The Commander told her that she had been under surveillance for quite some time and that it wasn't uncommon for that to happen because of the sensitivity of the secret codes that the Cryptology Installation guarded. He said that there were very good reasons for this that he wasn't to go into in this meeting. He told her that he had reviewed her Personnel File and that it showed that she had a fine record in her Navy Career and that was the reason that he chose to have this meeting with her himself. He then put some pictures of her and her SAS Soldier in front of her when they were at different parties of her friends and of his friends and also of them going into her Flat at night and of him leaving early in the morning with the dates and the times on the pictures.

Lorrie looked at them and blushed, because she knew now that her superiors knew that she had been having sex with this British Soldier. Her Commander was quiet for a moment to let her study the pictures so it would all sink in to her. He then told her that those pictures and the report that he had on her told the whole story and that if her record wasn't so good that he would recommend for her immediate discharge from the Navy. He told her that her SAS Soldier lover was at this same time in the exactly the same meeting with his Commanding Officer and being presented with the same choices that he was going to present to her. He told her that the United States Navy had very strict rules about their High Security Personnel fraternizing in that fashion with the Military Personnel of other Nations, even that of their Allies. He told her that she had three choices: 1. She could cut off her relationship with the SAS Soldier immediately and stay in London at her position, 2. He would transfer her to another Installation in another Country, or 3. She could apply for a Discharge from the Navy, it would be her choice, but he would have to have her decision immediately. Lorrie was stunned and knew that there was only one choice for her and that was to cut off her relationship with her SAS Soldier boyfriend. Lorrie told this to her Commander and he smiled for the first time and told her that she would have only one more phone call to her SAS Soldier and that it would be now from his phone to the SAS Soldiers Commanding Officers office where her SAS Soldier was waiting. He told her that after that phone call that there would be absolutely no contact of any kind between them and if there was then she would be Discharged from the Navy and was she perfectly clear on all of the points of their discussion. Lorrie told him that she was and her Commander picked up his phone and asked to be connected to the SAS Commander's office. He had a short conversation with him and then handed the phone to Lorrie and she heard her SAS Soldiers voice on the line and Lorrie told him that she had enjoyed their time together, but that it was time for them to move on to more important things and that she wished him the best in his Career in the future and that was what she was going to concentrate on for herself. He agreed and they hung up the phone. Her Commander told her that their meeting was confidential and that under no circumstances was she to discuss it with anyone. He then told her to report back to work and to put her mind at ease and concentrate on the work on her shift. He then stood up and Lorrie knew that the meeting was over and she stood at attention and saluted and he returned her salute and dismissed her. Lorrie felt so humiliated and distraught that she went as fast as she could to the nearest rest room and cried her eyes out. This had caught her completely off guard. Here she thought that she was going to be congratulated for the good job her Team was doing and she instead was almost tossed out of the Navy. When she thought of this she shuddered and started to vomit in the toilet. She knew she had to get back to her Team on Duty, so she washed her face and straightened her appearance and tried to collect her thoughts to get back to the job at hand. When Lorrie's shift was over she went back to her Flat and gathered all the reminders of her SAS Soldier and she took them to the trash, because he was definitely out of her life forever. Oh well, she thought that their relationship was going no where anyway. Lorrie thought that now that the distraction of her SAS Soldier boyfriend was gone she would definitely concentrate on her job and also on how to remain in England at the end of her Enlistment in the Navy.

Gus—1983 planting season was in full swing for Gus and he had successfully made loans to finance his operations for the 1983 crop year. The Banking situation was still extremely bad and Gus knew that he would have to continue to look for ways to buy time to see if there would be a big improvement in the price of farm products to be able to pay off his loans and if not then he would have to continue to sell off his assets, because it would be the only way to generate enough money to make a difference in what he owed. Also Gus was still taking care of his mother with all the full time help that she needed and her medical expenses which was a big outlay of money. Gus was having to factor all of this into his Farm and Ranch loans and it really made his profit and loss predictions look bad. Gus was still suffering from the loss of his fifteen year old son, but he was able to be productive and responsible in his business operations. It was just at night when he was off of work that he became morose. He had left his son's room just as it had been that last day when he was killed and it had been closed up with orders to everyone that no one should open the door and go in the room. Gus and his wife were getting farther apart in several ways. She was taking the kids side of discussions more and more and she seemed to always be looking for ways to be on the opposite side of a decision that had to be made, so the arguments went on and on. Also his wife was spending more time with her friends in El Campo, friends that Gus thought were, should we say, low class. He just couldn't understand it and the only thing that he could attribute it to was her desire to have friends that looked up to her as being somehow above them. There was no way that Gus could associate with them on a social basis, so this cut him off from her social life. There was so much conflict here that Gus finally just got to the point that she went one way and he went the other and they refused to discuss the situation with each other. Gus's crops were coming along fine, but crop prices were not good and cattle prices were stagnant. To Gus it looked like another year of trying to figure out how to survive. He saw more farmers being forced out of business and more suicides. It seemed to Gus that this Great Recession had gone on a very long time and he couldn't see anything that would bring it to an end and he felt trapped. The weight of tragedy, responsibility and marital conflict had now overpowered the happiness that Gus had felt when he had come back from his families vacation trip to Big Bend National Park. Gus still went to his son's grave and talked to him, but he didn't sleep there anymore. His friend that owned the Mexican Cafe had a short, but to the point talk with Gus one night when Gus was in the bar drinking whiskey. He came to Gus's table and sat down and looked Gus in the eye and told Gus that he had something to say and he hoped that Gus would take it as a friend caring for a friend. He told Gus that he had been watching him ever since Gus's boy had been killed and that he had seen Gus drink more and more and he was concerned for Gus's safety and his health and maybe Gus needed to think about what he was doing, because none of it was going to bring his boy back alive. Then his friend got up and put his hand on Gus's shoulder and smiled and went back to his other customers. This really got Gus's attention, because Gus hadn't any idea that his drinking had become so bad that it was worrying his friends. Gus really took it to heart and he started to be more aware of what he was doing, so slowly he was altering his destructive behavior and he much appreciated his friends frank talk to him. Gus and his wife were almost living two separate lives and Gus decided that most marriages were probably like his because he had heard many stories from other men about the discard between husband and wife in their homes. Gus thought that the old fantasy of true love and romance was just for love story books and movies and that there was no such thing in real life. Marriage was just a challenge every step of the way and always would be. Then he thought of Lorrie and her sweetness and the wonderful kisses she had given him on the beach in Corpus and he wondered if marriage to Lorrie would have been any different then the marriages he had experienced. Maybe Lorrie was just an aberration to him now after so many years, but no she couldn't be because he could still feel the electricity of her kisses. The subdivisions that Gus had developed were making money and he had calls almost daily with people wanting to buy residential lots from him. These subdivisions were almost like little gold mines for Gus. The payments from them quickly paid off the Notes that he had on them and they were free and clear of Debt. Gus thought that if he had stuck only to the cattle business and had the subdivisions and stayed clear of the farming he would have been a lot better off, however the large income from the farming at the time had allowed him to buy his land, but now the land had become a liability in a way, because of the huge debt that it was carrying. Gus knew of no other way to buy time then to keep borrowing back on his land to keep financing his operations and to keep his Mom in her home where she was happy. Gus was getting to the point that he was having real doubts that he could ever pay off his huge debts with the income that was being generated from his agriculture operations. He was simply trying to buy time long enough hoping that he could make an Oil Lease that would get a producing well drilled or something similar that would put a lot of income into his operations. This was the only thing that Gus could see that might allow him to at least save part of his farm and ranch operations. His crops and cattle looked good, but the prices were still depressed, so it looked like Gus might still be just in a holding pattern again. Harvest was coming up fast and that would tell him what he would have to do for 1984.

Lorrie—1984 began and Lorrie had kept her word and had not been in contact with the SAS Soldier. Instead her and her girlfriend resumed their day trips to Paris and different locations in England to enjoy the art Museums and historical attractions and of coarse the local parties that were held at Lorrie's Flat. Her and her Team at work were still doing an outstanding job, but Lorrie knew that every week that went by brought her closer to the time that she was going to have to make a major decision about her re-enlistment in the Navy and she was worrying about it more and more, because 1983 was her last full year of Duty in England. One weekend when she was off Duty some of the other tenants of the Flat building had organized a party, which was a usual thing that happened. Someone was always having a party and everyone in the building brought something for the party and their guests were always invited. There were a lot of people and always some that were new and had to be introduced around to the regular party guests. All of a sudden one of Lorrie's friends walked over to Lorrie with a tall dark and Lorrie thought handsome man and introduced him to Lorrie. She told Lorrie that he owned a Dry Cleaners and Laundry down the street from their Flats and she had been doing business with him for some time and she had invited him to the party. Lorrie, her friend and the Laundry Man stood and talked and had some drinks for a few minutes then someone came and got her friend and that left Lorrie and the Laundry Man to get to know each other a little more. Lorrie found out that he was a British Citizen and that peaked her interest even more. He told her that his parents were originally from Greece and they had come to England during World War 2 and that he and his Father owned the Laundry. Lorrie also found out that his wife had died and that he had a boy that was seven years old. Lorrie thought this man was very interesting, but she didn't want to appear to interested in him on their first meeting, so she was playing the small talk game all the time gleaning little bits of information to feel him out. They kept being interrupted by the party goers, so Lorrie could only get a little information from him, but he seemed to be easy to talk to and really forthcoming with his personal life. He hung around Lorrie for most of the evening except when her friend took him away to introduce him to others, but he always came back to talk and have drinks with Lorrie. Lorrie decided that she wanted to get to know this Laundry man better, so before the party broke up Lorrie told him that she would bring him some laundry. When he got ready to leave the party he went around and told some of the other guests good-by and came back to Lorrie and told her that he hoped that he would see her again and he held her hand a little longer then he needed to when they shook hands and said good-by. This Laundry Man had Lorrie's interest and she decided that she would take it slow to find as much about him as she could. When Lorrie reported for her work shift a couple of days later she decided that she was going to talk to her friend during their coffee break to see how much she knew about the Laundry Man. Lorrie's friend told her that she had been taking some laundry to him for several months and she had met his old Father and that they both seemed nice and that was why she had decided to invite him to the party. Her friend told Lorrie that she knew that the Laundry Man had lost his wife to cancer and that he had a young boy and he and the boy were living with his Father and Mother. Her friend thought they lived there so he would have help in raising his son. Lorrie thought about this and decided that him having a young son wasn't a bad thing, because it showed that he had some responsibility to him about family and he also had his own business and he was a British citizen. Lorrie thought that so far all the check marks were in the right box. The next day

Lorrie took him some laundry and he introduced her to his Father. His father had a very heavy Greek accent to his English and Lorrie had to listen carefully to him speak and she got a real kick of this, because she was actually getting a little more involved with true English and also immigrant English culture. This is what she was looking for ever she set foot in England almost four years ago and now at last maybe she would have a chance to have the experience she had wanted. Lorrie invited him to the next party a week from then and told him that he would be her guest and he seemed very pleased. The next day at work Lorrie told her friend that she had invited the Laundry Man as her guest to the next party and her friend laughed at her and told her to be careful, because she should know what they say about Greek lovers being very jealous and Lorrie told her friend that he wasn't close to being her lover yet that she had a lot more that she wanted to find out about him before it would get to that stage. He showed up to the next party and went straight to Lorrie and handed her a picture of him, his son, his Father and Mother and his sister and told her that he had told his family about her and he said that his Father told his Mother that they needed to invite Lorrie over for dinner some evening. Lorrie told him that she would accept and to let her know in time for her to make arrangements. She gave him her phone number for the first time and it was something that she hadn't planned on doing just yet, but why not, he would need it now. Now this was very exciting for Lorrie to be invited to a private home in England for dinner. Her Laundry Man called her and they made the arrangements and he told Lorrie that the dinner wouldn't be a traditional English meal, but it would be a traditional Greek meal and she should just dress casual and he would come over to her Flat after he closed the laundry and he would drive her to his Mother and Fathers house and return her to her Flat. Lorrie thought this was just perfect and that she couldn't ask for anything better then this. She was really looking forward to this evening out. When they arrived at his parents house Lorrie saw that it was just a small wood frame house that was well kept and it had a lot of flowers planted in beds in the front. As they got to the front door Lorrie could hear a lot of noise going on inside and her Laundry Man laughed and told her that his Greek family was not a quiet one and for her to get ready for a lot of talking and laughing at a dinner like this. He opened the door and his sister immediately greeted Lorrie with a hug and a kiss on both cheeks then introduced herself and took Lorrie by the hand in to the kitchen and introduced her to his Mother, his son, her husband and their two daughters.

To Lorrie it sounded like everyone was talking at one time and everyone came up to her and gave her a hug and a kiss on both of her cheeks except the Laundry Man's son. Lorrie noticed the slight, but said nothing. Lorrie thought that his sister was a beautiful woman a little older then the Laundry Man. She later found out that he was actually the baby of the family that he also had two older brothers. They started the meal with toast's to her with Greek ouzo, a traditional Greek liquor and toast's to his Father and his Mother then they had a clear vegetable soup, lamb shish kabobs and grilled vegetables, flat bread, cheese, red wine and then more ouzo. The conversation then found it's way to Lorrie's family and they wanted to hear all about them in Texas and about Texas itself. Lorrie saw that his son was pretty quiet and didn't warm up to her and she didn't push it. She noticed that he was very spoiled getting his way very easily. All in all though Lorrie enjoyed the evening and when the Laundry Man took her back to her Flat she let him kiss her good night. After she showered and dressed for bed she sat in her little kitchen and did a lot of thinking about him. Lorrie thought him handsome and he was just one year older then her, he had a nice family and a business, he liked to party, but he wasn't what she would call a good kisser. His kisses didn't come close to arousing her, but maybe she could train him a little to improve. Gus's kisses still haunted her and no one had ever gotten close to what his kisses had done to her and she shivered with delight while she was thinking of them. Oh well, that was many years ago and now she needed to decide if she wanted to pursue this Laundry Man to see if he was going to be the one that could insure that she stayed in England. They continued to be a couple at the parties at the Flat and they would go to his parents home on different occasions. It got so that Lorrie would let him stay in her spare room after the parties, because he would get pretty drunk and she was afraid for him to drive to his parents house. One night after a party and they had gone to their separate rooms to bed, Lorrie was almost asleep and she detected him standing in the doorway to her room. She asked him what was wrong and he asked her if they could cuddle. She thought for a minute and told him that she guessed it would be alright. She understood cuddling as when you lay and put your arms around the other person, but she found out that in England it meant to have sex. Well one thing lead to another and she found herself reaching down to see if he was hard and she was so surprised to discover that he had the largest male appendage she had ever known and she wondered if she could even handle it, she was kind if scared. His kisses didn't arouse her, but the thought of this very large penis did and she decided she had to find out what sex would be like with him, so she complied with his wishes. The next morning she sent him off so she could decide what she really thought about his sexual technique. She had to admit to herself that his large penis was really all that he had going for him in he sex department and she also knew that now since they had done it that they wouldn't stop, so where was all of this going anyway. Lorrie decided it was time to start working on him to see if their relationship was taking the next step, because the year 1983 was speeding by and her Enlistment would be up soon, so she had to know what to expect so she could make plans. She always was one to make plans. The next day at work she told her girlfriend that she and the Laundry Man had sex and her girlfriend told Lorrie that she had been wondering when it would happen, because they had been looking very romantic together at the last couple of parties at the Flat. Lorrie told her friend that she had decided to see where the relationship was going and that right now she only had two things that bothered her about him one was that he seemed to drink a lot and get really drunk and the other was that his son didn't seem to be warming up to her very much. Lorrie told her friend that the Laundry Man said that he had a house in Bromley and that it had been closed up since his wife had died and he and his son had moved back in with his Mother and Father, he told her that he wanted to show it to her soon. Her friend told Lorrie that if he was going to show her his house that he had some serious plans for her that sounded like wedding bells ringing. Lorrie told her friend that she had been thinking that maybe the Laundry Man could be the answer to her being able to stay in England. Her friend then asked her that if he asked her to marry him would she accept and Lorrie told her that she probably would. Lorrie told her friend that she only had a couple of more months left on her Enlistment and then she would have to RE-Enlist and the Navy would sent her no telling where and she wanted to stay in England. Her friend asked Lorrie if she could really do this and Lorrie told her that yes she could and that she had married twice for reasons that had nothing to do with love and that her friend should know by know that Gus would be the only man that she would ever love, so what difference did it make now. Her friend told Lorrie that she just couldn't understand the reason that she couldn't get over that guy Gus that it had been a lifetime ago and she was still pining for him. Lorrie told her friend that if she ran into Gus tomorrow and he said that he wanted her that she would leave with him immediately and go with him where ever he went and that was just the way it was and the way it was always going to be till the day she died and she couldn't help it because she could only love one man and he had always been the one. Lorrie told her friend that since she couldn't have Gus then she just had to do what she could to keep living her life with someone else in a place that she wanted to be and that place was England. Lorrie could see that the Laundry Man had been starved for sex, so she decided that she was going to give in to him often, plus she started to cook meals for him in her Flat every once in a while. She was starting to tighten the rope on him, so to speak and it was working, because he told her that the next time she was off that they would drive to Bromley and they would stay at his house there and she could look it over. A week later they planned to drive to Bromley and spend two days at his house. Lorrie had never been to the little town of Bromley and she thought that it was nice looking with a shopping district and a couple of Pubs for entertainment. When they pulled up to the house, it was on a hill in a subdivision with neighbors and it was walking distance from the little town. He unlocked the front door and they went in and it smelled very musky inside. He turned on the lights and Lorrie started to inspect the down stairs rooms. He told Lorrie that the house had been built in the 1930's and had been spared from damage during World War 2. There were beams in the ceiling in the living room and Lorrie liked that, but the furniture was old and very worn. The kitchen was very small, but OK with a breakfast nook and there was a real small room that could be a single bed room or an office. There was a down stares small bathroom by the kitchen with only a lavatory and a toilet. Also there was a dining room, but it was ill arranged for the down stairs floor plan. Lorrie noticed that the stares going up to the top floor were very steep and the Laundry Man led the way. Up stares were three bedrooms one of which was small and there was a nice bathroom. Under the eves was an attic that was small, but could be used for storage. They went out to the back of the house and there was a nice sized back yard that could have a garden and some fruit trees. Lorrie's inspection of the house was over and she could see that it could be made to be a very nice place to live. There were some things about the house that she didn't like, but really it was probably the best house that Lorrie would ever live in. The more she thought about the house the better she liked the idea of living there. Lorrie suggested that they live together there for a while to see how they all got along, but the Laundry Man said that they couldn't do that because he didn't want his son to tell his parents that they were living together without being married. He said that they could come there by themselves for romantic weekends and that would be good, but if Lorrie would marry him then they could start making plans to move in and renovate the house. Lorrie asked him if that was a proposal of marriage and he told her that it was. She told him that she wanted to think about for a couple of days, because it would be a major decision that would mean that she could no longer return to Texas to live. He told her that he understood, but he was sure himself and that he begged her to come to yes as her decision. He told her that as soon as she said yes that he would get her an engagement ring. Lorrie didn't want to jump for joy in front of him, because she wanted him to think that she wasn't sure, but she was sure. It was the only thing that could ensure that she could stay in England and she was ready to make any deal that could do that. Her time was short and this really came in the nick of time. Lorrie and the Laundry Man got one bed room ready enough to sleep in for that one night and they went into Bromley to eat and have a few drinks before going back to the house to have sex and sleep together for the night before going back to London in the morning. Lorrie didn't really like to sleep all night with her lovers. Most of the time when the sex was over with she would insist that they go their own way back to their own places, but she knew that she was going to have to make an exception here if she was to insure that everything ran smooth till they were married and then maybe she could find some way to have a separate bedroom from him. Lorrie didn't sleep very good and was glad to see morning come except that he wanted sex again and she felt that she had to comply with his desires. That over and she suggested that they go into town for something for breakfast before they drove back to London. After Lorrie got back to her Flat she couldn't wait to get a bath and go over all that she had seen and learned about the house in Bromley. Lorrie was excited about being able to stay in England after her Enlistment was over, not exactly about marrying the Laundry Man. She called her good friend and told her about their Bromley trip and her friend told Lorrie that she had said that the Laundry Man had wedding bells ringing if he was showing her his house. Lorrie giggled and told her friend that she had been right and that Lorrie had told him to wait a couple of days for her answer. Her friend couldn't believe that Lorrie was going to really marry him. Lorrie told her that she definitely was and that she would be able to make some changes as the marriage progressed to make the marriage more like she wanted it to be. Lorrie told her friend that she was going to tell the Laundry Man that she would marry him and he had promised to get her an engagement ring and that would seal the deal, because she would tell him to give it to her at his Mother and Fathers home some evening, so he would be to embarrassed to back out after that. Her friend laughed at her and told her that is why Lorrie needed the time to think was to think up some way that she had him trapped real good and then both of them laughed. The next day she called him and told him that she would come to the laundry after her shift to give him her answer. She knew that he would wonder all day what it would be and she wanted him to be nervous when she came in. Lorrie decided to go in the laundry without a smile and then give him the good news to see what his reaction would be. This she did along with telling him that she wanted him to give her the ring at his Mothers and Fathers house and he started screaming and hugging her and his Father came from the back room to see what all the noise was and the Laundry Man said that Lorrie was going to be his wife. His Father came around the counter and hugged Lorrie and kissed her on both cheeks then he hugged his son and kissed him on both cheeks and he told them that he and his wife were going to have a big celebration for them, but the Laundry Man told his Father that they all were going to a nice Pub for the celebration as a family and that it would be next week. Lorrie thought that next week was good, because 1983 was almost gone and they needed to start to make wedding plans as soon as possible. Lorrie, called her Mom and Dad and told them that she was going to Marry a British citizen and stay in England and her Dad told her not to do it that there were two hundred thousand American men in the Navy and why couldn't she find one of them that she could Marry, that she didn't need to Marry a foreigner. Lorrie told him that it was the only way that she could stay in England and that is what she wanted to do. Her parents were unhappy about it all, but they couldn't stop her. Lorrie had never taken the Laundry Man to the Military PX and she suggested that they go soon while she was still in the Navy, because when her Enlistment was over she wouldn't be able to go there any more and that they could buy so many things there very cheap because there were no taxes on them. Lorrie and her now Fiance made several trips shopping at the Military PX and her Fiance just loved it. He couldn't believe the cheap prices on things there. They bought quite a few things for the house in Bromley and also personal items that were so much cheaper then the stores in London. Lorrie and her Fiance had been spending a lot of their off work time cleaning and reorganizing the house in Bromley and they had set their wedding date just a few days before her Enlistment was up in the Navy in early 1984. Lorrie had already notified her Superior Officer that she wasn't going to re-enlist, so everything was going according to her plans and Lorrie was so excited to be staying in England for good that she almost felt like she was really in love with her Fiance. She had decided that she was never going to give up her United States citizenship or her US Passport no matter what so she would never be a British citizen, she would be classified as a resident in England. 1983 was over and everything was set for her wedding in 1984, she had a hard time believing it.

Gus—1984 was a year starting with no grand expectations for Gus. His 1983 harvest had been just an average one with low prices, so he was just barely holding his own with the Banks. He was able to pay back most of the principal on his loans, but not all of the interest, so he had to roll it into his new loans for the crop year of 1984. This made him have to put up even more of his land as collateral to support his loans. Gus's debt was slowly growing each year and he was very worried about it. Gus knew that if this trend continued that one day he would have to take drastic measures to pay off his debts. Gus was in the middle of his spring planting when he got a very distressing call one night. This call was from the wife of a very good friend that he had ever since he had been in Wharton County Junior College. She was crying and she told Gus that his friend had died from a massive heart attack. Gus could hardly believe it, because his friend was only forty-three years old. She asked Gus to be a Pallbearer and Gus said that he would be honored to serve his friend in that capacity. It would be the last thing that he could do for his friend. After the Funeral Service and Burial Gus was invited back to hie friends house by his Widow and Gus and another Pallbearer, a well known singer of Rock-N-Roll named Roy Head, were sitting in his friends bar area talking and his friends Widow came in and went behind the bar and brought out a bottle of Gus's favorite whiskey and told him that his friend had bought it for him and he should go ahead and take it home with him. Gus looked at it and he told his friends Widow that his friend had bought it for Gus to drink there and he asked the other Pallbearer if he wanted to help him drink it right then and the Pallbearer told Gus yes that he would. They sat at Gus's dead friends bar and drank the whole bottle that evening and then he gave the empty bottle back to the Widow signed buy both Pallbearers and dated for her to have for a keepsake. After Gus returned home he thought to himself that this was just another sign to him that he needed to try and rethink his life and the direction it was going. He had lost his oldest son in an accident and now he had lost one of his best friends. Gus was only forty-two and he knew that he was in good health, but his friend thought that he was too and what about those unexpected accidents that killed his son, so maybe if Gus could finally get himself out of all this financial mess and the strain of all his burdens, he would try to steer his life in another direction, someday, but when. Gus went about his farming and ranching duties as usual except that every-once-in a-while he would think about the years ahead and what they might bring. After all his Dad had died when he was only sixty-one years old and Gus being in his forties with the recent events of loosing his son and then his friend were casting a little different outlook on life for Gus. He had been having some different thoughts about which direction his life should go after his son was killed and the loss of his friend just added one more piece to this puzzle. Gus then got another call from the sister of his first wife that her Father had died and that she and the family wanted Gus to attend the funeral if he could. Gus told her that he would and the funeral was in the same church that he and his first wife had been married in twenty-two years before, so he knew where it was. Her Dad, his former Father-In Law, had stayed friends all of those years and had visited one another from time to time, so it was important for Gus to go and pay his last respects to him and his family. When the church service was over and Gus was leaving he was summoned to the family's car and they invited him to the church hall for the dinner that they were having there and Gus. They told him that the whole family wanted him to attend the dinner, because it had been so long since they had seen him and they wanted to get caught up on how he was doing, so Gus went to the dinner and they seated him right next to a nice looking boy that was seventeen years old. Next to the boy was Gus's ex-wife and everyone seemed real glad to see Gus. They all talked of the times when Gus was still part of their family and they made Gus feel very much at home in their company. Gus and the boy ate and made a little small talk until the meal was over, then Gus's ex-wife got up and went over to Gus and put her hand on his shoulder and she told Gus that this boy was his son. Gus looked at the boy and he could see then a certain resemblance to himself with the pale blue glassy eyes and the nose and ears and the skin color. Also they were about the same size, so Gus couldn't protest right then what his ex-wife told him and the boy had no surprise on his face so he must have know about this for some time. A few minutes later when everyone was standing and sitting in groups visiting Gus took his ex-wife by the hand and motioned for them to go by themselves to a place where they could talk without interruption. They found a quiet corner in the big room away from the noise and Gus asked his ex-wife what the meaning of this revelation. Gus told her that he had known that she was having sex with the College Boy while they were married and that she had never protested when Gus thought that the baby was the College Boy's and then after her and the College boy got married that she and her new husband adopted the baby and Gus had thought that everything was as it should have been and that was the end of it, so how did she think that the boy was his son when she was having sex with this other guy and she and Gus had almost stopped having sex and if this was true why bring it up after so many years? His ex-wife told Gus that at the time when everything was falling apart with their marriage she was so stressed out with it all that she was just ready to get it over with and that she had known that she had been the original cause for their trouble with the first time he had caught her with the Parts Man where she worked. She told Gus that she thought at the time that he would never believe her if she had tried to convince him that the baby was his, but that women know these things and she had known that it was his baby. She said that the reason why she had to reveal this to him now was that the boy and his adopted Father didn't get along at all and that she thought that if Gus and the boy would get together then it would do both of them some good. She told Gus to look at the boy and he would be able to see that the boy didn't look anything like the College Boy and that he had a lot of Gus's features. Gus had to admit that she had a point there. She told Gus that she had always thought that he was a good man and that he would be a good strong figure in the boys life if Gus would just have an open mind and try. She told Gus that she had told the boy who his real father was when the boy was nine years old, so this was not something new for the boy. She said that one of the times when the boy and his step father were having a big fight she took the boy into her bedroom and retrieved a picture of Gus that she had and she sat the boy down and showed him the picture and told him that this man was his real father and this was why he and his step father couldn't get along, because they were too much different in the way they thought. She asked Gus what he thought of the boy and Gus told her that he just didn't know yet that he would have to think about this, but that he knew one thing and that was that the boy needed to get that long hair cut off. Gus told his ex-wife that he would have to think all of this over and that he would need her phone number to talk to her, so she wrote it down for him and they got up to go and join the others, but first his ex-wife turned to him and gave him a firm kiss on the lips and whispered that she still loved him, then they joined the others. On the way driving back home Gus had a hundred different thoughts going through his mind. When Gus got home he sat down with his wife and told her all that transpired at the funeral and about the meeting with the boy that his ex-wife claimed was actually his and not the College Boys. His wife ask him what he planned to do about this and Gus told her that he was just going to let it rest for now and see what time would do with it. Gus then drove off to a place on the ranch where he could park under the shade of some trees so he could be quiet and think a little about what had happened. Here Gus had thought that his first marriage's troubles were behind him many years ago and all of a sudden they pop up again. He had thought that when his first wife had married the College Boy and they had adopted the baby that all was like it should have been with the right Mom and Dad then having the baby and the baby having the fathers name, but now if it was true that Gus was the father then the boy had the wrong name again, so what should be done now, after all the boy was seventeen years old and had been using the College Boys last name for all those years. Well just another mess in life to deal with. Gus was wondering what else would pop up in 1984 that he didn't know about yet. Gus thought to himself that he kept trying to straighten out his life so it would be like a normal persons, but there seemed no end to the complications that were arising. Then Gus thought about Lorrie. He thought about her so hard that he had actual visions in color of everything that happened on the beach in Corpus Christi and in her room and he could see every beautiful thing about her and he could recall the sound of her voice as she spoke the sweet words to him about how long and how much that she loved him. It was almost like she was in his truck with him and Gus was wondering how much better his life would have been if he would have taken the chance and married Lorrie when they were so young. He suddenly felt remorse for the decision that he made so long ago to leave her alone. All he could do now was to hope that her life hadn't been as complicated as his had been and that his decision had been good for her, because it sure hadn't been good for him. It seemed like he was constantly putting out personal fires in his life. In the days ahead Gus didn't dwell on the happenings at his ex-father-in-laws funeral. He went right back into his farming and ranching responsibilities and also taking care of his Mom. He heard no more from his ex-wife on the subject and he didn't contact her either. Gus was into the harvest season now and soon it would be time to put his budget together for the Banks for his 1985 crop year and he was already wondering what that would look like. The only bright side that he could see right now was that soybean prices were rising because Brazil was experiencing a drouth and the estimate on the country's crop had been dropping. Brazil was a major producer of soybeans and their crop had a lot to do with the price of soybeans world wide. Well Gus still had a lot to do in 1984 before the year was out.

Lorrie—1984 Everything was so exciting now in 1984 for Lorrie with all the plans complete for her wedding. They were going to be married in a nice non-denominational Church by a pastor that Lorrie really liked and she had bought her white wedding dress that had a small white brides veil adorned with spring flowers in a circle around the forehead. She was finally going to have the kind of wedding that she had always wanted. She had planned for a small reception after the wedding across the street in a hall that she had rented for the occasion and she had girlfriend and a couple of her co-workers for brides maids. Everything was set for the wedding and now all that was left was to try and get as much done in the Bromley house as they could so they could go directly there after their honey moon in Paris, which was another dream of hers as a little girl to have a romantic honey moon in the city of love Paris. Lorrie just couldn't believe that all her dreams as a little girl were about to come true in 1984, well not quite all, because she would like all of this to be her and Gus. If it would be her and Gus getting married and having a honey moon in Paris then Paris would really be the city of love, because there could never be a more pure love then the one that Lorrie had always had for Gus and for them to be there, well that thought just took her breath away. Lorrie's best friend that she worked with was to be her Maid of Honor and two girls on her team were Brides Maids. They had a small little party at Lorrie's Flat the night before the wedding day and Lorrie's Fiance got terribly drunk and repulsive. Her girl friends were appalled. Lorrie told him that if he was drunk for the wedding that she would walk off and not go through with the wedding. Lorrie called one of his friends to come and get him and take him to the Bromley house for the night. Lorrie's Maid of Honor told her that she couldn't see how Lorrie could get married to such a man and that if Lorrie wanted to back out that she would help her. The next day at the wedding Lorrie could tell that her new Husband had been drinking, but at least he wasn't drunk. The Pastor completed a nice sweet wedding service and then they all went outside to go across the street to the building that they were having the reception in. When they got outside they discovered that it was pouring rain and they all had to try to get through the traffic to the building and they all got soaked through and through. Lucky that Lorrie had put her change of cloths for the trip to Paris in the restroom there and she had something dry to change into. They had a nice wedding cake and punch and finger foods and of coarse beer and hard liquor. Well Lorrie's husband started sneaking to the bar and drinking the hard liquor in-stead of beer and Lorrie was furious at him, but he just kept it up till he was falling down drunk. She was so embarrassed that she kept her distance from him. They finally left the reception for their Honey Moon trip and her Husband slept almost all the way to Paris. They got to Paris and checked into their Hotel and the room had a stocked bar in it and immediately her Husband poured himself a large whiskey and after that he laid down on the sofa and went back to sleep. Lorrie just looked at him in disgust and he slept all night and of coarse there was no sex on the Honey Moon night. They stayed four days in Paris and her expectations of a romantic Honey Moon didn't play out quite as good as Lorrie wanted them to. They did have nice times at the sidewalk cafes with all the nice French coffee and their wonderful pastries. Lorrie did insist that they go to some of the great museums in Paris and they took in some of the nice floor shows that Paris is noted for. They went back to England and they stayed at Lorrie's Flat, because she was still in the Navy for a few more days. Lorrie was using up her vacation time to finish out her Enlistment in the Navy. They still had to do some grocery shopping to restock the Bromley house for them all to live there and they had to pick up her stepson who had been staying with his Grand Parents till everything was ready for the final move to the Bromley house. Lorrie had enjoyed her Honey Moon in spite of her new Husband, but she was also excited for all of them to start their life together in her new home in Bromley. She would finally have a stepson to raise to take the place of her own son that had been hidden away from her by her first husband and she was excited about having this opportunity. They would be a family, her family now. Lorrie and her husband went to the grocery store in Bromley to get everything they would need to start out house keeping there and when they got to the check out Lorrie was so embarrassed when her Husband kept watching the prices being rung up on the register and all of a sudden he started taking things off the check out counter and putting them off the side. Lorrie asked him what he was doing and he told her that they didn't have enough money to pay for all of the groceries. This was the first indication that Lorrie had that there were money problems and when they got home to the Bromley house she was going to find out what was going on. When they got to the Bromley house they unpacked the groceries and the few cleaning supplies that they bought and then Lorrie put some coffee on for them and she told her Husband that she wanted him to drink coffee and not beer or hard liquor, because they needed to have a serious talk and she needed to know what was going on with his finances. He went to the ice box and got a beer anyway and he told her that she could have the coffee. When the coffee was done Lorrie poured her a cup and one for him also, but he ignored it and got himself another beer. Lorrie told him that she didn't want to cause any trouble, but she needed to know about their financial situation so she could help and also to make a budget. Finally he sighed and told her that the Laundry wasn't making any money and that he and his Dad had been trying to sell it without any results. She asked him why it wouldn't sell and he told her that their was a lot of repair work that needed to be done on the building and they didn't have the money to repair it. Every time some buyer showed an interest in it the Inspectors would give them a bad report and they would back out. Lorrie ask him how they were supposed to make a living if the Laundry wasn't making any money and he told her that he had been a Tailor before buying the Laundry and he was still doing some of that work which was the main source of their income right now, but that he didn't have the time to do enough of it while they still owned the Laundry. Lorrie asked him why he didn't just shut down the Laundry and go back to Tailoring. With this question her Husband got up and got himself another beer. He sat down and looked a little peeved that she would ask this question, but he told her that there was still a big loan on the Laundry with the Bank and if he shut it down it wouldn't sell for enough to pay the loan back so the Bank would then come and take his house here in Bromley and sell it to pay off the balance of the loan, so he and his Dad were trapped into keeping it open. Lorrie just sat there for a couple of minutes not believing what she was hearing. While they were dating he had never let on to how much in trouble he was financially. She couldn't believe that he was stupid enough to have re-mortgaged his house to buy the Laundry. Lorrie was already seeing a much different side to this Englishman that she hadn't suspected and she was wondering what else was there that she would finally find out. They hadn't been married but a week and already things were tying her stomach up in knots. Lorrie thought that after hearing all of this that she was the one that need to get drunk. It looked like she had fallen into another mess. Oh well she would have to see what could be done to help out now that she was his Wife and also she had become a stepmother to his boy. Surly she could help him get out of this mess and they could save the house. They worked on finishing getting the house in order to pick up his son in a couple of days so they could start operating as a family. The next day Lorrie started to get together all the information she could from her Husband so she could see how to put together a budget for them to live by. He had no cash money left on him and all the cash that Lorrie had was in her purse which wasn't much. She had some in her account in the Bank she had used before they married and she knew that they would need it to live on till she could get everything figured out. She told her Husband that she needed every receipt that he got no matter how small or for what he bought, so she could put together a budget. She also told him that before they picked up his son she wanted to go to the Laundry so he could show her what need fixing there. Her Husband just nodded OK and went to the ice box and got himself another beer and Lorrie was shaking her head. The next day Lorrie went with her Husband to the Laundry to look it over and what she saw in the back, that you couldn't see as a customer, was depressing. She had never been a person that had been involved with any type if renovation of a building, but she could see so much damage, mostly from a leaky roof, to all the wood in the roof and the walls that she could see why the inspectors gave bad reports to the buyers. Also she noticed that the plumbing was in bad shape. Lorrie went to her Husbands little office at the laundry and started going through the invoices and paper work in there and she couldn't make heads or tails of it. It was an absolute mess and there was no organization at all to it. Papers were stuffed in drawers and in boxes that been wet from the leaky roof and some of them you couldn't even read them any more. Lorrie was at a loss to know how her husband could know how much money the laundry was loosing or making. She was determined to straighten it all out, she just had to if for nothing else, so she would know what was going on with the finances. Also she told him that she was going to work with him to try to fix the building. His Father had been a carpenter, but he was much to old to do that kind of work any more, but he could give them advice and they could work on the building after they closed the laundry for a few hours each night and Lorrie would put her money into it to buy some of the supplies needed to make repairs. Lorrie knew now that she had married into a total mess, but she was determined to get things running on an even keel so she could have peace of mind. Lorrie told her Husband that if they were going to work on the laundry at night that his son was going to have to stay with her Husbands parents a little while longer till they got things straightened out at the laundry, so that is what happened. Well after several weeks of working at night they had patched up the roof and the rotten lumber with caulking wood filler and paint so it looked OK, if you didn't look to close at it and they got the plumbing working if you didn't do two things at one time that would over load it. Maybe now if a buyer would bring in inspectors quick, before all this temporary patching came loose and pealed off, maybe they could sell it. Lorrie's Husband had been trying to sell the laundry for enough to pay off his total loan and Lorrie told him that she didn't think that the Laundry would ever sell for that much, because he had payed way to much for it in the first place and that he had better drop the price before all their patch work fell off, then maybe they could get rid of it and then they could make arrangements with the Bank to pay off the rest of the loan with money he would make from going back into full time Tailoring and she would start looking for a job to help out. Lorrie's Husband didn't want to admit she was right, but he had no other idea of what to do, so he told her that he would drop the price on the Laundry. With in a week there was a buyer that was interested and he did send in inspectors and they come up with some repairs that needed to be done, but it didn't discourage the buyer and he came back with another offer that if her Husband would drop the price a little farther then the buyer would take the deal. Lorrie encouraged her Husband to do it, because it would allow them to be able to work with the Bank on the rest of it and save the house in Bromley. Lorrie's Husband didn't want to go talk to the Bank about it, so Lorrie put together a plan that she could discuss with the Bank and she went in his stead. He used the excuse that he had to stay and work at the laundry. Lorrie met with the Bankers and brought all the paper work on the sale of the laundry and her plan for them to release the laundry to the new owner and then for them to keep the note on the Bromley house and the income that her Husband would make doing his full time Tailoring work would be able to make payments on the house note. The Bankers agreed to the transaction and the laundry was sold and her Husband then contacted his old friends in the garment business and started to receive Tailoring work on a steady basis every week and their income increased with each week, because her Husband had the reputation of being a very good Tailor. They were able to get his son moved into his own room in the Bromley house and finally they were able to start living as a family. Now Lorrie could finally get a handle on what was going on with the family finances and she could actually make a budget. She knew that she was going to have to put her Husband on a strict budget that he wasn't going to like, mainly because he wanted to buy so much beer, that they couldn't afford right now, but she could promise him to increase his beer allowance as his income from his Tailoring increased, this would give him incentive to take in more work. She thought that it was very much like dealing with children telling them that if they cleaned their room that they could have more ice cream. Lorrie thought to herself that it looked like they were going to survive 1984 and be in a much better position in 1985 which was almost there. Lorrie was thirty-nine now and it had been twenty years since she had left home and twenty-two years since she and Gus had been on the beach kissing in Corpus Christi. Lorrie bit her lip to choke back the tears of the disappointment that she still carried when ever she still thought of Gus not coming back for her at sixteen. She wanted to marry Gus and not this man she had married.

Gus—1984 The end of 1984 had good and bad for Gus. The soybean prices stayed up, so he made good money on them, but cattle, rice and milo maize prices were still lagging and interest rates were still outrageous. Also his Mom's health was getting worse. When Gus made out his Budget for his 1985 crop year and presented it to the Bank he knew that they would require him to put up more land for collateral to back up his loan. Gus and his Wife were still very much at odds and the deep divide between them seemed to be growing. Gus was starting to get to the point to where he really didn't give a damn. Gus had one main objective now and that was to try to hold on and try to save as much of his land as he could and hope he could figure a way to make enough money to do this. He decided that there was only two ways to be able to stop the bleeding that was going on in his operations and that was a big oil deal or a vast improvement in the prices of his agricultural products. If this didn't happen then he would have to start selling land to pay back loans and to cut off this high interest. Gus was having a hard time believing that this recession had lasted for so long and it wasn't over yet. He had already seen many big, good farmers whipped completely out and it was scarey out there. Banks and oil companies were also still going broke and laying off their workers. 1985 came in with nothing new to give any help to Gus with his business. It looked like he had just barely made enough money the previous year to hang on in 1985. A call from an Independent Oil Man in Houston gave Gus sudden hope for a good oil lease, but in talking with him Gus found out that he only wanted to lease forty acres. Gus tried to get him to lease at least one hundred sixty acres, but the oil man told him that he was very small and he only had the money for the forty acres, so had to do the deal for that. It was disappointing, but it was a little more money to add to his Budget. Gus's crops were getting off to a good start and that made him feel a little better, but he well knew that they had a long way to go. An Oil Company had been exploring an area between El Campo and the small community of Pierce and had discovered vase reserves of natural gas and petroleum liquids in a formation known as the Yegua Sand. Gus finally learned the name of the geologist and the Oil Company and he called the Geologist and talked to him and got his interest in the land Gus owned and also the surrounding farms. Gus made an appointment with him in Houston and showed the Geologist his maps and gave him some information and the Geologist told Gus that he would look into the geology of that area to see if it had potential. The crop year went along as usual for Gus and he could see that there wasn't going to be any big changes for the better in the agriculture business. He hadn't heard anything from that geologist, so Gus thought that he wasn't interested. Also the Independent Oil Man that had leased the forty acres hadn't done anything with it except put out a stake with ribbons on it and then nothing happened after that. It just seemed to Gus that no matter how hard he tried to make a good oil deal that he just couldn't make it happen and he knew that as time went on that his time was running out to save his land. Gus's crop yields were just average and so were the prices and this put Gus in the holding pattern he had been in for a long time. 1986 was looming in the near future, so what would it bring with it?

Lorrie—1985 found Lorrie getting many things finally organized in the Bromley house and with her new Husband. She had everything on a Budget and she was relentless in her strictness of keeping the Budget. She knew that their survival in that house was dependent on watching every penny that her Husband earned. Something else was troubling Lorrie and it was what was happening with her involvement in helping to raise her Husbands son. She had an agreement with her Husband on this subject before they were married and now it seemed as though her Husband was undermining her authority with the boy. If the boy didn't like some decision that Lorrie made on his behalf he would run to his Dad and complain and his Dad would overturn Lorrie's decision to the boys favor. This would happen almost daily and it was very disturbing to Lorrie and it was detrimental to the boy, because Lorrie was trying to solve the problem of the boy being spoiled by her Husband and also by the boy's Dad's parents. Sometime Lorrie's Husband would even sneak around to try and hide what he was doing when he was going against Lorrie's decisions. The boy finally understood that his Dad would do this all the time and he would tell Lorrie that she wasn't his Mother, so he didn't have to mind her. The boy had been terribly spoiled by his Grandparents when he and his Dad were living with them. Lorrie's Husbands sister told Lorrie that her Husband had been spoiled by his parents, so they were doing the same thing to their Grandson and her Husband couldn't see it, because he had been spoiled in the same way, so he thought it OK. Lorrie's Husband was starting to pick up more tailoring work that earned a better profit for them and Lorrie would let him buy a little more beer when that happened, so when he wasn't busy he would be on the phone contacting his old friends in the garment business trying to line up more work. Lorrie's plan to keep her Husband working was bearing fruit and because Lorrie was keeping tight strings on their finances they were keeping up with the house payments. Lorrie still had the problem of her Husband's son rebelling against her. She knew that the root of the problem wasn't the boy, but his Dad, her Husband, because he absolutely wouldn't back her up and they were arguing more and more about it. Lorrie knew that she couldn't just give up and let the boy rule the home. She had lost control of her own son and now she had a second chance with her Husbands young son to be able to guide him and be a good Mother to him and she was so looking forward to this responsibility of parenthood, if only she could somehow get her Husband to be responsible and become a part of the parenting, in partnership with her, with the same goals in mind for his son and her stepson. The boy was eight years old now and had been spoiled his entire life, so Lorrie knew that things wouldn't be turned around over night, but she knew that it could be done in time with the help from her Husband. Lorrie had her hands full and she knew it. The whole time she had dated her Husband she never suspected any of the troubles that she was having to deal with now, if she had she would have never married him. Lorrie started to resent what she considered to be an intolerable situation. She found out accidentally that her husband wasn't giving her all the money that he was getting paid on some of his tailor work. He would deliver a coat he had finished and sometime he would get paid cash. He would then give Lorrie two-thirds of it and he would spend the other one-third on beer and hide it in the little shop in the back of the house where he worked. She didn't really give a damn if he drank the beer, but she needed to know about the money, because they were just barely making it and she wanted to put some money back for emergency's if she could. Lorrie decided that she needed to have a good talk with her husband to get everything out in the open and she had to do it before he started drinking every afternoon. One day at lunch Lorrie told her Husband that after their lunch she wanted to discuss something with him and he looked at her like he had been caught at something. Because of the funny look on his face Lorrie was wondering what else she didn't know. She told him that she was over loaded and that she needed some help and support from him. Lorrie began to wonder if all men had major faults in their character that they didn't show you till you married them. All of the men she had been involved with so far in her life had these faults, well all but Gus. She hadn't known Gus all that good, but her inner soul told her, from when she had only been a young girl, that Gus was the one man on earth that she was really compatible with and she could be happy with and that all other men would be simply substitutes that she would fill in her life with. Lorrie thought, oh Gus why didn't you come back for me!! Lorrie thought that if her Husband could keep expanding his contacts in the Tailoring business then he would be able to pick up more work from different garment shops. She had him go to London and visit shops that he had never done business with before and take a sample of his work for them to look at and it was paying off with some new orders. Her Husband did do some excellent work and the word was beginning to get around to the places that mattered. Things were starting to look up for them financially a little and Lorrie thought that maybe they could make it to 1986 without loosing the Bromley house. Between the financial stress of trying to keep her Husband working and having to deal with her vary spoiled Stepson Lorrie was having second thoughts about her marriage. She contacted the Navy to explore the possibility of re-enlisting, but she found out that she was too old now. If she had stayed in the Navy it wouldn't have made any difference about her age, but since she had been discharged, that made the difference. Lorrie hadn't been even married quite a year yet and she decided that she had made a huge mistake, but what could she do about it.

She felt trapped since she was in a foreign country with no family around and really no good friends to lean on. She couldn't call her parents in Texas, because her Dad told her not to marry a foreign citizen and she hadn't listened to him, so now she was in a real fix. She decided that she would have to stick it out with this marriage and do her best to try to adapt herself to this stressful situation and maybe in time things would get better. Lorrie loved the Christmas season and she loved to decorate for it. She knew that she didn't have much money to buy decorations with, but she could get a few and she would choose them carefully. Her Husband hated Christmas and tried to discourage her in every way that he could to destroy her Christmas spirit, but Lorrie was determined to pay no attention to him. Lorrie made him go with her to buy a Christmas tree and as she and her Stepson decorated it, her Husband proceeded to get drunk and make fun of them for believing in a religious myth of Jesus birth. They ignored him and Lorrie had Christmas music playing as they decorated the tree and put up what simple Christmas decorations that Lorrie was able to buy. She went Christmas shopping and loved all the Christmas displays that the Shoppes in London put in their windows. Her train ride back to Bromley was pleasant with Christmas Carolers singing on the train. She had bought her Husband a special gift and she had bought her Stepson two gifts she knew that he wanted and along with what money she had saved for their Christmas dinner and treats was all that she could spend. A few of the Garment Shops that had hired her Husband to do tailoring sent them some wine, brandy and different types of cheeses which Lorrie was very grateful for, because she didn't have enough money to buy all that much booze and if they would have any guests come by then Lorrie could offer them some Christmas cheer. Lorrie loved to get gifts as well as give them and she knew that her Husband had rat-holed some money of his own, so she made several attempts of giving hints to her husband about some small things that she would like to have. She didn't know if he got the hints or not, but she was excited to see what he would get her for their first Christmas together. The closer it got to Christmas the more excited Lorrie got. She would hide the gifts that she had purchased for her Husband and her Stepson and when they weren't around she would carefully wrap them and then hide them again until a few days before Christmas, then she would put them under the Christmas tree. She noticed that they hadn't put any gifts under the tree either, so they were playing the same game that she was playing. Two days before Christmas two gift's appeared under their tree and they were from her

Stepson, one to her and one to his Dad. Lorrie could tell that the gifts were something that he had made himself in school. She decided that it was time to put the ones that she had bought and wrapped under the Christmas tree, so she slipped out of bed very early the next morning and placed the gifts to her Husband and her Stepson under the Christmas tree and she just knew that her Husband would then put the ones he had purchased for her there. Christmas Eve came and still no present to her was under the tree, so she knew that her Husband was really going to surprise her on Christmas morning. On Christmas morning Lorrie waited a little longer then usual to go down, so her Husband would have time to put her gifts under the Christmas tree. She put on her robe and went down to the kitchen and put on some water to boil for tea and she could hear her Stepson around the tree and he was calling for her to come in there so he could open his gifts, so she went in and first put on some Christmas music to play while they opened their gifts. When she went over to sit on the couch by her Husband she noticed that under the tree there was only the same gifts there that were there the night before and she was a little disappointed, but knew that her Husband must be hiding her gift till the last minute. She went in to the kitchen and poured them some tea and returned with the tea and some sweet rolls on a tray for them to enjoy and then she started passing out the gifts for her Husband and her Stepson. When they had opened them and given her hugs of appreciation and still no gift for her had materialized, it suddenly dawned on Lorrie that the only gift that she had been given was the one that her Stepson had made in school and she kissed him and thanked him for it, then she made an excuse and went up stairs to their bedroom and buried her head in her pillow and cried her eyes out. She had never been so humiliated at Christmas before in her life. Even her first husband had never forgotten her at Christmas and now her Husband acted like nothing was wrong. Lorrie just couldn't believe she had so misjudged the kind of man that he was. She knew that she was going to have to talk to him about this and find out what had happened and why he hadn't gotten her anything. She would wait for a few days though and let herself calm down so she wouldn't come to pieces when she was talking to him. She just had to find out what was going on with him. Later in the morning her Husband brought out more beer that he had hidden in his work shop and he started drinking one beer after the other and Lorrie could see that he was going to be very drunk and they were supposed to have some of his friends stop by and she didn't want to be embarrassed by his behavior, but what could she do. She was afraid to talk to him now and make him mad. Sure enough some of his friends and associates started coming by their house to visit for a while on Christmas afternoon and her Husband was already very drunk and crude in his language. Lorrie tried to quietly tell him to be careful of his language, but he only made fun of her in front of their guests. When the evening was over her Husband lay sleeping on the couch and Lorrie went to bed, very glad that he wasn't in bed bothering her for sex. Lorrie decided that a few days later was the time to talk to her Husband and ask him why he didn't get her a Christmas present. She confronted him with it and he told her that he didn't like shopping and wouldn't even begin to know what she would want. She told him that she had given him several ideas when they were talking before Christmas, so why didn't he choose one of them and he told her that he just didn't like shopping and to stop bitching at him, then he went to the ice box and got himself a beer. Lorrie saw that it was no use to continue this conversation, because he was getting aggravated and he was drinking again. Lorrie's thoughts now drifted to a few days ahead when it would be New Years 1986 and she was a little bit afraid of what might happen if her Husband got too drunk. They were invited to a New Years dinner and dance payed for by the wealthy owner of one of the well known Garment Shops in London. Lorrie was excited about going, because she had always loved to dance and also she would be able to meet some new people in the Garment Business. This was the first real social event that her and her Husband would be together at since they got married and she was really looking forward to it, because up till this time everything had been stressful with getting settled in the Bromley house and dealing with the Bank and trying to get her Husband more work and trying to deal with her Stepson. This New Years party would be the first really good social event that she would be able to enjoy and she was looking forward to attending it. It occurred to Lorrie that she somehow needed to hint to her Husband that he needed to try and pace himself on his drinking while they were there. She had been with him many times when he got very drunk and she didn't think much about it at the time, because they were partying, but now she could see that it looked like he might have a drinking problem and she didn't want him to get too drunk at the New Years party because of the bad impression it might leave with people that might want to send him work. Lorrie would just have to think on how to approach her Husband with this, because it seemed as though he could take things the wrong way real easy and she certainly didn't want to provoke a fight. The day before the New Years party Lorrie decided to approach her Husband with the subject of his drinking too much at the party. They were eating dinner at home and Lorrie eased into it by asking her Husband about the people that might be in attendance and what to expect. He told her that he had never been invited to one before, but that he had done business with the man that was throwing the party when he had been in doing tailoring before he had bought the laundry and he would know some of the other people there that were in the business, but there would also be people there that he didn't know, because he had been out of the tailoring business for several years. This was Lorrie's chance to bring up his drinking, so she told her Husband that it might be a good idea if he would pace himself on his drinking, so he would be able to meet and convince some new Garment Shop Owners to bring him business. He stopped eating and just looked at her for a minute and Lorrie thought that she had made a mistake, but then he grinned and told her that he might do just that. Lorrie was relieved that he took it so good. The evening of the New Years party Lorrie had made ready everything that she was going to wear. She didn't have a nice evening gown, so she had borrowed one from her Husbands sister and she had bought shoes and a small hand bag to match it. In the jewelry that she had before they married she found ear rings and a necklace that would go nice with the gown and she also found a nice neck scarf that would finish out her attire. Her Husband had arranged for a friend of his that owned a small Garment Shop to pick them up and they would go together to the party. Just before his friend picked them up Lorrie told her husband how handsome he looked and she noticed that he didn't make any comment on her appearance. She hoped that he was pleased with her, because she didn't want him to be ashamed to be at the party with her. She thought that it would have been nice if he had said something nice to her, but she didn't want to start the evening out on the wrong foot by mentioning it to him, so she just let it go. They got to the Hotel in London that the party was at and Lorrie was impressed by all the nice decorations and the way that the tables were arranged with white table cloths and napkins and candles. There were waiters with black pants and white jackets walking around with trays of different types of drinks and finger snacks and a live band playing soft music, so people could talk without a problem. This was the meet and greet part of the evening and Lorrie was nervous, but at the same time excited to be a part of this lovely evening. There were quite a few people that came by their table to talk to her husband and Lorrie was glad to be able to meet people that she hadn't known before. Lorrie noticed that her husband was doing real good pacing himself on his drinking, but that he was drinking whiskey instead of his normal beer and that worried her some. Finally their Host got to the microphone and welcomed them all to his party and announced that the dinner was served in a nice buffet that they could choose from and that after the dinner then the dancing would start. Lorrie made sure that her Husband ate a nice amount for dinner to help balance out for the whiskey. The music started and they danced several times. Everything was going as Lorrie had hoped. One of her Husbands friends asked her to dance and her Husband told her to dance with anyone that she wanted to dance with, so Lorrie whorled around the dance floor with several partners and it seemed that she was in demand, because she didn't sit out very many songs. What Lorrie didn't realize was that her Husband was taking advantage of her being away from the table and he was drinking a lot more then she knew. After one dance when she returned to the table she realized that her Husband was getting pretty tipsy and she suggested to him that maybe he should slow down on the whiskey and go to beer. He looked at her and then got up and wobbled off to the bar and sat there. Lorrie stayed at their table with some of the other guests that she had met and danced a few more times until the friend of her husbands that they came with, told her that he had taken her Husband out to his car to sleep it off, that her Husband had passed out in the bathroom. Lorrie was so embarrassed and this is how the New Year of 1986 started for her.

Gus—1986 New Year 1986 found Gus and his wife at a party and dance sponsored by one of the Rice Seed Companies that Gus did business with. They were late to this as usual and Gus was aggravated, because his wife could never get anywhere on time unless it was to her bowling team. No matter how much time she had to get ready for something she was always late. Gus was the kind of person that wanted to be prompt and he hated to have to go with his wife anywhere, because of her habit of being late. He sometime thought that she did it just to make him mad. Anyway this started out the night on an unhappy note. His wife was a pretty woman and she liked to flirt with all the men at all the functions that they went to together, and Gus was to the point that he didn't care what she did. He was tired of arguing with her and putting up with her neglect as a housewife and her disinterest in the stress he was having trying to keep his business together in the crazy business climate of the 1980's. The party was a good one and they danced to a few songs and then went their separate ways to talk to other people. Gus enjoyed himself talking to other farmers and found out that they were also having a hard time with financing and were looking for ways to bring some relief to their struggling operations. Every now and then some wife would come up and talk to her husband for a minute and Gus would speak to her about her family and compliment her on her looks and tease her husband about how lucky he was to have such a pretty wife, then Gus would walk over to another group and talk to them for a while. There were all sorts of people at this party which was the usual thing when one of these big parties was given. There were farmers, bankers, local town officials and business owners that were connected with the agriculture producers in the area. Some of these people you didn't see very often and it was nice to be able to visit with them again. One of the local machinery companies owners had brought his secretary as a guest and she asked Gus to dance with her and Gus danced two times with her and she did flirt with him very hard in a way that couldn't be mistaken for anything else then an invitation to have sex. When Gus dismissed her and went back to talk to the men they told him that he had better watch out for her that she looked like she was after him. Gus just laughed it off and the night ended with a lot of goodby's and good luck in the New Year. Immediately when he and his wife got into the car to drive home his wife started questioning him on who the girl was that he was dancing with and that he should have never have danced with such a bitch. This put Gus on the defensive and his wife liked nothing better then to get him on the defensive, so she could drill him even on subjects that didn't connect with the original subject that she started with. This way the argument could last for hours on end. Well this totally destroyed any good feelings that the nice party had produced and they went to bed in a sour mood. Gus thought well hell Happy New Year here we go again. The next several days were very cold and miserable and Gus was out feeding his cattle to help them through the bad weather. His thoughts were far away from the New Years party argument he and his wife had, because there were so many of those that he forgot them quickly as just another day of marriage with her. He had many more problems to think about then some trivial stuff that she wanted to argue about. The New Year of 1986 brought the same problems he had been dealing with for several years, except that now he was in some serious problems with the value of his assets. He had been depending on them for some time as a way to keep borrowing money to buy time to see if things would turn around and he could make enough money to pay back the Banks and get the Leans released on his land. Gus just kept getting deeper and deeper in debt and the value of his assets were falling which reduced his borrowing power. Also his Mom's health had been slowly getting worse and that was another worry. One night when he had just come home from work he got a call from her care taker and he was told that his Mom had died. This was January 9th and it meant that his Mom had died on his Dad's birthday. Gus was getting pretty good and efficient at putting together funerals, because this would be the third one that he had to do. First it was his Dad's, then his fifteen year old Son's and now his Mom's. A few days after the funeral his Mom's lawyer called his sister, her husband and their children in for a conference on his Mom's will. The lawyer told them that they would receive his Mom's house and her share of the cattle that she owned and any money that was in her bank account, but that Gus would be her Executor and that he would put the money in her account and any money from her cattle in an account that would draw interest till the youngest child was 18 years old before it was to be distributed evenly between them. Gus was glad that he had already bought the land from her years before, because he knew that he would have had trouble from his sister and her greedy husband. There wasn't anything that they could do now but live in the house and wait for several years till their youngest daughter turned 18. A couple of days after this Gus went out to the Grave Yard to talk to his family and now there was the new grave of his Mom's there. Gus would do this every-once-in-a-while just to be able to vent his frustrations and to think and he could say things to them now that they would have not liked to hear when they were alive, in short he could be perfectly honest with them like he would have liked to be when they were alive. His parents had been from the old school and some things just weren't talked about between parents and their children and his son had died at to early of an age for Gus to be completely honest and up front about what life might hold for him, so now there weren't any taboo's to overcome. The Grave Yard was the only place that Gus had anyone close to him that he could be completely honest with. The Grave Yard was Gus's only conference room where he could discuss the most private and the most worrying problems with people that were the closest to him that he could trust. If anyone had come up when Gus was doing this they would have thought that he had lost his mind. When Gus had finished his talk with his dead family he got into his truck and started the motor and immediately the radio started playing the song "In The Still Of The Night" by the Five Satins and Gus just sat there and listened to it and his mind went back so many years now, to he and Lorrie on the beach in Corpus Christi and those wonderful kisses that she gave him and he wondered if his life would have been better if he had gone back to her. It was too late for that now he thought, because he was now going to be 44 years old and Lorrie would be going on 41 years old and he hadn't heard a thing about her in 21 years. He just hoped that she was happier then he was. Gus drove away from the Grave Yard feeling a little better as was usually the case, but now he still had to go face the everyday problems with his marriage and his business and try to find solutions to those problems. Gus had his farming fields in good shape for the 1986 crop year planting season and it went about as good as he could have expected. When he had finished planting and was getting organized to start the spring round-up and working of his cattle herd he got an unexpected call from the Oil Company in Houston that the geologist he had met with months before worked for and they told him that they were interested in making a three year oil Lease with him on a large portion of his land. Actually it would cover all of the land at his Head Quarters which was seven hundred forty-one acres. The price Gus negotiated with them was a good one for the time and he knew that the money generated from this Lease would give his farming operation a new lease on life for a while. Also just think if they drilled a good producing well, what that would mean to him, well it could actually produce enough income to pay off all of his debts and leave his land free and clear once again. He had seen things like this happen to others before, not often that was for sure, but it wasn't impossible. It seemed like he was saved again and it wouldn't have happened it he hadn't done the research and looked up that Geologist and had that meeting with him. Gus had thought that his trouble in doing that had been wasted, but this proves that when you do things that others wouldn't think of that they can produce good results. This just lifted a huge weight off of Gus's shoulders, but Gus knew that the fight wasn't over that this Lease was only a temporary fix to a much larger problem of not having enough cash flow to handle his debt. Something else much more lasting would have to happen to be able to pull him out of the financial mess that he was in. As the farming year progressed the Bank's financing Gus's business operations noticed that he wasn't borrowing as much of the money that he had set up in his loans for that year and they questioned him as to what was going on in his business that he didn't need the money. Gus just told them that he was doing some of the financing out of other sources of income he had arranged and he didn't tell them what they were. The oil Lease Gus had made was a three year Lease and the big money had been the Bonus for the first year, but then there would be much smaller payments for the next two years, but Gus hoped that the Oil Company would drill sooner then later. This was usually not the case though. In Gus's experience the Oil Companies usually waited till the last year on the Lease to drill, if they did it at all and many times they never even drilled the leased property. During this first year on the Lease the Oil Company came in in the fall of 1986 after the crops had been harvested and did a seismic cross grid across his land and that was a good sign that they were getting serious. They had also Leased land from some of Gus's neighbors and the seismic grid covered their land too. Gus's crops in 1986 were average and the prices hadn't improved very much, but because of the oil Lease money Gus was able to pay down his loans some and pay up all the interest to date. This made his borrowing situation look a lot better for the next year of 1987 and if the Oil Company paid their rental for 1987 it would help a lot. Gus's old friend that owned the Bar called him and asked him why he hadn't been to see him for some time and that he hoped that Gus wasn't mad at him for some reason. Gus told him that he wasn't mad about anything that he had simply been too busy to do anything except work and try to keep everything going as smoothly as possible. Gus promised him that he would come in and have a few drinks with him and catch up with what was going on real soon and that it sounded like it would be a good way to let off a little steam and relax. Gus had really been too busy to even think about any recreation and enjoyment for himself, but now it hit him as a very good idea and he intended to do it as soon as possible. This would be a good time of year to go to his friends Bar, because it was real close to the holiday season of Thanksgiving and Christmas and maybe some people would be back in town for them that he hadn't seen for a long time and maybe even some friends that he had graduated from High School with. This all sounded real good to Gus and all of a sudden he couldn't wait to get things organized so he could go and visit. After a couple of weeks Gus finally was able to make the time to go to his friends Bar and it happened to be during the Thanksgiving holidays. Gus walked into the Bar and immediately his friend spotted him and came up and gave him a big hug and handshake. He told Gus that there was a long table in the next room that had several of Gus's old friends there and that they had been asking about him and his friend bought Gus a drink on the house and led him to the table and the whole table erupted in hoops and hollers to welcome Gus to their friendly gathering. Everyone wanted to know how things were going with him and they were telling him their own stories. Some of these people he hadn't talked to for fifteen years, so there was a lot of catching up to do. Also there were a number of people that were at the table that he had never met before and he was introduced to them. Two of these were women that came with one of Gus's friends that he hadn't seen since High School. One of them was his friends girlfriend and the other was her friend and they were from Houston, Texas. Gus found out that his friends girlfriend worked for Southwest Airlines as a Flight Attendant and she was absolutely beautiful, and her friend worked for a Mortgage Company in Houston and she wasn't very pretty, but she was, lets say a little on the plain side, but very interesting to talk to, because she worked in the Mortgage Companies Comptroller's Office and knew the details of how brutal the economy had been on the Banking business and the toll it had taken on the value of Real Assets like land, housing and the lack of investment Capital for investment in the Oil and Gas Business and the development of raw land. They were having a hard time hearing each other, because of the noise and they were sitting across the table from each other, so the girl changed seats with one of Gus's friends and she sat next to him so they could talk better. This conversation was right up Gus's alley, so to speak, because he had been dealing with all the problems that she knew about, for years and it had effected him, he found out from her, the same as it was effecting the business people in the big cities. This girl was a breath of fresh air to talk to, because he had never talked to a woman that had the business knowledge in finance that she had. She instantly became more attractive to him. It was the beauty of her mind and not her outward appearance that attracted Gus to her. They pretty much zeroed in on each other and she seemed interested in Gus's business history and the problems that he had been facing for years and the difficulty of trying to figure out solutions to those problems. She was telling Gus stories of situations she was involved in working for the Mortgage Company and they resembled what had been going on with the country people in agriculture. She said that her company had file cabinets with drawers full of keys that belonged to Motels, Hotels, Retail Business Malls and Housing Developments that nobody wanted any more, because the owners couldn't pay the payments and there wasn't any money to loan for anyone to buy them. She said that the owners would come into the Mortgage Company with a huge ring of keys and lay them on their desk and tell them that they had run out of money, so the owner was basically saying we are turning this property back to you, so you pay the taxes and upkeep on it, because I can't do it anymore. She said that the Mortgage Company would push the keys back toward the owner and he would push them back and then he would jest get up and leave. She told Gus that the Mortgage Company had hundreds of millions of dollars of this kind of Real Property just sitting there that no-one wanted anymore and that if he had some extra cash that he could pick it up for just pennies on the dollar no questions asked and that the owner of the Mortgage Company would take Gus to his private club and wine and dine him because he would be so glad to get the stuff off of his books. Gus told her that cash was his problem also and that he had been strapped for cash for a lot of years now and didn't know what was going to happen with his business that each year it was touch and go to see if he could last another year. She told Gus that she could understand that very well that he wasn't the only one, that several million business people were in the same fix. She said that the U.S. Government was calling it a recession, but everyone in the Banking business and the individual business owners knew that it was actually a depression that was as serious as the one in the 1930's. The evening was extremely enjoyable for Gus. He and this business woman danced a couple of times and she followed him pretty good. They drank the same drink which was whiskey and water and their conversation just flowed without any hesitations or misunderstandings, in short, they were talking the same language with the same intellectual understanding. Gus had never before talked to a woman that could relate to him on that level of business knowledge and she interested him very much. Certainly his wife couldn't even begin to hold a light to her on the subjects they were talking about and not only that she wouldn't even have the slightest interest in them. Needless to say that Gus stayed at his friends Bar until it closed down and when he said goodby to the Business women she kissed him passionately and gave him her card with all her contact information and told him to please contact her that she would love to continue their relationship on any basis that he wanted it. Gus took her card and told her that he would contact her and then he left and went home to a wife that he knew would be waiting to have a big argument with him, but right now he didn't care in the least, because he had just had the most enjoyable evening that he had in years and no matter what she did, he was determined not to let her spoil it for him. Sure enough when Gus got home his wife was waiting for him and she started in on him about where he had been and that he had been drinking and that he had stayed out so late without letting her know anything in advance. Then she asked him what he had to say for himself and Gus told her that what he had to say was that he was going to bed and that if she wanted to argue then she could look in the mirror and argue with herself and boy then she hit the fan and followed him around while he was undressing and washing up and getting into bed and Gus didn't say anything, he just closed his eyes and went to sleep while she was raving on and on. The next morning Gus got up normal time made and drank his coffee got ready and left the house, while his wife was sleeping and went to work as usual. Gus didn't know for sure if he was going to contact the Business Woman in Houston, but he knew that he would like to see her again. From talking with this Business Woman for several hours Gus found out that his whole mind and body had been yearning for some female companionship that he could relate to and relax with and not have to think about the stresses of his marriage and business. It was almost like a vacation that took his mind off of everything that had him tied in knots all of the time. The question to Gus was could he do this and not get emotionally involved and keep her from getting emotionally involved. Could they keep it on the basis that it started to be without taking it to a level of craziness, especially if there was sex involved and Gus was sure that sex would be part of the equation, because of the way that they ended the night and her last minute kiss and statement. Gus knew that in his heart that he wanted to be with her again, but that he would have to have a heart to heart talk with her before things went any farther. He would have to have an understanding with her that no matter what, their relationship couldn't and wouldn't go any farther then enjoying each other mentally and sexually. She would have to understand that no matter how his marriage was going and that included even if he got a divorce, that there would never be the idea of them being serious and romantically in love and getting married, because he was through thinking about being in love with a woman. He hadn't married his present wife out of love and he would never marry for love again. There was maybe only one woman that he could have married for love and that was Lorrie, but Gus wasn't ever sure that he knew the difference between lust and love, but he knew that if their was a such a thing as true love, that there had to be a big difference between lust and love. Everyone else he married for a reason and the Business Woman would have to understand all of this. Gus decided to call her and tell her that he wouldn't be able to see her till after the Holiday Season and the New Year of 1987 and that their first time together there were going to be some ground rules that they would have to live by. Gus called her and told her his thoughts and she agreed and she told him to call her after the first of the year 1987 and she would tell him how to get to her apartment where they would be alone and they could hash everything out to each others satisfaction. She told Gus that she was a grown, mature woman of forty-two years old and had been married twice before and that she had no allusions about what they were going to do and she only wanted to have an honest relationship with him and yes she also wanted sex to be a part of it. She told Gus that she had no desire to get romantically involved, that she had been looking for someone like him for a long time that could stimulate her mind and body and that she had gotten that feeling from their conversation at the bar that not only simulated her mind, but it had also sexually aroused her and that just talking to a man had never done that before and that she had been thinking of it ever since. She told him that he needn't worry about her being a sex maniac, because she had only been sexually involved with four men and two of them had been her husbands and that none of them had ever given her even a small orgasm. She told Gus that she hadn't been sexually involved with a man for three years and that this was a big step for her to take. They agreed to get together after New Year 1987 and they left it right there and said goodby.

Lorrie—1986 started as a disappointment for Lorrie because of the way her Husband acted at the wonderful New Years party that they had attended payed for by one of the rich owners of a large Garment House. Lorrie had a lot of mixed emotions about her marriage. It had been very stressful and disappointing for her from the start and there hadn't been very many happy times. Her Husbands hard drinking, the debt and trying to be the mother to her spoiled Stepson had taken a toll on her she knew, but at the same time she was very proud of her Husbands reputation of being one of the best Tailors in the Garment Business and he was beginning to earn a very good living for them, if she could only keep him under control on his drinking. Lorrie felt that if she could keep him working that soon they would be able to pay off the Bank Loan and the Bromley house would be free and clear. Lorrie thought that when they paid off that Bank Loan then they could start doing some of the things that they talked about. Her Husband wanted to get back into his ski vacations in Germany, because he had always enjoyed it since he was a young man and he had been an instructor at one time. He was used to ski the difficult slopes and he wanted to take her with him to the ski Lodges and teach her to ski. He also loved motorcycles and he had done the dirt bike races, but now all of that had been put on the back burner, so to speak, until their financial situation improved. He had his motorcycle in their garage but he needed to work on it, so it just would have to sit there until they had the extra money. They had also talked about getting a Volkswagen Travel Van to go camping in and Lorrie wanted to see more of Europe, so when the Bromley house was payed off they would be able to do the things that would add fun to their marriage and their relationship would be better and all this stress would go away and Lorrie was sure that her Husbands drinking would slow down when that happened. All she had to do was stick it out and things would improve. Lorrie became her Husbands secretary and with her guidance his business grew. She had a down to earth discussion with him and set down some rules that they needed to operate the business by in order for him to be able to ever expect to afford his expensive ski vacations and his motorcycle racing again, not to mention maybe loosing the Bromley house to the Bank and he seemed to be impressed enough to listen to her. Lorrie told him that number one he wasn't to drink during working hours, that after work and on the weekends he could drink if he wanted to, number two he was to be sure to give her every receipt on any money he spent, no matter how small it was, so she could keep track of all finances and expenses that could be used for tax deductions and number three he was to be relentless in using his time, when work was slow to contact Garment Houses that did business with very wealthy individuals to try to pick up some very high priced Tailoring pieces. She also told him that she was tired of him thinking that he was going to come in everyday from his little workshop out back in the evenings and drink till he was drunk and think that he was going to screw her every night and go to sleep, because she was tired and stressed from all the work she had to do every day. She told him that if he wanted sex, that was fine, but that they would have to agree on the time. She told him that if he didn't want to do these things then she was going to leave him. He agreed to this arrangement, but didn't look to happy about it. As the year of 1986 was slipping by Lorrie was surprised to see that her Husband was really trying to keep the arrangement that she had proposed to him. He did have a few slip ups, but for the most part he had done really good up to this point and she had become much more happy with their marriage. Her Stepson was ten years old now and still a real problem, because of the undermining of her authority over him by her

Husband. Her Stepson had a habit of openly disobeying her and throwing screaming tantrums until her Husband would give in to him or he would go to her Husband behind her back to get his way and it kept the whole house in a constant turmoil. If Lorrie's Husband hadn't been doing better keeping his end of the agreement that they had made she didn't know if she could have stayed with him. Her Husband was starting to do business with some very well established and expensive Garment Houses and he was picking up some pieces that he could demand a lot of money for the tailoring work, but this was not steady yet, because he wasn't their main Tailor. Lorrie predicted that he might become their main Tailor when some of the other ones decided to retire, because some of them were getting pretty old and the kind of work that they did required good eyesight and steady hands, because it required hand stitching that was perfect in every way. These Garment Houses did business with the Royal Family, Movie and Music Stars and the Leaders in Government and Foreign Dignitaries, so there was real money to be made there if you could get your foot in the door. Lorrie had three main worries in 1986 that put a lot of stress on her. First was the constant worry of making the Note payments to the Bank, so they didn't loose the Bromley house, second was trying to keep peace in the house between her, her Stepson and her Husband and third to keep her Husband from becoming belligerent toward her when he was drunk. Her Husband had a habit, when he was drinking, of thinking of something that had happened a day or two in the past and bringing it up and scream and cruse at her until she would cower down and and just try to protect herself in case he would get physically violent. These outbursts were usually brought on by something that had to do with Lorrie's Stepson. When her Husband had one of these rages he would scream and cruse so loud that their neighbors would call the Police to come and check on them and this was extremely embarrassing for Lorrie. He would even scream and cruse at the neighbors, when he was drunk, over trivial things. All of this kind of behavior was extremely hard on Lorrie. She was trying to cope with all this stress, but secretly she felt trapped. She felt that she had no one to turn to for help. During their first year of marriage Lorrie had discovered that she had made a mistake and she wanted to get a divorce, so she had made inquires to the Navy about enlisting again only to find out that she was now to old. This had not occurred to her and it really shook her to her bones. The Navy had once saved her after her first marriage ended in divorce and it had rebuilt her confidence in herself and her ability to survive in a very competitive environment. She had been counting on the Navy to give her this chance to extract herself from this marriage that she had jumped into without much thought. Now that possibility was gone. She couldn't go to her family in Texas for help, because they had cautioned her on marrying a foreigner and if she went to them now they would just gloat and tell her that they had told her so. She knew that they would help her, but she just couldn't bring herself to give them the satisfaction of knowing that they had been right. After all they had been trying to run her life all the time she had been living in El Campo, Texas and this would just prove to their satisfaction that someone needed to run her life, because it appeared that she didn't have enough sense to do it herself. She didn't have enough money to go it alone in England and she didn't have any close friends there to help her either, so Lorrie really felt trapped. Lorrie knew that her only alternative was to dig in her heals and try to survive until somehow things would improve. On the sly without her Husband knowing Lorrie started looking for a job as a way out to be able to support herself. Sometime she would momentarily think of Gus and wonder about him and get a little smile on her lips, the lips that yearned for the warmth and true love between them that had never come to pass, and the question was always why. All her life she had wondered why, but she knew that that question would always go unanswered. Now another unexpected problem popped up and that was about her husbands Father's health. It seemed to Lorrie that there would be no relief in the problems that she was going to have to deal with in this family. Her Husband's Father was a very sick old man and he had always been sweet to Lorrie. He had been the one to beg Lorrie to have patience with her Husband and her Stepson and he had tried his best to lecture her Husband on how he needed to listen to her and to respect her advice, because her Husband could never make a decision on anything. He couldn't even decide which table for them to sit at when they would go to the local Pub. Lorrie would even have to make that decision, that's how bad it was. Her Husband was good at his Tailoring profession, but he was no business man and couldn't cope with the stress of making even small decisions. Lorrie's Husband and his sister were trying to figure out what to do with their Father, because he was a widower and he could no longer live by himself, because he was very sick with heart trouble and really bad sugar diabetes. Lorrie listened to their back and forth on the subject for several days until she couldn't stand it anymore and she spoke up and told them that her and her Husband could take his Father in and make a place for him in a real small room that she had been using for an office and that she could give him his injections, because she had once been a nurse. She said that she knew how to bath him and take care of his needs and medicine as long as was needed, so that is what they did. This was just another example of how Lorrie would take control of a situation and find a solution that no one was able to solve. As time went on Lorrie had hoped for some help from her husband on this, but he left everything to her. In a way his Father living there was somewhat of a help for Lorrie, because he would intervene on her behalf when her Husband would start to be combative or when Lorrie was trying to get her Stepson to do his school lessons and he would try to throw one of his fits. Her Husband's Father would tell his Grandson that he needed to obey Lorrie and not cause trouble that she was doing things for his own good and this would help to keep peace in the family. Lorrie was glad when her Husbands Father would tell him that he was drinking to much beer and that he should use that time to help Lorrie. When her father-in-law passed away Lorrie felt that she had lost a great friend and she knew that she would really miss his support in trying to hold their family stable. 1986 had been a hard year for Lorrie and it wasn't over yet. Her Husband was earning more money now, but he was also using the excuse of his Father dying to drink more and now the old man wasn't there to help Lorrie with that. Lorrie's Husband had finally got his motorcycle fixed and he would ride it to deliver some of the work he had done until one day he had an accident on it and it had caused an old back injury from skying to cause him so much pain that he could do nothing but lay on his back. He was unable to work and yet again Lorrie had to go to the Bank and make special arrangements on their payments. Lorrie thought that they would never get the loan paid off to the Bank on the Bromley house at this rate. It seemed that there was always something that was putting their future in question. The only good thing that Lorrie could see about this development was that her Husband had to sleep in a bed by himself and that gave her the excuse to move into the spare bedroom upstairs. She was determined not to ever move back in his bedroom, because it made her to convenient for him to have sex with her and she was growing less and less interested in having sex with him, it had become more of a duty as a wife. This situation looked like it could last for the rest of the year of 1986 and Lorrie could see that they weren't going to have much of a Christmas 1986 turned out to have been a damn hard year for them and Lorrie was glad to see it go. She was desperately hoping for some kind of job in 1987 to help relieve the pressure on their finances since her Husband had been hurt and out of work for so long.

Gus—1987 At the beginning of 1987 Gus decided that he wasn't going to get in a hurry to get involved with the Business Woman that he had met in his friends Bar in 1986. He had to much to do to to be spending his time trying to development a relationship with another woman. He knew that he had no romantic designs on this woman and if they developed a relationship at all that it would be based on sexual pleasure simply for the relief of the stress that each of their lives had placed on them. Gus was hoping that the Oil Company would pay their rental on the Lease. It wasn't a lot of money, but things were still very tight and every dollar counted to let Gus make another year in business. Going year by year one year at a time was the only thing left for Gus to do to try and save his business. Gus knew that if buying time like that didn't work then selling enough land, equipment and cattle to pay off his debts to the Banks would be the next step and that would be the same as going out of business. He had been in the agriculture so long that he wondered what he could do for a living if it came to selling out and looking for a job. He had no trained skill like welding, plumbing or electrician. He decided that this was something that he would have to think about, because it could surely happen and quick. He had seen it happen to people that he knew and Gus knew that he had just been one step ahead of that several times. Gus had all of his financing lined up for his 1987 crop year, but he was always thinking ahead to the next year and how to manage it. His business was down to just him and one helper now and it seemed to Gus that his once thriving agriculture operation was just a shadow of it's former self. It was a depressing situation to behold for him. The situation at home with his Wife hadn't changed so there was no relief there and he was basically operating around her like she wasn't even there, because she had her own friends now and all she wanted to do was run to town to bowling and parties and she had no interest in what was happening with his business and he didn't even give a damn anymore. All Gus wanted was for her to leave him alone to try and solve his own problems and hoped that she wouldn't add anymore to them. Actually Gus hoped that she would get her a boyfriend and run off with him. Gus wondered why dealing with a woman in marriage was so difficult. His farm and ranch operation had been scaled down dramatically and he was able to handle it now with only one full time employee and some part time help when necessary.

Gus was getting older now and he was starting to experience some of the effects of the brutally hard, heavy work and the long hours that he had done when he first started his farming and ranching business. His body had taken a beating and he knew that his eyesight was suffering from cataracts at an early age due to the use of chemicals on his fields and he had trouble with his back. Gus was only 45 years old now and he wondered how much longer his body could stand up to all the physical abuse that farming and ranching dealt it. He had once thought that by this time in his life he could hire younger help to do the heavy work and he would be the brains, but the American economy had backfired on him and he found himself in the same place basically as when he was when he was 25 years old. His business had been loosing ground inch by inch for a long time and he was to the point that only something big like an oil well could pull him out of the hole he was in financially. Gus was into the planting season and it was progressing with it's usual ups and downs. But it was getting done. He received a card from the Business Woman, in his mail box, wondering if he had forgotten about her and for him to please call her. Gus was pleased to get the card, but he had no time to spend going to Houston to see her, but he thought that he would call her just the same. He did call her and she said that she needed to see him really bad if he still wanted her. Gus told her that he did, but that he had been too busy to be able to arrange a trip to Houston and that it would be some time before he would be able to break loose to do that. She asked him if he would be able to see her if she would drive to El Campo and rent a Motel room for the weekend. Gus told her that he would be able to do that, but that they couldn't go out anywhere, because he was to well known in town and that they would be seen together and the rumors would spread like wild fire. She said that she understood and that it would be fine with her if they spent the whole time in the room in bed. He told her that that is exactly what they would do and that he had a friend that owned a Cafe that he could get to deliver food to their room, so they wouldn't even have to go out to eat. That next weekend she drove to El Campo and Gus made arrangements to meet her at her room. When he knocked on her door and she opened it she grabbed him and pulled him in and started kissing him aggressively and unbuttoning his shirt. He told her that he hadn't even had time to say hello yet and she told him that he could say hello while he was getting his pants off, that she needed him now and very badly, so Gus obeyed and it didn't take but a moment for him to discover that this seemingly plain looking woman had a very inviting looking body and that she was in total sex mode not wanting to wait for any foreplay. She was just wanting to have immediate wild, hard riding sex. After their first sexual encounter she calmed down a bit and told Gus that she had been ready for him for months and that he had just given her her first big orgasm of her life and that she was ready for some more of that. After several hours of steady sex and finally eating the meal that was delivered Gus told her that he had to go, but that he would be back the next morning after he got things organized and she told him that she would be ready for him when ever he got there, so Gus left and went back to work with a smile on his face and a feeling of relief that he hadn't had for a long time. Gus did go back the next day and it was just as pleasing as it was the day before. He told her that as long as he was as busy as he was that he wouldn't be able to meet her in Houston. She told him that she understood and that she would drive to El Campo as much as possible and when he could get away then he could come to her apartment in Houston. She told him that no matter what else she felt that she would never press him on a deeper relationship and that if he would just give her what they were having and his time in conversation that it was all that she would need. Gus told her that he could do that and not to expect more and that he was really enjoying their sex and companionship. They had this agreement from the start and their relationship went forward on that basis without a hitch. Gus really felt lucky to have accidentally found a woman that didn't want to have anymore from him then he wanted from her. The Oil Company paid their rental for 1987 and Gus used this to pay on one of his land notes to the Bank, so it disappeared fast, but he wouldn't have to rely on proceeds from crop sales for at least this one note payment. Gus struggled through the 1987 crop year and barely secured financing for 1988. His relationship with the Business Woman went along as they had planned and she had been true to what they had agreed on. They had become very comfortable around each other and knew what to expect, so there weren't any hitches. It seemed that both of them had a need for this kind of relationship that was private and intimate and there was no need for it to go any farther. They avoided all pretense of being in love and never told each other that they loved each other only that they liked very much something about each other and that was as far as it went. 1987 slipped by with Gus hoping that the Oil Company would drill a well in their last year of their lease in 1988.

Lorrie—1987 As 1987 came in Lorrie was trying to cope with all the problems that followed her from 1986. Her Husband was trying to do some small tailoring jobs even though he hadn't completely recovered from his back injury. She was still sleeping in the spare bed-room and was now calling it her own. It had been months since her and her Husband had sex and Lorrie was thrilled about that. She knew that it wouldn't last forever, because he would eventually recover, but she was sure that she was never again going to move back into his bed-room. If he came to her she knew that she would have to give in, but she would never start it and she was always trying to think of a way to avoid the subject of sex. Lorrie was still looking for a job and she had her application at several places. After all she did have some good skills and she had one year of college. Her computer skills were very good thanks to all the Navy training she had and she was accomplished in leadership of personnel. Things were hard at the time in England and there were a lot of people out of work there, so it was hard to find a job. She found out when she called back to Texas to talk to her family that things were hard there too, with a lot of people out of work. Lorrie was going to be 42 years old this year and she was trying to figure out which way here life was going. She knew that she wasn't any spring chicken any more, but her health was reasonably good and she hadn't had any problems since that big operation when she was in the Navy. Her idea of marrying to stay in England hadn't worked out so good, because all she had done since then was to struggle to help him keep the family afloat. She cursed herself for not staying in the Navy for a 20 year retirement, but no telling where they would have stationed her. Hell she thought, maybe at least she would have been in Texas and had a chance to run into Gus, because 40 or 45 years old wouldn't have been to old to start over with someone you really loved. Her husband was improving now after several months so he could work several hours a day and they were able to start paying more on their Bank loan. He asked her when she was going to move back into his bed-room and she told him that she was all set up in her own room and she was happy there. Her Stepson was 11 years old now and since her Husband had been down flat on his back for months and couldn't drink and raise hell, they had been able to have a better relationship. It was a long way from perfect, but at least her Stepson was learning that Lorrie was trying to look out for him and he did less protesting when she asked him for some help with something or for him to clean up his room. He was still sneaking around and going to his Dad about some things, but not as bad as he had done before, which proved to Lorrie that her Husband was the heart of the problem with her stepson, but what could she do about it. She just hoped that after her Husband got back to his old self that things wouldn't spiral out of control again. Her Husband told her that he didn't want her to go to work when he finally recovered completely if he started earning money liked he had before the motorcycle accident. Lorrie told him that if she found a good job that she wasn't going to turn it down, because the way things had been she could never tell when the next disaster was going to happen and they would need the money anyway to pay off the Bank loan faster. He grumbled about it but he didn't say anymore. The months in 1987 were slipping by and her Husband was picking up more work and he was feeling good enough to slip into her room at night and bother her for sex. She didn't protest, but her heart wasn't in it and his wasn't either, because there were no kissing or sweet words involved. When he was through he would go back to his room and that would be it and Lorrie would just lay there and cry. She knew that it was her duty as his wife to provide him with sex, but she considered this almost as rape. In the mornings, when they were in the kitchen having tea and break-fast, after one of these episodes her Husband would just look at her with cold displeasure in his eyes and it would put a chill on her. He had started his drinking again, not as bad as before, but she could see that it was increasing slowly as time went on. During the whole time they had been married her Husband had never given her a gift for her birthday, for Christmas, for Valentines Day, for their anniversary or anything and she would try everything that she knew to inspire him to just get her any little thing, even a gift card to the local book store, but he did nothing. Things like that meant a lot to Lorrie, because she was and always had been an incurable romantic. She loved to give and get small gifts that would call attention to special private moments between a man and a woman and also she loved to give and get romantic greeting cards that had sayings that reflected deep thoughts of the heart that were hard to express and she would draw lines under some of the words and add her own thoughts to them. With her Husband all of this was impossible and she was the kind of woman that yearned for the kind of love that she and her mate could spoil each other with in a romantic way. To Lorrie romance was the spice of life that made life worth living and if she could ever get it somewhere she promised herself that she would run to it as fast as she could no matter what. Toward the end of 1987 Lorrie got a letter from one of the Government Libraries hiring departments that requested an interview with her after the first of the year in 1988 and for her to call them to make an appointment. Lorrie was thrilled to say the least and at a library at that. It was like a special present from God that knew that she had loved to read ever since she had been just a child and now to get the chance to work at a library, it was as the British would say "just lovely". Lorrie kept this letter and this secret to herself till this last minute, so her Husband wouldn't have time to think up something to ruin this chance. Lorrie thought that if the job payed enough money she might even be able to leave her Husband and get a divorce and that would be the answer to another prayer. Lorrie was able to cope with all her Husbands drinking during the holiday season better, because she knew that right after the first of the year 1988 she was going to have that interview with the Main Library in Bromley. It had fourteen Branches and it was huge with nine floors and she hoped that she could get a job there since it was close to where she lived. Lorrie was so excited and she would have loved to discuss it with her Husband, but she knew how he was and she felt that he would find some way to stop her from getting the job, so she kept it all to herself. She knew that she might not get the job and that was depressing to think about. She had no idea how many people would be interviewed for the job and she worried that her being an American citizen might leave her at a disadvantage over English citizens, but no matter she would have to try. This was the first job interview that she had been called for and she was praying hard for success and that God would lead her in the right direction on her answers. January 1988 couldn't get there fast enough for Lorrie. A lot was riding on this 1988 Library job interview.

Gus—1988 brought more business decisions on drastic downsizing from Gus. The business economy in the United States and the Banking system was still in a big mess. This had been going on for a lot of years now and it was something that Gus had never imagined could last so long. It had gotten to the point that Gus was ready to just sell out and do something else, but the big question was what were his options. What would he be able to do for a living after being totally involved as a owner and operator in agriculture for so many years. His mind was constantly spinning different ideas on the subject. All he knew was that there was only one thing now that could save him in the business he was in now and that was a good oil well or two. Things had gone too far in the wrong direction for his agriculture operations to pull themselves out of debt on their own. There was simply not the time left for them to do so. His Wife and family seemed to be oblivious to what was going on and they didn't show the least interest in caring. Her attitude was that it was his problem and it was up to him to solve it. Well he was thinking that one of the downsizing ideas he had was divorcing her, because she was just a liability to his way of thinking. That was just one thing on his list of ideas and he would just have to see how that was going to add up later on, but now would be a good time with all his debt to the Banks and the low value on his assets, she wouldn't have much stroke in Court on finances. The only bright side in his agriculture operations were that cattle prices had risen a lot from what they had been. He started putting out feelers that he wanted to sell his cattle. Gus knew that the best time to sell cattle was when the market was on the up-swing and it had been for a few months now. He wanted to sell to individual cattle men, so he wouldn't have to pay the commission that he would have to pay if he sold through an auction house. His idea was to sell the cattle and then lease the pasture to bring in a little more cash income. If he accomplished this it would be the first time that he would not own any cattle since 1961. Gus thought that this was a real mile stone in his life and now he wouldn't have any work for his horses any more. Gus was still farming Milo Maize and Rice on a much smaller scale then he had farmed in eighteen years. It was the final year of the Oil Lease and the Oil Company notified Gus that they were going to drill a well, but that it was going to be on his neighbors land and not his as they had previously thought. They told Gus that if they were successful that they would drill on his land next. Gus was disappointed in this, but it might give him the option to make a Royalty deal with someone else in the Oil Business. The reason that this idea made sense was that the original Oil Company, that had made the Lease, took in with them a Major Oil Company that helped to give this well the credit of being more of a sure thing and not just a long shot. The way that Gus structured his deal was that if an interested Investor would pay Gus $50,000.00 before the results were out on the well being drilled on his neighbors land then the Investor would have a 25% interest in the Royalty payments on 160 acre unit on the next well which was to be drilled on Gus's land. Gus would keep 75% interest in those payments. If that well was successful then the same deal would progress to the next 160 acres and so on till all of Gus's land had been drilled. If the neighbors well was a dry hole then all the Royalty would come back to Gus and his land, so Gus would loose nothing and it would be a hedge in case of a dry well. Gus shopped this deal around for several months and was having some interest, but no takers. The Oil Company started drilling and Gus was getting very anxious to find an Investor, because if they drilled a dry hole than Gus wouldn't get any more money and the Oil Company would pull out and everything would be over with. The Oil Company drilled to their bottom depth and they started testing the well. Gus had been keeping up with what was going on with the plans for the testing and found out that the Oil Company was to do extensive testing that would take about two weeks, so that is all the time that Gus had left to find an Investor to make a deal with. Finally Gus got a call from the President of a medium sized Oil Company and he wanted to be the Investor, so Gus made the deal with him and he wired Gus the $ 50,000,00 for the first installment on the first 160 acres. Two days later the testing was over and the well was designated as a dry hole. Gus breathed a sigh of relief that he had made, at the last minute, $ 50,000.00 that he wouldn't have made if he hadn't come up with this idea and made it happen. This $ 50,000.00 would make a big difference by giving Gus some back-up money when the time came to do what he had to do if things got tougher. Gus took this money and deposited it in an interest bearing account in an out of town Bank and kept this secret. Gus had continued to see the Business Woman on a limited basis as the year of 1988 progressed. The sex between them was fairly good, but what Gus really liked was the opportunity to discuss with her what was happening with the business and Banking situation in Texas. She was extremely astute in her knowledge of these subjects and their conversations on this could go on for hours on end. She related to Gus that the Mortgage Company that she was working for was in serious trouble, as were many at that time, and that it had begun to lay off a few people and that she predicted that it was only the beginning. She told Gus that she had already started looking for another job with something more stable, but that it was extremely difficult with all the people out there out of work. She told Gus that she was going to stay there until she was laid off or something better was offered to her. She felt quite confident, because she had some very good skills and she had been in the business for quite a few years. Gus had an idea for a new business venture that he wanted to discuss with her, but he wasn't quite ready reveal it to her yet. As the year progressed Gus was trying to gather his thoughts as how to exit the agriculture business and leave it behind. He was totally discouraged with agriculture and all the hype you would get from the agriculture supply companies and agriculture news magazines was to stick it out that it would be better the next year. They had been singing this same song for years now and guess what it might have been better for them, but not for the producers. Producers all over the United States had been dropping out now for years through taking Bankrupt options, foreclosures or even suicide because of loosing family farms that had been their family for generations. The Government had even passed a new Bankrupt law especially designed for farmers, because so many were going broke and even the Country Singer Willie Nelson got in the act by organizing concerts that would benefit farmers going broke. Gus had actually been doing a lot of things, for several years, that were designed to lead to a path of exiting agriculture if necessary, like releasing all of his leased land, reducing his farming acreage in crops and paring down his labor to a bare minimum. Now he could see that hiding cash was next step to being ready for the last decisions he would have to make when the time came pull the plug, so to speak, on the rest of his agriculture business and this had to be done in secret for two reasons, one was that the Banks that he had loans with couldn't know about it and second he felt that his marriage was so shaky that he might need cash money to finance a divorce. His Subdivisions were still making good profits and that was a good thing. Gus had no hopes left that he could pull his way out of this financial mess with agriculture and on top of that he had totally lost heart in it. Still the big question was what avenue would he finally take when he decided to get out and what would he do after that. He decided that only time would show him the way to the final resolution to this problem and that he would have to simply play his cards as the game of life unfolded itself for him, he only knew that he would need the right cards to play when that happened. Later in the year Gus got two cattlemen interested in buying his remaining cattle and he negotiated a really good deal with them, so they payed him cash for his cattle and then they would lease his pasture. Again Gus took this money and opened an interest bearing account at a different Bank in a different city. All of this cash that Gus had been banking in different places would be some of the cards that he would need to play in the final game, Gus new this to be a fact. Now what would be the next card to be played by Gus in this very serious game of life to survive or fail? Gus no longer had his cattle to take care of and his farming acreage was small now, so his harvest time was short. His Bankers had no idea that he had made an oil deal with a big cash payment and they had no idea that he had sold his cattle for cash, because they had never held a mortgage on his cattle. With his reduction in expenses he had borrowed much less money then he usually did and along with the revenue from his crop sales he fished some money out of the account with the oil money in it and he combined the two to pay down some of his debt. The Bankers never thought much of this, because they were in so much of a turmoil being under the close supervision of the Bank Regulators that any extra money they received was a welcome event. Gus succeeded in keeping his secret money hidden and he also kept his option of renewing financing for his small farming operations open. Both of these things were now part of the base plan he had for exiting agriculture completely. He knew that he had to walk carefully here and not to show his hand. Because the Banks might just decide to call his notes and then he would loose everything. Gus knew that he was going to loose more assets in land, but his objective was for him to save as many assets as he could and that would take a lot of stealth and reading the ever changing landscape if his position in connection with the Banking situation and also his personal life. It became more and more evident to Gus that he was going to have to divorce his wife. He knew that this was a decision that could have unwanted circumstances connected to it, so it would have to be handled in a delicate manner and that every detail would have to fall in place in it's proper order. He went to his Lawyer and told him of his decision and told him to go ahead and make out the divorce papers, but not to file them until Gus instructed him to do so. Gus was laying all the bricks in place as he went for a foundation to launch his final with-drawl from the life that he had lived for so long. This was an emotional and stressful time for Gus, but he knew that he wound have to muster all the strength of body and mind that he could, in order to survive it, because all the forces of finance, Banking, government and the courts could be mustered against him if he made just one misstep. Every decision from now on would have to be carefully made and thought out. No action on Gus's part could me made from emotion, it all had to be calculated and he only had a foggy idea of what might be ahead of him, but he knew that his very survival depended on every last decision that he would make. Finally in November of 1988 Gus decided that the time was right to tell his wife that he had decided to move her out of the house. She really didn't seem surprised and almost looked pleased about it. Her only response was that she wanted to take the children with her. Gus told her that he had anticipated that and that he had rented her and the children an apartment for that purpose. He then gave her receipts for paying four months in advance her rent, telephone, utilities. Then he told her to pick out all the things that she wanted out of the house and he would have them mover to the apartment for her. He told her that it was time for him to show her her where they were going to live then she would better know what she would need. He told her that he wasn't going to leave her destitute, but that she needed to start looking for a job to help out with her finances. This is what they did and Gus thought that this move might even shake up his wife enough to where she would change her ways enough so he wouldn't have to file the divorce papers. He was simply going to sit back and see what she would do before making any more moves. Gus knew that he was going to sell some more of his land to reduce his debt load, but he wanted to keep the debt where it was until he knew if he was going to finalize the divorce or not. He had been running a lot of numbers together creating a different picture each time for a different situation that might arise from an action that he would have no control over and these numbers would show him the probable outcome of that particular situation, so now Gus was starting to see how to steer his decisions in a possible direction that might be a better one for him, although none of them were very good, some were just better. The Thanksgiving Holiday came around and Gus got a call from his wife to see what he had planned for his Thanksgiving dinner and Gus told her that he had not planned anything. She told him that she had been thinking about fixing Thanksgiving dinner as a family thing just as she always had and wanted to see if he agreed with that. Gus told her that he thought that it was a great idea and that he would buy everything that they would need if she really wanted to prepare the meal and they would eat it as a family at her apartment, so it was all planned to do that. Gus was impressed with her move to do this and he thought that it was an excellent opportunity for his whole family to be together and enjoy each others company. Gus also thought that maybe she had been thinking things over and had to decided to use Thanksgiving as an opportunity to show him that she had decided to turn over a new leaf and be more of a partner in his life instead of a liability. They went to the grocery store together and bought everything that his wife thought she would need for Thanksgiving including a few decorations just to make things look more like the Thanksgiving Holidays for the children. They got along real good doing the shopping and Gus actually enjoyed it. Everything was all set and Gus had a good feeling about the whole thing. The day of Thanksgiving arrived and Gus went over to his wife's apartment early for the dinner to give her some help and also to be with the children. He helped his wife for a while in the kitchen and she told him that she had everything under control and for him to go in her living room and watch TV with the children and that when she needed him she would call him, so that is what Gus did. Gus was sitting with the children watching a show on the TV and all was fine for a while until all of a sudden his wife started yelling at him from the kitchen on some subject that had come to her mind and she continued cooking and complaining and fussing at him and he never responded to her, he just let her rant on and on until he just couldn't listen to it anymore, so he told the children that he was going to his truck to get some more cigarettes, but Gus knew that he had to get out of there before he exploded himself. He went out and got in his truck and drove back out to his house at the ranch and fixed himself a spam sandwich and a glass of milk for his Thanksgiving dinner and all was quiet, there was no fussing to listen to. His telephone rang and it was his wife telling him that Thanksgiving dinner was ready and what was he doing. He told her that he had decided to go back home and to have a spam sandwich and milk for his dinner. She was quit for a minute then she said well I have fixed all of this food what should I do with it and Gus told her that her and the children should eat and enjoy it and that they would have a lot of left overs, but he wasn't going to go back to town to eat with them. She was quiet again for a minute then she told him that she didn't understand why he was doing this and all Gus told her was that he realized she didn't understand and that he was convinced now that she never would, so they hung up and that was Thanksgiving. Gus knew right then that he would have to go through with the divorce, because she would never change. This had been the final test for her and she just couldn't restrain herself from trying to start a fight. He didn't need anymore of that kind of conflict, the last flicker of flame went out on his marriage for Gus and now there was no turning back. Time once again had shown Gus the way on his decision making. Gus bought a Christmas tree and presents for all of the children and gave his wife some money in a card, but he didn't celebrate with them, it was the time to start the realization of the painful separations at holidays that would be with them from then on. It was a sad time for Gus, but he knew that he had to make his decisions on reality and not emotions, so for him as well as his family he felt that this was the best coarse to follow. 1989 was upon Gus now and he knew that his divorce would be over in the first part of the year and after that he would proceed to doing what he had to do with that behind him. What the year 1989 would deal him he wasn't sure, but he knew what his objective was and that was to keep working toward a solution to his financial situation that would leave him enough assets to start a new life somehow.

Lorrie—1988 The New Year of 1988 had finally arrived and Lorrie had set up her interview with the Bromley Library for the second week of January and that was a good thing, because her husband had slapped her and knocked her down when he was drunk on New Years Eve and it had left a mark on her cheek that would have time to heal before the interview. She said no more to him about it hoping for it all to blow over. She had made up her mind not to tell him about the interview until one day before it happened. This would take him by surprise and he wouldn't have time to think up a lot of objections to discourage her. She knew that she didn't have his support and she was determined to go it alone. The time passed fast and the day before the interview Lorrie told her husband that she had to go to the Library for her interview. He looked at her shocked and told her that he really hadn't thought that they would chose an American for an interview for a job like that. The next morning she got ready and went to Bromley for the interview. She passed her verbal interview and went on to the computer part that she passed with flying colors. The supervisor had a conference with her and told her that she had the job if she wanted it and gave her all the required forms to fill out. They took her to lunch and then they took her on a tour of the Library and showed the sixth floor, her work station where she would be working and the smoking coffee room she would use on her breaks. They had separate coffee rooms for smokers and non-smokers. They told her to report to work on the next Monday. Lorrie was in seventh heaven and considered this to be a new and important chapter in her life. She could see that the pay wasn't going to be enough to be able to leave her husband and get a divorce, but it would give her a certain amount of independence. With this she planned to open a separate bank account for savings and to put as much of it in savings as she could each month and maybe some day she would have enough to get out on her own. The interview and the tour at the Library took most of the day and Lorrie arrived back home exhausted, but elated. She told her Husband the good news and he didn't even smile. All he had to say was how did she plan to work there and also be his secretary. Lorrie told him not to worry that she could and would handle both without a problem. Her Husband was quiet and sullen for the rest of the evening and of coarse he drank himself into a stupor and went into his own bed room and left Lorrie alone. Lorrie was 43 and going on 44 years old now and this job had given her a new lease on life. She was feeling better now then she had been in a very long time. There was so much to catch up on that had been neglected because of the shortage of money. She could now help pay off the Bank Mortgage on the Bromley house, the house it's self needed some repairs, their furniture had been worn and seriously out of date since they had moved in and maybe she could even afford to get herself a few new cloths, then also they needed to start thinking about saving money for her Stepson, who is now 12 years old, to go to the University some day and the list went on. For Lorrie this whole marriage thing had turned out to be completely different then she had thought it was going to be. As it is turning out she is the leader of the house instead of her Husband. He can't seem to ever be able to make a decision on anything. Lorrie started her job at the Library and soon became very accomplished and comfortable with her job. Lorrie's job, in the Bibliography Department, was to add books on the computer to the system, that had been bought by the Librarian. She found out that there were some advantages to her job that she hadn't dreamed of. Lorrie found out that in the Library Complex there was a theater named The Churchill and on press night the Library staff could get free tickets. This was right up Lorrie's alley, because she craved the distraction from her dismal marriage and she had always enjoyed cultural events. Lorrie was starting to enjoy a little of life again, because of this Library job. It got her away from her Husband and spoiled Stepson everyday and it provided her with an avenue to pamper her need to grasp for knowledge. Books, plays, music, and art were knowledge for Lorrie and her store house of knowledge had been depleted by being married to the man she had chosen. So far she had received nothing but problems with the marriage, but she was determined to over come that and some how be able to enjoy Europe, even in a small way, the way she had intended too. So Lorrie now had something to grasp to, to help sustain her even though her marriage seemed to be getting worse. Her Husband had recovered and he was gradually picking up more high priced garments to tailor, but it seemed like the more money he made the more discontent he was and he would take it out on Lorrie. The physical and verbal abuse was getting worse and more often. The Police were called to their home several times in 1988 and it was extremely embarrassing for Lorrie. She wouldn't file charges on her Husband though, because he had told her that if she did that he would find her and do her in and she was terribly afraid of him when he was drinking. This is the way that the rest of 1988 went and Lorrie was looking forward to her career with the Library in 1989.

Gus—1989 New Year 1989 found Gus by himself at home watching several programs on his TV and one of them was a music program that featured music and singing groups from the 1950's and 1960's. Gus was enjoying this very much, because he didn't have much time to sit and listen to music. This brought many good memories for him when he played in the band and of the times that he would have a date and go to all the country dance halls in those days. Gus could see that the bands and the artists were showing their age, but they were still damn good. He wished that he had one of those girls that he used to see at the dance halls to dance with right then. All of a sudden The Five Satins were announced and they sang "In The Still Of The Night" and the memory of Lorrie and him on the beach in Corpus Christi was vivid in his mind. Gus drank in every word of that short song and longed for those wonderful kisses that young, beautiful Lorrie had given him. His life now was a big mess and he wondered again if things would have been different if he had gone back to Lorrie and married her. Some how he always thought that they would have been or maybe he had just wished that it would have been, he wasn't sure any more. He only knew that any time he thought of Lorrie it had a special meaning for him and he couldn't account for that feeling. He had acquired a small amount of financing for the reduced acreage that he was putting under cultivation and he had his land work done for the winter. With his reduction in farming and no cattle to take care of, Gus had more time to think about what he was going to do after he liquidated enough assets to finish paying off his Bank loans. He had been thinking about an idea he had that was born out of the struggle he had to find to find quality help to take care of his Mom as her health became worse and she needed more and more help of all kinds. Gus had thought all along that if he had this kind of trouble then a lot of other people must have it also. Now Gus was actually writing down notes and doing some research trying to figure out what kind of business model he should use. He knew what kind of services that he wanted the business to provide and he was sure that it needed to be a corporation to limit his liability in case of a law suite, but exactly what kind of business model he wasn't sure of. He didn't like the idea of having to keep up with all the employee deductions and payments to the IRS. He wanted to avoid this if he could, but the question was how. He wanted to design this business as simple as possible. His all time favorite saying was simple is better and he wanted to use that idea to organize this business. Finally he settled on the idea of starting an Employment Agency that was actually a business that recruited people to do this type of work and then found placement for them with the people that need this work done. This model would eliminate his responsibility to the IRS, but it would also limit the amount he could collect from what the workers would be paid by their employers. There would have to be all sorts of forms for Gus to figure out that he would need to get the workers to sign off on so as to keep him within the legal limits of an Employment Agency, but at the same time to give him the right to collect the workers wages from their employers, so he could deduct his commission and then disperse the rest to them. Also he would need to get the workers to sign a form letting him do security checks on them to look into their background to make sure they were of good character. Then he decided that he would have to have forms that would list all the duties that the workers could provide and have a place that showed which ones that the worker had performed for their employer and this one needed to be in triplicate, so he could have one, the employer could have one and the worker could have one. Wow, there was a lot to think about and he was sure that he would come up with more as time went on. Any way this was a start. Spring came and planting season went quickly for Gus because of his reduced acreage. One afternoon Gus was going over to his wife's apartment to check on his stepdaughter, who was sick, and when he was pulling into the parking lot he noticed that his wife was in a car with an unknown man trying to pull out of the parking lot, so Gus stopped them and asked his wife how his stepdaughter was doing. He noticed that his wife seemed terribly uncomfortable and she didn't introduce him to the man driving the car. After Gus left he had to laugh at the encounter, because it was what he had been waiting for. He drove directly over to his Lawyers office and told him that now was the time for him to file the Divorce in the Court Docket to get it to a Judge, because he was certain that his wife had a boyfriend and now she would be distracted by him and would be easier to deal with on settlement terms. His Lawyer did as Gus instructed and the results proved Gus was right, because the settlement agreement went smooth without a great deal of difficulty and Gus used some of the money he had hidden in out of town Banks to pay her off and gave her two cars and settled on child support payments and his visitation rights rather easily and it was all over in about two weeks. Now one huge worry had been solved without a big squabble and there was still a nice friendly relationship with his now ex-wife. All of this was to the good and now he could concentrate on extracting himself from the grip of the Banks. Gus had been putting a lot of numbers together for a long time to reflect different outcomes according to what might happen with different situations that he didn't have the answers for at the time, but now he knew the answer to the outcome of his Divorce and this was a big one, so it really helped his planning on how proceed. It was true that he was still a long way from being free from the Banks control, but this was one big step forward to help him come to decisions on his next steps to take. He knew that these steps would have to be in order of their importance and be carefully executed in order for him to get the outcome he desired. He decided to treat himself to a trip to Houston for the weekend to see the Business Woman and just relax and enjoy her company. A weekend with her would relieve a lot of stress, at least for now. Gus took along with him his notes and ideas of this new business he was trying to organize, so he could discuss it with her and see if she had a different perspective then he did. He had held back from telling her about it for some time, but decided that now might be the right time to discuss it with her, after all she had been involved with business for many years and should have knowledge and instincts on small corporation business that Gus felt that he didn't have. He wanted a discussion on the possible pros and cons of filling this overlooked need for people and how best to do it. They had a wonderful weekend and she did come up with some interesting ideas that he would certainly use in his final organization of the business. She even came up with a possible name for the business, it being "A Care Concept". The year of 1989 was speeding by for Gus and he was spending his visiting days with his young son and also his older stepson had come back to live with him at the ranch, so he could finish school and graduate with his friends and Gus was real proud of him, because he had conducted himself wonderfully in all respects, not causing any trouble, keeping his grades up and taking care of his duties at home and he also had been elected as President of his Senior Class which was a real special thing. Harvest was coming up quick and it would be a short one for Gus, because he wasn't farming much acreage. After harvest Gus was prepared to launch another step in his quest to get out from under the Banks control. He started searching for a buyer for the last piece of property that he wanted to sell to pay off a large portion of his existing debt with the Banks. He knew that this would take some time and that he wouldn't get near what it was worth, because of the sorry state of the Banking and business sectors in Texas, but he had already allowed for that and if he got a figure anywhere near what he had used in the examples that he had put together, then he would be within range of taking control of his financial situation and the Banks would be at a disadvantage for once. Gus brought his harvest money to the Banks for payments on his loans and he added some of the hidden money to it to get his balance to line up to where he wanted it, so when he sold his land that money would give him control and if he needed additional funds he had a little hidden money left to add to that. New Years 1990 he spent with his Business Woman and she informed him that she thought that she might loose her job when the next group of employees were discharged and she said that it was surely coming, because the Mortgage Company was seriously insolvent and the next examination by the Regulators would show it and that would be it. Gus told her that if that happened and she didn't have another job by that time then she could come to live with him and she could help him set up the "A Care Concept" business and he would give her a 49% share, but that he was keeping the controlling interest. She said that it was an interesting idea and she would just have to see how things went, so that is how they left it and the year of 1990 arrived with Gus feeling a little better about his situation. He knew that he was going to have to farm a small amount in 1990 to keep the Banks guessing about what he was doing, but 1990 should be his last year in the agriculture business. If this would be the case then Gus would have been an agriculture producer for 30 years.

Lorrie—1989 started with trouble at home for Lorrie with her abusive Husband constantly tormenting her and the stress of trying to keep the peace between him and her spoiled Stepson. Lorrie was glad of two things though and they were that her Husband didn't bother her as much for sex anymore and that she had that good job at the Library. Lorrie was still sleeping in her own room and had decided a long time ago that she would never give that up. Actually she was looking for a way to discourage her husband on having sex even more and she was considering asking her Doctor to have a talk with him about it. Also she considered trying to gain a lot of weight and looking fat so she wouldn't be physically attractive to him. She had already almost stopped wearing makeup except for a little lipstick, but she was ready to do almost anything to keep from having sex with him. She had been working at the Library for a year now and just loved it and she had secretly been putting money away in an account for emergencies. The way things were at home with her marriage she never knew what could happen. Lorrie actually looked at her job at the Library as a sort of sanctuary from all the turmoil at home. She was in another world there and she loved the Churchill Theater in the complex. One day on her break she met a woman in the break room and struck up a conversation with her. They both discovered that they had a lot of interests in common and they got along very well. They both smoked, so they used the smoking break room and they decided to plan their breaks so they could take them at the same time. Lorrie's new friend worked on the seventh floor and was in the Home Library Department, where as Lorrie worked on the sixth floor in the Bibliography Department and her new friends name was Jill. Lorrie found out that her and Jill had similar marital problems and Jill had recently separated from her husband. Lorrie was very impressed with Jill and thought that she was one of the sweetest women that she had ever met. One weekend Lorrie's Husband was drinking and became extremely angry at her, because when he went into her bedroom to have sex with her he couldn't have an erection and he blamed it on her, so he started to beat her and he pushed her down the stairs and then he broke her nose and she had to go to the emergency room at the Hospital to get it set. This did it for Lorrie and she thought that if she didn't get away from him he might kill her the next time. When she went to work after the weekend everyone wanted to know what on earth had happened to her, so Lorrie told them that she had simply fallen and broken her nose, because the truth was embarrassing for her. When she had her break with Jill though she told Jill the truth. Jill told Lorrie that she had a room that was available to rent since she and her husband had separated, to help with her finances and she offered it to Lorrie. Lorrie accepted her offer and after work went home and started packing up some things to take with her. When her Husband came in from his work shop in the back and discovered what Lorrie was doing he begged her not to leave him. He said that he was so sorry for what he had done and he promised never to do it again. The way he acted Lorrie actually felt sorry for him, so she told him that she wouldn't leave this time, but that he needed to do something about his drinking and keep himself under better control or she would call the Police. He promised he would be a lot better, so they left it at that. The next day on her break she told Jill that she was not going to leave her Husband, so she wouldn't need to rent the room, that he had promised to reform his behavior. Lorrie's Husband did do a lot better with his drinking and his attitude toward her was more pleasant. This assured Lorrie that she had done the right thing by trying to leave him and it seemed to shock him into reality. Lorrie kept a keen eye on him when he came in from his work shop and started drinking his beer and she could tell that he was trying to limit how many beers he was drinking. This was nice, because they were actually being able to talk about some things that normally would throw him into a rage. Lorrie was very pleased, because she had finally found a tool that she could use that would bring her Husband to think about his behavior. Lorrie and Jill's friendship really blossomed and they started spending time together after work. They would go to the Pub or the Pizza Express and smoke and share a bottle of wine and talk over their problems. Sometime they would do shopping and then go to the Pub to share a bottle of wine and then they would go to the Theater to see the plays. Never before had Lorrie experienced the close friendship that Jill provided her. With Jill she knew that she could talk about anything personal and it wouldn't go any farther then that. On top of that they had so many common interests that it made for the perfect friendship that most people never really find. Her job at the Library and her friendship with Jill provided Lorrie with the haven she needed to escape the depressing disappointment of her marriage. The year of 1989 progressed and Lorrie and her husband had their ups and downs, but he hadn't beaten her anymore and she considered this a major victory. He was making more money in his tailoring business and they were doing well in paying off the mortgage on the Bromley house to the Bank. Lorrie was taking care of all the bills, the Bank account and financial arrangements of the house and her Husbands Tailor business and her Husband didn't seem to have an interest in any of the things that she was doing in their little office. When she would try to explain things that came up that she thought that he needed to know he would listen, but just look at her showing no understanding of what she was talking about. Lorrie finally came to the conclusion that her husband was incapable of understanding finance and the importance of being aware of even the small things that could effect a small business such as his Tailor business. Through her leadership and suggestions his business grew and he was continually receiving more and more expensive garments to tailor. Their prospects for financial stability were looking good with Lorrie having her job at the Library and her Husbands talents as a fine Tailor earning more money all the time. Lorrie felt that soon they would be able to afford some of the things that they had talked about when they first got married. Lorrie could start to see one drawback now though as things got better for them. Her husband had started slipping back into more of his old drinking habits and it was showing in his increasingly negative behavior toward her. She knew that she would have to watch him carefully and try to anticipate when he was going to explode, so she could avoid it. So 1989 was drawing to a close with an overall mixed feeling for Lorrie. They had a lot of success in 1989, but there was still the same old struggle with their dis-functional marriage. Lorrie had come to the realization that she was going to continue to keep plugging along and try to make the best of things, because she had made her own bed with her decision to marry this man, so she was going into 1990 with the attitude that at almost 45 years old she didn't have much choice but to try and make the best of it

Gus—1990 Gus had his crop land well prepared for planting in the spring of 1990. He was farming such a small amount of acreage that he could cover it quickly. He had planted 100 acres of rice on one farm, 120 acres of milo maize on another farm and 120 acres of cotton on another farm. Gus had never planted cotton before, but decided to, because the price of cotton had gone up dramatically and he had obtained an early contract for a very good price. The rice and milo maize prices weren't very good, but Gus new that he had to farm these crops to keep from raising a red flag and alerting the Banks that he might be making a major change in his farming plans. If that happened then the Banks might want to keep a closer eye on what he was doing and then they could discover his plan to put them at a disadvantage in the final negotiations of his payoff to them when the time came. It was great importance that he keep them in the dark until he had all the pieces of his plan in place to pay them off and get out from under their iron grasp. This would be the only way that he could save assets and keep the Banks from completely breaking him. Thank goodness his Subdivisions were still doing real good, because they were the only steady source if income that supplied him with living expenses and they were making him enough money, so he could also put some of it away in a safe place, for extra cash if needed. The Business woman called him and told him that she had been right about loosing her job at the Mortgage Company. She told Gus that they had just had another audit by the Federal Bank Regulators and it came out even worse then her bosses had expected, so they had decided to lay-off everyone except just a few employees that would work with the Regulators to close out the Mortgage Companies business and put the assets up for sale at a later date, so she was without a job now and didn't have any job waiting for her. She asked Gus if he still wanted her to move in with him and they could start the home care business to see how it would go. Gus told her yes and she could move in when ever she had everything taken care of in Houston. Gus was thrilled about this, because he knew that she would be a great asset in helping to get everything organized with "A Care Concept". Gus decided that it was time to step up his plan looking for a serious buyer for the last piece of farm land that he was going to sell. He knew that he couldn't advertise it in the normal way you would to attract attention to the sale of land, because it would also attract the attention of the Banks and that was something that he had to avoid. He also knew that it would probably take a lot of time to find a buyer, so now was the time to start looking while he had the time and he would also have the Business Woman there to help him with the rest of what he had going on. Gus had some business contacts in Houston, Austin and San Antonio that he could rely on to put the word out about his land for sale and maybe through them he could find a buyer with enough independent capital to buy the land in a timely manner with a simple private land sales agreement and then a cash payoff that wouldn't attract attention and Gus could deposit that cash in an out of town Bank to be used at the time of his payoff to the Banks that were holding mortgages on the rest of his assets. This would be the final piece of the puzzle that he could use at just the right time. The Business Woman did move in with Gus and when she got settled she immediately started to go over ideas about "A Care Concept" with Gus and they started to put together a business plan that would be an Employment Agency Corporation that specialized in the kind of personal care that Gus had wanted it to do. They made up all the forms that the business was going to use and the Business Woman typed them up and took them to the Printer to see if he could print them in duplicates and triplicates. While all of this was going on they got their Corporation License and then they started advertising for workers and also for clients to use the service. It wasn't long before there was response to both adds and they were signing up workers and checking their backgrounds. Then either Gus or the Business Woman would go to the prospective client with a worker that was qualified to do the service and they would make sure that the client was satisfied with the worker before a business relationship was started. Every day they were receiving more calls for the service and they were able to put more workers on the job. Some of the calls from people that wanted the service thought that the service was a free government program, but the government and insurance didn't pay for any of this type of service it was paid by the clients themselves. Even though the charges for the service was reasonable and the people wanted it and needed it, some of them wouldn't use it unless it was free and this was something that Gus couldn't understand. Gus had needed this same kind of service when he was taking care of his Mom and he just couldn't understand how someone with the responsibility of taking care of a loved one or friend could turn down the opportunity to have a service like this just because there was a small hourly charge for it. An RN Nurse called and signed up with "A Care Concept" and in just a few days she was hired by a client to check on a loved one twice a week. Gus's Business woman was impressed with the speed that the business seemed to get started and she thought that it might have the potential to grow. With her involved with the everyday running of the business it gave Gus more time to take care of his crops and to think about another business idea that he had put on the back burner of his mind and that was going to the Fort Bend County Court House and doing research on small tracts of land that he could buy that he could subdivide like he had done in Wharton County. His Wharton County subdivisions were doing very good and he thought that if he found the right tract of land to subdivide in Fort Bend County it might do good also. He knew that the land in Fort Bend County would cost more, but he could also sell it for a higher price. Fort Bend County land prices had suffered drastically during the big bust of the Banks because big Developers had paid huge prices for land that they developed into expensive housing developments and shopping centers, expecting Houston to expand in that direction and then the over priced land and developments sat empty, while the economy stagnated and they had to abandon them to Mortgage Companies and Banks that went broke. The Government had taken over these abandoned properties when they closed the Banks and Mortgage Companies and they were just sitting on them, because there was no market for them and this had depressed the land prices now for several years. This was just another idea that Gus had that he would have to take the time to research to see if it had possibilities, because he had only a small amount of money to risk and he had to be very careful how he used it. The first month of operations with "A Care Concept" were very interesting. When Gus and the Business Woman sat down to look at the income and the expenses for the month they discovered that the business was paying it's own way and this was encouraging for them. Their biggest expenses were advertising in the local News Paper and the printing of the forms that they had to use in the business. This had to be done every month and there was no way to get around it, so the only way to increase income was for the client base to expand. They had enough workers signed up, but they needed more clients to use their services. They thought that in time this would happen and the business was financing its self, so it wasn't costing them any money to run it, just their time. The Business Woman told Gus that she would work with it as long as she could, but if it didn't take off financially enough for her to start drawing money from it then she would have to start looking for another job. Gus told her that he understood and that was why he wanted several things going so that something might make some money. Gus and the Business Woman basically had a business relationship even though they enjoyed each others company sexually and there was no other ties between them other then this kind of special friendship. If the business "A Care Concept" worked they would stay together and if not then they would go their separate ways as friends. Gus went to the Wharton County Court House to talk to his friend there that was the Tax Assessor and Collector for the county to see if he would give Gus the name of the Fort Bend County County Clerk and to give Gus a letter of introduction to that County Clerk. While talking to him, his friend told Gus that he was going to retire when his term in office was up and that Gus should consider running for the office. Gus was taken by surprise by his friends statement. Gus told him that he had never thought about running for any political office of any kind and that he didn't know the first thing about running a political campaign. His friend told Gus that he should consider it, because he might be the perfect fit for the office, because Gus knew about agriculture lands, he knew about oil and gas properties and he knew about residential subdivision properties and he had been the head of a large operation that hired employees and knew how to deal with them, he had been the speaker at several public meetings, so he knew how to represent himself to the public and he had a University Degree to go along with his other qualifications. Gus had never considered himself in this light and he thanked his friend for these very nice compliments. His friend told Gus that he would be glad to give him a letter of introduction to the Fort Bend County Clerk, because he knew the Clerk personally. Gus thanked him and left his office with the letter and something new to think about. While driving back home Gus kept thinking about what his friend suggested to him about running for the office of Tax Assessor Collector Wharton County. Gus couldn't imagine how he would organize a political campaign. This he would have to think about and maybe he would come up with someone he had known that had some experience in this. Well right now he had other things to think about, so this would have to wait. That election wasn't until next year anyway, so there was plenty of time to figure out if running for that office was what he should do. Several months were going by in 1990 and Gus was taking care of his crops and he and the Business Woman were working together on "A Care Concept" and it was beginning to be a little disappointing. The business was still holding it's own, but it just wasn't making enough money for them to draw any money out of it. Each month after they dispersed the money to the workers and payed the bills there wasn't but a small amount of money left in the business account. They had tried to come up with ideas on how to increase their client list, but always hit a brick wall. The Business woman told Gus that she was going to have to start looking for another job and she would work with him on the business until she found one. Maybe it would pick up before she found one, because it was really hard to find a decent paying job in the economic climate that was persisting in Texas at that time. Gus had made a trip to the Fort Bend County Clerk's office and had a meeting there and explained what he wanted to do in Fort Bend County. The Clerk assured him that the Clerk's office would try and assist him in any way that it could locate small tracts that he might be interested in. This was a very satisfying meeting for Gus, because it opened the door for him to do research there when the time came for him to look for property there. It was the middle of summer now and Gus was starting to get ready for the harvest of his milo maize and rice crops. They looked pretty good, but the prices were poor and Gus knew that there wouldn't be a big profit in them. The cotton crop was at least another month away from harvest and it was looking real good along with a very good price on his contract, so it held the most promise for a big profit pay out. Late one evening Gus got a call from his friend in Houston that he had told a business associate of his about Gus's farm land for sale and he was very interested. Gus's friend told Gus that the man was going to call him and arrange a meeting with Gus to make a trip to El Campo to look at the land and negotiate a sales agreement if he was happy with what he saw and the price was acceptable to him, and he also told Gus that the man was prepared to pay cash when the deal was finalized. This was the kind of good news that Gus had been hoping for, because it would be the last piece of the puzzle that Gus needed to be able to have a complete plan ready to present to the Banks at the end of 1990. If this land sale went through in a timely fashion

Gus would be ready to spring his trap on the Banks to extract himself from their grip and at the same time to save some valuable assets in land, minerals, subdivisions and cash. Gus knew that he would have only one chance at this and from now on every decision and step that he took had to be in order of how he wanted his plan to play out and it had to be kept secret with only him knowing what end result he was trying to obtain from the Banks. He had to keep them in the dark until the last minute, so they wouldn't have time to figure out what he was doing to gain the upper hand in negotiations with them. If his plan worked liked he hoped it would he would he would be able to use the Banks own greed against them to gain an agreement that would keep them from completely breaking him financially. He had watched the Banks break several of his friends, so Gus had a healthy respect for what they could do. He noticed that the Banks seemed to pick out farmers and ranchers that still had some pretty good equity left in their assets and they would call their Notes to the Banks knowing that they couldn't come up with that much cash in a short amount of time. Then the Banks would sell out their assets for twenty-five cents on the dollar and use the money to make their books look better to cover for all the loans that they had that the assets wouldn't even begin to cover the original loan, much less the interest. Gus could see the writing on the wall that his loans were not far from being called by the Banks, because he still had some pretty good equity left in them. He felt that if he couldn't get in the position to make a good deal with the Banks soon that it would be too late for him to save at least a part of what he had been working for, for the last thirty years. The man from Houston called him and they made a date for their meeting in two days. Gus got all of his documents together on the land to prove that it was free and clear of any debts or attachments and he notified his Lawyer that he wanted a sales agreement ready for signing if his buyer was happy with everything. Gus's prospective buyer met him for breakfast at a cafe in El Campo and then they went on a tour of the farm land Gus wanted to sell him. This was the farm that Gus had cotton on at the time and the prospective buyer was impressed with the looks of the cotton crop and Gus showed him the contract Gus had on the crop which showed the prospective buyer that it would be possible to pay for the land with agriculture. Gus then produced all of his documents proving ownership and the absence of debt and then they started discussing the price of the farm. Gus had priced it with a healthy margin for negotiation, knowing what he would have to have for it, to be able to use the proceeds for his plan with the Banks, but it was still below what the market price should have been. It was priced to sell without the minerals, but Gus ended up giving ½ the minerals to make the deal and he ended up receiving more then enough to use the proceeds for the last piece of the puzzle for the plan with the Banks. They went to his Lawyers and signed the sales agreement and the buyer committed to paying the cash price within ten days. Gus thought that God was helping him put all of these final pieces together now just when the timing was right. The money from his crop harvests and the sale of his farm would be coming one right after the other so he could be sure of what he could do when the time came and that time was only a few weeks away now. He knew that he had to play his cards carefully and in order to get the outcome that he wanted. His other ace in the hole was a friend that worked for one of the Banks that he could get information from as to when and how desperate the Banks were for cash to make their books look better for the Bank Regulators. When Gus got that information he could schedule a meeting with the combined representatives of the Banks to put forth the final part of his plan to gain control of his financial situation and get out from under the dominating grip of the Banks. Gus finished harvesting his milo maize and then his rice crops and while he was waiting for the money from them he started harvesting his cotton crop which was turning out extremely good and the quality was better then expected, so he would receive a bonus on the original contract price. Then as expected the buyer for the farm paid the cash price and Gus signed the deed to him and Gus immediately went out of town to another Bank and opened another account and deposited all of the money from the land sale. Very soon now when he received all the money from his crops he could set up the meeting with the Bank representatives. Gus's friend at the Bank called him and told him that they got notice that the Bank Regulators would be coming in one week to make another audit and that the Bank was scrambling around trying to figure out how to present the best picture of their strength to the Regulators. Gus thanked him and when he hung up he decided that he would call the next day to schedule his meeting. Gus called the next day and talked to the President of the Bank and ask him if he could arrange a meeting with the representatives of the other two Banks in two days and that the Bank Representatives would have to have the authority to make and sign agreements that would be legal, binding and final on the Banks that they Represent. The President of the Bank wanted to know the subject of the meeting and Gus told him that it would be the settling of his accounts with cash to the Banks in return for some guarantees from them and also some guarantees from him to the Banks. The Bank President told Gus that he would call him within the hour with an answer to the meeting. Gus waited by the phone and sure enough he got the call and was told to be at the Bank at 9:00 am the following morning that all the representatives would be there ready to hear Gus's proposal for a final payoff. Gus was thrilled, but he was also afraid, because he knew that he had to do everything right in this meeting. He knew that they would try to read him and he had to appear to have every confidence and be in complete control and to lead the conversation in the direction that would catch the attention of their greed at a time when the Regulators would be breathing down their neck. Gus prepared his brief case with everything he would need to take to the meeting to complete the transactions he wanted. This included the checks from the sale of his milo maize, rice and cotton crops, a cashiers check for the land sale, an accounting of all the outstanding loans and their interest to all three of the Banks, a list of the guarantees he wanted from the Banks, and a small tape recorder. Gus had figured that if he would get from the Banks what he wanted then he would have enough cash with him to pay off all but one of the outstanding loans to them and also the interest for the year 1990 which was a much smaller amount then the outstanding loan was and here was where the hook would be bated. Gus was at the Bank at exactly 9:00 am and he was ushered into a conference room where the representatives of all three of the Banks were waiting along with an Attorney. They all greeted Gus and asked if he would like any coffee and pastry, but Gus declined and told them that if it was agreeable to them he would like to get to the business of the meeting. They agreed and the representative of the largest Bank spoke first. It seemed that he had been chosen to be the lead from the Bankers side of the meeting. He asked Gus to address his proposals on what guarantees he expected the Banks to give him in exchange for paying off his loans, which he was obligated to do by law anyway. Gus told him that he was prepared to do that, but first they needed to organize the meeting a little better to be able to document it from several sources so there could never be a misunderstanding from either side of the discussion in the future. Gus asked for a secretary to take dictation of the meeting and ask them to record the meeting. They agreed to Gus's request and then Gus brought out his own recorder and told them that he also wanted his own copy of the meeting and he also wanted a copy of the dictation that the secretary took. This is how Gus basically took charge of the meeting with out the Bankers realizing it. Gus brought out the list of guarantees that he wanted from the Banks and also all the checks that he was going to present to them. The list of guarantees from the Banks included : 1. a release of all Lien's and obligations to the Banks upon the payment balance, 2. a forgiveness of interest for the year 1990, 3. a promise not to send a notice to the IRS of the forgiveness of interest, because the IRS would classify it as income, 4. a promise not to expand the reach of the Banks into his assets that weren't named on his original loan documents, such as his subdivisions and his bank accounts. In return for these guarantees Gus would pay off his outstanding loans minus the interest for 1990 within ten days of the date of their agreement. The Bankers first looked at Gus with some frowns on their faces and then the lead representative told Gus that they had an updated summery of his obligations to them and he didn't see how Gus could come up with that amount of money in ten days to meet the time deadline that he proposed. Gus told the Bankers that if he couldn't meet the time deadline then they could always force a foreclosure on his assets immediately upon his default. The Bankers looked at each other and at the attorney and asked him if such an agreement would be possible. The attorney told them that it would if all of the parties were satisfied with it and would sign on to the agreement. They became quiet for a couple of minutes and then the lead Bank representative told the Attorney that he would be in favor of excepting this agreement and he could accept it for his Bank. He said that without this agreement that Gus might use the Bankrupt laws and that would delay a final foreclosure for more then a year. The other two Bank representatives nodded in agreement. Gus then told them that he wanted the agreement to be drawn up immediately, so all parties could review it and execute it with Notary. They all agreed to this and the document was reviewed and executed by all parties and then Gus handed over the checks that he had been covering under his legal pad for the Bankers and their Attorney to accept and compare with the summery of what Gus owed them. They came up with exactly the same conclusion that Gus had and that it still left a large Note unpaid. The lead representative asked Gus how he intended to pay off that large amount of money on that Loan in ten days. Gus told them that he was going to sell his farm machinery and that should cover the balance minus all the interest in 1990. The representative reviewed the inventory of Gus's machinery and told Gus that he didn't think that it would sell for enough money in the present economic business climate. He had a smile on his face when he said this revealing a feeling that he thought that the Banks had just put Gus's back against the wall. Gus just smiled also and told the Bankers that he thought that it would or he would have never made that agreement. They all got original signed documents of everything that had taken place in the meeting and Gus put it all in his brief case including his recorder and then he shook hands all around and exited the Bank with a smile from ear to ear, because he knew that no matter what his machinery sold for he had hidden money to make up the difference. Gus thought that in his brief case he had documents that ended one life for him and started another life for him that protected the balance of his assets and his cash for a new start. All he had to do now was sell his machinery and that would be done in one week he knew, so he would be able to beat his deadline on the balance of payments. He would have to keep all of this secret and only celebrate it by himself when he got all of the Release of Liens recorded at the Court House. A week later when Gus received the check from the sale of his machinery he saw that the Banker had been right about it not selling for enough to pay off the final balance on his loan, so Gus drew a small amount of cash on the hidden money from the Oil Deal to make up the difference and made his final payment and received his releases from the Banks and took them to be recorded. He felt like a big heavy bolder had been suddenly taken from his shoulders and a knife had been pulled from his chest. For the first time in many years he was out of debt and he intended to stay that way if possible. He had lost a fortune, but he had also saved a lot that he could use for a new start. He had saved 300 acres of land, all his mineral rights, his subdivisions, his home and vehicles, thirty thousand dollars in 1990 interest, two bank accounts with cash and also his reputation in business that he could use to his advantage when making any kind of business deal. No one that knew him could accuse him of not paying them by using a bankrupt law to dodge paying his bills. He also knew that the Banks would keep quiet about the agreement, so no one would know how Gus accomplished his payoff to the Banks. Now Gus could concentrate on "A Care Concept" and maybe he might even look into running for that Tax Assessor and Collectors position. The year 1990 had progressed to the fall season and it wouldn't be long till everyone was in the holiday spirit. This all gave Gus such of a strange feeling, because he felt so free from worry and stress that he became almost uncertain as to how he should be acting. He felt like jumping around and screaming and laughing like a school boy, but at the age of 48 he knew he needed to subdue himself. He did have a different feeling going into the holiday season this year and he wished that he had someone special he could love and share this feeling of freedom and a new beginning with, yes someone he could love, like that sweet girl Lorrie. The Holidays came and went and the home care business wasn't making anymore money then it had in the last few months. He and the Business Woman still couldn't draw any money out of it. It was disappointing and 1991 was right around the corner, so Gus would have a lot to decide on in just a few days to give his life a direction for 1991.

Lorrie—1990 Lorrie started the New Year with a positive attitude, because their financial situation was improving and her job at the Library was a salvation for her in many ways. Her friend Jill was also a major source of happiness for her that she could enjoy the cultural things that her and her husband couldn't enjoy together. Lorrie and her husband were keeping up with their bills and payments to the Bank on the Bromley house without any trouble now since she had added to their income with her Library job. She was actually starting to put some small amounts of money away in a Bank account that she had opened in her own name as a way of savings for important things that might come up in the future. They were also able to afford some better cloths for her Stepson who was now in High School and he was getting invited to some parties and outings by the kids of the more respected families. This made Lorrie feel good that they could finally afford to provide him with the things that would give him a better chance to make decent friends and a better outlook for his future. One day after Lorrie got home from work she was going through the mail and noticed a really nice envelop addressed to them from a well known Garment House that dealt with only wealthy clients. It hadn't been opened, so Lorrie opened it with curiosity wondering why they would be getting something from them. To her surprise it was an invitation to an Easter Gala Dinner and Dance sponsored by the Garment House. When her husband came in from his shop and got himself a beer she asked him about it. He told her that the Garment House had been giving this Easter Party for a number of years and that only wealthy people in the Garment and Tailoring business were invited. He said that he didn't know why they had been invited and that he didn't want to go and associate with those stuck up people. She told her Husband that they needed to go, because it was the perfect opportunity to make contacts and to tout his tailoring skills. He grumbled about it and said that they weren't wealthy and shouldn't have been invited, but Lorrie stood her ground and told her Husband that they needed to go and they would have to buy some new cloths that would be suitable for the occasion. He complained that he didn't have the money for cloths that they might not ever be wearing again and Lorrie told him that she would buy her own cloths and he could actually tailor his own suit and she would be sure to call attention to it when they were around the right people. She told her Husband that the party was still three months away so they could buy what they needed a little at a time and it wouldn't seem to cost so much money. She knew that she would have to work on him a little at a time to get him in the mood to attend, what she considered to be a great chance to socialize with important people in his profession that could boost his Tailor business. Lorrie began to plan what they would wear, because she wanted this whole event to be centered around a business promotion for her Husband instead of just a social gathering for them to attend and enjoy. She thought that if only she could get her husband to see it that way. Well she had some time to work on him, so maybe he would see the light before they went to it. Her job at the Library was going very good and also her friendship with Jill. She was discussing the invitation to the party they had received with Jill and telling her that she was going to have to buy something that would be appropriate, for the occasion to wear and that she needed to convince her Husband to Tailor himself a new suit to show off at the Gala. Jill told Lorrie that she knew the wife of her Husbands best friend that had died and that she would talk to her and see if she would convince Lorrie's Husband to go ahead and tailor himself a new suit for the Gala occasion. Lorrie thought it a good plan and thanked Jill for going to the trouble to do that. On their break at work Jill and Lorrie would look at ladies fashion catalogs trying to pick out evening gowns and accessories for Lorrie to wear to the Gala and it was so much fun. They decided that they would have to take the commuter train to London and do some shopping together. Lorrie could choose what she wanted to wear with accessories and she could put them on a lay-away program to be payed off before the Gala. This she did and it also had the advantage of staying out of sight of her Husband till the right time for him to see it. She didn't want it to set him off on a drinking and screaming rampage about spending that much money on useless cloths. Lorrie knew that her Husband was a very good Tailor and she thought that if he got the right opportunity to promote himself and his work that he could work himself up to being one of the most sought after Tailors in England and she was determined to do what she could to help him get noticed by the right Garment Houses that did business with the rich and famous, because these

Garment Houses were the ones that payed a premium to their Tailors to put out exceptional work and she knew that her Husband could do that kind of work. He had done a few small pieces of work for them in the past and these expensive Garment Houses had never complained about his work, but they had their special Tailors that they had been using for years and they even advertised these Tailors work in their pamphlets because for a Garment House to have a number of celebrated Tailor's of distinction associated with them gave them a reputation proclaiming superiority. They had been invited to a News Year Party by one of the better Garment Houses before and it didn't turn out very good, because her Husband got drunk and passed out in the rest room and his friend carried him to the car and that ended the night, so Lorrie didn't get the chance to promote his business then, but she was determined to turn this Gala Party into her own opportunity to promote her Husbands Tailor business. Lorrie was also planning a trip back to Texas to visit her family there. This was one of the things that she wanted to use some of the money that she was saving in her own Bank account for. She was shopping for the best air fare rates, which would be the most expensive part of her trip, because she had a sister that lived in Houston and her sister would pick her up at the airport and they would drive to El Campo. Once in El Campo Lorrie would stay with her Mom and Dad and she would be able to use their car to get around in, also she still had a couple of friends that still lived there that she could visit them and they could go out to eat and do some shopping together. She hoped to make the trip sometime in the summer and stay for two weeks. Lorrie had always been a planner and she was busy doing a lot of it now. For her she knew that constantly having several things to plan for helped to keep her mind busy and away from thinking about the more depressing side of her life. She felt like she always needed something new to plan for, be interested in, a distraction more or less from reality. In this way she could make her own reality and ignore the more unpleasant part. Suddenly the time had slipped by and it was the evening of the Easter Gala Dinner and Dance and Lorrie had already inspected her Husbands new suit that he had tailored for himself. Along with the suit he had also tailored a vest and a tie and she had to admit that he had done an outstanding job on all of them. She thought that he looked very handsome in them and she told him that she was going to be so proud to tell the owners of the Garment House that he had tailored everything that he was wearing. Lorrie put on her new evening attire and it consisted of a pale green silk evening gown that was off one shoulder with soft side silk medium heels for dancing and a matching green and gold small string purse. She wore small gold ear rings and a gold bracelet and necklace that she had owned for years and for a final touch she had bought herself a nice wrist corsage of spring colored flowers for a compliment to her gown and of coarse she wore Shalamar her favorite perfume. She joined her Husband in the living room to wait for his friend to pick them up and he told her that she looked nice. Looked nice is what he told her, not lovely, not beautiful, not delicious, not pretty, just nice. Lorrie smiled at him and thanked him, and thought that at least he had given her some kind of compliment, because he never did and she considered this as an improvement. She decided that maybe he had decided to make the best of this Gala and help her to promote his Tailor business. Before they left she told him that she hoped that he would pace himself on his drinking and that he would stick to beer and he told her that he had planned to do just that. Lorrie was very happy about this, but knew that things could change once that the party really got started. His friend picked them up and they went to London to one of the most fashionable Hotels and were ushered into its Banquet Room that was decorated beautifully and went to a table that had their personalized name tags ready and then through a greeting line that was made up of the Garment House Owners and their Families. After the Greeting Line they were met by waiters that looked at their name tags and took them to tables that were assigned to them with their names at their places of seating. At each place was a gift card to an expensive shop that had the value of $200.00 US, which Lorrie thought was an amazing gift. The waiters hovered around each table and announced the drink orders to subordinates who got the drinks and returned to the tables with them and the waiters made sure that the drinks went to the right person and that they were to that persons satisfaction. Lorrie had never seen anything like it and she almost started laughing out loud at what she perceived as the left over pieces of the famous British Class System. She thought, oh my, the rich here in England still see themselves back before World War 2 when England had been a dominate force in the world with all her Colonies of peoples that they dominated and expected them to look up to them. Lorrie thought in a way to put it in a British term that this was going to be a "jolly affair". A full Orchestra had been playing very softly, so as not to over power conversation and Lorrie noticed that there were fancy menus by each seating, so this dinner would actually be ordered from menu instead of being a buffet. Lorrie whispered to her Husband that this must be costing the Garment

House thousands and thousands of dollars and he told her that not to worry, because this was a small affair to them and not only that but it was coming off their taxes. The tables in the room were filling up now and Lorrie thought that there must be several hundred people there, because it was a big room. The Orchestra Conductor announced that it was time for the socializing between guests to start before ordering for dinner and people started getting up to go around to tables to greet friends and business associates. Lorrie didn't know any of them, but a few came by to talk to her Husband and to meet her. In their conversation they asked her Husband if he would mind if when the dancing started they could dance with his lovely wife. Lorrie really did look lovely. Even though she was almost 45 years old and had gained weight on purpose, she was still tall, with long, shapely legs and a great flawless complexion, glittering eyes and the same infectious beautiful smile that hinted of the sensual hidden portion of her that could grab the attention of a man in an instant. Actually Lorrie was one of the most beautiful women there and her Husband didn't seem to notice that. While Lorrie and her Husband were milling around in the room meeting and visiting with people, Lorrie came up with an idea when she was talking with one of the owners of one big Garment Houses. She noticed that his suit had a small thread that hadn't been cut short enough and it gave the appearance of it unraveling. She called the mans attention to it and told him that her husband would never turn in any work like that, because the client of the Garment House might notice it. The man saw what she was talking about and told her that she was right and that if a very particular client saw something like that he might not pay for the suit and Lorrie told him that, that client might also decide to change Garment Houses because of it. The Owner gave Lorrie his card and told her to have her Husband call him and they would set up a meeting. Lorrie was talking to another Garment House owner and called his attention to several stitches that were out of line on a button hole and she got the same response and a personal card with the promise of a meeting. She went around the room seeking out these important Owners and applied the same tactic with similar results and by the time the socializing period was over and it was time for dinner Lorrie had eight personal business cards of Owners of the big Garment Houses in her pretty little string bag. She was also trying to keep an eye on her Husband to see if he was still drinking beer and hadn't switched to whiskey and thank goodness it seemed like he was pacing himself on beer. She knew that if she could get him to eat dinner then it would help keep him sober for a couple of hours longer and he did make it to dinner and he ate a big steak with all the trimmings, so Lorrie felt better about the rest of the evening. When the dancing started Lorrie asked her Husband to dance and they danced two songs together and then Lorrie became sought after by other men as a dance partner, because they saw how wonderfully she floated around the dance floor. She would loose sight of her Husband with all of this dancing and was wondering about his drinking. After about an hour of the dancing she spotted him at one of the bars and he had a glass of whiskey in his hand. She knew that she would have to ease him out of the party soon before he got drunk and caused a disturbance and messed up all that she was trying to accomplish for him. Lorrie found her Husbands friend that had driven them to the party and told him her fears. He knew her Husbands drinking habits, so he told Lorrie that he would make an excuse to her Husband and tell him that he had an emergency call and would have to take them home. This worked and Lorrie and her Husband's friend saved the evening from the possibility of being a disaster, because with her Husbands drinking you could never tell how things would go. After they got home Lorrie showed the business cards that she got from the owners of the big Garment Houses and told her husband that they wanted him to call them for a personal appointment. He was surprised and told her that they would probably forget about it, so he wasn't going to waste his time being disappointed by them. Lorrie told him that she wasn't going to forget about it and that she would call for him and set up the appointments for the meetings. Her husband told her to do as she pleased, he didn't really care. They had a few more drinks before bed time and Lorrie, as usual, out waited her Husband till he went to bed first, hoping that he would go to sleep and not want to bother her for sex. When the weekend was over and Lorrie had time on her lunch break from the Library she called the Garment Houses and talked to the actual owners themselves and she secured five appointments for meetings with them. When she got home that evening and told her Husband that he had those appointments to go to he couldn't believe it, because he knew that it was next to impossible to get an appointment with them as a Tailor, because they each had their own Tailor's that were loyal to them and they used them in their advertisements. He became excited and knew that he would have to take examples of his work with him for them to examine. Lorrie made sure that her Husband would be dressed properly for his appointments by laying out everything that he was to wear and also making sure that he had a sparkling shine on his shoes, like she was taught in the Navy. As the week went on and her Husband completed his appointments she asked him what he thought the chances were that he would pick up some of the Garment Houses highest paid work and he told her that three of them definitely told him that they were going to send him some pieces that he would have to finish and that they would be judged very carefully before any formal agreement would be signed between them, but they were impressed with the samples he had shown them. Lorrie felt real good about this, but was careful not to take any credit from him for this success, because she knew that if he got in a bad mood and started drinking he would brood about her being too much in charge and he would end up having a drunken angry meltdown on her. Things had been going pretty good and she didn't want to make a simple mistake that would upset her Husband. Sure enough within a couple of weeks he started receiving pieces of very high priced work from the three Garment Houses and he completed them with time to spare and his work received very high marks and he was awarded contracts that would double their income. After a few months of working for them they started to use him in their advertising as one of their acclaimed Tailors. With this increase in their income Lorrie didn't need to use her money to help pay the bills, so she was able to save most of it in her own account. She had long term plans for her savings like her Stepsons University education, vacations back to Texas and helping to pay for her Mom to come to England to visit her. Things were really looking up for them now since her Husband had proved himself the equal of all the celebrated Tailors of the big Garment Houses. In the fall of 1990 her Husband bought himself some new ski equipment and scheduled two separate ski vacations, one in December 1990 and one for March 1991. Lorrie told him that she didn't want to go, because she didn't really care to learn to ski and she was better staying home, going to work and taking care of her Stepson that shouldn't be left at home alone for that length of time. Secretly she wanted time away from her husband and this would be the perfect time to start this tradition of him going by himself with a friend. This is what happened and Lorrie considered herself very lucky to get a vacation away from her Husband. Lorrie had been secretly starting to plan a New Years Eve Party and with her Husband gone she would have more time to work on it. She was very much pleased with the way 1990 had turned out and she knew that if she could just keep her Husband on track in 1991 that it would also be a good year and she was looking forward to 1991.

Gus—1991 New Years day 1991 was also a new beginning for Gus. He had a couple of options he could pursue. One was the buying of land in Fort Bend County to develop into another subdivision, but he hadn't located a tract as yet that he could afford that would be suitable, so he would have to keep going to the County Clerks Office there to research that and the other thing was to maybe look into the possibility of running for the Tax Assessor Collectors office in Wharton County. Gus had to laugh at himself for even thinking of this, because he had never had a very good opinion of politicians and now he was considering launching himself into that arena. Gus had to agree with his friend, that was retiring from that office, when he told Gus that he had all of the qualifications he needed to run for the office. Gus was still stumped though on who could help him organize a political campaign, even for an office on the County level. He decided that if he couldn't find anyone to help him then he wouldn't attempt to run for office. He had the immediate problem of what to do with "A Care Concept" to increase it's client list. It was so depressing to have a fare amount of money in it's Bank account at the end of each month and then when all the bills were paid and the Printing Shop was paid there was barely enough left to keep the Bank account open. He and the Business Woman still couldn't draw any money for themselves out of the business and the Business Woman had been in the process of looking for a job because of this and Gus couldn't blame her. Neither one of them had an answer to why the business didn't grow, it just didn't. It didn't make enough money and it didn't loose any money, but both of them were spending their time working with it for free when they could do something else that would generate some income. Sometime Gus wished that he had long ago learned a marketable job skill like welding, plumbing, electrician, something that he could just get a regular job with instead of always following this stressful entrepreneur idea of starting business. Gus thought that the trouble with him was that in the pursuit of developing different business he had learned many different important skills, but as the old saying went he was "The Owner Of Many Skills, But The Master Of Non" fitted him perfectly. He had never reflected on himself like this before and it disturbed him some that he had always had so much confidence in himself to be able to confront any difficulty and be able to overcome it that he had never looked at himself in the light of what if he just wanted to go out and get a regular job, what did he have to offer an employer to hire him. He thought that it was a little late in life to think of that now, because he was 49 years old, so he would just have to stumble along and somehow find his way as he had always done. Finally the Business Woman came to Gus and told him that she had found a job that looked like it would be stable and she wondered if Gus was still going to keep running "A Care Concept". Gus told her that he thought that he would keep it going as long as it didn't start costing him money, but that since she wouldn't be involved with it anymore that he needed to buy out her 49% interest in the Company. She agreed, so Gus wrote her a check for her shares at their face value. They kissed and shook hands, said goodby and promised to stay friends, but Gus felt that he would probably never see her again. Well that was one more thing behind Gus now and he was once again by himself. In the weeks that followed Gus kept thinking of who could help him organize that political campaign. One day he was in a local Drug Store drinking coffee with the Manager of a Department Store and he was discussing this problem with him and he came up with the name of a girl that Gus had gone to High School with. He told Gus that Ellen lived in Houston and had worked on several political campaigns for a popular United States Senator. He told Gus that her Mother was still living in El Campo and he should call her Mother and get Ellen's phone number to see if she would be willing to help him. Gus thought that this was a great idea, because he and Ellen had always gotten along well in school. He hadn't seen her in years, so he knew that she would be shocked when she got a call from him. He just hoped that she would consent to help him or if not maybe she could point him to someone else that he could ask for help, if not that then he guessed that he would have to give up on the idea of running for the Tax Assessor Collector office. Gus got Ellen's number and called her and she told him that her and her husband were planning on coming to El Campo on that next Saturday and if Gus would come over to her Mothers house they would talk about it and that it sounded interesting. Gus met Ellen and her husband at her Mothers house and after hearing Gus's plea for her help she consented to help him. She told him that she was indeed involved in the campaigns of the Senator and she was still working for the Senator, so she could give Gus advice and help him get organized, but she couldn't be involved on a daily basis, because of still being employed by the Senator. Gus was thrilled and told her that what she was offering was all that he needed, so with this the beginnings of a political campaign were born. They stayed in touch by phone and Ellen would give him pointers as to what his next move should be every few days. Gus's main campaign talking point was to restore the tax collecting responsibilities in the

County back to the Tax Assessor Collectors office. The office was established by the Texas Constitution and given the authority to collect the taxes. Since that time another Texas Government Agency had been established to be responsible for the equal assessed value of properties within a County to keep the County Tax Assessor Collector office from giving low tax value to big campaign supporters. This new Agency was known as the Central Appraisal District and it was also given the power to collect taxes if the Tax Assessor Collectors office failed to exercise it's powers and do so. Through the years the County Tax Assessor Collector let more and more of the taxes be collected by the Central Appraisal District office until it was collecting most of the taxes for the taxing entities in the County and in doing so that office had grown in staff and building requirements. To finance all of this expansion in the Agency it was charging all the taxing entities a fee for collecting their taxes, so these entities were not actually getting all their tax money. Gus's campaign talking point on this was that if the County Tax Assessor Collectors office would regain the collection of these taxes then the taxing entities would end up with all of their tax revenue, because County office was already financed to do this work. If Gus got in office he would present his case to all the taxing entities and the County Tax Assessor Collectors office would take back all of the tax collecting, the Central Appraisal District would shrink back to the size it should be and do the job of assessing value to property as it was originally mandated to do and the tax payers of the county would get the benefit of lower taxes in the process. This ended up being a popular debating point for the five contestants that ended up running for that office. Gus spent a lot of time visiting every town and small community in the County putting up campaign signs and posters and also going to every popular public event where he could meet people, shake hands, pass out his election cards, take pictures holding babies and buying beer at the local taverns. In the early voting he came in second which was supposed to be a good sign that his chances might be good to win the election, but in the final election results Gus only came in third out of five, which was the same as loosing completely. This little campaign cost Gus $5,000.00 dollars and he would never have imagined that a little County election would cost him this much. Gus was $5,000.00 dollars poorer for it and it also ended his political aspirations for good. Well he thought that he had learned something in this and that was that most voters had to be untrustworthy, because they all told him that they would be sure to vote for him after shaking his hand and drinking the beer that he had bought for them. That was over with and now Gus could go back to looking for land to develop in Fort Bend County and taking care of his disappointing Home Care Business. The year 1991 was speeding to an end and Gus was no better off now then he had been at the beginning of the year. He had lost the election and his Home Care business was still not making any money and he had not succeeded in finding any tract of land suitable for him to purchase in Fort Bend County to develop into a rural housing development. It seemed that he was simply marking time and in doing so his life was going by with him not accomplishing anything and for Gus that was exasperating. He was always one to be champing at the bit to accomplish something. Gus spent all the Holidays by himself and brought in the New Year of 1992 sitting in front of his TV with a glass of whiskey toasting the American Flag and the National Anthem and then going to bed.

Lorrie—1990 & 1991 Preparing for a New Years Party for 1991 took a lot of planning and work for Lorrie, but she enjoyed all of it. She had always enjoyed having parties and now with their income increasing, because of her efforts helping her Husband get those lucrative contracts from the big Garment Houses she had the money to do it right. As New Years approached her excitement grew and she was sending out invitations to friends and business associates to join them in the celebration. She even planned a separate little New Years Party for her Stepson, so he could invite a few of his school friends over. Lorrie was having her Husband clean out and rearrange a space in their garage for her Stepson's little party. Ever since Lorrie had married her Husband she had many ups and downs from the excitement of finally finding a British citizen to marry so she could stay in England to the disappointment of finding out how much in debt he was and the quirks in his disposition that made it extremely hard for Lorrie to adjust herself to. Not long after they had married Lorrie had tried to rejoin the Navy and leave him, but she found out that she had passed the age of induction, then because of his drunken physical and verbal abuse she had almost left him again and she had even contemplated suicide, but now was one of her up times and she was at her height of glory planning this New Years Party and looking forward to a happier and more prosperous 1991. Lorrie's idea of happiness now had nothing to do with loving her Husband, for she knew that she had never and would never love him and she knew also that he didn't love her, but having financial stability was the key to her happiness, because it would allow her to finally be able to experience

England and Europe in the way that she had dreamed she would as a young girl when she was reading and looking at pictures in the National Geographic Magazine. She would now be able to do and see things that her High School classmates would have never imagined her being able to do. She knew that many of them probably never would even live away from El Campo much less live in England and travel all over Europe. She planned on returning to El Campo for visits and maybe even her High School Class Reunions sometime and she would be able to boast about all she had seen and done in England and Europe. Lorrie was buying all kinds of party favors for their guests along with confetti, whistles and other noise makers to celebrate the actual arrival of 1991 at 12:01 am New Years Day. She bought a good supply of liquor and also a small bar to be well stocked so their guests could have any kind of drink that they wanted including some real Kentucky Bourbon Whiskey that was very expensive and was a sort of status symbol and conversation piece, because most people couldn't afford to buy it for a party. Lorrie would use it as a means to open conversations about the United States and Texas in particular. Everyone in England was curious about Texas and she was a living source of information for them on Texas. She had all sorts of decorations planned including her ever present Texas Flags that she stubbornly displayed around the house in defiance of her Husbands degrading remarks about Texas being a primitive land with primitive people. Her menu for the evening would include several kinds of dips and chips including Lorrie's version of a homemade spicy Texas chili dip, sliced ham, sausages, cold cuts and several types of cheese, white bread, rye bread, smoked fish, caviar and three different kinds of pizza. The invitations were professionally printed to Lorrie's satisfaction and they stated that guests could come and go or stay and enjoy the entire evening till the New Year and then a breakfast would be served of German pastries and coffee. All of Lorrie's free time was spent putting her party together almost to the point of exhaustion. Her Stepson was much more help then her Husband was, because for once he and his friends were going to be a part of it and he wanted it to be a success also. After her Husband had cleaned up the garage she and her Stepson decorated it and set up a table for his own refreshments and moved his stereo in there for the kind of music that the teenagers would like to play. He was very excited to be the host of his very own New Years Party and to be able to invite his own guests. Lorrie was excited for him and she enjoyed them working together with him on this party. It gave her a little bit of an ache in her heart to do this with him, because it would have been something that she would have liked to do with her own son that was lost to her now and she tried not to think of him, but from time to time she would in a private way and cry, but never when she could be discovered and she never mentioned him to anyone except to Jill. Jill was the only one that really knew the deep hurt that she carried with her about her only child. Lorrie's Mom once ask her, when they were talking on the phone, why she didn't have more children and Lorrie answered her that there was only one man that she wanted to have his children and that it would never be possible, because she had messed that up long ago. That subject was never discussed again. December the 31st arrived and Lorrie and her Stepson had everything ready. Their guests were to start arriving about 4:00 pm and some would stay and some would come and visit for a while and then go home or to other parties, because they had been invited to several and they would try to attend each for at least a little while before going to the next one. Lorrie's Husband wanted to start his drinking and Lorrie was having to watch him carefully to try to keep him sober, because she didn't want him drunk before their guests even arrived. She actually enlisted her Stepson to help her watch his Dad and he was prompt in reporting his Dad's sneaking around with his beer, because her Stepson also wanted to make a good impression with his friends. He knew that when his school started back again after the Holidays that his New Years Party would be their main topic of discussion and if it got a favorable review then even the older boys would hear about it he would want to be friends with him. Between Lorrie and her Stepson they were successful in keeping her Husband sober and shortly after 4:00 pm some guests started knocking on the door. There was a lot of come and go guest traffic through the house and her Stepson soon had some of his friends show up, so he took charge of them and they disappeared into the decorated garage and started their music and snacking. Their guests that were arriving later were prepared to stay till the New Year came in and they were very impressed with Lorrie's decorations and her display of liquor and food for their evenings enjoyment. All went well for the whole evening and when the New Year finally arrived everyone threw their confetti and blew their whistles and kissed who ever was handy close to them at the time. Her Stepsons friends parents began picking them up and they all seemed to have a good time. Lorrie's guests started thinning out, but some stayed to eat the breakfast and drink a lot of coffee to try and combat the liquor they had consumed. Lorrie's Husband had barely made it till New Years and she wasn't even sure that he realized what all the commotion was all about when everyone blue their whistles and started singing, because it startled him and he was so drunk that he jerked his arms back and threw his whole drink all over himself, so Lorrie took him upstairs to wash up and go to bed. After she got her Husband in bed she went back down to see to the guests that remained and to make sure that her Stepsons friends had all left. Everyone finally went home and her Stepson helped her do a few things to put up the remaining food and then they went to bed also. On New Years Day Lorrie and her Husband and her best friend Jill went out to lunch with some common friends and this was becoming a tradition for them to do. Sort of a standing New Years Day lunch date. Lorrie noticed that her Husband was unusually quiet, because he normally was real talkative with this group of friends. All of them, except for Jill, had been his friends even before he and Lorrie had met. Lorrie thought that it was because he had a bad hangover from the night before, so when they got home she asked him if he needed her to get him a pain killer for a hangover and he just glowered at her and went to the bar and poured himself a whiskey. She had no idea what was wrong with him, but she could see that something was bothering him. There was still a big mess in the kitchen, so she went in there and started cleaning it up when he came in and took his hand to push several things from the counter top off to the floor and he told her that she could clean that up while she was at it. Lorrie just looked at him and could see an angry look in his eyes and she knew better then to say anything, so she just kept up with what she was doing hoping that what ever it was that was bothering him would pass. Later in the day as he got drunker he started yelling at her and he told her that he never wanted her to belittle him again in front of his friends and business associates by accusing him of being drunk and taking him up to bed. He was so loud that Lorrie's Stepson came down from his room to see what was going on and he tried to calm his Dad down then his Dad told Lorrie that she was turning his Son against him and that he wasn't going to stand for that either. Lorrie and her Stepson just looked at each other and then her Husband slapped her hard and knocked her onto the couch and Lorrie started crying and her Stepson started crying and that sobered her Husband up enough to where he calmed down and walked out to the back yard and left them alone. This is the way the first day of the New Year 1991 went, but Lorrie wasn't going to let it ruin her outlook on the New Year. Lorrie now knew what her long game was, because she knew what those big contracts from the big Garment Houses could do for them and she knew that her

Husband was capable of producing the kind and quality of work that was needed, because he had already proved that. All she had to do was to steel herself against the occasional physical and verbal abuse and keep her Husband motivated to do the work that the Garment Houses required and then she would push forward with steady deposits in their savings accounts and also do all the things that they had talked about to make their lives better. They would get over this outburst just like they had done with many others. When the holidays were over and Lorrie went back to work at the Library everyone there was talking about her New Years Party and it made Lorrie feel so good to have positive things said about it. Nothing was said about her Husband getting so drunk and she was glad of that. Lorrie thought that she was about as happy as she could be under the circumstances and she suspected that most married people derived what happiness that they had in their marriage from having a nice income to supply them with the things that they needed and also the things that would occupy their interests, so they could over look the truth that their marriage was not built on mutual romantic love and respect, but upon what they could do for each other by staying together. She knew that was why her and her Husband were staying together. They were just tolerating each other because of the benefits of being able to live better together then if they were by themselves. Her and her Stepson had a much better relationship for quite some time because of the way that they had worked together to put on the party and he had seen a bad side to his Dad and what it had done to Lorrie, so he had grown up a little more now and recognized that Lorrie was someone that he could depend on to be there when his Dad through one of his fits. The year was progressing as Lorrie was hoping it would with her Husband having steady high paying work and them planning to do more and more things that they could now afford. She was planning a two week vacation for herself back to Texas. Lorrie knew that she needed to look good when she went back to El Campo to visit her family and friends. She didn't want to give them any reason to think that she had made the wrong decision to marry a foreigner and live in England. She had to present her marriage as a very happy one that was furnishing her with love and very good financial security. Lorrie bought herself some real nice cloths and luggage for the trip. She planned it for the Thanksgiving Holidays and she would stay two weeks. The flight was the most expensive part, because she wouldn't have to rent a car and she was going to stay with her parents. She was going to take plenty of cash with her and gifts for her family. Her plans were to put the gifts in two pieces of luggage and then to fill the two empty pieces of luggage, that had contained the gifts, with Texas style food products, that she couldn't get in England, and take them back on her return trip. Thanksgiving wasn't a holiday in England but Lorrie planned to have everything in order by the time she was going to leave so that she would be relatively sure that her Husband and her Stepson wouldn't get into too much trouble in the two weeks that she would be gone. Her Stepson had been doing good on his school work and had made some real nice friends that he could associate with and her Husband continued to turn out exceptional work for the big Garment Houses. He had his spells of drunken anger with her that he abused her verbally with all sorts of accusations and calling her terrible vulgar names, but at least he hadn't hit her in quite some time. There were times when Lorrie thought that he was going to beat her when he became so enraged and she would just curl up in a ball on the couch or the floor to try to protect herself, if he had started to beat her, but something would stop him. Several times the screaming became so loud that their neighbors would call the Police and they would come to their house to investigate, but Lorrie would never file charges on her Husband and the Police would just give her Husband a good lecture on wife abuse and threaten him with arrest if he continued this type of behavior. Lorrie knew that the Police were compiling a large file on her Husband and it was very embarrassing for her, but what could she do about it. She had tried everything that she knew to do, but at least she was in England, so far away from her parents that they would never know what was going on, because she wouldn't be able to stand it if they knew that she had married a foreigner who beat and abused her, when they had cautioned her against it. If they knew that they would never let her live it down, so she had to present her marriage as a very loving and caring one. Lorrie thought that she had become a pretty good actress and she would be able to make her marriage appear to be made in Heaven perfect. Lorrie had been gaining weight for some time now trying to discourage her Husband from wanting sex with her and she knew that her family and friends would see the change in her instantly. They remembered her as being tall and trim, but now her face was a bit chubby and she had spread out in the hips and butt and her stomach was pooching out pretty good. She had chosen her new cloths to hide some of this, but her increase in weight would be noticed quickly. Lorrie decided that to explain her weight gain she would tell her family that she was so happy that she had become "Fat and Sassy", as the old saying went, and that would throw a good light on it. They would never know that she had gotten fat for the exact opposite reason. The day for Lorrie's vacation flight from England to Texas arrived and Lorrie had her Husband take her to the Airport very early in the morning. She knew that it would take her some time to get her luggage checked, because she had four big suit cases, and also she wanted plenty of time to get to the Airport in case of some delay on the road. When they got there her Husband dropped her off, no kissing and hugging goodby and Lorrie got her luggage checked and her ticked checked and was assigned a seat she felt a big relief. She knew now that her adventure back to her old stomping grounds was about to begin. The flight was a non-stop one to Houston, Texas that would be many hours long, so she brought a nice book with her to read. Her sister, who was living in Houston was going to pick her up at the Airport and then they were going to drive to El Campo and then they were going to stay with her parents during the Thanksgiving Holidays. During the flight Lorrie got tired of reading and napping, so she went back to a little bar area and discovered some men there that were actually from Texas and she sat with them and had a few drinks and visited. They were working in the Oil Business for companies that were drilling in the North Sea and they were doing back to Texas on their month off time. Lorrie enjoyed listening to their Texas drawl, because it had been a long time since she had actually sat down with Texans and listened to them talk. Some of their words for things were so different then were used in England that she would have to think about their meaning, before commenting in the conversation, so she wouldn't look like she was stupid. After all she was a Texan and should have been able to fall right into the discussion with out a problem, but it had been so long since she had used some of the words that she had to hesitate for an instant to put them into meaning for her. At least she hadn't lost her Texas accent, because none of them sad anything about it and her friends in England would always make fun of her accent and tell her that no matter what she did to be English that when she opened her mouth she sounded like a foreigner. This used to embarrass her in England, but she was glad of it now. The few drinks relaxed Lorrie and she went back to her seat and started thinking about who she might see in El Campo, then her mind drifted to the possibility of maybe running into Gus there. She wondered what he would think of her now, because the last time he had seem her she had her school girl figure and now she was a fat middle aged woman, or maybe he wouldn't even remember her at all and that would kill her to find that out. At that she closed her eyes and went fast asleep. The next thing she knew the Captain was announcing for everyone to buckle their seat belts and to prepare for the decent into the airspace over Houston, Texas for their landing. Lorrie looked at her watched and discovered that she hadn't reset it, because the time difference between England and Houston was 6 hours. She disembarked from the plane and presented her American Pass Port and because of it she was passed through Customs relative fast and she was met by her sister for the trip to El Campo, Texas. As they drove to El Campo Lorrie was watching for familiar landmarks and new developments that been built since her last time in Texas. This part of Texas didn't have any natural landmarks to observe, because it was basically a flat coastal plain, but the ones Lorrie was looking for were the old buildings that she had known when she was young and had gone to Houston and other places in that area as a kid. The trip from the Air Port in Houston to El Campo only took about an hour and a half, but Lorrie was really tired from all the hours in the air from England, so she was really ready to just get settled in at her parents house and sit on their patio with a drink of whiskey and water her cigarettes and her family seated there with her so they could talk. Her parents phone kept ringing with friends wondering if Lorrie had arrived yet and her Mom had to tell them yes, but that Lorrie was too tired to talk and that the next day they could come by for a visit. Lorrie sipped on her drink and talked to her Mom about the plans for their Thanksgiving dinner and who all might be there. She told her Mom that the smells in the house of baking cookies had brought back a lot of memories. Her Dad told her that from the looks of her that being married and living in England had made her happy. Lorrie thanked him and gave him a big hug. Her little brother came over when he got off from work and he wasn't so little anymore. He was 12 years younger then Lorrie, but at 34 years old now he was over 6 feet tall and very handsome. He had a very cleaver dry sense of humor and sometime it took a while to catch on to what he he was making fun of. Lorrie really got a kick out of him. He was the one that she felt the closest to, because she had taken care of him so much when he was small and she knew that he had a soft heart and he was very easy going. The Thanksgiving dinner was planned for the next weekend, but all Lorrie could think about right now was taking a shower eating a light dinner and going to bed. She was looking forward to the next day, but she needed sleep. The next morning Lorrie was refreshed and was ready to go shopping with her Mom and sister for the rest of the things that they would need to cook a nice Thanksgiving dinner. Lorrie knew that off and on for the whole week they would be getting things ready for Thanksgiving, but when she had time she would borrow her parents car and go visiting. One of the first things she did was to drive around Gus's Mom's house and she discovered that there were people living there that she had never seen before. Lorrie wondered what had happened to his Mom and if Gus was even still living in El Campo. She decided that she would try to find out something from one of her friends. She drove around just looking at different places that she used to go to, to see how things had changed. She went by the old service station that Gus worked at when he was in High School and the memories flooded her about the times that she had gone there with her friends so she could flirt with him. She could almost see him out on that driveway putting gas in a car. She thought my, he was so damn cute and her eyes began to cloud up a little. Then she went over to the Beauty Salon that her friend Toodie owned to get a hair appointment before Thanksgiving. Lorrie had been going to this Beauty Salon since she was in High School. Her Mom would take her there on special occasions to get her hair fixed, like for the Prom and her Mom had a standing appointment for Thursdays at 9:00 am every week. Lorrie thought that wild horses couldn't drag her Mom away from that appointment. The Beauty Salon owner Toodie and Lorrie had developed a good friendship through the years and it was her that Lorrie did jogging and tennis with to get in shape when Lorrie signed up to go in the Navy, so many years ago now. Lorrie knew that Beauty Salons had all the local news and gossip pass through them, so they talked about who had died, who had divorced, who was having an affair with who that Lorrie might know. Lorrie really enjoyed this visit that lasted for two hours and she barely got back to her parents house in time for what they called their happy hour which was either a glass of wine, a beer or a whiskey around 5:00 pm on their patio. The days of Lorrie's vacation were flying by and her family's Thanksgiving Dinner went off very good. Lorrie planned to use the last week of her vacation looking up old friends and shopping for food items to take back to England with her. Lorrie ran across an old girlfriend from her High School days when she was in the grocery store and almost didn't recognize her. The girl had married her High School boyfriend after he had come back from the Viet Nam war and he turned out to be a total nut case, so she divorced him and went deep into religion. She married a self proclaimed Preacher, quite wearing make-up and was helping him gather a small group of believers to form his own ministry. Lorrie couldn't believe what she was seeing, because this girl had been a normal beautiful High School girl the last time she had talked to her and now she was this religious fanatic that sort of scared Lorrie and Lorrie decided that she didn't want anything to do with her. Lorrie next looked up another of her old High school girlfriends. She was the one that she had run around with when Gus was working for the girls Dad in the service station. They had a really good visit. This girl had also married her High School boyfriend and they were happily married with two girls. They talked about their High School days and what happened to the people that they knew. They laughed and they cried and had several beer's together and Lorrie asked her if she knew anything about Gus. Her old girlfriend told her that Gus's Mom had died and that Gus had moved somewhere out in the country, but she didn't know where, but she thought that he was still around and she didn't know if he was married or not. She asked Lorrie if she still had a thing for Gus and Lorrie told her that she had always loved Gus and that she always would and that she hoped someday to see him again, although she knew that it would be unlikely since she was living in England and she had no idea what Gus was doing or exactly where he was living. Lorrie used the rest of the week to buy the food products that she was going to take back to England. She bought wonderful Texas style foods that she couldn't get in England like Ranch Style Beans, Dry Pinto Beans, Taco Shells, corn and flour Tortilla's, Picante Sauce, Wolf Brand Chili and Sliced Pickled Jalapino Peppers. She took all of these products and packed them in the two empty pieces of luggage that she had brought the gifts from England to Texas in. They were heavy and Lorrie knew that she would have to pay extra to fly them back, but that was OK, to be able to have some of her precious Texas to take back with her. Lorrie's Sister drove her back to the Air Port in Houston and she boarded her flight back to England. As the plane took off and gained altitude Lorrie tried to look back in the direction of El Campo wondering where out there somewhere Gus might be and what he was doing and if he ever thought about her as she thought about him. Lorrie's Husband picked her up from the Air Port in England and they drove to Bromley and home. She knew that everything had to get back to normal now and she had a lot of catching up to do. It wouldn't be long until her Husband was going on his ski vacation and then Christmas and then New Year 1992 would be upon her. Lorrie rested for a couple of days and then started catching up on things that had been left for her to do when she got back. After a few days of catch up work Lorrie started to plan for their Christmas and all the decorating she wanted to do. It was a favorite time of year for her and she loved to decorate and do all she could to promote the Christmas spirit. Christmas came and went and as usual her Husband didn't get her a gift, so she bought herself one again and wrapped it and acted surprised when she opened it. This was the little game she played with herself. She wasn't going to have a New Years Party this year, but she would plan for friends to come by and have a drink and socialize. New Year 1992 arrived and Lorrie felt good about her future plans.

Gus—1992 New Years Day 1992 Gus sat drinking his coffee and trying to evaluate what direction was left for him to go in order to achieve a more stable financial future. His subdivisions were doing good, but one day all those lots would be paid for by their owners and then that source of income would be over. True that would be a few years down the road, but if he kept living on this income he wouldn't be able to save any of it or invest it in something else. This was the only thing right then that was keeping him afloat. His Home Care Business wasn't making any money and his mineral rights weren't making any money at present, so he needed to do something that would generate another source of income. The only thing that he could think of was to pursue his idea of trying to locate a small tract of land in Fort Bend County to buy and develop in the same fashion as he had done in Wharton County. He would still keep his Home Care Business open hoping for it to finally pick up some new Clients, but he didn't think that it would. Gus had really lost interest in it and he thought that he could do both without anything really suffering. Gus remembered a friend that was now the Fort Bend County Attorney and he hadn't seen him in some time, so Gus called him and told him what his plans were and invited him to lunch when he came to Fort Bend County Clerk's Office to do research for the land tracts. His friend accepted and they renewed their friendship over lunch. His friend lived in Sugarland and told Gus that anytime he was in town and wanted to spend the night that he would be welcome. Gus split his time between taking care Of "A Care Concept" his Home Care Business and the Fort Bend County Clerks Office doing research on possible tracts of land to buy. He would find one or two at a time and then he would have go find them and look them over to see if they might meet his criteria to subdivide. While doing this he would drive by farm and ranch land owned by the Texas Department of Criminal Justice. There would be prisoners on tractors working and State pick-up trucks with State Prison employees out in the fields making sure that the Prisoners were doing their jobs and what else Gus didn't know, but it was all very interesting. Gus had been going by the Prison land ever since he was just a child when he went with his parents to Houston to visit one of his Mom's cousins that lived there, but he had never taken the time to really watch and wonder what was going on there. This land was beautiful farm land, because it was very rich, red, Brazos River bottom land and it was known for being very good cotton, corn, milo maize and ranching land. After driving by it off and on for several weeks Gus became more curious about it and he wondered if the State Of Texas allowed common citizens to take guided tours of the Prison land. While Gus was doing this he got a phone call one morning from an old woman that had been a friend of the family for many, many years and she wondered when he was going to come over to visit her. She told Gus that he hadn't been over in a while and that she had been thinking of him and she wanted to talk to him. Gus told her that he would be over to see her that morning. When he got there she had coffee and cookies made as she usually did and they talked for a while and then she told him that she had something that had been worrying her for some time and she wanted to tell him who his real Mom and Dad were, but that she had promised his Adopted Mom never tell anything about it and she couldn't break her promise. She told Gus that everyone was dead now except his real Mom and she was in bad health. Gus asked her exactly what she had promised his Adopted Mom and she told him that she promised never to say anything about the whole thing. Gus thought for a minute and then he told her that saying something was talking, but if she wrote it down then she wouldn't be talking, so she wouldn't be breaking her promise. The old woman looked at him for a minute thinking about what he said then she got a pen and paper and wrote down the names of his real Mom and Dad. It turned out that his real Mom was his Adopted Dad's sister that he had been calling his Aunt and his real Dad was a man that she had worked for in his Department Store. This changed the structure of the family relationships, because his Aunt was now his Mom and his Cousin was now his Brother. Gus thanked her and he thought that that big family secret was over and it took him 50 years to find out the truth. He was Ok with it though and went about his life as usual. One night Gus remembered someone that worked at the Prison in Sugarland, but couldn't quite remember his name for sure. Gus had meet him when he called several years before wanting to do a day goose hunt lease. Gus had let him come hunting and liked him and had saved his name and telephone number. Gus kept a book with a lot of contact numbers and addresses and he got it out and found the mans name and number, but he decided it was too late to call him that he would wait till the next evening to call him. That next evening at 6:00 pm Gus called him and his wife answered the telephone and Gus told her who he was and he asked if James was at home. She told Gus that he was and she put James on the phone. They talked for several minutes and Gus told him that he was really curious about the Prison land and their farming operations and would it possible for him to take a tour of it. James told Gus that that could be arranged and Gus asked him when he could schedule a tour. James asked Gus if he could meet him at 7:00 am the next morning at the Prison and Gus told him that he could, so it was all arranged just that easy. The next morning Gus arrived a little early for their meeting and observed that there was already activity going on in the fields. Soon James drove up in a State pick-up and told Gus to be sure and lock his vehicle then to ride with him. Gus did so and the tour began. They rode for several hours through fields of beautiful red soil and visited hog raising pens and farm shops. It was spring planting season and tractors were moving everywhere. James introduced Gus to several different employees that worked under him on the Prison Farm. Gus was astonished to find out that the Prison Farm there comprised 10,000 acres and that it not only farmed cotton, milo maize and corn, hogs and cattle, but also raised many acres of garden crops that helped to feed the Prison population. Gus thought that it was an impressive operation. He never dreamed that it was such a large operation when he saw just a portion of it when he was driving by going to look at tracts of land. He was curious, so he asked James how the Prison Agriculture system hired employees and if they hired by advertising job openings or was it mostly a closed hiring system where friends and relatives were the first to be offered jobs. James told Gus that after lunch he would take him to the Southern Regional Agriculture Office right there on the Prison Unit and introduce him to the people there and Gus could find out more about it, but first it was time for lunch and James had planned to take Gus to the Officers Dining Room for lunch, where the Prisoners did all the food preparation, cooking, serving and clean up for breakfast, lunch and dinner each day under the supervision of the Mess Captain and several Prison Guards. They were checked through the Back Gate by Prison Security Guards and Gus had to sign as a visitor then they walked to the Officers Dining Room and Gus had to sign again as a visitor. Gus was impressed by the cleanliness in the dining room and the Prisoners waited the tables like a waiter would do asking what he wanted to drink, bringing a white cotton table napkin and stainless knife, fork and spoon. The food was served cafeteria style with a choice of pork or chicken, three different vegetables, bread, real butter, milk, tea or coffee and a dessert of cobbler or cake. The food was very good and Gus enjoyed his lunch and while they were eating several Prison employees came by their table to talk to James and to meet Gus. James told Gus that all the meat, vegetables and dairy products were grown by the Prison System and that there were many more State Prisons that produced many other things that were used in the Prison System. James told Gus that the State Prison System was almost self supporting, with agriculture and industry, construction and transportation. Gus was so glad that he had been curious enough to ask for this tour. He had learned so much that he had never realized about the Texas Prison System and it was impressive to say the least. Also right there at Sugarland there were actually three separate Prison Units and their were plans to build another one. They went back to James's office to see if there was any thing he needed to do there where he made some phone calls and had to review and sign off on some purchase requests. The afternoon was slipping away and James suggested that they go over to the Southern Regional Agriculture Office so Gus could talk to the secretary there and he could be introduced to the Bosses that actually made the major decisions on agriculture in the Prison System for the whole State of Texas. There were several in their offices and the rest were at different Prison Farms taking of their responsibilities through the State. While he was talking to the secretary there she told him that they were starting to advertise a job at another Prison Unit and that if Gus was interested he should make out an application for employment with the State of Texas, so his background could be checked and then he could apply for that job. She handed Gus the proper applications and also the requirements for that job and the job duties and the pay range for it along with the benefits that the State of Texas offered to its employees. Gus looked at James and James told him to go ahead and take all the time that he needed, because he needed to go and check on a few things and he would be back to take Gus to his vehicle. Gus wasn't sure that he wanted to do this, but he thought what could it hurt that he wouldn't be forced to take the job if he happened to be chosen. Gus read all the papers and was impressed with the State benefits, but had doubts about the pay for this particular job. He saw that he had all the qualifications for it, so he went ahead and made out the application for the job. The secretary made copies of all the papers and gave them to Gus and thanked him for his application and offered Gus some fresh coffee while he waited for James to return. James returned in a short time and returned Gus to his vehicle and asked Gus if he had made an application for the job and Gus told him that he did, but that he wasn't very impressed with the pay scale on it. James told Gus that the State of Texas wasn't the best on pay, but they had really good benefits and then he asked Gus how old he was and Gus told him that he was going to be 50 years old that year. James told Gus that he would be hitting the age requirement right for a ten year and age sixty retirement package that the State offered and where else could he retire after only working for ten years. Gus thought that it was something to consider. They said goodby and James told Gus he hoped he would consider a job with the State and Gus drove back to his ranch house. When Gus got back home and sat down to review all the papers he had filled out and the benefit list that went with the job, he decided that it might not be so bad as he first thought. He got to putting a few numbers together with his present income along with that of the State job. The State job also had a retirement plan, paid vacation, paid sick leave, a small paid life insurance policy and paid health insurance, all of these things Gus had never had working for himself and he knew that they added up to money, if he had to pay for them himself. He had no debt, but he did have a car payment and child support to pay. That was all his financial obligations, except for regular monthly bills. Gus thought that this job might be interesting and it wouldn't cost him anything to try it if he was hired and he could always resign if it didn't work out for him. A month later Gus got a call to appear for an interview on the job that he applied for. Gus thought this was exciting, because he had not had a job interview since he had been a senior at the University and that was 1964. When he arrived there he found himself sitting in a room with five other applicants for the job and all of them were much younger then him. It finally became his turn to be interviewed and he found himself at a conference table looking at six men that would be asking him questions plus a secretary that would keep a written account of the proceedings and a tape recorder to record the whole affair. The questions were fair and to the point and Gus felt good about most of his answers. The only ones he had any trouble with were the questions that concerned corn, because Gus had never farmed corn and he had limited knowledge on some of the questions asked of him on corn. When the interview was over they all shook hands with him and they seemed to want to just talk to Gus in an informal way with the recorder turned off and the secretary out of the room. They indicated to Gus that they were impressed with him and that if he didn't get this job, not to be discouraged, but to please continue to apply for others and he would certainly be able to land another one. Gus thanked them and then drove over to the Fort Bend County Court House to visit with his friend The Fort Bend County Attorney. They ate lunch together and discussed what Gus was doing about looking for small tracts of land. His friend told him that he was building a nice condo close to his house on some land that he bought next door and that his plans were to sell his old one and then move into the new one. They drove to Sugarland to see it and it was a beautiful place. Gus's friend told Gus that if he got that Prison job that he might be interested in buying the old condo to live in instead of driving all the way from El Campo everyday to work. Gus had not thought of actually living in Sugarland and he told his Attorney friend that he would just have to think about it if he ever got a job there. Gus then drove back to his ranch house that afternoon and took care of a few things that needed to be done with "A Care Concept. A week went by and Gus got a letter in the mail from the Agriculture Office at the Prison that told him that he hadn't got the job, but that when another job became available that they would be pleased if he would apply. On the bottom of the letter there was a hand written note from one of the big bosses that thanked him and encouraged him to apply again. Gus thought that was a nice gesture and decided that he would apply again if any job was brought to his attention. Gus went on about his business of searching for small tracts of land in Fort Bend County, taking care of his Home Care Business "A Care Concept" that was still not making him any money that he could draw on and looking after his Subdivisions. He also had been trying to get some Oil Company interested in his Prospects without any success. It seemed like he was in a holding pattern and not able to get anything to move forward in a positive direction. One evening Gus went to El Campo to a local restaurant and bar to eat dinner and have a few drinks and he ran into a nice looking girl there that was working for a communication company laying in buried cable and they stuck up a nice conversation and ended up back at his house spending the night together. She told him that she had a small bay house at Port Aransas and she invited him there for the weekend. Gus accepted and that weekend he drove there and they had a nice together until they were walking on the beach after dark and they stopped to kiss and all of a sudden Gus remembered this same type of encounter so long ago with a beautiful young girl named Lorrie. Those kisses were much different then the ones he was having with this girl and he discovered that he wasn't enjoying them like he should have been. His mind now was on the past with Lorrie and he just couldn't go on here on the beach with this girl any longer. He made up an excuse that he would have to leave early in the morning so he needed to get back to her house and go to bed to get some rest. While they were walking on the beach back to her house he decided that he was going to go ahead and leave as soon as he could get away from her. When they got back to her house Gus told her that he hated to cut their weekend short, but he was going to go ahead and leave and drive back in the dark because he was so concerned about his very early meeting in the morning that there was no way that he would be able put his heart into sex, so the both of them would have a memorable time together and that he would rather have a rain check for them to get together when he didn't have pressing business to deal with. He kissed her goodby and promised to call her and left. On the way back he felt bad about lying to her, but he just couldn't go on after remembering the wonderful time he and Lorrie had on a similar beach, and that made his whole desire for this girl disappear, because there was no comparison in the feeling he got from kissing her on the beach and kissing Lorrie. Gus just couldn't believe that he had given up sex with a good looking girl when he thought of Lorrie. He knew that he would never call that girl again, because it would just bring back the memory of Lorrie again since it happened this time and he knew that being with this girl again would only remind him of the time he and Lorrie were on the beach. Gus had to laugh at himself for letting a memory about a sweet young girl so long ago interfere with his ability to have a sexual relationship with a good looking available woman. The months of 1992 were going by and Gus finally got a call from the Agriculture secretary at the Prison informing him that she was sending him an application for the job of Supervisor in the Harvesting Department and with it would be an explanation of the duties required in the job. She told him that it was a higher paying job then the last one he had applied for and that it would require some traveling. Gus thanked her and waited for the packet to arrive. He got it a few days later and when he read through the information he was delighted at what he learned. It did seem like a much better job and he immediately filled out the application for it and sent it back to them. Gus got a call two weeks later for him to appear at the Southern Regional Agriculture Office in Sugarland for his interview. This was now July 1992 and the Prison System was into their harvest season. A few days later Gus got a call and was informed that he had been chosen for the job and could he report immediately. Gus told the secretary that he would need a week to get everything in order and she agreed to his request and that he would start that next Monday. The next day Gus called his workers with "A Care Concept" and told them that he was closing it down immediately and that they could go ahead and keep their clients and work with them just as they always had except now they would be in charge of collecting their own money and they would have it all without any deductions for the business. They all agreed, so that was done. Gus called his ex-wife and told her what had happened and that their might be times when it was his visiting weekend with his youngest son that he might not be able to pick him up because of his new job. She was very nice and that as done. Gus made sure that everything he knew of was in order, because he was familiar with harvest seasons and had no idea exactly how they would have him working. All secretary had told him was that there were five Supervisors in the Department including him and he needed to show up for work by 7:00 am. Monday arrived and Gus left his ranch house at 4:30 am so he could have extra travel time in case of trouble on the road. He sure didn't want to be late on his first day. If everything went OK it would take him 1 ½ hours to drive there, so it gave him an extra hour to find out how bad the traffic was going to be driving to Houston that time of the morning. Gus got there really early and had to wait for the rest of the Supervisors to arrive and unlock the door to the main shop and their office. One of the Supervisors went to check out their Prisoner Inmates that they were going to use as mechanics, parts men and general helpers around the shop. Gus was given the keys to his own State truck and the tool and parts boxes on it and also the keys to the shop, office, the tool room, the parts room and the Security Key Box. He was also assigned an Inmate mechanic to ride with him. He inspected his truck and saw that it had a powerful Motorola two-way radio and he was assigned his own call number and given a list of numbers to use to describe different situations on the radio when transmitting to different Prison units. Gus was familiar with these kinds of radios and also with some of the call numbers to be used. He was also given the call numbers of the other Supervisors and even the big bosses in case he needed them for something. They told Gus that he was to take his mechanic and go down to a Prison Farm south of Sugarland about forty miles and they were harvesting milo maize there and there were three combines there with one broke down. He was to make sure that it was repaired and then he was to stay there and supervise the harvest unless he was called to go to another Prison Farm and solve problems there. Gus told them that he didn't know the location of the Prison Farm they were sending him to and they told him that his Inmate mechanic knew where it was. Gus felt a little funny having to depend on a Prisoner to show him the way to this Prison Farm, but it all worked out fine. This first days experience reminded Gus of his own harvest operations, except his Prison Inmate mechanic did all the dirty hard work and Gus just made sure that it was done right which was a far cry from what he had to do when he was farming for himself. That first morning all the Supervisors, in the Harvesting Department, were in such a hurry to go in different directions that they had given Gus very limited information on how things really supposed to be done, because of having a Prison Inmate along with him. Gus decided to get information from Bosses on the Prison Farm that he was sent to and they were glad to tell Gus how everything worked when having an Inmate with you. This helped a lot and Gus made it through the first day without any trouble. Gus drove back to his ranch house after turning in his Inmate and parking his State pick-up. It was 10:00 pm when Gus finally got home and he knew that if this was a normal time to get home during the harvest season then he was going to have to move to Sugarland, because he wouldn't be able to get enough sleep living this far from work. They were working a schedule of 10 days on and 4 days off and there wasn't a set time to quit work each day, because it just depended on how the machinery was doing. If it broke down late in the day, then you worked late to get it fixed. Then you had to drive back to your office and check in and then you had to take your Inmate to the showers and search him to make sure that he didn't have any weapons or contraband, let him shower then go check him at his dorm. This all took time and it could really make you get home late. Gus was going to have to try and figure out something so he didn't have to drive so far to get to work, but he had limited time right now because of the long hours and working ten days before a day off. He knew that as soon as he could he would have to solve this problem. When Gus's first 4 day off period came he had to catch up at his ranch house with taking care of his yard, cleaning house and doing all the washing. He no longer had his Home Care Business to deal with, so it was just his Subdivisions and his new job with the Prison system. He called his friend the County Attorney of Fort Bend County and asked him if he knew of anyone that had a small apartment or a room for rent that was reasonable, so he didn't have to drive so far every day when he was working. His friend told Gus that he could stay with him until September if he didn't mind sleeping in a canopy bed with lace pillow cases. His friend told Gus that his daughter was away for the summer visiting her Mom and wouldn't be back until school started and Gus could use her room until then. Gus was delighted and told his friend that he would be there on his last day off to get organized. His friends condo was only five blocks from the Prison, so it was a perfect temporary solution until Gus could figure something else out. This would give Gus about a month and half to find lodgings that he could actually unpack his cloths in, because he was just living out of his suitcase in this situation. His friend was right about the canopy bed, because the first morning that Gus woke up in it he opened his eyes and looked up and thought where in the hell am I and then he remembered where he was. Gus went back to work on his next 10 day shift and he was learning fast about where all the Prisons were in Texas. He had previously had no idea that the Texas Prison System was so large and that it was spread out over the whole huge expanse of Texas itself. He found out that there were Prisons from the Panhandle in the North to the Texas coast in the South and from Fort Stockton in the West Trans Pecos to the piney woods of East Texas and the Harvesting Department traveled to many of these harvesting field crops and garden crops, that used mechanical harvesting. It was the job of the Harvesting Department to train Inmate machinery operators, train mechanics, repair harvesting machinery in the field and to bring it in the main shop to be completely overhauled when the harvest season for it was over. There were many other important responsibilities too numerous to talk about that Gus was learning about. When Gus got his 4 days off he would return back to his ranch house and take care of everything that had to be done there. Gus felt that he was temporary in both places and the back and forth was all work and didn't give him any time to have any kind of social life. Time was speeding by for Gus and he realized that it wouldn't be long until his friends daughter would be back to go to school and then Gus wouldn't have a place to stay. Gus's friend then came up with another temporary solution. He was having a contractor build a new condo right next to his and the contractor was living in a travel trailer while he was building it. Gus's friend asked the contractor if he would let Gus live there with him for a while until Gus found something else and the contractor was happy about this, because he would like someone to talk to and drink a beer with, so Gus moved in with him. The living quarters were small and cramped, but at least Gus had his own little bedroom. The contractor was a friendly man and he and Gus got along well. Gus was still needing to find something more permanent though. This was just a stop gap measure to buy some time till he could make different arrangements for something better. One night Gus's friend came to the travel trailer and told Gus that he knew a girl that Gus needed to talk to about a place to stay. His friend told Gus that he used to date this girl and that she was in charge of a Head Hunting Company and she might be able to find him a better place, because she had a lot of friends and contacts. He gave Gus her home and business number and Gus told him that he was going to call her on his first day off. Gus called her his next day off early in the morning and she told him that his friend had already contacted her, that she was getting ready for work and she gave Gus directions to her office and told him to meet her there at 10:00 am and just tell the secretary who he was and she would make time to talk to him. When Gus found it he discovered that it was on the 10th floor of a Bank building. He went up in the elevator and found her office and introduced himself to the secretary and she told him to make himself comfortable that her Boss was with a client and she would be through in a few minutes. Sure enough in a few minutes the door to her office opened and an older woman came out and Gus wondered if this was her, but then this beautiful lady came out and introduced herself to Gus and motioned him to enter her office and he heard her tell her secretary to hold all her calls that she would be busy for the next hour. This Head Hunter Lady was about Gus's age and of medium height with natural red hair and hazel eyes and her figure was perfect. Gus sat across the desk from her and she asked Gus to tell her what he had in mind. This he did and then she asked Gus all about himself and when he was through she opened up and told him about herself. Their conversation was flowing very good and the time was going by fast when her secretary buzzed her and told her that the hour was up and did she want to except calls now and the Boss told her no that she would let her know. She had a small bar in her office and she offered Gus a drink and he accepted a Bourbon and water and she had one also and then they resumed their conversation. She mixed them another drink and then she excused herself to her private bathroom connected to her office. When she came out Gus noticed that she had put on fresh lipstick, perfume and had unbuttoned the top two buttons of her blouse showing a very nice portion of her very nice breasts. Gus looked at his watch and noticed that it was close to lunch and offered to buy her lunch for all of her trouble and she accepted. When they left her office she told her secretary that she would be busy and out of the office for the rest of the day. They went to a real nice Mexican Cafe and had lunch and several more drinks along with conversation and then she invited him to follow her to her house to finish up the afternoon. This Gus did and after a couple of more drinks they ended up in her bed for several hours. Before he left she told him that she had a girl friend that had a room for rent and she would talk to her and call Gus. They kissed and Gus went from there to the travel trailer for the night, because he was going to his ranch house the next day to take of things there. It had been many months since Gus had been to bed with a woman and this was a very nice experience. The last time he was going to have sex with a woman he couldn't do it because the circumstances of being on a beach with her brought back memories of Lorrie and it spoiled all his desires for that woman. This was different, because there was nothing that could remind him of Lorrie. The next day she made arrangements for them to go over to her girlfriends condo after work and she introduced Gus to her girlfriend. She was divorced and had a job as a proof reader for a printing company. She lived there by herself and she showed Gus the bedroom that would be his with his own closet, chest of drawers, and his own connecting bathroom. It had a single bed and Gus thought that this was perfect. She wanted only a small monthly payment and Gus would pay his long distance phone calls on her bill. The arrangement was simple enough. Gus's new Landlady was about 45 years old and a little on the chubby side, but pretty in the face with very large breasts. She seemed to have a very good since of humor and she loved to listen to all kinds of music and have a few drinks. Gus thought that they would get along just fine, so he went over to the Contractors travel trailer and got his things and moved in to his new room. Gus was 50 years old now and was enjoying his single life, but he was well aware of his age and that his Dad had died at the age of 61. Gus thought that 61 was only 11 years away, so maybe he should start looking for someone that would make him a good partner to go into old age with. Actually Gus was tired of going from woman to woman in shallow relationships. He was starting to get interested in having a stable long term relationship with a woman that he could get along with easily. He kept seeing the Head Hunter lady off and on until she told him that she had a Doctor for her new boyfriend, then they just drifted apart. Gus's Prison job was going well and he had made friends with the head of the Harvesting Department and sometime after they got in from work they would meet at a B-B-Q place in Sugarland to drink a couple of beers and discuss what had happened through the day and what was lined up for the next day. Gus was still going to his ranch house on his four day off time to take care of things there, then he would drive back to Sugarland to have one day there before starting another 10 day shift. Gus had decided to surprise his Landlady one evening when he was off and have something for them to eat without making a big mess, so he went to a nice Grocery Store that had a great selection of wines, cheeses, pressed meats, smoked sausages, olives and some nice crackers and bought a selection of them to take back to the condo for their dinner. When his Landlady got home from work Gus told her to go ahead and have her shower, put on something comfortable and come to the kitchen that he had something for their dinner. She smiled and asked what it was and Gus told her that it was a surprise and she would find out after she cleaned up. She came into the kitchen after she had showered and dressed in her PJ's and housecoat and seeing what Gus had displayed on the table, she clapped her hands and laughed with delight. They sat down and Gus poured them a glass of German red wine and they started sampling all that was in front of them, sipping their wine and talking about their separate days experiences. It was very plesent and relaxing and his Landlady seemed to like everything that he had bought, because by the time they had finished the wine there wasn't much left on the plates of the meal. Gus told his Landlady that he was going to bed, it was 9:00 pm and he had to start his next 10 day shift early in the morning. She told him that she would wash up the few things they had used then she was going to watch the news on TV, before she was going to bed. When Gus was working he always went to bed at 9:00 pm, because they started work at 7:00 am and Gus was always up by 5:00 am or before to get ready and drive to work. This night Gus woke up and felt someone slipping into his single bed with him and it was his Landlady. It was 12:30 am and she told him that she was lonely and that she just wanted to sleep close to him for the night. This is what happened and there was no sex involved. Gus kept renting the room from his Landlady through harvest and they would enjoy those special little dinners with different wines while he was there and his Landlady would sleep next to him on occasion when she was lonely and there was never any sex involved with this. In October harvest was over and Gus was called in to the Big Bosses office to get instructions to report to the State Training Academy For Officers in Huntsville. He should have gone through that training as soon as he was hired, but he was exempted for a time, because of the harvest season and he had been declared to be competent to deal with the Inmate workers that he had to supervise. Now though he would have to go through the training that all of the Officers that dealt directly with Inmates had to pass. It was set up similar to Boot Camp in the Military. There was so many hours of class room instruction with tests and morning exercises along with hand to hand combat style instruction and finally firing range, live fire tests with pistol, rifle, shotgun and an experience of running through tear gas without a gas mask. If you failed any tests along the way you were disqualified and rejected from working for the State Prison System. Gus found himself the oldest one in the class, but he was one of the highest achievers to graduate that Officers Class. After graduating the class Gus went back to Sugarland and resumed his job at the Harvesting Department. They were now on a regular work schedule of five day weeks and this made things easier to plan what you wanted to do. Gus was still living in his rented room, but he had been wanting to look for a house to buy, because he could see that his job was going to be stable and he had become competent in what he was doing. He now felt very comfortable with this job. Gus found a Realtor that he liked and trusted through his Friend the County Attorney and he had been looking at different houses in the Sugarland area. Gus had also talked to his Attorney Friend about some Singles Clubs in the area and his Attorney Friend suggested one that met at a local Methodist Church. Gus got cleaned up and went to one of their meetings one night and they had a Halloween party going on, because it was just a few days away. Everyone there was dressed up in a costume except for Gus and they had a buffet dinner arranged on some tables. Everyone men and women came up to Gus and introduced themselves and invited him to eat with them and join in the party. There was no alcohol at the party and that was fine with Gus. The only thing that perplexed Gus was how was he supposed to be able to tell what the women looked like when they all had masks and make-up to make themselves into whatever character they were supposed to be. Gus figured what the hell they seemed like all nice people and he was just trying to get to know some new people from the area. He ate a nice little dinner with them and then they had some games and some lady was reading scarey stories to depict traditional Halloween villains. Gus thought that she did a great job of it acting out the voices of the characters as she read the story. Gus couldn't tell much about her, but she had a sweet young sounding voice and he could see her smile was nice and she was tall and thin. This was about all that he could tell about her. There were several women that were sort of flirting with him, but again he couldn't tell much about them. Just before the Halloween party was over they all got together to see how many wanted to meet at the

Movie Theater on Saturday afternoon to go to the Matinee, because it was cheaper and about half of them said that they would go and they invited Gus. He told them that he would have to see what was going on at the time, but he would keep it in mind and he might show up. He really didn't know if he wanted to go or not and anyway that was several days away anything could come up. Halloween came and went in the mean time and Saturday showed up with only laundry for Gus to do at his Landlady's, so he decided to go to the movie. At least this way he would be able to see what some of the women looked like. He showed up at the appointed time and everyone that was going was there and he remembered a couple of the men, so he followed them in and seated himself in the dark of the Theater and all of a sudden someone sat down beside him and introduced herself as the one that was reading the scarey stories. This was the beginning of a sweet relationship between them. They went out to dinner several times after that and Gus was invited over to her small house for a home cooked meal and they got to know each other. She had been divorced for 8 years and had a job supporting herself. Her children were grown and had moved on to pursue their own lives. She seemed to have a very sweet disposition and was easy to talk to, so Gus spent as much time with her as he could. Gus discovered that she had a lot of very good qualities and these were the types of things that he was looking for in a stable woman that he might decide to plan a permanent bond with. She was only one year younger then him so it put her in the same time frame of growing up years to have the same basic experiences and values. Gus continued to look at houses in the Sugarland area and in November he finally found one that he liked. It was in a small subdivision only about three miles from where he worked. The house was only six years old and it had a good price on it because of the depressed prices still on real estate. Gus put 25% down on it and he actually bought it for $ 25,000.00 less then it cost to build. Gus closed the deal in December of 1992 with a mortgage on it, but he had figured that his pay check after all deductions would pay for his child support, his car payment and this house payment with a small amount left over for groceries and utility bills. He was going to have to subsidize his living with some of his other monies until his car was payed off and his child support was over and that was only two and three years away, then his pay check would completely support him and he could save the money that his other investments were making. Maybe in the mean time he could make an oil deal or some other business deal that would make him money. Gus moved everything from his ranch house into his new one and put his ranch house up for rent which would pay for his child support and his car payment. His Landlady cried when he left, so Gus told her that he would come by to see her sometime and he handed her his key back. 1992 was almost over and Gus and his Girlfriend were invited to celebrated the coming of 1993 at a party with some old friends of his Girlfriends. Gus was looking forward to this, because he always enjoyed meeting new people and thought that he might gain some new knowledge that would be useful to him in the future, as was usually the case, when he talked to new people. He thought that he had come a long way in 1992 and had established himself in another town with a new job and now had a nice Girlfriend to spend time with. He could think of nothing that would keep 1993 from becoming a very good year.

Lorrie—1992 New Year 1992 came in for Lorrie easy with friends dropping by the evening before to visit. Now on New Years Day they were going to do what they always did and go out to lunch with friends. After they did that they returned home and Lorrie decided that she was going to call her parents, because she knew that her sister and brother would also be there and she would be able to talk to them all for a special New Years treat. She talked to each of them separately and they all discussed what they were hoping for in the New Year. Lorrie's Mom asked her if she was still happy living in England and Lorrie told her yes that she was. After their phone call was over Lorrie poured herself some Brandy and was sipping on it and thinking. She was sitting in her little office room and it was quiet there. Her Husband was taking a nap upstairs and her Stepson was visiting some friends. Lorrie didn't have a lot of quiet times to just think about things and she wondered why her Mom would suddenly ask her if she was still happy living in England. Of coarse she was happy living in England wasn't she? She sure was! Then her mind drifted to her Thanksgiving vacation in El Campo with her family and seeing a lot of the old places that she used to go and the streets that she used to ride her bicycle on, even around Gus's parents house just to catch a quick siting of him, how silly she was, she thought. She had been living in England now for almost 12 years and she had been married to her Husband for 8 years and yes she was happy in a sort of incomplete way, but why did she feel that her happiness was incomplete, was it because she still had things to see and experience in Europe and also that she had yet to take the University classes that were in her plans to get a more complete understanding of the art works of the Masters of Art in Europe. The more that Lorrie thought about it, she came to the conclusion that if she kept pursuing her dream of staying busy traveling in Europe, learning it's history, visiting their museums, National Monuments and gaining knowledge of the wonderful art works that this would do two things. It would be the fulfillment of her dream as a little girl and that is what would make her happy and where else could she get happiness like that except here in England even though she had a loveless marriage. Lorrie also knew that the key to all of this was to keep encouraging her Husband to deliver superior work to the Big Garment Houses and to be relentless in demanding and collecting the money he deserved for this work. She knew that she was the driving force behind his business and that she could not let up on it. She had to keep him sober and dangle enough apples in front of him to show him that the secret to him having the things that he wanted depended upon his success as a sought after Tailor by the Big Garment Houses. This also meant that the things that she was planning would come to pass too. Her Husband was starting to talk about his two week ski trip and Lorrie was glad to help him make the plans for it. When he left on these trips Lorrie and her Stepson always breathed a sigh of relief. Lorrie's Husband had a radio in his little shop behind the house where he did his Tailor work and he would listen to different talk shows while he was working and a lot of the subjects that they discussed would upset him and put him on a rampage and when he came in the house for lunch or after he finished work in the evenings he would rave and rant about what ever it was and then he would want their thoughts on it and if it didn't fit his thinking he would berate them about it and in the evenings after his work if he was drinking these episodes could get real abusive. When her Husband was gone on his ski trips Lorrie and her Stepson actually got closer to each other and were able to enjoy each others company. Lorrie's job at the Library and her friend Jill were still the main havens of sanity that kept Lorrie from the depths of despair. While her Husband was on his ski trip Lorrie and her Stepson got interested in the idea of them all going camping trips. This idea came from one of her Stepson's friends. He came over to visit and he was telling them about a Camper Van that his Dad had purchased and how much they enjoyed using it for outings and holidays to camp grounds and sporting events. Lorrie and her Husband had talked about buying one when their finances improved and Lorrie thought that it was time to look into getting one, so she and her Stepson started to do some research on which one might be the best and also one that they could afford. This also gave her and her Stepson something to do together that they could enjoy. They could put together some ideas on where they would like to go with it and how they could use it and imagine all sorts of good times spent camping. This was a fun time for them together and there were not that many that they could enjoy like this. Lorrie's Stepson was 16 years old now and he could be a big help on the camping trips. Her Stepson or her Husband didn't know a thing about camping, but Lorrie remembered a lot about the camping trips that her family went on when they owned a similar Camper Van and she knew how to organize one and what it's limitations would be. This was very important when choosing where to go, because different camping areas provided different amenities for campers and you had to determine which one most suited the Camper that you owned. When her Husband got back from his ski vacation Lorrie and her Stepson had already put together a whole folder of information on several different types of Camper Vans. Lorrie had even done extensive research on what the purchase prices of each would be and what the expected maintenance and gasoline mileage would be along with the finance costs of each one, so they were all ready to present their case to her Husband when the time was right and she knew that when he got back from one of his ski trips that he would be in a good mood for several days, so it would be an opportune time to talk to him about it. Her Husband usually waited several days before he resumed his Tailoring, so Lorrie and her Stepson used this time to show him all the material that they had put together on the Camper and they talked him into all of them making a trip into London to look at the ones that Lorrie had researched. This turned to being an all day trip that was very tiring, but they finally settled on buying the Volkswagen Camper Van. Lorrie thought that it was much like the one that her Mom and Dad had when she was young except it had a better design that created more storage and it was prettier inside. It didn't have a shower, but Lorrie knew that they could purchase a separate one that hung up outside on a frame that was like a surround shower curtain with a water sack hanging up inside that would be heated by the sun. It all just came apart and folded up nicely and could be stored in the Campers storage bin. They bought one of these also and made arrangements for the new Camper Van to be delivered to their house in Bromley. When it arrived her Stepson was on the phone calling his friends to come over to look at it and soon there was four of his boy friends lounging around in it talking about how much fun they could have in it at the Rock Concerts. Lorrie enjoyed watching and listening to them, because it made her feel good for her Stepson to be proud of something that they had and want to show it off to his friends. Lorrie had a good feeling about this Camper Van that it would draw the family closer together and give them many good times enjoying the same experience. They immediately started planning a weekend camping trip to try out the Camper Van to see if everything would work as it was supposed to work. Lorrie was also planning her next vacation trip back to see her family in El Campo, Texas. She wanted to stay longer this time. She had only stayed for two weeks for Thanksgiving before, but that went by pretty quick and the expense of traveling plus all the work of getting ready for the trip was the same no matter how long she stayed. Her parents were getting older and Lorrie wanted to spend more time with them. They had been extremely strict on her when she was growing up and especially when she was in High School, because they were afraid she might get pregnant, so they made her life miserable and she finally rebelled when they caught her and her boyfriend behind the stadium bleachers at Wharton County Junior College kissing. This is when she quit Junior College and they sent her to her Uncle and Aunt's in Florida. This was a big mistake on her parents part, because she really went wild when she had her first taste of freedom. That was years ago now and Lorrie hadn't forgotten what had happened, but she had a special way about her that would file all those unpleasant things away in a deep lock box that was hard for her to access. She wanted them to be proud of her and to see that she could run her own life and make good decisions. This is why they must never know about how bad she screwed up in marrying this British man, because her Dad had even warned her against doing it and she did it anyway just like she had always done after she got her freedom from them. There were many other things that she held secret from them also, in fact much of her personal life was unknown to them, because she knew that they wouldn't approve of it, so it was better that they not know. Now that Lorrie was older and she was living her life out of her parents view she had developed a closer feeling for them, especially for her Dad. He was a tough guy on the outside, but Lorrie learned that he had a very soft heart and would help her if he could, he had proven that to her when she was getting her first divorce. Lorrie didn't feel as close to her Mom for some reason and she couldn't really determine why she felt this way except that Lorrie had always felt that her Mom was colder to her then her Dad was. Lorrie and her parents had a real good relationship now, because she wasn't causing them any problems and they thought that her life was running smooth and happily.

Keeping them in the dark as to what her life was really like had produced good results for all concerned and Lorrie was determined to keep it that way. She had decided to see if she could stay a whole month this time. 1992 was going along real nice so far and the Camper Van was a very good addition to the activities of their family. They were enjoying the camping trips on the weekends and her Husband especially liked taking it to the motorcycle races. Lorrie's Husbands Tailoring business continued to see increases in revenue and Lorrie's job at the Library added to that. It was to the point that Lorrie was putting most of her money in her own account, because it wasn't needed to finance the families living expenses or social activities. Lorrie thought that this money might one day have to be used for a new start for her. With her Marriage having so many ups and downs it created a constant environment of uncertainty as to how long she could stay with her Husband. Lorrie had become resigned to dealing with her Husband's drunken abuse by herself, unless it got to the point where he would become physical, then she would call the Police or sometime she would leave him for a day or two and he would call her and beg her to comeback and swear not to do it again, just like he had done before. When this happened Lorrie knew that at least things would calm down for a time and she would get a breather and her Husband would slow down on his drinking and be easier to be around. Lorrie knew that she had to make the best out of the good times to be able to weather the bad times. At the end of summer and fall starting Lorrie was deep into planning her vacation back to Texas for the whole month of November and also planning for Christmas and New Year in England. This was a happy time for Lorrie, because she could keep her mind busy on many things that she loved like going home to Texas and planning decorations and friendly gatherings for the holiday season. Lorrie had the same basic plans for her Texas vacation that she had used before, because it had worked out so well. The only difference was that she was going to stay for a whole month this time instead of just two weeks. The flight was long and tiring as usual and this time instead of going directly to El Campo Lorrie was going to go to her Sisters house there in Houston for a few days to relax and then do a little shopping. From there Lorrie and her Sister were going to drive to El Campo and her Sister was to stay there for a few days before going back home and then return for Thanksgiving. Lorrie liked this month long visit much better then the two week one she had before. There was more time to just visit and be relaxed about it instead of trying to push so much into a small amount of time.

Lorrie's time there with her family and some old friends still went by fast and before she knew it she was shopping for her favorite food items to take back to England with her. This trip back to El Campo Lorrie had resisted the urge to drive by Gus's Moms old house and the Service Station that he used to work at, but it had been on her mind. She only had several days left on her visit and she decided that she couldn't go back to England without driving by the places that she used to haunt to catch a glimpse of Gus. Lorrie thought that anything could happen to her and she might never again get a chance to see those special places that she kept close to her heart, so she had better go by there when she had a chance. She drove her Dad's car by there very slowly and her eyes took in everything that the short time would allow and she saw that those places hadn't changed that much in 30 years, yes it had been 30 years. As Lorrie looked longingly at those places her heart was swelling and her throat was getting a knot in it, because her mind traveled back all those years and she could almost see Gus's red Hot Rod at his Mom's house and at the Service Station she could see him walking on the driveway to put gas in a customers car. Driving back to her Mom and Dad's house her eyes were so blurry with tears that she couldn't see to drive, so she pulled over and wiped them clean with a tissue and she sat there for a few minutes composing herself. Lorrie was aggravated at herself in a way, because she just couldn't understand why she couldn't get past the bitter-sweet memories of her and Gus together and what a life with him might have been like. Her mind drifted back to the question her Mom had asked her when they had talked on the phone on New Years Day and that was if Lorrie was still happy living in England. Lorrie had told her yes and later that day when Lorrie was thinking about it she even went to great lengths to convince herself that what she had told her Mom was true. Deep down though she knew that she would trade it all in an instant for a life with Gus if he would only love her. Lorrie drew in a big breath and put the car in gear and drove back to her Mom and Dad's house. Lorrie's vacation was over and she was back in England making plans for their Christmas and catching up on paper work in her little office that her Husband hadn't done. Lorrie was back at her job at the Library and she and Jill were enjoying some of the Plays at the Churchill Theater that related to the Christmas season and then Lorrie would do a little Christmas shopping buying gifts for her Husband and Stepson knowing that she would get nothing in return from them, but she enjoyed giving them gifts anyway and she would play the same old game of buying herself a Christmas gift and acting surprised when she opened it. She was also buying small gifts for her special friends and some new decorations. This was also the time of year that her Husband went on one of his ski Vacations and Lorrie and her Stepson could do things together that weren't possible when her Husband was home. Christmas had always been a special time of the year for Lorrie even back in the early years when she didn't have the money for nice gifts and Christmas decorations. Thanks to her Husbands continued prosperity with his Tailoring business she had all the money that she needed to decorate beautifully for Christmas and every other Holiday that they celebrated. Lorrie's house became known for it's beautiful Holiday decorations, for all Holidays and this was just another thing that Lorrie loved to do and of coarse it had the hidden benefit of masking the true relationship between her and her Husband to the outside observers and also a benefit was the pleasure that it gave Lorrie personally helped to fill in for the absence of true happiness that she secretly longed for. Yes, Christmas was a season that Lorrie looked forward to, to lift her spirits. Lorrie's house was filled with guests from time to time during the Christmas Holidays and she hardly had time to catch her breath when New Years Eve arrived. She had been busy preparing all sorts of snack foods and dips for friends that were expected to come by and her Husband was some help to her, because it always gave him an excuse to re-stock their bar with liquor and he sometime really enjoyed helping to prepare food in the kitchen. Their guests would come and go all evening and the ones that happened to be there when the New Year of 1993 arrived got whistles, caps and confetti filled eggs to add to the celebration. By the time the New Year arrived Lorrie's Husband was passed out on the couch and their friends took it as a normal happening, because they knew what to expect from him. This was OK with Lorrie and she was perfectly happy to start the New Year with him sleeping off a drunk rather then him bothering her for sex. Lorrie and their friends blew their whistles, threw their confetti, drank a glass of champagne and sang and shouted the coming of the New Year 1993 while Lorrie's Husband lay dead drunk on the couch. The party broke up later and after everyone left Lorrie threw a blanket over her Husband, poured herself some brandy in a glass and went upstairs to her bedroom. She sat on her bed and sipped the brandy and thought over the old year of 1992 and called it successful. She was now looking at a New Year and wondered what it would bring. She knew two things that would happen in 1993 and they were that her and her Husband would be married for 9 years and she would be 48 years old. As she was sitting on her bed she had her head tilted upwards as if she was seeing some vision and then she shook her head and lowered it and softly whispered, oh Gus it's New Years 1993. Then she lay down and slept.

Gus—1993 Gus and his new Girlfriend were invited to a New Years Party 1993 hosted by some of his Girlfriend's old friends. They were really very nice people, but not people that Gus had any thing in common with. Two of them had worked for major oil companies, before they had been given the pink slip, but they had been in departments that dealt with mundane regulations that Gus was unfamiliar with and were too boring for him to get interested in. The rest of them seemed to have had lives that the only excitement had been a divorce or the discovery of a gray hair at the age of 35. There were about twenty people at the party and all of them must have traveled down only a single path in life that was void of surprises, conflicts and adventure. There were some nice finger foods and chips and dips and some soft drinks and some non-alcoholic punch and a real nice fellow was sitting on the floor strumming his guitar. Gus was introduced to all of them and after about two minutes of where are you originally from, what do you do for a living and how do you like the weather, there was nothing else of interest for either him or them to pursue to keep the conversation flowing and it was all Gus could do to keep from screaming, because he had been used to being able to fit into any gathering because of all his experiences had gained him a lot of knowledge that he could use to converse with most anyone on any subject. The problem here was that every topic that Gus tried to start a discussion on no-one knew anything about, had an interest in or even cared to know. After a couple of hours of this Gus told his Girlfriend that he was going to find a Convenience Store and buy himself some beer and did she want him to get her a bottle of wine. She said no that he should be careful of drunk drivers when he was out. Gus walked out the door and wondered how long he could stay gone to let time go by till the time would be right for them to leave the party. Gus came back with a 12 pack of beer just in case someone else broke down and decided to drink one with him at the arrival of New Years. Gus sipped his beer and stood around and gave up trying to get into conversations. He just listened to his Girlfriend and her friends talking about different organizations that they had been belonged to that would help to build your self confidence and the different people that had known while attending those meetings. Gus was so bored that he couldn't even get interested in drinking his beer. While at the

New Year 1993 Party he only had two exciting times and they were going to pee and saying goodby to everyone about two minutes after the New Year 1993 arrived. Gus thought to himself that he had never been to a party as boring as this that was so devoid of anyone that had any knowledge anything interesting to talk about. The only thing that he could compare it to was a reception he had been to at a Baptist Church and even there he found a number of people that he could identify with and have a healthy intelligent discussion with. Well this party was the worst, but he wasn't going to tell his Girlfriend that. They went back to his new house and they took off their cloths and put on robes and Gus lit the fire in the fire place. He had put a bottle of red wine in the ice box before they went to the party and now he opened it and poured both of them a glass. They sat in front of the fire and toasted to the New Year of 1993 and kissed. Gus's new Girlfriend had never been one to drink alcohol, but with Gus she would drink one beer or a glass or two of wine. So far their relationship had been without any difficulty. Gus wasn't impressed with her friends, but she didn't seem that attached to them. Her kids were all grown and moved off, so they weren't being a problem. She had a steady job and was living in a small house that she owned in the country. They spent the weekend together and Gus had to admit to himself that she was nice to be around. Gus went back to work at the Harvesting Department with the Prison System. They were busy repairing the machinery from the 1992 harvest season and there were still some pieces of harvest machinery being delivered to their shop by the Transportation Department from Prison Farms around Texas. This time of the year the Harvesting Supervisors didn't do much traveling. They stayed at the shop and oversaw the complete re-building of the harvesting equipment by their Inmate Mechanics. This process would go on for six months until right before Harvest Season when they would start shipping out the harvesting machines to different Prison Farms that were first in line to use them. Gus had found a good renter for his ranch house in Wharton County, so he didn't have to worry about going there all the time to take care of the yard and the rent was supplementing his pay check so he didn't have to use much of his revenue from his Subdivisions. In fact he was putting most of that money in a interest bearing account and it was growing nicely now. He had to use some of that money to make a hefty down payment on his new house, but he was now replacing that money, which made him feel good. As the months in 1993 went by Gus was watching his Girlfriend closely as he was introducing her to a different type of life style then she had ever been acquainted with. She had slowly moved in with him and was now basically living at his house full time and after her work day she was assuming the roll of the woman of the house with grocery shopping, laundry, cooking and house keeping. Gus hadn't asked her to do any of this she just started doing these things on her own and he let her run with it to see if she was going to continue to be happy with this roll that she chose for herself or if she was going to get bored with it and start to let things go. When the weekends came they would usually go to one of four different eating establishments and make an evening of it first drinking beer for a while and visiting and then ordering a large dinner and that would end the night. Gus's Girlfriend wound never drink more then two beers and usually it was only one. She never complained to him about his beer drinking and Gus was glad of this. Gus loved to party, but his Girlfriend was more subdued, because she had never been around drinking, partying, boisterous people and she didn't quite now how to fit in with it. She had been raised around the Church group where a party was with cake, punch and quiet talk. She had only learned to dance after she had divorced eight years ago, so she had very limited experience with the rowdy type of crowd that Gus was used to being around. Gus also went to a little B-B-Q place after work every day with another Supervisor that he had made friends with and they drank keg beer there for a couple of hours. She didn't complain about this either. Gus was watching her reactions to things very closely and he had not detected her pouting, giving him the silent treatment or neglecting any of her usual duties when he would stay to long drinking somewhere or come home a little too drunk. Her attitude and disposition seemed to run steady all the time. If she became upset at him in any way she was doing an excellent job of hiding it. Gus decided that his Girlfriend was the first woman that he had been involved with that seemed to just let him be himself and this was a pleasant experience for him. He was constantly evaluating their relationship as they went along and so far there was no evidence of problems, in fact his Girlfriend was growing more accustomed to his ways and was anticipating what he was going to do and how he was going to do it, so she could be of assistance to him in any way that she could. She had not given up her more reserved way of living, but she wasn't trying to change Gus either. She had simply, mostly remained who she was only moderately joining in with his rowdy friends enough to be welcomed into the bunch as Gus's Girlfriend, knowing that she didn't look down them for the way that they liked to party. Gus introduced his Girlfriend to his Boys and they seemed to like her and she went out of her way to make them feel comfortable around her. Gus's job at the Prison was going very good and he was feeling like he had made the right decision to take the job there. It didn't pay a lot of money, but it was allowing his other investments to grow without having to use them for living expenses and also the Health Insurance Policy that the State paid for kept Gus from having to pay for any Doctor expenses. When Gus was at work he worked hard, but his days had a limit to them and he had scheduled days off. He had never experienced anything like that before and he marveled at the time he had to work on his own projects or just have leisure time with out having to worry about being absent from his business. He had worked for himself for so long and that required for him to basically be working 24 hours a day 7 days a week and if he took off he felt guilty of abandoning something that he should have been doing. He was finally getting use to the idea of off time from work that most people enjoyed because they worked for Companies and not themselves. This job gave Gus time to try and develop interest in some of his minerals for oil and gas drilling, but he wasn't having any luck, because the economy was still in a shambles and along with it so were the Oil Companies. Gus was leading a whole different kind of life in 1993 then he ever had before. Not since he worked at the Service Station when he was in High School did Gus have a job that he made money at without having to risk his own money and that was over 30 years ago. For the first time ever Gus had money that wasn't earmarked to pay on some business Note and he enjoyed landscaping his back yard by putting in a pond with a fountain and a flag stone patio with a covered area to grill steaks and B-B-Q on his days off. He also made flower beds with crushed rock walkways between them so he could use his back yard even when it had rained a lot. Everything was designed so he didn't have to worry about mud when he wanted to entertain guests. As the months of 1993 went by Gus was thinking more and more of a permanent relationship with his Girlfriend, maybe even Marriage. He realized that they were very different and they probably would never share the true same zest for life that inhabited Gus's Soul, but she had some very, very good qualities that he couldn't over look. As long as she wouldn't try to change him or create unnecessary problems Gus would trust her to be the sweet, caring person that she seemed to be. He thought that this year 1993 he was going to be 51 years old and his Dad had died when he was 61 years old and Gus had never let that age of 61 disappear from his mind as being a marker in his life of the possibility of all sorts of health problems that he might need personal help with. He couldn't think of a more caring person then his Girlfriend to have with him if he would need that kind of care. He knew that if he would expect her to care for him in old age then he would need to do the same thing for her. Now he was seeing their relationship as each other taking care each other going through old age. Gus thought that maybe this wasn't the exact ideal way of deciding to get Married when you should do it when being madly in love, but he had never Married for love before and this was a common sense reason for getting Married that would benefit both of them. Gus was thinking about the words in the Marriage Ceremony that were "To Death Do Us Part" and he thought that this might be his only Marriage that he would be able to keep that part, because he had certainly not done that before and besides at 51 years old he would be getting to old to be switching wives again. At work they were finishing up on rebuilding most of the harvesting equipment and they would soon be shipping it out to the Prison Farms that were going to be the first to harvest. It was May 1993 and Gus decided to go ahead and ask his Girlfriend if she would like to get Married and of course she excepted. Gus told her that she would have to select a date out of two different months, because he wouldn't be able to take off during the harvest season and that would be from July till the end of September. That left June or October to chose from and of course she chose June, Gus thought it was so he wouldn't have a lot of time to change his mind. It was now May, so it didn't give a lot of time to get a wedding organized. They weren't going to have a big elaborate wedding, but it still would take time to get it all organized. The wedding was held on the grounds of a Historic Home in Richmond, Texas and the Fort County Judge performed the ceremony. The only alcohol there was some Champagne to toast the Bride and the Groom. Gus's new Wife invited some of her friends that Gus had met at that New Years Party along with her daughter and her son and Gus invited some of the Supervisors he worked with, his sons, his real Mom and two of his ex-wives. Gus chose Laredo, Texas as there Honey Moon spot. He knew of a beautiful historic Hotel there that was right by the Rio Grand River and they would be able to walk to the Border Crossing there every day, so he could get his new Wife familiar with the customs of the Mexican people, because he was thinking about plans he had for the years ahead. Ever since he had taken his Mom out to the Chihuahua Desert and Big Bend National Park in far West Texas in 1962, he had been trying to think up a plan of how to eventually move out there, this was a dream of his. This far West Texas area had a very large population of Mexicans and if you weren't familiar with their customs you might end up not being happy living there, so this Honey Moon would also be a sort of field trip learning experience for Gus's new Wife. Gus gave her all the warnings about what to avoid when eating and drinking to keep from getting the stomach virus that eating in Mexico was famous for. They went shopping at the big Mercado and bought gifts for their friends and family and Gus started teaching his Wife some Mexican words. Gus wasn't fluent, but he had learned quite a lot of Spanish when he was farming and had Mexican workers. He could speak and understand Spanish well enough to be able to bargain at the Mercado, order food and drinks and deal with a Mexican Taxi Driver or ask for directions. He wasn't always correct, but he could communicate. They stayed there for a week and then they drove back to Sugarland to get back into the routine of the everyday life there. Gus had one more week off then he would be back at work with the beginning of the harvest season and that meant that he would be working long hours on a ten day on and four day off schedule and traveling all over Texas where the harvest was going on. Most of Gus's traveling for the State would be to Prison Farms that were close enough for him to be back in Sugarland at home at night, but there were some that were far off like the one at Fort Stockton in far West Texas and others up in the Pan Handle of Texas that would require him to stay away from home for up to two weeks at a time. While harvest was going on Gus would build up a tremendous amount of time he could take off, because the State didn't pay for overtime, instead they granted time and a half off that could be used like vacation time, so for every hour that Gus worked during harvest he could get 1 ½ paid hours off after harvest to use like vacation time and Gus liked this. He had made up his mind to use part of this time to go out to far West Texas and search for cheap land to buy as part of his plan to retire somewhere out there. He wasn't sure where he was going to go to look for the land he wanted to buy, but he knew that it would be out in the Mountains of the Chihuahua Desert. He had fallen in love with that area when he took his Mom out there in 1962 and he had never forgotten the feeling when he was out there. He knew that somehow and for some reason he was supposed to be there. It was a similar feeling that he had about Lorrie and both of those feelings seemed to be something that he couldn't forget, although he couldn't tell himself exactly why they were so special to him, they just were. He didn't know where Lorrie was, because she had vanished, but he knew where the Chihuahua Desert was and it would always be in the same place just waiting for him to be a part of it when he could get there. Gus thought that it was a good thing that his Dad wasn't alive, because if he found out that Gus wanted to buy land out there he would give him hell about it. Harvest started the second week in July with their combines harvesting Milo Maize on the Prison Farms between Sugarland and Brazoria down on the Coast. It was only about another week and the Prison Farms at Sugarland started harvesting and also the Prison Farms at Navasota and up around Huntsville. Eventually the Harvesting Department would have twelve combines running harvesting Milo Maize and Corn and then two cotton pickers and two cotton strippers harvesting Cotton and they would be spread all over the State of Texas. Gus had an Inmate mechanic that he took with him everyday in his State pick-up to service and repair the harvesting equipment. His pick-up was loaded down with tools and parts that would fix everything except the big most unusual break downs. If this happened then he would have to drive back to their main shop in Sugarland to get what they would need to do the job. Sometime he would even have to get the Transportation Department with their big heavy haul trucks and trailers to take the machine back to Sugarland to their shop if the break down was too serious to fix in the field. The Harvesting Department had between 45 and 50 Inmates under their supervision. The largest majority of them were harvesting machinery operators that the Harvesting Department Supervisors had trained to operate these machines and they would be transferred to the Prison Farms that were harvesting their crops along with the harvesting machines. The other Inmates were in the Harvesting Shop's own Parts Department at their shop in Sugarland and the mechanics that the five Supervisors had with them every day while the harvesting operations were in progress. While traveling with these Inmates Gus got to know them quite well and many times he even ate lunch with them in the field or at the Prison Farm Trusty Camp Mess Hall. They would have some interesting stories about their criminal lives and they came from all walks of life. The Inmates had all the skills that you found in the population outside of Prison, which was called the Free World, so there was some real talent there. There were Doctors, Lawyers, Policemen, welders, electricians, plumbers, mechanics, construction builders, bankers, farm machinery operators, truck drivers, heavy machinery operators and much more. There were also Inmates there that had never had a regular job and they were 45 years old. They had been selling drugs all their lives and had no skill at all except for trying to avoid getting caught by the Police. Some of them had been in Prison three different times and these were usually related to drugs. When Gus had his days off he would catch up on his yard work and plan and work on improvements to his patio area and closing in a side porch to make a museum room to hold all of his artifacts that he had collected over the years. Also Gus decided that he would introduce his new wife to a trip to Far West Texas, when harvest was over, to see her reaction to that rugged forbidding land. He had built up a lot of time to take off and he would use some of this for the trip. He knew where to go now, because of the original trip he had made there with his Mom in 1962 and he had been back there three or four times since then. Gus's secret idea was to be on the look-out for some land out there that he could buy for future retirement, so while he was on this so called vacation trip he would find out all that he could about the land prices, availability of water, electricity, access to the land, taxes and any other information that he could glean from ranchers, Game Wardens, Border Patrol Agents, Real Estate Agents or who ever he could talk to about the subject. When the Prison Harvest season was over in September Gus and his Wife took a week vacation trip to Far West Texas. Gus would have liked to spend more time out there, but his Wife only got two weeks of vacation time at the job she was working and this trip would take half of it. The travel time to get out there was a whole day and then a day to get back ti Sugarland, so really they would only be out there for five days. They left Sugarland very early in the morning and Gus had packed all sorts of extra equipment and supplies in case of flat tires or breakdowns and also hiking equipment that included some really good hiking boots, canteens and back packs. Their first stop for the night was in the little town of Marathon. They stayed at the same Tourist Cabins that he and his Mom stayed at 31 years before and Gus couldn't believe that they were still there and in good condition. The next morning they drove into Big Bend National Park and went into the Basin Headquarters and ate breakfast there then went hiking on a mountain trail for a couple of hours. Gus was keeping a close watch on his wife to see if she enjoying this outing and he was impressed that she didn't start making some excuses about the rough trail or how tiring the hike was. She seemed to enjoy it and along the way she called his attention to some small flower, wanting to know what it was or some interesting rock formation and she didn't complain when she had to go to the bathroom and Gus told her that no one was around and that she would have to simply squat on the side of the trail and do her thing. They made their way back to the

Basin and ate lunch there and then drove to Boquillas Canyon and walked a trail down to the Rio Grand River where Mexicans from the other side would paddle a small boat across and pick you up and take you to the Mexican side of the river for a small price. Then you had your choice, for a small price, of riding in an old pick-up truck up the side of the mountain to the little town of Boquillas or renting a burro to make the same trip up the mountain. Gus chose the burro's to see how his Wife would manage the ride up the mountain. Gus knowing something about those cute, big eyed, big eared burro's knew that they could be very mean and they would try to bite and kick you the first chance they got when you weren't looking. His wife thought that they were just darling and Gus told her what to watch for and to never take her eyes off of them when she was within close proximity of their teeth and hooves. They were traveling up the mountainside on the trail and his Wife was complaining that she couldn't make the burro speed up and Gus told her that the burro's didn't understand English that she would have to talk Spanish to them. She asked Gus what to say and he told her then her burro flapped his big ears and picked up his pace to keep up with Gus and his burro. When they got up the mountain to the little town, two small Mexican children ran up and Gus gave each of them 50 cents to watch the burro's while Gus and his wife walked the one dirt street to look at the town and then to sit at a local Cantina and drink a couple of beers and just rest. Gus talked Spanish to several Mexican men in the Cantina and then they went back to get their burros and found the Mexican children gone and the burros tied to a small tree. When his Wife went to untie her burro she forgot to watch out for his hoofs and he tried to kick her and his hoof just brushed her pants leg which gave her a start and a good lesson to remember that was to prove more enduring then just the warning that Gus had given her before. They left there the same way that they had traveled before and then drove to the town of Alpine. In Alpine Gus visited with Real Estate people and then they drove south to Study Butte and Terlingua which were old quick silver mining towns. Here they spent another night and Gus talked to several people there about the availability of land and the prices. The next day they drove along the River Road to Presidio which was a very beautiful drive along the Rio Grand. They ate lunch in Presidio and drove to the old silver mining town of Shafter and then on to Marfa where the movie of Giant was filmed. There they went to the old Pisiano Hotel where the cast of the movie stayed and had afternoon coffee on the Patio there then Gus met with some more Real Estate people there to discuss land and prices there. They stayed the night in Marfa and then drove to Fort Davis and visited the old 1840's Army Fort and the McDonald Observatory, did some hiking and talked to some more Real Estate people there and stayed there over night. Their last day sight seeing was spent driving a back road to the tiny town of Valentine where the US Post Office there is overrun each year with requests for a Post Mark with the familiar Heart Sign from that Post Office for Valentines Day cards to sweethearts, then to Van Horn and finally they got to Fort Stockton where they spent the night. Early the next morning they left on their drive back to Sugarland and arrived there in the middle of the afternoon exhausted, but happy to be back. They came back with a lot of pictures, pretty rocks that they picked up and information on land in a very large area in the Chihuahua Desert and also Gus paid for a subscription to the Alpine Avalanche news paper, so he could keep up with the news and land for sale out there. This news paper covered a very big area in Far West Texas, so it would be a good source of information to come. Gus was very pleased by the way his wife had taken to the rugged hiking, her appreciation of the desert landscape, and the way she seemed to enjoy picking up pretty rocks and noticing the beauty of the desert flowers and getting excited over the different colors of lizards and the horned toads that you don't see anymore on the Gulf Coast. They had crammed a lot into 1993 with their marriage, honey moon and now their West Texas trip. Gus was in a hurry to get this trip in to see his Wife's reaction to it, because her reaction would be used in the future to be a part of his plan of whether to include her or not in making a decision on West Texas. So far Gus was pleased in what he saw from her. The rest of the year they spent each doing their separate jobs and getting ready for Thanksgiving, Christmas and New Years 1994. Gus's new Wife was really into cooking the traditional meals for Thanksgiving and Christmas. She did some decorating for each holiday but nothing in the extreme. They were getting ready for New Years 1994 and had been married for about seven months now and they had lived together for five months before that, so basically they had been keeping house together for a year. Gus thought that his new Wife was more committed to the marriage then he was. Gus never got into any deep conversations with her about their relationship, but from bits and pieces of things that she would say about her previous marriage, it seemed that she was just grateful for someone that held a steady job, provided a nice house for her to live in, was neat and clean in the way that he lived and didn't scream and holler at her all the time and treated her with respect. They decided to have some snacks and drinks available to friends that wanted to stop by on New Years Eve, but not a party. A few friends came by for a short time, then Gus and his Wife watched TV for the announcement of the beginning of the New Year 1994.

Lorrie—1993 came in for Lorrie and her Husband as usual with them going out for lunch with old friends. This was always a pleasant event for Lorrie, because she enjoyed their company and it also was a way for them to spend time away from their house where their partying went on the evening before, because there was the mess to finish cleaning up and then it provided a time period of several hours that her Husband would be distracted from thinking of something that had happened the evening before that had irritated him and he could use against her in an argument. Lorrie had found out that sometime this was enough time for him to forget about what ever it was completely and they could end up having a pleasant New Years Day. Lorrie was feeling much more secure now with their financial situation being very good, in fact Lorrie had never had as much money to spend in her entire life. Her relationship with her Stepson had improved a lot and sometimes it almost seemed like a normal family lived in their house. She had also developed a real tough skin to overlook her Husbands abusive behavior towards her at times. Her job at the Library and her friend Jill supplied the real relief she needed from a usually tense home life. With her Husbands Tailoring business bringing in more income all the time, Lorrie was able to plan trips to France and Italy with friends to enjoy the rich culture and history of those countries. Lorrie started a little herb garden so she could have fresh herbs for the recipes that she loved to experiment with. She was really getting into Italian pasta and sauces and her husband liked to grow fresh vegetables. She thought that he still had some of the old Greek peasant blood in him, because he felt like he needed to be growing a vegetable garden. Lorrie was thinking more and more about going back to the University there in England to learn more about the history, the culture of the times that included the political and religious intrigues combined with the individual characters of each of the Great Masters of the European Art World that inspired them to create the art works that survived centuries and that were still admired for their beauty as well as the underlying message that they told about the times that they were created in. The art works by these artists gained Lorrie's thoughts and interest more and more. It seemed that the more that she looked at them and read about the Masters that created them the more she wanted to know. Since her Husband's Tailoring business had been generating a good stream of income now for a while, Lorrie's mind was drifting away from the years that she had spent in fear of their financial collapse, because that might have meant that she would have had to leave England and go back to Texas to her Parents to live. Heaven forbid that to happen, because the embarrassment of that at her age would have been something that she wouldn't have been able to stand. She was thinking more and more of improving her mind by enrolling in some of the University Classes and actually working toward a Degree. Her job at the Library subjected her to an environment immersed in books and learning and along with it was the Churchill Theater that her and Jill attended the Plays at and all of this was an extension of what Lorrie had been interested in as a young girl, so she was in her element, so to speak and she finally had the money and would somehow find the time to pursue her passion of learning all that she could about her childhood dream of European Art Works and the Great Masters that created them. Lorrie and her family were still enjoying their Camper Van on some of the nice weekends, but these outings were becoming shorter and less often now because her Husband was into his gardening and that took up some of the days that the weather was good and when in the winter months the weather was too bad to go camping, also her Stepson was having a lot of other interests now since he was in High School and Lorrie wasn't to excited about just her and her Husband going, because that would put them by themselves in too close proximity to each other and he might get sexual thoughts that she was trying to avoid. Lorrie and her Husbands relationship was still up and down depending on different happenings between her Husband and her Stepson or maybe some perceived wrong that Lorrie herself had committed without knowing it, because when her Husband would start drinking, which was everyday after he finished his work, he would brood about it until he would explode into a rage that would frighten Lorrie, because she knew that if she made the wrong move or said the wrong thing he could get physically abusive and she would always try to avoid this at all costs. She knew that she was trapped into staying with him if she expected to keep living in England and she had to live in England if she wanted to pursue her education like she always wanted to. The year 1993 was speeding along and Lorrie's life at home appeared to be following the same abnormal path that had become normal, for the way that she existed in her personal life with her Husband and her Stepson. It had become a known thing to her now and she just had to deal with it. She was still traveling back to Texas for her month long vacations there with her family during Thanksgiving and visiting her friends that she could still find in El Campo. While she was there Gus always crossed her mind, but she just couldn't ever get the courage to try and get in touch with him. She heard that he still lived there somewhere, but no body that she knew seemed to know anything about him. She even got the curiosity to look in the local phone book to see if his phone number was there, but didn't see one for him. She was puzzled then, because if Gus still lived there he would have a phone number in the El Campo phone book. She thought that if she had his phone number that she wouldn't have the courage to call him anyway, but it would be nice to just hear his voice again. When she got back to England she started her Christmas decorating and shopping and got herself in full swing organizing for the Holiday Season. She was looking forward to the New Year of 1964, because she was already planning something very special for it that would include the whole family. Christmas came and went and again she had to get herself her own present and now there would be getting ready for their New Years Eve celebration. This was always fun for Lorrie to plan, because she always loved to prepare all sorts of foods and snacks for the guests that would stop by and now it also included a lot of people that were in the Tailoring business that they had become friends with through the business. These were pretty good friends, but not the kind of friends that knew how Lorrie and her Husbands personal relationship was between them, this had to always be held as a secret away from his business, because it could very well have adverse affects if it was found out. When they were around these friends they had to appear to have a happy marriage and her Husband would control his drinking to a point and treat her with consideration. Lorrie enjoyed this, because she could socialize without worrying if her Husband was going to have a drunken outburst. Their New Years Eve celebration went off well and 1994 arrived right on schedule. They went to their regular lunch date with their old friends on New Years Day 1994 and Lorrie was thinking of the special vacation she was planning for later in the year.

Gus—January 1994 at the Prison Harvesting Department was a slow time as usual, because all that was going on was the tearing down and the rebuilding of the harvesting machinery. Most of their Inmate machinery operators had been transferred to other Prison Farms that needed them and that only left about 12 Inmates that worked with the rebuilding of the machinery. The head of the Harvesting Department and Gus became Friends just a couple of months after Gus went to work there and his Wife was managing a Day Care Center for an older couple that wanted to sell it. His Friend told Gus about this and Gus thought that it might be a good investment. His Friends Wife had been working there for years, so she knew all the in's and out's about the actual running of the business. They all had a meeting and the Owners made them an offer that Gus considered very reasonable. It would only require a small down payment and the Owners would finance the balance themselves for five years on monthly payments. They wouldn't own just the business, but also the building and land that it occupied and this was in a part of Sugarland that was beginning to increase in value. Gus his Wife and his Friend and his Wife would be 50-50 partners. His Friends Wife would be the day to day manager of the Day Care that was Licensed for 54 children. Gus's Wife would go there after she got off from her job at 5:00 pm and stay and help at the Day Care till it closed at 6:30 pm and Gus and his Friend would do all the repair work and maintenance and also all the shopping of the food and supplies that was required to keep the business running on a daily basis. Gus knew that things would work OK during the winter months, because things at the Harvesting Department were slower then, but it might get hard for him and his Friend to keep up their end when things got busy during the harvest season. His Friend told Gus that when that happened the women would just have to do it themselves when that happened. Gus knew that no one was going to get paid except his Friends Wife until the business was paid for in five years, because the monthly payments were pretty steep, Gus and his Wife would have to wait till 1999 before they could see any money out of it. Gus looked at it as an investment for the future, because he and his Wife didn't need the money to live and there were two different avenues for it to make money in five years. First was selling the whole business if it was doing good and then there was the value of the land and building that would be worth more in five years, so Gus thought that the chance for loosing money on it was small, but he also knew that any investment always had the chance of loosing money. With this deal done it added another facet to Gus and his Wife's lives. She was excepting of helping out at the Day Care, but she didn't want any responsibility in the management of it. Harvest season came around and things got pretty hectic sometime with Gus and his Friend trying to get back to Sugarland late in the day to go do the shopping and sometime they just couldn't do it and the women had to do it for them. To Gus the worst part of the Day Care business, he found out, was all the Inspectors that walked in from different Government Agencies to inspect you for anything and everything imaginable and you had to write them a check for inspecting and bothering you, so you had to pay them to harass you basically. Then they would always write you up for something silly just to show some paper work to some other Bureaucratic Boss and it would cost you in time, work and expense to correct something that didn't need correcting in the first place. This was very irritating for Gus and it was a constant thing that you had to deal with and you just had to smile and write the check or they would come down on you like a ton of bricks. Gus's job at the Prison Harvesting Department was going good and so far Gus was glad that he had gone to work there. He had more money and more free time on his hands without the stress and worry then he had ever had before in his life, well except when he had worked at the Service Station when he was in High School and Lorrie would come in there and flirt with him. Lorrie would come into his mind from time to time for no apparent reason and thinking of her was always pleasant, but it was also a mystery to him as to why she kept popping up in his thoughts. Gus had been receiving his subscription to the Alpine Avalanche Paper and was really enjoying reading all the news from out in Far West Texas. This news paper covered a real big area out there from Alpine, to Fort Davis, to Marfa, to Marathon, to Valentine to Study Butte, to Terlingua, to La Jatis and sometimes even to Van Horn. The classified section was especially interesting to Gus with the real estate for sale advertisements. He was sure that sooner or later he would discover a really good deal on some land out there that he would be able to afford to buy. The Prison Harvest Season had gone pretty smooth and Gus had built up a lot of overtime that he could take off from work, so he was planning another week vacation out in Far West Texas. This time he came up with an idea that would give him access to ranches that he would normally never be able to gain access to. He called several Real Estate Brokers in the area and made arrangements with them to tour ranches that they had listed for sale. He knew from the prices and the sizes of the ranches that he couldn't come even close to being able to afford to buying them, but when the Real Estate Brokers heard that he lived in the Houston area they presumed that he was a rich man and they were jumping at the chance to show him the ranches. He had it understood with them that after they took him to the ranches he would have the freedom to roam around on them without being escorted. In this way Gus would be able to hunt for semi-precious stones and Indian artifacts and also he would have the time to study the terrain and the wild life and plants to learn more about the whole area. Gus knew that other people would pay a lot of money to go to Guest Ranches and sign up for rock hunting expeditions and they would have to pay for what they found, but this way it wasn't costing him anything, just his Motel bill and his meals. His Wife took a week off from work and they really enjoyed their freedom to roam around all of these interesting ranches discovering ancient Indian camps and picking up arrow heads, scrapers and other stone tools along with fossils and all sorts semi-precious rocks. They went back to Sugarland with several boxes full of these. They also picked up some bigger rocks to use as landscaping. The Holiday Season was upon them and that was always a kind of low key affair with them. Because they didn't have any big parties, only a few friends might stop by or maybe Gus's boys might come by for a short visit. So 1994 slipped by quietly and they woke up in the New Year of 1995.

Lorrie—1994 was going to be a special year for Lorrie, because of what she was planning for her, her Husband and her Stepson. There were several things that would make 1994 special for them. It was their 10 year Wedding Anniversary, which Lorrie knew that her Husband didn't really want to celebrate, her Stepson was graduating from High School and would be enrolling in the University, it was Lorrie's 30 year High School Reunion and most of all was the surprise that she had been planning for them. She had secretly been making plans for all of them to fly to the United States for a whole month on vacation. Her Husband and her Stepson had never been to the United States and she wanted to take them to her home town in Texas to her 30 year High School Reunion, finally meet her family and some of her friends, then go on a driving trip to the Alamo in San Antonio, a special place for Lorrie, because it was the heart of the Texas Revolution from Mexico, then on to see the Grand Canyon in Arizona, to Disney Land in California, to Las Vegas in Nevada, Carlsbad Caverns in New Mexico and then back to El Campo, Texas for a couple of days before having to go to Houston for their flight back to England. Lorrie had been researching all of this and saving money for six months to pay for this vacation. She had put together all the information needed for the trip and had made all the hotel reservations, bought plane tickets, rental car reservations. Lorrie did all of this before discussing it with her Husband, because she knew that he would just argue about it. Now it was done and she would tell him about it at an opportune time when he was in a good mood even if she would have to have sex with him to seal the deal. Her Husbands Tailoring business was going great and Lorrie had already informed the Garment Houses that he was working for, that he wouldn't be accepting any work during the month that she had picked out for their vacation and she had the understanding with them that they would keep the secret for her. That spring they would go to different Universities looking around and getting all the information on each to see which one most suited them and her Stepson. Her Stepson had decided that he wanted to pursue a Degree in Economics and Finance, so this was a major consideration for them on making their choice. The year was speeding by fast and Lorrie's Stepson's High School graduation was upon them and she decided that it was the time to tell them about the vacation trip she had planned. They were all upbeat and in good spirits talking about what kind of graduation party and gift that her Stepson was to receive. Lorrie went into her little office and she got the folder out with all the travel brochures and the plans for their vacation and laid them out on the table in front of her Husband and her Stepson. She didn't say anything, but just watched their faces to see their expressions. Her Husband and her Stepson just watched her spread out the travel brochures on the table with a question on their faces and they started picking them up and looking at them and it finally dawned on them that these were from the United States. Lorrie's Husband looked at her with a frown and then her Stepson did what Lorrie had hoped that he would do and that was to get excited and hug her and state that this was the best graduation present that he could get and that his friends were going to be so envious of him getting to tour the United States. Her Husband looked at his Son and he opened his mouth to say something, but nothing came out, and then he just smiled and shook his head and asked when they were scheduled to go. That's when Lorrie put the plane tickets on the table and everything else that pertained to the trip. The rest of the day was spent on looking over all the material and discussions on the trip. Lorrie was real proud of herself for choosing the exact right time to let them in on the secret vacation that she had planned for the family. One of the questions they had was what kind of clothing they would need for the trip and Lorrie had the answers for that, because she had been to each of these places before when she had been married to her Air Force Husband, so none of this was a question for her. She knew exactly what they would need. Her Husband asked her what this was going to cost and she told him that she had already paid for everything except their traveling money. She told him that this was also going to be their 10 year Anniversary present and that they were going to attend her 30 year High School Class Reunion. Her Husband seemed just fine with all of this and Lorrie was so relieved that it all went so smoothly. She wondered if he would start thinking about something later when he started drinking and start a fight with her. Lorrie made her Husbands favorite supper for him and the whole evening went by smoothly. After Lorrie's Stepson's High School Graduation they made arrangements for his enrollment in the University and then their preparations began in earnest for their big vacation trip to the United States. They landed in Houston and their rental car was ready for them, so they drove to El Campo, Texas to spend a few days with Lorrie's family before setting out across the Southwestern United States. Lorrie's family greeted her Husband and her Stepson with loving hospitality. Lorrie's Dad had some of his favorite beer, so he shared it with Lorrie's Husband, but she could tell that he wanted more and was sort of frustrated by being limited to only three beers. Lorrie took him aside and asked him to please stay sober around her family, because they weren't going to be there that long and it would just ruin everything if he got drunk. The next day Lorrie took her Husband and her Stepson on a driving tour around El Campo showing them the High School she went to and some of her friends houses and she even took them by Gus's Mom and Dad's house and told them that the boy that lived there had built a red Hot Rod like in the movies. They had no idea that Lorrie was actually remembering riding her bicycle around that house looking for Gus when she was young. She took them to the local grocery store to see all the items that it carried that were never seen in England and of course her Husband had to buy a case of beer. Lorrie's parents had a little party for them the next day and Lorrie invited a couple of her High School friends over to meet her Husband and Stepson. Her friends were telling them funny stories on Lorrie when she was in High School and her friend that was the daughter of Gus's old boss told how they would go into the Service Station and flirt with that cute boy that worked for her Dad and Lorrie almost choked and tried to make eye signals to shut her up but to no avail. Her friends were amused by the British accent of her Husband and Stepson and of the different words they used and sometime Lorrie would have to step in on the conversation to clarify what a word meant in both directions. Lorrie's Husband had hidden the case of beer he bought in a little shed in the back yard and after the three beers that he drank with her Dad he would sneak out to that shed and guzzle a beer hot real quick before anybody missed him. Lorrie caught him at it, but was afraid to say to much to him for fear that he would go into one of his rages. She wanted everything to look like they were happily married, so she was extra considerate of her husbands comforts and moods. She even went with him to the grocery store everyday they were there to get another case of beer to hide out in the back yard shed. They finally set off on their trip and the first stop was the Alamo in San Antonio. Her Husband and Stepson had seen the " Alamo " movie by John Wayne in England and there had been a series on British TV by Walter Lord Titled " A Time To Stand " that they had watched, so they knew the history about the Alamo and the Texas Revolution from Mexico, but as a Texas girl Lorrie was now in her height of glory as she took them to different parts of the Alamo complex and explained what had happened in the exact same place they were standing. Lorrie had been to the Alamo many times and it was one of her favorite places, so her oratory on the thirteen days that the little band of Texans held out against the huge Mexican Army came alive for her Husband and Stepson and they really enjoyed that historical visit. Lorrie omitted telling them about the affair she had with her first Husbands friend and aid when she had lived in San Antonio, but she did tell them that this was the place that she had her horse. From San Antonio their plan was to drive through New Mexico to Arizona to see the Grand Canyon. Lorrie's Husband was driving through New Mexico and he was driving on these long open roads with no traffic, so he was speeding and Lorrie told him that he had better drive the speed limit, because she used to live in New Mexico, when she was married to her Air Force Husband and she told her Husband that in New Mexico they watched speeding traffic with a small air plane and if it noticed a speeding car it would call by radio to a State Trooper that would stop the car and write them a speeding ticket. Her Husband just laughed at her and Lorrie told him that she knew what she was talking about, but he just frowned at her and increased his speed even more. About five miles farther down the road a State Trooper was sitting waiting for them and pulled them over and gave her Husband a big speeding ticket for over a hundred dollars. When they drove off from the Trooper Lorrie just looked over at her Husband and smiled and he cussed and told her that he wasn't going to pay that speeding ticket. Lorrie told him that he had better pay it, because she didn't want to have that hanging over her head when she came back to the United States to visit and that if he didn't pay it she would pay it herself. They drove on to Arizona and Lorrie noticed that when her Husband was driving from then on he stayed within the speed limit. They rented a cabin at the Grand Canyon Park area and spent two days there and hiking and looking at the Grand Canyon and the wild river at it's bottom. Her Husband and Stepson were very impressed with it and really hadn't expected it to be so beautiful. They then drove to California and spent two days at Disney World there. They then drove back east through California to Lake Tahoe then Carson City, Reno and finally Las Vegas, Nevada. They stayed one day and night there playing the slot machines and looking at all the famous neon lights on the Strip that made the night into day. Lorrie's Husband got extremely drunk while in the Casino's because he was able to have all the whiskey free while playing the slot machines and it took Lorrie and her Stepson together to get him to their room. They left Las Vegas the next morning and drove back to New Mexico to Carlsbad and got a motel room there, so they could tour the Carlsbad Cavern the next day. This was the last big attraction that Lorrie had planned for her Husband and her Stepson, before driving back to Texas and El Campo. The rest of their vacation would be spent at her parents house and they would be attending Lorrie's 30 year High School Class Reunion, the Class of 1964. This was very important for Lorrie for several reasons. She knew that she would see friends that she hadn't seen in 30 years, and she could boast to her Husband that none of the men that he was going to meet there had slept with her, because she had not had sex with anybody while she had been in High School and also she could show all of her old Class Mates that she had amounted to something, because she had a Home, a Husband and a Stepson in England with a happy marriage and a secure future, she had also served for eight years in the United States Navy in a very High Security Job in their Cryptology (Codes) Division and she had been to Country's in Europe and seen things there that her Class Mates could only dream about. They would be able to see that Lorrie was no longer the small town girl that they had gone to school with. She would present herself as a woman of the World. Lorrie knew that no one there would have that kind of life to talk about and it made her glad that she had been able to stick it out with her difficult Husband and Stepson. She knew that her old Class Mates would talk about this for a long time. There time at Lorrie's parents house before the Class Reunion were spent going over her old scrap books and picture albums and in one of her picture albums was a picture of this young man standing by a chopped down red Hot Rod Coupe with a big engine and around the picture a big heart with an arrow through it was drawn and the names Lorrie + Gus written. Lorrie flipped passed this page fast and her Husband caught sight of the Red Hot Rod and turned the page back to see it. Lorrie turned red in the face and she could feel her heart pounding and her skin getting hot. Her Husband told her that he liked that car and that it was just like the Hot Rods that he had seen in some Movies that were made in the United States that depicted teenagers in High School back in the 1950's. He asked her if it had been her boyfriend and this was the question that Lorrie had been trying to avoid. Lorrie told him no that the boy had been too old and to wild for her, but that she had liked his car. Her Husband told her that if he hadn't been her boyfriend then why was her name on the picture with the boy's linked with an arrow and a plus sign. Lorrie told him that she couldn't remember, that someone had given it to her as a joke, then Lorrie got up and went out the back door and smoked a cigarette and cried. Lorrie had forgotten that the picture had been that picture album. Looking at it had brought back so many memories, some beautiful and some that still hurt deeply. Lorrie wondered why in the hell she couldn't get over Gus. He had always had this strange hold on her and when ever something brought up his memory strange things happened to her that never happened at any other time and it always took a little time for her to collect herself and get back to being herself. At times like this she would wonder just who she really was, because these memories brought her right back to being that small town girl that was in love with Gus and she didn't want to be, because she was now this Married woman living in England that had seen and done so much and she considered herself to be a woman of the World now, but somehow being in love with Gus and that small town, in those memories seemed much more appealing. Lorrie thought that she had better get back in or they would wonder what was wrong with her. Lorrie's Husband continued to hide beer out in the shed in the back yard and he would slip out there and drink it warm. Lorrie's parents never found out, but they mentioned that her Husband spent a considerable amount of time in the back yard, but thought that he just needed some time to himself since he might be a little uncomfortable being from another country that had different customs. When Lorrie would detect that her Husband was getting a little to unsteady on his feet she would quietly suggest that he take a nap and she would put him to bed for a couple of hours and thankfully he didn't cause a disturbance, so her parents never found out how much that he drank everyday. Lorrie's 30 year High School Class Reunion of the Class of 1964 was finally getting started and Lorrie wore an expensive silk dress and her dancing shoes along with a nice necklace, ear-rings and a couple of rings that included her High School Senior Ring. Her and her Husband and Stepson signed in and found a table close to where the dancing would be, so Lorrie could watch the people dancing and be able to talk to them as they would dance by and also it made it easy for her and her Husband to get up and get on the dance floor. Lorrie was having the time of her life visiting with old friends most of who she hadn't seen in 30 years. The organizers of the Class Reunion had put up a Memorial Board that had school pictures of Class Mates that had died and there were several that had been killed in Viet Nam and a couple of boys that she had dated. This Memorial Board surprised Lorrie, because she had no idea that so many of her Class Mates had already died from one thing or another. After the nice catered dinner there was a program that featured giving away different prizes and Lorrie won the prize for traveling the farthest to attend the Reunion. The the lights dimmed and the bar opened and the music started playing for those that wanted to dance to the 1950's and 1960's music that her Class had danced to at the country dance halls at Hillje and Taiton Halls. There was a lot of nostalgia that this music brought back to Lorrie and it washed over her as song after song played and brought back the people that she had known some dead now in their younger lives. The sadness of the War Years and the boys that she knew who left to fight the war, some of her girlfriends that had thought that their life was over when their boyfriends broke up with them, the times that she had been punished and grounded from going to the all important dances at the country dance halls and more and then " In The Still Of The Night " by the Five Satins was playing and one of her boy Class Mates immediately asked her to dance and she was so glad, because it got her away from her Husband, for she thought that she might cry in front of him. They danced to the other side of the dance floor and Lorrie was holding to him so tight and she had her face buried in his shoulder to muffle the sounds of her weeping. He knew something was wrong and ask her if she wanted to sit down and she told him no she wanted to dance and she did dance to " In The Still Of The Night " like she had never danced before, because all of a sudden she was in Gus's arms and dancing with him. When the song was over her dance partner noticed that his shirt was wet on his shoulder and he ask her what happened and she told him that she had always loved that song and always cried when she heard it. He returned her to her table and her Husband had been kept busy by some of her Class Mates and even her Stepson had been asked to dance. Lorrie danced a lot with her Class Mates and also her Husband and this kept her Husband from getting too drunk. They didn't get back to her parents house until 3:00 am, because after the main part of the Reunion was over a lot of them stood around outside talking, knowing that they may never see some of the other Class Mates again, for one reason or another. Lorrie enjoyed herself to the limit and was so glad that she had decided to do this vacation. It was almost over now, because they only had three more days before their flight back to England. This trip had accomplished everything that she had hoped it would do. Their last three days at Lorrie's parents house were spent mostly resting and of course Lorrie had to do her Texas food shopping routine where she bought foods that she couldn't get in England to take back with them. Her Husband kept extra beer in the shed out in the back yard and Lorrie tried to keep an eye on him so he didn't get to drunk and cause a problem. Lorrie knew that she had to do one more thing before they left and she had to do this by herself, so she decided to do it the last day they would be in El Campo. She had noticed that across the street from her parents house a teenage girl had a bicycle. She asked the girl if she could ride it for a while and the girl was happy to let Lorrie borrow it. Lorrie told her that she would bring it back in about an hour. Lorrie waited till her Husband laid down for a nap and then she went across the street and got the bicycle and rode off on it. It had been a while since she had ridden a bicycle, but after about two blocks she was peddling fine and she was heading as fast as she could toward Gus's parents old house that she used to ride her bicycle around trying to see Gus. Lorrie smiled as she looped around the block that Gus's parents old house was on and she craned her neck around looking just as she had done a hundred times when she was 12 and 13 years old knowing that he wasn't there anymore, but going through the motions and it made her feel young again for just a few minutes. She knew that this was just an exercise in sweet memories, but she had done it and now she was satisfied and she could go back to England with this memory to add to all the rest. She had taken a lot of pictures and had bought small gifts for her friends in England. They had a good, but long flight back to England and took a few days just to rest. Lorrie's Stepson was about to start University classes and her Husband was back at work doing his Tailoring business. Lorrie had been saving money for a long time to pay for her Stepsons University education. She had payed for his tuition, books, new cloths and the rent on a small apartment with a friend for the first semester along with some money in a Bank account for him have for spending money. His Dad also gave him the family Credit Card in case of emergencies. Lorrie was starting to think more and more about taking those classes on art, she just needed to research more on how she wanted to do it. It was getting into the fall of the year and that meant that Lorrie would soon be making plans for their holiday season. This Christmas her decorations would include some decorations that she bought on their vacation trip in the Southwest United States, such as a string of red Jalapeno pepper lights and several small Native Indian ceremonial dolls made out of corn husks. They were colorful and she would hang them on their Christmas tree as ornaments. Lorrie thought of these beautiful little dolls as Native American art works, so they fit in perfectly with her romance with art and the Jalapeno pepper lights were a direct connection to the Mexican flavor of culture that had influenced the roots of her beloved Texas and the Southwest ever since the Spanish had dominated that area 500 years before. The Christmas and New Years Holidays came and her Stepson was home on his Holiday vacation from University. He had been doing very good in his grades so far and they were proud of him. With her Stepson being gone to the University that fall Lorrie and her Husband seemed to actually be getting along better and that was a relief to Lorrie. Her Husband still didn't give her a present for Christmas and Lorrie went through the standard practice of buying and wrapping herself a gift and acting surprised when opening it. Her Stepson did buy her a book at the University Gift Shop though and that pleased Lorrie a lot. Their New Years celebration went as usual except that some of her Stepson's new friends that he had made at the University stopped by to visit and Lorrie enjoyed meeting them. The next day which was New Years Day 1995 Lorrie and her Husband went to lunch with their old friends as they usually did and so 1995 was officially underway for Lorrie and her expectations were upbeat for the New Year.

Gus—1995 January 1995 was a slow time at work in the Prison Harvesting Department. All that was going on there was in their shop where they were repairing the Harvesting Machinery that would be used for the 1995 Harvest Season. Part of Gus's job was to supervise the Inmate mechanics and keep them busy on the repair jobs. Gus was still getting the Alpine Avalanche news paper and it was his connection with what was happening in Far West Texas. He read every word of that paper trying to glean information that would be useful to him in the future, including people's names and what they did out there that might be good contacts. The towns in Far West Texas were small and far apart for the most part. People out there thought nothing about driving 100 miles just to go to a dance. The three largest towns were Alpine about 8,000 population, Fort Stockton about 8,000 population and the city of El Paso about 400,000 population. There were little towns in between these that the population was from 200 people to 2,500 people. The Alpine Avalanche covered stories and had advertisements from most of these towns, except El Paso which was so big that it was self contained and didn't need a regional news paper. Gus couldn't wait to get the paper each week to see what was going on out there. He and his wife were getting along fine and she hadn't changed a bit from when she had first moved in with him. She was easy going and predictable and totally dedicated to their relationship and marriage. Gus knew that he wasn't madly in love with her, but he was really fond of her and he was also very pleased with the way that she tried to take care of him. He had never had a wife that was so totally dedicated to being a wife, but still he could not bring himself to totally give his heart to her in a romantic love. It just wasn't in him to do that. He had never been able to do that with any of his wives. He had always shielded himself from this kind of vulnerability, because if you fell in love that meant that you automatically believed everything that your partner told you and you trusted them with everything without doubt and Gus just couldn't put himself in that position on purpose. He had seen men get taken to the cleaners and ruined by wives that supposedly loved them and men that had tried to commit suicide because of a lost love. No that strange thing love wasn't for Gus, because it was much too dangerous. Hell, he had never trusted a woman enough to even have a joint Bank account with her. He always insisted that she have her own account and he have his. Gus wanted everything separate in case of a split and he had already had plenty of splits with women. From what Gus had seen and been through it didn't make any difference how good a woman seemed to be, she could always turn on you like a mad dog and bite you. He thought about Lorrie then, and that when he didn't go back and face her like he should have been strong enough to do, she hadn't looked him up to find out what happened and caused him any trouble, maybe even got her parents involved. She could have easily done that, but she didn't. That was curious to Gus and he wondered why he was thinking of this now after 33 years. It was strange to Gus that every-once-in-a-while Lorrie always came to his mind through the years, that sweet pretty girl that had kissed him so wonderfully on the beach in Corpus

Christi in 1962. She had like, completely given herself to him and it had scared him for some strange reason that he still couldn't understand. That had always left a gap in his life that he couldn't seem to fill with any other woman. Strange, simply strange, no explaining it really. Gus thought that this is the way that life goes with so many things, that he didn't have the answers for and didn't have the time to search them out. The Day Care they owned was doing fine and they were keeping up with the payments and all the other obligations that were involved which there were many. Gus was starting to wish that he hadn't got involved in this Day Care business, but he was in it now and he would have to carry out his end of it. The spring of the year 1995 was speeding by and soon the Harvesting Department would be shipping out their equipment to the different Prison Farms for the Harvest Season and then things would really get busy. Gus was looking forward to the harvest season starting. Because he enjoyed traveling around to the different Prison Farms in different parts of the State of Texas. Gus always said that he would never have seen so much of Texas if he hadn't gone to work for the Texas Prison System. He was the only one that they sent out to Fort Stockton to stay for one or two weeks at a time, because no one else liked to go there. The Prison Farm was so far out there that it took six hours of driving just to get there and the town of Fort Stockton didn't have much to offer to most people as far as places to eat and attractions to see on days off. Gus liked it, because it was close to the area that he wanted to be someday. It wasn't in the real mountain country that was 100 miles farther west, but it had a very similar climate with a lot of the desert plants and animals that inhabited the Chihuahua Desert. They planted their crops about two months later then most of the other Prison Farms, so they were the last to harvest. By the time they were through with their harvest out there and their harvest machinery was shipped back to the Harvesting Department shop in Sugarland, Gus was ready to take another vacation out to Far West Texas. He discussed what they were to do and see with his wife and they assembled all of the things that they would need to do hiking and to take care of emergencies that might happen in an environment that could be very inhospitable to novices that didn't know what to expect. They would leave for a week at the end of September or the first week in October, because this was all of the time his wife could take off of work for vacation. She only got a two week vacation and she saved the other week to use for other things. Gus would have liked to stay much longer, but that couldn't happen for a while yet. Gus used his same ploy as he did the year before when he contacted Real Estate Agencies in the area to look at the ranches they had for sale. He also made friends with a ranch owner in the Alpine area that owned a ranch that was famous to rock hunters for it's wonderful agate and other semiprecious stones. Through him Gus met many interesting people that were interested the local gem stones and some of these people were locals that were from families that had been pioneers there when the Indians and Bandits roamed the area and they had a certain amount of notoriety because of this and also some of them were characters in their own right. Gus loved to sit and drink a few beers with them and listen to their stories and ultimately they would invite him to visit their ranches that had been their family for a century or more. Usually the ranch Head Quarters would be very rustic and mostly run down by the Eastern standards of Texas ranch country. The accommodations there would be classified as primitive by city people, but they were right up Gus's alley. Most of all is that Gus was making friends and contacts, along with learning all that he could from the people that actually lived their life on the land. This was the kind of education that had always interested Gus more then a University Degree and it was one that was never boring like a drooling, self important Professor going on and on about a subject that had minimal importance to the information that needed to be impressed on the student. Since this land and it's people were so much different then where Gus had grown up and lived most of his life he needed to learn all that he could and as fast as he could to prepare himself for the final decision to sell everything where he was and to move to the high mountain area of the Chihuahua Desert. It was a place where he had no relatives and no long time friends and he would have no one to depend on but himself to be able to live and survive there. If he failed he would probably loose what little that he had and he was of the age at 53 years old that he wouldn't be able to rebuild his finances, so he needed to learn all that he could and be careful in the investments he made out there. Gus knew that he wouldn't be able to move out there until he was 60 years old and had taken that early 10 year retirement that the State offered, but he needed to be on the look out for a house and maybe some ranch property that he could buy before his retirement time came up. Gus thought that you don't make a move like that all at once, you have to plan and be able to take advantage of property that was being sold that could be renovated for a reasonable price and that had the potential to increase in value, so he was on the constant lookout for something that would fit his price range that fell into that category, because his idea was to pay cash for everything and not have any debt. Gus bought an old 1953 Jeep that had been advertised in the El Campo news paper that was in good condition and he did some work to it to get it dependable to take with him on his West Texas vacation trip. A man that he worked with at the Harvesting Department had a trailer he wanted to sell and Gus talked him into letting him use it to haul the Jeep on his vacation. Gus had the idea of renting a room at a Motel between Alpine and Study Butte and using it for a base to explore a lot of unfenced land in the Southern end of Brewster County and this Jeep would give him the advantage of being able to look at a lot of that land that he wouldn't have the time to do by just hiking. The Jeep was made for that kind of terrain and it was a tough little vehicle that had enough room in it for him to carry extra gas, water and food. Gus had been interested in hunting for American Indian artifacts ever since his Grandmother had given him a flint spear point she had chopped up in her garden when he was six years old and he had found a lot of arrow heads and stone tools from them over the years. One of the things that he hoped for when he was looking for some land to buy out in Far West Texas was that it would have Indian camps on it so he could look for these artifacts. This Jeep that he bought to do his exploration with would allow him to go farther out into the Desert to look for Indian caves in the mountains he could crawl up to and hunt for these artifacts. Gus and his Wife had a real good vacation trip out in the Desert and they found some arrow points and stone tools along with some real nice agate, tiger eye and jasper that he wanted to polish. Gus's idea of renting that Motel room for a base of operation and the Jeep turned out to be a good decision and he decided that he was going to use this same plan every time he came out to Far West Texas. Gus hadn't found any ranch land to buy, but he was still looking for it. He went back to work and started to slowly make plans for the Thanksgiving and Christmas Holidays. Gus realized that the year 1995 was almost over and wondered how it had gone by so fast. He remembered a saying that his Mom used when she talked about how fast a year went by and it was that the older you get the faster the years fly by and Gus thought that she had been right. Gus woke up one morning and it was January 1, 1996 and while he was drinking his coffee he realized that he was going to be 54 years old in 1996 and that he would then only have 6 more years to go before his 10 year retirement. He knew that if his Mom had been right then that 6 years would go by quick, so he need to stay alert for land and a house out in Far West Texas.

Lorrie—1995 New Year 1995 was going to be a year of change for Lorrie and her Husband. Lorrie's Stepson would be away at the University finishing his Freshman Year, so they would be making an adjustment to being the only two people in the house most of the time. Her Stepson would only be back home on Holidays and for the yearly Summer Break. Lorrie knew that she would miss him some, because she had already experienced this when he had started classes in the fall of 1994. She hoped though, that by him being away that her Husband wouldn't have as much cause to get upset about some of the things that her Stepson got them involved in when he was living in the house. It seemed that when he was living in the house that there was a constant high level of stress that hung over her just waiting for something to happen that would set her Husband off on one of his verbal and physical abuse rages. Lorrie was sure that her stress level would go down now with Stefan living away from home. As her Stepson had gotten older her relationship with him had steadily improved, but there always seemed to be something in the relationship between the three of them that caused big problems and Lorrie could never really put her finger on what it was that caused this. Sometime the smallest thing could cause the biggest, scariest, most violent eruption from her Husband that would last for a couple of days and then again a rather big thing might only cause her Husband to rave and rant for a couple of hours. There seemed to be no clear pattern to his behavior. When Lorrie's Husband would have to go to London to deliver a finished garment he would stop by and visit with her Stepson on occasion and take him and one or two of his friends out for a meal. Her Husband was very proud of his Son going to the University, because he never had the chance to go himself. Her Husband had big ideas that his Son would someday become a rich Banker or Stock Trader, but Lorrie just stayed quiet and hoped that her Stepson would finish his education and get a good job that would have a future for him and then he could find a nice girl to marry and they could have a family together. Lorrie didn't have the grandiose plans for her Stepson that her Husband had, but if that made him happy then let him have them, she thought. Lorrie's experience in life, with herself as an example, told her that you could never tell what your children would end up doing. Lorrie was making her own plans and now that her Stepson was off at the University she had more time to research and collect information on how she was going to go back to school and try to obtain a Degree herself. There were several options that she had already discovered, but she had to find the one that best fit her situation. Lorrie's Husband was continuing to produce good Tailoring work for the Garment Houses and their income was to the point that Lorry was considering resigning from her job at the Library, but first she had to see how things were going to work with her Stepson at the University and if she had saved up enough money to carry him all the way through to get his Degree. Lorrie had also decided to get her some kind of sweet little dog to cuddle up to that she could show her love to, because she had a lot of love in her to share. She didn't want to pay a lot of money for one, so she went looking at some of the Animal Shelters that offered their pets at reasonable prices to be adopted out to loving owners. Lorrie finally found what she wanted and it was a sweet little Yorkshire Terrier named Mitzi. Little Mitzi took to Lorrie immediately and when she sniffed Lorrie's hand she wagged her tail and licked her hand, then looked up at Lorrie with sparkling eyes and Lorrie just fell in love with her on the spot. They became fast friends in about five minutes and Lorrie found herself talking to Mitzi on the way home like she was a human. Lorrie's Husband wasn't too surprised when she came home with the little dog and he accepted her, but Lorrie noticed that Mitzi didn't take to her Husband like she had to Lorrie. When Lorrie's Husband went back out to his shop Lorrie told Mitzi that it was OK not to like her Husband and it just showed that Mitzi was a good judge of character. Lorrie was having so much fun shopping for the things that Mitzi needed and for a lot of things that she didn't need, but that Lorrie just thought were pretty accessories for Mitzi to wear and of coarse Mitzi and to have the best toys that Lorrie could find for her to play with. Lorrie's Husband went on one of his two ski vacations for two weeks and that left Lorrie and Mitzi at home by themselves. Lorrie couldn't have been any happier. Her and Mitzi ate together, played together, slept together and listened to country music together. When the weather was warm enough Lorrie took Mitzi walking to Bromley and let her discover all the things like the Ducks that hung around the lake on the walk down. When Lorrie went to work she made sure that Mitzi had everything that she needed to make it through the day until she got back home. The first day that Lorrie came home after work and put her key in the lock on the door she could hear Mitzi barking and it sounded so sweet to Lorrie to have that sweet little dog there to greet her home and be glad to see her, because Lorrie wasn't used to having anyone at home that seemed glad to see her. This loving little dog was another piece of a puzzle that made life living with her Husband more pleasant. The first part of that puzzle was the job that she got at the Library in Bromley, then her friendship to Jill, then when she helped her Husband acquire the work from the big Garment Houses that payed so good that it brought their income up to a sound upper middle class status and now this sweet little Mitzi that she could love and be loved back. Lorrie thought that with Mitzi to love that she could survive almost anything abusive that her Husband could dish out to her. Her next plan was of course to start her University Classes on Art and to start extending her vacations back to Texas for a month at a time. Spring time came and when the weather was good Lorrie and her Husband would take their Camper Van and go on camping trips for the weekend. Lorrie loves these and of coarse she had Mitzi with them. Her Husband would sleep in one bed and her and Mitzi would sleep in the other in the Camper Van. This arrangement wasn't unusual, because Lorrie had been sleeping in her own bed room for several years, she just had a bed partner that she enjoyed now. When her Stepson completed his first year in the University Lorrie and her Husband had a party for him and some of his friends at a nice Restaurant in London and it all went off real well. Her Stepson came home for the summer off season and Lorrie noticed some changes in him that she was trying to organize in her mind to determine what they meant. He seemed more confident and also a little bit of a know-it-all. She thought that this is what happens when a young person gains a little bit of knowledge they begin to think they know everything. Lorrie was planning her month long vacation back to Texas and she was very excited about it. The only draw back was that she was going to be separated from little Mitzi. Lorrie made a very detailed day to day schedule of how her Husband and Stepson should take care of Mitzi. Her vacations back to Texas would be in the summer months now because her Stepson would be home on summer break from the University with his Dad. Lorrie was afraid that if her Husband was there alone that he would just stay drunk most of the time and then Mitzi would suffer and also he might even loose some of his business with the big Garment Houses and that would put all of her other plans in jeopardy. Lorrie told her Stepson, secretly, that she wanted him to watch his Dad, because if he stayed drunk and lost his business with the big Garment Houses it could affect his attending the University. She didn't tell him that she had already saved the money to pay for his University Degree. She wanted him to be diligent and if he risked loosing something important to him then he would more apt to do it. When Lorrie landed in Houston, Texas she stayed at her sister's house for a few days and mostly relaxed there before they drove to El Campo to stay with her parents. Lorrie's Brother was there also and they all had a great time talking about the new things that were happening around El Campo and Lorrie had pictures that she wanted to show them of Mitzi. She had pictures of Mitzi doing everything imaginable. Lorrie had always felt closer to her Dad then she had to her Mom and when their so called traditional happy hour started everyday about 5:30 pm her and her Dad took their drinks out to the patio in the back of the house so they could smoke and sip their drinks and talk. Lorrie thought that she detected something different about her Dad but dismissed it when she asked him if he was feeling OK and he told her that he thought that he felt fine for his age. Lorrie rested there for a couple of days then her, her sister and her Mom went shopping like they always did. It was a happy time for Lorrie and she would run into people she knew when they were shopping and talk to them a few minutes. Lorrie was anxious to see some of her classmates that had been at the class reunion the year before to hear their reaction of what they thought of her British Husband and her Stepson. Lorrie's chance came to get feed back on the last years class reunion when she was invited to a wedding of one of her old class mates. At the reception she had women coming up to her telling her that they thought that her Husband and Stepson were very handsome and then some of them were taken with their British accents. Some of her men classmates were impressed with the amount of beer that her Husband could consume and still be standing on his feet. They were also impressed with the fact that Lorrie had spent eight years in the United States Navy and that she had been the only girl that had served in the Military out of their class. They were talking about things that happened in the past and one woman that had been in the band with Lorrie asked her if she remembered the time that the band had made that trip to Corpus Christi and Lorrie and another girl had been kicked out of the band for staying out late with two older boys. Lorrie smiled and told her that she remembered it well and that the boy's name was Gus. Lorrie thought later that the famous trip to Corpus Christi story would follow her for life and she knew for sure that she would remember it for life, but in another light then other people would remember it. They hadn't been in love with Gus and she had, well she still was and knew that she always would be in love with Gus. But what could she do, she had to go on with her life. The time slipped by for Lorrie all to quickly and all of a sudden she realized that she needed to do her food shopping to take back all the Texas type food that she could stuff in her luggage. Her time with her family was finally over in El Campo and when her brother took her to the Air Port in Houston she ask him if he thought that her Dad was OK and he told her that he thought so, and that their Dad wasn't a spring chicken any more, so Lorrie thought that he was probably right. She hugged her brother goodby and walked into the terminal for the long flight back to England. When Lorrie arrived back in England she found that things hadn't gone as she had hoped they would. Her Husband had loaned out their Camper Van to her Stepson and a couple of his University friends to go to an open air Rock Concert and they had all but destroyed it. Lorrie didn't find out about this right away, it was a couple of days later when she wanted to get something out of it, that she noticed some deep scratches on the side of it and then she unlocked it and went inside to find the interior all torn up and dried up vomit, food and drinks spilled and holes burned in everything from cigars and cigarettes. It was Lorrie thought, beyond repair. She almost cried, because it had been very pretty and she had kept it clean and nice and stocked with everything that they would need to go camping and now just look at it a total mess. When she looked inside and saw what had happened what she had gone in there for completely escaped her mind and she walked out, locked it and went into the house crying. She questioned her Husband and found out what had happened and he defended her Stepson as much as he could by using his Son's story that his friends had actually caused the damage, but Lorrie didn't buy it and she told her Husband that he needed to just sell it, because she wasn't going to clean it up and it would cost to much to hire a company to go through it and completely redo it. She was discussed with it and she was through with it. Lorrie told her Husband and Stepson that she wasn't going to touch it and if they wanted to they could clean it up as best as they could and sell it. This is what they did and that was the end of their nice camping trips. Her Stepsons summer break from the University was over and he was back in classes. It was going into winter and Lorrie's Husband was planning his first ski trip that he always took in December for a week. Lorrie was back loving little Mitzi and she had turned 50 years old. She was back to planning for the Christmas and New Years Holidays and this was always a happy thing for her to do. Lorrie loved to decorate and make things around the house festive. She was still upset about the Camper Van, but she knew that between her Husband and her Stepson that she would never really know what had happened to it. She would simply block it from her memory like she had done so many other things. Lorrie was enjoying this Christmas more then usual, because she was buying Mitzi a lot of gifts and really Mitzi was the focus of her love and the little dog seemed to give all of her love to Lorrie. Mitzi slept on Lorrie's bed with her every night and on New Years night when Lorrie's Husband came into her bedroom to have sex Mitzi growled at him and he threatened to throw the dog against the wall and Lorrie told him that if he did he would never have sex with her again, so he took Lorrie like that, then went back to his room and then Mitzi crawled up close next to Lorrie and whimpered like she knew what had happened. This comforted Lorrie and her and Mitzi went to sleep. This is the way that Lorrie brought in the New Year of 1996.

Gus—1996 The New Year of 1996 found Gus very optimistic about his situation in life. Although he felt the pressure of getting older, in respect to the time he had to accomplish his dream of one day moving to the Mountain Region of Far West Texas in the Chihuahua Desert, along with the realization that with age his physical strength and ability would diminish with every year that passed. Gus knew that it would be at least six years before he could move to Far West Texas and he wondered what kind of physical shape he would be in at that time. When Gus made his trips out to Far West Texas he was careful to look around and ask questions about the land and housing in different areas, because he didn't want his old dream of living out there to blind him on exactly what it would take to move there and to set himself up there on a permanent basis. He understood that if he didn't do his homework on that area it could lead him into a disaster that he would never be able to recover from at that age. Gus could see from what he had learned that if you moved out there that you needed to take your money with you, because the opportunity of making a good living there was extremely limited. Most of the jobs out there were either for a laborer or they were with some sort of Government entity, like Federal, State, County or City. There was just very little opportunity for a good paying job. When Gus was looking around though he did see some opportunity because the land and housing were cheap and the taxes on Real Estate were very reasonable. The attitude out there on Real Estate prices and taxes reminded Gus of the Wharton County area where he grew up in the 1950's and also the area hadn't adopted all the regulations that made everything you did to build or improve your property expensive to do, like the rest of Texas along the Gulf Coast and back to East Texas. This was all a plus for Gus when he was making his plans, because it meant that you could take your money from the East part of the State and buy and do more in the West part of the State with it, basically multiplying its value and buying power. The problem for Gus was just how much money would he be able to take with him, and that would be a question that he wouldn't have an answer to for six more years. Gus's job at the Prison Harvesting Department was going along in a predictable way. Working for the Texas Government in the Prison System was extremely structured with rules and regulations that you had to follow and also the pay was very structured also. Almost the only way to get a pay raise was to apply for a job that would give you a promotion that carried a pay raise with it. The State was big on giving evaluations that changed your job title, but gave no pay raise with it, so Gus was pretty sure that he wouldn't be able to expect a big increase in money from that area. His wife was in a dead end job where she worked, so there wouldn't be any big increase in money there either, so everything depended on Gus and how much money he could put together from his Subdivisions, his Ranch Land sale payments, possible Oil Deals, the eventual sale of the Child Care Business and the sale of his house in Sugarland. Right now all Gus could do was to stay on the look out for some real good deals on land and housing through the Alpine News Paper. The Harvesting Department was finishing up on all the repairs to its machinery by late spring and preparing to start delivering the machinery to the Prison Farms in the early summer when they got the orders of which farm would began harvest first. This was always a big scramble to get the Inmate Operators transferred to different Prison Farms along with the harvesting machines they were to operate. Gus and the other Supervisors would have to visit these Prison Farms to help them determine when their crops would be ripe enough to start harvesting. Gus liked this, because by this time he had enough of just being around their shop and doing office work and was ready to get on the road and visit these other Prison Farms around the State to see who was new there and what was new on the Farm and also to see old faces that he knew well by now. The Harvest Season started as usual in July, first with the Milo Maize then the corn and finally the cotton. There were mechanical break downs for sure and also rains that would hold up the harvesting for a time, but they always finished around the middle to the last of September and then Gus could plan his next vacation to his beloved High Mountain area in the Chihuahua Desert of Far West Texas. This harvest season was no exception and Gus and his Wife were headed out West in the last week of September. Gus used the same plan that he had used in 1995, staying in the same Motel and taking the Jeep with him on a trailer. This time Gus explored a little different area that had been a very volcanic area at one time and it had a beautiful rock canyon with some Native Indian ground shelters, a seeping spring and some bed rock mortar holes that the Indian women used to grind up their seeds. He found several artifacts and it had a lot of different semi-precious gem stones and when discussing the place with the Motel owner he learned that the property was owned by an elderly lady that lived in Alpine. Gus found her name in the Alpine phone book and tried to call her without success, so he talked the Motel owner into letting him keep the phone book to take back to Sugarland with him. Gus hiked all around on this property not really knowing the extent of it or where property lines were. He drove to Alpine which was the County Seat of Brewster County to go through the records at the County Clerks office to see if there were any claims against the property and then to the Central Appraisal District office to find out the amount of tax on the property and the address of the woman that owned it. With his research at the Central Appraisal District office Gus discovered that two people besides the owner were paying taxes on the property. This meant only one thing to Gus and that was that each of these people were trying to obtain the ownership of the property by a little known Texas Law called Adverse Possession. This Texas Law was created back when a lot of Homesteaders came to Texas and stayed for a while and then left the land and no one was paying taxes or using the land. Under this Law if the land wasn't being used, and this land wasn't being used by the woman that owned it, someone could pay taxes on it and improve it a little, for several years and then they could file for ownership of it. Also in Texas the taxing Authorities weren't obligated to tell the owner that someone else was paying taxes on their property, so several people could be paying taxes on the same property and the owner would never know it and the State would be collecting multiple Taxes on the same property. He then contacted a Land Surveyor in Alpine to see how much it would cost to get a Survey of the property and was told that it would be somewhere around $ 1,500.00. Armed with all of this information Gus would be able to contact that woman from Sugarland after he got back home and make her an offer for her property. He found out that the property was 550 acres. When Gus got back to Sugarland he made contacting this woman a priority. After several days of trying to contact her by phone he finally decided to write her a letter and include a check for $ 25.00/ac or $ 13,750.00 just to see what would happen. Sure enough after about a week Gus got a phone call from the woman and she told Gus that she wanted $100.00/ac for the property and Gus told her that no way was the property worth that, then she went down to $50/00/ac and Gus told her that if she wouldn't sell the property for what he offered to just return his check. He then told her that she might have trouble with the other people paying taxes on her property and she needed to look into it. She was surprised and didn't know anything about the Adverse Possession Law and thanked Gus and she did return his check. This was Gus's first attempt to buy land in Far West Texas, but he had done his homework and he knew what that kind of land was worth and wasn't prepared to pay more, besides he knew that he really didn't have a lot of money to risk on this rugged land way out in the middle of the Chihuahua Desert. Gus would have liked to have purchased the property, because he had been familiar with that particular area for several years, but that High Mountain Chihuahua Desert region was a huge expanse that covered millions of acres and hundreds of miles and surely there was something out there that would suite Gus's Bank Account and his interest, he just had to keep looking. Gus kept up with his job and his responsibilities at the Day Care in Sugarland and the rest of 1996 was slipping by in an orderly fashion. He and his Wife made their usual plans for the Thanksgiving and Christmas Holidays and they had a very low key New Years Eve. Gus woke up to a New Years Day 1997 drinking coffee and reading the Alpine Avalanche to find out all the latest happenings and also if there might be some interesting land for sale advertisement in Far West Texas.

Lorrie—1996 started For Lorrie with the upsetting episode of her Husband satisfying his sexual appetite and threatening little Mitzi when she growled at him, but besides this Lorrie still felt good about starting the New Year of 1996. Lorrie always tried to have high spirits for the starting of a New Year, because to her it meant a new beginning that she could work with to improve what had been before in the year that had just passed. Her Stepson was in his second year at the University and they were having some trouble with him that started with the destruction that he and his University friends did to the family Travel Van. They had since sold it at a big loss and Lorrie still hadn't forgiven her Stepson for his disregard for their family possessions. In fact he acted like it wasn't any big thing and that if it was a family possession then as him being a part of the family he had every right to do what ever he wanted to do to it. Lorrie couldn't figure out why her Stepson had developed his arrogant disposition just because he was attending the University. All of a sudden he thought that he was smarter then anyone else and that everybody owed him something, like he was entitled to do what he wanted without regard for anyone else. Lorrie had always had problems with her Stepson, but this was a new one and she didn't like it a bit and again her Husband was making excuses and protecting his Son. Lorrie had been researching, for several years, what would be the best way to earn a Degree in Art from a University. Lorrie had decided that there was no way that she could go to a full time attendance University, because she would be away from home to long and she was afraid that if she wasn't around to do the billing, collect the money, keep the books for the business and try to watch her Husband with his drinking then everything that she had nurtured along with his Tailoring business would be ruined. She finally discovered what the British called Open University. This looked like it might be a perfect fit for her purposes. The Open University offered a Art History Degree by answering assignment essays sent by mail, going to see a Tutor on regular visits and field trips to Europe to visit the Art Galleries there as part of the overall Degree Plan. In the United States it would be called getting a University Degree by taking Correspondence Courses. She knew that this would take her several years, but this looked exciting to Lorrie, because it would give her the best of both worlds. She could stay at home and take care of her Husbands Tailoring business and get her Art Degree and also have the chance to visit the great Art Galleries in Europe with Instructors that would be explaining all that she would learn in an actual situation with the Art Works right in front of her. Lorrie started putting a pencil to the costs of this Degree Plan and discovered that it wouldn't be cheap, but that they would be able to afford it. If Lorrie decided to ultimately sign up for these University Classes it would mean that two people,in their household, would be working toward University Degrees at the same time. She had already saved enough of her own money, that she had worked for at the Library, to send her Stepson to the University, so that one was already paid for, now what to do about her Degree was the question. Lorrie knew that she was going to have to talk to her Husband about this and she wasn't looking forward to that. Lorrie still had some savings, but she wanted to keep a fair amount of money tucked away in case that she would have to run from her Husband at a moments notice. Lorrie was never sure what might be in store for her with regard to her Husbands angry rages that could get very violent and that money she had in her savings was a security to her that might mean her very survival. Lorrie felt like she was floating on air with finding this option of getting a Degree through the Open University system. She had been thinking of how she should approach her Husband with this. Lorrie wanted him to pay for it, so she could keep her savings, but how should she approach him with that proposition. She would have to be very careful and choose the right time and then soften him up otherwise he would just tell her that she had no need to wast the time and money learning about art or he might even throw a big fit and things would get out of hand and turn violent. Even after being married to him for 12 years Lorrie could never be sure how her Husband would respond to something. Lorrie went on about her normal daily life carefully keeping watch for the opening she needed to broach the subject of her desire to sign up and take classes through the Open University. Her little dog Mitzi continued to be a source of comfort and emotional stability for Lorry, because of the unconditional love and commitment the little dog showered on Lorrie. Lorrie would have so much fun telling everyone the latest things that Mitzi would do, just like Mitzi would be her child. Mitzi is exactly what Lorrie needed, which was to love and be loved. In the early summer of 1996 Lorrie finally got the chance to talk to her Husband about her desire to take the Art History Degree classes at the Open University. Her Husband had received a huge bonus check from three suit coats he had Tailored for the Royal Family and he came home in a very good mood waving the check around and telling her to get ready, because they were going out to their favorite Pub for dinner and to celebrate. Lorrie smiled brightly knowing her time had come to talk to him, but she would have to do it before he got drunk. She sat him down and got him a beer and had him tell her what all had happened when he had delivered the suit coats. After he told her his story and she had his attention she told him that she also had something very nice to tell him. Lorrie told him all that she had found out about the opportunity to take her Art History Degree through the Open University System and that she would have to resign her position at the Library to do it, but in doing so she would be home full time and would be able to spend even more time doing his secretarial work for his Tailoring Business. She told him that the only catch was that she needed him to pay for her classes and books, but he was going to save money with his accountant, because she would have more time to prepare the forms and organize the information his accountant needed to prepare his taxes. He was real receptive to all of this in his state of euphoria and he agreed to all that Lorrie proposed to him. Lorrie went to get ready to go to the Pub and she smiled to herself that finally she had made the move she had been wanting to make for years and that was to be able to learn more about the art and the artists that had produced some of the worlds most wonderful works of art. She knew that she would have to complete signing up as soon as possible so her Husband wouldn't have time to change his mind. She decided that she would start in the fall of 1996 and that would give her time to plan her month long vacation back to El Campo, Texas using her time off from work, before her resignation became effective at the end of the summer and then she could concentrate on her studies. Lorrie thought that it was a shame that she always had to resort to finding the right time to talk to her Husband about subjects that needed discussion between them so as not to provoke an outburst of anger from him. She had no idea why they had such a hard time relating to each other. She had learned from experience to wait for the right times to talk to him and to measure her words to frame her subject in the right way. Just one word out of place or the wrong timing and she could end up with her Husband in a rage that would build into verbal and physical abuse that would last for hours and maybe even days. Lorrie got her Open University Classes signed up and paid for to start in the fall and she also presented her resignation to her supervisor effective after her summer vacation to El Campo, Texas. Now all Lorrie had to do was to start planning her vacation back to her home town. Lorrie was feeling a little sad about resigning her position at the Library, because it had meant so much to her. It had come along at a time when she had needed it so bad for several reasons. The Library job had supplied badly needed income when they were about loose their house to mortgage debt, but it also gave Lorrie other things that improved her life dramatically like a friend in Jill that she had met there and also some badly needed cultural additions to her life with the Churchill Theater that was a part of the Library Complex. The Library job had given her so much to be thankful for and actually she thought that it had saved her Marriage and probably her life, because she had contemplated the possibility of suicide. Lorrie knew that now was the time for her to move on though, just as she had learned from other experiences to move on, she knew what the feelings inside her were telling her to do and there was no mistaking those feelings. Lorrie used her time now to keep her promise to her Husband by spending more time on his Tailoring Business office work to simplify the tax process for his Accountant and save him money and she also was in the process of planning her month long vacation back to Texas. Her vacation this year would end about two weeks before she was to start her Open University Art History Degree classes and she would need this time to catch up on her

Husbands Tailoring Business and also to prepare herself mentally for her classes to start. Lorrie's flight back to Texas was the usual long tiring one that it had always been, so she rested up for a couple of days before really getting into visiting with her family and friends. One of her main topics of discussion with her parents was her return to studying on the University level after leaving Wharton County Junior College after only one year. They were very happy that she had chosen to resume her education. They didn't exactly understand why she chose to study Art for a Degree, but they were proud of her for working toward a University Degree. Lorrie's friends were amazed that she would attempt to go back to school at her age of 51 years and also with everything else that she was responsible for doing, but they also thought that if she graduated with a Degree from a European University it would be something that they could never even think about doing. They knew her accomplishments in the Navy, so they had no doubt about her ability and determination to succeed and finish her Degree. Lorrie was so proud to tell her family and friends about her decision to resume her education, because in her past she felt that she had given them more disappointments in her then accomplishments and this would be viewed as a positive in her life. Lorrie's month long vacation back in El Campo, Texas was going by fast and before she knew it she was shopping for the food products that she always brought back to England with her. The last couple of days there she took the time to ride around Gus's Mom's old house and the Service Station that he had worked at and she wondered what he would think of her going back to the University. Would it make a difference to him, would he see her in a different light, maybe one that would make him proud of her, maybe even proud enough for him to love her. Lorrie knew that she was being silly even thinking like this, because there was no way that her and Gus would ever have the chance to get together. Well it was time to think about getting back to England and starting her University Classes and seeing her sweet little dog Mitzi and her friend Jill. When Lorrie arrived back in England she found out that her Husband and her Stepson had been at odds for several days about extra money that her Stepson wanted deposited in his bank account each month. He didn't really need it, but he thought that he deserved it and was demanding it to use for his social partying escapades. Lorrie's Husband wouldn't commit to it until he had a chance to talk to Lorrie, because he basically didn't know anything about their money situation. Lorrie had handled all of their Bank accounts and billing and collections ever since they had been married and her Husband was afraid to commit himself to something that he had no knowledge of. Her Stepson had been trying to convince his Dad to give him the money before Lorrie returned, because he knew that she would be against it. Now Lorrie was in the middle of the fight and this was something that she would have liked to avoid, because it could cause terrible trouble between her and her Husband. Lorrie's Stepson had been a source of trouble in her Marriage from the beginning. She could never depend on either her Husband or her Stepson to side with her on a decision that had to be made. They would change their positions in the middle of a discussion and make her out to be the bad guy and her Stepson would stomp up the stairs to his room and slam the door and then her Husband would start with his berating of her with some of the most ugly screaming, viscous, degrading language he could think of to call a woman and Lorrie and her little Mitzi would hunker down on the couch hoping not to be violently attacked after an hour or two of this vocal abuse. Lorrie was not ready for this, so she decided to suggest that they increase her Stepsons Bank allowance by twenty percent, which was about one third as much as he wanted, but at least he didn't stomp off to his room, instead he just sat there and pouted for an hour and Lorrie avoided a major confrontation in the family. This is how she was welcomed back from her month long vacation. In the fall she started her Open University Classes and she was very happy to be back in school learning things that she had only dreamed about since she was just a young girl. This really gave Lorrie a new lease on life and something to look forward to each day. It took the dark clouds away from her dismal Marriage and home life. Now Lorrie had three things that she could focus on that gave her happiness and a way to escape to a secret place that allowed her soul to heal from the reality of her everyday life. She had her friend Jill, her little dog Mitzi and now she could also escape into her world of the art of the Great Masters. As the months went on Lorrie studied and spent all the time that she could with her Tutor learning how to get into the minds of the Artists that produced some of the greatest art works in Europe. The Christmas Holidays came and she bought herself an expensive book containing pictures of many of the famous paintings that hung in the Art Galleries in Europe as a Christmas gift from herself to herself, since she never got anything from her Husband or Stepson. Lorrie was especially happy on New Years Eve this year, because she knew that she could look forward to continuing her Open University studies. All of her grades on the papers she had turned in had perfect scores for her first semester and this gave her a new feeling of accomplishment that brought back memories of her time in the Navy and how it had rebuilt her confidence in herself after her divorce and dismal two years back home living with her parents in El Campo, Texas. This was doing the same thing for her that the Navy had done and on New Years Day 1997 Lorrie was more then ready to meet any difficulty that 1997 could bring as long as she could continue with her studies in the Open University Art History Classes. When her and her Husband met their friends for the New Years Day 1997 lunch the talk was about her art studies and Lorrie was extremely animated as she related all that she had learned. Her friends were very interested and asked questions, but her Husband was bored, so he kept himself occupied by getting drunk. Lorrie ignored it and decided she wouldn't let it spoil the first day of the year 1997.

Gus—1997 New Years Day 1997 Gus was just relaxing and drinking his coffee and reading the Alpine Avalanche paper. He usually read it from front to back to help him gain information and learn more about the lives of the people out there, the weather, different businesses he might need to know about when he bought land there, the people that were leaders in their communities that he would need to know, problems in the individual towns and of coarse the advertisement section with Real Estate homes and land for sale. He was noticing a pattern about the different prices of housing and land that occurred in different areas. The Towns that promoted Tourism and had a lot of it, had prices on their housing and land that was a lot higher then the Towns that depended only on their traditional resources for their existence, such as ranching, mining and limited irrigated farming. Quiet times like this for Gus gave him time to reflect on the changes in his life over the years. He thought that he had so many changes, so much strife and conflict, so many financial wins and losses and he knew that if he could keep things going in the right direction that he was going to have another major change when he turned 60 years old and had worked for 10 years for the Texas Department of Criminal Justice. They offered a retirement for 10 years of service that he could take at age 60 that would guarantee him a small retirement check plus he could keep his medical insurance for him and his wife. That means that he could take it in 5 more years. Gus knew that if he didn't take this retirement and move to West Texas that it would be his last chance to be able to make his dream come true to live out there. He could take that retirement in 2002 which would be exactly 40 years from the time that he had taken his Mom out to the Big Bend in 1962. Then he thought that speaking of 1962, it brought back memories of that sweet, beautiful girl Lorrie. Gus was just amazed that thinking of the year 1962 had immediately brought back the memory of Lorrie. Sweet Lorrie, how many years now had it been since he had seen her or even heard her name, it must be 35 years, wow and he still remembered her like it was just yesterday that they were on that beach in Corpus Christy, Texas. All of a sudden her kisses seemed to still be on his lips, because he remembered exactly how they felt and how he felt kissing her. He had never experienced anything like it since. Gus knew that he had a very sweet wife now and that she was totally committed to making a good marriage and he felt a little bit guilty thinking about Lorrie again like this, but he couldn't help it. The memory Gus had about Lorrie no other woman he had ever met could compete with it. Something in him told him that maybe he had made a mistake in not following his heart back then in 1962 when he was 19 and Lorrie was 16, but it was much to late now. Well he still had his memories of her and that would have to do for him and he hoped that her life had turned out better then his had. He was going to be 55 years old this year and his objective now was to start putting together a plan to be able to move out to Far West Texas when it came time for him to retire from the Texas Department of Criminal Justice in five more years. This meant that he would have to own some ranch land out there, a home in the area of his ranch land, have enough cash money to do repairs and improvements and be debt free, so there was a lot to think about and plan for and he knew that he wouldn't be able to do it on short notice, so the five years he had left on the Gulf Coast in Sugarland needed to be spent putting this plan in action a little at a time as his money became available so when the time came all he would have to do was pack up and leave for Far West Texas. This time of the year was usually slow for the Harvesting Department at the Texas Department of Criminal Justice, because the Supervisors were not on the road every day driving to Prison Farms that were harvesting their crops. They were busy repairing all the different harvesting machinery that had been previously out in the fields on the Prison Farms, but had now been shipped back to their shop in Sugarland to under go the repairs that they would need to put them in top shape for their next harvest season. The Supervisors would also be training some new Inmate mechanics and operators, because every year some of their Inmates would be discharged for finishing their Prison Time or be Paroled Out for good behavior. This was a job that Gus was involved in, because he was familiar with how the Classification System worked and he could talk to them to Red Flag an Inmate that looked like he would fit into the Harvesting Department's Inmate training program. The Harvesting Department trained Inmates to be machinery and truck mechanics, welders, machinery operators, parts men and clerks in their office, so there were a variety of jobs that they were trained for and all of those jobs held opportunities for them when they were discharged from Prison. Some of these Inmates didn't work out and had to be transferred to other Prisons to be re-evaluated and placed in other jobs, but others turned out to be excellent workers and became dependable workers for the Harvesting Department until they were discharged. The Texas Prison System followed along the lines of Political Correctness advocates and succumbed to pressure to abolish the use of tobacco by the Inmates and this created a huge problem with the smuggling of contraband tobacco and also fights between the Inmates, because of the short tempers caused by the withdrawals from tobacco addiction. This really interrupted a lot of work that the Harvesting Department was involved in trying to get their machinery repaired before harvest. The Inmates would not be turned out to work many times so an extensive search could be made of their work stations to see if any tobacco could be found and if it was, then the Inmates that worked in that work station were brought up on charges and the would be transferred out of the Harvesting Department. This also applied to Inmates that got into fights, so all of a sudden there was a constant upheaval in the Harvesting Departments Inmate workers and new ones would have to be transferred in and the training had to start from the beginning. The people at the top that order these types of policies are insulated from the problems that they cause and the Supervisors that have to abide by these policies and see to it that the same amount of work is accomplished are not forgiven if the work slows down. They are still expected to have the same performance as if everything was the same as it had always been. Also there were a lot of good Inmates that for no other reason then a change in policy had charges placed against them that went against them when they went up for parole. This whole thing was a mess that Gus and the rest of the Supervisors had to contend with, not only in the Harvesting Department, but system wide. Harvest finally started and Gus and the rest of the Supervisors had to use some real green Inmates as machinery operators. It was really scary to have to turn them loose with one of those big pieces of harvesting machines when they weren't fully trained. Gus was reading an issue of the Alpine Avalanche when he saw an advertisement in the land for sale section by a School Distract that had over one thousand acres of land for sale, that they had taken back for unpaid taxes, and the interested buyers had to supply a bid for this land by a certain date. Gus looked at this bid deadline and saw that it was just a few days away which meant that he wouldn't have the time to drive out there to look at the land before the deadline came. It was July the 7th when Gus saw this advertisement and the Harvesting Department was in their harvest season full swing. No one was allowed to take off during the harvest season, so what was he to do about bidding on this land. This was very frustrating for Gus, because this was a real chance for him to acquire property out there and it was the right amount of acreage that he was interested in too. He decided that he would have to wait till the next day so he could call that School District and find more about where the land was located and that meant that one more day would be gone on the deadline for the bids to be in and he would be running very close on this. The next day Gus called the School District and talked to the Superintendent of Schools there and he told Gus the approximate location of the land. Gus looked it up on a map that he had and decided that it had possibilities. It was located directly west of the Sierra Viejo mountain range in western Jeff Davis County and it was approximately eight miles east of the Rio Grand River. Gus decided to go ahead and mail in a bid on the land with seeing it. He decided on a bid price of $ 17.50/acre, which he knew was very low, but without seeing the land he didn't feel comfortable bidding more. He filled out the bid form that had been in the Alpine Avalanche paper and put in a check for the full amount and mailed it off Certified Mail Return Receipt. After he did this he discovered that the day that he had seen the advertisement in the paper it was July 7th and that was his dead son's birthday. Gus thought that maybe that was a good omen that all of this would work out. A week later Gus got a call from the Superintendent of the school and he told Gus that he had won the bid for the property, but that after talking to his School Board they decided that to be fair to Gus, since he lived in the Houston area and the climate and land was so different there then it was in the Chihuahua Desert where he had won the bid on the property, they wanted to extend an invitation to Gus to come and look at the land before they cashed his check. Gus thought that this was a very honest way for them to treat him and he told the Superintendent that it would be a few days before he could manage a trip out there, because he would have to wait till his four day off period started and it would take a whole day to drive there and one day to drive back to Sugarland, so he would only have one day to look at the land he had bid on. He told the Superintendent that he would be driving in on a Friday and he could look at the land on a Saturday, but since it was a weekend would anyone be available to show him the land. Gus told the Superintendent when he would be able to come and the Superintendent told Gus that there was a man that worked in maintenance for the school and he knew the lands location and arrangements would be made for Gus to meet him at the school and he would accompany Gus to look at the land. Gus thanked the Superintendent and began making his plans to drive out to look at the land he had won the bid on in the Chihuahua Desert of Far West Texas. Gus was working a ten day on and a four day off schedule at the Harvesting Department, so he had to wait for a few days to get off his four days to drive out to look at the land. Even though Gus knew that he would be tired from his ten days of work he decided that he would leave the next day, a Friday very early in the morning, and drive to Marfa, Texas and get a Motel room for the night. The next morning, a Saturday, he would go to the small School in the little town about 35 miles north of Marfa to meet with the man that was to take him to see the land that he had bid on. He would spend that Saturday walking over as much of the land as he could and then he would spend the night in the Motel in Marfa and drive back to Sugarland on Sunday so he could still have one day, Monday to rest before he had to go back to work on his next ten day work schedule. Gus knew that this was going to be a grueling trip, but there was no other way to accomplish it, because he wouldn't be through with the harvesting season till sometime in late September. The small School was in a very small community named Valentine, so it was real easy to find the School and the man that was to be his guide. His Guide had lived in Valentine his whole life and he knew the land around there very good, because even as a young boy he had hunted it with his friends for deer, rabbits and quail. Gus and his Guide drove north of Valentine for ten miles and along the way Gus saw the Sierra Vieja Mountain range on his left and noticed that the land between the Mountains and the road they were driving on was relatively flat looking and Gus told his Guide that he hoped that the land he had bid on didn't look like that, he hoped that it was more rugged. His Guide just looked at Gus and didn't say anything and Gus wondered what he was thinking. His Guide motioned Gus to turn left on a narrow blacktop road and after four miles it went to dirt and rock and the Guide told Gus that the road was actually an old railroad bed that had been built with Chinese labor back in the 1880's that went to an old coal mine close to the Rio Grand River, but it had been abandoned and the rails had been pulled up for salvage. When they drove through a road cut and came out on the other side there was a big drop off and in front of them down in the drop off was a huge volcanic dike that went up a couple of hundred feet. It looked beautiful and Gus pulled up to the drop off to look at it and to survey the landscape. This landscape on the west side of the Sierra Vieja Mountains was completely different then on the east side. It was very rugged and had many signs of violent volcano activity. Gus told his Guide that this looked better to him and again his Guide didn't say anything, he just looked at Gus. Gus wondered what his Guide was thinking. They pulled away from the drop off and followed the very rough road at between five and ten miles an hour, because if you tried to drive faster then this you would tear up your car. About ten more miles down the rough road his Guide told him to stop. They got out of the car and his Guide told Gus that they were on the land, but that he didn't know where the boundaries where located. Gus knew that the land was a mile wide north to south and two miles long east to west, so he knew which direction that he would walk. Gus stood there and turned around slowly looking carefully and saw that the land was very rugged. He was immediately taken with it and was excited about doing some exploring to find out more of it's secrets. Gus told his Guide that he would take him back to the school and then he would come back to the land to look it over. On their way back to Valentine Gus finally got an idea about what his Guide had been thinking, because out of the blue he said that he wasn't for sure what good that land was but you might be able to put some goats on it. Gus had the feeling that his Guide thought him a stupid city boy and Gus knew better then to try to explain to his Guide why he wanted the rugged, sorry looking land over the much better looking land on the east side of the Sierra Vieja Mountains. Gus knew that his Guide would never understand. By the time they got back to Valentine it was lunch time, so Gus ate at a local Cafe and bought several bottles of water to put in his cooler that he had in his Jeep Cherokee along with some fruit, cheese and lunch meat. Gus also had a knife and a pistol. He drove back out to this wild land that was just eight miles from the Rio Grand River. It was crisscrossed with volcanic faults that zigzagged back and forth and you could follow them with your eye from the lower flats to where they went up the sides of the mountains. There were some mesas farther south that were just on the west side of the Sierra Vieja Mountains that were slanting at 45 degrees and showed the wild formation of this region by the tectonics and volcano's when they were erupting. He walked from the road going east toward the Sierra Vieja Mountains and 96 pass which was a saddle in the mountains. As he walked Gus picked up several semi-precious rocks a fossil of a shell and two Indian arrow heads. He made a u-turn after an hour and walked back west to a creek and found a small seeping spring there that came through fractures in a lava dam that crossed the creek. There was a large pool of clear water there that had tracks of deer and a very large mountain lion. Gus looked around that area for a while and found a lot of rock flakes and a few pieces of pottery shards indicating an ancient Indian camp. He also noticed some large pieces of coal laying on the old railroad bed that crossed this land. Gus knew that he had found the piece of land that he wanted even though it was extremely hard to get to and had no electricity. He went back to his car and drove to his Motel in Marfa. It was getting dark by this time, so Gus found a place to eat his dinner then he went to his room to clean up and go to sleep so as to be ready for his long drive back to Sugarland on Sunday morning. Gus went to bed early, because he knew how tiring his drive back would, but sleep evaded him. He was so excited about what he had seen on his hike around the land that he just couldn't settle down and sleep. He would lay there and open his eyes to look at the clock thinking that hours had passed and it had maybe been only fifteen minutes. Finally at 11:30 pm he decided that he had to do something that would take his thoughts off of the land. What finally came to his mind was Lorrie and the times he remembered her and this settled him down. Gus went through every memory that he had of her from the times that she had come to the Service Station with her girl friends, when he had worked there when he was in High School and the times he saw her walk around his Mom's house in her black stretch dancing suit, to the time he followed the High School Band bus to Corpus Christi and they ended up on the beach there kissing and talking and Lorrie told him that she wanted him to take her virginity, but not there, that she would let him know when it would be, to the last time he had seen her at her Mom and Dad's house in her bed room when they almost made love, but were interrupted by her little sister and brother. As he went through his wonderful memories of her their kisses stood out the most and as he drifted off to a sound sleep the last thing that he remembered was the feel of her hot, soft, wet lips on his.. He woke up on Sunday morning with Lorrie on his mind and smiled and thanked her memory for giving him the rest he would need for his trip back to Sugarland. While he was driving back he wondered what it would have been like to have had Lorrie with him walking over that rugged land with it's beautiful, but unforgiving landscape Would she have been noticing all the beautiful rocks and been picking them up to put in her pockets or been excited about finding an Indian arrowhead and a fossil and absolutely loving the experience that they were having together, well he could not know this, but somehow he had the feeling that she would have fallen in love with this rugged land just as he had done. Gus sped on down the miles and miles of highway toward Sugarland and home with the knowledge that he had found the land that he wanted and could afford to own. Now was the next step and that was to decide how he was going to develop it enough to be able to enjoy it. This was going to be a fun part for Gus. He knew that he was going to have to come up with ideas and research them to try and figure out the best ways that he could afford to use this land. He knew for sure two things and they were that he no longer was going to be traveling to different areas around Far West Texas, because he would be concentrating his efforts on his new property and that his first priority was to find the property lines which would involve hiring a Surveyor. Later in the summer Gus was sent to a Prison Farm over by Fort Stockton, Texas to supervise the harvesting of their cotton. He was going to be out there for at least a couple of weeks, so he used some of his off time to try and find a Surveyor in the area to survey his property. Fort Stockton was in the Chihuahua Desert, but it didn't have the big mountains that dominated the Desert farther to the west. Fort Stockton was a long drive from Sugarland and who ever went out there was going to have to stay for a while and the town didn't have a lot of the up-scale eating establishments and other attractions that the Sugarland area had, so none of the Supervisors really liked to go there. They were really glad that Gus always said that he would go there. Gus always enjoyed going there, because it was the Chihuahua Desert and he was familiar with it. While he was there this time he found a Surveyor in Fort Stockton that would do the survey of his land, but he wouldn't be able to do it until November. Gus would have liked to have gotten it done sooner before winter, so he could make other plans for a camp, but he had to take what he could get, so he hired the Surveyor for November. Gus also found a company there that did bulldozer and maintainer work and he talked them into going out there in October to build him a road and blade off a place for a camp. One morning while Gus was driving out to the Prison Farm he noticed a shipping container in a pasture on the side of the road and a phone number was painted on it plus containers for sale. He wrote the number down, because Gus thought that a shipping container might make a good sturdy camp house if modified right. He called the number and found out that the company selling these containers was located in Arlington, Texas close to Dallas. He talked to the owner and learned that the owner had a hunting lease not far from Fort Stockton and was coming out there in October and would be glad to deliver the container at a discount because he was going to be in the area. Gus agreed on a price and he made arrangements with the bulldozer company to come out a couple of days before the delivery of the container to make a road and smooth off a place for a camp to put the container. This trip to Fort Stockton had really made things come together quick, maybe to quick, because Gus wouldn't get the land surveyed till November, but he thought that he could find a spot for the camp within his property lines, because the property was one mile wide and two miles long. The Fort Stockton Prison Farm was always the last one to harvest, because the climate out there was about two months behind that of the other Prison Farms on the Gulf Coast and East Texas. The climate out there stayed colder longer making it a risk for frost if the crops were planted earlier. Gus's trip to the Fort Stockton Prison Farm's harvest season this year came at an opportune time that gave him the chance to line up the people he needed quickly to do the work he needed at his newly acquired property in Far West Texas. Gus had always been very good at organizing and timing work with personal and machinery in a step, by step program that made his operations work fast, efficient and smoothly. His only hitch this time was that the Surveyor should have been the first step, but it was going to be delayed till after the machinery work because he was going to have to take advantage of the weather and the vacation time he would take from his job. All of this was running close to the Far West Texas winter season and Gus knew how unpredictable that could be. He knew how severe those could be and those winter storms coming through the mountains could bring with them snow and ice and high winds. He didn't want to be caught in one of those in the middle of the machinery dirt work. He wanted to get the basic camp set up before winter. Gus finished the Fort Stockton Prison Farm harvest season and went back to Sugarland to get himself organized on his vacation time so it would be approved at the same time that he had scheduled the machinery dirt work and the delivery of his container that would be turned into his camp house. Gus bought ply board, 2x4's, insulation, wiring, switches, wall outlets, a window, a metal door, wood shelving, screws, nails and other supplies that he thought that he might need and he loaded them along with all the tools he would need in an eight foot trailer that he would pull out there with his Jeep Cherokee. He also looked up a Motel in Van Horn and made reservations to stay there for a week. He had never stayed in Van Horn before, but it was the closest town to his property which was 35 miles to the south west. Gus pulled into Van Horn and went to his Motel and checked in and unhooked from his trailer, so he could drive around town and see what it looked like and what it had to offer. He was a little disappointed at what he saw at first. There were broken windows on some vacant store buildings on the main street and he saw beer bottles and cans laying around stop signs along with old tires and car batteries strewn around vacant lots. Van Horn sure didn't look like a prosperous growing town. He thought that he would have to find out more about the town and maybe he would learn something while staying there for a week. The next day his bulldozer operator and the bulldozer came in to town and he checked into the same Motel that Gus was staying in. Early the next morning after eating a good breakfast they set out for Gus's property 35 miles to the southwest. It was mid morning by the time they had unloaded the bulldozer and Gus crawled on it with the operator and he told the operator that they were just going to drive around on the property and look it over, so he could decide where he wanted his first road and the camp. Gus wanted to do it this way, because this land had a lot of cactus and thorn bushes that would destroy tires, but they wouldn't hurt the steel tracks on the bulldozer. They spent about two hours exploring the land and Gus finally decided where he was going to build his first road. This road would be the main access to the interior of the property and to his camp. This road started from a road that went across the western part of his property and his new road climbed up from there about 100 feet to the top of a mesa that wound around what looked like the center of the property. After making this road Gus picked out the highest and the widest place on that mesa to bulldoze off clean of brush to make his camp where the shipping container was to be unloaded the next day. This was very exciting for Gus and even after a big dinner and three beers at a cafe in Van Horn that evening Gus was having trouble getting asleep. He remembered what he did that night when he stayed in Marfa and that is what he did again this time. As he went through his memories of Lorrie he drifted into a deep sleep and the next thing he heard was his alarm clock go off at 5:00 am that morning. Gus and the bulldozer operator ate a good breakfast and drove out to his property. When they turned off of highway 90 Gus started tying colored ribbons on posts and brush to mark the way for the truck that was to deliver the container. Gus knew the approximate time to expect the container delivery which was to be after lunch. Everything was ready at the new camp, so Gus decided that they needed to get on the bulldozer and bulldoze a road east toward the Sierra Vieja Mountains to see what they could discover there. They crossed two deep arroyos and after that the elevation of the land kept climbing slowly. Gus started to see some different kinds of cactus that he hadn't seen on the western side of the land, such as cholla and a beautiful fish hook barrel cactus. They came to a sudden drop off that went down about 150 feet into a canyon that was called 96 canyon, named for a famous ranch that once ran cattle on all of the land there and that ranch was called the 96 ranch, because it was made up of 96 sections of land and 96 sections is equal to 61,440 acres. When they stopped at the 96 canyon Gus got off of the bulldozer and walked around some just looking at the canyon and also at the ground to see what he could discover there when he saw a large rock that turned out to be a very big metate and beside it was the mano that went with it. This was a sign of an Indian camp that must have been used for years, because the metate and mano were used by the Indians for thousands of years to gring their seeds and grains to make meal for their breads. This was exciting for Gus and he wondered how many other interesting things he would discover in the future when he was learning out more about the land. He looked at his watch and decided that it was time for them to return to the camp, but by a different way then they had come, so they turned south for a about two hundred yards following the 96 canyon and then turned west back toward the camp. They arrived back at the camp about lunch time, so Gus opened up his cooler and got out everything that they needed to make sandwiches along with bottled water and tea and a thermos of hot coffee for later. They finished their lunch and Gus noticed a cloud of dust coming from a couple of miles away to the north and he hoped that it would be the truck delivering his container. About thirty minutes later the truck with the loaded container pulled up and Gus showed the driver where he wanted it positioned on the ground and the truck pulled over the spot and started tilting its bed. Gus had the bulldozer operator hook a chain on the container to get it started sliding off the tilt bed into place and then the truck pulled forward slowly until the container sat flat on the ground exactly where Gus had wanted it. When they were through and everything was picked up that they had used to unload the container, Gus got out the coffee and they all sat down in some lawn chairs that Gus had in his Jeep and they relaxed for about thirty minutes drank their coffee and talked. The truck driver then left and Gus helped the bulldozer operator load his bulldozer on his heavy haul trailer and Gus paid him and told him that he would have him some work in the future and said goodby. When the big truck left all was quiet and Gus was left alone there on that mesa in the middle of no where, but he was thrilled at what he saw and what they had accomplished in so short of a time. Now the work of turning the 40 foot shipping container into a camp house would begin. Gus was so glad to finally get a camp where he could unhook the eight trailer carrying all of his building supplies and tools from his Jeep. He had been dragging it around with him, because he was afraid to unhook it for fear that it might be stolen. He started by marking off where the front door would be installed and the front window. He used his cutting torch to make these openings and now he could start framing up the inside of the container just like it was a regular room in a house. He had to use all hand tools, because he didn't have an electric generator yet, but he was going to buy a welding machine that also would double as a generator. Gus kept his Motel room and drove out to his land for the rest of the week working on the container, soon to be the camp house. On his last day there he had finished installing the door and the window, so he made plans to spend his first night there sleeping on the floor in a sleeping bag and using a kerosene lantern at night for light and he could make coffee and cook on a camp fire. Late that evening Gus sat in a lawn chair in front of the container by his camp fire listening to the coyotes howl all around and he was in his height of glory. Early the next morning Gus made coffee ate a can of beanie-weenies for breakfast and then unloaded the rest of his supplies into the container for safe keeping loaded up his Jeep and drove to Van Horn to fill up with gas and headed out for the long drive to Sugarland. Gus's old body was very sore not only from all the hard work, but also his bones hurt from sleeping on that hard wood floor of the container all night. After all he wasn't a young man any more he was now 55 years old, but he knew that he would get over all of that soreness in a few days. The main thing was that he finally was making his dream from so long ago come true. He had a long way to go, but at least he had a good start now. Gus got back to Sugarland and had a couple of days to rest and catch up on things at his house before going back to work and he also had a lot of pictures that he needed to get developed that he took of everything he could think of. He was determined to make a picture book of this whole experience. One other thing he did was to decide on what to call this property and it was to call it the Blue Quail Ranch, because that was the first wild game he had seen when he had gone to see the land. When he had gone to see the land he crossed the big creek and a covey of blue quail ran across the road in front of him. So from now on it would be the Blue Quail Ranch when he talked about it. Gus had a lot of off time built up at work and this was their slow time, so he knew that he would be able to use a lot of this time to go to his Blue Quail Ranch and work on making it habitable enough for him, his wife and his boys to use in the future. His objective now was to meet the Surveyor in November to find the actual property lines and to work on the camp house to get it ready to use. The Surveyor was to meet him in Van Horn in the first week in November and Gus had already made a new list of supplies that he would need for the camp house and he was also looking for a welding machine to buy and take with him, so he would take his trailer with him when he drove out. The first week in November finally arrived and Gus had his trailer all loaded with supplies he would need converting his shipping container into a camp house. He also had acquired a new welding machine that had the capacity to generate more then enough electricity to power the whole camp house. Along with the welding machine Gus had also acquired a propane two burner camp cook stove and a propane heater to keep the camp house warm. He met the Surveyor at the same Motel in Van Horn that he and the bulldozer operator had stayed in October. The weather was cooler and it had rained some, but everything was still good enough to do the surveying. The Surveyor told Gus that he thought that it would take three days to complete the survey. The first couple of days went fine except they had to start about three miles farther from Gus's land then they had thought. They had to work their way step by step toward the land in a methodical way so as to tie the survey together with other survey markers. The night before the third day a strong norther blew in and it rained all night and the next morning was cold overcast, foggy with a fine mist. In other words simply miserable weather to be surveying in. The fog meant that the Surveyor wouldn't be able to see as far through his instrument and that meant the survey was going to take longer, because there were going to be more instrument set-ups and more rod shots taken. The survey ended up taking five days instead of three, but they finally got it done. Gus found out that the camp he had built for the camp house was about 150 feet off of his property line, which meant that he was going to have to pick out another location on the mesa for it and also have the camp house moved. This was aggravating, but what the hell, that is what happens when you don't have everything in order like he had wanted in the beginning. When Gus had the first camp built he knew he was taking a chance, but felt like he needed to while he had the bulldozer out there. There was no real hurry to move his camp, because the area he was in on the west side of the Sierra Vieja Mountains was like open land with no one around and no fences. He had not seen a single person out there since he had owned the property. Gus left Van Horn to go back to Sugarland the next day after they finished the survey, because it had taken longer then expected to finish the survey, which meant that he didn't get to do the work he had planned to do on the camp house. His next trip out there would be during the Thanksgiving Holidays and he would use six days of his built up off time along with the holiday time and the weekend to give him ten days out there, so he should get a lot done on the camp house, plus he could stay out there now since he had a heater, cook stove and electricity furnished by the welding machine. Gus got back to Sugarland satisfied with what he had accomplished and immediately started making plans for his next trip. The operations at the Harvesting Department shop and offices in Sugrland were going along as usual with the complete overhaul of cotton pickers and strippers, combines, carrot harvesters, green bean pickers and the repair and maintenance of their own trucks. There were also the never ending training of new mechanics and operators for the harvesting equipment. Gus was using his days off gathering up the supplies he would need to finish the inside of the camp house. With the new welding machine Gus could now use his power tools to work on the camp house which would make things go much faster. This time he had also bought insulation to completely insulate the walls and ceiling before he enclosed them with ½ inch ply wood. He was also going to install an AC unit that was like the ones in a big Motel room. The trip Gus was planning would be without anything else to do except to finish out the inside of the camp house just like it was a room in a house with electric lights, wall outlets and switches and a lot of shelving to hold everything that would normally be in cabinets, pantry's and chests in a regular house, but the space was very limited in the container camp house being that it was only eight feet wide, so there wasn't any room for furniture, only shelves were the solution. He had plans to wall off 13 feet on one end that would end up being a bath room area, but for now it would be used for storage of supplies and the welding machine. The idea that Gus had for his Thanksgiving trip to his Blue Quail Ranch was to get the camp house finished enough to use for him, his wife and any of his sons that wanted to come out during the Christmas Holidays. Gus was used to developing plans and acting on them with speed and determination and he was already developing a plan for their Christmas trip before he even went on his Thanksgiving trip. This was a pattern he had developed when he was an independent business man and entrepreneur so things would move forward with speed toward a planned objective. It had served him well and it came second nature to him now as he wanted to achieve as much as he could in a limited amount of time. Gus left for his Blue Quail Ranch loaded down with supplies and tools determined to finish the main room of the camp house. After working feverishly for eight days Gus had completed the main room of the camp house with electrical wiring, lights, insulation, ½ inch plywood walls and ceiling and he installed shelving all around the walls, a walled off room at one end of the camp house, to be a future bath room, the AC installed, a temporary kitchen table, a stainless steel double sink installed in a hand made drain board in front of the camp house to be for temporary all purpose use and he had even got the whole inside painted. He had brought along with him two used trundle beds and a futon so the camp house would be able to sleep four people. His eighth night there is the first night that he slept on a bed in his sleeping bag. The next morning Gus was so exhausted and his body so sore that he could hardly crawl out of bed. It was very cool in the camp house and Gus lit two kerosene lamps and the propane heater and also the propane camp stove for the first time in the camp house. He sat that the temporary kitchen table in a lawn chair. With the insulated walls and ceiling the camp house warmed up real quick and Gus made himself some cowboy coffee on the propane camp stove. The inside of the camp house smelled of fresh paint and now the smell of kerosene and strong brewing coffee mixed in to give a homey feel that Gus hadn't experienced since he had been a small child. When he was young his Mom and Dad had kerosene heaters and a kerosene cook stove and in the mornings his Mom was always brewing strong coffee for his Dad, so these smells brought back some nice memories of his child hood. Gus poured himself a cup of the strong coffee and sat in the warm camp house thinking back to those times. His mind drifted along memories of his young life and Lorrie suddenly came into his mind with those still sweet memories of her and Gus wondered if she would have loved this rugged desert land like he did and if she would have enjoyed this kind of camping. It was nice to think of Lorrie and just sit there for a while and enjoy his coffee in silence. He had grown up in a time when a lot of the old ways of living were still being used, so he was familiar with the ways of operating a house that didn't depend on electricity for all the power and conveniences that everyone thought that they needed. He was perfectly happy not having to use the electricity generated by the welding machine, because it made so much noise. He had even decided to cook himself bacon and eggs for breakfast instead of eating something cold out of a can or making a cold sandwich. This was his last day at his Blue Quail Ranch and he had to load up everything and get ready to leave early the next morning. His day was spent taking care of small details, cleaning up sawdust and storing away pieces of lumber that he might need later, nails, screws, etc., were all stored in the vacant room at the end of the camp house. It hadn't been framed in, insulated, wired or walled. That would have to be for a different time. It was just bare metal walls and a wooden floor like the whole container had originally been when he had first received it. For now it was a great place to use for storage. Gus was extremely satisfied with all that he had accomplished on this trip. The only thing that he was sorry about was that he had been so busy that he wasn't able to do any exploration on the land. He hadn't been any farther then the camp, because he had so much to accomplish that his time spent working on the camp house to get it ready for the Christmas vacation that he and he and his wife were going to spend there and now it was ready for that, but there was much more to do and that would have to wait for another time. Early the next morning Gus had everything loaded and had his Jeep Cherokee running so it could warm up and he walked to the edge of the camp mesa to watch the first rays of the sun come through 96 pass in the Sierra Vieja and just before he turned around to go back he looked down and right at his feet was an Indian arrow head. Gus picked it up and smiled, because he took this as a good omen. Gus arrived back in Sugarland late that afternoon with a lot of pictures of all that he had done to the camp house and with his arrow head. Gus went back to work at the Harvesting Department and also started planning for his next trip out to his Blue Quail Ranch. This trip he decided that he was going to take the old 1953 Jeep with him and he would leave it there, because he had room to store it in the room that would end up becoming the bath room. With the old Jeep there he would be able to do exploration of the land a lot faster and there was a lot of land there to explore. Those old Jeeps were famous for being able to advance across rugged terrain and through brush and this land had plenty of both. Gus talked to his youngest son and he wanted to come out to the Ranch with his girlfriend for three days during his Christmas Vacation from College. Gus told him that it would be OK, because the Ranch house would sleep four people, but that he need to tell his girlfriend that it was a little on the primitive side. Their baths would have to be done out of buckets of water and for bath room facilities there would be a potty chair like is used in a sick room for a patient. As the days passed Gus and his wife were getting together all the things that they had on a list to take with them. Gus had made arrangements to rent a tilt bed trailer to haul the Jeep on and it would also have room for a couple of big ice chests which would leave all the room in the back of the Jeep Cherokee to put the other things that they would need to spend a week out there. Gus and his wife left Sugarland a couple days before Christmas very early in the morning, because he knew that they would be driving a little slower since they were pulling the old Jeep on a trailer. They got to the Blue Quail Ranch without any trouble in the middle of the afternoon and unloaded the Jeep and then Gus immediately started setting up the camp and arranging things so they would be easy to use as the days went on. The weather was fairly mild and Gus was happy about this, but he knew how unpredictable the weather out there could be in the winter, so he had tried to prepare as best as he could for a bad winter storm that could drop snow and ice. They had brought a lot of food booth fresh in the ice chests and canned along with three 15 gallon barrels of water and four 5 gallon containers of water, extra supplies of kerosene and large propane bottles and four 5 gallon gas cans. They also had a good assortment of blankets and quilts for the beds and futon. This was the first time his wife had been out to see the Ranch. She had seen pictures, but this was her first real look at the land. After they unpacked, made the beds, hooked up the propane bottles, positioned the water containers to be used, took the welding machine out of the unfinished bath room and rearranged things in there so it could be used with the potty chair, Gus gathered wood and built a fire for them to enjoy and later they were going to roast some wieners for hot dogs. It took a while to get all of this done and it was approaching dusk. They both were very tired and sitting in front of the fire felt good, because it was starting to get very cool and the wind was picking up some. They were trying to stay outside long enough to gaze up at the beautiful night sky that this Far West Texas area was famous for, because of the amazing brilliance of the stars. They saw that it was true, but it got colder and the wind got stronger till they finally had to bundle up in their heavy coats and stocking caps with their hoods up and then the clouds started to cover up the stars and it just got to cold to stay out any longer, so Gus extinguished the camp fire and they went into the camp house lit the oil lamps and the heater then put the coffee pot on the camp stove to make cowboy coffee to warm up with. They put extra blankets on the beds and when they went to bed they could hear the wind picking up outside whistling around the camp house and through the brush. When Gus woke up the next morning at 6:00 am it was still dark and he didn't hear the wind blowing, but he could feel that it was pretty cold. He got up and lit the heater then took his flash light and went outside to check the thermometer and found it to be 26 degrees F, no wind, clear skies and snow on the ground. He quickly retreated back into the warmth of the camp house, lit the oil lamps and put the coffee pot on the camp stove to boil for coffee. It felt real good in the camp house now, because the propane heater warmed it up real fast. He thought that he also needed a thermometer inside so he could compare the inside and outside temperature. He wrote this down on a list that he would add to as their stay went on, because Gus knew that he would discover small things that he could do there that would make staying there more pleasant as time went on. By the time his wife woke up Gus had coffee made and was sipping on his second cup. She was commenting on how nice and cozy it felt in the camp house and Gus told her to stick her nose outside and she would be even more impressed. This she did and it was just getting light enough for her to see that everything was white with snow. She told Gus that when it got a little lighter she wanted to go out and get enough snow to make snow ice cream which consisted of snow in a bowl with cream, vanilla and sugar on it and they had everything to make it. Gus said that what he wanted to do was go out after it was light enough to see good to see what kind of animal tracks that he could find and identify. After their breakfast of fried bacon, eggs, potatoes and pan toast with jelly his wife gathered snow for their ice cream and Gus looked for animal tracks in the snow. He came back and told his wife that he had found coyote, rabbit and bob cat tracks close to the camp. This was Christmas Eve, so Gus cut a small bush and nailed it to a piece of wood to use as a Christmas tree and they decorated it with pieces of tin foil and card board that he spray painted different colors. It didn't look like much, but it was the thought that counted. The weather started warming up that afternoon and by evening most of the snow had melted. Gus decided that if Christmas Day was nice they would get in the old Jeep and do a little exploring to see if they could discover an Indian camp or maybe some fossils, if nothing else they could find out the directions that future roads might be made to other parts of the Ranch. That evening Gus cooked some thick pork chops on the grill outside over mesquite wood coals and warmed up a can of ranch style beans to go with them. After they ate their dinner Gus had his wife boiled some water for them to use in washing the dishes and cleaning up everything. They had the outside double sink that they could use, but the water had to be added to it by hand and it drained into buckets underneath that had to be dumped out after they finished. This was rather primitive, but it worked well and the dishes got as clean as they would have been if washed they had been washed at home. Gus then sat out by the fire sipping on a beer and just looked into the flames as if being mesmerized by them, but he was not mesmerized he was soul searching. The evening was quiet except for the distant howling of coyotes and the crackling of the fire. He thought that everything was wonderful except somehow he had the feeling that something important was missing. There seemed to be a missing part to this adventure and he couldn't for the life of him figure out what it could be. Gus wondered about himself and his feelings, because he had always felt that God had wanted him to do something important in his life and he could never figure out what that might be, and all through his adult life he had felt that no matter what he was doing or who he was with that something important was missing and he could never figure out what that was either. Gus was sitting there watching the fire and the sparks coming up from it wondering if those two things had a connection and if they did how could he identify what they were and if he ever figured them out would he be able to do what he needed to do to to make things right, so he could no longer feel that he had a missing part to his life, that it would then be complete. About this time his wife came out and ask him if he wanted another beer and Gus told her yes. Gus always woke up around 6:00 am and it was dark as usual. He lit the propane heater and put the coffee pot on the camp stove to boil for coffee then he went outside to look at the outside thermometer and he was glad to see that it had warmed up and was no longer freezing. He could see stars shining and that also was a good sign that Christmas Day had the possibility of being a good one. He was determined to use the old Jeep and go exploring. He had never been able to take the time to explore around the Ranch since he had owned it, because he used all the time that he had spent there working on developing the campsite and working on the camp house, so this was going to be an exciting adventure to see what he could discover. After their breakfast Gus and his wife made some sandwiches for a lunch and filled two canteens with water and started out in the old Jeep driving out the new road toward the west to find a way to get to the spring in the big creek. Gus had his pistol with him just in case he needed it, because he remembered that he had seen a mountain lion track by the spring when he had first walked on the land in July. He got off the road and wound around some large black lava that was pushed up like a fence and eased through the brush with the Jeep trying to be careful not to drop off into something that would give him trouble. He finally made it to the bank of the creek and drove along it looking for a place to take the Jeep down into it so he could drive closer to the spring. Gus finally found a break in the brush and a sloping place that wild game and cattle had been using to cross the creek and he eased the Jeep down it into the creek bed itself that was flat and made up of gravel and sand and was very firm to drive on. He drove to within fifty yards of the spring and they walked to it and found a lot of tracks of deer. It was a beautiful place with large trees on both sides of the wide creek and the spring water was dribbling through the cracks in the lava dam that was holding everything in place with a large pool of water at the base of the lava dam. The pool of water had minnows and leopard frogs swimming in it. Gus was convinced that there must be an Indian camp around close, because of the spring water, so they went back to the Jeep and drove back up the slope in the creek bank and worked his way back up the creek to a place that was clear of brush and then they got out and started looking around on the ground for evidence of an Indian camp ground. It wasn't long and Gus started to find chips of flint and larger rocks that had been flaked on to get pieces that the Indians could make into tools or arrow heads, then he found his first pottery shard. It was about 2 inches square and it was white inside and out with geometric lines on the inside in black. Gus had never found pottery like this, but he knew what it was, because he had read about it and had seen it in museums. Gus thought that this kind of pottery wasn't even supposed to be found this far south in Texas, because it was made in Northeastern New Mexico. This was very interesting and Gus was sure that there would be more very interesting discoveries made. It was lunch time, so they went back to the Jeep to sit and eat their sandwiches and rest. Gus's wife had found a nice selection of different colored flint chips and when Gus examined them he found that one of the larger ones was actually a nice scraper. They ate their lunch and then walked around a little more and found a metate and mano. Gus decided that it was time for them to work their way back to the road and go back to the camp.

He was going to try and find a different way back to the road, so he could get the feel of another area of the land and this he did. He noticed that this trail he was making went up a few feet and that it looked like he was driving on another part of the Indian camp, so this camp must be pretty big and it looked like it followed the creek for at least about ½ of a mile. They finally got back to the camp and they put all of the treasures they found except the matate, because it was to heavy, on a makeshift table outside, so they could sit and look at them. It was getting toward late afternoon and Gus knew that they needed to drive out to highway 90 and tie green and red ribbons along the way for his son to follow so he wouldn't get lost, because he was supposed to drive up there the day after Christmas and this was the only way that Gus could think of for him to find the camp without getting lost. It had worked for the men delivering the container, so it should work for his son. The weather had warmed up real nice and the skies were a beautiful blue. Late that evening Gus built a fire to sit by and watched the sun go down while he was drinking a beer and grilling some hamburgers for their dinner. He was excited about having his son out there, because he had taken him to the Big Bend for a week after his son's graduation from High School and he seemed to really like that Desert mountain country. The next afternoon his son and his girlfriend drove up and there was a lot of things that Gus was showing them about how the camp house was to operate. They were to sleep on the futon and Gus showed them where to store their belongings, because there had to be a place for everything since there was limited room in the camp house, then Gus and his son each got a beer and they took off in the old Jeep to look around a little before dark. After they got back to the camp Gus and his son started a camp fire, put out some lawn chairs and seasoned up some rib eye steaks to be grilled and then they sat down to talk, drink some beer together and just enjoy being together. Gus's wife and his son's girlfriend were in the camp house getting the side dishes ready for the steaks. After their dinner and the clean up they all sat out by the fire and looked at the beautiful sky full of stars and they watched several satellites cross the sky. His son and his girlfriend stayed there for three days and they all had a great time exploring, cooking out on the camp fire and visiting. After his son had gone back home Gus and his wife discovered a place to cross the deep arroyos that crossed the ranch to the east and he worked his way toward the Sierra Vieja mountains and Ninety Six Canyon that was located on the far east side of the ranch. They drove the old Jeep up on a high place over looking the canyon and the view was beautiful. Gus got out of the old Jeep and started looking around and he discovered another Indian camp. Also while he was working his way back to Ninety Six Canyon Gus had noticed something down low in a big flat stretch of ground below the mesa they were driving on that looked like it had levies on it and he was interested in taking a closer look at it to see exactly what it was, but this would have to be for another day. Gus and his wife spent the rest of their Christmas vacation at the ranch and Gus made a list of the things that he would need to get when he came back out and that wouldn't be until the next year after the Harvest Season of 1998, so it would be a long time. He knew that he was going to buy another container to use as a shop and for storage, so he could finish out the room at the end of the camp house and make it a real bathroom. He did a lot of measuring and drew up plans for how he was going use the new container. He would have plenty of time to figure everything out, because it would be almost a year before he would be back at his Blue Quail Ranch in 1998.

Lorrie—1997 was the beginning of a happy time for Lorrie, because she had convinced her Husband to let her enroll in the Open University System to study for a Degree in Art History. It was all she could do to contain herself, because she was so excited to be adding this very interesting cultural knowledge to her life's resume. When the Open University Courses started arriving and she had purchased the books that were required she was constantly reading ahead beyond the required reading for that particular segment. It was hard for Lorrie to limit herself to concentrating on just a small segment at a time, because she was so interested in the subject that she wanted to charge forward in an unrelenting quest for that knowledge. Lorrie and her sweet little dog Mitzi would spend hours studying together and writing her responses to the questions on the assignments and then mailing them in. As the classes progressed Lorrie was required to study twice monthly with a tutor on weekends. This was very stimulating for Lorrie, but the prize that she waiting for was still a year or more away and that was to go with a class group to different art galleries in Europe such as France, Italy and Holland where she could see the actual art and discuss it with experts on each artist. Lorrie's anticipation of visiting these galleries kept her enthusiasm bubbling for more knowledge. After a few months she was able to share some of what she had learned with her friend Jill. They would go to galleries in England and Lorrie would try to apply what she had learned to the art and the artist so as to get a greater appreciation for work the artist had produced. Jill liked this also, because it gave her a different perspective on some of the artists work that she had viewed before, it was like having her own tutor. When they would finish with their art gallery excursion they would go over to Pizza Express for pizza and share a bottle of wine. Lorrie and Jill had been great friends now ever since Lorrie had gone to work at the Library. Even though Lorrie was no longer working at the Library her and Jill stayed in touch and they spent as much time together as they could. Lorrie couldn't imagine her life without Jill, because they had confided in each other so many things that they wouldn't tell another person. Lorrie had Jill, her little sweet dog Mitzi and now the Open University Degree studies that helped her disregard all the unpleasantness that plagued her home life with her Husband and her Stepson. Her Stepson was in his last year of his University education and would receive his degree in the early summer. He had made excellent grades, but he had given them trouble from time to time. There was the time he and his friends had destroyed their Travel Van and all along his Dad had secretly been giving him more money on the side, but Lorrie knew about it and the latest was a scam that he pulled to get more money. He and his friends would go out to eat and party and he would collect money from them to pay the bill, then he would put their bill on his Dad's credit card and keep his friends money. Lorrie caught him doing this and she was very upset with him. Lorrie considered this to be dishonest and she wanted her Husband to take the credit card from him, but her Husband wouldn't do it and they had a big argument about it that her Husband later used as an excuse to get drunk and knock her around and break her nose again. The neighbors called the Police to their house again and the Police tried to get Lorrie to file charges of abuse on him, but Lorrie wouldn't do it, because she knew that it would end her chances of getting the Open University Art History Degree and that her Husband would become so violent that she would be afraid that he would hunt her down then things would be worse. She knew that with a little time the bad feelings at home would subside, but her husband was continuing to add scars to their relationship that would be with her forever. Lorrie's University education was in it's first year and her Stepsons was almost over. He now had the idea that he wanted to join the Royal Air Force as a fighter pilot after his graduation. Lorrie thought that it would be a great idea, because she knew how the military could re- make spoiled, young people into productive upstanding citizens and she knew that her Stepson was definitely spoiled and thought only of himself. Lorrie's experience in the Navy, first as a Drill Instructor training new women recruits and then as the leader of a Cryptology Team gave her first hand experience in seeing how the training changed the attitudes of young people for the better. She encouraged him to enlist, because she knew that it might be exactly what he needed to overcome his dependence on his Dad and his selfishness. Her Stepson did en-list and he passed his physical and all his tests with flying colors. His Degree from a University also gave him the opportunity to become an officer and Lorrie was very proud that her Stepson had decided to use the military to mature him and build his character. She thought that if this didn't do it nothing could. He went through his physical training camp and did well and then advanced to his Cadet classes teaching Cadets the beginnings of flight instructions classroom. Lorrie was also doing very good in her Art History studies and she discovered that the more she learned the more she wanted to learn. Her and her little dog Mitzi would study together and Lorrie would talk to Mitzi, about her lessons, like she was a human and Mitzi would look straight at her and have different expressions on her face and express different body language to what Lorrie was saying and Lorrie was convinced that Mitzi really did know what she was telling her. Lorrie really loved her little Mitzi and when she was at home they did everything together. Finding Mitzi and being able to shower her love on her and to get it back from Mitzi was a blessing for Lorrie. The closest thing like this that Lorrie ever had was for that one year that she had her horse when she had been married to her first husband when they were stationed in San Antonio, Texas. Lorrie was finishing some of her Art Degree work, so she could take a break to go back to Texas on her annual vacation for a month. The year 1997 was speeding buy for Lorrie and she realized that after her vacation back to her hometown to visit her family and friends in Texas the year would be ¾ over and then she would be starting her second year of her Open University Art History Degree. She was really farther along than that, because she had advanced so fast that she had exceeded the limits of each segment of study, so now she would be able to go on the Europe Art Gallery tours and that was one of the things that she had been looking forward to doing. Lorrie was busy getting everything lined up for her Texas vacation. She decided to take copies of some of the study material along to show her Mom and Dad what her Degree was going to be about. While Lorrie's plane was flying from England to Houston, Texas she, for the first time, felt sort of like her life was following a time warp. Lorrie had a sense of living in three different time eras. She had been submerged for months studying the Medieval Art from three hundred AD, Renaissance art and the Masters that produced it in the fifteenth century, so that her mind was beginning to be trained to think like theirs and now she was flying in a jet plane in 1997, to go to a place that she grew up in, in the 1940's and 1950's. Lorrie had to laugh at herself and then she thought that she wished that she could escape back to the fifteenth century or before, or better yet back to the 1950's in El Campo, Texas where she had first seen and fallen in love with Gus. Her thoughts were, that if only she had known then what she knew now, how differently she would have approached Gus. Lorrie knew that she had ruined that forever and her heart still ached for Gus when she thought of him. Maybe, just maybe she might get lucky enough on one of her vacations back to El Campo to get a glimpse of Gus, even from a distance, just to see if he was OK and how handsome a man he would be. She arrived in Houston, Texas and as usual she spent the first week with her sister that lived there, then they both drove to Lorrie's home town of El Campo to spend the rest of her vacation time with her family there. Lorrie was so happy to see them, and they seemed really proud of her now even though her and her parents had been at odds many times in their lives Lorrie loved and respected them. She had always yearned for their approval and that was the reason that she had kept a lot of what she had done in her life a secret, because she knew that they wouldn't have been proud of her for those things. She felt guilty about this, but she had always been the kind of girl that had to live her own life making her own decisions, right or wrong, in her own way. This was why she could never have admitted defeat in her decision to marry a British man and live in England. Her family had always thought that her marriage to him had always been happy, because Lorrie had never talked about the bad times and she wouldn't ever let them know. She lived one life in England and presented another life to them and this wasn't the first time she had done this. Really this was the model she had used ever since she had gone to Florida in 1965. The truth is that so much of Lorrie's life was only known to herself and she only reveled private things about herself to people she chose and even then only specific parts of her life that she didn't want connected to anything else. A couple of days after she arrived at her parents house she found the opportunity to get out all of her Open University Art Degree material and began explaining everything to them. She showed them her study subjects with her research and her test papers that had been graded with the perfect scores and then described what they meant, so her family could try to understand what she was learning about the famous art works of Europe and the Great Masters that had created them and why they had chosen the subjects to use for their masterpieces. She could see that they were having a hard time grasping the magnitude of the inspiration that had driven these great artists to produce art that had captured the attention of millions of people world wide for generations and generations. Lorrie told them that their art work was an everlasting thing that told stories through visual beauty and design that was so important that during World War Two there was a whole new Department created in the American and British Armies that was tasked with saving the Historical Art of Europe and North Africa. Lorrie's family was seeing a whole different daughter and sister when she talked about what she was learning and although they didn't quite understand it all they were happy for her and proud of her for continuing her education and striving for excellence in it. After being back in El Campo Lorrie made a hair appointment with her long time friend and Beauty Salon owner. Lorrie had put off getting her hair cut and colored in England so her friend in El Campo could do it. She had been going to her since she was just a girl and getting her hair done by her old friend was like an established ritual. Lorrie was getting quite a bit of gray in her hair now and she had been having color put in it from time to time. Her old friend the Salon owner was always trying to talk Lorrie into doing different colors, but Lorrie was resistant and felt better sticking to a color that she was used to seeing on herself. The problem was that her old friend the Salon owner would change her color without telling her and Lorrie wouldn't know it till she got out from under the hair dryer and looked in the mirror. Lorrie would then question her old friend why she did it and was told that she looked great and to just be quiet while she styled it and then she would realize that her old friend had been right all along and who knows, but Lorrie might accidentally run into her old flame Gus in the grocery store and he would fall down on his knees and ask her to marry him. Lorrie was completely taken by surprise by this and she asked her old friend why she had said something like that. She told Lorrie that she had seen Gus in the grocery store a week before Lorrie had come to El Campo, but he had a woman with him that she didn't know, so she was hesitant to ask him a lot of questions and besides she had been in a hurry to complete her shopping. The only thing that he told her was that he was in town for a funeral and then he was getting prepared for a trip out to West Texas someplace. Lorrie asked her what place and where did he live, but her old friend couldn't remember. Lorrie was exasperated, because this was the first Gus sighting she had heard of in years and by one of her best old friends and all of the information that it generated was that Gus was still walking and talking on the face of the earth, how ridiculous! Lorrie then wanted to know how Gus looked and her friend told her that he looked like a mans man with confidence, real good and sexy and that is why she needed that new color just in case she ran into him. Lorrie almost wanted to cry and felt herself getting short of breath and a little weak in the knees. When her old friend was through with her hair Lorrie had to admit that it did look good and before she left she told her that if she ever ran into Gus again to please find everything about him that she could. Her old friend told Lorrie that she would try to remember, but that it was the first time she had seen Gus in years and no telling if or when she would ever see him again. Now this had all of a sudden changed the complexion of her vacation and she knew that her every move in El Campo would be haunted with his memory and she would be secretly on the look out for him. She was sure that she would know him if she saw him even though it had been 35 years since she had seen him, but would he remember her, that was the big question. Lorrie left the Beauty Salon and fought the desire to drive by Gus's Mom's old house. She won out and concentrated on driving back to her parents house. When she got back the first thing her Mom did was ask her why she had changed her hair color. This aggravated Lorrie, because it brought back the conversation with her Friend the Salon owner and she was trying her best to forget it. She just told her Mom that she just decided to make a change to see how it would look and that she liked it. Lorrie's Sister was coming back to El Campo on the weekend, so, Lorrie and her Mom were busy baking cookies and a cake for her. When Lorrie's sister came it was standard procedure to have cookies and a cake for her, because she liked her baked sweets and Lorrie's Sister was considered to be the real baker in the family. When her Sister arrived and unpacked she looked at Lorrie and asked why Lorrie had changed her hair color and Lorrie had to go through the same thing that she had told her Mom, but Lorrie was really thinking that she was being reminded of her conversation with her Friend about Gus again and it looked like she would never be able to forget about it. Lorrie knew now that she was going to have to take a drive around all the places that she had seen Gus at in the old days the next time she had to go to the store for something. Lorrie's little Brother lived next door to her Parents and when he got home from work he always came over for their evening happy hour and conversation and usually stayed over for dinner, unless her Sister and him got into an argument. They had been at odds with each other ever since her Brother had been a little boy, because her Sister would me mean to him when she would baby sit him and he hadn't forgot about how she had treated him. Lorrie's Sister still tried to push him around, but now he wouldn't put up with it. He would just say what was on his mind and then go home leaving his Sister to be mad all by herself. That was his way to let her know that she wasn't in charge of him any more. This was very disconcerting for Lorrie, because she didn't like arguments, so she tried to keep the peace. Lorrie thought that nothing had changed all these years between her little Brother and Sister. The same animosity between them was still there that had caused her plans for Gus to take her virginity back when she was 16 years old to go wrong and then everything seemed to spiral out of her control even to this very day. She didn't have the backbone to face Gus again, because she couldn't take the chance on him rejecting her again. Lorrie would rather love him in secret as she always would. There seemed to be something about this particular trip back to El Campo that kept bringing up the memory of Gus and it started on the flight over from England when Lorrie was thinking that she wished she could escape back to the Medieval Period or the Renaissance and then decided that she would like to go back to the time she had first discovered Gus in the 1950's. This was the trouble with coming back to El Campo, it had all those memories about her and Gus. She would deal with that later, but now she wanted to visit a couple of friends that still lived in El Campo and then she would have to start thinking about doing the food shopping to take the Texas food items that she liked back to England. While Lorrie was back in El Campo her Dad always liked for just the two of them to go riding and then stop at one of his favorite places to drink a couple of beers and talk. Lorrie loved doing this with her Dad and they became closer every time that they did it, but Lorrie still avoided some of his more personal questions about her life in England with her Husband and Stepson. Lorrie always wanted to leave him with the impression that all was good in England. The last couple of years on her vacation when she and her Dad would have these times together Lorrie would notice small changes in her Dad physically, but she just brushed it off to him aging. She had mentioned this to her Brother and to her Mom, but both had said that they hadn't noticed anything alarming about him. She decided that she was just seeing things that weren't there. There were only a few days left on her vacation in El Campo, so Lorrie did her shopping and packed all that away. The next day she decided to do a go back in time trip and drive around to all the places that she had seen Gus back in the 1950's and 1960's. The first place that she went was to the parking lot where he pulled up to the School Buses that they were going to Corpus Christi on and she parked there for a little while visioning what had happened that Saturday morning in 1962. She could see it in color and could remember every detail. Then she drove around his Mom's old house slowly and remembered seeing Gus out working on his red Hot Rod, after that she drove around the corner to the Service Station that Gus had worked at and she and her friend would go there to flirt with him, then on to the last place and that was up town on the square where she had seen Gus's car parked and she had put the record of " In The Still Of The Night" in his car with the note of when to come over to her parents house for their love making to take her virginity. She saw a place to park that might even been the same place that Gus's car had been parked in and she pulled her Mom's car in the parking place and sat there remembering what she had done. She remembered that she had been looking for Gus for a couple of days to either talk to him or to find his car and put the record and the note in it for him to find. She bought him the record with her baby sitting money, because she knew that it was his favorite song and she had already written out the note just in case that she saw his car, because she didn't want to wast any time trying to write out a note in a hurry and forget something. In the note she had written down the day and the time that he need to come to her parents house for them to be together, so she could keep her promise to him that he was the one that she wanted to have take her virginity and let her pass from being a girl into being a woman. In the note she told Gus that if he didn't want to date her after they were finished then he was free to go his own way, but that either way she would love him forever and she signed it and drew a heart with Lorrie and Gus written in it. Lorrie sat there and remembered this as it had just happened. She smiled and put her Mom's car in reverse and backed out to go back to her parents house. Her remaining time in El Campo was spent with her family savoring their companionship. Her long flight back to England brought her back to the present and her studying for her Art Degree. She had met another woman that was studying for the same Degree and they had struck up a new friendship, because of their same interest and Lorrie was wondering if this woman might become another good friend similar to Jill. The woman's name was Carol and she liked to party some too like Lorrie did. Lorrie arrived back home in Bromley and unpacked her luggage which included the usual big one with all the canned and packaged food products from Texas that she couldn't get in England. Another one of her bags contained a few gifts to to friends like Jill and her new friend Carol that were little souvenirs from Texas and she had a special gift for her sweet little dog Mitzi that was a sweater with a Texas flag on it. As usual Lorrie found the house in a mess and there was a lot of paper work stacked up on her desk that hadn't even been looked at. Lorrie stood there and looked things over and thought that, yes this is my house, because it looks the same as it always does when I come back from my Texas vacation. She knew that she couldn't let any time go by resting, because she would have to get caught up on everything before her fall semester started with all the studying she would need to do on her Art History Degree with the Open University. This semester was going to be a lot of fun, because they were going to start taking the field trips to famous Art Galleries and Museums in different countries in Europe and now Lorrie had a new friend to share that with. Lorrie knew that their research and study lessons would cover the Art and the Master that had created it prior to their actual visit to the Gallery or Museum to see the Art and have on site discussions about it with experts on the Art Work and the Artist, discussing everything about the work from the frame, canvas, how it was stretched and attached, to the mixture of the oils and the style of the Artist along with the reasons for the Artist choosing that particular subject for the Art Work. Lorrie knew that her Degree studies were now going to take on a whole different excitement and meaning for her and she couldn't wait to get started on them. Her fall semester was going to start in only two weeks, so she had to get all her house and their business straightened up quickly, because she didn't want any of that hanging over head to worry about. Lorrie's Art History class made their first Art Gallery trip to Holland for a weekend. Her and Carol shared a room and had a great time. The Art Works were absolutely wonderful, and after the Art Expert's lecture and insight Lorrie saw and understood so much more about the Great Art Works and the Masters that created them. She was so glad that she had chosen this subject of Art History to base her Degree on. They had free time after the lectures and they would do a little shopping for souvenirs to remember their trip and then they would go to a cafe to eat and have a few drinks and party with local patrons. These Art History field trips were not only interesting and educational for Lorrie, but they also gave her the chance to get away from home with a good reason and let off a little steam with people of her same mind set. These field trips were an extension of the escape process that she had devised for herself when she was looking for some way to generate happiness in her life. While she was at home she escaped the oppressive and abusive drunken behavior of her Husband and the selfishness of her spoiled Stepson by lavishing her affections on her little sweet dog Mitzi and also burying herself in studying for her Art History Degree and the Art History field trips were the icing on the cake to get away and forget all about her home problems for a couple of days. All of this was a big boost in helping Lorrie to cope with her Marriage and stay in England, for many times she had longed for some way to leave it all behind, something that she could use to save face, so her family wouldn't be able to tell her that they had warned her not to marry that man in England. She could never think of any thing that would work, so she developed ways of dealing with her situation and also she thought that she was getting to old to be starting all over again. The year of 1997 was slipping by now at a fast rate and the Christmas Holidays were almost on Lorrie. Lorrie had even more Christmas spirit then she usually had and she was planning to buy some new decorations, because decorating with new decorations always helped to build the excitement in her for this most special season. Her Stepson would be home on leave from his Royal Air Force training, so she was going to include some British Military Patriotic items in with the Christmas decorations. She wanted her Stepson to have the feeling that she was proud of him and his service to England and she thought that Christmas would be a good time to do that. She got her Husband to take her to the Christmas Tree Market to buy just the right tree. Lorrie already had all the measurements memorized from buying trees for past Christmas's. Her Husband left everything up to her just like he did on other things, because he could never make even the simplest decision, such as where to sit in a Cafe and this really aggravated Lorrie that she had to always make the decisions about everything. Lorrie sometimes wondered what he would do if she ever left him for good. She found her perfect Christmas Tree and they brought it back to the house and put it up in the place that Lorrie had prepared for it. Lorrie wanted her Stepson to help decorate the Christmas Tree, so she timed the decorating so he would be home on his Christmas leave from the Royal Air Force Academy. She had prepared her Stepsons favorite dinner for his home coming and she waited and waited and while she waited her Husband drank more and more beer. Her Stepson finally showed up two hours late and she could tell that he had been drinking. They finally all sat down to the special dinner that was good and dried out now, but her Stepson and her Husband were so drunk that they never noticed.

After dinner she wanted them all to decorate the Christmas tree together while listening to Christmas Music, but her Stepson and his Dad got into an argument and her Stepson stomped up the stairs and slammed the door to his room and her Husband sat on the couch and brooded while Lorrie went about the decorating of their Christmas Tree. She thought that it was really hard to try and have something nice for the family to do together. Well Lorrie wasn't about to let them ruin her Christmas again if she could help it. She had already bought all the gifts including her own as usual and as usual she would act surprised when she opened it. They had a few friends and business associates come by on Christmas Eve for snacks and drinks and her Stepson had two Royal Air Force Cadet friends show up for a few minutes then he and them left to go to another party. Christmas morning Lorrie and her sweet little dog Mitzi got up and put on some spiced tea to heat then turned on the Christmas Tree lights and some Christmas music. Lorrie was in a good mood and thought that as long as she had Mitzi at home it would be all the family there that she would need. Lorrie made Mitzi some warm milk to lap and got one of Mitzi's presents from under the Tree and tore the paper a little so Mitzi could smell that it was some of her favorite treats Mitzi sniffed it then looked up at Lorrie and Lorrie told her to go ahead and open it and that is all it took for Mitzi to tare off the paper and nibble at the treats and lap the milk. Mitzi would jump on Lorrie's lap and give her a kiss then jump down and nibble the treats and lap the milk. Lorrie got such of a kick out of this to see Mitzi so happy that it also made Lorrie happy on this Christmas Morning. Lorrie thanked God for this sweet little dog and wondered what she would do if she didn't have Mitzi to love and Mitzi to love her. It was just her and Mitzi in front of the Christmas Tree this Christmas Morning because her Husband hadn't come down yet from his bed room and her Stepson had stayed some where else for the night. Lorrie thought that this was going to be the best time she would have on Christmas, before any one else caused a disruption that would break her and Mitzi's feeling of peace and happiness on this Christmas Morning. Finally her Husband came down and went into the kitchen and poured himself a mug of hot spiced tea then added a shot of whiskey to it, so it would ease his headache. Her Stepson came home later and wanted to know what she had cooked for their lunch and that is the way that Lorrie's Christmas 1997 went. Their New Years Eve was mostly quiet with a few friends stopping by to wish them a Happy New Years. Her Stepson didn't come home for New Years, so it was mostly just her and her Husband and he told her that he wanted to have sex to bring in the New Year, but Lorrie made sure that he was to drunk to come to her room, so she once again dodged the degrading sex act that her Husband liked to perform on her. New Years Day 1998 they had their traditional lunch with their friends and Lorrie was looking forward to 1998 spending her time with her friend Jill, her new friend Carol, studying for her Art History Degree and loving her little dog Mitzi. Lorrie was happy, because the thought that she had a lot to be thankful for with all of those things to look forward to in 1998.

Gus—1998 Brought a change to the Harvesting Department at the Prison. The Southern HQ decided it was time to modernize, so they bought computers for all the departments and they hired a young man for the Harvesting Department to do the computer work there. His main job was to keep track of parts inventory, purchase orders and work-orders on equipment and vehicles. The problem with their new computer expert was that he knew absolutely nothing about machinery or the parts used to fix it. In other words he was constantly lost, because you need to have a mechanical type of background to understand what you need to do. All the Supervisors at the Harvesting Department agreed that this was a typical mistake made by personal departments when developing the requirements for a job. Instead of collecting information from the department that the job was to be opened for they simply advertised for someone computer literate. Until this new computer man learned a lot about equipment the whole repair operation would be slowed down to a crawl. This meant that the Supervisors would be aggravated and the Inmate mechanics would be aggravated and the Inmate parts men would be aggravated. In other words there would be tension all around and this would have the potential to cause dangerous problems of fights. Everyone was glad that the computer man came in so early in the year, because it would give them time before the actual Harvest Season started to get him trained and up to speed. If he would have been hired right before harvest it would have been a disaster. There were arguments all around, but the Supervisors succeeded in keeping the peace until things in the office improved to the point that there was very little slow down. The one last problem was that no one in the Harvesting Department knew anything about a computer, so when their computer man was off from work, there was no one to take his place and the work for him was stacked up sometime to the point that it took him two days to catch up on it. During all of this slow time before the real harvest season started Gus was making his plans for his Blue Quail Ranch. He knew that he was going to buy another 8 foot x 40 foot shipping container to be delivered to the ranch. He contacted the same man that he had bought the first one from and made the arrangements for him to deliver the new one on a tilt bed truck with a wench. The reason for this was that Gus knew that he was going to have to move the one he now called his camp house, because the Survey had shown that it was off of his property line. When the new container was delivered then his camp house container could be moved to it's proper location next to the new one. Gus actually drew out a plan for his new campsite with the containers located twenty feet apart, so a roof could be erected over them to produce a 20 foot x 40 foot carport covering and on the camp house front he drew a 10 foot x 40 foot porch, also he drew out the design of a railing around the porch and gates for the carport to keep out cattle that roamed the open range. He also designed a twenty foot tower to be welded to the camp house container that would hold a 350 gallon water tank. He wanted all of this made out of steel, so he determined the different types of tubing, angle iron, strap iron, hinges, springs, horse wire, to go around the railing on the porch, bolts, screws and a multitude of accessories. Gus called the man that he bought the new container from and had an agreement with him that he would buy the list of the big, long iron and put it in the container for transport and Gus would pay him for it when he delivered the container. Gus told him that the delivery date would have to be sometime after the middle of September 1998 and Gus would tell him two weeks ahead of time to give the man time to get everything together. Gus could haul the rest himself, but that iron came in 24 foot lengths and Gus didn't have a trailer that long. Putting all of that iron for Gus's building project solved a big problem for Gus. Gus also knew that he was going to have to get a Bulldozer and a Maintainer along with a man that could do the welding and another one to help him out to the Ranch a few days before the new container was delivered, so a new camp site could be ready when the truck pulled in with the new container. All of this would have to be organized and the timing would have to be perfect, so as not to have the expensive equipment, the operators and the welders doing nothing waiting for the container truck to show up. Gus called the man in Fort Stockton that had done the first road and camp site to tell him what Gus had in mind and he told Gus to let him know at least two weeks in advance so he could make his plans. Gus thought that he had done all that he could do for then except to start buying and loading all the small supplies that he was going to haul out to the Blue Quail Ranch and scratch them off his list. Gus's Wife had to get another job, because the company that she had worked for sold out to another company and they were closing their office in Houston, so she got a job working as a teachers aid for Fort Bend School District. She wasn't making as much money, but she had more time off and her Holidays fit better with Gus's. She also got the chance to stay on during the schools summer vacation by working with their summer school and that gave her some extra income. That worked out well, because the summer months were Gus's busiest time at work, because of the Prison's Harvest Season. The whole time the Harvest Season was going on Gus was buying what he needed to take with him to his Ranch and loading everything in his 8 foot trailer. The Prison's Harvest Season was going along on schedule and Gus learned that he was going to be sent out to the Fort Stockton Prison Unit to supervise the harvest there. That was going to work out perfectly for Gus, because the Fort Stockton Unit was always the last to harvest and Gus would be right there, so he would know the exact time the harvest would be over and then he would be able to calculate the timing to tell the man that owned the heavy equipment business and the man that was going to deliver the new container. In fact the man that owned the heavy equipment business was right there in Fort Stockton, so Gus would be able to visit him in person to get it all lined up and also meet the operators and welder that was to go out to his ranch. This was a welcome situation that fell right into place that even Gus couldn't have planned any better. Gus was out at the Fort Stockton Unit for about two weeks supervising their harvest and three days before he was finished he had his meeting with the heavy equipment owner. Gus explained to him all that he wanted to do and the owner called in two of his workers to meet Gus, so Gus could talk to them and explain what he wanted and also to give then directions to his Ranch. One of the workers was the welder and he would be driving a welding truck and the other worker was a heavy equipment operator that would be operating the Bulldozer and the Maintainer and he would be driving the heavy haul truck and trailer loaded with the Bulldozer and the Maintainer. Gus told them to be prepared to stay out for five days and he would supply the place for them to stay in the camp house, the food and some beer for everyone at their quitting time happy hour every day. They seemed happy to get the opportunity to get out in the wild mountain country for a few days and were anxious to go. Gus planned it so they would be out at his Ranch for two days before the delivery of the new container, so they could have a new road built to the location of the new camp site and to level off the campsite for both the new container and the Camp House. The Harvest Season for the Fort Stockton Unit was over the second week in September, so Gus notified the man that was delivering the new container to come in the middle of the last week and at the same time he notified the owner of the heavy equipment to send out his equipment and his welder and operator at the first of the third week. Gus was planning to go out two days before they came so he could put out colored ribbon to mark off the new road to the new Campsite which was going to be ½ mile long and to mark off the outside boundary of the new Campsite, so the inside could be cleaned of brush by the Bulldozer and leveled by the Maintainer to have a nice clean place to position the new container and the Camp House. When Gus finally left Sugarland for his Blue Quail Ranch he had his Jeep Cherokee and his 8 foot trailer loaded down with everything that he would need. He even had the 350 gallon water tank that was to go on the 20 foot stand in his trailer. It took Gus about nine hours to get to his Ranch, because he was pulling a heavy load. He pulled up to his Camp House and unloaded what he would need for the time he and the welder and the operator would be there till the new container would be delivered. He was tired and it was getting late in the evening, so Gus built a camp fire, put out his lawn chair and opened himself a cold beer to relax for a while before he fixed himself a grilled pork chop and ranch style beans with chili peppers and onions for his dinner. After his dinner Gus sat out by the camp fire and listened to the coyotes howl and yip for a while then he went into the Camp House and lit a couple of kerosene lanterns for light so he could get everything arranged for the night and go to bed. He sat in his lawn chair at his little table in the camp house with the light from the lanterns flickering and throwing shadows on the white walls. It was quiet and Gus had time now to think and what he was thinking about was everything that had happened in his life that had brought him to this rugged unforgiving place in the Chihuahua Desert, at this point in time and at his age of 56 years old. He had never imagined himself being married four times and how in the world had that happened anyway. As Gus thought way back into secret corners of his memory and starting opening forbidden doors that he hadn't visited in many years he started to find evidence that he didn't like the look's of, but it was there and he knew that what he was remembering was the truth as bad as he hated to admit it. He could see that he had come way short on good points when he looked on his relationship with women. True, he hadn't been mean or abusive to them and he had done his best to financially support them, but was that all it took to make a good relationship? He knew that it took more then that, but what exactly was it and why couldn't he provide the rest of what it took, that seemed to be the big question. He thought that maybe he should look closer by opening another forbidden door to see what it might reveal to him. Gus decided that he was much to tired to be trying to figure out something that it was to late to fix anyway, so that would have to wait for another time. Tomorrow he would mark off the new road and the new camp site and that would take a lot of walking, so he decided to turn out his lantern and go to sleep. Gus woke up the next morning with some sore muscles and a little stiff from the trip and unloading things, but he had slept good. He fixed coffee on his camp stove and boiled some eggs for breakfast. After getting dressed he set out with his colored ribbon to mark off the new road and the new camp. Marking the new road would be rather simple, because it would follow the top of the mesa. The mesa narrowed after the first campsite, but then it widened again to form a bulge that he thought would make an excellent campsite. The top of the mesa rose about 100 feet above the land below it and would provide an excellent view to the east and the west. He marked the outside boundary of the campsite with everything within it to be Bulldozed and then smoothed with the Maintainer except for a few desert plants that he wanted to leave for landscaping that he marked with a different color ribbon. The interior of the campsite would about one acre in size. This would give him plenty of room for the new container and the Camp House plus a lot of space for parking. This took him till lunch and he walked back to his Camp House to rest and eat. After his lunch Gus organized the Camp House so the welder and the equipment operator would be able to sleep in there. They would be coming in the next morning and they would unload the heavy equipment at this old campsite and leave the big truck and trailer there to use as their base of operation while getting the new campsite ready. Early the next morning Gus made coffee and cooked himself a good breakfast of sausage and fried eggs with pan toast grape jelly. He knew that he would need this, because they would be working as soon as they got the equipment unloaded and they would work till close to dark. Sure enough they drove up not long after Gus got his dishes washed and everything started moving at a fast pace. When en the equipment was unloaded they took a break and drank some ice tea that Gus had made then Gus started the Bulldozer making the road. He rode on it with the operator to make sure that he understood what

Gus wanted. The welder was preparing the Maintainer for operations while the Bulldozer was working and as soon as the Bulldozer was finished with the road the welder crawled on the Maintainer to smooth the road while the Bulldozer was working on the new campsite. At dusk they shut down their dirt work and went back to the old campsite to start a camp fire and sit around it drinking a couple of beers and talking. While Gus was preparing some steaks to grill the men took their sleeping bags and kits into the Camp House then washed up and they ate a nice dinner made some coffee and talked a while before they went to sleep. Gus was glad that they got some of the work done and he knew that they would finish the next day, because the day after that the new container would arrive and then they would also move the Camp House to the new campsite. The next morning Gus and the men made coffee and egg, bacon and potato burritos for breakfast then they went back to the new campsite to finish it and and make sure that everything there was ready for the new container and the Camp House to placed on it. When they finished everything Gus got out his 100 foot tape measure and wooden stakes and they measured and staked off the locations for the new container and the Camp House they were to be set parallel to each other 20 feet apart, so that a frame could be welded overhead to serve as a roof to cover the 20 foot by 40 foot area and provide some shade when covered by the horse wire and over-laid with ocotillo stalks. Ocotillo was a tall stalked woody desert cactus plant with the stems covered with thorns and the stalks could be 20 feet tall. When laid side by side across the top they would provide a dappled shade for his Jeep Cherokee. He had also planned to weld a 10 foot by 40 foot framework on the front of the Camp House for a porch and to cover it the same way. He had already talked to a man in the little town of Valentine that would cut the ocotillo on the Blue Quail Ranch and stack it in piles so when Gus came out in October he could lay it on the roof of the car port between the two buildings and the porch in the front of the Camp House. On the rear of the Camp House he was going to weld a stand 20 feet tall to hold the water tank, so it would have gravity flow into the Camp House and it would be welded on to where the bath room would be inside, so the water pipes could go through the wall directly into the bath room. Gus had already drawn up all the plans for this. When they finished all of this they went back to the Camp House for lunch. After their lunch Gus organized the two men into helping him to move things that were big from the first campsite to the new one. They unloaded the water tank out of the trailer at the new campsite, so they could load Gus's welding machine into it and take it to the new campsite and leave it there, then they moved all the propane tanks that Gus used with his camp stove and heater. Then they loaded the double sink stand and moved it along with all the water barrels that Gus used filled with the water that he always brought with him and finally Gus took his old Jeep down there and left it. All this moving took the afternoon up and they were exhausted, because there was a lot of lifting of heavy stuff. Gus hurt his back doing this heavy lifting and he was limping around in a lot of pain, but he knew that he had to keep going, because there was just to much that he was going to have to see and make sure was done the way that he had planned for it to be done. They fixed some beef stew for dinner and then sat around the camp fire sipping on beer till bed time. The next morning they didn't have to get in a big hurry, because they had gotten everything ready the day before, so they sat around longer drinking coffee waiting on the big truck to arrive with the new container. About mid-morning they saw a lot of dust rising from the road a couple of miles to the north and they knew that it must be their expected truck. They were all excited to get started and Gus was still hurting and stiff in his back, but his excitement was overriding his pain. The big hauling truck pulled up in a big cloud of dust and the man that Gus had bought the container from stepped out and shook Gus's hand and Gus pointed toward the new campsite and told him to go down the new road to the new campsite and Gus would follow him then Gus would line him up to unload the new container. Gus had the Maintainer operator bring the Maintainer the new campsite in case they would need to move the new container a little ti line up in it's place, because they could do it with the Maintainers blade extended out to one side. This was a good way to move heavy things just a little at a time to get them in line, because the blade was controlled by hydraulics and they were very good at precise movements. The truck hauling the new container drove into the new campsite and Gus got out of his Jeep Cherokee and started directing the truck driver around to the location that he had marked off for the new container. After he had the truck in line he went to the front of the truck to hand motion the driver as the truck pulled forward slowly, so the truck would be in the center of the marked location. When the truck was close to being perfect Gus told the driver to slowly tilt the bed, so Gus could see where the rear of the container would touch the ground. He saw that the truck would need to move back for three feet, so he hand guided the driver to that spot, then the driver leveled the bed, so the container could be unchained and then tilted the bed back again and the container slid slowly down the bed and the rear end rested on the ground, then the truck pulled slowly forward till the container rested completely on the ground. Gus sent the truck back to the first campsite to get the Camp House and while he was doing that Gus motioned the Maintainer operator to put his blade on one end of the new container to slowly push the container a few inches to square it with the location that it was on. They waited for a few more minutes until the truck brought the Camp House then Gus lined it up the same way and the driver unloaded it. Gus then got out his tape measure and measured between the two buildings to see if each end was 20 feet from the other and he had to get the Maintainer to adjust them a small amount till they were exactly parallel and even. Gus then paid off the truck driver and owner and thanked them and they went on their way. Gus then opened the double doors on the new container and showed the welder all the metal that they had to work with. The rest of the morning was spent marking off buildings where the metal was to be welded to form the carport, the front porch and the 20 foot stand to hold the water tank. They grilled some sausage for lunch and made wraparounds with bread and B-B-Q sauce and cold pork and beans. Then the welder and his helper that had been the Maintainer operator started cutting and welding the iron between the two buildings that would become the framework for the roof for the carport. Gus helped them lift and position the pieces that were welded to the top across the buildings. Gus was trying to determine how much longer it would take for them to get all the welding done by that evening at their quitting time. They had finished the overhead framework for the carport, but they still had to make four gates, two for each side, so they could be closed to keep out cows that grazed the open range there. He was taking inventory of his food supplies and his ice supply. He had been lucky that the weather had been cool, so the ice had been lasting real good, but he was a little worried about the food. If they ran out he could drive into Van Horn to the grocery store there, but that would take half a day, because of the bad road and it was almost 40 miles from the Blue Quail Ranch to Van Horn. Gus estimated that the welding would take at least two more days if everything went well and he had gotten enough iron and other supplies to do the job that he had planned for them to complete. That evening they put together some big rocks to form a raised three sided platform to support the heavy iron grill, that they had used at the first campsite. That gave enough room underneath to put a good supply of fire wood to cook on. Gus put out three lawn chairs and the small ice cooler with the beer in it, then started the fire for them to sit around and sip there beer and rest before they started cooking their dinner. Gus had planned fajitas for dinner and he had brought the meet with him from Sugarland that had already been seasoned and was ready to be grilled. The next morning they welded together the four gates that went on the carport and mounted them on hinges that were welded on them. They then started on the tower that was to hold the water tank. It was going to be the hardest of all the projects that Gus had planned for, because it had a lot of iron in it that made it heavy and it had to be built on the ground and then lifted by hand into place so it could be welded onto the side of the Camp House. It took them all afternoon to build it and they barely were strong enough to get it lifted up in place so the welder could weld it into place. Gus's poor back was killing him, but without him helping to lift it they would never have been able to get it upright and into place. After they had it welded in place they all took a break for a while and drank some ice tea that Gus had made, then they put the boards up on top that the water tank would sit on. It was time for them to stop work and they were to tired to put that big water tank on the tower, so it would have to wait till the next morning. Gus had an extension on one side of the tower that was taller and it was made into his flag poll that he raised his Texas Flag on and he was proud of his Texas Flag. Gus woke up the next morning stiff and sore in his back. He had hurt it a couple of days ago and there was no way that he rest it so that it might stop hurting him. There was just to much to do that required him to lift things or be in positions that hurt his back. After their breakfast and coffee they proceeded to get the 350 gallon poly water tank on the tower stand. They tried several ideas that failed, because the tank was to slick and big to simply get a hold of and lift it by hand. Gus finally came up with the idea of making a sort of rope harness to go around it and tie another rope to it, then Gus would get up on top of the tower stand and pull it while the other two men pushed from the bottom and they finally, after much effort, succeeded in hoisting the tank into it's place on the stand. This took much longer then Gus had thought that it would and now he wondered if they would finish building the porch that day, because it was supposed to be the last that the men were there. The men were wondering if their boss had lined up something for the next day for them and were worried about it, so Gus told them that he would drive out toward Van Horn till he got cell phone service and call their boss to see they could stay another day and that is what he did while they were working on welding up the frame for the front porch. Gus got about half way to Van Horn before he got cell service and by the time he got back it had taken him three hours to make the round trip Their boss had given them an OK to stay another day, so that took some of the pressure off. They got most of the frame of the porch built and welded that day and knew that they would finish by lunch the next day. The next morning they had their coffee and Gus discovered that he was almost out of food of any kind, so instead of everyone having two fried eggs they each only had one with a little more bacon and two pieces of pan toast. All Gus had left in his ice cooler for food was two eggs, some bacon a small chunk of cheese, some jalapino peppers, onion and a tomato. He had no idea what they were going to do for lunch, but they had to finish all their work that day. They did finish a little before lunch and the men proceeded in picking up all their tools and loading everything in their welding truck, then they went up to the other camp and loaded up the Bulldozer and the Maintainer. Gus told them what he had left to eat for lunch and the said wait just a minute and one of the men went out to their pick-up and brought in a huge can of sardines. They said that they were going to use them to make burritos. Gus never heard of sardine burritos, but he decided to try one. The two men chopped the onion, tomato, jalapino and the sardines and mixed them up in a bowl with some salsa and they wrapped that in a tortilla and to Gus's surprise it was real tasty. Gus would never have believed that a sardine burrito would be goon. He thought that he had learned something here and it would make a good story to tell in the future. After their lunch Gus had them help him put things in the new shop, new container, and load some things in his trailer, because his back was still hurting and he wanted as much help as he could get, so he would have a minimum to do the next day when he left to go back to Sugar Land. The men then left that afternoon and Gus was there alone to look over what they had done. What he saw he was proud of and when he came back the next time he could build on what they had accomplished this trip. That evening Gus boiled the two eggs and fried up the rest of the bacon. He had a bacon sandwich for his dinner and saved the two boiled eggs and the rest of the bacon to eat for breakfast the next morning with coffee. Gus slept poorly that night, because his back was hurting him so much. The next morning after his coffee and his breakfast he loaded up everything and started out for Sugarland. The farther he drove the more his back hurt and Gus was starting to wonder if he was going to be able to drive back home. When he got to Fort Stockton, which was about 150 miles from his ranch, he knew that he could go no farther that day and that he had to rest his back, so he got a Motel room and called his wife and told her that he wouldn't be home until the next day, because his back was hurting so much. The next morning after a fitful sleep he decided that he was going to have to drive back regardless of the pain, so he started out and from time to time he would have to pull over and get out of his Jeep Cherokee and stretch his back before starting out again. He finally made it back to Sugarland later that afternoon and only unloaded just what he had to and left the rest for the following day which was his last day at home before returning to work. After several more days of pain Gus decided to go to a Chiropractor to get some relief. He has had to do this through the years when he was farming and ranching, so he had a good idea what to expect. Sure enough two days after his visit to the Chiropractor his back started to feel better. His work at the Harvesting Department at the Prison went along as usual for that time of the year with the repair of all their harvesting equipment and the training of the new mechanics and new operators. Gus was always planning his next visit to his Blue Quail Ranch and when he had been out there this last time he had done a lot of measuring on the inside room that was to become the bath room, because he had plans on framing it in like the main room and wiring for lights and plumbing in water pipes to install a shower, sink and toilet. He also needed to cut through the tough outside metal wall to install three small windows. He planned his next trip for a week during the Thanksgiving Holidays, so he was buying all the materials that he would need to do the framing, insulation, ½ inch plywood for the walls and ceiling, electrical wire, light fixtures, water piping, toilet, shower stall, propane hot water heater and a double sink that he was going to install in an old cabinet that he had salvaged from the Prison trash dump, windows, a big assortment of screws, nails, pipe fittings and black metal pipe to run for propane. He also salvaged two poly water drums that he was going to convert into septic tanks. The next things he needed to acquire were a water trailer with a pump and a 250 gallon propane tank and he had seen an advertisement on an auction with a list of the items to be auctioned and there was a water trailer and several 250 gallon propane tanks on that list. Gus went to that auction and and the water trailer was just what he needed. It was a 500 gallon poly tank mounted on a 12 foot trailer with a large box installed in the front of the tank that held a water pump and a small pressure tank. It was perfect and Gus bought it for what the trailer alone would cost. It needed new tires and to be cleaned up and washed up, pumped out with clorox and vinegar to kill any germs and fungus, because it looked like it had been sitting up for a long time. He also bought a 250 gallon propane tank and an old style propane heater for future use out there. He wouldn't take the water trailer out on his next trip, because he would have to have his 8 foot trailer with him with all the supplies and tools he was taking with him. He would wait till another time to take the water trailer. There was no hurry, because he had a lot of work to do before he would need to haul that much water. The Thanksgivings Holidays finally came around and Gus had everything loaded that he could get into his 8 foot trailer and the Jeep Cherokee. He knew that he wouldn't have enough time in one week to get everything done, but now with the other container at his Ranch he had a place to store the supplies that he couldn't use right away. Gus arrived at his Blue Quail Ranch that afternoon and he immediately set up everything that he needed to stay in the Camp House, then he unloaded all of his supplies in the other container that was going to be a work shop and storage for tools, parts and supplies. By this time it was getting dark and Gus started a camp fire to sit by and sip on a beer and relax for a while before fixing himself a little dinner. While he was sitting there looking at the Sierra Vieja Mountains he was thinking that what he would really like to do was to go exploring on his Ranch to see what else he could see and find that was interesting, but that would have to be somewhere in the future, because he would have to use all of his time to work on the Camp House to make it more livable. It seemed that all he ever did when he came out was work instead of have a good time out there, but he also enjoyed seeing the difference when he made something better through his work. He didn't know how long it would be before he had things finished enough to where he could just come out and use it like a regular house with electric lights, refrigerator and running water to take a shower, flush a toilet and wash dishes. He knew that he had started from scratch and even with the time off from his Prison work that he had built up to use to come out and work on the Camp House it was going to take him a long time to get it like he wanted it. Gus worked furiously on the bathroom in the Camp House. He was so determined to get a lot done in it that he didn't even cook like he usually did. He made a lot of sandwiches and opened cans and heated their contents up instead of cooking to also cut down on the time spent washing dishes. Gus was getting a lot of work done. First he cut holes in the outside metal wall for three small windows. Then he framed up the inside walls and ceiling just like a house would be, then installed the electric wiring and installed the wall outlets. Then he insulated the walls and double insulated the ceiling. Next he built the stand for the shower stall and toilet that would raise it two steps from the floor, because the plumbing for the shower stall and toilet would have to go under it. Next he screwed up the ply board to the ceiling and nailed the ply board to the walls. He left the end wall of the bathroom unfinished, because he would have to use that end to bring in the big old cabinet that he had installed the double sink in and the shower stall. Gus opened up the double doors on the end of the Camp House and backed up the trailer to the opening and then unhooked the trailer so it would tilt down and he could slide the big old sink cabinet out and right onto the floor of the bath room. From there he could push it to the location on the wall next to the main room where it would permanently remain. Next he unloaded the shower stall and placed it on the stand where it wound be plumbed in and be permanent. The last big thing he brought in was the toilet and he placed it on the stand next to the shower where it would be plumbed in and be permanent. He was so glad to finally get these big bathroom. Items inside the bathroom in the Camp House where he could finally get them plumbed in and water piping to them. Gus knew that the hardest part of plumbing in the shower stall and the toilet was going to be working under the cramped space below the stand that he had built to support them. He could barely slide under there up to his shoulders, so he made sure that he would have everything underneath the stand that he would need to finish the job. He had already cut the holes through the lower outside wall, so he could pipe through there without any trouble. This plumbing took him the rest of the day, but he was glad that he was through with it. The next morning Gus was stiff and sore from working in the space under the platform stand for the shower stall and the toilet and while he was drinking his morning coffee he was planning how he was going to run the water pipes to the bathroom sink, shower stall and the toilet. Gus had all of that done by lunch and after lunch he started building a small closet on the outside of the Camp House under the water tank tower to house the hot water heater. He got this all framed up by evening and the inside water pipes were stubbed out to the hot water heater closet. He decided that he would sit by the camp fire for a while and sip on a couple of beers to rest and celebrate what he had accomplished. Gus was exhausted from being on a whirlwind work schedule ever since he had arrived at his Blue Quail Ranch and he had only eaten hastily fixed meals and needed a good bath to make him feel better, but he would have to stick to warming up water and continuing to wipe himself down until he got everything finished for the bathroom, which wasn't going to happen this trip. He decided to take the time to fix himself a good dinner with a small steak grilled on the open fire and a salad and a potato baked in the coals. After this he washed up his dishes and heated up water on his camp stove and washed himself out of buckets. It wasn't very glamorous, but it did the trick and he fell into bed feeling much better. The next morning he nailed up the ply board over the framing and made a door for the front of the closet, then he rested with a big glass of sun tea he had made before he moved the hot water heater into the closet and hooked it up to the inside plumbing that had been stubbed out for that application. He also ran the water piping from the overhead water tank to the hot water heater and to the inside piping that had been stubbed out for that application. Now everything was hooked up to supply water inside the Camp House to the bathroom where all water would be used inside. All that was needed now was to bring out the water trailer and fill it in Van Horn for the Ranch and to set up the 250 gallon propane tank and plumb it into the Camp House, with metal black pipe, for the camp stove, the heater and on the outside to the hot water heater closet. Gus would also have to hire a backhoe to come out to install the septic tanks and dig the trenches for the sewer line and the drain line for the shower and bathroom sink. That would have to wait till his next trip for his Christmas vacation of ten days. Gus took the next day to clean up the inside of the bathroom and painted the ceiling and walls white just like the rest of the Camp House, then he gathered up all the wood that he had left over and stacked it in the shop, storage building along with the tools that he was going to leave there. He put his old Jeep in the shop and after it the welding machine. By the time he had everything put up and organized it was time for him to start his last camp fire of the trip to sit by and sip on a beer and just rest before he fixed himself some dinner. Gus sat there and looked out over the Sierra Vieja Mountains and 96 gap and watched the sun go down while listening to the coyotes wild howls. He loved this primitive rugged, unforgiving, high Chihuahua Desert mountain country. He knew that he wasn't a young man anymore, but somehow being out here in this Desert made him feel more viral like the young man he used to be. Gus thought about how it might feel for a young man and young woman that were truly in love to live together out in this Desert country. He asked himself if they could make it living out here and stay deeply in love just depending on each other to do what it took to survive and also if he had been given the opportunity to do that as a young man what young woman would have he chosen to be with him that would have been his other half committed to the land and to their life together through the rough times which surely would have been more numerous then any good times. He sat there sipping on his beer in deep thought about that going through the list of his ex-wives and ex-girlfriends and none of them, he was sure would measure up to the task it would take, then he remembered that beautiful Lorrie and her wonderful kisses, her beautiful body and her commitment to him even when she was so young. Would she have been the one he wondered, but he really didn't know, but there had always been something special about her that he could never quite figure out. Lorrie had always been with him in some way that he couldn't explain and when he had the time to think about her he was always perplexed as to why the vivid memory of her had followed him all these years when he had forgotten so many other women and many of them a lot more recent then Lorrie. Gus thought that it was strange the way that Lorrie's memory would appear to him at unexpected times, like it was hiding in ambush to find the right time to shoot back into his mind to give him sweet memories and to align itself with whatever he was doing. Strange, very strange, but now he had to eat, clean up and get everything packed and ready to leave early in the morning to go back to Sugarland. The next morning Gus fixed himself a little breakfast, a sandwich and snakes for the trip then washed up his dishes, loaded up the last of what he had to take back with him, hooked up his 8 foot trailer, looked around one last time then drove down his Blue Quail Ranch road toward the highway on his way back home. Gus went back to work at the Prison Harvesting Department where everything was running about as smooth as could be expected and he thought how much different this was compared to when he was working for himself. In the first place he would never have had this much time to go out to a ranch in Far West Texas and work and another thing is that when he did take off for even two or three days he never knew what to expect when he returned, usually something was wrong that he had to attend to immediately. Actually this was the perfect job that he needed to make his transition from living on the Gulf Coast to Far West Texas which was probably only four years away. Gus had been thinking about getting a pick-up truck because of everything that he needed to haul out West. He just couldn't keep doing it with his Jeep Cherokee and that 8 foot trailer. Also the pick-up he needed would have to have four wheel drive because of the terrain and the possibility of snow and ice in the winters. He wanted to get one before his next trip out there in December, because he wanted to pull the water trailer with it and the Jeep Cherokee could pull the 8 foot trailer that would have the propane tank and other supplies in it. Gus went around to car dealerships looking at their new four wheel drive pick-ups and their used pick-ups and they wanted a lot more money then Gus wanted to pay for one, but he finally found a small independent used truck dealer that had a nice 1997 Chevrolet ½ ton four wheel drive pick-up that had belonged to a major oil field service company. It was in good shape and it had heavy duty springs, an extra large fuel tank and the dealer would throw in a good headache rack. Gus test drove it and was pleased and paid him cash for it and drove it home. He told his Wife that she needed to sell her Toyota and he would give her his Jeep Cherokee, because it was more suited to what they were going to do out in Far West Texas, so that is what she did. Now Gus could pull trailers behind both his pick-up and the Jeep Cherokee which solved the problem of getting the water trailer and the rest of the supplies and the propane tank out to the Ranch at the same time. All the time Gus had been back in Sugarland, since his last trip out to his Ranch, he had been planning what he was going to do next and he was acquiring the supplies to get the job done. He also called a Backhoe operator in Fort Davis and made arrangements for him to meet Gus at his Ranch during his Christmas trip out there. Gus wanted to get his septic system installed and the propane tank set up and piped into the Camp House and the hot water closet, then to fill the water trailer in Van Horn and take it out to the Ranch and pump it up into the water tank on the overhead stand. Then he would have running water in the Camp House and propane to his water heater the Camp House heater and the camp stove used for cooking. He was hoping that he could get all of this accomplished with a few days to spare so he could enjoy the Camp House being more like regular house. They were going to be out there for ten days instead of two weeks, because that was all of the vacation time that his Wife had left for the year. Gus and his Wife left Sugarland with his Wife driving the Jeep Cherokee and pulling the 12 foot water trailer and Gus was driving his 1997 Chevrolet pick-up truck pulling the 8 foot trailer with the propane tank and loaded down with all the extra supplies he would need to finish everything he had planned to accomplish. He was going through San Antonio when he had a blow out on the 8 foot trailer and had to pull over to the side and change the tire to put on the spare tire. He then had to look for a place to buy two new tires for the trailer so they would match each other, because he knew that he had a long way to go and with the weight that he was carrying in the 8 foot trailer he didn't want any more trouble. This slowed them down for about two hours which was a big deal on so long a trip, because they couldn't drive as fast as usual pulling the trailers and this extra delay would throw them late getting to the Blue Quail Ranch, but Gus figured that they would make it before it got dark. They just wouldn't be able to get everything unloaded before dark like he had wanted to do. They got to the Ranch about two hours before dark and unloaded what they would need to set up the camp for the night. They still had to use water out of the barrels they brought and keep the food in the ice coolers, because they were in a transition stage out there until they got the water in the overhead tank and the propane tank piped in and hooked up so Gus could use the used propane camper ice box that his step brother had given him. The only thing that they could use was the electric lights that he could hook up to his welding machine for the generator. Gus hated to use it, because it made so much noise and it used 10 gallons of gasoline every eight hours, so he only used it when he had to. The next day the Backhoe operator drove up about mid-morning and he and Gus got busy digging the hole and trenches for the septic tanks and the four inch and two inch drain lines. They finished this and had everything covered by 4:00 pm that afternoon. Next Gus had the Backhoe operator unload the propane tank from the 8 foot trailer and Gus positioned cement blocks to lower it on that would serve as it's base. With this finished Gus paid the Backhoe operator and now it was time for a camp fire and a beer. While Gus was sitting by the camp fire he was also planning the next day and he thought that he would be able to get the shower stall and the bathroom sink plumbed into the two inch drain line and the toilet plumbed into the four inch to the septic tanks, by early that next afternoon, then he could drive into Van Horn and fill up his 500 gallon water tank trailer and get back to the Ranch in time to pump water into the overhead tank. Then they could use the toilet, the bathroom sink, the shower. They wouldn't have any hot water for a shower or to the bathroom sink until he got all the piping done to get the propane tank plumbed into the Camp House and also drive to Van Horn get the Propane Company there to bring out a load of propane to charge Gus's 250 gallon tank. Gus thought that it might take another three days to get all of that done. Gus was able to get a lot more done with his wife along, because she took care of most of the cooking, except on the grill, and she did most of the dish washing and she would even help hold something for Gus or hand him something and all of this saved Gus time, so he accomplished things faster. She was a great help and she didn't seem to mind helping Gus when she was needed. That next morning Gus started all his plumbing to hook up the water to the Camp House and the sewer line to the Camp House. Everything had been stubbed to the outside of the Camp House on his last trip, so it was just a matter of making the connections fit up and running the outside lines. This took Gus a lot of time to get everything to line up so there wouldn't be any leaks, but he finished by lunch time which was a couple of hours earlier then expected. That was good, because it gave Gus more time to get the water in Van Horn and he also needed to go to the store for some more ice and a few other food items. After their lunch Gus hooked his pick-up to the water trailer and they drove into Van Horn. The Water Department in Van Horn was real nice helping him to fill up out of their commercial valve and the charge for the 500 gallons of water was only $5.00. They went to the store for ice and a few more food items, filled up with gas and they got back to the Ranch by 4:00 pm. Gus unloaded the ice cooler and the food and then he pulled around between the Camp House and the Shop Container beside the water tower and the welding machine that he had put there the evening before. The welding machine would be used to power the electric motor for the water pump. This was all exciting for Gus, because this was the first chance that he had to see if he had any water leaks in his plumbing and also just the idea of having running water in the Camp House way out here in the middle of the Chihuahua Desert was something to be proud of. Just think now they could use the toilet instead of the potty chair. Wow, what a luxury. Gus started the welding machine for power and then crawled up the ladder with a hose to fill the water tank. He secured it in the tank then came back down to open the valve to pump the water up into the tank and it all worked like it was supposed to. It took him about 30 minutes to pump the 350 gallon tank full and that left 150 gallons of water in the trailer tank to be pumped up later. Gus then opened the valve on the bottom of the over head tank and went into the Camp House to bleed the air out of the lines and to check for water leaks. All the connections were dry with no leaks and Gus told his Wife that he would give her the first chance to use the bathroom toilet as a present for helping him and they both got a laugh for that statement. Really though it was a great improvement to have a working toilet and running water in the bathroom sink that was actually a double stainless steel kitchen sink that could be used to wash dishes in bad weather, so it served two purposes. While they had been in Van Horn Gus had talked to the owner of the Propane Company and paid him in advanced to bring a load of propane out to the Ranch the next day. Gus had to pay him $ 100.00 extra, because the road was so bad and it was so far out to the Ranch. Gus knew that he was going to be cutting and threading pipe the next day, for the installation of propane into the Camp House the next day, but for now it was late in the evening and it was once again time to rest in front of a camp fire and enjoy a beer and then grill some pork chops and some squash with onions and bell pepper for their dinner. In the morning Gus actually filled the coffee pot with water from the sink faucet in the bathroom to boil for their coffee. He thought that this was really nice not to have to go outside to get water from their water barrel. While Gus was sitting at the kitchen area table he was wondering what time the propane truck would arrive, because he had a lot to do after the truck filled his 250 gallon propane tank, but until it arrived he would stay busy measuring, cutting and threading the propane pipe and attaching it to the outside of the Camp House, boring through the walls to install the valves in the places to serve the propane heater, the propane cook stove, the ice box that was either propane or electric and the hot water heater. Gus had all the pipe, fittings and valves that he would need and the pipe cutter and threader and pipe wrenches, so he would start on it as soon as he finished breakfast. He worked hard as the morning progressed and he was almost through with the front side of the Camp House piping when the propane truck drove up. It was a real relief to see this truck pull up. The truck finished filling the tank and drove off, so Gus decided that he was going to go ahead and pipe the propane tank to the regulator that he had already attached to the Camp House. After that he started on the piping for the back side of the Camp House that would supply propane to the cook stove and the water heater. Gus didn't finish that before it got dark on him, but he knew that he would finish it the next morning before lunch. The next morning Gus started the final part of his piping on the back side of the Camp House. This took him a little longer then he had thought that it would, because he had some trouble hooking up the propane line to the water heater and also his boring tool was getting dull and he had trouble boring through the outside wall to install the valve for the cook stove. All in all though he did finish all of the piping and installing the interior valves by lunch time. After his lunch Gus disconnected the cook stove, heater and refrigerator from their propane bottles and attached them to the propane wall valves. He sat at the kitchen table and rested for a while with a glass of tea before he would start to bleed the air out of the propane line and light all the appliances that would be served by the propane. After he bleed the line and lit the heater, water heater, cook stove and the refrigerator that now would be on propane, he went out with a container of soapy water and a brush to check all of his connections for leaks. He would brush the soapy water on each connection and if there would be a leak then it would make a soap bubble, but there were no leaks. The Camp House was now provided with the same civilized conveniences that a regular house would have, except that Gus didn't want to run the welding machine all the time for electricity, so they would still use kerosene lamps in the Camp House most of the time for light at night and they would use the kerosene lanterns out side when they needed them, but from now on they could have good showers and hot water in the double sink for washing dishes and for Gus's shaving in the mornings. Gus had a couple of days left before they would have to pack up to go back home to Sugarland, so he knew that he wanted to do some more exploring on his Ranch. Exploring on his Ranch was a slow process, because the terrain was so rugged that you had to find ways to drive his old Jeep and then hike after that, but he always seemed to find all sorts of treasures, like more Indian Artifacts, fossils, semi-precious stones and even old ammunition casings from the 1800's era. Exploring on his Ranch was always an exciting time for Gus and the time slipped by before he knew it. All of a sudden it was time for them to pack up and drive back to Sugarland. They would celebrate New Year 1999 in their home in Sugarland and it would be a time to look back at what they had accomplished at the Ranch in the high mountain Chihuahua Desert of Far West Texas. They were taking back some arrow heads and fossils and pretty rocks to look at as the year of 1999 would go by along with the large amount of pictures that they always took, because it wouldn't be until sometime in September 1999 that Gus would be able to go back to his Ranch. From now on going out to the Ranch would be a little easier and staying there would take less work and it would be more pleasant. Also there would be more time to go exploring since so much of the work had been done to make the Camp House more like a regular house and there would be less time spent on things like burying the waste from the potty chair, hauling in water from the water barrels on the porch boiling water to shave and bathe and changing the small propane bottles that were used for the cook stove, heater and refrigerator. Gus knew that there would always be work to be done, because he was already planning some things for the container that was the shop and storage building now and he wanted to put up more shelving in the camp house along with towel racks and things like that, but they would be small improvements compared to what he had been doing. Gus was barely able to get the pictures developed before the New Year Holiday and he was looking forward to looking at them and sipping on a whiskey to bring in New Year 1999 and that is exactly what he did.

Lorrie—1998 had the potential for being a very good year for Lorrie. Lorrie thought that she had more to look forward to in this New Year of 1998 then she could remember for a long time. The only depressing parts for her to contend with were her dismal marriage and her scheming Stepson, but as long as she had her little sweet dog Mitzi, her long time friend Jill, her Art History Degree to work toward and now a new friend Carol that was also studying for the very same Art History Degree, then Lorrie thought that she could put up with almost anything at home. After New Years Lorrie dove back into her studies with a passion. She was always ahead of the other students and was already planning on trying to finish her Degree in three years, which would be one year early and she was well on her way to doing that. She would meet Jill for lunch sometime and they would go to some of the Art Galleries in the afternoon and Lorrie would show Jill what she had learned while they were viewing and discussing the art work and the Artist. Jill was very impressed with Lorrie and she thought that it was like having her very own private Art Tutor and of course Lorrie loved to show Jill what she had learned and it also gave Lorrie a chance to revisit the Lectures and the Museums and Galleries she had been to in her classes, so as to bring it all back to life for her again, thus helping to cement it in her mind, so it was also a benefit for Lorrie too. After that they would usually go to Pizza Express and eat pizza and share a bottle of wine. While they were at Pizza Express they would talk about more personal matters. Jill was the only person in the world that Lorrie would discuss personal problems with and there were even some things that Lorrie didn't talk to Jill about. Lorrie was notified that the art class was going to take their next field trip to the Galleries in Milan, Italy. Lorrie thought WOW Italy was the heart of the Master Sculptors and Painters of the Medieval Art Period and the Renaissance Art Period, with Masters such as Di Vince, Michael Angelo and Rafael. Lorrie could hardly contain herself to wait for the trips to Italy to began. These field trips would also take them to visit the actual living quarters and work shops of some of the Artists, so the students could get the feeling of their living conditions and experience the surroundings of where they produced their work with their tools displayed there, in essence they would be walking in the footsteps of the Great Masters. The purpose of this was to give the students even more appreciation of the Great Masters work that they produced by seeing how and where and with what tools that they accomplished such Great Works of Art. Later in the spring of 1998 Lorrie and Carol made this trip with their class and Lorrie as usual took a lot of notes. When they got back to their room to clean up, before going out for dinner and party with the class and the locals, Lorrie wanted to compare her notes with Carols and she found out that Carol didn't take any notes and Lorrie was shocked, because she knew that there were going to be questions on their next examinations that would cover this trip. Carol just brushed of Lorrie's concerns and said that she would remember enough to pass the examinations. This gave Lorrie a pause to re-evaluate Carols sincere interest in the Art Classes. Lorrie thought that it was Carol's business, so why should she worry about it. Carol was fun to be with and they were about to go have some Italian food and wine and maybe dance and flirt a little with the local dark, romantic men. They got a kick out of flirting with them and letting the men pick up the dinner and bar bills and then excusing themselves to go to their own rooms and leaving the men to wonder what had happened to cool things off. Lorrie and Carol would have several laughs about these excursions when they got back to England. Lorrie simply loved the trips, because they not only put the icing on the cake when it came to her Art History Degree, but it also gave her a chance to temporarily divorce herself from her home life in England, by transporting her into a completely different environment and sometimes even into a different time period that would allow her to almost forget who she was, so she could pretend her life was different. These times didn't last very long, but they were just long enough to raise her spirits enough to go home and face her disappointing marriage. Lorrie's spring Open University Classes were going very good and she was always asking for advanced material to study with her Tutor. She was now months ahead of where her schedule showed that she should be and her grades were excellent. It wouldn't be long until she would be moving into the summer vacation season and she was already thinking about her next trip to her home town of El Campo, Texas. She was keeping in touch with her family there every week through Trans-Atlantic phone calls to Texas and she placed special emphasis on having a long conversation with her Dad, so as to determine if she detected any changes in him. After talking to him she would talk to the rest of her family and ask them questions about him, but they didn't seem to be concerned that there was something was changing about his health. Lorrie had been trained as a Nurse and something had been worrying her for some time about her Dad, but she just couldn't put her finger on what it was. She had come to the conclusion that either she was loosing her mind or there were such small, slow changes happening with her Dad's health, that since her family was around him all the time they didn't recognize them. She was determined to try to get to the bottom of it when she went back to El Campo in the summer. So she could quit worrying about him. Lorrie's Stepson was still doing his trailing at the Royal Air Force training Academy and they didn't see much of him. When he did get a leave he either didn't come home at all or he only spent one night at home and then he was off with someone else. This was OK with Lorrie, because he usually only came home to get money from his Dad and that always put Lorrie in a bad mood. She thought that he should be doing just fine on his Military pay and learning how to budget it responsibility like an adult. Since he had been gone Lorrie and her Husband had less friction and her Husband's drunken, abusive outbursts hadn't been as frequent. Her Husband was still doing very well with his high end Tailoring Business and Lorrie had been able to get their collection schedule on track so that everyone involved knew what to expect and if one Garment House was a little late with payment then Lorrie would send them a Registered Business Letter with a veiled message that they would have to look at that account more carefully in the future and the account would be paid quickly. They were being invited on a lot of mini-holidays to Spain and France paid for by the owners or representatives of the Garment Houses and that was a lot of fun and a pleasant distraction for Lorrie. Lorrie needed a lot of distractions from her home life and when she was at home too much with her Husband it would get to the point that she would drink right along with him and when she did that then she might slip up and say something that would set him off on a tirade that she would regret. Lorrie's Husband was still doing his two ski trips a year and that was always a welcome relief for her. It was the first of June and time for Lorrie's annual month long vacation back to see her family and a few friends in El Campo, Texas. Lorrie's Sister picked her up at the Houston Intercontinental Airport as usual and Lorrie spent a few days with her and her Sisters Husband before both of them would drive to El Campo. When Lorrie was alone with her Sister she questioned her about their Dad's health.

Lorrie told her Sister that when she was down on her vacation last year she had noticed something different about their Dad, but couldn't figure exactly what it was and that lately when she would call back to El Campo and talk to him that he had a little different sound to his voice. Lorrie didn't know if it was because of the phone or if her imagination was playing tricks on her and she wanted to know if her Sister had noticed anything since she wasn't around him all the time either. Her Sister told Lorrie that she hadn't noticed anything, but she would try to pay special attention when they were in El Campo this time. Lorrie had brought one of her luggage cases with her little gifts for everyone from England like she always did and when she went back she would fill it with Texas food products that they couldn't get in England. This was always her routine on every trip. Her Dad was 74 years old now, but Lorrie thought that he was still one of the handsomest men she had ever know. When she was just a young girl she would sit on his lap and try her little flirtations to see if she could get her own way about something. Lorrie always said that Texas girls learned to flirt by starting out on their Dads to perfect their flirting for later use on their boyfriends. She said that for Texas girls flirting was a science and it had to be worked at to be effective. Lorrie and her Sister arrived in El Campo and everyone was there to welcome her. Her Mom had been baking cookies for several days because she knew how much Lorrie and her Sister loved them. Lorrie's little Brother was there also, but he wasn't so little any more, because he was 41 years old and well over six feet tall and he towered over all of them. Lorrie's Brother had a very sweet disposition and usually got along well with everyone except Lorrie's Sister and he tried to let old dogs lay between them until she would make some sort of sly remark that brought back old memories for him of when she would baby sit him when he was a little boy and she had enjoyed being mean to him. When this would happen he would simply excuse himself and go home rather then to cause a big argument there at his Mom and Dad's house. Lorrie always held her breath hoping that her Sister would behave herself, so everyone in the family could enjoy each others company. Late that afternoon at around 5:00 pm, they always called their happy hour, they all went out on the patio and enjoyed a beer, a glass of wine or a mixed drink, before dinner and Lorrie gave her a Sister a look that meant to watch their Dad and her Sister nodded her understanding. They sat and talked about what had been happening England and about Lorrie's Art History studies and then about what had been going on around El Campo and the people that Lorrie knew that still lived there. Lorrie kept observing her Dad closely and she noticed that he had a slight twitch in his hand when he brought up his beer for a sip and a little lisp in his speech, but other then that he looked fine. She didn't know what to think of it and didn't want to jump to any conclusions, so she decided that she would talk to her Sister and her Mom in private when she got the chance. The next day Lorrie's Dad wanted to do one of his favorite things with Lorrie and that was to go riding and buy a six-pack of beer, just the two of them, so he could talk to Lorrie in private to find out what her life was really like. What her Dad didn't know was that Lorrie would closely guard her secrets about her private life, just as she had always done and he wouldn't learn much of anything that would throw a bad light on the way that she had run her private life. This was the way she had been ever since she had been a young girl, because they had been so strict on her, so she started hiding what she was really thinking and doing from her parents to keep from being punished in some way and this continued throughout her whole life. Because of this her Parents never truly knew who their daughter was, they just knew the daughter that was presented to them in carefully thought out and planned performances by Lorrie. There was no way that Lorrie would let her Parents know the truth about the turmoil that her private life existed in. She wasn't about to let them know that she needed a lot of diversions from the reality of her Marriage so she could stay with her Husband. Lorrie always enjoyed these private drives with her Dad, because she always learned more about him and what had been going on with people in El Campo then she would otherwise and also now it would be the perfect chance to observe him more closely. They went to her Dad's favorite little Beer Joint and visited there for a little while then they bought their six pack and drove around and just talked. Lorrie thought that her Dad seemed mostly fine except that the little changes that she had observed at their happy hour on the patio were still there and that bothered Lorrie, but what could she attribute those to, was it just old age or something else. The next day when Lorrie, her Sister and her Mom went shopping Lorrie discussed this with them and they were of the impression that it was just the progression of aging. Her Mom told her that she was noticing changes in herself as she was getting older that came on a little at a time and she was sure that it was just the aging process. This somewhat satisfied Lorrie and she decided to stop worrying about it and enjoy her vacation with her Parents and friends in El Campo. Lorrie's visits to El Campo always had bitter-sweet moments to them. Not only did she revisit some of the places and memories about Gus, there were also things there that brought back painful memories of her only child, her Son, that basically had been lost to her through a temporary child custody agreement with her first Husband. While she was in El Campo she had to drive by the Elementary School that he attended almost every day, because it was on the same street that her Parents house was on and she would remember the times that the Principal of the school would call her to come up to the school to meet with him about some trouble that her Son was in because of his over active behavior. He had attended this school for two years while he and Lorrie were living at her Parents house and she was working at the Hospital as a Nurse, after her divorce from her first Husband. It was during this time that Lorrie decided to join the Navy and the Navy rebuilt her confidence in herself and gave her a career for eight years, but in doing so, she lost her Son. Since then she had only had bits and pieces of information about him and what she had learned about her Son she didn't like. Lorrie thought that there were so many things about her life that she would like to change, but she couldn't live her life thinking, what I should have done was this or that, because that would just drive her crazy, so she had developed a way of closing all of those unpleasant memories behind thick doors and most of them were locked there, not to resurface, except for those of her Son and those of Gus. Lorrie's month vacation back in El Campo, Texas was speeding by and she had enjoyed it, but now she was beginning to think about resuming her studies on her Art History Degree in England. She thought that if everything went well this next year would be her last year and she would Graduate a year early. Lorrie's last few days in El Campo, Texas were spent with her family going through old picture albums and remembering family vacations and past holidays. Two days before she was to leave for her flight back to England Lorrie always did her shopping for the Texas food products that she always liked to pack to take back with her to England, because there was no getting them there and if she stretched them out after she got back they would last a long time and give her her favorite taste of Texas to enjoy. Along with this shopping trip for the groceries she always had to make her final trip on memory lane around Gus's parents house just to look at it and remember the feeling she had when she had been a young girl riding her bicycle on the street around it looking for a glimpse of Gus and it always put butterflies in her stomach when she saw it, just like it had always done so many years ago. She thought about Gus every time and hoped that he was happy and her heart always ached a little in the remembering. Lorrie would just bite her lip and drive on to the grocery store wondering if something would keep her from continuing to make the trip back to El Campo each year to see her family and of course to see her old stomping grounds and the house that Gus had lived in when she had first fallen in love with him. Lorrie said her goodby's and her Brother took her to the Houston Airport for her long flight back to England. Lorrie had many hours to think on her flight back to England and some-time she wished that there would be a good reason for her to go back to live in Texas. After all she had accomplished her dream of living in England and she had been able to see quite a lot of Europe and now she was on the verge of completing her Art History Degree, so she thought that her childhood dream was basically complete. Lorrie wondered if she could rebuild a life for herself back in Texas at the age of 53 years old. It seemed much to old to start over and that would mean that she would have to get a divorce from her Husband and that would be a big thing in England, because the English Courts always leaned toward the men. Oh well, she put that out of her mind and decided to sleep for a while to pass the hours of the long trip. Lorrie's first few days back at home in England were always spent unpacking, resting from her trip, checking out her sweet little dog Mitzi to make sure she had been treated properly and getting back in touch with her best friend Jill to catch up on what had been happening while she was away. There was always the jumble of mail that her Husband had piled on her desk that she had to sort through to pick out the bills and other mail that would be important, because he didn't have a clue what to do with them. She contacted the Open University to make sure that her admissions for the fall of 1988 were all in order so she could start on her final year of her Art History Degree which would start in only one week, but Lorrie was ready to get back in the saddle, as they would say in Texas. She asked her Husband about her Stepson and he didn't have much to tell about him, because he hadn't seen much of him, so Lorrie figured that all was good there. Lorrie finally got in touch with her new friend Carol that was taking the same Art Degree and found that she was also signed up for the fall Semester, so they would be seeing each other from time to time again. Lorrie made arrangements for her and her Husband to meet Carol at a Pub that Lorrie liked to frequent and they talked about their fall Semester classes and wondered which Museums and Art Galleries they would be visiting. Lorrie's Husband was really putting on a show for Carol spending a lot of money, much more then usual, on expensive drinks and dinner for them and Carol was really impressed with him and showed her pleasure with animated conversation that Lorrie recognized from her experiences with Carol when they went out in the evenings after their field trips to the Museums and Galleries in Holland and Italy. Lorrie wasn't really jealous, but she thought that Carol was showing disrespect toward her by the way she was acting and Lorrie didn't appreciate it a bit. Lorrie's fall semester was in full swing and she was loaded down with her last years work to do and she wanted to do the very best she could on her assignments and with her Tutor, so when it came time for her to go to the last field trip she would be fully prepared, because it was going to be the big one in Paris, France which was the Louvre and an Annex Museum named the jeu de Paume, that had the distinguished history of being the secret beginnings for the saving of the Art Works of Europe after World War II, from the German looting during the War, because of the covert work of an obscure, dedicated Assistant Curator staff member named Rose Valland. Lorrie was always excited to make these field trips, because of being able to see the Art Work in person and have everything explained to her by the experts, but this had even more of an interest with the World War II connection, because her Dad had served during World War II and anything connected to that held a special interest for her. This field trip was going to be something real special for Lorrie to look forward to in the spring, but now the Christmas and New Years Holidays were getting close and she had to devote all her energy to studying, doing the office work for her Husbands Tailoring Business and shopping and decorating for the Holidays. Lorrie liked for her life to be busy, because that kept her mind diverted from her unhappy Marriage and as a result it made living with a man she didn't love easier. Lorrie had lost all respect for her Husband other then the fact that he was a superb Tailor and at the top of his business. She did all of her Christmas shopping for their gifts and food she would prepare for guests that would stop by on Christmas Eve for drinks and snacks. Her and her Husband were invited to several Christmas Parties that were sponsored by the big Garment Houses during the two weeks before Christmas as usual, and Lorrie had to always watch her Husband closely at these, so he didn't make a fool of himself by getting too drunk and causing trouble. This was nothing new for Lorrie and she always asked one of her Husbands friends that was in attendance at the party to help her, because sometime it was hard to keep track of him for he would slip off to take extra fast shots of whiskey that she didn't notice and his friend would call her attention to her Husbands behavior so Lorrie could put an exit plan in action to get him home. Lorrie would buy gifts for her Husband, her Stepson, herself and of coarse for her sweet dog Mitzi. When Christmas Eve arrived Lorrie had everything beautifully decorated and had Christmas music playing with all of the special food arranged in a decorative fashion, with their bar stocked with the usual assortment of alcoholic beverages, gifts under their Christmas tree and she also had a pretty little Christmas costume on sweet little Mitzi. Everything was ready for Christmas Eve, to entertain friends and business associates that would stop by during the day and early evening to visit. Lorrie's Stepson called and said that he would be late and she could tell that he was drunk, so she didn't expect him till Christmas day. Her Christmas Eve open house celebration was a success as usual and Lorrie finally closed everything down about twelve midnight and her and Mitzi went up the stairs to her bed room leaving hr Husband passed out on the couch. Sometime in the early morning hours Lorrie heard noise down stairs and after listening she heard her Stepsons voice and her Husbands voice in an argument, so she turned over and hugged Mitzi and went back to sleep. Lorrie got up on Christmas morning looking forward to the day, that as a child she always remembered as being filled with excitement, and she put on the Christmas tree lights started some Christmas music softly, put the tea pot on to boil and was warming up some Christmas sweet pastry for her and Mitzi's breakfast. Her and Mitzi ate their breakfast and they sat on the couch in front of the Christmas tree enjoying the glow of the beautiful lights and decorations with the pleasant soft Christmas music with Mitzi nuzzling her head on Lorrie's lap and Lorrie softly stroking Mitzi's head. Everything was quiet in the house except for the soft sounds and smells of Christmas. Lorrie loved times like this, just her and Mitzi to love each other in piece. Lorrie was in the kitchen fixing herself another mug of tea when her Husband came down with swollen eyes and she could tell that he had a hangover from his drinking on Christmas Eve. He went over and cut off the Christmas music and that irritated Lorrie, then he asked her to fix him a mug of tea, which she did. Lorrie asked her Husband what time her Stepson had come home and he yelled at her that it was non of her business and then he picked up her mug of tea and threw it to the floor breaking the mug and splashing tea everywhere. Lorrie just looked at it and said nothing. She got the dust pan and broom and swept up the broken mug and got out the mop and some water to mop up the tea. Her husband went into the living room and sat on the couch and little Mitzi got up and went into the kitchen to lay close to Lorrie's feet. Lorrie thought that she could never remember having a really sweet Christmas since she had Married this man and wondered if she would ever experience a wonderful Christmas again. Her Husband pouted the rest of the morning and her Stepson finally came down at lunch time. Her Husband just glared at him and said nothing and Lorrie kept quiet afraid to ask any questions. After her Stepson had a mug of tea he started complaining about how stupid and unprofessional his Instructors were at the Royal Air Force Training Academy, he went on and on and Lorrie just listened, not really understanding why he was so upset with them and she was afraid to ask any questions, so she just let him exhaust his displeasure until she could have the chance to divert the subject to something more Christmas like. This seemed to work pretty well, because she avoided a fight between her Husband and her Stepson that would have probably ruined the whole of Christmas day. They finally sat down in front of the Christmas tree and the first gift was for Mitzi which was a new snuggle bunny toy for her to carry around and lay down with. Lorrie got her Stepson a new electric shaver and some expensive shaving lotion that she knew that he liked and she got her Husband new pajamas and slippers and a fancy cigarette roller. Lorrie got herself a present from Santa Clause that was a gift certificate to the local Book Store in Bromley. Lorrie noticed that her Husband and her Stepson were rather cool to each other and that was fine with her, because she sure didn't want any big arguments during Christmas. After they opened their gifts they ate the Christmas dinner that Lorrie had prepared and her Husband went up to his bedroom and her Stepson went up to his bedroom and that left Lorrie and Mitzi by themselves to enjoy the rest of Christmas night together. Christmas was over and Lorrie was preparing for a small gathering of friends for New Years Eve. It would be mostly a come and go affair with finger foods and a variety of drinks to choose from. Her Stepson's holiday Leave from the Royal Air Force Academy was over and he had gone back so he wouldn't be there with his friends and their absence would make things a little more low key. She still hadn't learned what the big argument had been between her Husband and her Stepson and also why he had been so angry about his Instructors and she decided to just let it all go by the wayside. New Years Eve came and Lorrie's little party went off without a hitch. Her Husband even behaved himself and there was a nice gathering of friends and business associates that came and went through the evening. Finally right before the New Year was to enter her Husband decided that he was going to go to bed and that suited Lorrie just fine, because then she could bring in the New Year with Mitzi. Lorrie and

Mitzi sat on the couch together and Lorrie was sipping on some brandy and listening to music on the New Year television show when all of a sudden they played "In The Still Of The Night" by the Five Satins and a lump in Lorrie's throat got so big that she couldn't swallow her brandy. She set the glass down and stroked Mitzi's head with one hand and wiped a tear from her cheek with the other hand, held her breath and listened to each word. When the song was over she whispered only four words and they were, where is my Gus. New Years morning 1999 Lorrie was getting ready to meet their friends for their annual New Years lunch and she was thinking of all the things that she would be thankful for in 1999. She was sure that if everything went well on her studies that she was going to be able to graduate with a Degree in Art History and that would be a major accomplishment for her. Also she was looking forward to her Stepson completing his training to be an Air Force Pilot and she could pin his wings on him at the Military Ceremony. That would be a proud moment for her. Yes 1999 had the possibilities of being a banner year.

Gus—1999 New Years day was a day to reflect on all that he had accomplished in 1998 and he was going through the picture album that he was making on his Blue Quail Ranch in the Sierra Vieja Mountains in the Chihuahua Desert of Far West Texas just eight miles from the Rio Grand River. He was adding the new pictures and writing the captions under them like he had done all the others. These pictures would document everything that he was doing there and some day his kids and grand kids would cherish this album. Gus was thinking that it wouldn't be many more years before he would be able to retire from the State Prison System. He would be 57 years old in 1999 and he could retire when he was 60 if he wanted to take a 10 year retirement from the Texas Department of Criminal Justice. The 10 year retirement wouldn't be a full retirement for Gus, but he would be able to keep his health insurance and there would be a small monthly check, about enough to pay the grocery bill. He would have to be there for another 5 years to hit the rule of 80 if he wanted a full retirement. The rule of eighty was when your age and your time served added up to 80 and if Gus stayed till he was 65 he would have served 15 years and that would put him at the rule of 80 and not only that, but it would put him at his maximum on collecting his Social Security. This would be the smart thing for Gus to do for his retirement and he knew it, but Far West Texas was calling his name and also that extra 5 years would mean a lot physically at his age as to how much work he would be able to do and Gus knew that he would have a lot of real hard work to do if he moved out there, because he didn't have the money to buy or build a new house which meant that he was going to have to renovate an old house and he would have to do most of the hard work himself like plumbing, electrical, carpentry, painting, etc.. He would have to make a decision on this real soon and he was leaning toward the 10 year retirement, but if something very good happened with his job at the Texas Department of Criminal Justice, like a promotion to a real higher paying job that he liked he would consider staying until he hit the rule of 80. Gus was taking two news papers from out in West Texas now, the Alpine Avalanche and the Van Horn Advocate. Gus decided that he needed to start paying more attention to the house for sale advertisements in these papers, so he could get an idea of the prices and also what towns they were located in. The Alpine Avalanche served Alpine, Marfa, Valentine and Fort Davis mostly. The Van Horn Advocate served Van Horn and Sierra Blanca and that was about it. Alpine was 95 miles from his ranch, Marfa was 75 miles away, Fort Davis was 70 miles away, Van Horn was 35 miles away, Sierra Blanca was 70 miles away and it didn't have much to offer, it even got it's water supply from Van Horn, Valentine was 35 miles away, but you couldn't even buy gasoline or groceries in Valentine, so that canceled out Valentine. The closest town was Van Horn and it was a town with a population of about 2,500 and it was on Interstate Highway 10 and El Paso was only 120 miles to the West on I-10 if you needed something that you couldn't find in Van Horn. Van Horn looked like the most likely town to look for a used house, but that all depended on the price. The work repairing and rebuilding the harvesting equipment at the Prison Harvesting Department went on as usual. Gus would get on the road in the winter and go from Prison Farm to Prison Farm and invoice anhydrous ammonia equipment repair parts to the Prison Farms that used anhydrous ammonia for fertilizer and this was about the only time Gus got away from the Harvesting Shop, for a few days in the winter. In the spring of the year Gus and his Boss would go on the road to the Prison Units in East Texas and apply fertilizer to their hay meadows with a huge machine called a Terragator. The tires on this huge machine were taller than a man and it had a big hopper on it that held the fertilizer and there were two propellers that spread the fertilizer out the back of the machine. They would go from Prison Farm to Prison Farm until they had fertilized all of the meadows and this was the only time they would leave the Harvesting Shop for a few days in the spring, before the Harvesting Season. Gus was saving up enough money to hire a Bulldozer and a Maintainer to build a couple of roads on his Ranch that would lead to the east side and down into 96 Canyon. This was an unexplored side of the Ranch and Gus wanted better access to it and he intended to do this as soon as he could get out to his Ranch after the Prison Harvest Season was complete. The Prison Farms Harvest Season started off really good and the Harvesting Department's Inmate crews and machinery were making great progress harvesting the milo maize, corn and cotton until the middle of August and the hurricane season started to produce a lot of low pressure areas in the Gulf of Mexico right off the coast of Texas that were moving inland and dumping a lot of rain. These showers and thunderstorms were slowing down the harvest on all the Prison Farm Units along the Gulf Coast of Texas and inland into the Prison Farm Units of East Texas. Almost everyday it was raining on one of the Prison Farm Units and it was creating a huge problem. The quality of the grain and cotton was going down with all the moisture and delay in harvesting and it was taking a toll on the harvesting machinery with constant breakdowns because of operating them in the heavy mud. Also Inmates and Staff were wearing down with all the extra stress of the situation and sometimes tempers were short and apologies had to be made to keep everything under control and running as smooth as could be expected under the circumstances. Gus began to see that he wasn't going to be able to take his usual vacation at the end of September and go to his Ranch in West Texas. He was going to have to alter his plans and call the man with the Bulldozer and the Maintainer and tell him that he would be out there later then he had expected to be and that he would call him and set up a new time as soon as he could determine when that would be. The 1999 Harvest Season for the Harvesting Department was a struggle all the way to the end and it was the middle of October before they were finished and bringing all the machinery back to their Harvesting Shop in Sugarland so they could repair it during the winter and there was going to be a lot of repair work to do, much more then usual. Gus finally saw some light in his schedule and he lined up everything and left Sugarland to take a week of vacation out at his Ranch the last week of October. He took with him all the supplies that he had been buying for the Ranch in the back of his Pick-up and his 8 foot trailer. He unloaded and set up his Camp House which took a lot less time and work now that he had completed most of the improvements. It was getting colder out there now and he was using his propane heater at night and in the early morning. After a good breakfast Gus set out in his old Jeep with some colored ribbon to tie on the brush to mark the way for the roads he wanted the Bulldozer to blade. This took him all day to do and he was glad that he had finished them, because the Bulldozer and the Maintainer were to arrive on the Ranch the next morning. Making roads and doing dirt work with heavy machinery was always exciting to Gus, because he liked to see improvements that made the land better. He had always liked this ever since he had been a young man improving the land when he had been farming and ranching. This was just an extension of that only in a much smaller way. In a lot of ways Gus had never changed, but his location and his objectives had changed. He was simply using things that he had learned many years before to his advantage when he was working with the land. It had warmed up some during the day and Gus was able to wear a lighter coat, but as the afternoon went to evening he had to put on his heavier coat with a stocking hat so he could sit at his camp fire and drink a couple of beers and reflect on what he had done during the day. Whine he was marking the path for one of the two roads he had caught a glimpse of something from the top of another Mesa at the far east side of his Ranch that he wasn't sure what it was. There was a deep depression of maybe 200 acres on the east side that was surrounded by the Mesa that looped around it and the depression was on one side and 96 Canyon was on the other. There was something at the bottom of the depression that didn't quite fit there and Gus would have to wait till the Bulldozer made a good road before he could see better and also to Bulldoze down into the depression so Gus could drive his old Jeep down into it and explore it. Gus sat in front of his camp fire warming his hands and sipping his beer and planning his supper which would be a mesquite fire grilled T-bone steak along with fried potatoes and onions and ranch style beans fixed on the camp stove in the Camp House. Gus got up early the next morning and fixed himself cowboy coffee on his camp stove. He was excited about the Bulldozer and the Maintainer coming out and getting started on building the new roads. For breakfast he fried up two eggs and then warmed up a piece of his left over T-bone steak along with some of the left over fried potatoes and onions then he made some pan toast with butter and topped it off with grape jelly. The truck with the heavy equipment loaded on it pulled up to the Ranch about 10:00am and the excitement in Gus was building as he watched the Maintainer and the Bulldozer being unloaded. He told the Operator that he had water and lunch packed for them and that he would be following the Bulldozer as it made its way to the east side of the Ranch. As the Bulldozer cut it's way through the brush and rock mixed earth Gus kept his old Jeep a respectable distance behind the Bulldozer, because it raised up huge clouds of dust that he wanted to stay out of as much as he could. Along the way behind the Bulldozer Gus would stop at different interesting locations to look around for Indian Artifacts, Fossils, beautiful semi-precious stones and cactus that he hadn't seen on the other part of the Ranch. Some places he found noting of interest and at others he would make interesting finds that he knew he would have to exploit sometime later. It took them all day to make this first road, because it was the longest and they figured that the last road would only take till lunch the next day to rough in, then after that the Maintainer would be able to do the finish work on both roads in the last half of the day. Late that evening the Bulldozer Operator drove the Bulldozer back to the Ranch Camp and he and Gus started a camp fire to enjoy while relaxing with a couple of beers before their dinner and making plans for the next day. The next morning Gus made coffee and breakfast for them before they went out to finish the second road. They had been right in their estimate of the time it would take to finish the second road and they brought back the Bulldozer to be loaded on the heavy haul truck and then eat a lunch before taking the Maintainer to do the finish work on both of the roads. They finished with all the work on the roads late that afternoon and the Maintainer was loaded and Gus paid the operator and he drove off with the heavy machinery and Gus was left alone at his Camp House. It was too late for him to start any exploring, so he made himself some dinner, washed up and got everything prepared to start out the next morning on his new roads that he hoped would give him access to new discoveries. Gus woke up the next morning so excited that he just made himself some coffee and he ate some fruit for breakfast, then made a lunch to take with him in the old Jeep. He discovered some barrel fish hook cactus and dug up a couple to replant as landscaping at the Camp House then he stopped at a couple of other places and walked around and found some flint flakes as evidence of Indian Camps and he did pick up a few chipped tools and decided to explore these places more the next day, because he wanted to drive down in the depression he had seen to see what he might discover there. When he reached the bottom of the depression he was, at first, perplexed at what he saw. There was a 5 foot deep channel that bisected the depression, but on each side of it appeared to be terrace levies 2 feet high and 5 feet wide that were spaced about 50 feet apart. Gus left the old Jeep and started walking to be able to get a better look at the whole basin. He looked in the length of the channel and discovered that there were large boulders at intervals that might have been used to dam water in locations all along the channel and they corresponded with large rocks that were stacked at the ends of the terrace levies and all the terrace levies came up to the channel. Gus had been a rice farmer, so this started to look like an ancient irrigated field to him. He searched around some more and he found a chipped stone hoe and a ground stone wedge shaped tool that could have been tied to a shaft that would have been used to make holes in the ground to plant seeds. There was a little high spot on one side that he found a flint knife and some other stones that had been chipped on. The more that Gus looked at it he was convinced that it had been an irrigated field of some sort. The channel must have been shallower one thousand or two thousand years ago and it must have had live water running in it from a spring or maybe several springs for these ancient peoples to depend on the water to grow their crops. According to archaeological evidence that had been discovered in other areas of this Desert Region some of the Native Indians farmed beans, corn, squash, gourds and melons and they could very well have farmed them here. Gus was well pleased with this discovery. Gus drove back up on the Mesa and just looked all around him in every direction and thought that this Ranch was really a kind of enchanting place that held a lot of secrets from the ages. He drove back to his Camp House and started packing up things that he was going to take back with him. He had taken a lot of pictures as he always did and would put them in his picture book on the Blue Quail Ranch. Early the next morning Gus drove out on his Ranch road to make the trip back home to Sugarland. When he got back to Sugarland and went back to work they were in the process of tearing down all the Harvesting Equipment that needed the most repair, because of the rough use it got during the muddy Harvest Season. That machinery would be repaired first then they would go through the rest of it and put it back in good operating order. Gus would be going back to his Blue Quail Ranch in just a few weeks, because he had taken his vacation time late. The delayed Harvest Season caused by the wet weather had delayed him by almost three weeks and he would be going back for the Thanksgiving Holidays for a week which also included the first week of the Far West Texas Mule Deer Season. This meant that two of his boys were going to come out to hunt, drink beer, have shooting contests and cook on the open camp fire and just generally act like Mountain Men did at a Mountain Man Trapper gathering back in the 1700's and early 1800's. They had a lot of fun doing this and Gus's youngest son always called this High Mountain Desert rugged, unforgiving land Man Country. While they were there they killed a Mule Deer, a Javalina and some Blue Quail. There wasn't any work done on the Ranch with this trip, because there wasn't time to focus on any. Everything went at break neck speed, because his boys only had a few days to be there and they all stayed up late at night and the rest of the time was spent hunting, drinking beer, telling stories and just being a Dad with his grown Sons together. They all went back to their homes tired and tried to get back in the rhythm of their regular lives as soon as possible after living for a few days as pioneers out West. Gus went back to the Harvesting Department at the Prison System until the Christmas Holidays and then he and his Wife went back out to his Blue Quail Ranch for a week. Their week at the Blue Quail Ranch was mostly spent exploring and hiking around the Ranch that had been hard to get to before the roads had been made. Now Gus could drive to places he wanted to explore, then get out and hike the rest of they on foot. The weather was cold and windy most of the time, but Gus did manage to erect some simple quail feeders that he filled with milo maize for the quail to scratch and feed at. He found that that the quail found them in a couple of days and learned how to use them quickly, to his satisfaction. He found a lot of painted and unpainted pottery shards along with some that had been decorated with the finger nail impressions of the potter put into the wet clay in lines prior to the pot being baked to hardness. Gus thought this was very interesting and he placed his finger nail in the impressions which fit him and he felt a sort of connection with this ancient artist that mastered his or her work 2,000 years before. They went into Van Horn and filled up the 500 gallon water trailer and took it back to the Ranch before they left to go back to Sugarland. They got back to Sugarland a couple of days before New Years and stayed home for the coming of the New Year of 2,000. Gus was no longer into big New Years celebrations, so he just worked on the picture album of the Blue Quail Ranch and cleaned up the artifacts that he had found, so he could admire them and spent a quiet time on New Years Eve reflecting on all that had happened in 1999. He went to bed before the New Year came in, but on New Years Day 2,000 he was already thinking that he only had three years to go before he could retire from the Texas Department of Criminal Justice and he needed to find a place out in one of the towns close to his Ranch to buy a house to move to when he did retire. Finding a house out there was going to be his next big objective and he would intensify his search in the year 2,000.

Lorrie—1999 The 1999 New Years Day lunch with their friends went off well for Lorrie. This was always a time for all of them to reflect back on the nice things and sometime funny things that they had experienced together. They would also discuss subjects that they thought were to be important in the New Year. One of these was Lorrie's Graduation from The Open University with her Art History Degree. They decided that they were going to have a Graduation Party for her when that came about, but type of party they would have for her would be a surprise. Lorrie told them that she was always uncomfortable with surprises, but that she would allow them this latitude since she knew that they would never do anything to embarrass her. Lorrie went back to work on her University Degree studies with a passion. She was certain that she could complete her Degree by the end of the spring semester and that was just 5 months away. During the early spring Lorrie arranged for her Husband to take her, Jill and her Art Degree friend Carol to France. They drove to the Euro Star and went on the car train through the tunnel under the Thames to France and went to the huge Hyper Market buying all sorts of groceries and her Husband was interested in buying a lot of his favorite commodity which was whiskey. They then had lunch and came back to England on the Euro Star car train. During this excursion Carol was ugly to Jill and told her that her and Lorrie were joined at the hip and that Jill wasn't needed as a friend anymore. This so surprised Jill and hurt her feelings deeply, but she knew in her heart that Lorrie couldn't feel that way about their friendship. Lorrie eventually found out about this and she started to distance herself from Carol. There was no way that she was going to risk her friendship with Jill and there were other reasons for Lorrie's displeasure in Carol being her open flirting with Lorrie's Husband and Carol's lagging interest in her studies for her Art History Degree. Lorrie was loosing her patience with Carol and included her less and less in her personal life. Lorrie's Stepson came home on Leave in the spring and he was extremely upset, because his Air Force Instructors had rejected him for his training a to fly a Fighter Aircraft. He wouldn't give Lorrie or his Dad any reasons for his Instructors decision other then the Instructors were a bunch of idiots and didn't know what they were doing. His Instructor told him that he could still be in an Air Force Plane as a Navigator, because he was good at his math and Navigation needed strong math skills. Lorrie tried to talk and console him, but he was beyond any rational reasoning. All he wanted to do was to drink and berate his Officers. When he returned to the Royal Air Force Training Academy he was still upset. It was time for Lorrie's final field trip to the Art Galleries and Museums and this one was going to be the best, because it was to be the big one in France to the Louvre and the Annex the jeu de Paume. Also there would be some wonderful party time in some of the famous old night spots in Paris. Lorrie and Carol traveled together as they usually did, but Lorrie had cooled off on Carol being a special friend. She now only thought of her as an associate studying for the same Art History Degree. In the Paris Museums and Galleries listening to their Instructors explain in detail each art work and the Master that created it Lorrie took extensive notes to review, but noticed that Carol wasn't taking any. Carol had done a similar thing the year before in Milan and Lorrie had wondered how she would be able to pass her exams without the notes to study. Lorrie got the impression in Milan that Carol had lost interest in her Art History Degree and now she was sure of it and decided that Carol was just along for the fun she could have on these field trips. Lorrie started going her own way on this field trip and was evasive when Carol would ask her what she had planned for the evening. Lorrie had decided that she was going to accompany the Instructors when they went out for dinner, drinks and entertainment in the evenings instead of her and Carol going their own way to different night spots hoping that this would send a message to Carol to quit hanging on to her. When Lorrie told Carol that she was going with the Instructors, Carol looked perplexed and she told Lorrie that they would have a lot more fun if they went on their own to some different places and Lorrie told Carol to go where ever she wanted to go, but that Lorrie had made her mind up to accompany the Instructors. Carol went with them at first, but then she split off with a couple of other students and left for another night spot and this made Lorrie happy that Carol was starting to get the message that their relationship had run it's course. This field trip was the last one that Lorrie would attend that was required for her Art History Degree and after she returned home she had many pages of notes to organize and study for her test on the field trip. When she received her test and reviewed it she was astonished to see how much it covered. It was much more in detail then the others had been and she knew that if she hadn't taken so many complete notes that she would never be able to pass the test. Lorrie made a very high score on her test and this made her very happy. Now all that she had left was a few more lectures and Tutor study periods before her Final Exams. Lorrie needed a few things from the store and it was a beautiful spring day, so she decided to walk down the hill from her house past a little park that had a nice small lake where a flock of ducks swam around with their ducklings and she liked to watch them. A group of them crossed the path in front of her with their ducklings following behind and they waddled through the tulips to get to the lake. Lorrie smiled and thought that this was one of the small things that she liked about walking to Bromley. She did her shopping then huffed and puffed back up the hill with her purchases and when she was at her front door she could hear loud talking inside. Lorrie unlocked the door and picked up her packages and entered right in the middle of a angry confrontation between her Husband and her Stepson. She was shocked to see her Stepson, because he was supposed to be at the Training Academy and wouldn't be up for a leave until the end of the month. They quieted down when she walked in, so she put up her purchases and went in to see why he had come home so early and then she noticed that he didn't have on his Air Force Uniform, he was wearing his civilian cloths. Lorrie asked him why he was home so early and he told her that he was home for good that he had been Discharged from the Air Force and he didn't want to talk about it. She told him that he would tell her what was going on and that she deserved to know what had happened. He snapped back at her and told her that it was non of her business and he turned and went up the stares to his room and slammed the door. She looked at her Husband sitting on the couch now bent over with his face in his hands and asked him to please explain and he said nothing. He got up and went to the refrigerator and got himself a beer. She asked him again and he was still silent. Lorrie asked her Husband if he knew what had happened and he finally told her that he did, but it wasn't any of her business and not to ask him again. Lorrie was furious and felt that she deserved to know what had happened for her Stepson to be Discharged from the Air Force. She had so proud of him and had been patiently waiting to do the honors of pinning his Wings on him. This was to be one of the high points of 1999 for her. She needed to know what it was that had cheated her out of this honor. Lorrie thought for heavens sakes was she a part of this family or not. All the time she was fuming and trying to get answers, her Husband was making trips back to the refrigerator getting more beer to drink. Lorrie was to the point that she didn't care if she got into an argument with her Husband. She usually tried to avoid arguments with him, but now she felt that this needed some explanation. Her husband was steadily sucking his beer down one after the other and Lorrie was standing with her hands on her hips in front of the fire place when he slapped her so hard that he knocked her into the fire place and she hit her head on the mantel as she fell into it. Now he was screaming at her at the top of his voice that she would never know what had happened and if she knew what was good for her she would just shut up and go about her own business. Then he marched out of the room and got another beer and went up the stairs to his room and slammed his door. Lorrie was left trying to extract herself from the fireplace and crying and she called a Cab to take her to the Clinic in Bromley to see the Doctor there. She had a purple spot on her face where he slapped her and a lump with a small cut on her forehead where she hit the mantel and thankfully it didn't require any stitches. After Lorrie got back home she made up her mind that she was through with the idea that her Stepson was going to accomplish great things. She had always wanted him to be a great success in life and he had shown great promise, because he was at the top of his class with everything he had ever been in and now this was going sour too, just like when she had lost her own son to her first husband. Lorrie thought that if that was going to be the way of it, then she wouldn't ask again and she wouldn't have any more hi-powered dreams for her Stepson. The next day she told her Stepson that from now on she would cook for the family, but that she no longer would clean his room and do his laundry that he would have to do it himself and he had a University Degree to help him go look for a job. He sulked around the house for a couple of weeks mostly keeping to his room and coming down to eat when her and her Husband had finished and then he would take a plate to his room and stay there. Lorrie paid him no attention only asking him to bring down his dishes to be washed. Lorrie worked hard to finish up the papers on her Art History Degree so she could take her Final Exams. That day finally came at the end of the spring Semester and she passed them with flying colors. At Lorrie's Graduation Ceremony Jill, Lorrie's Husband and her Husbands best Friend, who had died, Wife were in attendance. Lorrie took pictures in her Graduation Gown with her Graduation Mug that had the Universities Insignia embossed on it and she was so proud of her accomplishment. It had been 35 years since she had enrolled in Wharton County Junior College, when she had lived with her Parents in El Campo, Texas and now she was a University Graduate at the age of 53 in England. After the Graduation Ceremony and the pictures they all went to the Pizza Express to have pizza, wine and celebrate. Lorrie didn't know it yet, but Jill had arranged for an extra big special surprise for Lorrie in recognition for all of her hard work and the excellent scores she had made for three years to finish her Art History Degree. Jill had arranged to get tickets to take Lorrie to an

Equestrian Performance featuring the Spanish Horses, because Jill knew how much Lorrie loved horses. Lorrie was overwhelmed with emotion when she found out what Jill had organized just for her and she couldn't help but weep a little. Her own Husband had never done anything so sweet for her and he wouldn't even get her a gift certificate for her Birthday to the local Book Store. It was summer now and her Stepson had found a good job at one of the big Banks in London. He had an apartment there and Lorrie was glad that he was out of the house. She never did learn what had happened for him to be Discharged from the Royal Air Force Academy and she didn't really care any more, the main thing was that he was finally out on his own now and would no longer be a problem between her and her Husband. Lorrie actually felt a little lost since she had Graduated from the Open University with her Degree in Art History. She had dedicated so much time and energy for three years to her studies that she felt that something was missing from her life. She was forced to slow down now and she didn't know if she liked that or not. Her Art Degree studies had given her the opportunity, not only to enhance her love for art, but to also use them as a supplement for happiness that she was lacking in her Marriage. Now without the dedication to her studies she was experiencing a kind of depression similar to the breakup of lovers. It was time for her to start to focus on her next Vacation back to El Campo, Texas and this would give her something extra to think about that would relieve her of the anxiety she was experiencing. While Lorrie was packing for her Vacation back to Texas she had all the pictures that she had taken on her field trips to the Museums and Galleries in Europe developed along with the ones of her Graduation, so she could show her family and friends back home in El Campo, Texas. Lorrie's long flight from England to Houston, Texas was exhausting as usual and her Sister picked her up at the Airport and Lorrie spent several days in Houston with her before they drove to El Campo to her Parents house. They got to her Parents house before lunch and Lorrie unpacked and gave them the little gifts she always brought them from England. They all then had a light lunch and sat down to talk. Lorrie showed them all of her pictures and they had all sorts of questions to ask her that she was pleased to answer. Lorrie was a little puzzled, because her Dad asked the same question twice and she also noticed that he still had that quiver in his hand when he would lift it to sip his iced tea, also she was sure that his speech was not like she had remembered it. The more that Lorrie looked at him she thought that he looked a little drawn in the face with his facial expressions not as pronounced as they had been. Lorrie decided not to say anything about her observations on her Dad till she could get a private time with her Brother and Sister. The thing that Lorrie couldn't understand was why they couldn't see what she was seeing. That afternoon they all had their usual Happy Hour on the Family Patio at the back of the house. Lorrie kept a close eye on her Dad, but tried not to be obvious about it. After their Happy Hour her Dad cooked some hamburgers on his grill outside and her Mom made homemade french fries to go with it. When their dinner was over Lorrie and her Sister cleaned up the kitchen and washed the dishes and they all retired to the living room to visit. It didn't take long for Lorrie to start getting sleepy and her Mom suggested that she go on to bed. This she did, but she lay in bed for a while thinking about her Dad. She had been worried about his health for a couple of years and she was still seeing things that bothered her about him that she considered unnatural. Her Sister had told her the last time she had been down on her vacation a year ago that it was just that their Dad was getting older that it was to be expected for him to show signs of old age. Lorrie had hoped that old age was the only problem, but something kept telling her that there might be more to it then just old age and she was determined to get to the bottom of it. The next morning was Sunday and after coffee and breakfast Lorrie asked her Sister to go with her next door to her Brother's house. The three of them discussed Lorrie's observations about their Dad and came to the conclusion that maybe they hadn't really noticed what Lorrie had, because they were around him more and if his symptoms were only slight then it was possible that they wouldn't notice them. Lorrie asked them if they knew when their Dad had been given a good physical examination and they told her that they had no idea how long it had been since he had had one. Lorrie thought this was good, because it would give her something to work toward. She would find some excuse to get her Dad to get a physical examination and before he went in for it she would talk to his Doctor and tell him what she had observed. Lorrie was home for a few days and suggested to her Dad that they get a six-pack of beer and take a ride around and look at the town and talk. She knew that this was one of his favorite things to do with her when she was down on her vacation, so he accepted the invitation immediately. They road around El Campo and discussed the few changes that had happened there since Lorrie had been down one year earlier. They finished their six-pac of beer and her Dad turned the car to go back home and Lorrie told him that she wanted to take him to his favorite little Bar where they could sit and enjoy a beer and visit with the owner. He thought that it was an excellent idea and they went there. This gave Lorrie an idea and a way to follow up on it. She knew that the owner of that Bar had some bad problems with skin cancers on him and she wanted to get him in a conversation about them. They entered the little Bar and sat down in their favorite place and right away the owner came over himself and brought them each a beer, because he knew what they always ordered when they were there. They invited him to sit with them and he was glad to see Lorrie and wanted to know what all that she had been doing in England. Lorrie brought him up to date on herself and then she pointed to some new places on his arms and face that had been operated on and some of them even had stitches in them. He sighed in resignation that he had an ongoing battle with some bad skin cancers and that his Doctor kept telling him that he should have come in earlier for an examination, because they would have been easier to control if he could have caught them earlier. He told Lorrie that he wished that he had payed more attention to them earlier, but had simply thought that they were spots created by aging. This gave Lorrie the opportunity she had been waiting for and she started pointing out dark spots and some rough spots on her Dad's arms and face and the owner of the Bar looked at them and he told her Dad that he had similar spots that had turned out to be bad cancers and that he needed to have a Doctor look at them. This pleased Lorrie and it gave her the opportunity to suggest to her Dad that he needed to make an appointment with his Doctor to look him over real good. Her Dad started looking at his arms and the spots on himself and agreed that it might be a good idea, because he sure didn't want to be cut and stitched up like his friend the Bar owner. They finished their beer and left to drive home and Lorrie knowing that she needed to strike while the iron was hot told her Dad that it was still early enough for her to call his Doctor for an appointment for the next day and he agreed. She wasn't about to let it rest over night, because he might decide to put it off and then he would never go to the Doctor. When they got back home her Dad told her Mom that Lorrie was going to make him a Doctors appointment to have some of his spots on his arms and face looked at to see if they might be cancer and she thought that it might be a good idea. Lorrie then called and made the appointment for the next morning and she told her Dad that she was going to go with him. He was glad, because he knew that she had been trained as a Nurse and he would want to know what she thought about the Doctors diagnosis. Lorrie was pleased with herself and the way that she had maneuvered her Dad into getting a Doctors appointment without having to reveal her real reasons for it. Lorrie didn't feel kike she was being dishonest or sneaky about it, she just knew that if she had told her Dad that she suspected something was wrong because of a few obscure observations, he would just have laughed at her and that would have been the end of it. Now the only thing else she had to do before the appointment was to talk to his Doctor in private and relate to him what she had observed and let him take it from there. She went over to her Brothers house next door and called the Doctor back and told him what her main objective was for the appointment for her Dad and that she would appreciate it if he would keep it a secret. She told the Doctor all that she had observed and the Doctor listened attentively and then he told her that he would indeed keep it secret and that she was doing the right thing, because he was well aware how stubborn her Dad was about having medical examinations. The next morning Lorrie went with her Dad to the Doctors appointment. The Doctor looked at all the dark spots and rough spots on his face and hands and then had him take off his shirt so he could look at his back. The Doctor found several of the spots that he was concerned about and told Lorrie's Dad that they needed to be burned off, so that is what he did, then the Doctor asked her Dad if he had any other problems they needed to discuss and that is when Lorrie spoke up and mentioned several of her observations. Her Dad looked surprised, but went along with the conversation by blaming those things on aging, but the Doctor told him that it might be something else and the Doctor asked him to take a few simple tests that were easy that tested his speech, his reflexes and his retention of memory. After about thirty minutes of these the Doctor told her Dad that he wanted to refer him to the Diagnostic Center in Houston for more extensive tests just to make sure that he was healthy for his age group as a man. Her Dad said that he would go and so the Doctor set up his appointment in Houston. Lorrie was so glad that her Dad had decided to go to the Houston appointment. The Houston appointment was set up for the next week, so the whole family had the time to reflect on Lorrie's Dad's physical health. Lorrie's Sister was to meet them at the Diagnostic Center in downtown Houston for the examination. The day of the appointment they left El Campo very early, because the examinations would go on all day. Lorrie's Dad was examined and tested by three different Specialists in their Fields of Medicine. Lorrie, her Dad and her Sister were all exhausted by the end of the day and Lorrie drove her Dad back to El Campo. The results of the tests would take several days to be evaluated and then sent to her Dads Doctor and he would then set up an appointment to discuss the results. All of this was consuming the days that Lorrie had planned for her month vacation, but that was alright with her, because she had the feeling that there was more then just aging that was wrong with her Dad and she wanted to find out what it was. The next week her Dad's Doctor called them and told them that he had received the test results and that he had also talked on a conference call to all three of the Specialists that had examined and tested her Dad and that it was time for them to talk about the results and that her Mom also needed to be there to hear the diagnoses. When Lorrie heard that they needed to include her Mom in the discussion she knew that something wasn't good in the diagnoses. They all went to the Doctors appointment and the Doctor explained the reasons for each of the tests that her Dad had taken, then he told them that it was the decision of all three of the Specialists that her Dad had Stage 3 Parkinson's Disease. The Doctor told them that there were 5 stages to the disease and that there were some drugs that could help, but that there wasn't a cure. He also told them that no Doctor knew the cause of the disease. He told them that the disease progressed so slowly that it almost always was misdiagnosed as simply aging, but that it wasn't that and that her Dad's Parkinson's could have been coming on for maybe ten years and no one ever suspected it even him being a Doctor. Her Dad was given a copy of the results along with a list of things that could be done to lesson the effects of the disease plus what to watch for in its progression. The Doctor suggested that her Dad schedule regular appointments, so the Doctor could keep a record of the diseases speed of advancement to the 4th Stage. The Doctor then asked for questions and all of them were speechless. They all looked at Lorrie, because she had always been the strong one of the siblings and she told them that they had found out what they needed to know and now it would be up to all of them to start adjusting to the new found facts. They went home and that evening their Happy Hour wasn't happy, it was more of having a couple of drinks as a bracer for what what they had learned about Lorrie's Dad. The next Day Lorrie called her Husband in England and told him about the Doctors Diagnosis and that she was going to extend her vacation and she wasn't sure how long it would be. He wasn't very happy about that, because he said that there were going to be bills and business things that only Lorrie knew how to deal with and what was he supposed to do about it. She told him that she would call everyone in England Trans-Atlantic and tell them what the circumstances were and that she would arrange everything so her Husband wouldn't have to worry about it. Lorrie knew that her Husband had always been inept at anything to do with business. Then as an after thought her Husband told her that something was wrong with her sweet little dog Mitzi that she seemed to be getting stiff in her back legs. Lorrie was shocked and asked if some accident had happened to her and her Husband told her that he didn't know of anything. Lorrie told him that she was going to call the Vet in Bromley the next day and that he should take Mitzi there as soon as he could and no excuses about it. Lorrie told her Husband that she would call him to find out what the Vet told him about Mitzi. Lorrie had decided to stay longer in El Campo for two reasons. First she was determined to do her own research to find out as much as she could about Parkinson's Disease and second to make sure that her Mom would be organized with everything that she would need to be able to deal with her Dad's physical limitations in the future. Lorrie went to the local Library and found a couple of Medical Journals discussing Parkinson's Disease and she had the Librarian order several Medical Books that were written by Specialists on the Disease. Lorrie was going to learn all that she could and through her Nursing training she knew the medical language that would help her to understand the technical side of the disease without any problems. She knew that if someone without medical training tried to read these books it would be like reading a foreign language for them, but she could read them and understand them. When Lorrie was with her Dad now it was hard for her to be cheerful, because she could almost see the hands on the clock moving toward the sunset of his life as she looked on his face. She knew that she had to hide this fear like she had hidden most of the hurts and disappointments in her life. It reminded her of the very first major hurt she had when she had been rejected by Gus and she had never gotten over it, instead she had stored it behind very thick doors deep within her heart, so she could try to resume living her life, but it would reappear from time to time just to remind her how much that she still loved him and always would, for he was the only one she would ever love and she knew this without a doubt. Lorrie called back to England checking on her sweet little god Mitzi and her Husband told her that the Vet had diagnosed Mitzi as having a degenerating nerve disorder that would permanently paralyze her in a short time. He told Lorrie that the Vet said it was a disorder that was common to the breed Yorkshire Terrier. This through Lorrie another curve that didn't help lift her spirits any from the already depressing diagnoses of her Dad. Now she was going to have to try and determine how long she was going to stay in El Campo, because she was sure that she would need to get back to England to care properly for little Mitzi. There was no way that she could depend on her Husband to do the right thing when it came to making decisions on something like Mitzi's well being, because he had never been able to make a decent decision on anything, ever since she had known him. Lorrie did all the research that she could on Parkinson's Disease and made a simple list of physical changes in her Dad that might occur, that her Mom needed to look for and also a small list of devices that could be of help to compensate for her Dad's physical inabilities. Lorrie was leaving El Campo with a sad heart as her Brother drove her to the Airport in Houston, Texas. She knew that when she got back to England that she had to face the depressing sight of her sweet little dog Mitzi dragging her back legs around. Lorrie's flight seemed three times longer then usual, because she was leaving one depressing problem and coming back to England to another depressing problem. She would find out when she got back if there could be anything done for Mitzi that could heal her. Surely there was something and Lorrie knew that she would not spare any cost to find it. When Lorrie returned home the first thing that she did, even before unpacking anything, was to go to little Mitzi and see how bad she was. Lorrie found Mitzi trying to make her way to her when she heard Lorrie's voice come in the front door and Lorrie could tell that the poor little sweet thing was in pain and she was partly trying to walk and drag herself along wagging her tail and whimpering at the same time. Mitzi looked so pitiful to Lorrie that she broke down and cried as she picked Mitzi up and hugged her to her breast and let Mitzi lick her face. Lorrie found that Mitzi could no longer follow her up the stairs to Lorrie's bedroom, so Lorrie had to pick her up and carry her. Lorrie didn't quite know what she was going to do, because Mitzi had been the object of her love at her house for a long time and if Mitzi died Lorrie would be without the returned love from Mitzi that she had depended on to get her through the rough times that she would experience with her Husband. Lorrie slept fitfully that night with little Mitzi checking on her ever so often to make sure she was not in a bad position to hurt her. The next morning Lorrie briefed her Husband on her Dad and then she called the Vet in Bromley that had examined Mitzi. Lorrie decided to take Mitzi to London to get the opinion of two different Vets there. After an exhausting all day trip to London Lorrie came home with the same diagnosis about Mitzi's condition. She found out that Mitzi's condition would degenerate rather quickly until the nerves in her back would deprive her bowls from working and that she would die of internal infection. Lorrie couldn't even stand to think of this, much less watch it happen. The Vet had given Lorrie a sedative that she could give Mitzi for pain, but nothing could be done to relieve the progressing paralysis. A few days later her Husband was complaining to Lorrie that she cared more for that dog then she did for him and Lorrie told him to remember back that she had taken care of him when he was down several times and taken care of his Dad till he died and that quieted him down. After another month Lorrie could see that it was no use to hope any more and that she was going to have to take Mitzi to the Vet and have her put down. Making that decision drained Lorrie of strength so bad that she had trouble getting dressed to go to the Vet's office and she let sweet little Mitzi lick her face for the last time and she stroked her head and told Mitzi that she would always love her and that she would never forget her then she let the Vet put her down. Lorrie was cried out, so she didn't cry any more. She had brought a little box with her to put little Mitzi's body in and she took Mitzi back home and they made a grave for her in the back yard of the house and there she rests for all time. There were so many things in the house that reminded Lorrie of Mitzi and it took a long time for her to start to get rid of them, just the same as if her child had died. The months that were passing were hard for Lorrie, with the death of Mitzi and the worry of always calling back to El Campo to check on her Dad, Lorrie finally decided that she had to put Mitzi behind those big thick doors in her heart that she hid all of her other tragedies and that is what she did. Lorrie would do the best that she could to prepare for the Holiday Season, but her heart wasn't in it. As Lorrie was shopping for a few new Christmas decorations and some gifts she kept seeing some very cute gifts that she would have bought for her little Mitzi that was now deceased and this brought back the sadness to her that was helping to damped her Christmas spirit. Lorrie's Stepson was living and working in London now and that had been a big relief for Lorrie, because he had always been a source of conflict between her and her Husband that could break out at any time for the smallest of reasons. Now that he was out of the house and making good money working for one of the big Banks in London Lorrie could breath a little easier. He would be coming home for Christmas, but Lorrie didn't expect him to stay more then a couple of days. She had already decided that she wasn't going to do anything big for New Years Eve. Lorrie's Stepson arrived home on the afternoon of Christmas Eve and he and his Dad started celebrating early with mixed drinks. Lorrie, not really being in the Holiday mood, dodged the offers from them to mix her a drink. Instead she was sticking to eggnog with a little Brandy topped with whip cream and nutmeg. She was trying hard to elevate her spirits for Christmas, but it was a hard, hard thing for her to try and accomplish. She would feel better for a few minutes then she would slide back to where she had been and that surge and fall of emotions would last all evening on Christmas Eve. Lorrie got up before her Husband and Stepson on Christmas morning and she turned on the Christmas Tree and put the tea pot on to boil along with assembling some sweet pastries for their breakfast. Usually she would have put on some Christmas music, but she really didn't feel like listening to it. Everything was just to different now that her sweet little Mitzi was not there with her and her worry about her Dad in El Campo, Texas. Her Husband and Stepson finally came down and her quiet time was over. They made fun of her for being so subdued on Christmas morning, but Lorrie didn't care what they said, because she was in another world from them and their remarks didn't effect her one way or the other. Christmas afternoon a few friends came by to visit and late that evening Lorrie decided it was time for them to open their gifts. She had bought her Husband and her Stepson gifts as she usually did, but this Christmas she didn't even buy herself a gift certificate to the local Bookstore. Lorrie passed the gifts out to them and they set their beer down to open them and were pleased at what she had bought them, but they never even noticed that she didn't have anything under the Christmas Tree. Her Stepson stayed Christmas night and he went back to London the next day. Lorrie thought that this Christmas was one of the worst that she had ever had, but she kept trying to think of all the things that she should be thankful for to keep herself from being so depressed and she knew that they were many good things for her to thank God for. That week went by in a semi-fog for Lorrie as she tried to boost her spirits up for New Years. She finally succeeded in brushing off some of the doom and gloom that had been dominating her ever since her little Mitzi had died and she had received the depressing Doctors report about her Dad's Parkinson's Disease. Lorrie knew that she needed to have a better attitude for the start of the year 2,000, so she decided to invite a few friends over for New Years Eve to keep her busy, so she didn't think about the depressing things that had happened and it seemed to be working. She spent a lot of time cleaning and decorating the house for New Years Eve and she even started eating some snacks and sipping on some Brandy a little early on New Years Eve afternoon to help get her in the mood to celebrate. Friends came by and visited and some stayed while others were committed to go to other parties, so Lorrie's New Eve Party ended up to be just the size and with the kinds of friends that she needed for the evening. The party broke up right after the New Year of 2,000 came in and Lorrie was ready to put all of the left over snacks and go to bed. Her Husband had gone up-stares to his own room and she sat down on the couch and thought back to when the New Year of 1999 came in and what she had thought then. She had high hopes for 1999 and even remembered thinking that it would be a banner year, thinking that she was going to finish her Art History Degree and Graduate, and she was going to pin the Wings on her Stepson at his Royal Air Force Academy Ceremony, as a proud Stepmother, then she would have a wonderful month Vacation in El Campo, Texas with her Mom, Dad, Brother and Sister and be able to bask in the feeling of achievement of what she had accomplished. How wrong she had been on everything except for her Graduation from the Open University with her Art History Degree. After that everything else went to hell, because her Dad has a disease that has no cure, her Stepson was, for some reason, Discharged from the Royal Air Force without earning his Wings, her Husband and her had a big fight over that and he knocked her into the fire place and her precious, sweet little dog Mitzi had died, so how wrong could she get. Lorrie went on to bed missing the warmth of Mitzi's little fuzzy body snuggled up to her, but she knew that she had better get used to not having her close to her. New Years Day 2,000 Lorrie got up an showered and while she dried off she was observing herself in the full length mirror, seeing the changes in her body as she had grown older. She saw a woman that was going to be 55 years old this year and had put on a lot of weight, some of it on purpose to discourage her husband from wanting to have sex with her and that had served it's purpose, because he came in her room now for sex only once every month or so and the rest of it from just getting older. Her face had always been sort of round, but now it was even more so, because her cheeks had collected their share of the fat that she had gained, her lips were no longer full and supple, they had become thinner, her neck had a ring of fat around it that hid what used to be a thin well formed neck, her small well shaped, firm breasts had become a little bigger from being fatty and they were sagging some now, her once flat stomach now looked like a pot belly, and she had not worn any cloths in a long time that would show her stomach, but her legs were still long, smooth and shapely and about the only thing that Lorrie did to improve her looks was to keep her hair colored. Lorrie just smiled and the thought crossed her mind wondering what Gus would think of her naked body now after seeing her naked when she was 16 years old. Lorrie decided that Gus would freak out and run away as fast as he could. Lorrie and her Husband met their friends at their annual lunch on New Years Day. This was always a nice occasion for Lorrie and she needed it more this time then she ever had. She excused herself to go to the restroom and her friend Jill went with her. Jill told Lorrie that she wanted for them to talk in private for a few minutes and Lorrie was grateful for that. Jill hugged Lorrie and told her that she knew all the sorrow and disappointment that Lorrie had endured toward the end of 1999 and she just wanted to reassure Lorrie that she would always be there for Lorrie to lean on if she needed it. Lorrie looked Jill in the eye and smiled sweetly, then put her hand on Jill's cheek and told Jill that she didn't know what she would do without her as her friend. They went back to their table and resumed their conversation with the others. That night after Lorrie went to bed she knew that she didn't know what the New Year of 2,000 held in store for her, but she decided that what ever it was she would accept it good or bad and continue to go on. The year 2,000 was the turn of the Century and Lorrie was going to be 55 years old.

Gus—2000 New Years and the turn of the Century morning 2,000 Gus was up early drinking coffee and thinking that he was going to be 58 years old and he had about the three years left working for the Texas Department of Criminal Justice before he could take a 10 year retirement package from them. He thought that actually it was less then three years, because he would have his 10 years of service in at the end of August 2002, so that was only two years and eight months. The time had really flown by for Gus and he was going to be 58 years old this year and he would be 60 years old if he took the ten year retirement package. Gus had felt himself slipping a little at a time physically through the years and only hoped that he would be in good enough shape physically to be able to handle all the work that he knew he would need to do if he moved to Far West Texas. His hair was mostly gray now and his fore-head was receding, he had a pot-belly because he still drank his beer and he also had quite doing a lot of the heavy work that he had done while he had been farming and ranching. Other then having to buy pants with bigger waist sizes and longer belts, Gus had changed little. Gus had spent just about all the money that he was going to spend on his Blue Quail Ranch except for small improvements and the general upkeep of his roads that would only require maintaining if there was enough rain to wash out places. Gus knew that his next big expense was going to be buying some sort of house in one of the towns out close to his ranch. He didn't have a lot of money and he wanted to be able to pay cash for the house, so he knew that it would have to be an older house that probably would need a lot of work. Gus went back to work at the Harvesting Department and each week he would receive two news papers from out in Far West Texas that he would read carefully and look over all their ad's on houses for sale. These papers were the Alpine Avalanche in Alpine, Texas and the Van Horn Advocate in Van Horn, Texas. Between these two papers they covered almost all of the area that Gus might be interested in looking for a house. Gus had been trying to save money for making this investment in a house out there and he was beginning to replace the money that he had spent on his Ranch and all the different improvements that he had done out there. He looked at his Ranch primarily as an investment for the future and not a way to make him a living, so he wouldn't be using it as a means of income to live on once he moved out to Far West Texas. He knew that everything that he did out there he would have to be payed for with cash and that money would have to be built up from sources that he already had that were available to him. He was going to have to take his chances out there and look for opportunities to make some money there, as the opportunity presented itself and who knows when or how long that would be. He calculated that he would have enough income to live on for several years, derived from a few of his residential lots that he was still receiving monthly payments on, the payments that he was receiving on the farm land he had sold, the payments on the ranch house in Wharton County he had sold and what ever he would receive as a small retirement check from the State of Texas. The trouble with this was that in time all of these sources of income were going to disappear when the Notes were paid off, then he would only end up with Social Security and his small State of Texas retirement check, so he would have to always keep his eyes pealed for opportunities to make some extra money once he got established out there. He hoped to take between $90,000.00 and $100,000.00 in cash with him, but that remained to be seen depending on how things went in the next two years. The Prison Harvesting Department had started their Harvesting Season on the Southern Prison Units as usual and the yields of Milo Maize and Corn were turning out good so far. Every few days another Prison Unit would start their Harvesting and Harvesting Equipment and the Inmate Operators would have to be moved to those Units until all of the

Prison Units that were farming Field Crops were Harvesting, then Gus and the other 4 Supervisors were stretched from the Gulf Coast in the South to deep East Texas and out all the way to Fort Stockton in West Texas. When the Harvesting was at it's peak they were on the road to different Prison Units everyday and sometime not getting back home until late at night. It was a grueling task and the only salvation in it was the four days off after a ten day work schedule. In the late summer Gus and his Boss were sent all the way up to Amarillo in the Texas Panhandle, to Harvest Wheat and then to LaMesa, Texas close to the New Mexico Border to Harvest Green Beans. Gus liked his job, because you really did get to see a lot of Texas that you would have never visited other wise. Before the Harvest Season was over they had Harvest Machinery and Inmate Operators spread all over Texas on Prison Units and all of this had to be brought back to their Harvesting HQ and Shop to be rebuilt during the winter months to be ready for the next Harvest Season. Few people realized how big the Texas Prison Agriculture System was and Gus was shocked to learn it when he went to work there. In a way Gus was proud to be a part of it and it was just another sign that Texas always did things in a big way. Gus continued to save his money for his anticipated move to Far West Texas after his retirement and his cash was slowly building in his savings account. The value of his house that he bought in Sugarland in 1992 had been growing, because he had hit it lucky and bought it when the prices of all Real Estate were very low because of the Banking bust in Texas and the Nation, but things had been improving for several years and it looked like Gus might make a nice profit when he decided to sell it and this might be the only thing that would get his cash up to his projections when it came time for him to leave Sugarland for the West, because the Oil Business was still down and he had no chance of making any Oil Deals and he had all but given up on that. The middle of September Gus got his notice that his El Campo High School Class of 1960 was going to have their 40th Class Reunion. Gus decided to go, because he thought that it might be the last time he would get to see some of his oldest friends. They had been having their Reunions every five years and Gus had attended most of them. His Class had been pretty close, so they usually had a good turn out of Class Mates at these Reunions. He was making the rounds talking to his old friends when someone called his name and there was one of the guys that he had worked with at the Service Station with in El Campo when they were in School. They went to the Bar and ordered beers and talked old times. This was the first time this friend had been to a Reunion and he was really enjoying it. He asked Gus if his wife was the girl that they followed to Corpus Christi that time in 1962 and Gus told him no that he hadn't seen that girl, Lorrie, since then. His friend looked at him a little strange and told Gus that he was surprised, because after Gus and Lorrie had returned back to the car, after their long walk on the beach, Gus had seemed so different and all the way driving back home Gus had not spoken of what had happened on that beach, other then commenting that Lorrie was the sweetest and most beautiful young girl he had ever been with. His friend told Gus that he just figured that he had ended up marring her since he was so taken with her. Gus told his friend that life has strange twists, but that he probably should have married her since he had been married four times now, maybe if he had married Lorrie they would have stayed together. Harvest Season this year was finished about the usual time, because they had been blessed with decent weather and Gus got to take some Vacation time and go to his Ranch for a week in late September. During this time at his Ranch Gus decided to take time to drive to the three towns that were the closest to his Ranch, Fort Davis, Van Horn and Marfa, and take the time to look around in the towns and talk to people that live there to get a perspective of what was going on there and what the people thought were the towns biggest advantages and it's biggest disadvantages. In some instances Gus found this questioning to be very interesting. He was asked by several people if he was a reporter of some sort, some people thought that their town didn't have any disadvantages, some people thought that their town didn't have any advantages and some people actually tried to lay out the picture that told the good, bad and the ugly. Gus did this for three days and he got a much better idea of what was going on in the towns that he might one day live. Gus wrote down notes on each town and when he reviewed them he came up with a distinct difference in the basic character of the people in each of these towns. One town had a definite arrogance, in it's population, that felt they were a little better then that of the other towns in the area, because of their tourist attractions, in another town their population held to a past feeling of economic importance that had been long gone, but still seemed to blind them to the poverty that surrounded them and the third town had no allusions as to what was needed to improve the conditions of their people that lived there and some of their citizens were looking for ways to improve their lot. The differences in these towns was an amusing exercise in learning for Gus. He was glad he had undertaken this quest for information, because it might just make the difference in his decisions one day when he decided to buy a house and move from Sugarland. The rest of his time was spent doing small things that would make the camp more organized and therefore easier to stay at and he also used some of his time to explore and hunt for Indian artifacts, which was one of his favorite things to do. He also discovered a large outcropping of lava that contained mica and several small veins of silver intertwined in it. Gus was always amazed at the amount of the different things that could be discovered out in this Chihuahua Desert region. He had grown up and lived on the Gulf Coast of Texas most of his life and he considered it an unimpressive place to live with mostly flat land, with terrible weather and climate consisting of rain, more rain, mud, more mud, fire ants, mosquitoes, high taxes, traffic and oppressive regulations and fees for anything you wanted to do. The up-keep and on property on the Gulf Coast was expensive and time consuming. There was always grass and weeds to mow, spray and weed eat, ant beds to poison, mosquitoes to spray, termites to eat your buildings up, leather products to mildew in your closet, your B-B-Q pit to rust down and everything that could rot, did rot. Gus decided that he was going to make his last trip to his Ranch for the year at Thanksgiving, because this was when two of his Boys would come out to hunt Deer and stay for a few days. He and his wife would stay out there for two weeks and be back in Sugarland for Christmas and New Years of 2,001. Gus's youngest Son was the one that loved to hunt the most and he reminded him of the Son that had been killed in the accident with the Honda three-wheeler. Gus had only had that Son out to the Mountain Region of the Chihuahua Desert one time and that was when he had taken his only Family vacation to the Big Bend of Texas in 1982 and that Son seemed to like it out there a lot and that was only two months before he got killed. Gus had always wondered what he would have thought of the Ranch. The loss of that Boy was something that Gus had to deal with all the time within himself in order to keep going forward with his life. His Boys didn't kill any Deer again this year, but they did kill some Blue Quail that they put on the B-B-Q pit for dinner one night. His Boys went home after a few days and Gus and his Wife did their usual exploring and looking for semi-precious stones to polish and also Indian artifacts. They drove back to Sugarland before Christmas and got everything ready there for the Christmas and New Years 2,001 Holidays. They had a few visitors during the Holiday Season, but the Holidays were mostly low-key for Gus. Gus worked on refinishing an old secretary desk that he had salvaged from an old house that he had bought and sold in Danevang,

Texas a few years before and he got it finished before New Years Eve. He bought in the New Year of 2,001 sipping on a glass of eggnog spiked with some whiskey and watching old movies on TV and thinking about his conversation with his friend at their 40th Class Reunion about the trip to Corpus Christi and his question about Gus marring Lorrie. Gus thought that it was a damn good question, why didn't he marry Lorrie.

Lorrie— 2000 The year 2,000 would no longer have the distractions available for Lorrie that she had depended on before to make her life feel more fulfilled. Her sweet little dog Mitzi had died and this had been a great loss to Lorrie, because now she had nothing to lavish her love on and on top of that she had finished her Art History Degree and there were no more field trips to other Countries in Europe and no more academic research to take her mind off of the ever persistent dreary, disappointing and abusive marriage that she felt trapped in. Lorrie had no idea what she was going to use as a distraction to better cope with her everyday life. The more she thought about it books seemed to be the answer. She remembered that when she was a girl she would read books all the time and through them she could disconnect from her life at home with her strict parents and be in another world every time she picked up a good book and started to read it, so she started ordering all sorts of interesting books on different subjects along with novels and scarey zombie books. Lorrie found that this did work to a certain extent for she could hide in these books when things got to be depressing and when she had an interesting book on order it gave her something nice to look forward to when it was delivered. Sometimes Lorrie felt like she was just wasting her life on an hour by hour basis, because her life seemed like it had, had all the color washed out of it and that it had turned a shade of gray and there were times that she contemplated suicide, but she knew that she was going to be needed one day to help take care of her Dad with his debilitating disease. She was already planning to lengthen her vacation time in El Campo to three months and this would give her something to look forward to. Her Husband was still taking his two ski vacation trips each winter, one for a week and another for two weeks, so that would give her a break from him in the winter and the three month vacation she was planning would be in the summer, so that would provide her with an escape from him in the summer. Well, she thought that maybe she could continue living with her Husband like that with the help of her books and the winter and summer absences from her Husband.

She would be able to do the three months in El Campo, Texas, because her Husband already knew that her Dad had an incurable disease and that she wanted to spend as much time as she could with him and helping her Mom and also her Husband knew that she had taken care of his Dad until he had died, so he couldn't reasonably protest her going there for three months. Just knowing that she was going to be away from her Husband for three months gave her a big lift to her spirits. Now that was something to really look forward to. About a week before Lorrie was to leave on her vacation trip back to El Campo, Texas her Stepson shows up at their house with all of his cloths and tells them that he quit his job and vacated his apartment in London, because he was tired of taking orders from a Boss that wasn't as smart as he was. Lorrie was so shocked that for a minute she just stood there without saying anything and then when she was about to ask a question she stopped herself with the thought that this could get out of control and she didn't want to get beat up by her Husband in an argument right before she was going back to El Campo, Texas on her vacation. Lorrie walked off the restroom and closed the door so she could think in private. She sat down on the toilet and gazed at the wall in thought. It came to her that there was a pattern developing with her Stepson that she didn't like at all. First was the time he came home on Leave from the Royal Air Force Academy complaining that his Instructors didn't know what they were doing and then he was Discharged from the Air Force for reasons that she was never told and now he quit his job, because his Boss was stupid. Lorrie made a growling sound deep in her throat in disgust. She knew better then to believe everything that her Stepson told her, because he had lied to her a lot through the years and never seemed to be sorry for it. He could lie to her and his Dad with a straight face and had done it many times. She knew that there was more to it then he was telling, but she wasn't going to make any waves now. Lorrie had been proud of her Stepson for getting the job he had at one of the Biggest Banks in London and he had been paid a very big salary with bonuses. She knew that he had saved a little of it, but she also knew that he had lived the high life taking expensive trips to island retreats and wining and dining girlfriends, so how much money he had left she didn't know. Lorrie left for her vacation trip back to El Campo, Texas to see her family and friends the first of June and wouldn't return back to England until the end of August and she was so glad to leave and get as far away from that mess as she could that she felt a big sigh of relief when she boarded the plane for the long flight. Normally Lorrie dreaded this flight and it always produced a little bit of fear in her that the plane wouldn't make it, but now she was ready to take that chance over what was going on at her house in England. Lorrie's Sister picked her up at the Air Port in Houston, Texas as usual and Lorrie stayed with her for several days and they did some shopping together and discussed her Dad's health, so Lorrie would have a better idea what she was facing when she got to El Campo and her parents house. Lorrie's Sister drove her to El Campo and her Family was waiting for her. The stay at her Sisters house in Houston for several days helped to refresh Lorrie from her long flight, so she was ready for a lot of catching up on everything that had been going on for the whole year that she had been gone. They ate a lite lunch of a sandwich and chips and then Lorrie caught them up on all that she had been up to in England, except she left out all of the disturbing facts about her life in England just like she had always done. As far as her Family was concerned Lorrie had a wonderful life in England with a loving Husband a smart and successful Stepson and not a worry in the world. She had perpetuated this vision of her life there to her Family, because she couldn't stand to think of them knowing that she had made a huge mistake and she didn't want to hear, I told you so from them. That evening they all went out to a local Mexican Cafe, so Lorrie could get her Mexican food fix. Lorrie missed her Mexican food when she was in England and she couldn't even buy what she needed there to prepare it herself, so when she got back to Texas she ate it often. She had been keeping a close eye on her Dad to see if she could tell the difference in his appearance and movements from a year ago. Lorrie noticed that her Dad was not steady when he walked now and that he dropped things often when he was using his hands to eat. He also seemed to be eating slower and taking more time to swallow his food. As she observed all of this she remembered that her research had given all of these things as the result of the steady progression of the disease. A few days later Lorrie made an appointment with his local Doctor to discuss her Dad's condition and the Doctors assessment of how fast the disease was progressing. Lorrie told the Doctor that her Dad loved for her and him to go riding and drink a six-pack of beer and should they continue to do this. The Doctor told Lorrie that it was getting to the point that alcoholic beverages were going to add to his instability, so she should probably limit him to only one beer and there would be a time come not to far away that he wouldn't be able to have any. This was sad for Lorrie to hear, because those times had always been very special times that only her Dad and her did together and that is when they would be the closest to each other talking about things that no one else would know. When she was home her Dad always grilled some hamburgers on his outside grill, but when he tried to do it this time his coordination was not up to handling the cooking tools and meet patties, so her brother had to take over and she could see the disappointment in her Dad's face as he sat down and lowered his head looking down at the ground. Lorrie got a big lump in her throat and she wondered what her Dad was thinking at that moment. She went over and put her arm around him and told him that she loved him and that there were things that she couldn't do anymore herself either, so it was just simply time to let others do what they could no longer do and that seemed to brighten his mood some. When Lorrie stayed a few days with her Sister in Houston, after her flight from England, they had done some shopping and Lorrie bought a few cloths that she intended to wear during her three month stay in El Campo. She had brought some cloths, but not enough and she had planned all along to build a wardrobe of cloths to leave at her Parents house in El Campo for two reasons. First was so she wouldn't have to pack so many and bring them from England, because it was expensive to check in more luggage then was allowed by the Airline and second she had been thinking for some time that she could one day need to leave England quickly to escape her Husbands brutality and these cloths would be a great thing to have waiting for her at her Parents house, because that is where she would have to come to. Lorrie was also planning to give her Mom some extra money to save for her just in case, but she wouldn't be able to actually tell her Mom what the money was to be for. Lorrie thought that she would tell her Mom that she just wanted her to save it for her in case she needed it for something that she hadn't planned for. Lorrie decided that she was going to do this every time that she came home for a visit to build up enough money to give her a small new start if she needed it. She would then have some money and some cloths that she could depend on to be there in an emergency trip back home. Also this way her Husband would never detect the missing money or suspect that she was planning to leave him for good. Lorrie was doing a little shopping from time to time during her stay in El Campo. She was noticing what other women her age and with her body shape were wearing and using that as a guide to try and choose clothing that she thought looked on her for different occasions. She realized that she was visiting El Campo in the warm summer months and that if she did, one day, come back to live for good that she would need some cloths that were warmer then she was buying now, but there wasn't much in the

Department Stores at this time of the year that would do for cold weather. Lorrie thought that she might even have to pack a few winter things, that she didn't need in England, to bring with her when she came back next year to leave for the winter months in El Campo. Lorrie had been in El Campo for a month and decided that it was time for her to visit her favorite hairdresser Friend that owned her own Salon to get her cut and colored. They had been friends ever since Lorrie had been a young girl, because Lorrie's Mom had been using her for her hairdresser for many years and her Mom had a standing appointment for every Thursday. The hairdresser was several years older then Lorrie and she had already graduated from El Campo High School before Lorrie had entered as a Freshman student, but they non the less they had developed a strong friendship. The hairdresser Friend was not really aware of what had happened between Lorrie and Gus, because Lorrie had never told her the story. The hair dresser Friend just knew that Lorrie had known Gus, she didn't know that Lorrie had fallen in love with Gus and was still in love with Gus, so she had thought nothing of it when someone had come in her Salon saying that they had seen Gus or that Gus had been in town. Lorrie didn't know that her hair dresser Friend had been friends with Gus ever since they were just small children. They had grown up in the same Church and had been only one year apart in school and had even played in the Junior High and the High School Bands together. Had Lorrie known this she would have probably been pumping her hairdresser Friend for all the information she could get from her about Gus. Here was a connection that Lorrie had never dreamed of and there would be a time in the distant future that, that connection, unknown to her now, would be the vital link to changing the lives of Lorrie and Gus forever. Lorrie went with her Mom to the hair appointment and had a good reunion with her hairdresser Friend that she hadn't seen since her last trip back to El Campo a year ago. Lorrie was anxious to catch up on all that the hairdresser had to tell her about the local gossip. All women knew that the Beauty Salon was the hot bed of all news that went around a community. If you wanted to find out anything then just go to the Beauty Salon and you were sure to learn everything that was going on in the town. There was a lady sitting in the chair next to Lorrie getting her hair cut by one of the other girls that worked there and she was telling her that she had a very pleasant experience a couple of days ago when she had attended a funeral of a friend at the local Grave Yard. She had accidentally run into one of her old boyfriends from High School. He had been out to the Grave Yard visiting his son's Grave when she turned around to go and noticed him standing there and she walked over there to talk to him. He introduced the woman with him as his wife and they talked briefly, but when he took her hand to tell her goodby she still got tingles in her breast from the touch. She told the girl cutting her hair that at her age she didn't think that she would respond like that to a mans touch, but that she thought that he was as sexy as he had always been. Lorrie was getting a kick out of listening this old woman telling this story and thinking that she wished that she could get tingles from a mans touch and then the woman told the girl that she had ridden in that red cut down Hot Rod of his several times and man would it run fast. Lorrie almost fell out of her chair with shock, because then she realized that the old woman was talking about Gus. She told her Friend to stop cutting her hair for a minute and she leaned over toward the old woman and asked her how the boy died and the old woman told her that it had been a great tragedy, that he had been killed in an accident with one of those Honda three wheelers and at just about the whole town had turned out for his Funeral. Lorrie ask her if the man still lived in El Campo and the old woman told Lorrie that he didn't, but she couldn't remember where he had moved to, because they just talked a few minutes and since his wife was with him she didn't want to be around him too long or she might have grabbed him and kissed him. Lorrie thought that she sure understand that, because she still remembered well the effect his kisses had on her and that was 38 years ago, but it might have been just yesterday. Lorrie would have liked to asked the old woman more questions about Gus, but her Mom was sitting in a chair looking and listening to her and she didn't want to have to answer any questions that she might ask later. Lorrie fell silent after that and her Friend that was cutting her hair noticed it and asked her what was wrong. Lorrie told her that she was just thinking about that young boy that had been killed and that he could have been their boy. Her Friend stopped cutting her hair and turned her around and looked her in the face and asked her what she was talking about. Lorrie felt stupid all of a sudden and told her that she meant that she could have had a boy that got killed like that and how bad that would have been on her. Her Friend told her that she guessed that something like that must be one of the worst things that a parent could go through. Lorrie told her Friend yes, but she was thinking, O My God Gus it could have been Our Son. As Lorrie's time went by on her vacation she had developed a planned program that would help her Dad and also relieve the burden on her Mom. She learned to sleep with one ear tuned to the sounds of her Dad moving around in the night and would quickly don a robe to help him to the bathroom or to bring him a drink of water, anything to give him comfort and a secure feeling. She never seemed to get enough real rest, but she was glad to be able to help her Parents. A few days before she was to fly back to England Lorrie went through the same routine that she had developed during her other visits and that was to go grocery shopping for all the Texas food products that she couldn't get in England, so she could pack them and take them back with her and also to make her yearly pilgrimage around Gus's Mom's old house and all the places that she used to see Gus. This was always a bitter sweet time of memories pouring over her and now she even knew that he had lost his son to a terrible accident. She knew in her heart that she would probably never see him again, but he remained as alive to her now as he had been when she was just 16 years old on the beach with him in Corpus Christi in 1962. The old woman at her Friends Beauty Salon said that he was as sexy as he had always been and Lorrie smiled at the thought of that. Lorrie boarded the plane to flt back to England, at the end of August 2,000, wondering what disaster she might encounter when she arrived back home. She thought that she would just have to face it and make the best of things as they came along. She still had her books and she hoped that her Husband would keep taking his ski vacations and that was something to look forward to. Lorrie returned back to England and found that her Stepson was still living at their house and spending most of his time in his room. He didn't even come down to great her when she got home. Lorrie questioned her Husband to find out if her Stepson had been looking for another job and her Husband told her that his Son wanted to take a break from the stress of working in the high pressure London Banking system and he had told him that he could live at Home until he felt that he was ready to go back to work. This burned Lorrie up, because her Husband had always been so lax with her Stepson, that he just did as he pleased regardless of the difficulties he put everyone else in. Lorrie thought of him as a grown up spoiled brat. Her Stepson didn't start looking for a job until late in the fall and she knew that her Husband was slipping him money and trying to hide the fact from her. She went up to her Stepson's room when he was gone one day to see how it looked and was dismayed at what she saw. There were beer cans and wine bottles scattered everywhere and she saw a bottle of pills that she was curious about and she jotted the name down, so she could find out what they were. Lorrie took her Husband up to her Stepsons room and showed him that it looked like ma pig pen and she told him that she wasn't going to clean it up. She told her Husband that he needed to have a talk with his Son and have him clean up his own room. Lorrie also showed her Husband the pills and asked him if he knew what they were for. He told her that they were for depression, that her Stepson had been seeing a Psychotherapist, because he had been so mistreated by his Bank Supervisor that he needed to get himself straightened out before finding another job. It was right before Christmas before her Stepson found employment with another big Banking Firm in London. He still lived at Home with them and rode the train to London everyday to work until he could save enough money to get his own apartment in London. Lorrie had checked out the medicine her Stepson had been taking and found that the pills were not to be taken while drinking alcohol. She thought about all the beer cans and wine bottles that she had seen in his room and wondered if he was mixing pills and alcohol for drug Hi. New Years Eve found Lorrie and her Husband quietly watching the programs on their TV and having a few drinks. They didn't have a party this year, because Lorrie didn't feel like doing a lot of celebrating. Her Stepson was out with some of his friends and her Husband got drunk and barely made it to watch the New Year 2,001 program before he went up to his room and went to bed. Lorrie sat there a while longer sipping on a glass of brandy and thinking about the previous New Year 2,000 when she had wondered what it would bring with it. Now it was the year 2,001 and she was hoping for a better year than 2,000 had been.

Gus—2,001 was the year that Gus had to make the final decision of weather he was going to stay for 5 more years, working for the Texas Department of Criminal Justice, till he would be 65 years old, or to take the 10 year retirement at his age of 60 in 2,002. His decision would be based on two different circumstances. If he was given the chance to advance in his career to a point where his salary would make a significant improvement in his retirement pay then he would stay, but if not then he would take the 10 year retirement and also there was the problem of finding a house out there that he could afford to buy and renovate. If he couldn't find a house in time for his 10 year retirement then he would have to stay until he located one that suited his situation and who knew how long that would be. Gus and the other Supervisors were busy taking care of the repair work on all of the Harvesting Machinery. It had all been brought in now from all parts of Texas and each piece would be looked over and taken apart to recondition it to be ready for the 2,001 Harvest Season. It was a slow process and sometime it was made slower by the transfer or release of an Inmate Mechanic that had been working on a certain piece of machinery and then trying to find another one to replace him. Then there are the times when the whole Prison Unit is locked down for one reason or another and no Inmates are turned out to work for two or three days. That also throws everything behind, but they have always gotten everything repaired one way or the other and Gus expected them to get the job done this time too. During this time Gus kept scanning the Classified Ad's in both of the news papers that he got every week, to see if he could find a house for sale that was in his price range. He had called on a couple of them, but when he found out more about them he decided they weren't right for him. Gus thought that it might be nice to have an adobe house, because he had always heard that they were very cool in the summer and warm in ght winter, because of their 14 inch to 18 inch thick adobe brick walls. Gus knew that there were a lot of adobe brick houses out there in Far West Texas, but he really had never had any experience with one. They seemed perfect for the climate out there. Gus got the chance to apply for a Prison Farm Managers job at one of the Prison Farms south of Sugarland, which would have jumped his salary enough for him to consider staying until he was 65 years old. He knew that he wouldn't enjoy this job as much as the one he presently had, because he would be stuck on that Prison Farm and been able to travel around Texas. As it turned out he wasn't chosen for the job, so that solved that problem. Later in the spring Gus ran across an Ad in the Van Horn paper about a house for sale, that sounded interesting to him. The Ad stated that the house was a Historical two story rock home in the town of Van Horn and gave a telephone number. Gus called the number and a lady in Rio Rancho, New Mexico answered and told Gus that the home belonged to her 97 year old Aunt that was presently residing in a Nursing Home there in Rio Rancho and there were no family Heirs to lay claim to it and that all the contents would be sold with the house. She told Gus that there were two of her Aunts step nephews living in the house and they had done some damage to it with their drunken and drug parties and she wanted to sell it for her Aunt as soon as possible. Gus asked what she wanted for it and she told him that she didn't know what to ask and that he would have to bid on it, that she had one bid from a woman that lived in Oklahoma now but she had been raised in Van Horn and knew the house well. Gus told her that he would have to take off of work and drive to Van Horn to look at the house before he could present a bid and the lady told him that she would wait for him to do that. Gus showed the Ad to his wife and told her that he was going to go that next weekend and take one more day of vacation leave to make it a three day trip, because it would be a hard trip to drive up one day 600 miles and then drive back the next day 600 miles and that if she wanted to accompany him on this trip she would have to use up one of her vacation days. They set out that next Friday driving to Van Horn and arrived there in the middle of the afternoon, got a Motel room and drove around to find the location of the house and to see what kind of neighborhood surrounded it. Gus liked what he saw of the house from his drive by, and noticed that it was the only two story house for several blocks and also he noticed that there were all kinds of older, smaller houses that occupied the neighborhood. They also contacted a woman that worked at the local Bank who was to meet them at the house on Saturday morning and show the house to them. Gus and his Wife went to a local Steak House Cafe for their dinner and then went to their room. The next morning they ate a good breakfast and met the woman from the Bank at the house at 9:00 am. She had the keys and told Gus that she instructed the nephews of the old woman to be away from the house when she was to show it, so on one was there. Gus first walked around the outside of the house looking at the yard then he made a second trip around the house on the porch that was on all four sides supported by six big round column's on each side. In the back of the house there was a 10 foot by 20 foot cinder block storage/shop building that was connected to the porch with a 20 foot by 20 foot car port roof on a cement slab. That was pretty nice. He was looking at the outside walls and the ceiling of the porch which was closed in with ply wood. The house had the big old wood sash windows, but there were also modern storm windows over the outside of them. The cement porch had some pretty big cracks in it on each side, but it was a nice wide porch that would shade the walls and also protect the windows from the rain when it came. The walls were made of solid sand stone block 10 inches thick and there was no wood in them except for the old window frames and Gus didn't see any cracks in the outside walls. The yard was a mess, but that was a minor thing. The house had two dormer windows in the front and one dormer on each of the other three sides. The roof was of composition shingles that Gus didn't like and he wondered where the old chimneys were, because he could tell that the house was old enough to have at one time had chimneys. He surmised that they must have removed them when they replaced the roof, for he was sure that the house had been built with a cedar shake shingle roof. He didn't really know how old the house was, but he guessed that it must have been built at least in the 1920's or 30's. There were several huge old mulberry trees and a big desert willow that would be worth saving, but everything else in the yard needed to go. When they entered the inside Gus was disappointed to see that the outside looked better then the inside. It didn't take long to be able to see that it had been mistreated inside. It was dirty and smelly with grease stains on the old carpet and even a motorcycle parked in one bedroom that was dripping oil on the carpet. There were some wall electrical outlets that were hanging out of their boxes and an old gas wall heater that served the kitchen and living room that looked like it had never been cleaned and was smoked up looking, the down stairs bath room was tiny and the bath room fixtures were filthy and old probably dating from the 1930's, with tile falling off of the wall and the sink barely hanging on the wall. The bath room had a small pantry to hold towels and bedding. The two down stairs bedrooms were large, but had no closets and this was another clue as to the age, because way back they used an wardrobes to hang cloths and a cedar chest for woolen cloths. There was a nice sized utility room and the kitchen was a mess. The old woman had built a large bar with cabinets under it across part of the kitchen that would have to be torn out, because it restricted the proper use of the floor space and left the big round oak antique table and matching buffet and leaded glass china cabinet crammed in the corner and on part of one wall. There was a GE electric kitchen range that wasn't to old, but it was filthy with grease and it had a cast iron skillet on the burner that had three dead 2 inch long cock roaches laying in the grease in the bottom. The cabinets weren't to bad just greasy and filthy with an old cast iron ceramic double sink. The floor was filthy with a place that looked like it had received repeated water damage from an old dishwasher. The front door was the beautiful original with the original oval window in it and the original brass hardware, real nice stuff. The entry way was about 10 feet wide with the stair case 12 feet inside and going up a wall on the left side and a short hall leading to a closet built for coats. The stair case was 3 feet wide with a beautiful hand rail supported with turned spindles and it climbed at a nice easy angle to a small landing where it turned to the left and climbed to the top landing that was huge. This whole landing was surrounded by a nice wooden rail supported by turned spindles to keep someone from falling down and from there you could look down on the entry way, real nice. It was actually large enough to be a loft bedroom or maybe a library. To the right was a small bathroom, in terrible condition, that was made out of one of the dormers that was in the back of the house roof and there were three upstairs bedrooms that were small, but big enough and they had doors that opened to the landing, but they also had doors that opened between them, very strange. From this top floor you had a view of the whole town to the south all the way past I-10. All in all the top floor was impressive and had a lot of room. There was no central air conditioning or heating in the house and that would have to be done the old way with gas heaters like he grew up with and maybe window air conditioner units. It could all be done and the house looked solid and it had a lot of potential, but there was a work to be done on it which ment that it would have to be bought real cheap. Gus guessed that there was about 4000 square feet of living space plus the storage, shop building and the 20 foot by 20 foot car port and the big porch on all four sides, so it was a big house that was sitting on three town lots that were fenced. Really not bad for the right price. Now to try and establish what price that he wanted to pay for it. That afternoon Gus and his Wife road around town some more looking things over and Gus thought that the town looked like it had been left behind and had been trapped somewhere in the 1950's or 1960's which meant that the economy and average income there was a lot less then back along the Gulf Coast where he had grown up. That night they went to the local Steak House again for dinner and asked the waitress some questions about what kinda of jobs were available in the area and what the jobs were paying. What Gus found out was that if someone there was making as much as $25,000.00 a year they were considered to have a very good job and that was much less then people were making back where Gus was living. This would help him to make his decision on how much to offer for the house. Gus and his Wife left the next morning for Sugarland and all the way home Gus was rolling over figures in his mind, this was the way he had always been when considering to make an investment of a considerable amount of money. He didn't want to get more money tied up in repairs then the house and property was valued at. After they arrived back in Sugarland and unpacked, Gus sat down with a note pad and made a list of all the supplies he could think of that he would need to renovate the house. The list was a long one that filled three legal sheets. The only thing that he couldn't figure was the replacement of the roof, because he would have to hire that done by a contractor. The roof was much to steep for him at 60 years old to do himself and he knew that there would be many other things that he hadn't planned on that would come up to spend money on. The Monday after work Gus went to Home Depot in Sugarland to put dollar prices to the items on his list and that took him five hours to complete. That night he added them up for a total and then he doubled that amount to come up with an approximate renovation cost. When looking at this he determined that he was going to offer $25,000.00 for the house, three lots and all of the items included inside the house. This was his base price, but he decided that if he had to he would go up to $30,000.00. He then checked his savings and found that he only had $32,000.00 in his account which meant that it would leave him almost nothing to start purchasing supplies if he won the bid. Gus knew that he couldn't save enough in a little more then a year to do all that he needed to do and he didn't want to borrow any money, so he would have to think of another way to get it done. Well first he would need to talk to the niece of the old woman that owns the house to see if he can win the bid. Gus called the old woman's niece the next day and said he was prepared to bid on the house. The niece told Gus that he would have to beat a $30,000.00 bid that the lady from Oklahoma had bid, so Gus hesitated a few seconds, gritted his teeth and bid $31,000.00 and became the proud owner of an old house in Van Horn, Texas. Gus had decided at the last minute to over bid the other bidder. He knew that it would basically take all of his savings and not leave enough money in the account to even keep it open. He told his Wife what he had done and she offered a solution. She offered to take $15,000.00 from her savings and basically pay for half of the original cost of the house. Gus really disliked this idea and had to think it over. He had never taken any money from his Wife for anything not even for monthly bills and as a matter of fact he had never taken any money from any of his Wives for anything. The truth now was he couldn't come up with any other solution to his immediate problem, so he swallowed his pride and told his Wife that he would accept her solution. His Wife gave him a check for $15,000.00 and Gus deposited this and then drew $16,000.00 from his savings and wrote a check for $31,000.00. Gus mailed the check to the old woman's niece and she sent Gus a Deed to the property in return. Gus decided to make another trip out to Van Horn, before Harvest Season started, so he took four days vacation time and went out to see how secure the house was. He got the keys from the lady that worked at the Bank min Van Horn and bought three big pad locks with hasps and a box of big nails. He installed two hasps and locks on the front and back door and then went through the house and drove in the big nails on the top of the wood windows, so they couldn't be raised easily, then he installed the last hasp and lock on the door to the storage/shop building. This was all he could do to help and secure the house and storage/shop building from thieves. In June of 2,001 the Harvesting Department was shipping out Harvesting Equipment and Inmate Operators to different Prison Farms getting ready to start on the 2,001 Harvest Season. Gus's Wife had just finished working the School Year, so she would be free for the summer. Gus had a plan to use her to start getting things arranged for him to slowly start to move things from Sugarland to Van Horn. His Wife had a Daughter that was married and her mother-in law didn't work, so Gus told his Wife to see if the woman wanted to make some money traveling out to Van Horn and working with his Wife at the house there. Gus told his Wife that he would pay all expenses, Motel bills, meals and pay the woman $50.00 per day if she would help. Gus knew that the storage/shop was empty and he told his Wife that his plan was for her and the other woman to go out there and rent a Motel room for a week and do all of their eating at Cafes so they wouldn't have to wast time doing any cooking. They were to take as much furniture and other things out of the house and stack them in the storage/shop building, then do as much cleaning as they could in the house and then before they left to set of a bug bomb in each room of the house. He told her that he had gotten the serial and model number from the GE electric kitchen range and he would buy new burners, drip cups and oven elements before they went out in the fall and they would work on things more then. Now though all he wanted was to have room in the house to start taking a few things out there when he made a trip out there. Gus was busy with the Harvest Season and his Wife and her Daughters Mother-In-Law went to Van Horn for a week and accomplished what they were sent out to do there. She came back and told Gus that the storage/shop building was completely full of things that they had moved out of the house and there was plenty of room in the house now for him to use to store things that he wanted to take there from Sugarland. The house would just have to sit there for now, because Gus wouldn't be able to make a trip out there before the end of September. During the summer months Harvest Season Gus had little time to think about the house In Van Horn. He did buy the parts needed for the kitchen range there though. Gus planned his next trip out to Van Horn to basically be a trip that would give him more time to look over the house more closely and try to determine what it was going to take to fix it up enough for them to stay there while he was doing the overall renovation that might take several years, he just didn't know enough to even speculate on how long it would take to complete what he had to do there. Also he wanted to look at the small locally owned Hardware Store there to see exactly what they offered in their stock that he could depend on to purchase for his renovation work. He already knew that they didn't handle much in lumber supplies, because he had been there when he was working on his Ranch Camp House. Gus knew that he would have to go to El Paso to get a lot of what he would need. The Harvest Season on the Prison Farms was going about as good as could be expected with the occasional rain storm building up from tropical storms that would pop up on the Gulf Coast to delay the harvest on one of the Prison Farms in one place then in another place that would keep Gus driving from one Prison Farm to another trying to keep the harvest moving. The Harvest Season finally came to a close and Gus prepared to make his trip out to Van Horn and then on to his Blue Quail Ranch in Jeff Davis County. Gus's Wife had left one old full sized bed in the house just in case he would need to spend the night there. When Gus was packing things to take with him he decided to take some bed sheets, a pillow and a blanket for that bed. He also took the parts that he had purchased for the GE electric kitchen range and white paint, paint primer brushes, scrapers, sand paper and ammonia to clean grease. He was going to unload that stuff there to use another time to repaint the cabinets inside and out and to clean the electric range and repair it. He had notified El Paso Electric Company to turn on the power and The Town of Van Horn to turn on the water so he could use them when he was there. Gus also took some tools with him to dismantle the big bar that had been built in the kitchen. He left early in the morning and got to Van Horn about 3:30 pm. Unlocked the house and went inside to check out the bed. It looked terrible and thought that it was a good thing that he had brought a mattress cover, but he still wasn't satisfied, so he went to the store and bought a couple spray cans of disinfectant to spray on the mattress and let it dry before he put on the mattress cover and made the bed. He planned on spending at least two nights there before going out to his Ranch. That afternoon Gus took a lot of time looking through the house again before going to dinner at his favorite Steak House Cafe there and having a couple of beers. He didn't sleep very good that night because the house was stuffy, the mattress wasn't comfortable and some bug crawled on his face when he was sleeping and he slapped it squashing it on his cheek. The next morning he saw that the bug was roach and it gave him the shudders. He had turned on the water at the meter the even before, so at least he had water to wash off his face and brush his teeth. He went out to a small Cafe for breakfast and coffee then went back to the house to start tearing out the big bar in the kitchen. He couldn't wait to get that thing out of the kitchen to clear the room so he could move the big round table out of its confined corner and get a better idea of what the kitchen would look like. Gus worked the rest of the morning getting the Bar dismantled down to it's framework and found that it could be moved by sliding it a little at a time He measured the door and the Bar frame and he had just a couple of inches of clearance to get it through the door. The Bar was very heavy even after all the outside walls were removed along with the doors and drawers. He left the top and the middle shelf intact, because he could see that it could be used as a work bench in the storage/shop when it would be cleared out in the future. Gus went to lunch for a hamburger then went back to the house to move the stripped down Bar to the back porch and out of the way. The Bar was still so heavy that it took Gus two hours to get it moved out on the porch. He rested and then decided that he needed to go to the store and do his grocery shopping to stock up for his stay at his Ranch. Gus finished up his shopping and iced all his cold food down in a cooler and filled an extra big cooler with sacks of ice then went to his Steak House and ate a good dinner. After that he went back to the house and walked around the yard before dark. Now he discovered some more problems that he hadn't known about. He saw that the sewer line for the downstairs bathroom was bubbling up in the back yard and he could also see big wet spots in several places in the yard that indicated that the water lines were leaking. He remembered asking his Wife when she and the lady helping her were out there working if the toilet flushed ok and she said that it did, but she never knew that it was going out in the back yard. Gus thought that he should have known that a house that old would have a lot of sewer and water pipe problems, so not to be upset with about it. He knew that from now on when he was out there that he couldn't leave the water on at the meter for very long. In fact he went over and pulled the cover off the meter box and the meter needle was going around and around and he didn't have any water running in the house, so he got the water valve shutoff tool and shut off the water st the meter. He would turn it on in the morning so he could use the bathroom then shut it off again. The next morning Gus was grateful that nothing had crawled on him during the night and he he had survived the bad mattress except for a stiff back. He ate a good breakfast before he left town to drive to his Ranch that was about 35 miles south of Van Horn. It was a nice day and he couldn't wait to get there to see how everything looked. Gus drove up to the Ranch house and opened the door to unload his supplies and he immediately saw that there had been either mice or rats that had entered somehow. He had thought that those metal containers were rat proof, but they got in some how and he would have to find out how they did it. After he had unloaded everything, made his bed and turned on the water and lit the hot water heater he started to look around to find the place that the rats got in the Ranch house. He looked everywhere and couldn't fine any place that he even suspected as a place of entry. He remembered that he had brought a couple of mouse traps out a while back and had never used them, so he went into the work shop to get them, because he knew that he was going to need then during the night. He swept up the mouse droppings that he found and noticed that they had nibbled on some cheese crackers and a box of breakfast cereal, then he found a nest they had made on a shelf in his little pantry and it had three little mouse baby's in it that he took outside and disposed of. He was perplexed about where they got in and went around moving everything and still found nothing. That night Gus cut a couple if small pieces of bacon from a strip and secured each of them to a mouse trap and placed them in separate locations on the floor. He was asleep when he heard the traps snap shut, so he got up with his flash light and sure enough he had caught two rats, not mice. They were pack rats and Gus discarded them outside and reset the traps. Later in the night he heard one other trap snap shut and he had caught one more pack rat. He reset the trap, but he didn't catch any more. The next morning while he was drinking his coffee he was trying to figure out where in the world they were getting in the Camp house at. He walked outside to sit on the porch and finish his last cup of coffee when he noticed something he hadn't noticed before. It was rat pellets on top of his air conditioner unit. He started looking at it carefully and then he saw that the outside back louvered access panel that was screwed on to the unit had a ½ inch gap when it was mounted and screwed tight and there was no way to close the gap. He got dressed and went out and started his welding machine/ generator to have power in the Camp House and then he turned on the air conditioner and chewed up insulation plus rat pellets blew out, so now Gus knew for sure how they were getting in the Camp House. He turned the air conditioner off and shut off the welding machine/generator and proceeded to try to come up with a solution to that problem. Everything he thought of had a bad aspect to it, but all of a sudden he came up with the idea of making a sleeve out of 1/8th inch hardware cloth that would fit tightly over the whole outside of the air conditioner unit. The small square 1/8th inch holes would allow the air into the unit so it could breathe and it would close off the access of the rats to enter the unit and then the Camp House. He knew that he had to do it that day or he would have more rats in the Camp House that night. He remembered that he had seen some of the hardware cloth in the Hardware Store in Van Horn, so he drove into Van Horn which took him an hour and a half. He bought what he needed there and even though it was a little early foe lunch he found a Cafe and had a hamburger then drove back to the Ranch and got organized making the sleeve and fitting it. It took him all afternoon to finish it. He was always amazed to find out how long it took to do something that looked like a small job, but when you were hand making and fitting something it always took much more time then you would estimate. He was proud of his idea and his work, but a few nights would tell the tale to see if the Camp House remained rat free. Gus spent three more days there before going back to the House in Van Horn for the night before driving back to Sugarland and no more rats had entered the Camp House. Gus was sure that he had solved that problem and it made him feel good. Gus sat on the back porch of the House in Van Horn late that evening sipping on a beer and was reflecting on his life a little when he started thinking of why the kisses he had received from women in his past never really satisfied his yearning for just the right, deep feeling that he needed to be totally complete and tied to that woman. The only person that he could remember that had kissed him like that was that sweet 16 year old girl Lorrie on the beach in Corpus Christi in 1962 and why hadn't he been able to find another one that could match that he didn't know, because he had kissed a multitude of women since then and there was just none that could come close to the kisses that Lorrie had given him. He longed for her kisses, or someones that could match them, but he realized that those days were over and they would never happen again. His trip back to Sugarland was long and tiring as usual and he was glad to be back home. He knew that he was going to make two more trips in 2,001, one for Thanksgiving and one around Christmas. Gus went back to work at the Prison Harvesting Department and started making plans on what he would take out to the Van Horn House and what they would work on while they were there, because his Wife would go out with him on the next trip at Thanksgiving. Work at the Harvesting Department late in the fall always consisted on choosing which piece of equipment they would rebuild first and then the equipment would be lined up in the order of it's repair needs. The Supervisors had all of this organized even to which Inmate Mechanic would work on which piece of equipment. This all went on as usual until it was time for Gus and his Wife to take their Thanksgiving vacation trip to Van Horn. They loaded some furniture that they could do without into his 8 foot trailer, so he could tarp it down in case of rain and the rest of their things went in the back of his Pick-up Truck. He had received a huge water bill from the Town of Van for the three nights that he had stayed in the House the last time he was down there, so he had a plan now on what they would have to do. It would be inconvenient, but they could do it and that was that he had 6, five gallon buckets that they would fill with water, plus two five gallon containers with spigots to use at the sink and for cooking, then he would turn off the water at the meter till they needed some more water. They got out to Van Horn and unloaded the furniture in an out of the way place in the House, then they went to eat and buy some food supplies for sandwiches and lite meals that didn't take a lot of preparation or cooking. His goal was to clean and repair the kitchen range to make sure it worked properly and to clean, scrape, sand and put a good paint job on the kitchen cabinets inside and out. This would be the biggest job and it would take the most amount of time to complete. Gus wanted to get these two jobs done, so when they were ready to move they wouldn't have to work on the kitchen range and the cabinets would be all nice and clean and painted ready to put the dishes in them. They would have plenty to do without having to worry about the kitchen range and the cabinets. They cleaned the kitchen range first with ammonia and Gus replaced all the burners and the drip pans, then he turned each on to see if they worked properly and thank goodness they did. Gus and his Wife got a system going on the water. They would fill the buckets and containers in the morning, then again in the late evening. This gave them water during the day for some dish washing, a little cooking, hand washing, toilet flushing, then at night they would heat water on the kitchen range and mix it with cold water in a two gallon watering can to take showers with. It was surprising how good a shower you could get with two gallons of water. Cleaning the kitchen cabinets was a time consuming and tedious job. First they had to use straight ammonia and a scrub brush, because there was so much grease that had stuck to them for so many years. The grease was even inside the cabinets and it was a terrible job to get in there and work. They had to go over the cabinets three times with straight ammonia before they could try to scrape and sand. They worked two days cleaning with straight ammonia, one day scraping and sanding and three days applying a primer and top coat of paint. Everything in the kitchen looked and smelled good now. All of this work took up all of their time they had allotted for their trip, so they didn't have any time to drive out to the Blue Quail Ranch. The next morning early Gus hooked up his 8 foot trailer to his Pick-up and they drove back to Sugarland. Their next trip would be during the Christmas Holidays and they would take another load in the trailer to the Van Horn House. Gus went back to work for three weeks before they went back out to Van Horn. This time Gus loaded up his office file cabinets and two desk's and office chairs along with his Wife's piano and a bedroom set in his trailer. Then he loaded some pots and pans and dishes they had boxed up, some of his tools and three cement bird baths along with an assortment of things that he had been saving for yard decorations, in the bed of his Pick-up. When they were driving through San Antonio they had a blow out on one of the tires on the trailer and Gus had to put on the spare tire, then he had to look for a place to buy a new tire. He found a place and decided to buy three new tires, so they would all match. Two for the trailer and one for the spare tire. They were then back on their way and this had cost them several hours, so they would be getting to Van Horn much later in the afternoon then usual. By the time they got to Van Horn it was getting late, so Gus decided that they would go through the routine of filling the buckets and containers with water then go to a Cafe for dinner and wait until the next morning to unload everything. It took them all the next morning to unload the trailer and the Pick-up. They had sandwiches and chips for lunch and then Gus decided that he was going to spend some time locating the outside water leaks to see if he could fix them so they could leave the water on while they were staying there. It was easy to locate the leaks, because the ground was wet there. Gus got the shovel he had brought and dug down in two spots that were wet and found water pipe that was so rusted that he could grab it in his hands and break it into. It was thin and riddled with rust holes. He dug back farther till he found some pipe that looked like it was a little better and then he took his hacksaw and cut it off there. He went to the local Hardware Store and bought some PVC pipe and some rubber hose that would slip over the PVC and the rusty pipe along with several hose clamps. It took Gus a couple of more hours to get the repair work done and he turned on the water to see if he had stopped the leaks. He watched it for a few minutes and didn't see any leaks, so he decoded to leave the water turned on. Just before dark he went back out in the yard to check things and he saw two more wet places not far from where he had repaired the old line, so he cut off the water for the night. The next morning Gus got dressed and went out to dig the two wet spots up and find the pipe. Gus found the leaks and he saw that when he fixed the other leaks that it put pressure on these spots and made them leak, so from this he knew that there was no use trying to fix that old water line. He wold have to replace all of it from the meter to the House, but that wouldn't happen until they moved out to Van Horn for good. They stayed one more night in Van Horn then they bought groceries and ice and drove to his Blue Quail Ranch. He was hoping that there wouldn't be any rats in the Camp House and that the 1/8 inch hardware cloth sleeve he had built to go over the outside the air conditioner had kept them out. They pulled up in front of the Camp House and Gus unlocked the door and went in to look around. He saw that the two mouse traps that he had set before he left the last time were still just the way that he had left them and he didn't see any sign of rat's in the Camp House. They unloaded and Gus turned on the water, then they made the beds and got everything ready to stay at the Ranch for a few days. As he sat in front the camp fire that evening he thought that it was good to have fixed the rat problem, but he didn't fix the water problem at the Van Horn House. Their Christmas vacation was a pleasant one and when they woke up on Christmas morning there was even a little snow on the ground. Gus and his Wife spent a lot of time exploring and looking for artifacts, fossils and semi-precious stones for Gus to take back to Sugarland so he could polish them. They both enjoyed their stay at the Ranch and on their way back to Sugarland his wife started crying. Gus asked her what was wrong and she said that she was just thinking that it was her last trip to the Desert for the year and it made her sad. Gus told her that 2,001 was coming to a close, but that they would be moving out to Van Horn permanently in just 8 months, so it wouldn't be long until she would be living in the Desert. New Years Eve this year was a time for Gus to reflect on his years of living in Sugarland and working for the Texas Department of Criminal Justice. This was the last New Years Eve he would spend in the House he had bought in Sugarland 10 years before. It was the last full year he would work for the Texas Prison Harvesting Department. He would be leaving the Gulf Coast of Texas, where he had lived all of his life and move to a completely different climate in a small town that had a population with a whole different culture. He would be leaving the El Campo area where he had Ranched and Farmed and he had started several businesses and had several divorces and his Son had been killed. He was leaving all of his Friends behind to chase the Dream he had, had ever since he was 19 years old. Thinking of when he was 19 years old brought back sweet memories of Lorrie and he thought that he was also leaving behind all the places that he had seen her, like the Service Station he had worked at and the time she had waved at him when she was going on that Band Trip to Corpus Christi and them on the beach kissing and kissing and kissing, then the time he was at her Mom and Dad's House and she was beautiful standing naked in front of him in her bedroom until her little Brother and Sister came home unexpectedly. Sweet, beautiful Lorrie, he wondered what had happened to her. He hoped that she had a great life and if he didn't have her at least he had all of those wonderful memories that would come to him in private times for him to enjoy for just a few minutes. The morning of the New Year 2,002 dawned and Gus was drinking his coffee making a list of all the things he needed to do to get ready to Retire and move from Sugarland and one of the first was to find a Real Estate Broker and put his House up for sale, because even though the housing market was good now it could take a while to get a buyer with the money and Gus didn't want to leave with having his House sold. January 2,002 had arrived and Gus was going to be 60 years old.

Lorrie—2001 The New Year of 2,001 had arrived with Lorrie sitting in front of the TV wondering what it would bring with it. She got a little sleep and now she was getting ready to go meet their friends for their annual New Years Day lunch. Their New Years day lunch was always a nice gathering and of coarse Lorrie's best friend Jill would be there and for her to see Jill on the first day of the New Year meant a good start for the year. Their conversation always covered a lot of subjects and Lorrie was waiting for someone to ask about her Stepson and how he was doing. She had already anticipated this and had a fine answer thought up. When she was asked about her Stepson and his Banking job she told them that he had felt that he had been placed in a dead end position that didn't create much chance for fast advancement, so he had resigned to accept a new job with another big Banking Firm that promised more of a challenge. Lorrie had to bite her tongue to get this untruth out, but she just couldn't let them know what she was really thinking. She told them about her Dad's illness and her stay back in Texas for three months, but most of the talk was cheerful and she went back home that afternoon feeling pretty good. Lorrie's New Year 2,001 afternoon was a quiet one and she went to her room to read and nap. At times like these she really missed her sweet little dog Mitzi, because Mitzi would curl up by her while she would read and when she got to an interesting part of the story she would read it out loud and Mitzi would look at her and cock her head to the side like she was really understanding her and Lorrie sometime thought that maybe she really did. Lorrie had thought that when her Stepson got his first job at that Big Bank in London that her worries were over about him and that he would go on and build a life for himself like most other young men, but now she was not so sure. The pills, alcohol and this Psychotherapist thing had her puzzled. She decided that she needed to talk to her Stepson about it so she could get a better understanding of what had happened, because she had been gone to Texas and had been left in the dark about the whole thing, just like when he had been Discharged from the Air Force. Lorrie's Husband was still making a very good living in his Tailoring business and when she had left for three months to Texas she had made arrangements to take of everything in advance of her leaving. She had made out checks for the bills that she knew were going to come on and addressed the envelops, so all he had to do was to fill in the amount of money and mail the check. She had also made out deposit slips so all he had to do was to fill in the amount and take them to the Bank. This system had worked out pretty good except when he would forget to leave cash receipts on her desk and she wanted all of them, even the ones for just a few cents, because she hated it when the Bank accounts didn't balance. It had taken her several weeks to get all of that straightened out when she got back from Texas, because there was a pile of papers on her desk, some on the bar and some in the kitchen. Her Husband never seemed to understand that keeping all paperwork in the same place was important. She finally got it all straightened out and now it was time to give it to his Tax Accountant to do their Taxes. She had waited for a month to talk to her Stepson about why he was seeing a Psychotherapist and taking those pills for depression. She had waited until her Husband had left for his ski Vacation, so he wouldn't step in and try to keep her from finding out the truth, because if that happened then there would be a big fight and she wanted to avoid that if she could. Her Stepson had been coming home from work in a good mood and exclaiming how much he liked this job and the Supervisors over him and that already they were talking about giving him a big promotion. Lorrie was hoping that this was the truth and not just something in his mind. One evening when her Stepson had come home from work, she had prepared his favorite dinner for him, to have him in a good mood for her to question him about the pills and the Psychotherapist. During dinner their conversation was about mundane subjects while Lorrie waited for the right opportunity to broach the subject she wanted to know about. Lorrie was clearing the dishes from the table and she asked her Stepson if he had any dishes up in his room that needed to be brought down to be washed, because she was going to wash the dishes and she would wash them with the ones from their dinner. He told her that he thought that there might be some up there and he would go up and bring them down. With this said it brought up the subject of his room and she waited for him to return with the dishes to ask him about the pills that she had seen in his room and that his Dad had told her about the Psychotherapist. He stared at her for a few seconds then slammed the dishes down on the counter top and accused her of snooping in his room and into his private business. She thought that he might be resistant to her questions, but this accusation shocked her. She knew that he was smart and he had proved himself capable of turning around a question to put her on the defensive before, but she wasn't falling for that this time, because she wanted to know what the hell was going on with this Psychotherapist. Lorrie told him that she hadn't been snooping and that he was now a grown man and should be living in his own apartment and that if he wanted his privacy he shouldn't have moved back in their house. Now she wanted to know what was going on. He told her that his Dad shouldn't have told her anything, because he knew that she would make a big deal about it and that it wasn't a big deal. He told her that at his old Bank job he had a big argument with his Supervisor and it got sort of out of hand so in order for him to stay employed there he was required to go to this Psychotherapist for evaluation and to have therapy for depression and extreme behavior tendencies. She asked him why he was still going since he wasn't working at that Bank anymore and he told her that he was required to go through all the treatment, so it wouldn't be reported on his work history to the Government. She asked him about the pills and he told her that they were also part of the treatment, so he had to take them. She told him that he didn't have to take them, that he could throw them away if he didn't need them and also she knew that they shouldn't be mixed with alcohol and she was sure that he had done that, because she had seen all the beer cans and wind bottles in his room. He bristled up and told her that she needed to mind her own business that he wasn't a little boy anymore and that he would find his own place as soon as he could afford it, then he marched off to his room and slammed his door. The next day Lorrie got an angry call from her Husband, in response to a call he had received from his Son, demanding that she quit berating his Son about his medical condition and that when he got home from his ski Vacation he would straighten her out about it, then he hung up the phone while she was trying to explain things to him. Lorrie thought that she was in for it when he got home. Her Stepson was still a problem between her and her husband and it had been that way ever since they had been Married and her Stepson had been 8 years old. She wondered why they had never been able to work together to try to solve problems with her Stepson. Everything that she had ever tried to do to correct him or to guide him had always back fired on her and it had caused her grief. Her Husband had always protected him from her and had taken his side even though he knew it was wrong and there had always been a secrecy between her Husband and her Stepson that would undermine what she was tying to do to help. Lorrie would never understand it, but she knew that she would probably get another beating when her Husband got home from his ski Vacation. Lorrie was keeping track of her Dad's health problems, by weekly phone calls back home to Texas. The reports she was getting indicated that the advancement of his Stage 3 Parkinson's disease was slow and she had even convinced her Dad's Doctor to send her a copy of his examination after each of his appointments and this way she could keep up with it through the medical language that she had been taught in when she was a Nurse. The next few days her Stepson was cool to her and they said very little to each other. He would come home after work and get a plate of food and go up to his room and that was about all that Lorrie would see of him. When her Husband came home from his ski Vacation he just looked at her with a skoal on his face, but didn't say anything, which she was glad of, because she had prepared for the worst. Lorrie didn't even ask him how he did on the slopes, because she didn't want to give him an opening to scream at her for ruining his Vacation. Her Husband and her Stepson would stop talking if she came into the room, or they would change the subject, so she knew that something was happening that they were keeping from her. Her Stepson finally got his own apartment and Lorrie decided that if he wasn't living with them then she wasn't going to worry about what he was doing. They didn't see a lot of him after he got his apartment, just a call now and then. One day he called and told them that if they were going to be home he wanted to introduce them to a girl that he had been dating for two months. Lorrie told him to bring her to dinner and they would be delighted to meet her. Lorrie cooked a pork loin roast on the rotisserie with a dressing and brown gravy, asparagus and split carrots brown wilted with butter and herbs in the skillet and a cherry cobbler with whipped cream for desert. Her Stepson and his girlfriend arrived on time and when Lorrie first saw her she thought that she was lovely. Her name was Cheryl and she had a sweet smile that gave away an inner goodness about her. Her manner of speaking was polite with a soft clear British accent that had a comforting sound to it. Lorrie took to her immediately. Cheryl was a Registered Nurse that worked at one of the major Hospitals in London and she came from a working family with good values. Lorrie's Husband behaved himself and drank coffee with them, instead of beer, when they were having their after dinner conversation. They stayed for three hours before leaving to go back to London to a concert with friends. After they left Lorrie told her Husband that she was very impressed with her Stepson's girlfriend and that she hoped that he would keep this one. Lorrie knew that she could be wrong especially after only one meeting, but everything about this girl was different then any of the other girls that her Stepson had brought home for them to meet. Lorrie hoped this would become a serious relationship for her Stepson, because it might be the thing that would make him into a responsible man, nothing else had up to this point. It was getting time for Lorrie to be thinking about her trip back to El Campo, Texas. She had started staying in El Campo for three months the last time she was there and she was planning on doing the same this year. Lorrie had two feelings about her trip back home to her parents house this year. One was that she was glad to get away from her Husband and the problems with him and her Stepson for three months and then there was the depressing sight of seeing the decline in her Dad's health. She knew that he wasn't going to be alive forever of coarse, but to know that he was slowly wasting away was hard for her to accept. He had been such of a physically active man all of his life and now she knew that he was probably feeling very useless to his family. Lorrie took extra money with her again to have her Mom put it in her Bank Account for her, just in case she had to leave England in a hurry. She was picked up by her Sister at the Houston Airport as usual and stayed with her for several days before going on to El Campo. Her Sister told her that she would see a definite difference in what her Dad could do for himself, although he could still take care of a lot of what he needed to do for himself, there were things that he couldn't quite manage on his own and he was starting to use a cane some to make himself more stable when walking, especially on uneven surfaces. Lorrie's Sister drove them to El Campo from Houston and Lorrie unloaded all her luggage and then sat down to visit for a minute with her family before unpacking. When she went over to hug her Dad she noticed right away that his face was drawn more then it was a year ago. She knew from all the research she had done on Parkinson's Disease that this was one of the effects that it produced, because of the nerve damage that kept his face from responding in a normal way. He smiled a little crooked and his eyes told her how glad he was to see her. Lorrie almost broke down, but kept her composure so her Dad wouldn't see her sadness. They talked for a while before it came time for their usual Happy Hour on the back patio. Lorrie helped her Dad out the back door, because it had a step down to the cement patio and he used his cane to keep him steady. Her Mom and her Sister brought them their drinks and this was the first time Lorrie had seen her Dad drink iced tea from a glass with a handle on it instead of his usual Shiner Bock from the bottle at their Happy Hour. No one said anything about it, just like it was a normal thing, but this also saddened Lorrie, because it was just one more indication that he was slipping slowly down a one-way tunnel. Lorrie's Brother went to the local Mexican Cafe and brought back a Mexican dinner for each of them and Lorrie got to sink her teeth into some real Tex-Mex food for the first time in a whole year and she loved every bite of it. After their dinner Lorrie got out the little gifts that she always brought them from England. She brought her Dad a couple of books to read that she thought that he would enjoy and she brought her Mom some real special chocolate from Paris. She also always brought gifts for her Sister and Brother. Lorrie's Sister stayed for several days then went back to Houston. Lorrie did a little shopping, again buying things that she planned on leaving at her Mom's house, so she would have cloths to wear if she had to flee England fast and not have time to pack. It was time for her to go to her favorite Hair Salon Friend to get her hair cut and colored and Lorrie wondered what color it would be this time. Every time her Friend mixed up color for her hair it turned out a little different. Lorrie would tell her Friend what color she wanted and her Friend would try and convince Lorrie that she should try another color, but Lorrie didn't want to change, so her Friend would say ok, but Lorrie thought that her Friend would use the color that she wanted anyway and that is why it always turned out different then Lorrie thought it should. While Lorrie was at her Friends Hair Salon she kept her ear tuned for any talk about Gus, but there wasn't anything mentioned that could have been about him. She had heard things there before and everybody knew that the Beauty Salons were the hot bed of gossip to find out what was going on in a town. She still had a lot of her Vacation to go and would be in the Salon several more times before she had to return to England, so there was still a chance that she might pick up some information about Gus. Lorrie would go with her Mom to do the grocery shopping and she would get a chance to look at all the new food items that would appear on the shelves that were different from the last time she had been El Campo a year before. She loved to go each row of shelves to inspect the new items. They were so different from what was offered in the Super Markets in England. The main Grocery Store in El Campo had a much bigger selection then in England and the meat department had much more to offer and at much cheaper prices. Lorrie would never completely adapt to the food in England although there were some things that she did like. She spent most of her time at home with her Dad and she insisted on being the one to take him to his scheduled Doctor's appointments. While she was there she would organize the closet that she kept her cloths and shoes in to see what else she might need to buy to give her a full complement clothing to start out with in case she would have to flee her Husband in England at a moments notice. This was also why she had started giving her Mom money to save for her. It wasn't a lot of money, but she would add to it every time she came back to El Campo, because she felt that sooner or later her Husband would get so abusive that she would have to leave him and she felt that she wouldn't be able to stay in England because of the way the Laws there favored the men. El Campo was her only safe haven, she thought. Lorrie's vacation stay in El Campo with her family was coming to an end and she had been to her Friend's Hair Salon for the last time and hadn't heard a word about Gus. Now that she was staying in El Campo for three months every summer she thought that she might run into Gus when he came back to town for a visit. She didn't know what she would do if she actually came face to face with Gus, probably pass out or say something stupid that would cause him to be glad that he hadn't fallen in love with her in 1962. She would have to cross that bridge when and if it ever happened. She had mixed feelings about seeing Gus again, but she knew that she would always love him. He was the only man that she had ever loved and she knew that he was the only man that she would ever love, but it was just so impossible. She did her grocery shopping that she always did to take her Texas food back to England and the last day before her flight back she took her Gus tour to make a quick visit back in time to look and remember all the wonderful dreams she had about her and Gus being together as she looked at the different places that reminded her of her precious Gus. The next day Lorrie said good by to her Mom and Dad and took a longer time then usual to look in her Dad's eyes and hug him extra hard, then her Brother drove her to the Airport in Houston, Texas for her long flight back to England. Lorrie's arrival back in England was always an adjustment after being in Texas for three months. It always took her a couple of days to get back gear, so she could go through all the mail and figure out if her Husband had done what he was supposed to do. She found out that her Stepson was still dating that Nurse Cheryl that she liked so much and that pleased her. Her Husband was all upset, because he thought that he had been cheated out of some cash money that one of the smaller Garment Shops had owed him. He worked for them sometime when he had time and they payed him cash, which he hid at home. Lorrie really wasn't in the mood to hear him rave and rant about it for hours on end and she couldn't even make a judgment on it, because she had been in Texas when her Husband made the deal and she new nothing of his conversation with the other party. For all she knew her Husband might have done the deal when he had been drunk and really didn't remember what he had agreed to, because she had seen him do that several times and when this happened she always wrote down what was said and the date, so she could go back to her Husband and show him what he had agreed to and this would calm him down, but he had done this while she was gone, so all she could do was to listen to him raise hell. She thought that at least he wasn't raising hell with her, at least not right now. Lorrie's Stepson was beginning to act more like a grown up man should act. He and his girlfriend Cheryl would even come to Bromley for the weekends sometime and they all would go to a local Pub they liked and have dinner and drinks for an enjoyable evening. Lorrie also noticed that her Stepson had been working at the same Bank now for most of the year and wasn't complaining about how stupid his Bosses were. Lorrie attributed all of her Stepsons newly acquired good disposition to the obvious example that his girlfriend Cheryl was exhibiting. He was actually a pleasure to be around for the first time in his life. Lorrie was so pleased that she took Cheryl in the Ladies Room with her and told her that she was hoping that one day soon Cheryl would become her Daughter-In-Law. Her Stepson's girlfriend Cheryl was a breath of fresh air that gave Lorrie renewed hope of a better home life with her Husband. She thought that maybe, just maybe finally, Cheryl would be the driving influence that could turn things around and make life more pleasant. A beautiful, smart, level headed, young woman like Cheryl could make a positive difference in her Stepson, which would make a positive difference in her Husband, which would make a positive difference in Lorrie's home life. Well, Lorrie would be really looking forward to the Holiday Season this year, for the first time in several years and she could now enjoy buying gifts for someone new that she liked. Christmas suddenly had a new excitement to it. Lorrie had a new interest in getting everything ready for the Holidays. She got out all her old decorations for Christmas and went through them and discarded some of the older ones and made herself a list of the new ones that she wanted to buy to replace them. She was going to go all out and had started early playing Christmas music while she was doing all of this. Her Husband thought that she had lost her mind and it irritated him some for her to have that Christmas music playing so early, but Lorrie shrugged his comments off and continued her planning. Lorrie's Stepson and Cheryl came over on the weekend and Cheryl helped Lorrie decorate the house with the new Christmas decorations while Lorrie's Husband and her Stepson went to the local Christmas tree lot and bought a Christmas tree and brought it home. Lorrie hadn't had this much fun in years getting ready for the Holidays. Lorrie and Cheryl got along wonderfully and while they were decorating they also discussed her Stepson and Cheryl's relationship. Cheryl told Lorrie that she really liked Lorrie's Stepson and that they were talking about getting another apartment and moving in together. This pleased Lorrie and she told Cheryl that she had no objections to it and that she thought it a good idea to see if they would be compatible living together. Lorrie was careful not to tell Cheryl any of the negative points that she knew about her Stepson hoping that he would mend them to please Cheryl. Lorrie remembered her own experiences living with two different men at two different times and not being married to them, so how could she protest and beside she had already seen such a marked improvement in her Stepson that she wanted to encourage it. Their Christmas 2,001 was the best that Lorrie had experienced in many years and Lorrie even received a Christmas gift from someone besides herself as the giver. Cheryl and her Stepson gave Lorrie two great books, one on the History of the Roman Empire in England and one on the Texas Revolution from Mexico. These were books that Lorrie would enjoy reading and she knew that Cheryl must have chosen them, because her Stepson would have never gone to that trouble. Cheryl also had helped Lorrie to plan and prepare their Christmas dinner and Lorrie had never before had any such experience that pleased her more for Christmas. This Christmas was one that Lorrie would remember for a long time. Cheryl noticed that her and Lorrie's Stepson's gift was the only one that Lorrie had received except the one that Lorrie had given to herself. Lorrie asked Cheryl if she and her Stepson would come to a New Years party at Lorrie's house and Cheryl asked Lorrie's Stepson about it and he thought it would be nice, so Lorrie decided to have a New Years party and invite just a few friends so she could introduce them to her Stepsons girlfriend Cheryl. Cheryl would be the guest of honor. Lorrie's Husband was even putting an extra effort forward to better behave himself when Cheryl was around. Her New Years party was a success and almost every guest stayed till the New Year of 2,002 arrived and they all toasted the New Year and also they toasted Cheryl and her Stepson. After the party Cheryl helped Lorrie clean up a little and put things away then she and Lorrie's Stepson left to take the train back to London. Lorrie was so proud of her Husband for not getting falling down drunk at Christmas and at the News Years party, so after everyone left she went up to him and gave him a kiss that he didn't return. They hadn't kissed in years, so Lorrie thought that he would be pleased and respond to her kiss, but he just glared at her. She went on up stairs to bed and left her Husband sitting on the couch in the living room. The next morning was New Years Day 2,002 and Lorrie went down to put on a pot of tea and warm a few sweet pastries for breakfast. She found her Husband asleep on the couch and thought that he must have stayed up and drank himself into a stupor, because she saw a partial glass of whiskey on the coffee table by the couch. She drank two mugs of tea and ate a couple pastries, then woke her Husband up and told him that it was getting late and they needed to start getting ready for their New Years Day tradition of meeting their old Friends for the New Years Day 2,002 lunch. While Lorrie was getting ready for their lunch she looked at herself on the mirror and thought my goodness it's 2,002 and this next May it would be 40 years since her and Gus had been kissing on the beach in Corpus Christi, Texas. She smiled to herself and puckered her lips in a mock recreation of her and Gus kissing and she thought that it was much better then the kiss she had given her Husband the night before. Lorrie was more upbeat for the New Year 2,002, because of the positive effect Cheryl, her Stepsons girlfriend, was having on her Stepson and her Husband. For the first time in a while she had a positive outlook for the year of 2,002.

Gus—2,002 was going to be a year of great change for Gus. This would be his Retirement year and his focus was going to be on getting everything done that needed to be, so he could leave Sugrland as soon as he could when his Retirement date arrived. He had a local Real Estate Agent that he had used when he bought his house there in Sugarland 10 years ago and he went back to him to sell the same house. His Real Estate Agent told him that that were going to put the house on the market for $98,000.00 and that the way houses were selling in Sugarland he should get that price. This made Gus happy, because he had only paid $60,000.00 for it when he bought it. He still owed some money on it, but there would be a large equity balance in it for him to add to his cash for him to take to Van Horn, Texas when he moved out there. Gus was hoping to take $90,000.00 total cash with him to Bank in Van Horn. This would give him enough money to finish renovating that old house there and money to have on hand plus the income he would still have from a few lots in the Subdivision he had developed in Wharton County and the payments from the sale of his Ranch House and the rest of his Farm Land in Wharton County and a small Retirement Check from the State Of Texas. The next thing that Gus needed to do was to make a trip to Austin, Texas to make out his Retirement Papers and get a definite Retirement Date. Gus went back to work, but he would be taking a lot of time off to start making trips out to Van Horn with his 8 foot trailer hauling loads of home furnishings to the house in Van Horn. He already had that agreement with his Boss, so he wouldn't be surprised at Gus using a lot of Vacation and banked Overtime in doing this. Gus told his Boss that he would work a couple of weeks and then he would take four days off then come back to work and keep repeating this schedule until he had everything that he needed to move. At home Gus and his wife started to box up things that he would need to move and that would include some furniture. The Real Estate Agent already had his house advertised on the market and Gus had included in the in the Real Estate Contract that he would have the right to keep living in the house until his Retirement Date was reached. The first of March, when most of the bad winter weather, snow and ice, was over Gus left Sugarland with a load to take to Van Horn. He had made arrangements for a man there to help him unload the heavy furniture. He arrived in Van Horn in the middle of the afternoon without any problems on the road and contacted the man that was to help him. They unloaded everything then Gus handed him a $20.00 dollar bill and then they sat on the back porch and shared a six pack of beer and talked. Gus liked this man and he gave Gus a lot of information about different people and the goings on in the small town of Van Horn. Gus felt that all of this would be important for him to know, being new in town. While Gus was on this trip he had instructed his wife to start going through other things and pack them with labels, so he would know what was in the boxes, because when he got back he could start loading them in his trailer for the next trip. Gus was stacking boxes and furniture in different rooms in the Van Horn House out of the way, just so he could move around. Nothing would be arranged where it should be for two reasons. First every room would be completely redone and secondly he had no idea yet where the furnishings would fit. He knew that he was going to change the location of several doors, which meant that he was going to have to close up some door openings and open the walls for others. His plans were to take one room at a time and complete the renovation on it then move on to the next room. He wanted to do the downstairs bathroom first then the kitchen and go from there, but he know knew that he would have to replace all of the water pipes outside that supplied the house and he thought that he needed to replace them inside also. He also knew that the downstairs bathroom sewer line would have to be replaced. Gus estimated that he might be able to get the downstairs bathroom functioning enough to take a shower and use the toilet in two weeks, until then things would be a little primitive. Gus drove back to Sugarland to work a few days before he loaded up to make another trip to Van Horn. Gus continued this schedule of trips moving most of what they could to Van Horn and keeping a bare minimum in the Sugarland House so they could still live there. The Real Estate Agent had showed Gus's house to several prospective buyers and had received some bids in line with the asking price. Gus had received his Retirement Date of August 31st, 2,002, so he had to be able to live in his house till September 1st, 2,002. One of the buyers wanted to give Gus a bonus if he would move before then, but Gus turned him down. Gus didn't want to have to move twice in a short period of time. In May Gus was sent down to one of the Prison Farms to get the Self Propelled Carrot Digger set correctly and to start their carrot harvest and while riding on the outside of it giving instructions to the Inmate Operator a big wind caught the open door to the cab and blew it into Gus's face and knocked him off to the ground on his back and it injured his back and neck with severe pain. Gus was driven back to Sugarland by another Supervisor and he went to see a Doctor. The Doctor ordered x-rays then sent him to a Laboratory for a cat-scan and an appointment with a Neurologist. They decided to try muscle relaxers, pain medicine and Chiropractor treatments to see what the results would be before considering surgery. This helped, but the pain was still there and Gus would have help when he loaded his truck and trailer to make trip to Van Horn and then he had the man in Van Horn to help him unload. It was a good thing that Gus had made so many trips hauling things out there before his accident, because he only had a couple of those trips to make after he got hurt and he had moved everything that he could until the last day that they left Sugarland for good. Gus finally decided to take a bid from a woman that was moving from California to the Houston area and it was for $104,000.00 dollars, which was $6,000.00 above his asking price and she was fine with him living in the house till September 1st, 2002. Their last day in Sugarland Gus rented a covered U-Haul trailer, that would be pulled by his Jeep Cherokee to haul all the rest of the things that he couldn't get in his 8 foot trailer and the bed of his Pick-up. They slept on the floor that night, because the bed was loaded, and they left the morning of September 1st, 2,002 at 5:00am and never looked back. He had closed the book on his life in Sugarlnd and on his work career with the Texas Department Of Criminal Justice. He was leaving the Gulf Coast where he had lived for most of his life and Ranched, Farmed, married, divorced, buried his Dad, Mom and oldest Son, started businesses in Residential Development, Oil & Gas, Home Health, ran a campaign for Public Office and had been an intricate part of the Business and Social fabric of the area for so many years. He was looking ahead to finally fulfill the final step in a dream he had 40 years ago, (1962-2002), to live in the high Mountain Chihuahua Desert Region of Far West Texas and now he was going to do it and not look back. Gus was 20 years old when he first developed his dream to live in Far West Texas and now he is 60 years old. He realizes that he has a big task ahead with all the work he has to do on the old house that he bought in Van Horn and that most of it will be done by him and he also knows that the work isn't the only thing that he will have to do, because the culture in Van Horn is completely different then where he has lived most of his life, it is a culture that is based primarily on the customs from south of the Texas border in Chihuahua, Mexico and he knew that he had to learn the culture and adapt to it. All of this was quite a chore for an older man, but Gus felt that he was up to it. After they arrived in Van Horn they unloaded just what they would need for the night and the next morning and then went through the system of turning on the water at the meter to fill their buckets and containers, then turning it off again, because of all the leaks in the outside water pipes. They then went to the Grocery Store to buy the food that they would need for a few days. The old House had a refrigerator left in it that was working fine and they had brought their refrigerator with them from Van Horn, but they wouldn't unload it till the next day, then they would have two refrigerators and freezers going. They made the bed, put out clean towels and wash cloths and unloaded pots, pans and dishes and put these things up in their painted cabinets. After getting a little organized they went to a local Mexican Cafe and ate their dinner, then went back to the House to look things over and choose the first place to start working. Gus's next day was mostly taken up with unloading the rest of their things out of the U-Haul trailer, the 8 foot trailer, the Jeep Cherokee and his Pick-up truck.. Then he was trying to move some furniture so they could use their chest-of drawers for some of their cloths and the hanging cloths were scattered around where ever they could put them, because there were no closets down stairs except for a entry closet by the staircase. Gus could see that they would be living in an unorganized house for many months to come and this aggravated him, because he had always been such of an organized person, but he could see no alternative to this situation when everything was going to have to be moved around all the time as required to allow for work to be done in each room. His plan for the next day was to go outside and try to figure out just what he would have to do to replace all the water lines to the house and the ones that serviced the faucets in the yard. He was going have to do that before he could renovate the bathroom and have it serviceable. The next morning Gus was walking around outside looking everything over and what he noticed made him shake his head wondering why he hadn't noticed it before. The yard was so uneven with low's and high's that you had to be careful how you walked, so you wouldn't stumble. There were patches of Bermuda grass here and there interspersed with bare ground and rocks, but what struck Gus was that the dirt level of the yard was the same height as the cement porch all around the house and is some places even a bit higher. This was why when it rained hard that dirt would be washed across the porch. Gus saw that there was no way that he could simply dig trenches and replace the water supply lines. He was going to have to somehow remove six to eight inches of dirt from the entire yard before he could replace the water supply lines, because if he replaced them first he would tear them up when he was removing the dirt. This was going to slow him down in getting running water in to the house. This was a big lot 100 feet wide and 100 feet long inside the fence, so he couldn't do this by hand with shovels and wheelbarrows. What he would need was someone with a backhoe front-end loader tractor and a dump truck to do the big work and several men with shovels and wheelbarrows to work where the tractor couldn't work. Also he would need to set up his surveying instrument to make sure the level of the yard stayed level as the work proceeded. Gus also noticed that the shingles on the roof looked fairly new, but several had been blown off in high winds, so he knew that he would need to replace the roof with metal, so it would withstand the high wind better. It was September and Gus knew from experience how quickly the weather could change in late October to winter storms, so that meant that he would have to get as much of these big outside projects done before November hit and even late October weather could be unpleasant for outside work. Gus contacted the friend, Walley, he had made in Van Horn when he had been hauling out furniture that he needed help to unload. Walley gave him the name of a man, Henry, there in Van Horn that did heavy machinery work with a backhoe tractor, maintainer and bulldozer. Gus went and talked to Henry and invited him to come to the House to look over the job ahead. Henry told Gus that he could do the job and that he could dump the extra dirt that he removed from the yard across a low cinder block fence, that divided the yard from Gus's vacant lot and then he could load it into his dump truck and take it to a hole on his own property that he wanted to fill up. Gus still needed some men on the ground to do the work that the backhoe couldn't do and he asked Henry if he knew any men he could trust to do the work. Henry told Gus that he did and that he would get him four men. Gus already had the shovels and two wheelbarrows, so he was ready. They set up the start day on the next Monday. They worked for two weeks on this dirt work and they ended up removing ten, ten yard dump trucks of dirt from the yard and that is 100,000 cubic yards of dirt. In the mean time Gus located a man that did roofing in El Paso that came out to give Gus an estimate on the new metal roof and said that he could start the second week of October. Gus also wanted him to replace all the warped wood on the dormer's and insulate them then cover them with hardy plank, because it wouldn't rot or warp. The estimate was $10,000.00 and Gus signed off on the deal. Well Gus's estimate that he would have the downstairs bathroom in service in two weeks was laughable, because he didn't even have the new outside water service lines installed by then. Gus had been working on the little upstairs bathroom while the dirt removal had been going on in the yard.

He had completely torn everything out of it. The old shower, the toilet, the sink and some of the flooring. He had also torn out all the water lines and drain lines that were under the floor, because they were either plugged up or leaking. To do this he had to work on a ladder in a small pantry that was very cramped for space which gave him limited room to use pipe wrenches that had handles long enough to use sufficient force to break loose the old rusted pipe and this gave him a lot of trouble, but after several days he succeeded in removing all of the old piping. Gus drove to El Paso and bought a new toilet, small shower, vanity, light fixture, exterior plywood for the flooring and enough plywood to cover all the walls. Then he started to completely redo the upstairs bathroom and by the time all the dirt work had been completed he was ready to start painting the walls and then installing all the bathroom fixtures, which would take him another two weeks. As soon as the dirt removal was finished Gus rented a trencher and made the trenches for the water supply lines and the Roofer showed up and he started on the roofing. Gus was working on putting in the water supply lines and their shutoffs and drains and the risers for the outside faucets while the Roofer was working on the roof and the dormers. Gus stubbed out the water line for the downstairs bathroom and installed the hot and cold water lines to the upstairs bathroom, so it was ready to use before the downstairs bathroom was ready, which was exactly opposite of what Gus thought was going to happen. He also ran the hot and cold water lines to the kitchen sink, so for the first time in over a month they had a bathroom that they could take a good shower, use the toilet and a kitchen sink that they could use without having to haul water by hand to use them. This was a real blessing in comfort, plus the savings in time and work. Sure enough the third week of October a cold Norther blew in and it even rained a little and that made it hard for the Roofer to continue his work. Gus was working inside the House now renovating the downstairs bathroom. It had been a tiny thing with barley enough room to have a bath tub, toilet and sink and to use the toilet you had to sit a little off center, because the sink protruded out to close to it. There were tiles on the wall about half way up from the floor that were falling off, so Gus took all of them off and there was a wall that separated the little bathroom from a little room that had a linen pantry and a door at each end giving access between the two downstairs bed rooms. This space was totally useless and Gus tore all of that out and made the whole thing a bathroom. He cut new doorways in the walls on either side and closed the old doorways in and he found out that the old floor in the bathroom had been rotted out and cement had been poured in it's place with the original wood floor in good shape in the area that he included in the new bathroom space. Well he had to do something with this, because he was going to have to run new water lines and a new sewer line out of the bathroom, because he had found that when he flushed the toilet that it was draining out in the yard, which meant that it was stopped up or broken underground and the cement in this old floor would either have to be broken out and removed or he would have to build a floor above it with enough room for him to crawl under it and work to run the sewer drain line and the water lines. He opted to build a raised floor above the old cement floor. This construction went really good for Gus and the raised floor fit perfect. It gave him eighteen inches of work room under it so he could make all the holes through the exterior rock wall that he would need and also he could run all new water and sewer lines. All of Gus's new water and sewer lines outside and inside were to be PVC, so there would be no rusting through or corrosion. While he was doing this his wife accepted an invitation to visit part of her family out of state for two weeks, so Gus took her to the Airport in El Paso and he continued to work on the downstairs bathroom. During this time he installed the new toilet, big shower and sink vanity. He was in the process of cutting fitting and gluing the PVC together when he became violently sick, so he had to stop working. He became very weak and his fever climbed as high as 105* degrees. He was having chills and fever and he thought that he had the flew. He was much to weak to go to the little Clinic to see a Doctor Assistant, because there were no Doctors in Van Horn at the time. He doctored himself with Alka Seltzer, aspirin, whiskey hot toddies and finally felt like he could make it to the Clinic. They sent him to the Hospital for blood and urine samples that were sent to Laboratory in El Paso and it was 10 days before he got the results from the Laboratory. They found nothing wrong and by this time he had completely overcome what ever was wrong with him and had been back at work on his House. Gus came to the conclusion that he had gotten poisoning from the PVC glue when he was working under the bathroom floor gluing all the pipe together. That's why the Laboratory didn't find anything, because they were looking for infections and not chemical poisons. He learned a valuable lesson there and vowed to never work in a small area gluing PVC again without adequate ventilation for fresh air. Gus then went outside and dug out the old sewer drain pipe all the way to where it connected into the sewer drain from the upstairs bathroom and the kitchen and washer drain.

He replaced this with new PVC and his downstairs bathroom was ready to test for water leaks. This done and no leaks found Gus then built a two step stair case to go up to the bathroom from the entry that was at floor level and he had left a crawl space to one side that he covered with a panel that could be removed if need be to access the plumbing under the new bathroom floor. After Gus did his masonry work on the walls and repainting everything it was time to do the floor tile that he had purchased for the downstairs and up stairs bathrooms. Gus finished both bathrooms and took a day off from his renovation work to just rest and read a good book. Since moving to Van Horn and not having any TV Gus started reading books when he had time to rest from his renovation work and he discovered that he enjoyed reading much more then he liked watching TV and he also realized that through reading that he was educating himself on a lot of subjects that he hadn't known much about before. Reading good books became a great enjoyment for Gus that he looked forward to each day. They were like a good friend that was there just waiting for him to go to for relaxation and companionship. He could put his book mark in the book and lay it down and go do what he had to do and when he returned it was laying there waiting for him to pick it up and resume reading where he had left off even several days before. Gus found that doing without the TV was a blessing and he had lost all interest in watching Television. Reading had opened new worlds for Gus and he found himself devouring books on many different subjects. It was the middle of November now and the Thanksgivings would be upon them soon. Gus was glad that he had accomplished so much in September and October because now he could concentrate on working on the inside of the House during the bad weather of the winter months. Two of his boys and their families were coming for Thanksgiving and the House was still a mess, but at least he had the bathrooms ready for them to be used. Now he was going to at least try to get a little organization into the bedrooms so they could spend a couple of nights in the House then they all would go to the Blue Quail Ranch for several days to hunt and have a good time together. After the Thanksgiving Holidays were over and his boys had gone back to their homes Gus decided to work on their bedroom which required building two closets one for him and one for his wife. Now they had to take everything out of their bedroom and put it in the living room, so Gus had room to work and then he would also be able to patch up places in the wall with stucco and caulking and then repaint the whole bedroom. When remodeling the whole House moving everything around from room to room was a constant thing and sometimes Gus couldn't remember where his chest-of-drawers was so he could get cloths out to put on and he would have to go from room to room looking for it. Gus got their bedroom ready just before Christmas, so they moved all of their bedroom furniture back to the bedroom and were able to get it all arranged with clothes hanging in real closets for a change and that gave them some room in the living room to be able to put up a Christmas tree. Gus was feeling pretty good about what he had accomplished by Christmas 2002. He had three rooms completely renovated in the House and two of them were bathrooms which had to be completely torn out and redone, which was a big job. He had also had all the dirt removed from the yard so he could replace all the water service lines and do some sewer replacement and he had a Roofing Contractor put on a new metal roof. He thought that for an old man of 60 years of age he had done real well. Gus's next room to renovate would be the kitchen. Gus took out an old leaky dishwasher and built another cabinet in it's place. They needed the extra cabinet storage space more then a dish washer. He then boxed in the vent from the old water cooler that he decided not to use and he put a shelf there for his wife to store her cooking spices. He cut out a place in the ceiling that had been ruined by water leaks from the upstairs bathroom and replaced it then he filled in a place left open in the kitchen ceiling and the kitchen and also the living room walls from the removal of the old defunct wall heater. He did his caulking and stucco work and then it was time for painting. The painting would have to wait for the New Year of 2,003, because he had run out of time and it was now time to be thankful for all that he had accomplished. He decided that he was going to stop work for a couple of days for New Year 2,003 and just relax. It was hard for Gus to do because he could see how much he had left to work on. New Years Eve Gus and his wife drank a couple of egg-nog's and Gus put a shot of whiskey in his and then they went to bed. New Years 2,003 morning Gus went upstairs and lit the gas heater to warm it up there, because he had plans to go up later and plug in his record player and listen to old music and sip a few whiskey's and water. He had saved a lot of his old 45 rpm records from High School days and he just had a sudden desire to play and listen to that old Rock-N-Roll again. After lunch Gus went upstairs and turned on his record player, got out his old records, opened the record box and decided that he was going to just reach in and play the record he took out and it was "Rock Around The Clock" by Bill Haley and The Comets. Gus poured himself a whiskey and water and sat back in his chair to listen and think back about those times. The next record was "Blue Berry Hill" by Fats Domino, then he played "The Great Pretender" by the Platters, then "Wake Up Little Susie" by the Everly Brothers, then he pulled out "In The Still Of The Night" by the Five Satins. Gus looked at the record for a long time and it still had Lorrie's writing on it. She had written <u>With Love, Lorrie</u> on it and Gus ran his fingers over her writing softly, almost treating the writing as if it were a precious historical document. He poured himself another whiskey and water, then he put the record on the turntable and started the record. As it started playing the memories flooded over him and he lost himself in those times so long ago, wonderful times, young times in his life filled with Hot Rods, great music like this and beautiful young girls like Lorrie. The song ended and Gus started it again and sipping his whiskey, listening carefully to the words, "that night in May" and it was a night in May that he and Lorrie were on the beach in Corpus Christi in 1962, "I held you tight" and they did hold each other tight and the words went on and Gus was right back on that beach with Lorrie kissing her and her kissing him back and molding her young firm body against his so as to be one body. The song ended and it was a minute before Gus could shake off the feeling of being by himself and that Lorrie wasn't there with him. Gus was thinking about Lorrie's sweet kisses and that he had never, ever kissed a girl that could kiss like Lorrie. Why, he wondered had her kisses been so special and why hadn't he been able to be satisfied by other girls kisses. Gus still yearned for those kinds of kisses and no girls kisses since then had ever come close to satisfying his desire for them. He softly ran his fingers over Lorrie's writing again, <u>With Love, Lorrie</u>, then he smiled, shook his head, kissed his fingers and blew Lorrie a kiss, just like she had done to him when she had walked around his Mom's house in her black dancing stretch outfit when she was about 14 years old. Well it was a very nice memory to start the first day of the New Year 2,003 for Gus.

Lorrie—2,002 had the possibilities of being a good year for Lorrie and the main reason for this was the positive influence her Stepson's girlfriend Cheryl was having on her Stepson and her Husband. Lorrie was all smiles and happiness at their traditional New Years Day lunch with their friend. She was really enjoying it more this year it seemed like to her. Lorrie's mind felt clearer and without the usual heavy dread of starting a New Year wondering what was going to happen to her Stepson and if she was going to be able to stay with her Husband. They had Cheryl now as a part of their family and Lorrie's

Husband even liked her, which made things much easier. The talk around their lunch table was happy talk and the others were asking if Lorrie's Stepson was going to marry Cheryl. Lorrie told them that she would like that and time would tell, but she did know that they were talking about moving in together to see how things worked and to her that was a good sign. After their lunch they went back home and Lorrie got comfortable and decided that she was going to start reading on one of the books that her Stepson and Cheryl had given her for Christmas and she chose the one on the Texas Revolution From Mexico and took it upstairs to her bedroom to read and take a nap. Lorrie read for a while on the book and became sleepy and drifted off. She woke up suddenly when her Husband shook her and told her that he wanted to have sex. She told him that she was sleepy, but he insisted and she did as usual which was to turn over and pull her gown up and he crawled in her bed with her. This was hurting her real bad and she was becoming sick at her stomach listening to him grunt like an animal. It didn't last long and he got up and left her room and then Lorrie wept in her pillow. He hadn't been in her room for sex in a long time and Lorrie had hoped that he had lost his desire for sex, because she had tried to discourage him in ways that wouldn't create a violent reaction from him. Lorrie knew that her Husband was aware that she didn't want sex with him anymore, so she considered his rough sex acts, that contained no kisses and no sweet words, to satisfy himself nothing more then rape. Rape that she could do nothing about, but hope that he finally he would loose all desire for sex. This ruined her first day of the New Year 2,002. Thank goodness her husband left on his ski vacation and she was shed of him for two weeks. She decided that she needed to go to her Doctor and talk to him about it and maybe he could do something to stop it. She had talked to her other Doctor about this a few years ago and was told that he couldn't interfere, but she had a new Doctor now and would discuss it with him. A few days later Lorrie did make an appointment with her Doctor and she discussed her problem with him. He told her about the same thing that the other Doctor had told her, that sex with her Husband was expected of her and all he could do for her was to recommend a lubricant that would help to relieve her pain. He told her that he understood what she was experiencing and that there were many married women that came to him with the same problem. He could only a recommend a lubricant to help relieve her physical pain and maybe suggest her and her Husband go to a Marriage Consular for help. Lorrie thanked him and left knowing that if she suggested a Marriage Consular to her Husband that he would fly into a rage. Well this was just something that she would have to put up with, but on the bright side her Stepson had chosen a real winner for his girlfriend and Lorrie could finally have pride in him finally finding stability as a man. While her Husband was on his ski vacation Lorrie spent some time with her Stepson and Cheryl when they were looking for an apartment and when they decided on one Lorrie helped them move in and she even cooked them their first dinner there. Lorrie left them after Cheryl helped her clean up their kitchen and they were starting to sort through their packed belongings to figure where to put them. Lorrie felt real good about their relationship and she went home with positive attitude about their future together. The winter passed and spring brought better weather that raised Lorrie's spirits. She saw an advertisement that was announcing the organizing of a Country and Western Dance Club. This really caught Lorrie's eye, so she read more and the ad. explained that the members would be required to wear authentic Texas style Western Wear of Cowboy Hat, Western Shirt, Western String Tie, Blue Jeans, Western Belt, Cowboy Boots. Pistols, Gun Belt, Holster and Spurs would be optional. All the music would be Classic Country and Western and also the latest Country and Western Hits. Couples only would be admitted into membership. This was right up Lorrie's alley and she couldn't wait to find a way to approach her Husband with the idea of joining this Dance Club. That evening Lorrie cooked her Husband his favorite dinner and she even brought him beer from the refrigerator before dinner was ready. She listened to him complain about what he had heard on the Radio Talk Shows that he listened to while he was working in his shop in the back yard and this was something that she hated to do, because he went on and on about things that he could do nothing about, but this time Lorrie pretended to sympathize with his views. Lorrie had written down all the advertisement on the Country and Western Dance Club and she had conveniently placed it where he could see it. He went into the living room after his dinner and saw it laying on the coffee table and took it back into the kitchen to ask what it was Lorrie said that she had seen the advertisement and thought that he might be interested in it, because one of his friends in the Garment Business loved Country and Western Music and he could show the advertisement to him and also the Dance Club was serving actual Kentucky Whiskey at their Bar. Lorrie was clever enough to plant a seed that would grow into this being her Husbands idea. She had already talked to his friends wife and she was excited about joining the Club if Lorrie and her Husband were to also. Both wives had designed this plan together so each could support the other in getting their Husbands to commit to joining. Their Husbands talked about joining, but left the details to their wives, which is exactly what Lorrie wanted to happen. The women promptly joined and payed the membership fee then met to go shopping for Western attire for themselves and their Husbands. Within two days the Wives had everything done down to the last detail and were ready for their first Country and Western Dance. The met at the Dance Club and were pleased to see some many members dressed up in their best Western Regalia. Some of the men actually wore gun belts featuring two Colt six shooters just like the old Western Gun Slinger in the Western Movies, that people in England loved. The music was very good Country and Western and the members were doing the Western two step and then there was line dancing and, yes the Bar did sell real Kentucky Whiskey. Lorrie's Husband really enjoyed himself and the Kentucky Whiskey and he told her that he was glad that she had seen that advertisement and that he wanted her to buy him some more Western clothes so he have a choice of what he wanted to wear each time. Lorrie and her Husband's friends Wife just smiled at each other with the knowledge that they had accomplished a job well done. Lorrie looked at this Dance Club as a small connection to her past life in Texas listening to the music and going to those dances, when she was a young girl, at the country dance halls around El Campo, Taiton and Hillje. She felt that this would be another good distraction to take her mind off of how miserable she was being married to her Husband. Summer would soon be arriving and that would mean that Lorrie would be going on her annual three month vacation back to El Campo, Texas. She was busy planning for that now. The planning for her summer three month vacation back to El Campo, Texas took much more time now then it did when she was only gone for one month, because it also involved making special arrangements with Business that they used and the way the bills were going to be paid. Lorrie always had to make out checks in advance to all the businesses and utilities for the three month period and put them in order along with their addressed envelopes, so her Husband could simply mail them as they came in and she had to do a similar thing for Bank deposits that they were expecting for work he was doing for the Big Garment Companies. All of this would be lined up in order so her Husband wouldn't get confused on what to do. She also had to make her Flight arrangements well in advance so she could get the best price on it. Lorrie and her Husband were still enjoying their new membership in the Country and Western Dance Club and Lorrie was spending as much time as possible with Cheryl, her Stepson's girlfriend. The day finally came for Lorrie to fly to Houston, Texas for the start of her three month vacation in El Campo, Texas. On Lorrie's arrival at the Houston Airport her Sister picked her up, as usual, so she could stay with her for a few days before they both drove to El Campo to their parents house. Lorrie rested up for a day, because the long flight seemed to take more out of her each time now. She was going to be 57 years old this year and she thought that sometime she felt every day of it and the fatigue these long flights brought on proved it to her. The next day her and her Sister went shopping and Lorrie bought a couple of things that she would wear while she was in El Campo, but she would leave them there when she went back to England, because they would be a part of her emergency clothing stash in case she had to suddenly flee England from her Husband. Lorrie and her Sister arrived at their parents house in El Campo and her Sister was going to stay for the weekend and then drive back to Houston. They pulled up in the driveway of her parent's house and the first thing Lorrie did was go in to hug her Dad. He was sitting in his easy chair waiting for Lorrie and the first thing different that Lorrie noticed was that he had given up his walking cane for a walker. She knelt down by his chair and threw her arms around his and hugged him, then gave him a kiss on the cheek and looked him in the eyes with that dazzling, big smile and sparkling eyes and told him that she loved him and had missed him. He looked at Lorrie and she could see that his eyes were beginning to moisten up and a small tear started seeping from the corner of one eye. She quickly wiped it away and told him that she would be there for a long tine, so they could spend a lot of time together. The next two days Lorrie stayed close to her Dad and also ate all the Mexican food that she could acquire. The whole family even went out for a Sunday lunch to a local Mexican Cafe before her Sister left to go back home in Houston. The next week Lorrie took her Dad to his scheduled Doctors appointment and she had a lot of questions for the Doctor about what she had already observed about her Dad's physical condition. Her Dad's Doctor told Lorrie that he thought that her Dad was moving into the beginnings of Stage 4 of Parkinson Disease, because he now needed a walker instead of a walking cane and his facial expressions were starting to change, because muscles in his face weren't reacting the way that should to normal emotions such as smiles and her Dad was suffering from more trimmers in his hands and sometimes his head would shake without her Dad being able to control it. The next few days Lorrie payed very close attention to everything her Dad tried to do for himself and she found that he needed more help then he did when she was with him the year before. Lorrie was at the grocery store doing grocery shopping for her Mom and she ran into the Commander of the local American Legion Post and he was asking her about her dad. Lorrie's Dad had once been the Commander of that Post and he had many friends that belonged to it. The Post Commander told Lorrie that they were having a meeting and wondered if she could talk her Dad into coming to the meeting. He told her that he and some of the members had tried to get him to come to the meetings, but without results and he didn't know why her Dad wouldn't come. Lorrie told him that she would try to convince her dad to go and that she would go with him. After Lorrie got back home from the grocery store and put up all the groceries she approached her Dad and told him about the conversation with the American Legion Commander. Her Dad just shook his head no that he didn't want to go. Lorrie started to open her mouth say something to try and convince him that he needed to go, then thought better of it and decided that then wasn't the time to have that discussion. Lorrie decided that her best chance of convincing him to go to a Legion meeting was to have patience and lay the ground work by having interesting things to tell him about the Legion from time to time. She decided that she was going to start going to some of their meetings and that way she would have first hand things to tell her Dad, after all she was going to be in El Campo for a couple of more months before she had to go back to England. Lorrie stayed in touch with the Post Commander so she would know when to go to meetings that would have something interesting for her Dad to know. Lorrie had developed a kind of routine that devoted most of her time that revolved around her family from the everyday housekeeping of sweeping and mopping of floors to laundry and grocery shopping, then running small errands. All the time she was doing these things she wanted to get her dad out of the house so he could have some sort of social life other then just sitting at home and reading or watching TV. She would take him riding, but they no longer went to drink beer at his favorite little Bar and they didn't tale a six-pac with them when they went riding. The Legion Post had been doing some remodeling and it was complete now, so Lorrie used this as her plan of attack to get her Dad's curiosity up enough to encourage him to commit to go with her, so she could show it to him. She would help him out on the patio so they could talk in private when the weather was good and he finally admitted to her why he didn't want to go to the Legion Post meetings. She told him all about how nice all of the new remodeling looked and that she really wanted to show it to him and he just hung his head. Lorrie asked him if he would go with her so she could show it to him and he finally told her that he didn't want to go because he had changed in appearance so much because of the disease and also he was using a walker now and it didn't look very manly and they wouldn't know him because of his looks now. Lorrie almost broke down in tears to hear that her Dad was keeping himself at home like a hermit, because he was ashamed of how he would appear to his old friends at the American Legion Post. She got up and gave him a hug and told him that she had been to the meetings and has seen old Veterans there that had part of their faces cut off, because of cancers and some there that had strokes and were in wheelchairs and couldn't talk good and none of the members shunned them or acted any differently to them then they did to each other and besides he was in much better shape then some of them and she really wanted to be with him there, because after all they were not only Dad and Daughter, but that they were both United States Military Veterans. Her Dad looked up at her and his eyes began to tear up and he nodded his head that he would go to the next meeting with her. Lorrie went over and hugged him and they both cried. Lorrie went about her time with her Parents with a much lighter heart and the time went fast now till the next week and the evening of the Legion meeting. She helped her Dad shave and laid out some nice cloths for him and when he was ready she put his American Legion Garrison Cap on him, which serves as a uniform, and helped him in the car. The Commander already knew that she was bringing her Dad, so he organized a special welcoming party for her Dad, the former Post Commander. Her Dad was so surprised that everyone wanted to greet him and even a member that was in a wheel chair that couldn't speak and could only use his left hand wanted to shake his hand with his left. Her Dad tried to smile, but his facial muscles had limited response, because of the disease, but he did manage a slight crooked smile in appreciation. He was pleased with what he saw that had been done on the remodeling. The whole evening was a wonderful change of pace for her Dad and before leaving to go back home her Dad promised the members that if someone would take him to the meetings that he would come again if he was able. Lorrie was very pleased with the way everything had turned out. When they got back home her Dad had to tell her Mom all that he saw and the members that he had seen, but that it had really tired him out and he wanted to go to bed. After everything settled down and got quiet Lorrie mixed herself a whiskey and water and went out on the patio to relax and she sat there thinking of the evening with her Dad at that Legion Post meeting and thanking God that it had all finally came to pass. After a while sitting there in the dark the mosquitoes found her and started buzzing and biting and she had to cut her time of reflection off and go in to bed. Lorrie thought that this was one of the drawbacks to living on the Gulf Coast of Texas was those damn mosquitoes. Lorrie went to her friends Hair Salon with her Mom for a haircut and color. As usual there were several women of all ages there enjoying their time at the beauty salon sharing the local gossip. The Legion Post Commanders wife was there and she told Lorrie's Mom how much the members enjoyed seeing Lorrie's Dad at the meeting. This really pleased Lorrie, because she knew that her Mom would tell her Dad and it would give him more incentive to attend the meetings as long as he could. She tried to listen intently to the numerous conversations going on to see if she could pick up any information about Gus, but nothing was said about him. Her last week in El Campo was spent with shopping for some other things that she intended to leave there for her get fast get away plan from England and also she did her Texas food shopping that she always did to take back with her and she left the rest of her money with her Mom to deposit in her Mom's account for her emergency funds if she had to flee her Husband and leave England short of money. This was a contingency plan that Lorrie suspected she might have to use one day. Her last evening in El Campo Lorrie made her yearly pilgrimage, she called it, to drive around Gus's Mom's old house and to all the places that she had seen Gus when she was just a young girl. If she looked hard enough, she thought, she could almost still see him there working on his Red Hot-Rod, or pumping gas at the Service Station he used to work at. This complete she went back to her Parents house to finish packing, because her Brother was going to pick her up the next morning and take her to the Houston Airport. Lorrie's long flight back to England was uneventful and she arrived tired as usual. She got home expecting a big mess but was surprised to find her Sons girlfriend Cheryl there cleaning up the place so she wouldn't have to worry about it. This was a wonderful surprise for Lorrie and she couldn't believe how lucky the family would be to have this wonderfully sweet young woman for a future Daughter-In-Law. Lorrie unloaded her luggage then tried to help Cheryl, but Cheryl told Lorrie that she had it all under control and for her go unpack and relax for a while while she fixed a little dinner for everyone.

Lorrie's Stepson came in a little later and they all had a nice dinner cooked by Cheryl. After dinner Cheryl and Lorrie's Stepson cleaned up the kitchen while Lorrie sipped on some brandy and her Husband drank beer. Lorrie looked at her Husband and told him that for her it was hard to believe how much her Stepson had matured since he had been with Cheryl and even her Husband commented that Cheryl had made a big difference in his Son. The next few days Lorrie got back in the feel of things at home and she finally cleaned up her desk from all the paper work that had accumulated in her absence. It was getting to the end of September now and it dawned on Lorrie that at the end of October she would be 57 years old. She thought that no wonder that her Friend that owned the Hair Salon in El Campo had trouble with the color on her hair, because she must have a lot of gray in it now. Lorrie thought 57 years old, where in the hell has her life gone so fast. The weeks were speeding by and Lorrie realized that she needed to start getting organized for the Holiday season of Christmas and New Years. She had bought a lot of new decorations last year, so she wouldn't need to do that this time. She would have to figure out what kind of parties she wanted for Christmas and New Year's Eve and that would tell her what she would need to do. Lorrie was scurrying around getting the Christmas decorations from the attic and digging through boxes to see if they were all still in good order. She had been fighting a urinary tract infection for several days and Doctoring herself by eating yoghurt, cottage cheese and not eating any spicy foods, acid foods and carbonated drinks, but she was really feeling sluggish and she decided to go to her Doctor and get a shot and some anti-biotic pills to cure it fast, because she had a lot to do to get ready for the Holidays. Lorrie went to her appointment and the Doctor took a blood and urine sample and she had a little fever, so he did give her a shot and some pills then she went home to rest for a while. Two days later her Doctor called her and told her that the results had come back on her blood and urine samples and they showed a high level of sugar in both, so he had made an appointment for her with a Laboratory close by to run further tests on her. Lorrie knew what this meant, because she had been a Nurse in the United States, her Doctor suspected that she had Sugar Diabetes and these tests would take most of a day. A couple of days after the tests her Doctor called her to come in for a consultation. Her Doctor told her that the tests showed that she definitely had Sugar Diabetes, but that they had caught it early enough that she should be able to control it pills instead of the insulin shots used on the more advanced cases. Lorrie was very glad that she didn't have to have the shots, because she had given many of them when she was a Nurse and also to her Stepfather when he lived with her and her Husband till he died and having to take those shots was very inconvenient when you traveled or were out and around trying to be around other people. Lorrie thought that there might be a bright side to this, maybe she could use it as an excuse not to have sex with her husband. After about a week she had finally cured her infection and she was on schedule with her Diabetes pills. She would still have to do her Doctor for scheduled Laboratory tests to make sure that her Diabetes was under control and she guessed that that would go on for the rest of her life. She was feeling a lot better now and her Stepson's girlfriend Cheryl had volunteered to help her do the decorating. Lorrie had decided not to have a huge Christmas or New Years celebration again. She wanted it to be just family and close friends and business associates. Another one of those come and go affairs. She guessed that she was just getting to old to put up with all the drunken people and mess of the big parties. Lorrie and Cheryl did the decorating while Lorrie's Husband and her Stepson sat around and ate snacks and drank beer. She finally convinced them to go to the local Christmas Tree sales lot and pick out a good Christmas tree. This got them out of Lorrie and Cheryl's hair and gave them something productive to do. While the men were gone Cheryl told Lorrie that her and Lorrie's Stepson were planning on buying a house together. She said that they had been living together for about a year now in that apartment and decided that things were working for them, so it was time to take the next step and invest their money in a house together. Lorrie asked her if they had decided to get Married and Cheryl told her that they had talked about it, but that they didn't see any need to get married right now, because they didn't want to have children for several more years and they still wanted to have their freedom to vacation in far away lands and then be more financially secure before finally settling to family life to raise the children. Lorrie thought that Cheryl and her Stepson had made a wise decision since they both realized they weren't quite ready to have a family yet. Lorrie did worry a bit though about them buying a house together, because she knew how the history on how irresponsible her Stepson had always been with his money, but she didn't want to put doubts in Cheryl's mind to cause trouble. Lorrie thought that maybe Cheryl had influenced her Stepson enough to get him to be better in handling his finances, she certainly had made significant positive changes in him in some other ways. Cheryl told Lorrie that she had been saving her money for several years and about

$50,000.00 in savings that she could use for that purpose. Lorrie wondered how much money her Stepson had saved, because he had never saved any money before. He had always spent everything acting like a rich big shot taking expensive vacations to exotic places and buying expensive gifts for his girlfriends and throwing big parties, so when he was out of work he had to come back and live at home till he started another job, then he would start spending his money crazy again. Lorrie hoped that he had changed for Cheryl's sake. Lorrie's Christmas Party was a little larger then it had been in 2,001, because her Stepson and Cheryl had invited a couple of their friends over also. Lorrie got another Christmas present again this year, thanks to Cheryl. That is two years in a row that Lorrie got a Christmas present and she made a point of really making over it in front of her Husband who never got her a gift for anything. He simply glared at her, as if to leave the impression that he would settle with her later. She immediately thought that maybe she shouldn't have done that. As the evening went on her Husband stopped drinking beer and started drinking whiskey and that is when Lorrie tried to get Cheryl and her Stepson to spend to night, because she felt trouble brewing. They told Lorrie that they had to go to Cheryl's parents house before going home, so they couldn't stay. After they left her Husband sat on the couch and brooded for a while all the time drinking whiskey and then when Lorrie said she was going up to bed he jumped up and started screaming at her that she loved making him look bad in front of his Son and he had enough of it and he was going to stop it, then he grabbed her and shook her so hard that it put a crick in her neck and she thought that he was going to squeeze her arms into, until he threw her on the couch and stomped up stairs to his room and slammed the door. Lorrie was so frightened that she started crying, but she soon regained her composure and was thankful that his attack wasn't any worse. After all he didn't hit her as he had done before. Lorrie sat on the couch for a while making sure that her Husband had enough time to go to sleep before she quietly went up to her room and closed the door and went to bed. The next day they avoided each other as much as possible and after that things got back to their old depressing self. Lorrie was dreading their New Years Eve party because what had happened at Christmas, so she was extra careful to walk on egg shells in the way she acted around her Husband. She watched him carefully all evening to see how he was acting around their guests and also around her Stepson and Cheryl till they had to leave to stop by another New Years Eve party on their way back home. When the New Year 2,003 arrived and the last of their guests left, Lorrie didn't even pick up things like she usually did, because she was in a hurry to go up to her room and not be alone with her Husband while was drinking like he had been, because she was afraid that he might remember the Christmas fight and decide to start on it again. The morning of the New Year 2,003 Lorrie got up and went down to make some tea and she found her Husband asleep on the couch and a spilled glass of whiskey on her coffee table. Lorrie took her time and sipped her big mug of hot tea and ate a pastry before she woke her Husband up to see if he wanted tea and pastry. He got up wobbly and drank a mug of tea that she fixed for him then he went up to take a shower, because they were going to go to their annual New Years Day lunch with their friends. They had a nice New Years lunch with their friends and caught up on a lot that had happened to everyone, but Lorrie noticed that her Husband was mostly quite and she thought that he must have a bad hangover. When they got home he told her to bring him some aspirin and he took four of them and went up to his room and went to sleep. This was just fine to Lorrie, because now she could spend the rest of the day going over the events of the past year in her mind without being interrupted. This is how Lorrie started the New Year 2,003 and she thought that it could have been worse. She was looking forward 2,003 to seeing what kind of house her Stepson and Cheryl would end up buying and that would be a fun thing.

Gus—2,003 started slower for Gus, because he decided that he and his Wife would go to his Blue Quail Ranch for a couple of days. The weather was mild, for a change, and he wanted to take advantage of it to get away from the work he was doing in the house and get out and look for some Indian artifacts. When Gs woke up the next morning at the Ranch it was cold, so he lit the propane heater and then started the water boiling to make his cowboy coffee. He looked at the outside temperature and saw that it was 35* and there was no wind and the sky was clear, so he knew that it would warm up about mid-morning to 50* or 55* and with no wind that would be real good. They would eat a good breakfast before the left in his old Jeep and take a lunch with them, so they could stay out and explore as long as they wanted without getting a hurry to come back to the camp house. He always took two canteens full of water, two pistols with extra ammo, first aid kit, snake bite kit, walking sticks, tire fix-a-flat and a camp shovel. The terrain on this Ranch was beautiful, but it was in a wild and dangerous area not far from the Rio Grand River that through history had been the haunt of bandits and smugglers and it was no different today with the drug smugglers and the illegals that were walking through and then there was the possibility of running into a mountain lion, black bear, javalina or rattle snake, so it payed to be cautious, prepared and aware of your surroundings at all time. He planned to go to the far east side of the Ranch next to the Ninety Six Canyon and the Sierra Vieja Mountain Range and explore there first to see what he could find and after that he wanted to explore some areas that he hadn't had the time to walk around on to check them out. Gus discovered a Indian camp right on the banks of the Ninety Six Canyon that he hadn't found before. He found several stone arrow heads, some broken, and a couple of scrapers. They ate their lunch and went to another place to look around and there in the side of a hill his Wife found what looked like the end of a petrified tusk about 6 inch's long and 3 inches thick. They had found fossils before, but nothing like this. Most of the fossils they found were of sea shells and mollusks. They spent most of the day exploring around and they gathered some dry mesquite to build a fire to sit by and then to cook some steaks for their dinner. Gus washed off all that they had found and placed it out on a table to admire while sipping on a beer. Late that night a new winter storm blew in and the wind howled all night and the next morning it was still, but there was about 2 inches of snow on the ground. Well this wasn't good to be looking for Indian artifacts, so Gus decided that he was just going to drive around and see what kind of animal tracts he could find. His Wife stayed in the Camp House because she didn't like to get out in the cold and snow. She had grown up in Colorado, so she had seen a lot of snow and she told Gus that she wasn't impressed by the snow, she would rather stay warm in the Camp House. Gus found bobcat, coyote, deer and rabbit tracks and then he got cold, so he went back to the warm Camp House to make some hot coffee and warm up. Gus decided that they just as well go back to Van Horn the next day, because it was really too cold and windy to enjoy hiking around. The next morning they packed up everything including the artifacts he found and drove back home. Gus took off one more day after they got home from his Ranch, before he started back on the kitchen. He had finished three rooms, two bath rooms and the master bedroom and now he was going to put the finishing touches on the kitchen with the painting. All the rooms in the house had dingy walls and ceiling along with repair work that Gus had done or was going have to be done. The paint job to cover all of this would require two coats of primer and two coats of top coat, so it was a major undertaking that would take the best part of the week, because the paint took longer to dry in the cold weather. While he was doing this paint job it was a real problem to cook meals in the kitchen, because he would have to cover and uncover counter top and sink and move the electric kitchen range back to be plugged into the power outlet then out again and covered, so he could have room to work around it. All of the other kitchen furniture, two china cabinets, buffet were moved in the center of the room and covered and the kitchen table and chairs were in the living room till he finished the kitchen and the refrigerator was in the living room being run from an extension electric cord. He was so glad that they had cleaned and painted the cabinets before they had moved in the house, because he wouldn't have to unload them to paint them, all the contents could stay inside them with being splattered with paint. Gus finally finished the kitchen and it could be put in order. His next room to do was the living room, so everything had to be moved out of it into the entry way from the front door and the kitchen. The living room was going to take quite some time because it had some masonry work to be done repairing some bad places in the stucco. The days were slipping by as Gus was working on his House. He worked on it like it was a job and hardly ever took off work. Sometime he would go to a local Cafe early in the morning, that he knew the men in town liked to go frequent to drink coffee and talk. He used this to get information on what was happening in town and around the area and also to meet new people in town that he hadn't met before. This is how Gus started weaving himself into the fabric of the town. Gus finally finished the living room and moved the furniture back into it. February was giving way to March and the feeling of spring would appear on some days while others would still be cold and blustery. Out in the high Chihuahua Desert Mountain region of Far West Texas winter lasted a little longer and was colder then where Gus had lived on the Gulf Coast of Texas, because the winter storms could build up quick and move fast through the mountains and they could be unpredictable as how bad they would really be. Gus finally finished the living room and got all the furniture moved back in it. There were only three rooms left to do down stairs and one was the back bedroom another was the laundry room and the other was the large front entry area that he planned on doing last after he finished all the rooms upstairs and the staircase. One afternoon Gus got a visitor that was in charge of Economic Development Board and the Main Street Program Board for the town of Van Horn. He introduced himself and visited for a while then he asked if Gus would like to become a Board Member on both Boards. Gus asked him what was required of the Board Members and he replied that they were required to make monthly meetings and look for ways to promote the economic development of Van Horn by developing ideas to attract new business and also tourism. Gus asked him why they wanted him on those Boards and the man answered that the members of the Boards had been watching the way he had been renovating the old House that they considered one of the best properties in Van Horn and thought that he might be interested in helping to improve the town. Gus told him that he would have to think about it and let him know because he was so busy renovating the House that he didn't have much time for anything else. Gus told the man that he didn't even have the time he would like right then to go to his Ranch and spend a lot of time there. The man asked Gus if he could stop by again in a few days to see if Gus had decided what he wanted to do and Gus told him to stop by when ever he wanted to. Gus was working on the back bedroom when the man with the town of Van Horn came back to get Gus's answer. Gus had decided to tell him yes, because Gus felt that he had a lot of qualifications and experience in the business world to be an asset on the Boards and also it might give him an inside look at how the town operated and the new things that were coming to town. Gus went to the two Board meetings when they were scheduled and was warmly greeted by all of the Board members and listened to the up coming plans that they had for improving the town. The Main Street Board was planning the first town clean up that would enlist as many of the local civic organizations they could convince to help. It was to be scheduled for April and that was just a couple of weeks away. The Board was going to give four money prizes for the most trash to be collected by organizations or citizens. It was going to be judged by weight and Gus was going to be in charge of weighing the trash at a local scale, keeping a ledger of weight on what each participant brought in and then tabulating the total find the winners. Gus was glad to be a part of this, because trash laying around town was one of the first things that he noticed about Van Horn even before he had decided to move there. There was a lot of excitement about the cash prizes and most of the clubs in town wanted to sign up, because if they got a cash prize they could add it to their funds for the charity projects they supported. The clubs signed up were the Lions Club, Rotary Club, 4-H Club, Boy Scouts, Girl Scouts, Ladies Auxiliary, American Legion and several others along with individuals. A whole day on a Saturday was dedicated to the clean-up and tons of trash were collected including old tires, batteries, old motor blocks, beer cans, bottles, plastic shopping bags, old carpet, old hot water heaters, washing machines, refrigerators, dish washers, water coolers and much more. Gus road around Van Horn and through the alleys and vacant lots the next day and you could see a very real difference in the appearance of the town. He was pleased, because it had worked. The citizens of the town had actually got out and gathered up junk that in their minds they hadn't seen, because it had been laying everywhere for so long that they were used to it being there and had become accustomed to just passing it by with actually noticing any more. The next step on the Main Street Boards agenda was to get the owners of down town businesses that had broken windows or business buildings that needed painting to fix those problems and they had some push back from the owners, because they said that if they fixed up their property then their taxes would go up and they had a point. Gus had always thought that property taxes were designed wrong and that was why slums existed in big cities and that small towns had neglected areas. When property was kept in good shape then the taxes were high on those and when property was allowed to degenerate the taxes went lower, because taxes were calculated on property value. Gus always thought that there should be a reverse scale for degenerating property, in other words when property degenerated to an unacceptable point then taxes should be raised on it instead of lowered. Gus believed that it would give the owners an incentive to keep their property in good shape. The Main Street Board finally convinced the owners of these properties that needed repair, by actually buying the paint and the window panes for them and then paying a portion of the costs of the labor to do the repair work. All of a sudden the downtown area started looking better and the citizens noticed and started taking more pride in the town. All of this had a lasting effect, because now the town Council now set dates for next years clean up and the Chamber of Commerce started to advertise the neatness of the town. There were still some run down buildings down town however, but you couldn't expect to get it all done at one time. These two Boards hadn't taken up to much of Gus's time so far and he actually enjoyed being a part of something that was making a positive difference in the small town of Van Horn. He was still working on his House and he went back to work on the back bedroom. This room had some unique things to fix. It had some masonry to fix, but it also had an old in the wall air conditioner unit that Gus needed to figure out how to conceal it, so it might be able to be used at a later date after Gus had time to clean it up and see if it would even turn on and there was also there was an open electrical breaker box that was mounted in a hollowed out place on the inside of the outside wall that was part of the new big double closet he had built and it needed to be closed in also, so that it could be accessed when needed. Gus did the masonry work first and then he tried several ideas before he settled on ways to fix both problems. Now it was time for him to concentrate on the painting and that took him the rest of the week. Gus really liked the Economic Development Board meetings, but the ideas the board were concentrating on were primarily to do with tourism and really Van Horn didn't have anything to draw tourists to the town. Actually Van Horn was in the middle of nowhere and it was about 100 miles in every direction to the tourist attractions. Trying to make Van Horn into a tourist town was going to be a real problem. Almost all of the old original historic buildings had been torn down or redone to the point that they would no longer be useful as a draw for tourism. The original old huge sandstone block Court House had been torn down in the 1960's and replaced with a building that looked like a Doctors clinic and the only thing left at that location was the small old brick original Jail and a Historical Marker denoting the location of the original Court House. The only buildings left that would be interesting to some tourists were one old Hotel that had a good museum housed in it and a really nice old Hotel that had been built in the 1930's by some renowned Architects that were famous for designing and building Hotels using the Spanish Colonial designs inside and out. It was a really nice building, but it had been bought by a Bank and the downstairs had been occupied by it along with offices for the CAD and a Office Supply business. The whole upstairs had been ignored except for one Lawyers Office and an office occupied by the biggest Rancher in the County. Actually Gus's House was one of the oldest original buildings in the town, being built in 1906, by the towns first County/District Clerk for his family. Right now Gus had a very hard time seeing Van Horn as a tourist destination, he saw it more as a working class town that desperately needed good paying jobs and it had Interstate Highway 10 running right through it from east to west and Highway 90 to the south and Highway 54 to the north along with the Railroad, a lot of reasonable priced land, good water and reasonable taxes. These were the things that could be used to try and attract business that paid good wages and tourism usually only paid minimum wages. Gus decided that if somehow tourism got started, well fine, but he was going to try to concentrate on attracting other businesses. Gus went back to working on his House. He had finished the back bedroom and was now able to furnish it with his Dad's bedroom furniture that was left to him in his Mom's Will after she died. It was solid walnut and something that his Mom had bought for his Dad when they moved into another house in 1957. The next room he was to work on was the laundry room and he was going to have to do some electrical work in there first. He started with this on the back porch, by installing another electrical breaker box, because the old one was experiencing problems with all the hap-hazard wiring additions that someone had done. Gus installed the new box and conduit piping to run the new wiring in to inside the laundry room and install a new wall outlet for the cloths dryer. Then he reworked the two light switches and wall outlet and re-stuccoed them in. He then repainted the walls and ceiling and mounted shelves to hold what ever was needed to do laundry and for canned goods and supplies for the kitchen. There was only one more room down stairs to be done and that was the large entry area and that would have to wait till he had finished the up stairs. It was in the middle of the summer of 2,003 now and Gus was again yearning to take a break and go to his Blue Quail Ranch. The next day Gus and his Wife packed up enough food and ice in two big coolers to last for five days at his Ranch. Gus loved it at the Ranch it was a sort of therapy for him, because while out there he forgot everything else that he had to do and everything that might be bothering him. He stood out on that mesa that was the location for his camp and his mind wandered back thousands of years to the primitive occupants of that rugged area. He was sure that they had more resources of wood, water and wild game then were there now, but it still had to be extremely hard to make a living in this unforgiving environment. He thought that he could have fit in there in this place and in that time as well as they had done. After all he had learned how to find water where there was no water and how to make fire the way they made fire, to make the type of shelters that they had lived in, how to make their weapons for hunting and defense and how to use the herbs in the Desert for healing and cooking, how to track game and set home made traps and these were the basic ingredients of knowledge that it took to live in this environment. All other knowledge needed was only the refining of each of these to fit a certain situation at a certain time of the year. After his five days at the Ranch Gus was ready to go back to town and start on the upstairs of his House. The work upstairs was slow, because there was so much to do to get the three bedrooms and the big landing ready. There were no closets in the upstairs bedrooms and Gus needed to close two doorways between the bedrooms so the entry to each room came from the landing. He had no idea why the builder would have put the extra doors between the rooms, because it only made the rooms harder to arrange with furniture and they certainly weren't needed. The rooms were small, because of the roof line and the big landing that took up a lot of the upstairs room. Gus thought that the landing was big enough to make a loft bedroom if he wanted to, but he would have enough bedrooms and he would rather have the landing be a library. He was going to have to choose one of the upstairs bedrooms to turn into an office and that would still leave him two bedrooms upstairs and two bedrooms down stairs and four bedrooms was enough. The three rooms were of different sizes and he picked the smallest for his office. One room was big enough to build a double sliding door closet and still have enough room for a full size bed and a chest of drawers and night stand with a lamp and an antique oak wash stand and a chair and the other smaller room would have a smaller closet with an over head cabinet to store bedding and under that was room for a chest of drawers and the other furnishings would be a single bed with a night stand and a lamp and a desk that would hold a sewing machine and a chair. There were no wall mounted light switches in the rooms upstairs, so all lighting would have to be from lamps. There had been an old defunct gas heater on the landing and Gus removed it leaving a big hole in the landing wall that went into a space behind the wall that needed to be closed up also. Gus worked upstairs and also went to the Main Street Board and Economic Board meetings trying to put together ideas that might work for Van Horn and the weeks went by until it was the Holiday season again. Thanksgiving was upon Gus when his Sons would be out to stay at his Ranch for a few days and hunt. This had become a tradition for his Family and it was really the only time that they came out to Van Horn to visit, because it was 600 miles from where they all lived and it took the best part of a day to drive out and also to drive back which used up two days of their vacations just driving out to Van Horn. Gus was getting things together to go to his Ranch in order start getting everything ready for his Sons to come out to hunt right after Thanksgiving. He went to the hardware store to buy some more kerosene for the lamps and the lanterns, then he went to fill up his pick-up with gasoline and also three five gallon gas cans for the Ranch and while he was filling up a car pulled up at the next gas pump and a man got out then a young girl got out and she had on cowboy boots, blue jeans, a western blouse and a cowboy hat covering brown hair with a long brown pony tail held together with a green ribbon. She had a round face with generous full lips, small breasts and long slim legs and she almost took Gus's breath away, because he thought that is exactly how Lorrie would look in western clothing as a cowgirl. He couldn't believe how much she looked like Lorrie when Lorrie was sixteen years old. He couldn't take his eyes off of her and when he went in to pay for his gas she and the man was stand in line to pay also and Gus struck up a conversation with the man and he was the girl's Dad, so Gus talked to him for a minute then he complemented the girl on her western outfit and he asked her name and she told him it was Mauri and Gus had to ask her again, because he thought she told him Lorrie and she repeated Mauri. Gus told her that he thought she said Lorrie and then he ask her her age and she told him sixteen and Gus smiled and told her that he had once know a lovely young girl by the name of Lorrie that looked exactly like her and that she had been sixteen when he had last seen her. Then Mauri and her Dad paid their bill and left and Gus watched them walk all the way to their car while he was actually seeing Lorrie in his mind and all of a sudden a loud voice from behind the counter called his name and he snapped out of his daydream to pay his bill and leave. Gus's plan was to drive to the Ranch and unload what he had bought and then check out everything there to see what else he might need and make a list then hook to the 500 gallon water trailer to bring it in to town and fill it up, so they wouldn't run out of water when his Son's came out. The girl Mauri was on his mind all day long. Gus's Son's came out to his Ranch the day after Thanksgiving and stayed for four days and as usual they had a real good time, but again no one killed a deer. His Sons had a great time exploring along with their hunting and one of them even found an Indian arrowhead. Their visit was over and Gus stayed at his Ranch one more day to make sure everything was cleaned up and shut down. The last morning before he left he was standing outside drinking his last cup of coffee and looking toward the east and the Sierra Vieja Mountain 96 Gap thinking about that pretty girl Mauri and how much she resembled Lorrie and suddenly he wondered if something had happened to Lorrie and her spirit had been transferred to this girl. He realized that it would be what was called reincarnation and he wasn't sure that he believed in something like that, but then he was never sure how things worked as far as stuff like that, because he believed that God could do anything that he wanted to do, so why not that. Then Gus started wondering how old Lorrie would be if she was still alive and he started doing the math from 1962 to 2003 and he knew that she had been 16 years old in 1962, so she would be either 57 or 58 years old depending when her birthday was. Wow, Gus thought, because he still had the vision of her being 16 years old and now he wondered what she looked like if she was alive. He thought that if she was alive that she was still sexy and beautiful. He and his Wife spent a week at Christmas at the Ranch and they stayed at Home in Van Horn for New Years 2004. New Years Day 2004 Gus remembered what he had done the year before playing the record that Lorrie had given him so long ago, so he went upstairs and got "In The Still Of The Night" by the Five Satins out of his record box and turned on his record player and put it on the turn-table, lowered the needle on the record and sat down to relive his times with sweet Lorrie.

Lorrie—2,003 was a New Year starting for Lorrie and she was going to try and concentrate on the pleasant things in her life. She had her long time good friend Jill, her Stepsons girl friend Cheryl and the Country and Western Dance Club that they belonged to. She was so glad that despite her Husbands heavy drinking that he had maintained his ability to do excellent tailoring work and keep up with the orders that the Garment House were giving him. Really she couldn't understand how he could do it, because he had been drinking heavy for so long that she was surprised that his liver wasn't pickled. Cheryl, Lorrie's Stepsons girlfriend was keeping in contact with her about their house hunt and was asking her for advise from time to time about different things and Lorrie told her that she had never bought a house, but that she had dealt with Bankers a lot on her Husbands house when they were about to loose it when he was behind on the Bank Loan when they first Married and the time that he was out of work for so long because of his hurt back. Finally in March her Stepson called Lorrie and his Dad and told them that he and Cheryl had settled on a house that both of them liked and they would get together and have dinner then go look at it. Lorrie and her Husband met them for an early dinner and then drove over to look at the house that they had picked out. Lorrie could see that it was in an expensive neighborhood. After taking a tour of the house and the grounds Lorrie asked her Stepson how much it cost and what the payments would be. Her Stepson looked at her then barked that she shouldn't worry about it, because they could afford it. Lorrie took this rebuff in stride, because she knew her Stepson and his superior attitude when things were going good for him, but she was also skeptical of everything that he said, through experience. After her Stepson and Cheryl acquired the house Lorrie and her Husband bought some of the furnishings for them as a gift. Lorrie was never sure how much money that her Stepson put into the down payment, but she knew that Cheryl had $50,000.00 that she was ready to put into the down payment if needed. Lorrie just hoped for Cheryl's sake that her Stepson stayed stable enough to be a good partner for her and that they would finally get married and then maybe Lorrie would finally have some grand kids to spoil. It was the last week in May and time for Lorrie to leave for her annual vacation trip back to El Campo, Texas and she had purchased her round trip ticket a month earlier so she could get a good price on it. She was looking forward to this three month vacation away from her Husband, but it also held a sort of dread for her because of the disease that her Dad was suffering from and she didn't quite know what she would see when she would first encounter her Dad. Lorrie had taken pictures of her Stepson and Cheryl's new home to show her family. Her flight was long and tiring as usual and her Sister picked her up at the Houston Airport to stay a few days with her before they both drove to El Campo. Lorrie quizzed her Sister about her Dad's condition and she didn't like what she heard. Although Lorrie knew that there would be a steady decline in her Dad's physical condition she had a hard time grasping the magnitude of his present situation. After a few days of rest and some shopping as was their usual thing to do Lorrie and her Sister drove to El Campo to her Parents house. They were met by her Brother that helped them with their luggage. Lorrie had brought gifts from England for everyone in one piece of luggage that would hold Texas food when Lorrie flew back to England in three months. Her Dad was sitting in a wheelchair with his head down dozing when Lorrie came in to the house. She squatted down by his wheelchair so she could look him in the face when she woke him by placing her hand on his. When he opened his eyes and raised his head to look at her he looked puzzled for for a minute before he realized who she was but then he took his other hand and covered her's, but he didn't smile like he usually did, he just said Lorrie in a sort of shaky voice. Lorrie was very disappointed at what she saw, but tried not to show her emotions about her Dad's appearance. She put her arms around his shoulders and kissed him on the cheek and told him that she loved him and missed him. Lorrie noticed that there was no walker close to his wheel chair, but kept this to herself, because she wanted to ask her Mom some questions before she said something that might make her Dad feel bad about himself and also she wanted to look around the house to see what changes had been made to accommodate her Dad's increasing poor physical health. After she unpacked her Brother went to a local Mexican Cafe to get Mexican food to take back for them to have for dinner, except this time he didn't bring any back for Lorrie's Dad, because he no longer could eat these kinds of foods. Everything that he was eating now was either cut into very small pieces or it was soft food like cereal. Lorrie felt guilty eating her Mexican food dinner while her Dad was eating oatmeal with some cut up bananas on top. She had not seen him ask to use his walker and this disturbed her. When she made a little tour of the house she noticed a bedside commode next to his bed and a little bell on his night stand for him to ring for assistance. They all went to the living room so everyone could talk and enjoy each others company. Lorrie's Dad didn't carry on a conversation, he just would answer yes, no or shake his head and Lorrie noticed that his had slight quiver to it all the time now. Also her Dad would hold his hands together so they wouldn't shake so much. Lorrie brought out the pictures she had taken of her Stepson's new home for everyone to see and everyone wanted to know how much it cost, but Lorrie couldn't answer that question, because her Stepson wouldn't tell her. After her Dad went to bed Lorrie ask her Mom if her Dad was still using his walker and she told Lorrie that most of the time now he didn't, but that sometime he would have a good day that he wanted to use it for a little while, but he tired out quick. Lorrie then ask about his Doctors appointments and her Mom told her that they still took him to the Doctors office, but it was in the wheelchair now and Lorrie's Brother had to help her with it. While in England Lorrie would call back to El Campo to talk to her family and ask about her Dad and she understood from what they would tell her that he was getting weaker, but seeing this was worse then she thought it was. After everyone went to bed Lorrie got herself a beer out of the refrigerator and went out on the patio to sit quiet and think. She was glad that the mosquitoes weren't out and while she was sitting there she could hear the familiar sounds from her childhood of the cicadas and watch the lightning bugs blinking lights bobbing around the back yard. Lorrie started softly weeping and wondered how everything in her world got so screwed up. What started it, where did it start anyway. Why wasn't she like most of her friends that had nice husbands and good children and a stable life, maybe not exciting, but something that they could depend on and somebody that they truly loved and got love in return. It seemed that a life like that might have been better then what she had spent most of her life chasing. Lorrie thought way back to when she was just a young girl looking through magazines and reading articles and looking at pictures about the beautiful cities in Europe, Paris, Rome, Venice, Florence, Milan, Berlin, Vienna, Madrid and London to name a few, with their beautiful old buildings and museums with the most wonderful art works in the world and thinking that she wanted to see those things some day and maybe she would even live there and marry one of the handsomest men in Europe and live in his family's centuries old castles. Well she had been to all of these places and even lives in one of them which completed part of her girlish dream, but she certainly didn't marry her prince and live in the castle, although she did marry a man that had a nice house, but she actually had to do drastic things to save it so the Bank didn't take it away from him. Now after all of the years, 24 to be exact, living in England and experiencing her so called dream life, why was she so miserable with her life. When ever she came back to El Campo and ran into any of the old friends or class mates that were still around she acted like she was living a dream life and they all were in awe of the things that she had seen and experiences that she told them about and they made her feel like she was important and special because of this, but in her heart the whole time she was talking to them she secretly wanted what they already had which was a husband that truly loved them and the life that they had built together. Then she thought about Gus and the love she still had for him and that if he had come back to her and claimed her for his own that she would have never seen or lived in England or Europe, except in those magazines, but she would have had something so much more important and that was the same thing that those girls had that stilled lived in El Campo and that was a husband that truly loved her and that she could truly love. That part of life she had let pass by now and she would never have it and too late she had learned that her European dream was no replacement for what she could have had, but would never be now. Lorrie had sat out on the patio much longer then she realized thinking back, because when she snapped out of her deep thoughts she looked at the sky and saw that there was a faint glow in it and she looked at her watch to be surprised that it was nearing 5:30 am. Lorrie looked at her beer and discovered that she had only sipped half of it, so she poured it out in the back yard went in the house and washed up a little, slipped on her night gown and went to bed to get about 2 ½ hours of sleep. Lorrie's days in El Campo had evolved into a schedule that primarily fitted around how she could be of assistance with her Dad. She gave her Mom a break by being the one to get up at night when her Dad would ring his bell for assistance of one kind or another. Being around her Dad now was so different then it had been a year ago that there was no comparison and she was glad when the day of his Doctors appointment came so she could take him and be able to have a talk with his Doctor. When the Doctor finished the examination and had asked all his questions Lorrie quietly motioned for a short private meeting and the Doctor told Lorrie to meet him in his private office for a minute. Lorrie asked him what he thought and she told him that her Dad needed so much more help now then he had needed when she had been with him one year ago. The Doctor told Lorrie that her Dad's disease was progressing at a steady rate that was consistent with how most patients that had Parkinson Disease would progress. He told Lorrie that he was sure that her Dad was now entering the last stage which was Stage 5 and that this would be the most difficult for not only her Dad, but for the whole family, because he would need even more help and it would finally toward the end be 24 hour a day constant personal management of her Dads needs. Lorrie asked the Doctor how much time her Dad had left and he told her that it was up to God, because this could last a long time, maybe even a year or even two years. Lorrie took her Dad through the drive through at the Dairy Queen for an ice cream cone before they went home and after she got him in bed for a rest she told her Mom what had transpired at his Doctors appointment. Lorrie told her Mom that basically the most time that her Dad had to live was two years and maybe not but one and things would get steadily worse. Lorrie went to her Friends Hair Salon for her usual haircut and color. Lorrie was telling her about the Doctors appointment and what the Doctor had told her about her Dad and her friend was applying the color to Lorrie's hair when a woman cam into the Salon and went over to a woman in the next chair and told her that she had seen Gus at a dance the night before and Lorrie swung her head around so fast that the color solution on her hair slung off all over her friend Toodie the Salon Owner and she screamed making everybody in the Salon look around. She asked Lorrie what in the world she was doing and Lorrie told her that the woman was talking about Gus and the Salon Owner told Lorrie that she was talking about a different Gus that was the other woman's son. Lorrie looked embarrassed but settled down and apologized and finished her hair appointment that ended up again to produce a slightly different color to her hair then it was supposed to be, but that was her friend and you couldn't do anything about the color she wanted to put on your hair. The months were slipping by in El Campo for Lorrie now and she had been trying to do all that she could to relieve her Mom and Brother from having most of the burden of care for her Dad. Her Sister came down sometime from Houston when she could to help, but most of it was on her Mom and Brother. Lorrie almost felt like she was back in the Nursing profession that she had been working at in Albuquerque, New Mexico in 1973 and that was 30 years ago. She was doing all the grocery shopping also and when her Brother or Sister could stay with her Dad for a while she would take her Mom with her so she could have a outing also. She took her Mom with her when she did her Texas food shopping to take back with her to England, so she couldn't do her complete annual Gus memory run, all she could do was to drive by where Gus used to work at the Service Station and look over there and silently remember times there. Lorrie's time in El Campo was over and she dreaded telling her Dad goodby, but there was no getting around that and when it was time for her to leave, it was a real hard thing, because he held on to her and didn't want to let go. When her Brother was driving her to the Airport in Houston she told him that their Dad might not make it till she came back, so if things got to that point that he should call her and she would come back no matter when it was. When Lorrie got back to England one of the first things that she had to do was to go for a Doctors appointment check up on her Diabetes, so she could get her medicine renewed, because she had used almost all her pills on her El Campo trip. She couldn't get but three months supply at a time, so she had to do this quick. This time the tests showed that her Diabetes was under control with the medication she was taking, but now her Blood Pressure was much to high also. She told the Doctor about her Dad and he told her that maybe that was causing her high Blood Pressure, so he wanted to see her again in a week to take her Blood Pressure again and if it was still high then he wanted to start her on Blood Pressure medication. Lorrie still had a lot of her office work to straighten out at home with her Husbands Tailoring business, because she hadn't had the time when she first got back. It was September now and she was finally getting everything straightened out. Everything seemed to be going fine with her Stepson and Cheryl in their new home. She had only talked to them on the phone, because everyone had been too busy to get together for a visit. Lorrie was so relieved that her Stepson had found Cheryl and had bonded with her, because she had lost hope that he would ever be stable enough to be a success in his life even though he was very intelligent and seemed to have a lot to offer an employer. Cheryl had made all the difference not only in her Stepson's life, but for Lorrie and her Husbands also. Lorrie went back to her Doctors appointment to check her blood pressure and sure enough it was much too high, so her Doctor put her on blood pressure medication. Lorrie thought that she must be getting old, because now she was taking pills for two different ailments and in her mind that was an indication of aging. This fact did nothing to raise her spirits, because she had just come from El Campo where she stayed depressed over her Dad's steady decline in health and death that could come at any time now. Lorrie suddenly realized that she that ever since she had returned from her El Campo trip she had been feeling sorry for herself with a pity Lorrie attitude that must be getting on peoples nerves and her sweet friend Jill hadn't even scolded her about it. She told herself that she was going to turn over a new leaf and start thinking of all the things that she should be thankful for. She actually sat down in her little office and started writing a list of all the positive things that she should be thankful for. #1. Jill her sweet friend, #2. a nice house with a roof over her head, #3. a Husband that was still making a good living, #4. Cheryl her Stepsons girlfriend, #5. her Stepson still had his good job, #6. her Dad was still alive, #6 her Husband was still taking his ski vacations, #7 the Country and Western Dance Club social life, #7. her books that she liked to read, and #8. her sweet memories of her only love Gus. When she looked at this list she brightened up some, because seeing this she thought that she had a lot more to be thankful for then a lot of people. She decided that she was going to keep this list out on her desk, so that when she started to get down she could look at this list and brighten up. Fall was going into winter and the Holiday Season was coming up fast. Lorrie needed to start doing her planning for the Holidays, so she was going to call and talk to Cheryl to see what they had planned. Lorrie called Cheryl and talked to her a minute about planning for the Holidays and Cheryl seemed a little distant, so Lorrie asked her if there was something bothering her. Cheryl told Lorrie that her Stepson was having trouble at his job with the Bank. He was coming home telling her that he had the stupidest Bosses in the world, that they wouldn't listen to him and that he was thinking about looking for another job, because they didn't appreciate him. She told Lorrie that he was drinking a lot now when he came home and was disagreeable, so she didn't really know what to plan on for the Holidays. This shocked Lorrie to her bones. Never had she suspected this, because she thought that Cheryl had gotten her Stepson beyond this kind of behavior, but this resembled the old Stepson that she had always known and she knew that no good would come of it unless he could be persuaded to see how lucky he was to have this great job. Lorrie told Cheryl that she would talk to her Husband and see if he could talk to her Stepson. Lorrie thought that this constituted a family emergency, because this wasn't only about a job it was also about the big investment that just not long ago went to buying that house and also her Stepson's career in the Banking and Investment Business World. Lorrie knew that Cheryl had invested almost her entire savings in it and she also knew that her Stepson didn't have much to invest in it, because he had been a spendthrift, so her Husband had secretly, he thought, given her Stepson enough money to finish getting a Mortgage to buy the house. She knew better then to try and talk to her Husband while he was still working in his shop in the back yard, so she needed to wait till he came in for the day and that was going to be hard for her to do. She was so afraid that her Stepson would do something on impulse that would be utterly stupid at work and knowing him that could happen at any time and at a moments notice. This was going to be a long afternoon for Lorrie, but she had no choice, she just hoped that they could be in time to avoid a big mistake by her Stepson. Lorrie was going to have to figure out how to start this conversation with her Husband when he came in from work. Lorrie decided to make some special snacks for her Husband to eat while he was drinking his beer, so it might soften him up to some reasonable conversation on the subject. He always listened to those controversial talk radio programs while he was working and sometimes he would come to the house already all upset from what he had heard on the radio and he would be impossible to calm down for a long time and she just hoped that he wasn't like that when he came in this time. Looking out the kitchen window she saw him making his way to the house. Lorrie was dreading this conversation, because she never knew how he would respond, she just knew that she had to do it before he drank too many beers. He came in and washed his hands, opened the refrigerator, got out a beer and Lorrie asked him how his work was going, so she could test his response to see if it was testy or just a normal response. Lorrie decided that he was in a decent mood, so she got out the snacks for him and poured herself a glass of wine to join him. After listening to him talk about his progress on a sport coat for a Member of Parliament Lorrie got up to get him his second beer and decided it was time to open the subject that she dreaded. She told him that there seemed to be the possibility of a big problem on the horizon with her Stepson and he might need to have a talk with him to find out what exactly was the problem at his Banking job. Her Husband just looked at her for a minute, then he got up and got himself another beer. He asked her to be more specific, so Lorrie told him about her calling Cheryl to find out about planning for the Holidays and Cheryl told her that her Stepson was planning on quitting his job and she was very upset about it and that she couldn't make plans for the Holidays because of that. Lorrie asked her Husband what should be done about this. She knew that he had a hard time making decisions, but she wanted him to have the first opportunity to make a suggestion. Her Husband drank his beer really fast and went and got himself another one and then he hem and hawed around not saying much, so Lorrie finally suggested that he call her Stepson that evening and try to find out what the problem was before it was too late. Her Husband paced around the room for a while and told her that he would but she needed to get her Stepson on the phone and talk to him first and then he would take over from there. Lorrie kept watching the clock hoping to get the call in before her Husband got drunk and she convinced him to eat his dinner before they called. After their dinner Lorrie called and talked to Cheryl for a minute then she talked to her Stepson and could tell that he had been drinking, but what could she do but continue, so she broached the subject of how his job was going and he proceeded to tell her how disappointed he was with his Supervisors and the stupid decisions that they were making and that he could do much better then they were doing, but they wouldn't listen to anything that he suggested. Lorrie listened and then told him that his Dad wanted to talk to him and handed the phone to her Husband. He asked his Son what the trouble was and listened to what he said and then Lorrie heard her Husband tell his Son that maybe he was right and that getting a different Psychotherapist might be the right thing to do, then he hung up. Lorrie was mortified by this, because she knew that her Stepson would be back on those dangerous pills again. Her Husband told her that his Son needed to have some relief from the stress of his job and if the Psychotherapist could provide that then all would be just fine. This is what happened and at least they avoided her Stepson quitting that great job that he had and things moved quietly into the Holiday season. Lorrie's plans for their Christmas went well like they had ever since Cheryl had become a part of the family and after that her Husband went on his first ski vacation of the season which allowed Lorrie a reprieve from him and a chance to organize their New Years celebration to include a few friends. Cheryl came over to their house to help Lorrie with the decorations and prepare the dips and finger foods for the guests. Lorrie asked her how things were going and Cheryl hesitated to tell her that her Stepson had convinced his new Psychotherapist to put him on those same pills that he had been on before. Lorrie told Cheryl not to let him drink when he was taking them and Cheryl told Lorrie that she couldn't stop him and that she had warned him that drinking with the pills would destroy his health, but she thought that he was hiding his pills so she couldn't monitor them. Lorrie knew how sneaky her Stepson could be, so she told Cheryl that maybe things would turn out all right in time. Lorrie's New Years party was a small affair that turned out really good without any problems and Cheryl and her Stepson even spent the night which Lorrie really enjoyed. The next morning New Year Day 2004 Lorrie and Cheryl were up first and they fixed a big pot of tea and fresh fruit and sweet pastry for their breakfast and had a nice visit before the men got up to join them. During their breakfast Lorrie's Stepson started complaining about his job and that he wasn't looking forward to returning to work after the New Year Holiday and that he was still thinking about finding another job where they would appreciate his ideas and his worth. They all kept quiet to keep the peace until her Stepson and Cheryl left, then Lorrie and her Husband got ready to go to their annual New Years day lunch with their friends for New Year Day 2004. After their lunch they went home to take a nap and Lorrie couldn't go to sleep, because of the things that were worrying her that could happen in 2004 and they were that her Dad might die and that there might be some big family upset with the way that her Stepson was acting. Lorrie's outlook for the New Year of 2004 wasn't positive.

Gus—2004 New Years Day 2004 Gus was upstairs playing his record, "In The Still Of The Night", that Lorrie had given him so many years ago. He loved that song and he had liked it before Lorrie had given him that record, but after she gave it to him it took on a even more special meaning. It was a solid connection to the past that had such sweet memories that he had to play that record only when he had the time to listen to all the words and be able to let himself drift back in time for a few minutes so he could again savor the taste of Lorrie's hot, wet, sweet kisses. Those kisses he would never forget and he had yet to kiss another woman that could come close to Lorrie's kisses. Gus enjoyed his walk down memory lane on New Years Day 2004, but he knew that reality was waiting for him to get back to work on his House renovation, because he was up stairs playing that record and up stairs was where he was going to be working, so everywhere he looked there was work to be done. The next day Gus went upstairs and decided that the first thing he needed to do was to take the doors off between the bedrooms and tear out the door frames and close in the openings. He had already renovated the little upstairs bathroom, so that job had been done a while back. Gus had already anticipated this, so he had all of the lumber on hand to do the job. It took him all day to close in the two doorways and make two solid walls separating the three bedrooms. Now looking at what he had done he was pleased with the outcome. This would allow him to build two closets, one in each of two adjoining bedrooms, that he had envisioned when he had surveyed what to do to the rooms and now he was sure about the plan that he had for their construction. In the small bedroom he was going to build a smaller closet that would have a portion of it that went under the roof line and it would be walled off with a overhead extension two door cabinet that could hold bedding with room under neath it for a big chest-of-drawers and wall mirror that would fill out that one wall in the small bedroom. On the opposite side of the room from this was enough room for a single bed and night stand with a lamp and he would build a shelf all across that above the bed to hold what ever items that they decided need to be kept there. That left enough room on the wall that went to the dormer window to hold the desk with the sewing machine and it's accessories. Now the room was all planned out. Gus started working on this little bedroom first and it took him over a week to finish the construction. The next room was the big bedroom that was large enough to hold a full size bed. Gus measured everything off and decided that his original idea of building a big double folding door closet was possible. This closet would go from the bedroom doorway toward the dormer window and like the closet in the small bedroom, it would include the small space under the roof line. This would make a nice size closet and he already had the doors that he had salvaged from downstairs and they were real nice wooden slatted folding doors that were expensive when they were bought 40 years ago. Gus was glad that he had all of this inside work to do during the winter, because he could keep working without the bad winter weather stopping him. This closet was the only real construction that he needed to do in the big bedroom, because the doorway had already been closed in that would have led to the smallest room that he was planning to use as his office. This closet was a little more difficult to build, because of the way that the doors needed to fit and also there were problems with the old construction being out of square. Finally after two weeks struggling with it, the closet was ready to hang cloths in. Gus then did some work on the walls on the big landing and then he was ready to start painting the upstairs. The upstairs was taking the same amount of paint that the downstairs took which was two coats of primer and two coats of top coat, so it was a slow process. The weeks were slipping by and when March arrived anr the first good sign of warmer weather came, he decided that he and his Wife needed to take a few days off and go to his Ranch in the Sierra Vieja Mountains. They spent four days out there doing what Gus enjoyed to do the best which was to look for Indian artifacts and explore more parts of the Ranch that were hard to get to. When Gus got back to Van Horn his next project was to build a big book shelf that would hold a couple of hundred books that he could place on one wall of the big landing. He had an old small door that had been in the storeroom that was made in the old way with inset panels that he cut in half length ways to use for the two ends of the book shelf and then he would build the shelves to go the length of ten feet and all the screws would be counter set, so the holes could be capped with pegs to give the book shelf a more professional appearance. He finally finished it and painted it with the same powder gray paint that he had used on all of the trim around the doors and windows and base boards in the rest of the house and this project took him two weeks from start to finish. Gus continued to go to his Main Street and Economic Development Board meetings and there were always rumors of something good happening that would bring prosperity and good jobs to Van Horn, but they always fizzled out when they were investigated. Gus had started hearing about Oil and Gas Companies experimenting with new drilling and completion technique called hydraulic fracturing. He didn't know much about it, except what information he was gleaning from travelers that he would talk to that were working in the Oil and Gas industry that came through town and he would see them at a service station or on a cafe and get a chance to talk to them, because Gus was still interested in the Oil and Gas business, he just hadn't been around it much in several years and had lost all contact with his old contacts. The people he was talking to were describing oil and gas formations that Gus was unfamiliar with, because these formations were located in the Texas Panhandle and West Texas and he had never worked in those areas. He was used to the formations along the Gulf Coast of Texas and he knew those good, but these were all new to him and he thought that he needed to learn more about these. The months had gone by and it was now in the middle of the summer and Gus was about to start on the last big part of his House that needed renovation and that was the stair case with it's turned spokes supporting a very nice ash handrail and the front entryway room. The handrail on the big landing balcony was loose and it had a turned spoke that had been kicked out at some point in time, but he had found the broken spoke and thought he might be able to fashion a new piece to replace the broken part to the spoke. This would be tricky to do, but he was going to try to do it. Downstairs the entry way room had a large place where the stucco was missing and there were several cracks that could be fixed with caulking and also there was a narrow window by the front door that was broken along with some problems with a transom window above the door. The end of each stair had trim pieces that were missing, so Gus was going to have to make these to fit each stair and this he knew was going to have to take a lot of time and patience. Gus was now 62 years old and working on this staircase was not only slow work it was also very hard on his aging body, because much if the time he was working down on his knees at different levels that put his body in difficult positions for long periods of time, but he was determined to get the job done if it took him the rest of his life to do it. He would have to take more rest breaks because he would get cramps in his legs, or his knees and back would hurt so bad that he would have to stand up to relieve them. It seemed to Gus like he had been working on his House forever and he would wonder from time to time if he had taken on more then he should have, but he was coming to the final stages now after two years and could see the light at the end of the tunnel. He was wanting to take a break and go to his Ranch in the Sierra Vieja Mountains, but he knew that before he felt good enough to do that very physical few days there he would have to rest up for a couple of days, because there was a lot to do out there to just set up the Camp House for them to use it that required a lot of physical strength and if he wasn't rested he would have a lot of trouble doing what needed to be done. He decided to take a week off to rest and then to go out to his Ranch for a break from the House renovation. Even after resting for two days Gus had a hard time setting up everything so that the Camp House could operate without problems. All of this tired him out again, so he decided that he wasn't going to do a lot of hard hiking around this trip out. Gus still got up early in the morning, but took his time drinking his coffee and sitting out under his brush arbor porch roof in the mornings watching the quail come to eat grain at the feeder that he had put up and drink at a pan of water hr had put out for them. There were two different types of quail on the Ranch and sometime they would both coveys would come at the same time and then the cocks would fight and the hens would run around making a lot of noise while that went on and it was amusing to watch how nature would work. He also had a little bird house on one end of the porch that a pair of fly catcher birds were raising their young one and he would watch them both fly off then return with some kind of insect to stuff down its throat. Eventually Gus would get in his old Jeep and drive around the Ranch roads just to look around and maybe see some wild life. In the evenings he would start a camp fire and sip on a beer or two before grilling some meat to have for dinner while his wife was cooking something on the camp stove in the Camp House to go with dinner. He would sit out out after dinner by the fire and watch the stars and listen to the coyotes bark and howl, then he would go in a d go to bed. After a few days of this he was ready to go back to Van Horn and continue work on his House there. It was late in the fall when Gus finally finished all of the work on his House. All that was left was miner things like hanging curtains in some of the rooms upstairs. He had started putting books on the big book shelf upstairs and hanging old pictures, paintings and old framed documents on walls in different rooms in the house to make it have a sort of museum atmosphere. Antique guns and old framed News Papers were also hung. He had a mix and match arrangement of furnishings that were part antique and more modern, but all in all it was a comfortable house that was more like living in one back in the 1950's. This Thanksgiving Gus was glad that he could go to his Ranch with his boys and not have to worry about coming back to work on his House. They had a good time out there as usual and Gus wished that they could come to Van Horn more often through the year, but it was just too far for them to be able to do that. Again this year no one killed a deer, but they always killed some quail and everyone seemed to have a good time. Christmas was always a quite affair for Gus and his Wife, because no family came to their House for Christmas. They had gotten to the point that they didn't buy each other much for Christmas gifts, because there wasn't really anyplace to do a lot of shopping, so they would get each other something like a used book from this used book shop in Van Horn. They never had New Years Eve parties either, so really the whole Holiday Season except for Thanksgiving was a very quiet affair. New Years Eve Gus stayed up by himself and sipped on a little whiskey when the clock brought in the New Year of 2005 and people in town started setting off fire works and shooting the guns off in the air. When he would tell his friends back in El Campo about people in Van Horn shooting off their guns in the air for the New Year they didn't believe him, but in so many ways this West Texas town was still back in the old days on how it operated and no one thought anything about it. Yes the year 2005 was here and Gus didn't have to worry about the big renovation on his House anymore. In 2005 he could concentrate on something else.

Lorrie—2004 The New Year of 2004 was starting with some trepidation for Lorrie, because of her Dad's continued downward spiral in health and her Stepsons attitude toward his job and his responsibilities toward his finances. Lorrie was hoping for the best in both cases, but she had a gut feeling that there was going to be trouble sooner or later. Lorrie knew that there wasn't much that she could do in either case. She would just go from day to day and try to take it as it came. Lorrie called Cheryl and told her to keep her updated on what her Stepson was up to and that she would try to help her if she could. Lorrie felt some relief now, because her Husband was off on his two week ski vacation and she could do things like she wanted without having to worry about how he reacted to things. Lorrie was calling back to El Campo, Texas more often then usual now trying to keep up with her Dad's medical condition. It was spring time in England now and Lorrie had already booked her round trip flight to Texas, hoping that she could get there before her Dad died, because she had been getting some really disturbing reports on him. Evidently he was to the point now that he was having trouble eating and swallowing food and sometimes even water. He was having trouble controlling his muscles in his legs and arms, so most of the time he would have to use a bed pan and a urinal, but some days were better than most. One of those phone calls checking on her Dad her Mom told her that she had a breast exam and that it showed some lumps in both of her breasts and that she was going to have to have a biopsy on them to see if they were cancerous. Her Mom told Lorrie that she would call her back when she found out the results of the biopsies. Lorrie thought to herself that what a year this might be with her Stepson threatening to quit his good job, her Dad on what looked like deaths door and now maybe her Mom has breast cancer. Lorrie's Mom called her about a week later and told her that the test results came back positive and that she was going to have to have breast surgery, but that she had decided not to have it just now because Lorrie's Dad was so weak that he might worry too much and it could cause his death. Her Mom told her that the family had decided not to tell her Dad about the cancer. Lorrie was also trying to keep track of what was going on with her Stepson and Cheryl. Her Stepson was starting to worry her a lot again since he had started his complaining about his job and bosses there. She had seen similar behavior from him like this before and she could recognize the familiar evidence that had lead up to some of his bad mistakes in the past. She was hoping that it could be avoided this time and that he would come to his senses if he had any left. Lorrie knew that her husband had secretly put money into the down payment on that expensive house that her Stepson and Cheryl had bought, because her Stepson had never been inclined to really save any money no matter how much he made, he always wanted to act like he was rich and he would let his money run through his fingers like water. He could be so exasperating sometimes and hard headed to the point of his own self destruction and when he got like that he didn't seem to care who he hurt or brought down with him. Cheryl told Lorrie that her Stepson was still complaining about his job, but that he was still going to work . She told Lorrie that what was worrying her now was his drinking and taking those pills that the Psychotherapist had given him. He had been warned about mixing alcohol with them, but he was doing it anyway. Lorrie called him and tried to talk to him about that and when he realized what she had called him for, he hung up on her. Lorrie was getting to the point with her Stepson that if he wanted to destroy himself then she guessed that he could, but she didn't want him to take them down with him. She didn't have time to worry about that right now, because she had to get everything ready for her trip back to El Campo, Texas. There were more serious things there to worry about then a prodigal Stepson in England. Lorrie's plane was putting hundreds of miles behind it from England and Lorrie was doing the same thing with the worries she had there. She was now focusing on what was ahead and that was the problem with her Dad and with her Mom. She had already told her Sister that she didn't want to stay with her in Houston like she always had done on these trips, but that now she felt that it was better to go immediately to El Campo, so she could be with her Dad and her Mom. Her Sister picked her up from the Houston Airport and they drove to El Campo to her parents house. There she went directly to her Dad's bedroom to hug and talk to him even before she took her luggage from her Sisters car. Lorrie was shocked, to say the least, at the way that her Dad looked and he was even having trouble trying to talk to her. Lorrie thought that her Dad looked bad on her last trip a year ago, but that couldn't come close to the way he looked now. She wanted to cry, but knew that she couldn't and she had to be strong for her Dad. Lorrie unpacked and they ordered her favorite Mexican food for dinner and her Brother brought it back to her Mom and Dad's house. After their dinner her Sister sat with her Dad and Lorrie her Brother and her Mom went on the patio to talk. Lorrie wanted to know everything about her Mom's cancer diagnosis and what the Doctor was saying about how much time her Dad might have left to live. Her Mom told her that as far as her cancer was concerned her Doctor wanted her to have the operation as soon as possible, but that she couldn't figure out a way to have the operation, because it meant that she would be in the Hospital for two weeks and there was no way to hide that from her Husband, so she had decided to take her chances and wait to have it later. She told Lorrie that her Dad's Doctor told her that her Dad could die at any time and that he was surprised that he had lasted this long and that he would soon need shots to dull extreme pain and he would be completely bed ridden if he didn't die first. Lorrie was hearing very depressing reports on her first evening back in El Campo. She lay awake a long time that night and thanked God that she had been able to come back before her Dad had died and she asked for strength and knowledge and promised God that she would use all her skills as a Nurse to try and make her Dad's last days on earth as pleasant as they could be. She also asked God to have mercy on her Mom to give her time to be able to have her cancer operation in time to stop it from spreading. The next morning Lorrie was surprised to find herself refreshed and rested. She went into the kitchen and put on the coffee and look in the refrigerator to see what she could rustle up for breakfast. After everyone had eaten breakfast and got dressed for the day Lorrie got them all together to find out exactly what the schedule had been on everything that had to do with her Dad from the first thing in the morning till the last thing at night and everything in between. She wrote it all down including all the times, so she could compare what had been going with her Dad to possible changes from day to day. Basically she was going to make a Patient Record Chart on a clip board that any Doctor or Nurse could read to be able to track absolutely everything about her Dad from how much time he slept to how much he urinated in 24 hours, his temperature, blood pressure, pulse, skin coloring, medication, food and liquid intake, etc.. Basically Lorrie had become her Dad's full time Nurse. She consulted with his Doctor everyday reading the Patient Chart to him and administrating medications to her Dad at his Doctors directions. She had a hospital bed brought in so she could do a better job of handling her Dad. She took her Dad to the shower in his wheel chair and bathed him like she was taught in Nursing School and he was embarrassed that his Daughter had to see him naked. Lorrie told him that he had done all of these things for her when she was small and now it was her turn to do it for him, so he need to think nothing about it. It wasn't hard for Lorrie to see how much that her Dad's health had deteriorated in the year that she hadn't seen him. There wasn't a thing about him that hadn't changed drastically, his physical appearance, his strength and even his speech were totally unlike they had been the year before. As the weeks went by Lorrie worked with her Dad in an endless cycle and was sure that it wouldn't be very long until her Dad would have to be fed through his veins because he was having trouble swallowing even the thin broth now and that he would have to be catheterized because he was becoming too weak to urinate on his own. She was having to administer a lot of antibiotics now through injections to help combat infections in his chest and lungs and also pain injections to help with his muscle spasms. Lorrie would take little breaks and go to the Library to get books to read while she was sitting with her Dad and keeping an eye on him. Every once in a while she would go to the Dairy Queen to get her a ice cream Sunday and sit there to eat it, just to have a little change of pace and break her tension. Just thirty minutes away from her vigil and Nursing responsibilities would refresh her and give her renewed determination to do the best for her Dad that she could. The weeks were going by and Lorrie had seen almost no one except her family and her Dad's Doctor and his Church Pastor. There had been a few people that she knew that would come by and visit for short periods and a couple of them were girls that she had gone to El Campo High School with. They had married local boys that Lorrie had known and their children were grown and away from home now. These women had grand kids now that were married and their conversation centered around their family and what each was doing and how proud they were of their accomplishments and how thoughtful their children were of them since they were getting older. They would compliment Lorrie on how wonderful it was of her to come back to El Campo all the way from England to help out with her Dad and they knew that their children would do the same thing when it came time for them to need help in their old age, then they would look at Lorrie to tell them about her children and Lorrie had nothing to say. The conversation faded out there, because what could Lorrie tell them, that she had been married three times and had not loved any of her husbands and her present Husband abused her physically, mentally and sexually, that she had one Son that she hadn't seen or talked to in years and she was actually ashamed of him and she had a Stepson that was brilliant, but was so unstable and selfish that she wished that she could be done with him, because of all the problems that he caused. There was no way that Lorrie could talk about her Married life and Son and Stepson to these old friends. They would just look at her and feel sorry for her that her life had been such a disappointment and failure. Lorrie was glad to end these visits, because they made her think about her own life and where she had made the mistakes that had taken her down the wrong paths and now as she was growing older, 59 years old in 2004, she wished that she had the life that these women had. At one time she would have called their lives dull and meaningless, but not now as she surveyed her own life, she found that yes, she had done and seen things that they had never done or seen and the only way they could come close to her experiences was to look at pictures and read books on those subjects, but by the same token those women have something more precious then anything that Lorrie ever had and that was a loving Husband that she could truly love back and loving, responsible, successful children that they could count on to be there when them and their husbands needed them. Lorrie knew now which one was the better life, without even asking herself that question, because she now yearned for the kind of life that her friends had lived and were continuing to live now, but she also knew that it was much too late for her to try to start over and build a similar life like they enjoyed, because for one thing she would need Gus to do it and that could never be in this life, maybe God would grant that to her in her next life. The months had gone by and it was getting close to the end of August now and she usually flew back to England the last of August. Her Husband was calling twice a week now wondering what he was supposed to do if she didn't come back when she had planned, because he knew nothing about how to bill for his Tailoring Business and he had no idea of want she had set up for paying the bills. Lorrie finally told him that she really had no idea right then when she was going to return to England, because her Dad was very critical and that she was about to put him on a catheter and maybe any day now he would have to be fed through his vein, because he couldn't swallow without choking and getting fluid in his lungs. Lorrie told her Husband that she was going to call his Accountant and see if he would send someone over to their house to pick up the check book and her ledger, so they could see how things were arranged to work ans she would give them instructions that they could follow so that all would be taken care of till she got back that it would cost him extra money, but that couldn't be helped and then he could stop worrying about it. He calmed down then and she told him that she was going to call the Airline and put her return flight on hold till further notice. Lorrie was right about her Dad's condition and she called in his Doctor for a consultation, before she did anything new and he agreed with her that she should put her Dad on intravenous feeding and catheterize him. His Doctor also wanted to increase her Dad's antibiotic injections and try to give him breathing treatments to bring up some of the congestion that was bothering him. Lorrie's Dad had been having a low grade fever for a few days and it was starting to increase slightly, so they wanted to try to get the infection under control that was causing the fever. Lorrie was afraid of pneumonia, because she had seen several patients die of that when she was Nursing full time for a living. September was a very rough month for Lorrie's Dad and also her Mom, Brother and Sister, because he went down really quick on a daily basis and finally on October 4th Lorrie's Dad took his last breath, he was 80 years old. Lorrie helped her Mom make all the funeral arrangements and the next day she called her Husband to tell him and he didn't seem to care about anything she had to say, all he was interested in was if she was coming back to England right after the funeral. This really aggravated Lorrie and she told him that she wasn't, because now they had to schedule her Mom's breast surgery for the cancer removal and that she wasn't going to come back to England until she knew that her Mom was going to be alright. Her Husband told her that he was hoping that she was coming back soon, because Cheryl was having trouble with Lorrie's Stepson and maybe she could help Cheryl. He told Lorrie that her Stepson had quit his job and that he was drinking a lot and Cheryl didn't know how she was going to deal with it all. Lorrie asked her Husband why he didn't help and he just got quiet for a minute and then he told Lorrie that he had tried, but he and His Son had got into a fight and he wouldn't talk to him any more. Lorrie told her Husband that right now she didn't have the time to deal with her Stepsons crap and they would have to do the best that they could till she got back to England and she hung up the phone and thought to herself that maybe she wouldn't go back and how about that. One of the things that Lorrie was dreading worst in England had finally happened. Her Stepson had quit his big job at the Big Bank. This was the second time he had pulled this stunt and Lorrie knew that it was going to cost her and her Husband no telling how much money to get things straightened out. Lorrie's Mom got her breast surgery scheduled really quick and she came through it remarkably well even though she was 82 years old. Lorrie and her Sister and Brother had the house all back in order by the time her Mom was released from the Hospital, so there weren't all of the medical devices laying around that were reminders of the struggle that went on to take care of her Dad. Lorrie was so glad that her Mom had come through the surgery so good and taking care of her was much easier then taking care of her Dad. Her Mom improved everyday on a steady basis, so she was able to do more for herself as her recovery progressed, whereas with her Dad his health deteriorated everyday, so his care got more intense all the time and that was a major difference. It was getting close to the Holiday Season in Texas and Lorrie had decided to stay in El Campo for Thanksgiving. She hadn't had Thanksgiving with her family in many years. She called her Husband to break the news to him and she knew that he wouldn't like it, but there was a hell of a lot that she didn't like about what he did and what could he do about it anyway way over in England. Lorrie's Mom was completely healed up from her breast surgery and she didn't even have Radiation Therapy or Chemotherapy, by the time Thanksgiving had arrived. Lorrie had a wonderful time at the family Thanksgiving dinner and she even saw some of her old girlfriends in the grocery store when shopping for the turkey and side dishes. Lorrie was feeling free again since her Dad's death and her Mom's surgery was over. In a way she was hating to fly back to England, because she knew that things were in a super mess there. It was almost December and Lorrie had scheduled her new flight for December the first. The last couple of days in El Campo Lorrie had her hair cut and colored by her Friend that owned the Hair Salon and as usual her hair came out a different color then she thought that it would, but even this made her happy, because she thought that some things stay the same even though there is a lot of unhappiness and sorrow that goes along with living your life. Her last day there she did her usual Texas food product shopping to take back to England and of coarse she had to take her yearly Gus memorial drive to all the places that she had seen Gus when she was just a young girl. When she got in front of his Mom's old house she pulled over and looked at it and remembered all the times that she had walked and rode her bicycle around it hoping to get a glimpse of Gus working on his Hot Rod. She had a big knot in her throat and an ache in her heart and she sat there and told Gus everything that she had gone through on this trip back to El Campo. She knew that this was silly, but somehow it made her feel closer to him and she needed to feel close to her true love right then. She started the car and drove back to her Mom's house and spent the rest of the afternoon packing to fly back to no telling what in England. Lorrie arrived back in England and found the house a complete mess with beer cans overflowing every trash can. She didn't say anything about the mess, but just went about getting unpacked and walking around to all the rooms trying to figure which one she needed to start working on first. While she was doing this her Husband was following her around with a beer in his hand and telling her about what her Stepson had done. What he was telling her sounded similar to the way he had quit his other good Bank job, but she knew that the only way that she would know everything was when she talked to Cheryl. Lorrie talked to Cheryl that night and invited her over a couple of days later after Lorrie had time to put the house back in some kind of order. Cheryl came over and Lorrie had prepared a salad and a pizza for their little dinner while they discussed the situation and Lorrie found out that her Stepson had been abusing the pills he had been given by his Psychotherapist by drinking while he was taking them and it had been getting a little worse for a while when he suddenly realized that his supply of pills was running out and he would have to go back to the Doctor to get them renewed. The Doctor denied him a renewal of the pills and her Stepson threw a fit and that was the last straw, so he quit his job in a way that they had to provide him with medical benefits to go to a new Psychotherapist and have treatment sessions for a period of months, before he could be considered to be ready to either be re-instated at the Bank or to be moved to an affiliate of the Bank. Cheryl told Lorrie that it was a terrible strain on her to try and keep up with the monthly payments on the house and she had taken so much of her vacation time and sick leave herself to watch over Lorrie's Stepson, because he had mentioned taking his own life. This was the first time Lorrie had heard about her Stepson threatening to commit suicide. Lorrie made arrangements for her and her Husband to get one on one with her Stepson the following weekend and her Husband let her handle the whole conversation like he wasn't even there and she thought that he should have been the one to actually lead the conversation with her Stepson, because he was his Dad and supposed to be the man of the house, but no he wouldn't say a thing. Lorrie thought that this was just like her Husband, because for as she had know him he could never make a decision, not even to where to sit in a Cafe. Lorrie basically told her Stepson that if he didn't watch himself that he was going to loose his home to the Bank and that if he cared about Cheryl then he should think of her more then himself and straighten out his behavior before he looses her, because a woman wouldn't put up with a man acting like and putting their future in jeopardy forever. Her Stepson tried to come back at her by talking about how bad he had been treated by his Boss's and Lorrie told him that she didn't want to hear that talk and that she was just telling him how life was and that if he wanted to ruin his life then just keep up with his selfish behavior and he would get what he deserved and that he wouldn't like it when he got it. With that she ended her meeting with her Stepson and they left to go home. Since Lorrie had been back in England her time had been taken up with getting the house back in shape, catching up on her Husbands Tailoring Business office work and dealing with her Stepson's stupid decisions. Lorrie was running behind on the time she usually used to get everything ready for Christmas, so she told her Husband to get his Son to help him go pick out a good Christmas tree, because she didn't have the time to go with him. That weekend they had her Stepson and Cheryl over for dinner and then to decorate the Christmas tree and to put up more decorations in the house. Lorrie told her Stepson that since he was on the medication that she wasn't going to offer him any alcohol to drink and she could see the resentment in his eyes, but she didn't care. They had a family Christmas and Lorrie got a gift again from Cheryl and her Stepson, but Lorrie knew that it was Cheryl that had actually got it for her and everything went off without any trouble. Her Husband went on his first Ski Vacation for a week and this gave Lorrie a breather from him which she always enjoyed. While he was gone Lorrie was getting everything ready for their New Years party that was going to be a very small affair this year. Lorrie wasn't in the mood to do to much to get together a very festive party. She just wanted something low key, so she just invited a very few friends. Everyone that Lorrie invited came to her little party except for her Stepson. Cheryl came and told Lorrie that he wouldn't come with her because he said that Lorrie would embarrass him in front of the other guests by not allowing him to have a few drinks to celebrate the New Year. Lorrie called him to try and convince him that if he wasn't taking his pills that he would allow him a few drinks, but he was stubborn and resisted her invitation, so she let it be. They had a good time without him and Lorrie had no doubt that he was drinking at his house, but she would have no part in that, after all he was supposed to be a grown man, but in her mind that was debatable. New Year 2005 was brought in at Lorrie's house in a rather subdued manner, with her Stepson absent and also everyone knew of the hard time she had in 2004 with the death of her Dad and the cancer operation with her Mom, so there was mostly a feeling that they were glad that 2004 was gone and maybe 2005 would be a great improvement to look forward to. The only one that got really drunk was her Husband and he went to bed shortly after the New Year of 2005 was announced. After her Husband went up to bed Cheryl helped Lorrie straighten up her kitchen then she went up to bed in the spare bedroom and Lorrie poured herself some brandy in a glass then went into her little office and looked at the list she had made in 2003 about the things that she was thankful for, so she could look at it when she was feeling low and it would remind her and lift her spirits. There were eight things on the list and now she was going to scratch to of them off, because they weren't there any more and they were her Dad still being alive and her Stepson still having his job. She read over the rest of them and she smiled and knew that no matter if they somehow all had to be scratched off some day, that one would remain and that was #8 her sweet memories of her only love Gus and she thought that with that memory in mind that she could go to bed on the first morning of the New Year 2005 feeling better, so she could rest before she had to go to their usual annual New Years lunch with their friends.

Gus—2005 New Years Day 2005 Gus sat around watching movies on his video screen. He didn't have TV, but he could watch movies when he was tired of reading. He was also restless now that he was through with all the renovation work on his old House in Van Horn. He thought that now he could spend more time at his Ranch in the Sierra Vieja Mountains in Jeff Davis County. This he decided was going to be one of his primary objectives, after all isn't that one of the main reasons that he moved so far out to the high mountain region of Far West Texas, but he also needed to think about a way to make some money. He wished that there was some oil drilling going on in the area, so he could try to get into it, but there wasn't anything going on any closer then around Midland which was 250 miles from Van Horn. He had invested a good part of the cash money he had brought with him into renovating his House and he would like to replace that money. He still had income coming in from his little retirement from the State of Texas, the sale of his Ranch House and some of his Ranch in Wharton County, but all of the Residential Lots he had developed were paid off now and one day the Notes on his Ranch House and his Ranch Property would also be paid off and the clock was ticking on those, so he needed to figure out something to replace that. What he didn't know he would just have to keep his eye open for opportunities. Gus decided that he needed to go back to visiting a local Cafe in the mornings where he knew that a lot of the local men went to drink coffee in the mornings and discuss what was going on in the town and the surrounding maybe he would be able to gain information that he wouldn't be able to get otherwise. He knew that going there was just about as good as going to a ladies beauty shop to find out the local gossip and information. Gus started going to the Cafe in the mornings and he soon made some friends there that invited him to sit at their table that had eight or ten men there each morning including the local County Sheriff that he already knew. Gus did learn some interesting things at these morning sessions, but best of all is that he met a local Rancher there that had a 30,000 acre ranch 35 miles northeast of Van Horn in the Apache Mountains. This Rancher was a few years older then Gus, but they came from they same era in time and had the same love of the land. They became friends and Gus went to his Ranch in the Apache Mountains with him from time to time. Gus was also still involved with the Main Street Board and the Economic Development Board. He and his wife would pack up and go to his Blue quail Ranch for a few days at a time when he didn't have any meetings with the two boards that he belonged to and these were real enjoyable to Gus. He would explore all that he wanted to and the more he looked around the more artifacts, semi-precious stones and fossils he would find. He was amassing quite a collection that he took back home with him to Van Horn. One morning when he went to the Cafe for coffee his Rancher Friend was sitting at a table with an older man and his son with a map between them and Gus was invited to sit with them. The man was looking for a 640 acre section of land that was somewhere close to Gus's Rancher Friends land and they were trying to find it on the map. They thought that they had it located, but there was no ownership designated on the map. He and his son had been out there the day before and had tried to identify the location of it with a GPS device were not sure of it's property lines. The man indicated that he would like to sell it and asked Gus if he might be interested and Gus asked him what he what price he wanted and the Man told him $150.00 per acre and Gus told him that he wasn't interested, but that wasn't true. The real reason was that Gus simply didn't have the money to pay $96,000.00 for land at that time. The Man and his son left after giving Gus his contact information and Gus asked his Rancher Friend if he would take him out to where they thought the land was located so he could look around at it. After they finished their coffee they drive out to where his

Rancher Friend thought it might be, but he also didn't really have any idea if the property lines. What Gus saw didn't really impress him. The area was not as beautiful as where his Blue Quail Ranch was located. The land did have very good easy access with a State of Texas black top road and he thought that he saw electric power lines way off that might be located on the land, but at that point who knew. Oh well he thought maybe he learned something that would come in handy in the future. A few days later when Gus was reading his local town news paper he noticed an advertisement by the Town of Van Horn that they wanted to give free rent to someone that would renovate a small adobe building on the main street and start a business in it. This really caught Gus's attention, because he was always on the lookout for opportunity. He called the City Hall and found out the address of the building and then went to look at it. It was on the main street in Town and really right in the middle of town, which could be considered a prime location. The building was in terrible condition, in fact it was scarey to enter the building. The lot around it was grown up waist high in weeds with all sorts of junk laying around in it that could hide a rattle snake or two and there were two old elm trees next to the building and hanging over the rotten roof that were half rotten and one of them had a big killer bee hive in it's trunk. Gus got out his flashlight and ventured inside. The two front plate glass windows had been broken out and in places the ceiling was falling in. There were all sorts of scattered trash on the floor that had floor tile pealing up and there was sheet rock on the walls that was yellowed, gray with mildew and had holes knocked in it. There was a back room that at one time had a fire started on the floor and tin cans scattered around, probably by some vagrant that was staying there during the winter. He noticed a lot of spider webs that were inhabited by Black Widow spiders and that gave him a chill. He started feeling things crawling on him it seemed like. The smell in there was appalling. He went back home and loaded his extension ladder so he could take a look at the roof. What he saw up there confirmed what he had suspected and that was that the building would have to have a complete new roof, because it was so rotten and sagging that he only made a few steps on it before he became wary and decided that it wouldn't be wise to proceed, because if he fell through there wasn't anyone to rescue him. Anyway he had gained the information that he needed to understand what the building would need and it was a lot. He saw that there was a restroom in the building, but it was old fashioned and in pitiful condition and he looked over the electrical boxes and wiring and decided that none of it could be saved, it would all have to be new. Gus didn't know how much property was in the lot that the building was situated on and he would have to find that out, but there was also an old empty Service Station next door that looked like it had been built back in the 1950's and the lot in between it and the building was the one that was so grown up and full of junk. Gus went back home and started thinking about what he could do to the old adobe building to bring it back to life and then what sort of business would it be suited for. It was a small building only 16 feet wide and 50 feet long, basically only 800 square feet inside. He had never owned any downtown business property any where he had lived before and the idea intrigued him. Gus thought that if he could get it for the right price then he might be willing to invest his limited funds in it and put it back in shape. The next few days Gus went back to look at the building several times and the more he looked at it the more he was convinced that he would be able to do much of the work himself. He decided to go to the City and see what kind of deal he could make with them. He had a meeting with the Mayor and the City Manager and they brought out the Map of City Property along with the survey of the building and the size of the lot it was situated on. Gus found out that the building was actually sitting on part of an old alley that had been closed years ago and that the actual lot was only a few feet wider then the building. Gus didn't like this, because it didn't give any room for a parking lot or even room to park machinery to work on the building. They told Gus that if he renovated the building the City would give him two years rent free. Gus looked at them and asked them why they would want to rent the building when they could sell it, because then it would go back on the City Tax Rolls. They looked at each other and the Mayor asked Gus who in the world would buy such of a run down building and Gus told them that he would for the right price and deal. Gus told them that from what he had just seen on the City Property Map was that there was a big lot between the Adobe Building and the old Service Station that the City also owned and that if he could acquire another 50 feet of that lot along with the Adobe Building to be included in the same deal then he was willing to make an offer. They asked Gus what sort of offer he proposed and Gus told them that if he could buy the Adobe Building along with the extra 50 feet of the adjoining lot for an entire ground space lot of 60 feet by 100 feet he would pay $500.00 dollars cash and he would start the renovation within one week of receiving a Recorded Deed and the City would pay for all legal work and not put the property on the City Tax Rolls until it was completely renovated. This would give Gus 60 feet of frontage on the main street and it would go all the way back to the other street in the rear of the building. They were agreeable to the deal and told Gus that they would have to get it passed through the City Council at their next meeting. While Gus was waiting for the City Council decision he was trying to determine what plan he would have for the Adobe Building if he bought it. Hid first thought was to fix it up and rent it, but for what that was the question, then he started thinking about opening a business in it himself. Gus got the idea of a Coffee Shop-Cafe combination. Something that wasn't offered in Van Horn, something that might attract tourists and travelers. He started to envision a retail food business that offered fresh ground coffee, specialty teas from all over the world, 1950's banana splits and ice cream Sundays, soup of the day, B-B-Q brisket, ham, roast beef, turkey, and spam sandwiches, jumbo shrimp cocktails, fresh garden and shrimp salads, wines from a local vineyard and imported beer from Mexico. He thought that he might put in a small breakfast selection also. He didn't want to get into the heavy grease frying steak and potato menu. Gus knew that he didn't know the first thing about the retail food business, but he thought that he could learn and if this worked it would be the answer to his problem of developing a source of future income when some of the others he had would be gone. He begin to gather all the information that he could on the retail food business. The City Council met and approved his deal on the Adobe Building and the additional 50 feet of the connecting lot. Gus immediately started to make plans to clear the ground of the lots and to have the property surveyed to establish its property lines. He hired a local dirt contractor to bring in his backhoe-front end loader tractor to do the work. They pushed all the brush, weeds and trash in a pile and loaded then in a dump truck to be hauled off, then Gus waited till late the next evening when all the killer bees were coming back to their hive in the hollow tree. When it was very close to dark and he had been watching the bees come back to the hive they had in the hollow tree for some time he saw that they had stopped flying in and decided that he had to go ahead and kill those that were in the tree, before it got to dark for him to see anything, so he pumped up his sprayer that he had gasoline in and started spraying in the hole in the tree and he could hear the buzzung commotion going on inside and a few would fly out, but not many, but then all of a sudden there were more Killer Bees coming back to the hive and it was to dark for Gus to really see them, but he had to protect himself by mostly listening to their flying buzz and shoot the gasoline spray in that direction and this went on for nearly an hour before it finally stopped. The Killer Bees had been attacking him from several directions and he did get stung three or four times, but to Gus it was like he was standing in a fixed defensive position, because he dare not run and he was shooting at an enemy with superior numbers and he ended up with a few wounds, but he won the battle. This tree had to be removed because it was growing by the foundation and it was hanging over the roof and nothing could be done until it was removed, so Gus had to get rid of the killer bees in order to do it. He was glad that this was over with. He had tried to get a Bee Keeper to come and remove them and he did come and look things over, then he told Gus that he wouldn't mess with those Killer Bees. Gus went to the Adobe Building the next morning and found his foot prints in the dirt where he had been standing the night before when he was fighting the Killer Bees and he was surprised to see literally hundreds of dead Killer Bees surrounding his foot prints. They were within two feet of where he had been standing and he had no idea how close they had been, because it was dark and he was shooting spray at them by their buzzing sound only. He had the Dirt Contractor dig out the Killer Bee tree along with a smaller one and haul them off. Now Gus had the Dirt Contractor level the lot with the aid of Gus using his surveying instrument to shoot the grade. Now the Gus was ready to start working inside the Building to basically gut it and save what he could to maybe use later. February had gone into March but it was still pretty cold when Gus started working inside the Adobe Building. He started tearing down the old ceiling that was falling down in places and he discovered that the 2x6 ceiling joists that were the main support for the roof that spanned the width of the building were sagging a lot and he would have to figure out how to solve that problem without having support post's from the floor to a support beam, because he wanted a clear floor space especially since the building was so narrow. After cleaning out all the debris he started tearing out the sheet-rock walls that had been built over the original adobe-stucco walls and he found that there many good 2x4's that he would be able to save for use later somewhere. The stucco behind these sheet-rock was still in pretty good condition, but it didn't extend any farther up then the bottom of the ceiling joists and above that the adobe brick was showing all the way to the flat roof. Gus now had a plan to use the old roof as the ceiling and stucco over the adobe brick and around the ceiling joists to the bottom of the old roof, that was to now become the ceiling and that would make the ceiling joists go through the stucco to give the inside of the building the southwest Santa Fe look. He had to rip out all the old electrical wiring and get rid of the outdated fuse boxes. Gus was now involved in another major renovation project and he had only finished his House renovation a few months before this. He looked at this project as being different though, because this one might be able to make him some money and his house wasn't that kind of an investment. Gus had completely gutted the inside of the building and cleaned it out so it would be ready for the new remodeling to begin. Spring was turning onto summer and Gus knew that he had to do something about those sagging ceiling joists, before he tackled his idea of installing a new all metal roof above the old roof with a crawl space in between the two. There was an adobe wall at the back of the first room and that wall was the original back wall of the old building, but someone had built a smaller cinder block room behind that and connected it in a fashion that they made a door between the two rooms, to extend the building. Gus had figured out what he was going to do to solve the sagging problem with the ceiling joists and that was to run a six inch steel I-beam as a support from the front door all the way through the length of the first long room then knock a hole through the back room adobe wall and T that into another six inch I-beam that would run crosswise behind that wall that would support the roof of the cinder block addition, These I-beams would be welded to four inch square tubing that went to the cement floor and were secured by masonry bolts. The ceiling joists were jacked up six inches and the I-beam slipped under them for the support to keep them from sagging again. It was tricky to get all of this in place, but it worked perfectly and looked good and stable. Now that Gus got the old building in a stable condition he could concentrate on the new roof and an addition that he had been drawing out on paper that consisted of a patio in the rear of the building that would be as wide and long as the building itself with eight foot cinder block stucco walls that have small barred openings that resembled the ones that were in Spanish Presidio walls and the patio would have a flagstone floor with a flower bed to one side, a water fountain, over head colored fiesta lighting and piped out music. Gus located a small time local contractor that he had met and hired him to do most of the cement, masonry and interior remodeling. Gus also needed to get the new roof on the building and get the windows in so the building would be dried in for winter so work could be done during those months. Gus found another local contractor that would install the new all metal roof, but first the other contractor had to raise the outside walls of the building with cement and cinder blocks, so the new roof could be recessed behind them to block the wind that sometime could be very strong. This would lessen the chances of the wind gaining an entrance under the roof and blowing it off. Gus was having trouble here with trying to get the two contractors to schedule their separate work so that when the contractor that was doing the masonry to raise the walls, to accommodate a new roof, was finished the other contractor would get started with the new roof. He finally had to get both together and tell them that if they wouldn't work together on this that he would fire them both and find some others that would do the job. The two contractors then agreed to do the job like Gus wanted and there wasn't any more problems. It was late summer by the time the new roof was in place and Gus also had new window plate glass that he installed along with a new back door, so now the building was secured and dried in for the winter. During the fall months they worked on the eight foot high wall surrounding the big patio area and Gus located some flag stone on a ranch 50 miles to the southeast of Van Horn that he bought, then loaded and hauled to the Building location to be used for the patio floor. During the winter they worked and finished the interior except for the new wiring, painting, plumbing and he decided to wait till spring and better weather so when he started they could also do all the outside wiring at the same time. The Holiday Season slowed down everything, so Gus decided that he would stop all the work until after New Years. Thanksgiving was always a happy time for Gus, because he got to see and spend some time with his boys at his Blue Quail Ranch in the Sierra Mountains in Jeff Davis County 35 miles south of Van Horn and only 8 miles from the Rio Grand River and Mexico. This was the only time that they came out to see him and they all enjoyed them selves to the limit. When it was all over Gus always felt a little lonesome for a few days until he got back into his normal routine. Christmas was it's quiet self as usual, because neither Gus or his wife did much in the way of shopping. They weren't into buying things just to have them, they were more of the kind of people that bought what they needed and what they bought they had a specific use for it. The only deviation from this was books. They both liked to read and they would go to two different places in Van Horn that sold and traded in used books. When they bought each other presents it was usually used books or something the other one needed. Gus spent a quiet New Years Eve as usual and stayed up reading to listen for the fireworks and the gun shots in Van Horn that would announce the arrival of the New Year of 2006. When they started booming and popping

Gus looked at his clock and sure enough 2006 had arrived. He closed his book and went to the refrigerator and got out a bottle of whiskey, Gromes & Ulrich 1936, that had belonged to his Dad, who had died in 1971. It was his Dad's private stock, he use to call it, and Gus poured himself a double shot of it over some ice. He would drink it only on special occasions and he deemed this one of them, because he could see now that he was going to be through with his renovation of his old Adobe Building down town, sometime in this New Year of 2006, which meant that he would be able to open his first retail business establishment in this New Year of 2006. He had never started or run a retail business before. He had started a Home Health Care Business that hadn't made any money and he had been a Partner in a Child Care Business in Sugarland that didn't really make him much money, but never a real retail business selling a product to customers on a daily business. Gus was sipping his Dad's whiskey and thinking back on all the different business that he had been involved in even his little lawn mowing business when he was 9 years old that he did with that old push mower without a motor on it and it had made him money. This had been his first taste of thinking up a business for profit. He had also worked for several other people when he was young, like when he worked part time for a local News Paper in El Campo when he was an 11 year old kid and his first Service Station job that allowed him to buy his first car when he was 13 years old, then there was his real good Service Station job when he was in High School that paid him $75.00 per week and that was when Lorrie and her friends would come in to flirt with him. Lorrie, all of a sudden Lorrie dominated his thoughts. He discovered that it seemed that he had been so busy that he hadn't taken the time to think of her. Well it wasn't like he thought of her all the time anyway, it was only when he slowed down that she would seep back into his thoughts and then memories would wash over him and seem like they just happened yesterday. Why was that Gus wondered. On New Years Day a little after 12:00 am Gus sat in his Grandmothers old rocking chair, sipping on his Dad's old whiskey thinking about that sweet Lorrie and those wonderful Corpus kisses, he called them, that she gave him on the beach in Corpus Christi in 1962. That was 44 years ago and that would make her around 60 years old now and Gus would be 64 this year. Gus thought my goodness how time goes by so quickly and that time on the beach seemed like only yesterday it was so clear to him. He could almost taste her sweet,soft, liquid lips touching his as he remembered every detail of that time, then he snapped out of it like he had been in a trance and discovered that his whiskey was gone and the ice had melted and that it was now 12:30 am on New Years Day 2006 and he had been in that trance thinking about Lorrie for almost 30 minutes. Well the New Year of 2006 had started and Gus was ready for it.

Lorrie—2005 New Year 2005 Lorrie had gone to bed thinking about Gus and for her that was enough to give the New Year a good start. Lorrie and her Husband had their annual New Years Day lunch with their Friends and that was a pleasant relief for Lorrie to have a conversation with old Friends and enjoy their company. This pleasant time helped to momentarily shut out the looming problem that her Stepson was causing again. Lorrie went for a scheduled Doctors appointment to check her Diabetes and High Blood Pressure. Ever since her Dad had been diagnosed with Parkinson's Disease and her Mom Breast Cancer, Lorrie had been more attuned to her own health symptoms and she sometimes wondered if she wasn't getting a little paranoid about them. Lately every time there was some different feeling in her she wondered if there was a terrible health problem starting, after all she was almost 60 years old. A few days after her Doctors appointment her Doctor called her to come back in to get the results of her Laboratory Tests. He told Lorrie that her medication for Blood Pressure and for her Diabetes was doing an adequate job, but the Tests showed that she had a big increase in High Cholesterol and he want her to start on medication to combat her High Cholesterol. Lorrie picked up her Cholesterol pills and placed them on the table with her High Blood Pressure pills and her Diabetes pills and then sat down to look at all the bottles of pills that were building up on the table and they were all hers and not a single bottle of pills were her Husbands and he was the one that drank alcohol like a fish everyday, so you would think that he should be the one with health problems. He never went to the Doctor, so maybe he did have health problems and he just didn't know it. Lorrie just shook her head and wondered what else would the Doctor find wrong with her next year, because it seemed like every year now he had found something else wrong with her health. She guessed that this was the way things went as you were getting older. Lorrie's Husband went on his two week Ski Vacation and Lorrie was relieved to be away from him for a while. He had basically had been no help with the turmoil that her Stepson was causing. Lorrie was afraid that two things were going to happen if he kept up his erratic behavior and they were that he and Cheryl would eventually loose their house and then

Cheryl would finally get tired of his selfishness and leave him. Lorrie felt that if Cheryl left her Stepson that it would be his final undoing, because there had never been anyone but Cheryl that had brought stability to his life, not even Lorrie herself and certainly not his Dad, her Husband. She didn't know what to do about it and decided that she would just have to float along with what happened on a day to day basis. Her Husband came back from his Ski Vacation and went back to work with his Tailoring Business and he had orders for garments waiting for him. Lorrie was so glad that even though he drank so much he was still able to keep a steady hand and turn out excellent work and was a sought after Tailor. Her Stepson was called back in to the Bank in the early spring for a Review and Conference with their Personal Department. They had found that he had completed all of his appointments and therapy examinations with the Psychotherapist he had been assigned to and their decision was that he be reinstated as an employee of the Bank, but at an Affiliate Bank that was smaller and serviced a different market. They told him that his salary and commissions would be somewhat smaller, but he would retain the same employment benefits as before if that position was acceptable to him and that he would have the weekend to think it over and if all was satisfactory to him that he should show up for work at their Affiliate Bank on the next Monday morning. Cheryl had called Lorrie and told her that her Stepson was having that meeting and Lorrie had her fingers crossed that it was going to go well and that the Bank wouldn't fire him. Later that day Cheryl called Lorrie and told her the results of the meeting her Stepson had with the Bank and this gave Lorrie a lot of relief until Cheryl told her that her Stepson was infuriated that the Bank would basically demote him when he was the best, smartest employee that they had and that there was a conspiracy against him at the Bank to get rid of him before he showed up all of his Bosses to the Board of Directors. When Lorrie heard this from Cheryl she rolled her eyes back in her head and she wanted to scream at her Stepson to get in the real world, but she knew that she had to control herself. Lorrie told Cheryl to let her speak to her Stepson and when he got on the phone Lorrie congratulated him for retaining a position with the Bank and that this would give him an opportunity to improve the other Bank that he was being assigned to. She thought that talking to him first in a positive manner would defuse any thoughts that he would be harboring about her scolding him, which is exactly what she would like to do. He told Lorrie that he wasn't sure that he wanted to take the position at the Affiliate Bank and Lorrie told him that he better think about that long and hard, because if he lost his job completely at the Bank then he would also loose his House and Cheryl would leave him and that he could count on that happening, because her and his Dad weren't going to pay the payments and that Cheryl had just about had her fill of his foolishness and what he needed to do now was to concentrate on going to work and taking care of his responsibilities. Her Stepson was quiet for a minute and he told Lorrie that he would try it at the Affiliate Bank to see how he would fit in there. Lorrie was relieved and wondered how long this job would last him, before he found something wrong with it. Lorrie was starting to make plans for her annual three month Vacation with her Family in El Campo, Texas, so she booked her round trip tickets on her flight early as usual to take advantage of the discounts for early reservations. Her Husband complained that she had been over there for half of the year before, so why did she have to go for three months this time and she told him that she was simply getting back to her regular schedule. Lorrie thought to herself that she had to keep her three month trip away from her Husband other wise she would simply loose her mind if she had to be around him and the problems that her Stepson were causing. When Lorrie boarded the airplane in England for her flight to Texas she was overwhelmed with relief to get away from the tension at home and this time there weren't any problems in El Campo that she knew of. This trip back to Texas would be like they used to be before her Dad was diagnosed with that terrible Parkinson's Disease that had gone on for several years and had finally killed him. Her Mom had done well after her Breast Cancer surgery and she had been Cancer free on all of her tests this year so far. Lorrie was looking forward to visiting her Dad's grave site and talking to him there like she used to do when they did their drives around El Campo with a six-pac of beer. She landed in Houston and her Sister picked her up and she went with her to her house for a few days like she had always done before. They did some shopping and Lorrie rested for a few days then they drove to El Campo to her Mom's house. They were met with enthusiasm from Lorrie's Mom and Brother. Lorrie unpacked her luggage and then they all went out for lunch at their favorite local Mexican Cafe. This was so relaxing for Lorrie, because for a very long time there had been trouble and worry in El Campo and England both and now there was none of that just good conversation with teasing between Sisters and their Brother and laughing and of coarse good old Tex-Mex food with plenty of spicy salsa and beer to wash it down with. Lorrie's Mom was enjoying it also and Lorrie was so glad to see how well her Mom had adjusted to her Dad's death and to her own Breast Cancer operation. She was in good spirits and she was also getting around very good for her age. This break from the troubles in England is exactly what Lorrie needed. She didn't do much of anything for the next few days. Lorrie would get up in the mornings and make the coffee then go out on her Mom's patio to drink it and stare off out in the back yard and remember all the sweet times that she and her Dad had sat back there and sipped their beer and talked. She was going to go out to his grave in the next few days to visit and talk to him about a few things that she didn't want to talk to anyone else about. Right now though Lorrie was just enjoying not having any real responsibility and not having to deal with the endless problems that her Stepson produced and having to look at the scowling face of her Husband. This was the first time in years that she felt so good and free and away from burdens. Lorrie almost felt like a young girl again, if it wasn't for the reality that she had to go back in the house to take her three pills that marked her as not being young, but a woman that had a body that was aging. One of the first things that she was going to do was to get an appointment with her Friend that owned the Hair Salon to see if she could get in when her Mom went on Thursday which was her Mom's standing appointment every week and had been for many years. Lorrie went with her Mom the her Friends Hair Salon and let her Mom get in the chair first while she was looking at a magazine that had different hair styles in it, because she had decided to try something else and was having trouble making up her mind what he wanted. She finally picked out two different ones that she liked and called them #1 and #2 then wrote those numbers on two different small pieces of paper and rolled them up and placed them in a candy dish on the table there then closed her eyes and felt around till she felt the papers and picked up one and unrolled it to find out that it was #2. Well that was the one that she was going to show her Friend that she wanted to try. Her Mom got out from the chair and went under the hair dryer and Lorrie got in the chair and showed the hair style to her Friend and told her that she was sure that she wanted to try that hair style with the same color that she usually used. Between Lorrie's Mom and herself she spent about two hours in her Friends Hair Salon and she didn't hear anyone say a word that could lead to any information about Gus. While Lorrie was at her Friends Hair Salon her Friend told her that every Monday her and some old friends met for lunch at different Cafe's and wondered if Lorrie would like to meet them on the next Monday and Lorrie accepted with joy.

This was exactly the kind of socializing that Lorrie liked to do and no telling what she might learn out of the gossip that those women would talk about. Before Lorrie met them for their Monday lunch she wanted to get her toes manicured and painted so they would look good in the new sandals she had purchased when she and her Sister had gone shopping before they drove to El Campo. Seldom could she wear sandals in England, because it was to cold most of the time or to wet, but here in El Campo she could wear them everyday if she wanted to unless it was raining a flood, which it sometimes did. Lorrie met them on Monday at a favorite B-B-Q Cafe that had been in El Campo for years and she was really enjoying herself eating B-B-Q ribs, pinto beans, rice salad, pickles, iced tea and banana pudding for desert. She had decided to surprise her Mom by bringing her some banana pudding back home to her, because she knew that her Mom loved it. While they were eating and talking, a group of Cowboys came in and brought their heaped-up plates of B-B-Q over to a table next to Lorrie and the other women and they were talking about the cow work that they had been doing and their horses and of coarse Lorrie was all ears when it came to hearing about cow work and horses, so she had tuned out the conversation that the women were involved in and she was listening to the Cowboys. Who ever they had been working for didn't seem to know what he was doing, according to their thinking and one of the oldest Cowboys started telling stories of Ranchers that he had worked for many years before when things were done differently. He was telling stories about a Rancher that was the last one that he had worked for that still drove one pasture full of his cattle a long distance to get to his working pens at his HQ so he could work them and the different things that happened on those cattle drives. He said that Ranch was the Open Pitchfork Ranch and the Rancher was Gus and that he always knew exactly what he wanted to do and had everything organized and not only that, but when it came time to take off time for lunch he would bring the Cowboys into El Campo to the old B-B-Q place next door and tell the Owner of the B-B-Q Cafe to fill up the Cowboys plates with what they wanted and he would pay for it before they left to go back to the Ranch to finish working the cattle. That oldest Cowboy told them that Gus fed better then any of the other Ranchers he had ever worked for. Lorrie was stunned, because she had no idea that Gus could be a Rancher. She always thought that he might have a car repair shop or something like that. When the Cowboys finished eating and were getting up to leave Lorrie stopped the older Cowboy and asked him if she had heard him right about Gus being the Rancher that owned the Open Pitchfork Ranch and he told her that yes that was who he was talking about. Lorrie asked him how long that he had known Gus and he told her that he had known him for years ever since he had been a young man himself and that he and his brother had worked cattle for Gus far a long time until Gus had sold out and moved away. Lorrie asked him if he knew where Gus had moved and he told her that he really didn't know. Lorrie thanked him and went back to the table where her friends were sitting and her Friend that owned the Hair Salon asked her if she knew those Cowboys and Lorrie told her no, but they knew someone that she had known and she was just trying to find out what had happened to him. Lorrie's Friend asked her who it was and Lorrie told her that she was asking about Gus and her Friend told Lorrie that no one seemed to know where Gus was, that he had just moved away from El Campo. All of this made Lorrie a little sad, that Gus had seemed to just vanish into thin air. Surely someone knew where he was and maybe someday she would run into that someone. Lorrie's three month Vacation in El Campo was coming to a close and she was a little sad about that, because it had been very pleasant and she had also been able to see a few of her old High School friends. Lorrie also really liked the Monday lunches that she looked forward to with the other women along with her Friend that owned the Hair Salon. It was time for her to get herself organized on leaving, so she did her usual Texas Food shopping to take back to England with her and she went out to her Dad's grave one more time to say goodby to him and talk to him just a little. She told him things that she couldn't tell him when he was alive about the life that she had hidden from ever since she had been just a young girl and asked him to please forgive her for that, then she told him the whole story about her and Gus and that if they would have been together that she knew that her life would have been one that he and her Mom would have approved of. She told her Dad that if she ever had the chance to find Gus again that she wouldn't pass up the chance to find out what happened, that was if Gus was still alive, but she felt in her heart that he was. The next day Lorrie did her Gus drive around to all the places that she had seen him and while she was driving she told Gus that she had talked to a Cowboy that had know him, so now she knew that he had once had horses and cattle and that when she was young she would have loved that. Lorrie then drove back to her Mom's House to pack up everything and get ready for her Brother to take her to the Airport in Houston the next morning for the long flight back to England. When Lorrie got back in

England she found out that Cheryl was having trouble with her Stepson again complaining about his new job. Lorrie thought that this was the same old pattern that her Stepson always used before he finally found an excuse to quit his job. He would go along good for a few months then he would start complaining about one thing and then another thing and finally he would build a case for himself that his Bosses and Supervisors were ganged up against him because they realized that he was much smarter than they were, so they were trying to keep him from advancing. She had heard it all before and could almost quote him word for word. She didn't want to even hear it and she decided that she was going to wash her hands of it this time and gust see what was going to happen. Lorrie took her time catching up on her Husbands Tailoring Business paper work and they even got back into going to their Country and Western Dance Club dances. Lorrie really liked these and they were a pleasant diversion from the reality of her everyday life. She started making plans for the Holiday Season and as usual had Cheryl help her, so they could plan things that would include her Stepson and Cheryl. As the Holidays got closer Lorrie and Cheryl got together to make all their plans first for Christmas then for New Years Eve. Lorrie could tell that Cheryl wasn't her usual easy going self and asked her what was bothering her. They sat down with a fresh pot of tea and some cookies and Cheryl started pouring out her heart to Lorrie. Cheryl told her that she was afraid that Lorrie's Stepson was starting to pull some of his old tricks about his job and that she didn't know if she could take much more of it. She told Lorrie that she loved him, but if he quit his job this time that she would loose all faith in him and she didn't want to get trapped in Marriage with him when he was going to do that all the time. She was wanting a more stable life with someone that would make a good husband and father and that there was no way that she would consider getting pregnant and having children with her Stepson as long as he was so selfish and unstable. She told Lorrie that her Stepson had become addicted to those pills that the Doctors had been giving him and that is why he always wanted to change his Psychotherapist so he could start all over with a new program that required him to have access to those pills. Lorrie told Cheryl that she understood perfectly and that if she decided to leave him that Lorrie would never think bad of her and that she had tried to talk sense to her Stepson, but it went in one ear and out the other and it had always been like that ever since he had been eight years old when she and his Dad got married. Lorrie told her that she had done all that she could with him and that now all of them would just have to see what was going to happen and wish for the best. Lorrie knew that she hadn't helped Cheryl very much with that statement, but she had to tell her the truth. Lorrie also knew that if her Stepson didn't straighten himself out that she was going to have to have a talk with her Husband about him and she sure wasn't looking forward to doing that. She could see the handwriting on the wall, so to speak, that time was running out on her Stepson and his realizing how life really worked. He had been pampered all his life and even before Lorrie had Married his Dad he had been spoiled by his Grandparents and his Dad, because his Mom had died of cancer when he was young and now all of that was coming back home to roost, unless her Stepson miraculously turned over a new leaf. Lorrie thought that it could happen, but she wasn't going to hold her breath waiting for it to happen. They had a nice, quiet Christmas and Lorrie tried to get everyone a gift that they would want. Cheryl and her Stepson got Lorrie some Country and Western music albums by the artists that she liked the most and Lorrie was really thrilled, because she loved her Country and Western music. After their Christmas her and Cheryl started putting their plans together for the New Years Eve party. They wanted to keep it small again like they had done for the last several years. Cheryl helped Lorrie get everything ready for it and just a few friends of Lorrie and her Husband and also a few of Cheryl and her Stepson's were invited. The whole evening went very well and most of the guests left before the New Year came in, but a few stayed for the champagne toast at 12:01 am. 2006. Lorrie's Husband went up to bed and Cheryl helped Lorrie clean up some after everyone left, before she and Lorrie's Stepson went to their own house. After they left and everything was quiet Lorrie poured herself a small amount of brandy and put one of her new Country and Western albums on to play softly. Lorrie sat there listening to the music and thinking about last year 2005 and decided that it had been much better then 2004 had been and that the worst part had been the stunts that her Stepson had done that put the whole family in stress. Lorrie thought that this New Year of 2006 might be a good one especially if her Stepson would behave himself and if not then it would turn everything upside down. Also she needed to have talk with her Husband about what she was thinking and that would be hard. She decided to wait till after he returned from his last two week Ski Vacation when he would be in a good frame of mind. Starting a New Year was always a little mysterious to Lorrie, because what you might think it would bring could end up being just the opposite, but what ever happened she still had Gus's sweet memory to take her into the New Year of 2006.

Gus—2006 New Years Day Gus had been sipping his Dad's whiskey and remembering all the business and jobs he had been involved in his past and also thoughts about Lorrie. The weather had been so cold in January that Gus didn't do any work inside the building, because he didn't have any heat in there. February was just as bad, so it was March before any real work could be done. Gus decided that it was time to do all the electrical work and after that he would do all the plumbing, then the flagstone patio floor and all the other details that he would need before the building was ready to put in the furnishings and equipment for his Coffee Shop. Gus decided on doing the electrical work before the rest so they could stop using a generator and have the electric power for their tools. He had made a friend in town that had moved back to take care of his Stepfather and he had been a licensed electrician in Austin, Texas. Gus had made an agreement with him to furnish all the supplies and tools to do the work and to also be his helper and to pay him by the hour for his work. This suited Gus just fine, because it not only would save Gus money, but he would be able to learn some tricks about wiring a building that he didn't know and Gus was always interested in learning new practical skills that might help him in the future. When Gus thought about the future he also thought about his age and that was that he was going to be 64 years old this year and he didn't think many men 64 years old were considering learning new work skills for manual labor at 64 years old. His Dad had died when he was 61 years old and Gus had always used that as a sort of bench mark to use when thinking about how much time he might have left. Gus had already passed that mark and he had thought about that when he had done it, but it didn't slow him down and he just couldn't help thinking things that had a future to them. Gus had purchased a big breaker box and from there he wanted to run all the wiring in conduit tubing and this is what they did all through the building and the patio and outside for the flood lights. Gus bought a tubing bender and learned how to use it and he learned a trick in pulling several wires through a long length of tubing, with curves, which can be very hard. You can squirt dish washing liquid in the tubing before you start pulling the wiring and it makes the tubing slick inside and reduces the friction so the wires slide easier. Gus learned several tricks to electrical work from this friend and that alone was worth money to him. The next project that Gus was going to tackle was the plumbing and that was going to be a big project, because it required running water and sewer lines all the way from the sewer main and the water meter to the inside of the building and hooking up the toilet and all the sinks, hot water heater, valves for an ice machine and Gus was going to do all of this himself. He first hired the man with the backhoe to dig the trenches for the sewer line and the water line and he had him dig a deep hole by the foundation of the building right next to the outside wall where the bathroom was going to be so Gus could dig under the foundation, by hand, so give him access to work in a hole underneath the building to do the plumbing to connect the toilet to the maim sewer line. It took Gus till the end of April to finish all of the plumbing. His next project was to lay the flagstone on the patio floor and he knew that was a back breaking job. Gus first had to level the dirt on the patio and then water it down so it would settle and be firm. Then came the job of sorting through the different sizes, thicknesses and shapes of the individual flagstones and separating them into piles so he could be able to choose what he would need as he went along laying them out. Gus had done some of this kind of work before when he lived in Sugarland, but nothing that was as big of a job as this was going to be. He found out after the second day that he wasn't going to be able to work on this but about half a day at a time, because of the extreme strain on his back, so this process went very slow. Some of the stones were thicker and he would have to dig under them to make them level and others that were thinner he would have to build up under them with mortar mix to make them level. When he was finished laying all of the flag stones he poured sacks of mortar mix all over them and took a broom and swept the mortar mix into the spaces that separate the stones and then he put a sprayer on the water hose and he washed and swept the stones and soaked the mortar mix till there was water standing in puddles all over the patio, then he left it to firm up for three days before returning to walk on it. The flagstone patio turned out real nice and along with the stucco wall with it's small barred mission style windows gave it a real Southwest look. Gus was pleased with it and this and it was the last big project to do except for buying all of the tables, chairs, etc. that he would need for the actual operation of his Coffee Shop Cafe. Gus applied for his license to sell food and also for a license to sell beer and wine. It was now the end of May and Gus was getting the finishing touches done along with advertising for staff and putting together a menu, checking prices, ordering beer, wine, food products and driving to El Paso to get all of the specialty teas and coffee and fresh baked buns for the sandwiches. Gus opened the bank account for the business and decided to name it the Blue Quail Coffee Shop. He finally opened up on July 1, 2006. His business hours were from 9:00am till 10:00pm at night. Opening day was an exciting one for Gus and he was expecting a lot of people to come in just to see what the place was like. He had the patio all set up with eight tables with umbrellas the fountain going and music piped out to the patio which gave it a real nice ambiance mix of music and the sound of water splashing. The patio was Gus's favorite place. Gus's opening day was a big disappointment for Gus, because there were very few people that came in. Most of the time Gus and the staff just sat around and twiddled their fingers. When he got home with the days receipts and figured what the day had cost him to operate he had lost $ 130.00 dollars. He thought that it would pick up when word got around. The next morning he was up at 5:00am, so he could get down to the Coffee Shop by 7:00 am, because he had a lot to do before opening time at 9:00am. He had to wash off the patio, set up the outside chairs and umbrellas and turn on the water fountain, then he had to thaw out five pounds of shrimp to boil for the shrimp cocktail's and shrimp salad, then he had to slice up a B-B-Q beef brisket and get it into a crock-pot with sauce to stay hot for his B-B-Q sandwiches, then set up the cash register with the money to start out the day, re-stock the cooler with beer and chilled wine. His first staff would come to work at 8:30 am to start making the fresh garden salads and peal the shrimp that Gus had boiled earlier, fill the salt and pepper shakers and refill the napkin holders, put out cream for the coffee, grind the fresh coffee beans and make the first pots of coffee for the day. The second day went a little better and by the time Gus got out of the Coffee Shop to go home it was 11:00 pm and than he had to take all the receipts home to his office there to get everything figured out and make his report for the sales taxes and the report to the Texas Alcoholic Beverage Commission, so by the time he was through it was 1:00 am and then Gus still had to take his shower before going to bed. This same schedule went on day after day and Gus wasn't getting but about four hours of sleep each night and sometime less if there had been mistakes made on the cash register that he had to find and straighten out. His Wife was helping also by making the soup of the day and baking cakes to sell slices for desert and working to make the food for the orders of customers. The months went by and every week he would have to take money from his personal Bank Account to add to that of the Coffee Shop. He wasn't very happy about this, but he had been told that often it took six to eight months before a business would start to make money. Gus was prepared to give it a year, but having to work that hard with only three to four hours of sleep a night and loose money was hard to do. He was tired all of the time and he lost 30 pounds in his weight, but was determined to stick it out for a year. He found out that he had very few tourists as customers and most of them were locals, but when there was a football game or a wedding or some benefit for someone almost the whole town went to these and no one showed up in the Coffee Shop. Some days were very good and some days were terrible. On top of all of this he didn't have any time to go to his Blue Quail Ranch in the Mountains. He was closed on Sundays and Mondays, but there was no rest then, because on Sundays he was up at the Coffee Shop fixing something and n Mondays he and his wife went to El Paso to shop for all the things that they had to buy there, so basically it was a seven day a week business that had been loosing money every week. They were closed three days for Christmas and Gus decided that they would go to his Ranch for a couple of days. When they got out there they found out that drug runners from across the Rio Grand in Mexico had broken down the front door of the Camp House and broke out a window and stayed there a couple of days, steeling several things and leaving the Camp House open to the weather and rats, snakes and all sorts of varmints. He had to drive back into town to get the hardware store owner to open for him so he could buy a new door and something to close up the broken window till he could get a new one installed. Gus was so mad that he could hardly work to try to repair the damage enough to secure the building. The one good thing that happened during this time was that the oil business in the oil fields of Far West Texas started booming again and some of these oil people would come in the Coffee Shop and Gus would get information from them. He soon learned about the new oil and gas structures that he previously had no knowledge of and the Oil Companies that were active in the area. He ran an advertisement in the Van Horn news paper as Blue Quail Oil & Gas. This prompted him to start back into the Oil & Gas business and he used the Coffee Shop as a place for these people to come and also for people that wanted him to help them secure a lease, so slowly he was starting to build up a reputation in Van Horn as a man that knew the Oil & Gas business and he started to make a little money at it. New Years Eve came and went for Gus and all that he wanted to do was to get a little more sleep, so he had that opportunity to go to bed at 8:00 pm New Years Eve and he slept till 8:00 am the next morning New Years Day of 2007. He went up to his office after he had his coffee and thumbed through his bank statements on the Blue Quail Coffee Shop for 2006 and found that for that six months he hadn't made a single dollar for the whole six months, but he had put money out of his own pocket back into the business every month. He was wondering if he could hold out for another six months. The only bright spot about the Coffee Shop was that it was a place that he was using to get his Oil & Gas Business going. Maybe the year 2007 would see both the Coffee Shop and his Oil & Gas Business make some money. He would just have to wait and see what was going to happen in 2007.

Lorrie—2006 The New Year 2006 had begun for Lorrie with her deciding to hold a firm line with her Stepson if he kept up his foolish behavior. When her Husband got back from his two week Ski Vacation she had a good talk with him. Lorrie just laid it all out to him about what might happen if her Stepson quit his job with this Bank. She knew that her Husband liked Cheryl as much as she did, so that was the first thing that she stressed was that she knew that Cheryl was going to leave his Son if he quit this Job, that she had all that she could take of his needless instability. She told her Husband that it was past time for him to take a firm hand on his Son and have a man to man talk with him about how life worked. He told Lorrie that ever time he tried to talk to him over the past several years they ended up in a big fight and it just got nowhere, so what was he supposed to do. Lorrie asked him what he was going to do when Lorrie left his Son and then he lost his house and all her Husband did was to go to the refrigerator and get himself another beer. Lorrie thought to herself that both her Husband and her Stepson were impossible. Lorrie decided not to worry about it until and if it happened. They continued to go to their Country and Western Music Dance Club which Lorrie really enjoyed and they tried to meet friends at the local Pub they liked for dinner and drinks once a week. Things were going better at home for Lorrie now and she was grateful for the opportunity to live without being under stress all the time. True that there was no sweet talk, kisses or real love making between her and her Husband, but at lest they were not screaming and fighting as they had been for most of their Marriage. Lorrie wondered how long it would last till it all blew up again. There had been times like this before, but they never lasted for very long. With the winter over and spring warming things up Lorrie's Husband was out planting herbs and tomatoes so she could have them to cook with. Lorrie loved to cook and she really liked to use fresh herbs in her recipes. Lorrie also liked to walk down the hill from her House past a lake and watch the ducks with their ducklings wattling across the sidewalk nipping at the new fresh green grass and going to the lake for a swim, on her way to the store in Bromley. She considered this as exercise and also a way to clear her mind of things that were troubling her. Spring time brought with it this relief outlet that helped to flush out the drab overcast feelings that the long, nasty winters in England built up in her, so she could look at her world with a fresh feeling of goodness. She would stop for a minute to watch them and talk to them like they could understand what she was saying. With her arms loaded with groceries she would huff and puff going back up the hill to her House with a better feeling in her then when she had left her House before. There was just something about getting outside and away from her House on a pretty spring day that really refreshed Lorrie. Her health had been holding it's own with the medication that she had been taking, so she was becoming more resigned to the fact that her age was working against her in some respects. Inside her mind she still thought like a young girl, but when she undressed in front of the mirror all of her youthful thoughts faded away at the image in front of her. She wondered if she had taken the decision of putting on weight and not making herself attractive to far, in order to discourage her Husband from approaching her for sex. Lorrie thought my goodness what would Gus think if he saw her like this, because her only memory of him was as a viral young man with a strong, slim, muscular body and she couldn't imagine him any other way. Her Vacation trip back to Texas was still two months away, but Lorrie was already thinking about booking her Airplane round trip ticket to get the best price. She was changing cloths to help her Husband do some planting when the phone rang. Cheryl was on the phone and she asked Lorrie if she could come over that evening that she wanted to have a serious discussion with both of them. She told Lorrie that she would be by herself and Lorrie told her to come on over for dinner and that she would fix something special for them. Cheryl didn't tell Lorrie what the subject was that she wanted to discuss, but Lorrie got a kind of sick feeling in her stomach when Cheryl told her that she would be coming alone. Lorrie went outside and told her Husband what her conversation was with Cheryl and that he should be prepared to hear the worst and that Lorrie would appreciate it if he would refrain from getting drunk while Cheryl was there, because they both would need to listen carefully to what she said.

He told her that he would finish the beer that he had and not drink any more. Lorrie thought that he looked a little stunned and was worried about what she was going to say. That evening Cheryl did come alone and both Lorrie and her Husband felt very meek in her presence, because they could see that Cheryl had a determined look on her face and that she was carrying a folder of papers wit her. Lorrie had prepared a beef stew and garden salad with French bread and garlic butter and tea for dinner and Cheryl suggested that they go ahead and eat their dinner before discussing the subject that she had come to talk to them about. After their dinner they retired to the living room with coffee. Cheryl told them that she was sorry to have to come to them to talk about a subject that they were all hoping never happened, but that things had getting to the point of no return with the relationship between her and Lorrie's Stepson that she felt that she had no choice but come to them, so they wouldn't be surprised and also so they could hear the whole story. Cheryl told them that one of the reasons that she had held on to her relationship with Lorrie's Stepson was the love that she had for them, but she was at the end of her rope with him. Cheryl told them that he had quit his job at the new Bank the day before and that she had told him that she would give him one month to find another job and stay with it or she was going to leave him for good. Cheryl started to cry quietly and Lorrie got her a napkin to dry her eyes then she continued and Lorrie and her sat quietly and let her pour out her heart to them. Cheryl told them that she really didn't expect him to get a job in that months time so she needed to start making her plans to get back on her own and that included talking to them. She told them that Lorrie's Stepson had ruined her financially by demanding that they buy such an expensive house that it took all of her savings to make the down payment of $ 50,000.00 and he only put in $ 5,000.00 on it and then every time he had quit his jobs she was the one to have to pay all the bills and the Mortgage payments on the House, because he had never saved any money. Cheryl told them that all of his wild spending was so he could impress his friends and make them think that he was rich. She told them that he had ruined her emotionally, with all of his instability, wild spending, his addictions to his pills and alcohol and he had also ruined the love she had for him. Cheryl spread the papers she had brought with her out on their coffee table and showed them what she had put into the Down Payment and the money she had paid on Mortgage Payments and what Lorrie's Stepson had put in and she told them that she was preparing to take Legal Action against him to recoup her $ 50,000.00 savings, because she was going to need it to start over and that she was sorry to have to do it, but she felt that she had no choice if he didn't make some arrangements to pay her. She told them that he didn't want to sell the house to settle the debt on it and even if they did that it wouldn't sell for enough to pay off the Bank Note, so she told Lorrie's Stepson that he could keep the House, but she wanted her $ 50,000.00 savings back. Lorrie's Husband stayed quiet, but Lorrie asked Cheryl what she was going to do if her Stepson got a job by the end of the month and Cheryl told them that she didn't see how that could happen when he stayed drunk and hopped up on those pills like he was now. She told them that she had given him a month and would see what happened, but while that month was going on she was continuing to make her plans to make her break from him and that they were even sleeping in different bedrooms now. Lorrie didn't tell Cheryl that her and her Husband hadn't slept in the same bed for 20 years. Lorrie asked Cheryl if she thought it would be alright if they talked to her Stepson and Cheryl told them that was fine, because she wasn't afraid that he would hurt her, that she was just through with him. Lorrie's Husband finally spoke up and told Cheryl that if it came to it they would see to it that she got her money. When Cheryl was standing to leave she thanked them for being so good to her and that she had hoped that things would have turned out better, but she wanted to always be friends with them. They hugged and Cheryl left. Her Husband went and got himself a beer and Lorrie poured herself a glass of wine and they both just sat there quiet for a while not knowing what to say. The gravity of the conversation with Cheryl finally wore off of Lorrie and she told her Husband that she didn't want her Stepson to move back in the House with them and become a big baby to take care of. Her Husband told her that if Cheryl left his Son that he would probably move in with one of his friends. Lorrie convinced her Husband to call his Son and invite him over to talk. He came over that next week and Lorrie asked him what he had planned to do about a job. Her Stepson told them that he needed to talk to his Psychotherapist about getting his benefits extended so he could keep paying the Mortgage payments on the House. Lorrie looked at her Husband and saw that he was just looking down at the floor. She then told her Stepson that he was ridiculous and that he was loosing the best thing that had ever happened to him. He then tried to put blame on Cheryl telling them that she was against him just like the people at the Banks were against him. Lorrie stopped her Stepson and told him that they weren't stupid and that she knew him like a book and that this was only his fault, so not to try to blame Cheryl like he had done to other people all of his life when he was at fault. She asked her Stepson how he planned on paying Cheryl back her money she had put into the House and he said that he would pay her. Lorrie came back to him and asked him how he was going to that when he had no money and no job and not a damn thing to sell to get the money. At that he looked at his Dad and Lorrie told him that he had better start looking for some kind of job the next day and forget about that Psychotherapist stuff, because that wasn't real life it was only an excuse. He screamed at her to shut up and then he stormed out of the house. She looked at her Husband and told him that he knew that her Stepson would never have the money to pay Cheryl and that she wasn't going to pay it, so was he planning on taking it out of his savings since he had told Cheryl that he would see to it that she got her money back. Her Husband just glared at her then got up and got another beer. All of Lorrie's hopes for her Stepson were going down the drain and she had now lost all confidence in him. She knew that he could be brilliant, but he also had a self destructive side that she couldn't understand. Lorrie told her Husband that no matter what happened about this she wasn't going to let it stop her from going back to Texas for her three month Vacation. In fact she was thinking to herself that she couldn't wait to get away from all this unnecessary trouble that her Stepson was causing again. Before Lorrie left for her Vacation her Husband had told his Son that he would pay the Mortgage payments for a couple of months for him if he needed it. Lorrie left with that going on and glad to be away from it. The airplane landed in Houston and her Sister picked her up as usual for a stay with her for a few days before driving to El Campo to her Mom's House. They did their usual shopping with Lorrie buying some cloths that she would leave at her Mom's house when she returned to England. Lorrie stayed at her Sisters for a few days mostly resting and trying to get the troubles behind her before she got to her Mom's in El Campo. They drove there and were met with delight from Lorrie's Mom and Brother. Lorrie gave them the gifts that she always brought with her for them and then they all went to their favorite Mexican Cafe for Lorrie to get her annual Mexican food fix. This was always so special for Lorrie to sit around a table at this Mexican Cafe with her family sipping beer and eating Mexican food spiced up with hot salsa talking and laughing till her sides hurt and she had tears in her eyes. It was so sweet, but she missed her Dad at this special dinner every time she came back to El Campo now. This was her second trip back since he had died and it was hard for her to believe that it had been almost two years since he died. Life goes on she thought, but things are never quite the same when you loose someone so important to you. Lorrie went with her Mom to her usual Thursday hair appointment at Lorrie's Friends Hair Salon. She intended to get her hair cut and colored also. While Lorrie was sitting in the Hair Salon chair her Friend was cutting her hair and talking as usual when she told her that she had purchased herself a computer and she was having a hard time trying to learn how to use it. Lorrie told her that she had purchased one also about a year ago and she had paid to take a class that taught you how to use your computer. Lorrie told her that it helped her a lot and maybe that is what her Friend should do. They decided to trade e-mails so they could stay in closer contact when Lorrie was back in England. Her Salon Friend told Lorrie that the only information she got about Lorrie, when she went back to England, was when her Mom came in for her hair appointment and told her what Lorrie was doing from when they had talked every Sunday on the telephone. Now they could stay in touch with their e-mail. This made Lorrie real happy, because she had known this woman since she had been a young girl. Although her Salon Owner Friend was four or five years older then Lorrie they had been close friends a long time and she knew some things about Lorrie that her Family didn't know. That Monday she went to eat lunch with them at the local Dairy Queen and caught up on the town gossip. Lorrie ordered a foot long chilli-cheese hot dog with onions like she always got there when she was in High School and that always brought back pleasant memories when she was young and thought that she had problems, until real life slammed her in the face and real problems presented themselves. These lunch outings with the girls on Mondays were really fun for Lorrie. She had been in El Campo now for a month and it suddenly dawned on her that she hadn't even thought about all the mess that was going on in England with her Stepson. She hoped that him and his Dad hadn't killed each other by now. Well she wasn't there to suffer through it and she hoped that by the time she got back there that everything would be resolved. In the mean time though she was determined to enjoy herself and have a nice visit with her family and maybe she could see some more old friends also. Lorrie bought some flowers and went out to her Dad's Grave to talk to him. She sat down on the ground next to his Grave and talked to him like she had done when they had driven around with a six-pac of beer, except now she could even talk to him about things that she could never have before. Things that would have been embarrassing to her and things that would have been disappointing for him to hear about her. Lorrie was baring her soul to him about her secret life in England that they didn't know about. She only told them the good parts and even had made up good things at times when there weren't any good things to tell them. They had always thought that she had the near perfect marriage to the Englishman. Now she could tell her Dad the truth, so she poured out the years of secrets she had held back from him right up to the present with the trouble with her Stepson. Lorrie asked her Dad to please forgive her for not being honest with him about her life and that she knew that he would be angry with her for putting up with the abuse that her Husband inflicted on her, but she just couldn't make up her mind what to do about it. She told him that she had wanted to leave her Husband many times, but didn't want to admit to her Family that she had made another mistake, so she had stayed there and she told him that she had even thought about committing suicide before, but couldn't decided on the way that she wanted to do it. Lorrie told her Dad that she was going to be 61 years old, so she would die in England and be cremated then her ashes would be sent back to El Campo for her Brother to spread on the beach at Matagorda where they used to go as a Family and she had so much fun there as a young girl. That is what she wanted. Lorrie got up and looked at her watch and couldn't believe that she had been talking to her Dad for two hours. When she got back to her Mom's house it was time for their happy hour on the back patio. Her Mom asked her where she had gone in the afternoon and Lorrie told her that she had visited a friend that she hadn't seen for a couple of years, then the conversation drifted to other subjects. Lorrie's three month Vacation at El Campo went by much to fast for her and it was time for her to get things ready to leave. She still had two important things that she needed to do and they were doing her Texas food shopping for the things that she always took back to England and to do her annual Gus drive around pilgrimage, as she called it. She didn't hear a word about him this time and wondered if he was even still alive, because she knew that he was a few years older then she was. When Lorrie arrived back in England she wanted to turn around and fly back to Texas. She brought her luggage in the House and there was furniture stacked everywhere. While she was gone her Husband had let her Stepson move back in his old room and they had brought what furniture he had from the house that he and Cheryl had and just stacked it in her and her Husbands house. Her Husband couldn't make up his mind where to put it so it just sat where ever they had stacked it. Lorrie didn't ask anymore questions right then, because she was so tired from her trip and aggravated by what she was seeing that she didn't think that she could handle any more bad news. She told her Husband that she didn't want to talk about what had happened till the next day, that all she wanted to do was unpack, shower, get something to eat and relax some before she went to bed. She didn't even see her Stepson, because he was in his room with the door closed and that suited her just fine. Lorrie knew that she would have plenty of time to see him the way it looked. Lorrie woke up after a restless sleep late the next morning and went down the stairs to the kitchen to have some hot tea and cereal for her breakfast. Her Husband was in his Tailor Shop in the back yard and she guessed that her Stepson was still sequestered in his room upstairs, because she didn't see him. She finished her cereal and got herself another mug of tea and her husband came back in the house. He didn't say anything at first and Lorrie just looked at him then she held out her hands to the sides palms up as if to ask what happened. He stammered around trying to tell Lorrie what had transpired without making without ever getting to the point, so finally Lorrie just started asking him questions so she could get the real picture of what had gone on while she was gone. She found out finally that her Husband had paid Cheryl her money out of his own savings and that he had been paying the monthly payments to the Bank, so the Bank hadn't foreclosed on his Son's house. He told her that his Son didn't want to loose the house, so they had moved all of his share of the furniture to their house and put his Son's house up for rent. Her Husband told Lorrie that he thought that his Son could rent it for more then the monthly Bank payments. Lorrie ask her Husband what he planned to do with all that furniture that was cluttering up the down stairs rooms. He told her that he didn't know that he had thought that maybe she would want some of it to replace some of their furniture. Lorrie looked at him like he had fallen on his out of a tree. She told him certainly not and that they could put what could fit in the attic and the rest her Stepson would have to sell. Lorrie told her Husband that she hoped that he had learned something about his Son from this terrible experience that he had put them in and just because of his selfish attitude to everybody and everything. She asked her Husband how long he thought that her Stepson would be living with them and he told her that he was already looking for another job, so it shouldn't be to long. Lorrie looked at her Husband in disbelief and told him not to hold his breath. After a couple of more months trying to rent her Stepson's expensive house out for enough money in monthly rent to cover the Bank payment and repairs they gave up and went to a

Professional that told them that renting it for that price was impossible, so they had to lower the price of the monthly rent payment and it wouldn't even cover the payments that they had to make to the Bank. Lorrie's Husband had to make up the difference and that really burned Lorrie up. She told her Husband that her Stepson had been nothing but trouble to them ever since they got married and that was 22 years ago. She told him that he had been soiled so that he would never grow up to take responsibility for himself and that if things kept up like this that they would be stuck with him for the rest of their lives. Lorrie told her husband that her Stepson was nothing but a big over groan, spoiled baby and that if he would have let her alone with him when he was a small boy she would have trained him to be responsible. She was furious at all of the sacrifice that they were having to make for this big spoiled brat at their age when he had been making more money then they did and he had thrown it all away with his stupid ideas of superiority. At this her Husband, who had been drinking one beer after another, became angry and he screamed at her to shut her damn mouth and he lunged at her and grabbed her, shook her and slapped her real hard and threw her on the floor. Lorrie laid there crying in frustration as much as being physically attacked. A little while later there was a knock at their door and Lorrie opened it to find three Police Officers standing there and they asked to come inside. Lorrie stepped back and let them in and they told her that they were responding to a call that a domestic disturbance was in progress and they wanted to know if there had been a problem at this address again, because they had been called here several times in the past. Lorrie called her Husband to come and talk to the Police. He came into the room weaving trying to keep his balance and Lorrie told him why the Police were there. One of the Officers told him that they could see that Lorrie had been crying and that it looked like she had been physically abused and that when neighbors report loud domestic violence there is always something to it. The officers told her Husband that he was getting quite a large Police file built up on himself and that he had a real nice home there and probably a good income, so he should think more about behaving himself before he ended up in jail. At that the Police excused themselves and left. Lorrie's Husband turned around and went up to his room slammed the door and went to bed. The Holiday Season was around the corner now and Lorrie no longer had Cheryl to help her with it and also it was always so much fun planning things with her. Lorrie messed her a lot, but what could she do. Lorrie thought that everything had turned upside down this year and they had ended up with her Stepson back living with them. Their Christmas came and went and her Stepson still had no prospect of a job. He was out from under the employment umbrella of the Big Banks now, so his possibilities of a real good job in his area of experience was smaller. Lorrie knew that sooner or later her Stepson would have to take what he could get and not wait around for the big job. His house was still vacant, so they were still paying the whole Bank payment. Lorrie did some decorating for New Years Eve, but it sure wasn't the same without Cheryl. She fixed some dips and finger food for anyone that wanted to stop by, but really her heart wasn't in it for several reasons. They had a few people stop by to wish them a happy New Year, but none of them were her Stepson's friends. Most of them had disappeared after he quit his job, lost Cheryl and moved out of his house. He stayed in his room most of the time unless he went for a job interview and then his Dad had to give him money for his train and bus fare. Lorrie's Husband got drunk and went up to bed before the New Year of 2007 came in and she stayed up to watch the festivities on the TV. Thinking of the New Year 2007 Lorrie tried to get positive remembering that she still had her wonderful friend Jill and her sweet memories of Gus.

Gus—2007 New Year Day 2007 passed and Gus opened up the Blue Quail Coffee Shop hoping that it wouldn't take to much longer for it to start to make a little money. The long sleep he had refreshed him so it wasn't as hard to get up so early and do all that he had to do to open by 9:00am. He had been having trouble with one of his waitresses and he was wondering if she was going to show up for work. She was a pretty little gal that was a good worker, but she was wild as could be and stayed out at night partying, drinking and many times didn't show up for work. This January it was cold as a wedge and the snow was coming down in big wet flakes building up on any surface that it could cling to. The tables and fountain on the Coffee Shop patio were covered with 12 inches of snow by the time the snow had let up and they looked like giant white marsh mellows. Travelers were coming in for the warmth and hot coffee and they told Gus that both highway mountain passes on I-10 interstate highway were closed with black ice, so everyone in Van Horn was trapped for as long as it lasted. As things turned out the highway was closed for almost a week before they opened it and all the travelers left town. This was an interesting time, because there were several Oil Company Land Men trapped that came in and Gus and them had a lot of discussions on where the Oil Companies were interested in Leasing in Culberson County. This was good information for Gus and he started to contact Land Owners in that area to see if they would let him represent them in negotiating a Oil and Gas lease with the Oil Companies. Gus also decided that he needed to invest some money in Oil and Gas Ownership Maps of the County so he could locate the tracts of land and the owners to have more information to develop a plan of putting together tracts of land to form a Oil and Gas Prospect to present to an Oil Company for their consideration. He also composed a simple Letter Agreement Document for the land owner to sign that gave him the right to represent the owner in negotiations with the Oil Company. This was the real beginning of Blue Quail Oil & Gas. Gus soon had an interest from an Oil Company in Denver, Colorado and negotiated an Oil Lease between them and three different land owners. He didn't charge the land owners any commission, but instead got a nice Bonus Commission from the Oil Company of $ 73,000.00. The winter drifted into spring and his Coffee Shop was still loosing money every week, but at least he was using it to make contacts and get information about the Oil and Gas Business. Gus was buying more Oil and Gas Ownership Maps now on the Counties that joined Culberson County, because there was activity in several and these Maps were very expensive ranging in price from $ 300.00 to $ 550.00 each, but he needed them. The local News Paper contacted Gus to write a weekly Oil and Gas article discussing the Leasing and Drilling in Culberson and the surrounding Counties. Gus was very busy with the Coffee Shop, his new Oil and Gas business, the Main Street Board, the Economic Development Board and writing for the News Paper. Through all of this Gus was becoming to be known as the local authority on many subjects and anytime someone from out of town would call or go by the County Court House, the Chamber of Commerce or the City Hall and they didn't know the answer to what that person wanted they would send them to Gus for the answer and most of the time Gus would supply them with an answer to their questions and each time this would give Gus even more information as to what was going on in the area. In May Gus noticed that the Coffee Shop was making enough money to finally pay it's own way. After paying all the bills and labor there was just enough money left each week in May so that Gus didn't have to add money out of his pocket. This also happened in June and Gus decided that maybe the Coffee Shop had turned the corner and was going to start making enough money so he could take out some for himself. Then in July his Business

License was coming due and he would have to re-new it and that would be several hundred dollars, but first the Texas Alcoholic Beverage Commission was going to have to audit his books. Gus got all his paper work together along with all his Bank Statements and went through the audit with flying colors. When the Auditor was through they sat down to some coffee talking and she told Gus that he had done a great job because she hadn't found any infractions and that was a rare occurrence. Gus told her that he was considering not renewing his License, because he was so tired and that the business just wasn't really making any money and he had been running it now for almost a year. The Auditor tried to talk him into renewing his License and Gus told her that he had another couple of weeks on it and he would think about it, but if he decided against it he would mail in his License to them. She told him that he couldn't mail it in that he had to hand deliver it to their office in El Paso. Gus thought about that for a minute and he went to the framed License on the wall, took it down and took the License out of the frame and handed it to the Auditor. She asked him what he was doing and he told her that he wasn't about to make a special trip to El Paso which was 120 miles one way just to bring the License to them, so he just as well give it to her at that minute. She didn't want to accept it and told Gus that he might change his mind, but Gus shook his head and told her that he was to tired to keep working at the Coffee Shop when he couldn't put any money in his pocket. She took the Business License and left. Gus felt better by making that decision although he was a little embarrassed that he couldn't have made a success of the business within a year. The good part about closing the Coffee Shop was that Gus could now spend a lot more time at his Blue Quail Ranch. Now he needed to try to figure what he was going to do with the building that the Coffee Shop had been in. Gus was going to the Ranch and doing a lot of maintenance that he had let go while he was so busy with the Coffee Shop. Now he and his wife could go out there for several days at a time and work at his own pace along with continuing his search for Indian artifacts, semi-precious stones and fossils. She was getting more involved now with her Church since she wasn't having to help with the Coffee Shop. That was that was fine with Gus. He knew that she had always been a more active Church person then he had been and now she was enjoying her Church family and volunteering for different Church functions. Gus's interests were down a different road. Gus and his wife had always left each other alone to decided what they wanted to do, so they pretty much let each other live their own life. Gus was still working with his Blue

Quail Oil & Gas business when there was an opportunity to get a deal going and he was using his office upstairs in his House for that purpose. His computer was up there, but he really didn't have everything he needed to operate as an Oil and Gas business office should. He used the local Office Supply Store to do his copies and to fax documents that needed to be sent fast. He really wanted to get some more office equipment of his own to take care of all of this. In the middle of September he got a call from a Relator in Fort Davis that told him that she had a Client that wanted to buy his Ranch west of the Sierra Vieja Mountains and this took Gus by surprise, at first he didn't know what to say. Gus had never really thought of selling his Ranch, but he remembered the lesson he had learned many years before when he was offered $ 3,000,000.00 dollars for his Ranch and Farm in Wharton and Matagorda Counties and he turned it down, then when he needed to sell it the price had gone down 2/3 in value. He told the Relator that he would sell for the price he wanted and not a penny less. He told her that he wanted $ 150,000.00 net for it and would not settle for any less. Gus thought that no one would pay that much for that rugged land out in the middle of nowhere. After all he had only paid around $ 19,000.00 for it and it probably wasn't worth much more then that. A few days the Relator called Gus and told him that her Client had agreed to take the deal. Gus told her to tell her Client that he was going to take all of the improvements off of the land and that he needed ninety days after the closing date to accomplish that. The Relator told Gus that there wouldn't be a problem with that, because her Client bought land just for an investment and would probably never even see it. Gus got his check for $ 150,000.00 and signed the Deed in the middle of October. Gus took this money and split it between his Blue Quail Oil & Gas and his La Mirada Land Bank accounts that earned interest. He immediately started looking for a Trucking Company that could move his Camp House and his Shop-Storage Building. He also would need to find a place to store them and everything else from his camp. Gus also needed to find some help he could hire because when the time came he would have to work fast to get everything torn down, loaded on trailers taken to the place for storage and then go back to load again and unload at the place of storage until everything was moved off of the property. Gus knew that he would need all of that ninety days to get everything off of the property, because of the Thanksgiving, Christmas and New Years Holidays and bad winter weather. Gus had a friend that had bought some land in the Lobo Valley south of Van Horn that would let him store everything there till Gus could by another Ranch. Gus started taking everything down from shelves inside the Camp House and putting them on the floor. He did the same thing in the Shop-Storage building and even took the hot water heater and laid it down in there. Gus ended up hiring five men to help with all that had to be done, so several things could be worked on at the same time. Just as Gus had thought bad winter weather and the Holidays was slowing him down on getting everything done. He located a Trucking Company in El Paso that had a truck with a big tilt bed trailer and wench and scheduled them for the first week in January to haul the Camp House and the Shop-Storage building to the Lobo location. Gus could do the rest with his truck and eighteen foot trailer. Getting everything ready to move is what Gus concentrated on during the Thanksgiving and Christmas Holidays. He did take off on New Years Eve and New Years Day 2008. New Years Eve Gus was waiting to hear the fireworks and gun shots that always signaled the New Year in Van Horn and he was sipping on a glass of his Dad's Gromes & Ulrich 1936 with water thinking about selling the Ranch that he had dreamed of having ever since he had gone to Big Bend National Park with his Mom in 1962. He had a hard time believing that he had sold it. If he hadn't had that bad experience 20 years before he probably wouldn't have sold it. That experience taught him that when someone is waving good money in your face you should take it, because it might not happen again. Gus had made his dream of owning a Ranch out in the high Desert Mountain Chihuahua country come true after he saw that kind of country in 1962. He remembered that it was right after he had been with Lorrie on the beach in Corpus Christi. Yes he had made his dream come true and he suddenly wondered what that dream would have been like if he would have had Lorrie in it with him. The fireworks and gun shots were going off and Gus knew that the New year of 2008 had arrived, so he drank the rest of his whiskey and went to bed.

Lorrie—2007 arrived with Lorrie trying to find a way to be positive about it. The longer she lived with her abusive Husband and now her Stepson was back in the house it seemed that staying there just got harder all the time. She was looking forward to their annual New Years Day lunch with old friends, because the conversation and being with all of them would be a pleasant break from the tension that she was experiencing at home. Lorrie had was going to be Married to her Husband for 23 years and from the very beginning she had hidden his physical and verbal abuse from her family, his business associates and their friends except Jill knew some of it, but even she didn't know everything. Lorrie was having a hard time trying to figure out how she was going to crawl out of this depressive pit since her Stepson had moved back in with them. She could see nothing but a steady stream of trouble ahead that always associated itself with him. Lorrie had a talk with her Stepson and told him that he was a grown man and he should take care of himself, so she would expect him to wash his own cloths, clean up his room and wash his dishes. He didn't have any money except what he got from his Dad and Lorrie suspected that her Husband was giving him more money then she knew, because her Stepson would tell them that he had a job interview and he would be gone for the afternoon and into the night, then when he came in and walked by her she could smell alcohol on him when he was on his way to his room. He spent most of his time in his room on his computer and his cell phone and came down mostly to get something to eat and drink then back up he would go with the food and drink to his room. Lorrie started missing some dishes and she went up to her Stepson's room and in there she saw plates silverware and glasses that had been there for no telling how long. When he came home she told him to get all those dirty dishes out of his room and bring them to the kitchen and wash them up. He told her that she shouldn't have been in his room looking around and Lorrie just stared him down till he went up to get the dishes. Her Husband had a friend in the Garment business that bought a Condo in Spain and he invited Lorrie and her Husband to go there with him and his wife for the Easter Holidays and Lorrie was really looking forward to this trip. She had always liked Spain and it's history, because Texas was originally colonized by the Spanish and there were many Spanish Missions in Texas along with rivers and old towns named by the Spanish. Heck the town she grew up in, El Campo, was a Spanish name meaning "The Camp". It was named by Mexican cowboys that were driving cattle to be shipped on the railroad and they camped there waiting on the train. The man's wife had pictures that she showed Lorrie and from them the countryside around it looked like it was mountain and desert. It kind of reminded Lorrie of Albuquerque, New Mexico and she loved it around there better then any place she had lived in the United States, so Lorrie was really looking forward to that trip at Easter. Her Stepson finally got a job at a small Bank as a Loan Officer. It didn't pay much, but at least he had his own money to blow and wasn't mooching off of his Dad. Her Husband was still having to pay part of the Bank payment on her Stepson's house, because the rent wouldn't cover it and that was a real sore subject for Lorrie to think about. Lorrie and her Husband were still going to the dances at the Country and Western Dance Club and this was at least a little pleasant distraction from her depressing home life. She was looking forward to the Easter trip to Spain for the same reason. The day finally got there and she loved the looks of the Condo with it's Spanish style architecture and the rugged setting in a mountainous area. The interior was very pleasant and comfortable with a patio viewing the mountains. They were shown to their bedroom and that was when Lorrie saw something that she hadn't thought about. There it was right before her eyes and it repulsed her to look at it. Only one bed in their bedroom. This meant that she was going to have to try and sleep with her drunken Husband . Lorrie hadn't slept in the same bed with her Husband for many years, so she wasn't looking forward to it know. She knew that she would be much to handy for him to want to have sex with her. Well what could she do anyway. She thought that maybe toward the end of the night she could get him so drunk that he would just fall asleep. They were supposed to be there for three days and that would present a problem. That evening they went to a real nice Spanish Cafe that had wonderful food and then to a Club featuring Spanish Dancers both in the more Classical style and also the Peasant style that had developed in the Village Cantinas hundreds of years before. Lorrie loved both examples and the music for each was wonderful. Somehow it just got your blood flowing and you had to clap and yell to the stories that the music and the movements of the dancers were telling. Thankfully that night when they got back to the Condo her Husband didn't bother her for sex. The next day they all went shopping and Lorrie was buying small gifts from Spain to take with her when she went to Texas during the summer, to give to her family and friends. They went to sidewalk Cafe for lunch and enjoyed watching the locals walk by and drank some real good Spanish red wine then after the lunch they sat and talked enjoying the Spanish strong sweet chocolate-coffee. They went shopping for some clothing in the afternoon and then back to the Condo to clean up and get ready to go to another Club that was a dinner and dance Club with a full orchestra. They had a very nice dinner and Lorrie and her Husband danced a few times before he started to get a little to drunk to keep off of her toes. This was their last night in Spain and Lorrie could see that her Husband had a good start on getting drunk, so she thought that she had a good chance of finishing him off when they got back to the Condo by mixing his strong drinks. That is exactly what she did and it worked beautifully. She helped him up to bed and he was to sleep when his head hit the pillow. The next morning they all went down to Cafe for a late breakfast then a little more shopping before lunch then back to the Condo to pack and get to the Airport for the short flight back to England. Lorrie was proud of herself for being able to dodge her Husband for two nights sleeping the same bed and not have sex, because that would have ruined a nice trip. Back in England she had to get out of her make believe world she experienced while in Spain. Lorrie was beginning to think of a plan she might use to run away from her Husband now that she had been in Spain. She would have to find out more and do some research about it. It was just a thought right now and she would work on it sometime later. She needed to get her flight tickets reserved pretty quick for her annual three month Vacation back to Texas, so she could get the big discount on them. Taking that three month Vacation back to her home town of El Campo, Texas was something else that she was really looking forward to. It gave her so much relief from her constant stress. While she was there she never even thought of the problems she left behind in England. It seemed to Lorrie that her life had been split between two emotions ever since she had married her Husband and tried to raise her Stepson. These emotions were stress and relief. Everything to do with her marriage always built up stress and she was always searching for some way to get relief from that. Lorrie was having trouble with all kinds of skin spots now ans she needed to go to her Dermatologist again to have him look them over and see which ones needed to be taken off, so those places could have time to heal up before she left to fly to Texas. She had little scars all over her, mostly on her back and arms from these spots that had been removed in the past and she blamed them on her wearing bikini bathing suits when she was young. She had been very white skinned and she always wanted a good sun tan, so she wore those bikini's and now she was paying for it. She thought that when she was a young girl no one ever said anything about getting skin cancer from a suntan. All everyone was worried about was getting burned to a crisp and your tan peeling off, so you put on suntan lotion and that was all you did and since she was so white skinned she burned a lot. Lorrie was flying away from England to Texas and she was wondering if her Stepson would still have his job when she got back in three months. Well she was flying away from that problem and all the other ones at that House. Lorrie landed in Houston, Texas and as usual her Sister picked her up. Her troubles were thousands of miles away now and Lorrie felt liberated. After a few days with her Sister in Houston they drove to El Campo and her Family was ready to go the Mexican Cafe for lunch so Lorrie could eat her fill of good old Tex-Mex food. When they got back Lorrie unpacked and gave them the little gifts that he had bought in Spain and then she showed them all the pictures that she took while she was there. Her Dad had been dead for three years now and Lorrie was surprised how good that her Mom was doing even though she had been two years older then her dad. Her Mom was still doing her own grocery shopping and cooking and a lot of her own washing and cleaning, although there was a lady that came in to help one day a week. That evening they all went out on the back patio for their Happy Hour to talk and catch up on everything that had been happening in El Campo. As usual there were questions about how her Husband and Stepson were doing and also as usual Lorrie gave them flowery answers that painted a picture of tranquility and happiness with her Family in England. It hurt Lorrie to keep the truth from them, but she could not let them know how miserable she was living there with them. Lorrie had told herself that she had become accustomed to the abuse and the dis-function that represented a major part of her everyday life living with her Husband and Stepson. She had given up on trying to bring about a positive change in the way they lived their lives. Lorrie was a strong woman and she had gone through a lot of hard situations where she was the one that had to take charge and be a positive force to see things through to a good conclusion, but her Husband and her Stepson had worn her down and smothered her. Even when they were first married she had fought hard and used her wits to keep them from loosing everything. All along the way she would have to devise ways to compensate for her unhappiness by such things as taking University classes, having her little dog Mitzi to lavish her love on and the Country and Western Music Dance Club among others. They would soften the hurt that she absorbed on a daily basis, but now she was getting old and she didn't have the resilience she once had as a younger woman. Lorrie knew that one day it would come down to one of two decisions and they were to find a way to leave her Husband and vanish so he couldn't find her or to commit suicide. She had left him several times for only three or four days at a time and he would call her and stalk her relentlessly until she gave up and went back to him, so she knew that if she ever decided that she was going to leave her Husband for good that she would basically have to disappear, vanish, to someplace that he couldn't find her. She knew him and how violent he could get when things didn't go his way and this made her afraid of him that if he found her and she wouldn't come back that no telling what he would do to her. Lorrie knew that if she ever left him again that it would have to be done with a good plan and that is why she started getting an idea when she was in Spain. Lorrie would go to different stores, shops and the Library when she was in El Campo for her three months Vacation and she had secretly had always hoped to accidentally run into Gus. Now as an old woman she thought that she might have the courage to approach him and ask him if he knew who she was and what had happened that he didn't come back to her so long ago. Every place that she went she tried to keep a lookout for some man that might be him. It was hard for Lorrie to picture how Gus would look as an old man, because her memory still held him as 19 years old and how do you imagine that same person 45 years later, she couldn't figure out, but somehow she knew that she would know him by the feeling that would be immediately generated within her when she saw him. Lorrie had been in El Campo now for two months and she had been with her Mom to the Hair Salon that her Friend owned for two appointments without hearing any news about Gus. She had also attended two funerals of people that were of the age of people that Gus could have known and she hadn't seen Gus there. When it got to this point in her El Campo Vacation that it was 2/3 over she started feeling a little reluctant about getting on the plane and flying back to that mess she had to put up with in England. Lorrie made her last visits of old friends and told them that she would be back to see them next year and with each of them she asked about several people that she knew lived out of town, trying not to be obvious as she asked if any of them had heard anything about Gus. She always got the same answer that they hadn't seen him in a long time. Lorrie couldn't believe that Gus had fallen off the edge of the earth. She decided that either he didn't ever come back to El Campo, or if he did it wasn't very often, but she felt that he was somewhere and somehow she would find him. Lorrie did her annual Gus drive around pilgrimage and the next day she did her Texas Food Shopping to take back to England. When she got back to England she found the house in a mess, but was pleasantly surprise to learn that her Stepson still had his job. After unpacking and taking a day of rest Lorrie began getting all the paperwork on her desk straightened out. She got to examining all the credit card charges against the receipts that she always had her Husband put in a basket on her desk and there were quite a few that were missing. She had a sinking feeling about these. It was true that her Husband didn't always bring back his receipts and that she had to stay after him about it, but there were way too many missing and from what she could determine the charges were from business that her Husband wouldn't normally go to and if he did he would have paid cash, which meant to Lorrie that someone other then her Husband was using their credit card. She would bet that her Husband had given their credit card to her Stepson and he was using it to party and act big to the friends that he had left. Lorrie was determined to stop this and get that credit card back if this was the case. When her Husband came in for his lunch she asked him about all the missing receipts and he shrugged off the question as not being important. She asked him if he had his credit card and he told her that he did, then she asked him if she could see it and he told her that he didn't have it with him. She wanted him to go and get it and that is when he had to tell her that he had given it to his Son to use so he would be able to buy his lunch and his train fare to work. Lorrie got quiet, then asked her Husband what her Stepson was doing with his own money if he wasn't using it for his own expenses. Her Husband told Lorrie that what his Son did with his money wasn't his business or for that matter Lorrie's business either. Lorrie told her husband that if he didn't get that credit card back from her Stepson that she was going to have the cards canceled. Her Husband did get his credit card back from Lorrie's Stepson. She found out a few days later that Stepson still didn't take on his own responsibilities though, because she over heard her Husband talking to his Son and telling him that he was going to give him cash, so Lorrie wouldn't know about it. Lorrie decided to just let this go without saying anything. She wondered why there was always a secret between her Husband and her Stepson to undermine what she was trying to do to help the family. The whole time they had been married it had been like this and look at her Stepson how worthless he was and why couldn't her Husband see the results of what he had enabled. She knew that it was much to late to change any of it, but she didn't have to like it or approve of it. It didn't take vary many days back in England, for depressive feeling to come back on Lorrie. She had enjoyed the relief from this for those three months in Texas. Lorrie realized that she was back in reality as long as she was married to her and she fully expected that her Stepson would never be back out of the house on his own again. Christmas came and went and Lorrie did all that she could to get her Christmas spirits up, but it was hard for to do. Nothing for her was the same after Cheryl had left. Her Husband went on his week long ski vacation and Lorrie was glad that he was gone. She planned what they would have for New Year Eve, but her heart wasn't really in it. All of the excitement for the Holidays that Lorrie had always had, even as a young girl, seemed to have vanished somehow and she was struggling to try and maintain her feeling of strength in an environment that constantly worked against her day after day. Lorrie had always been fun loving and would drink alcohol when partying or during social gatherings, but now she found herself using it to relive her anxieties, so she could relax and be able to withstand the constant verbal abuse that her drunken Husband would berate her with, using terribly degrading, nasty words delivered only toward women starting with the letters B, W, and C. She had no choice but to just sit there and take it hoping that he would finally get drunk enough to go to sleep. She dare not dispute him and risk a physical beating. She made her mind up that if her Husbands Friend invited them to go back to Spain for another Easter Holiday that she would have something arranged with his Wife to take a tour around the country side to see some of the small Spanish Villages and try to ask some questions of the locals there. It would be a part of her plan that she had conceived on their first trip with them for Easter Holiday. Lorrie's Husband returned from his ski vacation and Lorrie had everything organized for their little New Years Eve celebration. For the last few years Lorrie's New Years Eve celebrations had been getting smaller and smaller. This year was an extension of that with her cutting back more on their alcohol selections for guests and also she didn't even buy any confetti or little horns to toot. She had prepared a few dips and finger foods and that was it. She had no help from her Stepson because he was too busy in his room. New Years Eve was pretty calm with only a few friends there and them being older so not as rowdy with their partying as they once had been, but of course her Husband still got falling down drunk before the New Year even arrived, so she and a friend took him to his room and laid him on his bed. Everyone left right after the New Year of 2008 came in and Lorrie cleaned up a little then sat down to think about her life. She sat with a glass of brandy with water and keep repeating 2008, 2008 to herself over and over. She was wondering if 2008 was going to be the year when she finally built up the gumption to leave her Husband and start a new life at 63 years of age. Lorrie didn't know how much more she could take from him and her Stepson. She felt like she was certainly feeling her age, because she was always able to pull herself out of her down times, but it was getting harder and harder to do. She still had her good friend Jill though and her sweet memories of Gus and their wonderful kisses on the beach in Corpus Christi in 1962. If only Gus would have kept kissing her for all of these years she knew that she would have been so happy and she would have loved to have his children, not like that first mistake with her first Air Force Husband and she had never been with a man since that she wanted children with. Lorrie whispered to herself Gus, oh Gus it's 2008 and I am old, would you even look at me now, I doubt it.

Gus—2008 after New Years Gus got a break in the winter weather to get his workers and trunking company organized and they finished moving everything from his Ranch that he sold in on the west side of the Sierra Vieja Mountains to his friends land at Lobo. Now Gus had to keep his eye out for another ranch that he could afford to buy and spend some money on to fix it up. He was still getting calls from people about his Oil and Gas Business and all of a sudden he thought what a numbskull he had been. The old Blue Quail Coffee Shop building was sitting vacant and it was on the main street in town. It would make the perfect office for Blue Quail Oil and Gas. Gus got busy on it and sold most of the cafe equipment and gave away some stuff to get the room for the office. He went to El Paso and bought a copy/fax machine, business desk, two office chairs, a conference table and a map table to store his oil field maps. He also bought three used filing cabinets and started to put his office together. He realized that he still had the Coffee Shop sign painted on the side of the building and the neon one up on the front of the building, so he got an artist to alter the one on the side and to add an oil pump jack to it and he took the one down in front and took it to El Paso and had Coffee Shop taken off and Oil & Gas added. Now he felt like he was really in the business with a down town office and all the equipment to make it work. Gus got a call from some land owners in the Texas Panhandle that had been contacted by an Oil Company that were leasing in Reeves County to the east of Culberson County and they wanted Gus to negotiate the Oil Lease for them. Gus negotiated with the Oil Company and got them up from the $ 200.00 per acre, that they had offered the owners to $ 500.00 per acre and Gus also got $16,000.00 from the Oil Company for doing the deal, so he added this to his Blue Quail Oil & Gas Bank Account. Gus had decided to take some oil and gas related classes at Midland College to update himself and this is what he did. While doing so he met several people that he thought might end up being an asset to know in his business. He knew that what he did was largely about contacts and getting a deal between them, so the more contacts he developed the better it was for him. The Oil Companies were Leasing up large tracts of land in Culberson County and they were looking for natural gas production in several different shale structures that they had to use hydraulic fracking to make them produce. Gus learned that an Oil Company out of Colorado had Leased a ranch not far from some land that he knew was not leased yet, so he called them and they showed a big interest in it. Gus then saw another section of land that connected it and called the owners to see if they would Lease it and they told Gus that they would. Now Gus had his Lease Prospect together and he presented it all to the Colorado Oil Company and they accepted it. With this Oil Lease Gus made the seven land owners each $ 100,000.00 and for a Bonus Gus made $ 78,500.00. This money he added to his Blue Quail Oil & Gas Bank Account. Gus went to his Blue Quail Oil & Gas office everyday never knowing what he might be doing there. There were days when nothing happened and all he did was to send e-mails to different Oil Companies or call them trying to get them interested in some Prospect of his. He would look up their drilling permits and track them on his ownership maps to see if any were close to his Prospects. He never knew who would walk in off of the street, call on his phone or e-mail that might make him some money. He did a lot of free work for people that didn't have any money and sometime the job was so small that he would tell the person to just give him $ 100.00 and that would take care of it. Gus had a lot of deals fall through also and that was always disappointing. There were a lot of young Oil & Gas Land Men working in the Court House for different Oil Companies and Gus was meeting them after work and drinking beer with them getting what information that he could from them. Some of it was helpful and some wasn't. He would also make field trips out to drilling locations to get information right from the drilling rig site about how the wells were producing. Gus tried to learn and keep up with all the information that he could. One evening when Gus was home he got a sort of strange phone call from a nice sounding lady that asked him if he was who he was and then proceeded to ask him if he knew a certain lady from many years ago. Gus almost told her that he didn't know the name, but he remembered that she must be talking about one of his old girlfriends that used a nickname instead of her given name and he told her that he had known her. The young lady then told him that he might be the father of her husband. This took Gus by surprise and he told her that he guessed that it could possible, because he had dated her for two years, but she had never mentioned being pregnant to him. The young lady asked Gus if he would like to meet her husband and then they could talk and decided what they wanted to do. Gus told her yes that he would be interested in seeing her husband. She told Gus that her husband was working in Denver at that time with a Telecom company and she would have him call Gus. Gus hung up the phone and told his Wife what the call was about and he wondered if those people were after money. The next evening Gus's home phone rang and it was the man that was presumed to be Gus's Son by an old girlfriend. They had a pleasant conversation and avoided the obvious pitfalls that might pop up because of the touchy situation. They made a date to meet at a local Mexican Cafe in Van Horn on the next weekend. Gus didn't invite him to his house, because he needed to have more time with him to get a better feel for the kind of person that he was. They met at the Cafe and it was a good day to sit outside drink beer and visit even though it was cool fall day. They sat out and talked for hours and Gus got a good feeling about this young man. The young man told Gus that he traveled all over with a company that did the wiring on cell phone micro-wave towers and that he had been working in Denver on one there. He told Gus that he lived a few miles from Ganado, Texas in the country and was going to be driving home there for a few days before going on another job. They talked about the young mans Grandfather, his Mom and one of his Aunts that Gus remembered. When they parted Gus felt a little funny for not inviting him to stay the night at his house, but Gus wasn't quite sure enough yet. They agreed to meet another time without naming a date. Gus needed more time. Gus always thought that time solved a lot of problems if you gave it a chance and that is what he was going to do in this situation. The Holiday Season was getting close, but Gus could no longer have his Son's out to hunt, because he didn't have a Ranch to take them to anymore. He was constantly on the lookout for a section or two of land to buy in a nice area to turn into another Blue Quail Ranch. He got a Christmas card from the new Son and his wife and also a framed picture of them and their son. Gus didn't send them anything or even recognize their gift to him. He decided to let time do the deciding on all of this, so he just stayed quiet about it all. Gus had a little Christmas party at the Blue Quail Oil & Gas office while the town's annual Lighted Christmas Parade was underway and he served homemade chili and rice in cups as long as it lasted. The people in Van Horn had never tasted chili and rice together and most of them that had a cup of it fell in love with it. Some even added a few jalapino peppers on top. New Years Eve came around and Gus still hadn't the slightest idea where he might find the right parcel of land that he was looking for. He and his Wife stayed home as usual for New Years Eve and again Gus was upstairs playing his old records and sipping some whiskey waiting for the fireworks and gun shots to announce the New Year 2009 had arrived in Van Horn. Gus was sitting at the little table upstairs on the landing/library by the big heater and it was very cozy up there. He was by himself enjoying the old 1950's and 1960's music and thinking about all that had happened during the year. Gus had actually made more money then he had anticipated in his Oil & Gas Business and was very glad of that, but at the same time he knew from experience that it sure wouldn't be like that all the time. He knew that the kind of Oil Business he was in was deal making and brokering and it just came and went, so you had to be ready to take advantage of it when you could and save the money you made, because there could be a lot of time between deals. He also was thinking about his new Son that showed up and wondering what was going to become of that. Heck that young man was already 34 years old, so that just goes to show you that no telling what will come back to see you from your young life. Gus wondered why the boys Mom never told him about this boy. Well Gus thought that you could never know what was on a woman's mind or exactly what was in her heart, just like what had happened to him with Lorrie back in 1962 when she wanted him to take her virginity. She had been only 16 years old then and he had turned his back on her and walked away. He thought that if he hadn't walked away from Lorrie then this boy probably wouldn't be wanting to know if Gus was his Dad, because Gus was sure that he would have married Lorrie and then none of this would have happened. Then Gus heard all the fireworks and gun shots going off and knew that the New Year of 2009 had just arrived and as he checked his watch his first thought of 2009 was that it only takes one small decision like walking away from Lorrie in 1962, to change a whole life like his.

Lorrie—2008 January 1, 2008 Lorrie was getting ready for their annual New Years lunch with their friends. Her Husband had a big hangover and Lorrie was trying to straighten out some of his cloths so he would look more presentable at the lunch. Lorrie always looked forward to these New Year day lunches, because the friends that were there and the conversation were a pleasant break from her everyday life. Lorrie knew that the sweetness of this lunch wouldn't last very long, but it was more then she would get from any other source. January for Lorrie was always a kind of depressing month, because it stayed overcast, cold and wet most of the time. Lorrie spent a lot of time on her computer looking up books to read and now she was doing research on small villages in Spain. Spain had become an interesting country for Lorrie. Her Husband was taking his two week ski vacation, so just Lorrie and her Stepson were at home. They could be civil to each other when talking about mundane subjects, but Lorrie had better not try and bring up a subject that might degrade her Stepson in an way, because he would just bite back at her and seclude himself in his room for the rest of the evening. He was becoming more and more touchy about subjects that had a relationship to how he handled his life. His room was becoming his cave hideout from reality. Lorrie's Husband's Tailoring business was still earning them a very good living and he was able to pay in the maximum each month for his pension and also deposit more in a Savings Account that he had at one of the Banks. A couple of weeks before Easter his Friend that had the Condo in Spain called them to go to Spain again for a Easter Holiday. Lorrie had her fingers crossed on this for a year. Lorrie had always been a planner and she would go to great lengths researching something and making plans. Lorrie and the Wife of her Husbands Friend were making plans to visit several villages while they were in Spain, but only Lorrie knew the real reason she wanted to do this. They went to a real nice modern Cafe and Club in the City that was a lot of fun and then they rented a car for their tour of several small villages in the area that had local histories of interest. They ate in the very small local Cafe's and enjoyed the local wine, cheese, olives and breads of each village. The centuries old Churches and buildings most even before Columbus sailed for America were very interesting to Lorrie and she wanted to see the schools and inquire about the prices of everything from food at their Markets to cost of rent and medical expenses. Lorrie told them that she was very interested in the common people that lived in the out of the way mountain villages in Spain, because she had read so much about them through the years and that is where the Spanish soldiers had come from that had conquered the New World and that had held a lot of interest for her for many years. She hoped that this explanation would be enough so they would let her to explore her interests without any more questions. Lorrie took detailed notes in a small notebook that she carried in her purse. She was using a Spanish to English conversation book as a helper and found it to be useful, but irritating to use. She could see that eventually she would have to do something better than that. Their Easter trip to Spain ended up being more of an educational experience for Lorrie and she had gained a lot of information that she was going to add to her file on each small village town. Their last days in Spain were spent doing a little shopping and then a real nice evening at a well known Dinner and Dance Club. Back in England Lorrie was secretly gathering and storing her information for later use. Spring was coming to an end and it was time for Lorrie to put all of her plans together for her three month Texas vacation. Lorrie had been putting up with her Husband and her Stepson now for 24 years and she was going to be 63 years old, but it was getting harder for her and at times she felt like she was suffocating and she just had to get away from them for a while. Her three month Texas vacation was the perfect thing that cleaned out her system of all the ugliness that she had to endure the rest of the year living with them. Her friend Jill and her books helped to keep her sane until she could purge her system again in Texas each year. She made her flight reservations and had her Doctors checkups so she could get the three months of medications she would need while in Texas. Her diabetes, high blood pressure and cholesterol were shown to be stable in the tests, so there was no change in her medication. Lorrie landed at the Houston Airport and then spent several days with her Sister like she always did. They enjoyed shopping together and Lorrie almost always bought a new purse. She loved purses and had been like that ever since she had been a little girl. They drove to El Campo and Lorrie unpacked then gave out the little presents that she liked to bring her family from England. She usually brought her Mom some real nice chocolate candy. Her Mom was a real chocolate lover and Lorrie always got her some chocolate candy that she couldn't get in Texas. They visited for a while then they went to their favorite Mexican Cafe so Lorrie could stuff herself with her favorite Tex-Mex Mexican food. That evening they sat on the back patio where Lorrie and her Dad had always liked to sit and talk. They called this their happy hour and Lorrie decided that she would drink a Shiner Bock beer, because it had been her dad's favorite and for some reason she felt very sentimental about it at that moment and it gave her a feeling that he was close to her sitting out there. She had the urge to talk to him about what was happening to her in England and so wished that he was still alive so she could discuss it with him. She didn't know why she felt like she could talk to her Dad, about those things now that he was dead, because she could never have brought herself to talk to him about it when he was alive, in fact she had hidden it from him. Well her Mom, Sister and Brother were out here on the patio, so why didn't she bring up the subject and talk to them about it and she knew the answer to that also and it was always the same. She could never let them know how bad she had messed up her life. Lorrie was a very strong person, but she simply could not face telling her family the truth about her life, so she was stuck with only being able to talk to her dead Dad and she could face him with it now. She knew that when she got the time that she would go to his grave and sit and discuss things with him there where no one else would hear them. Lorrie woke up the next morning feeling so wonderfully free. All her problems that she knew of were several thousand miles away and across the Atlantic ocean. She could drive where she wanted to, go shopping where she wanted to, eat where she wanted to, and go see who ever she wanted to and no one was going to call her nasty names and threaten her with a beating. Lorrie decided that she was going to go through the closet that she used when she was there and get rid of some of the older cloths she had left there and replace them with new ones. She would give the ones that she took out to the re-sale shop. Lorrie called a couple of her old High School girl friends and they went shopping and then ate lunch together. They had to show Lorrie their pictures of grandchildren and this made Lorrie feel a little funny, because she didn't have anything to show them. She didn't even show them the pictures of her Stepson. She had long ago taken them out of her picture folders, because she had not been proud of him in a long time. Lorrie went to her Hair Salon Friend with her Mom for a hair appointment and was interested in listening to all the gossip that the different ladies were talking about. This happened to be one of those days that the whole Salon was full and there was so much going on that it was hard to keep up with all the conversations. Lorrie then caught part of a conversation about one of her school girlfriends and that her husband had been diagnosed with a real bad cancer that he had supposedly got from being around asbestos when he was in the Navy. Lorrie asked some questions and decided to contact her Friend to see if she could visit her. Lorrie talked to her Friend on the phone and her Friend told her that it wouldn't be a good time to visit, because her husband was going back and forth to Houston taking some real hard chemotherapy and that they both were staying exhausted. She told Lorrie that she would call her when things got better. After Lorrie hung up from talking to her she remembered that this school friend of hers was the daughter of Gus's boss that owned the Service Station that they would go to and flirt with him. That was how long that she had known that girl. Lorrie was going to the girls Monday lunches at a different Cafe each time and she was loving this social gathering. When her Sister was down while Lorrie was in El Campo she attended these lunches also. Lorrie had long ago learned to hold her tongue around her Sister, because her Sister could start up trouble faster then anybody she had ever known and Lorrie hated confrontations. During a conversation Lorrie could tell when her Sister was going to add something that would cause an argument and Lorrie just hated it. Her Sister had a way about her that would try to draw you to her side of the argument even when you didn't want to be in it at all and she would do it about family matters also. This was upsetting for Lorrie and she tried to avoid these circumstances. There was enough fighting going on in her life in England and Lorrie sure didn't need it here in El Campo, Texas. This is where she came to be in her world without fighting and confrontation. This was Lorrie's world where she could bring up memories of things and just sit and study those memories to get the full flavor of them. Lorrie had lived in a lot of places, but this was the place that she always came back to and it was the place that she wanted so desperately to get away from when she was young, it was something about feeling safe, now wasn't that a confusing feeling. No matter how many times Lorrie thought about this feeling she couldn't bring herself to understand it and if she thought about it to long it would blur in her mind and confuse her. Lorrie finally got to visit her Friend and her Husband that was taking the chemo treatments for his cancer. Lorrie remembered him from High School and knew that her Friend had dated him then and married him right out of High School. They had a nice visit, but he really looked bad and his arms had blue-black spots all over them and he had dark circles around his eyes. After the visit her Friend walked her out to the car and she told Lorrie that her Husbands cancer was terminal, but they were trying to prolong his life with the chemo. She told Lorrie that he would have to have these treatments as long as he lived. Lorrie hugged her and they both cried a little before she left. Lorrie's Mom was still doing real good and she was doing most of her grocery shopping, driving and cooking, but she was getting weaker and had trouble with her balance and her eyesight. It was a good thing that Lorrie's Brother lived next door, because he would check on her everyday when he came home from work. Her Brother was a really good man that had to divorce his wife and raise his two children. It was a good thing that they had him for their Dad, because he was steady and had a loving disposition. Lorrie's time in El Campo had gone by fast and she just had a few days left to savor the freedom from the troubles that she knew waited her back in England. She did her Texas food shopping to take back to England and then she went out to sit by her Dad's grave and talk to him. She told him that she was working on a plan to get away from her

Husband and that he probably wouldn't approve of it, but it was the only thing that she could think of to do and that if he had a better idea that he should let her know what it was. She stayed close to her Mom's house except for the last day and then she made her annual Gus pilgrimage drive to see, once again, all the places that she had seen Gus at when he was in High School. She couldn't explain why she felt like she had to do this, but she just did. It's was like she couldn't go back to England without revisiting these places and for just a minute thinking about those times. Her Brother took her back to the Airport in Houston and Lorrie kissed him goodby then boarded the flight for England. All the way back Lorrie was wondering what she might find when she got there. She knew that her biggest mental purge of the year was over, which was her three month Texas trip, so she should be able to be strong enough to put up with the mess in England till her Husband went on his first ski vacation and that would give her enough relief to be able to last a little longer and she would go step by step as long as she could. When she got back she was pleasantly surprised to find out that her Stepson still had his job as a Loan Officer at that small Bank. Lorrie thought that maybe this is what he needed, a job that didn't require a lot of stress on his system. She went about her normal routine of going through mail, catching up on business affairs and house cleaning. Lorrie realized that the Holiday Season was coming up fast and she hadn't even thought about it. A lot of the fun went out of the Holiday Season for Lorrie after Cheryl left her Stepson. Cheryl just made the Holidays seem like they were more of a real family and now they were back to being just of a bunch of unhappy pitiful humans living in the same house together. They had their normal Christmas where Lorrie bought herself her Christmas gift and then her Husband went on his ski vacation. Their New Years Eve was just a small get together like it had been for several years now and Lorrie's Stepson stayed up in his room most of the time and her Husband got drunk as usual and went to bed which left Lorrie by herself to observe the arrival of the New Year of 2009. Lorrie sat there in front of the fire in the fire place sipping on a glass of brandy and watching the TV New Year program and tipped her glass to 2009 and whispered that maybe 2009 would be her year, with luck.

Gus—2009 had come in for Gus while he was upstairs playing his old music. He had gone to bed after the fireworks and gun shots signaled that 2009 had arrived. He was drinking coffee after he woke up and thinking about the new things that he was looking forward to in the New Year. He was going to have to learn more about his new Son and his family. He was going to have to keep looking for a new ranch to buy. He wanted to take some more Oil and Gas classes at the College in Midland and now that he had made some good money and felt secure he wanted to do something that he had been thinking about for some time and that was to go back to his home town of El Campo and go to the Funeral Home there and pay for his Funeral in advance. He also wanted to go to the local Memorial Grave Stone Dealer there and have his headstone made with all the writing that he wanted on it and have it placed at his grave plot, so it would be ready when he died. Gus was 66 years old now and his Dad had died when he was 61, so Gus always used that age if 61 as a sort of benchmark on things to remind him how far along he was in life. Gus already had to take care of the funerals of his Dad, Mom, his Son and non of them had been planned in advanced, so he had to do everything while under pressure right after the death of his loved ones and he didn't want anybody to have to do that for him. He had the Family Grave Plot that had his Grandmother, Granddad, Dad, Mom and his Son buried there and his head stone would be in place right below his Son's waiting for him. There was room in the Family Plot for 10 graves and Gus's would be the sixth one, so there would be room for four more Family members if they wanted to be there. Gus signed up for another class at Midland College on Unconventional American Shale Plays, which were becoming the most productive type of oil and gas structure to drill and it required horizontal drilling and hydraulic fracturing of the shale structure to make it release its oil and gas. Gus wanted to learn more about this and also what effect it might have on these types of Leases being negotiated with land and mineral owners. He met some interesting people in the business at this class and he always had a list of his Oil & Gas Prospects with him ready to present to any Oil Company Representative that he might run into while having lunch or a beer in a local bar after the classes. He did catch the attention of a Land Executive for a medium sized Oil Company and Gus ended up doing some work for them that made him $ 12,000.00, so his taking that class was not only educational it was also productive. That spring Gus drove to El Campo and got his Funeral and Head Stone all paid for and at the same time he visited as many of his old friends and business friends as he could. Finally the last day he was there his Head Stone was put into place and he was able to see what it looked like at the actual spot of his Grave. He was standing there looking at it and thinking that he was the first one to be buried there that was seeing his Grave Stone, because all the rest of his Family were buried first and then their Grave Stones were put down later. He was also the first one to pay for his Funeral, because he had to pay for his Dad, Mom and his Son's Funeral. Well it was taken care of now and it made Gus feel a lot better. His Head Stone was different, because it told a story of who his real Mom and Dad were and half Sister and it also had the name of all his Boys on it and each of them had a different Mom. Gus looked at it as a way for someone to use to make a connection if they were looking for family, years in the future. He didn't want his real blood line to be a secret any longer. Gus decided not to go see his new Son while he was down in El Campo even though it was only 20 miles from Ganado, because he felt that there was still to much for them to learn about each other before they could be totally comfortable about their relationship. Also Gus's other Sons didn't know anything about this new Son that just showed up. Gus just wanted to make sure that everything was good before he included this new Son into their Family Circle. The Stock Market was plunging down almost everyday and it seemed that the new Democrat President didn't have a clue what to do about it. People were selling their Stocks for what ever they could get for them and Gus's Wife did that also. She asked Gus for advice on it and Gus told her that he really didn't know much about the Stock Market. He had never really owned any stock, because he had heard so many horror stories about the stock market crash of 1929 from his parents friends that he had never bothered to learn much about it and that he had always just considered it to be something that was manipulated by the super rich to their their own advantage. His Wife had obtained her stock from a Company that she had worked for as part of their benefits to their employees. It had increased in value at one time till it had been worth over $100,000.00, but by the time she sold it she got about $70,000.00 and she put it into a interest bearing account at a Credit Union. She said that she was happy to get it out of the Stock Market even though she had lost a lot of it's value. That summer Gus's New Son called and said that he would be coming through Van Horn from New Mexico and wondered if it would be alright for him to stop and visit. Gus told him that it would be nice, so they spent a couple of days together visiting and talking and getting to know each other better. Gus decided that his New Son was a good man and he told him that maybe sometime he could bring his Wife and little Son out to see him. September of 2009 the man that Gus had met with the Rancher friend of his that had the 640 acres of land that Gus had turned down because he didn't have the money to buy it, called Gus to see if he was still interested in buying it. The man had wanted $150.00/acre or $96,000.00 when Gus had talked to him before, but now the man told him that he had lost so much money in the Stock Market that he wanted to sell his 640 acres and what would Gus pay him for it. Gus thought about it and told him that he would Give him $60.00/acre for it and the man told Gus that he couldn't accept that, because he had $110.00/acre in mind. Gus told him that he would think about it and that he wanted to go out to see if he could locate the land and then he would call him back about it in a few days. Gus got with his Rancher Friend and followed him out to where he thought the land was, but he told Gus that he didn't know where the property lines were, but that the land was on both sides of the paved Texas Farm Road. Gus had brought a canteen full of water and a walking stick along and decided to walk on the south side of the road first. Gus walked and walked and the land sloped down from a big hillside into some big thick brushy draws that Gus could see that drained a lot of water runoff at times and in the brush there were cow and deer trails and places where the deer had bedded down with a lot of their pellets everywhere on the ground. The land then rose back up again into some rocky ridges with some white gypsum spotted land and some big ceder trees. Gus walked most of the afternoon and by the time he returned to his truck he was exhausted, so he went home and decided to go walk the land on the north side of the road the next day. Gus went out the next day and this time he took a lunch with him and a thermos of coffee along with his canteen of water. He could see what looked like a electric power line way to the north and decided to walk that direction first. This was higher land on this side of the road and it dipped down into a deep draw with brush, but then it immediately climbed again back onto a high rocky hill that went all the way back to the electric power line and a fence. Gus walked east from there going parallel to the power line and finally came to a dirt stock water tank. Gus turned to the south and walked in the direction of the State of Texas Farm Road and then curved back to the west crossing two brushy draws before arriving back at his truck. Gus didn't see any roads on the land, but he did see what looked like an old abandoned road bed at one place. He had a good idea now what the land looked like and in a way he was disappointed but in another way he was excited about it. The land had good points and bad points. First it was only section of 640 acres and Gus really would like to have two sections, second he didn't see any of the beautiful rocks that his other ranch had on it and these were the bad points. The good points were that he had already picked up a small Indian arrowhead, so there must be some Indian camps on the place and there was the possibility of having electric power, there was some real high places to make a camp, there was a beautiful view of the Apache Mountains, there were two good roads for access, one State and one County, that would never be closed off by a big landowner and it was located only 35 miles north east of Van Horn on a hard surface road that only required 35 to 40 minutes to get there. Gus decided that it had a lot more pluses then minuses, so he was going to call the Man that owned the land and make him an offer while he was in a hurry to sell. Gus drove back to town and started running figures through the calculator to see what they would look like. He really wanted to buy the land, because his Camp House and Shop/Storage building and a lot of other things had been stored for almost two years and needed to be moved on to his own land. This was the first land that even came close to what he had wanted to by to replace the Ranch he had sold. Gus decided that he needed to get pretty close to what the Man wanted for the land and still be able to save some money on it, so he decided to offer him $90.00/acre for it or $57,600.00 and that was $20.00/acre less then the man wanted or $12,800.00, but Gus thought that if the man really wanted to sell then he would take it and that money saved would go a long way into the improvements that Gus would need to do to make a nice Camp out of it. Gus called the man the next day and told him what he would pay for the land and the man thought about it for a few minutes then told Gus that it was close enough to what he wanted if Gus could pay cash for it. Gus told him that he could and that he would write the man a check and send it to him that day and Gus wanted a clear Deed in return. The man agreed and so the deal was done and three days later Gus got his Deed and he filed it at the County Clerks Office and then Gus started to get things moving to find out where his land property lines were by hiring a local Land Surveyor that he knew and they surveyed and marked the land property lines. Gus then hired a local Dirt Contractor that had a bulldozer, maintainer and backhoe and while he was bulldozing and smoothing off the property lines Gus was marking off interior roads with ribbons and a place for the main Camp. This was in the fall of the year and Gus was trying to get as much done as he could before the weather got bad in the winter. It was already October and Gus hired hired three men to help him do all the manual labor that he knew he had to do to get everything set up. He took his welding machine trailer and the water trailer out there to use for electricity and for water for finishing the cement slabs that he was going to have poured for the Camp House and the Shop/Storage containers he was going to bring from where he had them stored. He also called back to El Campo to a Friend if his that had a Machinery Dealership and he bought a knew Kubota tractor with a front end loader and a box blade to use when he was working with things setting up the main camp. Gus knew that he would have plenty of work for it to do moving dirt around and also lifting up the iron tubing that had to be re-welded together for the porch roof and railing and the 20 foot x 40 foot roof between the two buildings. He arranged for a friend of his to haul it out to Van Horn on a trailer. Gus brought his surveying instrument out to level the two forms for the cement slabs that he needed to pour that were going to be each 9 feet wide and 41 feet long and 4 inches thick. Gus had bought this surveying instrument in 1971 when he was farming rice, so he could survey his own irrigation levies and canals to carry water to his fields and now 38 years later he was still using it for his benefit. This was the way Gus liked to operate. He liked to invest in tools and things that would last a long time if you took care of them and he had learned back when he was young that if you were careful with your things and took good care of them then they would be useful to you for many years and you wouldn't have to keep spending your hard earned money to replace them. Gus and his help set up the cement forms and put the re-bar iron in them and then ordered the cement from a local cement plant. It was delivered and poured and then Gus started his welding machine and hooked up the electric cord to the water trailer pump so he could spray the cement in the forms with water, so it wouldn't dry to fast before his help could get the cement spread and smoothed. After the cement was finished Gus waited two days for it to cure hard then he hired a tilt bed truck from a neighboring town and a big wrecker from Van Horn and they went down to Lobo to where Gus had stored all of the buildings and things from the other Ranch for two years and he brought the Camp House and the Shop/Storage building and had them each set on the cement slab poured for them then he took his 18 foot trailer and hauled everything left there at Lobo, to the new campsite which took him and his help another two days. Gus now called his youngest Son and told him that he needed to make arrangements to take four days of vacation time from his job and come Van Horn to do a lot of welding to put everything back together. Gus wanted to have his Son to do it, because most of the welding was going to be overhead and Gus's neck couldn't take that kind of work anymore. Gus went to Pecos, Texas and bought all the roofing metal and all the extra two inch angle iron and two inch and one inch square tubing and welding rods that they would need and hauled them back to the new camp. His youngest S0n came down and did the welding and then they put up all the metal roofing on the 10 foot x 40 foot porch and the 20 foot x 40 foot covered area between the two buildings. Gus, his youngest Son and his helpers got all of this done including all the eight miles of roads, before the Christmas Holidays. Gus had been lucky with the weather so far, but the winter weather was making it hard for him do much work out at his Ranch. He was just able to do small jobs and one of them was to use his tractor and move dirt to a place that he had chosen to build a cook shed. He had to move a lot of dirt, pile it up and spread it out, so it would be level with the surface that was right in front of his Camp House. He would have to wait for better weather to build this, so that wouldn't happen till the spring of 2010 and the dirt would have time to settle, so he wouldn't have any trouble with it when he started digging holes and cementing pipe to make the framework for the cook shed. Gus also had a lot of electric wiring to do, water lines to run and cement to pour for the porch and under the big covered area, so there would be a lot of work to do in the New Year. He was satisfied with all that he had achieved in just three months and now it was just a matter of waiting for better weather to finish his camp. He had the money thank goodness to do a real good job of things. It wouldn't be anything fancy, but the way he planned the place, it would be a place that he could actually live at if he wanted to do so. He would go out and piddle around on some small things when he would get a decent day, but they were rare and he would just have to wait to get any real work done. New Years Eve finally got there and Gus went to bed early and was awaken with the gun shots and the fireworks that always went off in Van Horn to signal the coming of the New Year, so Gus knew that the New Year of 2010 had arrived and he just turned over and went back to sleep.

Lorrie –2009 came in and Lorrie finished her Brandy and went up to her room and went to bed. The next morning she was getting ready for their annual New Years Day lunch with their friends. She had to wake her Husband up and he was slowly getting ready, because he was nursing a pretty big hangover, so he took a big shot of whiskey to help him get over it. There was food in the refrigerator that her Stepson could eat, so they weren't planning on bringing him back when they came home from their lunch. They finally made it to the lunch and this was always something that Lorrie loved to go to on New Years Day. The conversation with good old friends was always a pleasant way to start the New Year. After a while the conversation shifter to questions about how Lorrie's Stepson was doing and Lorrie looked at her Husband, but he didn't offer any answer, so Lorrie answered with a short description of her Stepsons life after his girlfriend Cheryl had left him and Lorrie noticed that her Husband was glaring at her, but he didn't say anything. She wondered what kind of omen that was and if she was going to hear about it later that day. She thought, oh well, what ever it was that her Husband didn't like that she said she had said it and it was the truth and she couldn't take it back now, so she just went on with her conversation like nothing was wrong. After their lunch on the way back home her Husband was quiet and Lorrie just thought that he was still feeling bad from his hangover. When they got home Lorrie went into the kitchen and saw dirty dishes that signaled that her Stepson had eaten his lunch then she went to go up stairs when she saw her Husband pouring himself a big glass of whiskey, so she passed him and went to her room to change cloths into something that she could just be comfortable in around the house when all of a sudden she heard her door open and her Husband came in at her and grabbed her blouse and tore it off of her screaming at the top of his lungs that he was tired of her degrading his Son which was the same as degrading him and that he was going to teach her a lesson, so he then grabbed her bra and tore it off of her and when he did his fingernails put long scratches in her breasts that started bleeding, then he slapped her and pushed her on her bed and hit her on her back with his fists several times before he stomped out of her room and back down stairs. Lorrie just laid there shaking and crying wondering what in the world had brought on this violent attack. She stayed in her room for the rest of the afternoon, because she was afraid to go down stairs. Late in the day Lorrie began to feel weak and a little dizzy, so she tested herself for her diabetes and found that she was having a reaction and she needed to eat something to get her sugar back in balance. She tried to go down the stairs and found that she was loosing her balance, so she had to sit down on them and go from stair to stair until she got down, then she held on to things as she went into the kitchen to fix herself some cream of wheat. Thank goodness her Husband was passed out on the couch and he didn't move when she went by. Cream of wheat was the only thing that she could eat when she was upset, because anything else just wouldn't go down her throat. She had experimented with other foods, but cream of wheat was her stand-by and it always worked when her Husband had her so upset that her whole system was screaming for relief. No-one would ever know how terrible it was to go through one of her Husbands verbal and physical abusive rages that sometime could last for an entire day or until he drank himself into a stupor and fell asleep. These seemed to be getting worse for Lorrie to be able to overcome or maybe it was just that she was getting older and she wasn't as strong as she had once been. Lorrie fixed her cream of wheat thin so it would slide down her throat easily and she fixed herself a big mug of hot tea also. When she finished this she went back to her room very carefully and laid down to sleep, thinking that this was not a good start to the New Year of 2009. Lorrie's Husband finally went on his two week ski vacation and this gave her the time she needed to be away from him and rebuild her self confidence a little. She also used this time to do some more research on Spain. She was discovering some interesting programs that the Spanish Government was sponsoring, but she had to do more research on them and she was also looking into two other small Spanish villages to visit when they went to Spain on Easter vacation with her Husbands Friend. While her Husband was on his ski vacation her Stepson came home from work complaining about how stupid his bosses were at the Bank where he was a Loan Officer. Lorrie could see the old pattern starting to play out again with her Stepson. He always started doing this every time he was planning to quit his job. She wondered if he really believed that he was fooling her. She didn't say anything and kept preparing the food for their dinner. There wasn't anything that she could say that would divert him from quitting his job. She had tried and tried to talk to him in the past to get him to see reality and all it did was get her into trouble with her Husband. She had gotten to the point with him that she really didn't give a damn if he worked or not, all that she wanted to do was to try to keep a little peace in the house so she could survive herself. She seldom even went up to his room, because she was afraid of what she might find up there. She had found those bad pills up there once before and she knew that he was drinking a lot in his room, but she was trying to forget about the pills and she didn't know what he did with his money, but he seemed to never have any when it came for him to pay for something for his own benefit. He always had to go to his Dad for money which made Lorrie wonder as to what he was spending his money on, maybe those pills and alcohol, because he had no expenses living there with them. She just let him go on and on and finally told him that if he wanted to eat dinner that it would be ready in about an hour. That shut him up and he went up to his room. Lorrie had called and talked to her Husbands Friends Wife about the other two small villages in Spain that she wanted to visit when they were there during their Easter Holiday and his Friends Wife was excited about visiting them. She was really into the historic ancient Churches, Shrines and Government buildings like Lorrie was, so it was easy for Lorrie to get her interested in them without having to reveal her real reason for doing all of this. Lorrie's Husband came home from his ski vacation in a good frame of mind that pleased Lorrie, but she thought that wasn't going to last very long when he learned that his Son was working up excuses to quit his job. Their Easter Holiday in Spain was nice as usual except for Lorrie having to be careful what she said around her Husband when he was drinking. Her and her Husband's Friends Wife had a real good adventure visiting the two small villages and they were up in very beautiful areas of the mountains with breath taking views, small olive groves and fruit orchards, red tile roofed houses and churches and municipal buildings that were hundreds of years old. Almost all of these small villages that they had been visiting on their Easter Holidays could be on postcards. Lorrie had fallen in love with them and her plans were becoming more and more vivid in her mind. She had to hire a person in each village that could understand a little English so she could communicate with some of the educated people of the village to find out things that she couldn't research about each one. She needed to learn Spanish she knew and she was determined to do so, in fact she had to learn Spanish if she was going to put her plan into action. Lorrie felt lucky that she had avoided sex with her Husband again on this Easter Holiday in Spain, because they always had to share a bed there. She always managed to see to it that he was very drunk by the time they were to go to bed, so he would fall asleep immediately. When they got back to England Lorrie took all the notes that she had made and added them to the file that she was building on each village and the people of importance there that she had made friends with. All hell had broken loose when they got back home, because they found out that her Stepson had quit his job while they had been gone and all he had done was to drink up all of the liquor of any and every kind that they had in the house and there was empty bottles and dirty dishes all over the house. Lorrie was furious and her Husband was upset also, but he still took his Sons side and he and Lorrie got into a big fight that got very loud and the neighbors called the Police again to knock on their door and came in the house to investigate what was happening so they could make another report to put in their growing file of domestic abuse. It was now getting close to the time that Lorrie needed to make her plans to go to Texas for her annual Vacation of three months there. She booked her airplane tickets for the discounted rate and she made her Doctors appointment to get a complete check-up so she could get three months supply of all her medicine to take to Texas with her. Lorrie went in and had all the tests made on her blood, urine and chest x-rays. A few days later she got a call from her Doctors Office to come in for a consultation. Lorrie thought that something didn't sound just right about this call. Her Doctor brought out all of her test results and they all showed that her medicine for diabetes, high blood pressure and high cholesterol needed to be increased to keep up with the advancement of these diseases and to bring them back to a normal level. Her Doctor questioned her extensively about her diet and her stress levels and then she told him about her troubles with her Husband and Stepson. He was quiet for a minute as if he was deep in thought and then he looked up and told her that her health was at a critical juncture and that she somehow would need to try and keep her stress level as low as possible and he didn't know how to advise her on the trouble she had with her personal life other then to tell her that it could continue to be a major factor along with her age that helped her health to decline at a more rapid rate then normal. He increased the strength of all of her medicines and told her that he wanted to see her as soon as possible when she got back from Texas. This was very depressing for Lorrie and actually it really knocked the blocks out from under her. She thought that she had been doing pretty good with her pills keeping her health regulated. Lorrie had kept her health problems secret from her Husband. He knew that she was taking some medication, but he didn't know the extent of her health problems and she didn't want him to know. Lorrie felt that she couldn't trust him to know about her health problems, because he might use that knowledge to somehow hurt her. Lorrie's Texas Vacation time finally arrived and she flew into Houston Texas where her Sister picked her up at the Houston Airport as usual. Lorrie was so glad to get away from her Husband and her Stepson. While at her Sisters house in Houston her Sister told Lorrie would have a surprise when she got to her Mom's house in El Campo. Lorrie cocked her head to the side and asked her Sister if it was a good or bad surprise and her Sister told her that she would have to make up her own mind about that. Lorrie told her Sister that she knew that she was dying to tell her, so go ahead. Her Sister told Lorrie that their Brother had a woman move in with him and was living there with him now. Lorrie was surprised, because her Brother was living right next door to her Mom and was sure that her Mom wouldn't like him to be living with a woman and not be married. Lorrie, her Sister and her Brother had always been very careful about upsetting their Mom and Lorrie knew that this was one of the things that would do it. Lorrie was really surprised at her Brother for being so bold, because he had always been very easy going with a real dry, quiet since of humor and had always been very respectful of his Mom and Dad's lings on everything. Lorrie asked her Sister what their Mom had done about it and her Sister told Lorrie that she really didn't know, but that their Mom wasn't very happy about it, but that their Brother wasn't going to send the woman away. Lorrie had all sorts of questions she asked her Sister about this new woman of her Brothers. Her Sister told Lorrie that she didn't know much, but that the woman had been married and divorced and she had some grown children. Lorrie thought that she would meet this woman in a few days and then she would make up her own mind about her. Lorrie just hoped that the woman was good to her Brother, because he had always been a sweet little Brother and his wife had hurt him real bad before they divorced, so Lorrie didn't want her Brother to have to go through any more hurt because of a woman. Lorrie was thinking quietly to herself and what she was thinking was that she had hidden things about the way she had lived her private life from her parents, because she had always been told by them not to shame them or the family with the way she conducted her personal life. They had impressed on her ever since she had been just a young girl not to embarrass them by making bad grades, flirting with boys, getting pregnant without being married, drinking, taking drugs or anything else that they considered not proper to do. She had been afraid of their disappointment and rejection all of her life and now her little Brother does something that there would have been no way in the world that Lorrie would have had the courage to do. She had to smile about her little Brother having the courage to do something that his brave older Sister would have just shuttered when thinking about doing it and her Mom and Dad finding out about it. Well she thought that she was really interested in meeting this woman and she was probably really nice if her Brother was taking this chance with her. Lorrie and her Sister drove to El Campo and was greeted at her Mom's house by her Brother and his Girlfriend. Lorrie thought that she was really pretty and she could tell that she was very in love with her Brother by the way that she cold not keep her hands off of him and that she would look at him and smile when she was talking. Lorrie told her that she was sorry that she hadn't brought her a gift, because she had just found about her when she got to Houston and her Brothers Girlfriend told Lorrie that the very best gift was that she finally got to meet her after hearing so many wonderful things about her. Lorrie had a good impression of her Brothers Girlfriend right from the start and she was enjoying being around her. They all went to the local Mexican Cafe for Lorrie to get her annual Tex-Mex fix and then they all went out on her Mom's patio for a drink and to talk. Lorrie was tired from all her traveling, so she went to bed, but before she went her Brothers Girlfriend told her that they wanted her and her Sister and their Mom to come over the next evening for dinner. Lorrie was impressed and was interested in talking to her about cooking, because Lorrie was interested in cooking. That next evening when Lorrie was over at her Brothers house she was watching her Brother and his Girlfriend cooking together and Lorrie was so pleased to see how well they worked together. They had a great evening there and Lorrie was looking forward to spending more time with her Brothers Girlfriend while she was in El Campo. Lorrie went about her stay with her Mom as she usually did when she was in El Campo. She went to the Monday lunches with the girls and listened to all the local gossip that went on in town. There were so many people in town now that Lorrie had never heard their names and the familiar names were becoming fewer and fewer. The older people were dying off and a lot of the younger ones that Lorrie had known had moved off somewhere to make a living. Lorrie took her Mom to her Friends Hair Salon on her standing Thursday appointment and got herself a haircut and color and as usual the was different then it was supposed to be, but Lorrie thought so what that is just the way that her Friend did things. While she was there she listened carefully for the mention of Gus's name, but there wasn't any talk of Gus from anyone and there wasn't anyone there that Lorrie thought might even have known Gus. While Lorrie was in El Campo she learned that her Brothers Girlfriend liked antiques and she loved to decorate with old things. Lorrie saw that she was extremely talented in doing this, so Lorrie went with her to several garage and yard sales looking for old items to decorate with and furniture that she could refinish and Lorrie was having the best time with her Brothers Girlfriend. She was so glad to see that her Brother was happy again. When Lorrie's vacation in El Campo was almost over she took her Brothers Girlfriend with her to do her Texas food shopping to take back to England with her. Her Brothers Girlfriend thought that this was the funniest thing, but Lorrie told her that she couldn't get any of this stuff in England and being a Texas girl she wanted to take as much of it back to England as she could get in her luggage. Lorrie also did her annual Gus drive around pilgrimage and her Brothers Girlfriend asked Lorrie what she was doing and Lorrie told her that she would think that she was crazy, but it was just something that she had to do before she went back to England each year and then Lorrie told her about Gus and that she had been love with him all of her life and that she had always hoped that she would be able to see him again. Lorrie told her that this was just a way for her to keep feeling connected to Gus. Lorrie flew back to England and had a good feeling about her Brothers Girlfriend. She had the usual catch up work to do and then she made her Doctors appointment like he wanted her to do. Lorrie wanted him to look at a spot on her forehead that she had been itching for quite some time. It was a little pink bump that would itch and then peal and Lorrie had been putting make-up on it for several months so it wouldn't be so noticeable. She would see if he would give her some salve that would heal it up, so she could quit messing with it. Lorrie had her Doctors appointment and he told her that the tests showed that her medication was doing it's job, so he wasn't going to change it. He looked at the bump on her forehead and told her that he didn't like the looks of it and that he was going to refer her to a Dermatologist. She had him make an appointment with the one she had been using for years. He was very busy though and she couldn't get an appointment to see him until January of 2010. That was just fine for Lorrie, because it wasn't bothering her that much, it just looked bad right there on her forehead, but she would keep it hidden as much as she could with make-up till the Dermatologist could do something with it. Lorrie finally got the courage to ask her Husband if her Stepson had been looking for a job and all she got in response was for him to bare his teeth and make a sort of growling noise, so Lorrie took this as a no and left it at that to try to avoid a fight. The Holiday season was coming up fast and Lorrie had been researching when she could start taking Spanish lessons through the Open University System like she had done with her Art History Degree. She couldn't start until the next Semester started after the New Year of 2010, so Lorrie signed up and paid her fees and ordered her books. This Spanish Degree would take her two years for her to complete it and she would be learning to read, speak and write Spanish. This was something for her to look forward to and she thought that it would be good to be back in school again and besides this was something that she needed so she could make her plan work to leave her Husband. Lorrie had found out that the Spanish Government was actively looking for English Teachers to go out into the countryside to small villages and teach English to the school children there and they were paying a good wage and furnishing a place to live. Lorrie thought that this would be a good way for her to leave her Husband and live in obscurity, out of the way in one of these small villages and just basically disappear so he couldn't find her. This is what she had been thinking about for several years ever since that first trip that they had come to Spain on Easter Holiday. Now since she had done enough research to understand how it was going to work she could start seriously working on her plan and learning Spanish was a major part of it. When Lorrie was getting ready for Christmas she remembered her Brothers Girlfriend and how nice it would be to have her with her now to decorate and get things ready for Christmas with like when Cheryl was still around. Lorrie did it all by herself and she bought everyone including herself a Christmas gift. Her Husband went on his one week ski vacation and that left Lorrie home with her Stepson, but Lorrie seldom say him because he stayed in his room most of the time. Their New Years celebration was small just like Lorrie had been having for the last few years and she sat up to watch the New Year of 2010 come in on the TV programs. Her Husband had gone to bed early because he had been having trouble with bronchitis and he had only drank whiskey toddies with a lot of lemon and honey in them. Lorrie was thinking about the different things that had happened in 2009 and also about what she was looking forward to in 2010. Lorrie was looking forward to starting her Spanish classes that would take her 2010 and 2011 to complete, but that was alright, because then she would be able to officially apply for a position as an English Teacher and be placed by the Spanish Government in one of the villages that she would choose and then she could disappear out of the life of her Husband and Stepson that she felt so trapped in. This Teaching job would be her way out and she was looking forward to that. It was 2010 now and Lorrie would be 65 years old. New Years Day 2010 Lorrie was getting ready to go to their annual New Year Day lunch with their friends and she was in a good mood for a change, because she was starting something in 2010 to look forward to.

Gus—2010 January and February of 2010 was slow for Gus. The weather was not good enough to work at the Ranch and he wasn't making any Oil & Gas deals either. He went to Pecos with his 18 foot trailer to get all the pipe and c-iron that he would need to build the cook shed and he had bought some used metal roofing for the walls and the roof. He now had all the building material that he needed to build the 20 x 20 foot cook shed when the weather got better. The first part of March when the weather improved his new Son called him to see if he, his Wife and his Son could come to Van Horn, so they could meet Gus for the first time and Gus told him that it would be nice to meet them. They came to Van Horn the next week and stayed at a Motel for a couple of days and they went to the Ranch with Gus. Something happened at the Ranch that no one noticed but Gus and it helped to convince Gus that this young man really was his Son. They had brought some hot dogs along to roast over a fire outside and Gus's new Son asked Gos what he could do to help. Gus gave him an ax and told him that he could chop up some wood for the fire if he wanted to and then Gus went get some water from the water trailer, because he didn't have the water piped to the Camp House yet. When Gus got back to the Camp he noticed that his new Son had three separate stacks of wood chopped and they were separated according to size small for kindling, medium to build up the fire and large to finish the fire for final use. This is exactly the way Gus would have done it himself and he didn't mention that to his new Son, so this meant to Gus that this young man thought the way he did, which was a good sign. Gus didn't mention any of this, but kept it to himself for now. This young man also had those glassy blue eyes like Gus and the rest of his Son's have. Things were sure adding up to where Gus was feeling comfortable that this young man was his new Son. He had a nice family also with a pretty and intelligent wife and a young boy. He seemed to be easy to talk to and he liked the out doors and owned and liked to shoot guns and drink some beer and listen to country music and this sounded just like what the rest of Gus's boys liked to do. Gus finally told him about the family deer hunting at Thanksgiving and asked him if he would like to attend and meet the other two boys that would be there and his new Son jumped at the chance. So it was settled now and Gus was going to have to tell his other two boys about this new Son that showed up after all of these years. There was one more Son that Gus would hold off telling about this new one and he was the Son by Gus's first marriage, because he wasn't as close to the family as the others were and Gus decided to let time tell him what to do about it. Right after his new Son and his family left to go back to Ganado, Texas Gus got things organized to pour the cement for the porch and under the big covered area between the two buildings. Gus told his helpers that they all were too old and that included him, to be pouring that much cement. He told them that the two 9 x 41 foot slabs that they poured for the two buildings almost killed them, so he had hired a local contractor to pour and finish this cement. He told them that he still had plenty of work for them to help him with. Before the cement was poured Gus and his helpers laid the water line from the 500 gallon poly water tank that was on a stand up on the rock outcropping up above the camp area and brought it all the way down and in between the buildings to furnish water to the camp House and to the hot water heater that was located in the Shop/Storage Building. They also buried a electric cable that would supply power to the Shop/ Storage Building and the camp House. The cement was poured and Gus and his helpers had to wait for two days for it to dry before they could return and start working on running all the electrical wiring and installing all the lighting fixtures. When that was finished, they finished the water pipes and the camp House and the Shop/Storage Building were ready to use. Now Gus was ready to build his 20 x20 foot cook shed. He kept two helpers on the payroll to help him with this. He had already moved the dirt there with his tractor and front-end loader and smoothed it down several months before, so it was set up and ready for him to do his construction work. They dug eight holes for the pipe uprights to be cemented in and then they started welding up the six inch c-iron for the framework. Gus did all the welding and then they all worked on putting on the metal roofing and the partial walls on the east and west sides to help to block some of the wind. Gus built two gates for the front that could swing open and open up the whole front and built a framework covered with horse wire for the south side so it could be seen through to view the Apache Mountains. This would keep the cows out when it wasn't being used. Then Gus started doing the masonry work building the cement block fire box that would house the B-B-Q grill and next to it a smaller one to use for dutch oven cooking. Gus built these right in the middle of the cook shed so that wood could be stacked on the south wall and a small bar could be put on the northeast side and a table and chairs could be on the north and west side and there would still be enough room to walk around the B-B-Q grill and the dutch oven cooking fire boxes. Everything could be used now and it had taken Gus and his helpers from October of 2009 to May of 2010 to get everything to this point. Gus payed the helpers and told them that he wanted to do some more work, but that he would need to make some more money before he could hire them to do it, so he turned them loose for the time being. There were still several things that Gus wanted to do and the biggest was to completely redo the inside of the camp House, but Gus wanted to try to make some more money before he spent any more out at his new Blue Quail Ranch. Gus got a notice that his High School Class of 1960 was going to have their 50 year Class Reunion in October of 2010. Gus called two of his Sons and talked them in attending with him and his Wife. He didn't tell his new Son about it, because he wanted him to meet these two sons at their annual deer hunting at the Ranch on Thanksgiving. Gus sent in his money for all of them to attend and he was glad that his Sons could meet some of his class mates and hear their stories of those school days. In July Gus made another Oil and Gas Deal that made him $9,000.00, so he decided that it was time for him to redo the inside of the camp House. He put half of the money in his Oil and Gas Bank account and the other half is what he was going to spend on the redo of the inside of the camp House. Gus contacted the two helpers that he had worked with before and hired them to help him with the inside of the camp House. They took everything out of it including the shelves on the wall and the toilet and they stored everything in the Shop/Storage Building and under the big covered area between the two buildings. Inside Gus put the two helpers to work in the big room cleaning the ceiling and walls taping off windows and caulking cracks and flaws in the plywood wall. While they were doing this Gus was finishing some work in the bathroom that he had never finished. His helpers put on a coat of primer then a coat of white paint while Gus was working in the bathroom, then Gus put one of them to painting all of the shelving a soft light gray and the other helper he put to painting in the bath room. When they had finished all of the painting Gus had them sweep the old plank floor good and make sure that there wasn't anything on it that would keep a sub-floor from laying down flat and smooth. Then they started installing a ¼ inch plywood sub-floor over the old planks and then marked off the starting point for the floor tile that Gus had bought. It was real hot working in the Camp House in July, but Gus didn't want to turn on the air conditioner and close up the camp House because he was afraid that the fumes from the glue would make them sick. He remembered well that time he had been so sick from doing the plumbing under the floor in the bathroom at his Van Horn House and he didn't want anything like that to happen again. They did the big room first and then the bathroom. When they were finished Gus was so pleased that he told them that the next day they would put everything back into the camp House and then the next day when they came back to the Ranch to get the tools and a few other things that they needed to take back to torn that Gus would grill each one of them a big rib-eye steak on the new steak grill and he would have some beer iced down. The next day with everything back inside the camp House it all looked so nice and clean and organized that Gus would have liked to move there to live. The next day after that like Gus had told them after they had loaded everything in his pickup Gus started the fire for grilling the steaks and he and his two helpers moved the cooler under the Cook Shed and they sat there and drank beer and enjoyed the fire and then they ate their steaks with baked potatoes in the coals and drank their beer. This was the first little party that was put on under the Cook Shed. Gus knew that his Sons would be surprised when they saw the new camp and the camp House with all the nice metal roofing and all the cement poured and the Cook Shed, because at his other ranch everything was sort of primitive. Gus spent time out at the Ranch now in more comfort with electricity and a shaded place to put his pickup under so it wouldn't get so hot in the sun and the cement front porch that he could sit on in the mornings and drink his coffee. He would go exploring looking for Indian artifacts and had identified three Indian campsites with two of them having bed rock mortar holes where the Indian women pounded their seeds to make flour for their tortillas. October came around and Gus and his wife met his two Sons in El Campo for his High School Class of 1960, 50 year reunion. That afternoon when they were there he took them all out to the Grave Yard there to show them his grave stone and tell them that he had already prepaid for his funeral. They saw that their names were on Gus's grave stone. He just wanted them to know what he had done and then he told them about his new Son that had turned up and told them the whole story and that he was invited to come out the annual Thanksgiving hunting get together and for all of them to meet and get to know each other. This surprised them and they had a lot of questions for Gus and Gus tried to answer them, but some he told them that they would have to ask the new Son, because Gus didn't have an answer for some of those questions. His 50th Class Reunion was a great success and Gus was glad to have seen Classmates that he hadn't seen in years, he also learned of several that had died. When he arrived for the Reunion and went in to register the girl classmate that was registering him handed him a slip of paper that had an old friend of his, name on it along with her cell phone number and her e-mail. His classmate told him that she had gone in to Gus's Friends Hair Salon to get her hair done for the Reunion and the Owner of the Hair Salon asked if Gus was going to be at the Reunion and Gus's classmate told her that he would and then she gave her the slip of paper and told her to tell Gus to e-mail her. Gus was glad to get this contact on his old friend, because he had known her since they were just very small children. They had grown up together in the same Church and she had taught Gus to tie his shoe's when he was in the first grade and Gus hadn't seen or heard from her since he had moved out to Van Horn. They decided at the Reunion to have the next one in three years, because so many of them were getting unstable physically that five years seemed to long. The Thanksgiving Holidays finally came and Gus sent an e-mail to his Friend that owned the Hair Salon wishing her a happy Thanksgiving, also Gus was excited to see what his Sons would say about his new Ranch Camp and also how the meeting with his new Son would turn out. Everybody stayed at the Ranch for four days and no one shot a deer, but they saw several doe's and cooked some good food, drank a lot of beer, listened to country music under the Cook Shed and everybody got along great with Gus's new Son, in fact it went better then Gus could have imagined with all of them inviting each other to their separate houses for visits. Gus thought how wonderful that all of this has worked out so nice. Now all of his three Sons had exchanged phone numbers and e-mail addresses before everyone went their separate ways back home. Gus stayed out at the Ranch one more day and cleaned everything up, loaded the trash into his pickup to throw away in town, then he cut off all the water from the main water tank on the rock outcropping and drained the water getting ready for the cold winter season. Gus went back to Van Horn feeling real good about how his Sons took to each other and this was from them having different Mom's except for the two that were ½ brothers with the same Mom. Gus thought that said a lot about the character of the three Sons. Christmas came and Gus and his wife had their simple little Christmas like they always did eating leftovers from Thanksgiving and then watching three of the same old Christmas movies on their VCR. Gus sent his Friend that owned the Hair Salon a Happy Christmas e-mail. He was enjoying being back in touch with her again and through her he was finding out about things in El Campo that he never would have known. New Years was coming up fast and Gus had made a habit of not going out for New Years ever since he had moved to Van Horn and this year wouldn't be any different. The afternoon on New Years Eve Gus decided that he was going to smoke two chickens and five links of good sausage that he had brought back with him from El Campo when he was there for the 50th Reunion, so he sat out by his big B-B-Q pit in the back yard and drank beer and smoked the chickens and sausage. All turned out real good which would give them a lot of left overs to freeze and they had a real good dinner with potato salad that his wife made then Gus went up stairs to the landing Library to play his oldies music and re-live some of his youth. When the song "In The Still Of The Night" played Gus got real quiet and all through the song Gus was remembering things about Lorrie and when it finished Gus heard the fireworks and the gun shots going off and knew that the New Year of 2011 had arrived and he held up his glass of his Dad's whiskey and gave a small toast to Lorrie telling her that he hoped that she had lived a good happy life where ever she was, then he drank the rest of the whiskey in the glass and turned things off and went to bed. New Year Day morning 2011 Gus sent his Friend Toodie that owned the Hair Salon a Happy New Year e-mail.

Lorrie—2010 The annual New Year Day 2010 lunch with their friends was very pleasant for Lorrie and it went off without a hitch. Lorrie's Husband was getting everything ready for his to week ski vacation and Lorrie was looking forward to him being gone for a while. While he was gone Lorrie had her Dermatologist Appointment and he removed the bump on her forehead with surgery and then told her that he was sending it off to the Lab to get it tested to see if it was a malignant cancer. Lorrie didn't think much about it and went home to continue with her normal routine. She had also started her Spanish Classes and was really enjoying them. Her classes were very interesting and stimulating, but Lorrie could see that learning to read, write and speak Spanish was going to be more challenging then she had thought. Her Dermatologist called her about a week later to come in to his office for a consultation. He told Lorrie that her bump turned out to be a malignant skin cancer and he recommended for her to go to a Radiation Treatment Facility in London for a series of radiation treatments on the skin area after it had healed. He told her that they couldn't do the radiation until it healed, because the radiation would kill the skin cells and then the incision wouldn't heal properly. Lorrie told him to go ahead and set up the appointments for the radiation treatments and he did that while she was still there with him. It took two more weeks before the incision was healed enough and then Lorrie went into London everyday for a week to take her treatments that only lasted a couple of minutes. It was all a lot of trouble for Lorrie to do, but thinking of a malignant cancer on her face brought on all kinds of terrible thoughts for

Lorrie to imagine about having different parts of her face cut away with surgery to remove cancer. It gave Lorrie a shudder just to think about it. Lorrie thought that it would be the final straw for her, because she was having enough trouble being married to her abusive Husband then to also have to put up with her face being cut away with cancer it would put her over the top and she knew that she would definitely have to find a way to commit suicide. After she had completed all the radiation treatments all she noticed was that there was a small red spot on her forehead for several days, then it went away and all that was left was a small little white scar that she could hide easy with makeup and letting her bangs grow a little longer to cover it. After a few weeks Lorrie didn't even think about it anymore. Lorrie was studying real hard on her Spanish. She was trying to learn how read and write it and was having difficulty learning how to switch the words around from English to Spanish, because a lot of the Spanish had the descriptive words after the nouns instead of before the noun it was describing like it was in English. The exercises she was doing were still fairly simple, so she was becoming aggravated with herself that she was still having trouble, because she knew that the exercises were going to get more complicated in the near future. Lorrie thought that this was a must for her to learn if she ever expected to get a job teaching English in the Spanish School System. She was getting ready for the Easter Holiday that her and her Husband were invited on each year with her Husbands Friend in the Garment Business. This year she was going to try out some of what she had learned in Spanish and read the local signs and the Public Notices that would be posted at different locations. This she thought would be fun and different then trying to talk in Spanish, because she hadn't actually gotten to the correct pronunciation of the Spanish yet in her classes and she wouldn't get into that till later in the class study. They were going to revisit two of the first small villages they had gone to, because there were some really interesting historical places there that her Friend was especially interested in seeing again and also Lorrie now had a better idea of what questions to ask then she had on their first visit. They drove in to their Friends Condo from the Airport and Lorrie always just loved this drive, because in a way it reminded her of Albuquerque with the rugged mountain terrain and its desert appearance. They had a nice time in a couple of clubs there and then Lorrie and her Friend wanted to take a day to visit one of the small villages, so they drove up in the mountains to it and parked to stroll around and visit the historical sites and for Lorrie to practice her Spanish reading skills. She found out that she was better then she had thought when she was actually doing it for real. That evening they went back to their Condo and got ready for dinner and dancing at a real nice Dinner Club that had live music. Their meal was excellent and Lorrie danced a couple of songs with her Husband until he got to drunk and then she danced one with his friend then by that time her Husband was starting to get a little loud with his talk, so they decided to go back to the Condo to finish the night out. Her Husband then started drinking straight whiskey and it didn't take long for him to pass out, so his Friend had to help Lorrie get him upstairs to their room. The next day he was feeling so bad with a hangover that Lorrie and her Friend went shopping by them selves and Lorrie did real good reading all the advertisements on different products for sale. She was real proud of herself and this was giving her more confidence in what she could do. When their Easter Holiday was over and Lorrie was back home she found herself in a much better frame of mind and she attacked her Spanish assignments with a renewed spirit of purpose. It was time for Lorrie to start making plans for her three month vacation back to El Campo, Texas and she was really looking forward to it. Lorrie and her Friend that owned the Hair Salon kept in touch with e-mails and Lorrie would ask her how Lorrie's Mom looked when she would go in each week for her hair appointment. Her Hair Saloon friend would also send Lorrie jokes via e-mail sometimes too. Lorrie e-mailed her to let her know when she would be coming to El Campo, so all the girls would know when to expect her for the Monday lunch. Her Brothers Girlfriend gave Lorrie another reason to be excited about her Vacation back to El Campo, because she truly liked her and also her Brother seemed so much more happy now. Lorrie wished that she could have found that kind of happiness with a Husband, well she felt that she could have with Gus, but that would never happen, and she was way too old for something like that anyway. For heavens sakes she was going to be 65 years old in October of 2010. She laughed at herself for even having something like being in love with a man cross her mind. She had always been in love with Gus and that was the problem and had always been the problem, because there was never any room in her heart to love another man. Gus had rejected her, so she had to go and try to live her life as best as she could and she had made a lot of mistakes with it along the way, but what else was she supposed to do anyway. Lorrie thought that life was life and you just had one and you had to live it and that is what she did. Lorrie finally left England on her long flight to Texas. Her Sister picked her up at the Houston Airport as usual so she could spend a few days with her before they would drive to El Campo. While Lorrie was staying with her Sister she was asking her about her Mom's physical well-being and her Sister told her that as far as she knew that their Mom was doing pretty good for being 88 years old and that their Brother would know more, because he saw her every-day. Lorrie and her Sister did their usual shopping and Lorrie found another purse that she liked, so she bought it. Every time she bought a new purse she thought why did I do that when I don't need a new purse, but she loved purses and what the hell she was 64 and going to be 65 years old, so why not enjoy her little weaknesses, they didn't hurt anything. They drove to El Campo and were met at her Mom's house by her Brother and his Girlfriend. They helped Lorrie unload all of her luggage and her Brothers Girlfriend helped Lorrie hang up all her cloths that needed to be unpacked and put on hangers. They sat around for a few minutes and then Lorrie got up and brought out all the little gifts that she had bought for them from England and also from Spain. She had even bought some special gifts for her Brothers Girlfriend, so she would know how much that Lorrie liked and approved of her being in the family. Lorrie then announced that she was ready to go to the local Mexican Cafe to get her Tex-Mex food fix. Late that afternoon they had their Happy Hour on the back patio and Lorrie was noticing that her Mom's hands were shaking more then she had remembered from a year ago when she was home to visit. She was wondering about Parkinson Disease like her Dad had, but didn't say anything then, because she wanted to talk to her Brother first. The next evening her Brother was going to have them over for steaks that he was going to cook on his charcoal grill along with baked potatoes and a fresh salad and a good red wine. Lorrie went over next door to his house early so she could talk to him about their Mom and she again observed how nice he and his Girlfriend worked together preparing all the food. Her Brother told her that he had talked to their Mom's Doctor and he had told him that it wasn't Parkinson Disease that it was just some kind of a Palsy that made her hands and her head shake, but it didn't affect anything else and it might get bad enough one day that she would have trouble writing and maybe eating liquid from a spoon, but that would be about all. Her Brother told Lorrie that the Doctor told him that their Mom was in very good health for her age and that he thing that they needed to watch was that their Mom might fall because of poor balance and that maybe she shouldn't drive, because of the way that she was shaking. They would have to watch her and then make the decision to talk to their Mom about it when the time came. Lorrie was glad to get this information and also glad that her Brother and his Girlfriend had been keeping such a good eye on their Mom. That next Monday Lorrie and her Sister went to meet the girls for their weekly Monday lunch gathering and she had such fun with them. Her Friend Toodie that owned the Hair Salon always had some real funny slightly nasty jokes to tell and Lorrie always enjoyed them. Her Hair Salon Friend even sent the jokes to her e-mail to England and she had been like that ever since Lorrie had known her. She was so much fun to be around. Lorrie told her that she would be coming in with her Mom for her weekly hair Appointment and that she also needed a haircut and color. Lorrie's Friend Toodie got out her appointment book from her purse and she wrote it down so she didn't forget it. She told Lorrie that she was having trouble remembering things now that she was 69 years old. That next Thursday Lorrie and her Mom went to the Hair Salon for their hair appointments and Lorrie picked out the color that she wanted on her hair then she sat still pretending to read a magazine, but she was actually listening to the different conversation\s around her to see if she could pick up the sound of Gus's name. There was all sorts of gossip going on, but nothing that had a Gus connection. When Lorrie and her Mom were through and Lorrie's hair was dried and brushed she discovered that her hair color was different again and she asked her Salon Friend about it and she told Lorrie that she thought would look better with it being a little lighter. Lorrie had to laugh, because she knew that her Friend Toodie would do what ever she wanted with her hair no matter what Lorrie said. Lorrie took her Mom to local B-B-Q Cafe for lunch and got her some of their banana pudding for her dessert, because Lorrie knew that she liked it so much, then they went home to take a nap. Lorrie was invited to go with her Brother and his Girlfriend to Canton, Texas for what was called the biggest garage sale in Texas. People from all over Texas and even other states come there to either buy or sell all sorts of things. Her Brother and his wife liked to go, because they both were into antiques and different odd things to decorate with. It sounded like fun to Lorrie, so she went with them and she had a wonderful time, but was so tired from all the walking. She had never seen so many stands selling so many things in her life. Lorrie liked this sort of thing also and she was tempted to buy several things, but how would she get them back to England. Lorrie's vacation time in El Campo, Texas was running short now. She had been observing her Mom ever since she had been there and was satisfied that she was doing real good for her age, but like the Doctor said, Lorrie had noticed that her Mom probably needed to use something better then a walking cane to make her more stable when she was walking and Lorrie had talked to her about that, but her Mom was embarrassed to use anything like a walker. She thought that it made her look like she was an invalid, likewise on her driving, Lorrie had talked to her about her not being able to see good enough to drive and her Mom refused to listen to her. Her Mom did give up one thing though while Lorrie was there. She let Lorrie write all the checks paying her bills and also she let her balance her checkbook, because she was so shaky with her writing that it was getting hard to read what her Mom had written. Lorrie told her Brother that he was going to have to take over that when she went back to England and he said that he would. It was time for Lorrie to get everything ready to fly back to England and she thought that the time had gone by really fast. She did all her Texas food shopping and had it packed up and then the last day she went to her Dad's grave again and talked to him then she did her annual Gus drive around to look at all of the places that she had seen Gus when she was young and now she was ready to fly back to England. She said good-by to everyone and her Brother drove her to the Airport in Houston, Texas for the long flight back to England. When she got back to England to her surprise she found out that her Stepson had gotten a job at a local Bank as a Teller. She was glad that he was working, but being a Teller was quite a fall from being the high powered Finance Investor for one of the most powerful Banks in the world. She guessed that he had finally gotten tired of doing nothing with his life. Lorrie immediately got back into her Spanish lessons and she realized that she didn't have a lot of time left on the reading and writing Spanish part of her class. She had been getting passing grades on all the papers that she had submitted, but they weren't as good as she had done on her Art History Degree. This part of it would be over at the end of December and then she would start the final year of actually speaking Spanish in January of 2011. That was exciting for Lorrie, because now she would be able to practice not only her reading and writing Spanish, but also speaking it on their next Easter Holiday in Spain. It was time again for her to get things together for the Holiday Season. As usual she wasn't getting a lot of help from her Husband or her Stepson. Lorrie sure missed Cheryl and things around the Holidays were never the same after Cheryl left Lorrie's Stepson. Lorrie did get her Husband and Stepson to go and buy a nice Christmas tree and bring it home and set it up in the living room. Lorrie would decorate it herself while she played Christmas music sung by some of her favorite Country and Western Artists. She bought all the presents as usual and hers also. After Christmas her Husband went on his ski vacation for a week and then it was time for their New Years Eve Party. Lorrie had planned a small get together again and she felt that it wouldn't be to many more years until she wouldn't even have any kind of party. They weren't much fun anymore like they had been when she was young. Now she felt like she was just going through the motions from habit. Their party was quiet with a few friends and they left early for different reasons, but mostly because they were all getting older and more cautious about drinking too much alcohol, that is except Lorrie's Husband who was still drinking like a fish. Lorrie's Husband went up to bed before the New Year of 2011 arrived, but Lorrie was determined to sit up till the New Year arrived. She watched the TV till they announced the arrival of the New Year of 2011 and Lorrie finished sipping the rest of the brandy that she had in her glass. Lorrie thought that 2011 was going to be the last year of her Spanish classes and then she would be qualified to apply for a English Teaching position with the Spanish Government and as soon as she got that job she would plan her disappearance from her Husband, so he wouldn't find her. Lorrie went up to her room and went to bed and woke up in the morning of the first day of 2011 getting ready for their annual New Years Day lunch with their Friends.

Gus—2011 started for Gus with nothing happening in the oil and gas business for Gus to do. He had a friend back in El Campo named Skeeter that had bought 40 acres of land down at Matagorda Bay at a place called Port Alto that he had been wanting Gus to come and look at. It seemed that he wanted to develop it into an RV Park and wanted Gus to give his opinion on it and maybe even invest money in it. Gus told Skeeter that he would come and look at it when the weather got better sometime in the spring or summer, but he didn't think that he would put any money in it, because he needed his money just in case that he would have to put up money for Oil Leases until he could get payed back by the Oil Company. Skeeter told Gus that the land would work good as a RV Park, because he owned the water system and the sewer plant for the small community of Port Alto and all he would have to do was to expand it to include the RV Park. Gus was going out to the Ranch every couple of weeks to put out rat poison and moth balls in the old Jeep to keep the rats out of it and to just check things out in general. That spring two different Oil Companies called him about leasing his minerals on his old ranch in Wharton County and Gus negotiated with them until one of the Oil Companies out bid the other one and Gus settled with an Oil and Gas Lease that paid him $ 70,000.00 Bonus. Gus put this in his Blue Quail Oil & Gas Bank Account so it would earn a little interest for him. Gus's friend Skeeter kept calling him to come down and look at his land until Gus finally told him that he would drive to El Campo in May and stay for five days and look around and that would also give Gus time to visit some old friends. Skeeter told Gus that he could stay with him, so he wouldn't have to spend money on a Motel. Gus called his New Son in Ganado and told him that he would be driving down and maybe they could meet for lunch or dinner someplace. He told Gus that he would like that, so Gus arranged it with Skeeter so he and his Wife could meet Gus's New Son and his Wife. May arrived and Gus kept his word and drove down to El Campo. He stayed with Skeeter and his wife and he and Skeeter drove down to Port Alto to look over the 40 acres of land and see what Skeeter wanted to do with it. Gus could see the potential that Skeeter was talking about with an RV Park, but the 40 acres that Skeeter had bought didn't have a view of the water and there was no boat ramp for the occupants to use to access the Bay waters and that concerned Gus. He told Skeeter that he would work with him and help him if he wanted Gus too, but that he wouldn't invest any money in it. Skeeter told Gus that when he got ready to start work on it he would call him, so they left it right there. Skeeter and his Wife got to meet Gus's New Son and his Wife and there were a lot of questions that both Gus and his New Son had to answer about how all of this came about and who his Mom was, but it all was in a friendly manner and everything went fine. While Gus was in El Campo he went by the Grave Yard to see his own head stone and to visit the grave of his Son that had been killed in 1982 at the age of 15. There were five graves in the family plot and that took up the top half of the plot, so Gus's head stone had started on the lower half of the plot right under that of his Son and that left enough space for four more graves other then that of Gus for a total of ten to fill the plot. Gus did all the visiting that he had time for. He visited his Friend that owned the Crop Dusting Business, another Friend that owned a Farm Tractor Machinery Business, a Friend that owned a Dirt Construction Business, another Friend that was an Oil and Gas Land Man and then he went to see his old Friend that owned the Hair Salon and she gave him a haircut. It was good to see her again and it was the first haircut he had from her in a lot of years. They laughed and talked about old times together and Gus told her about his New Son that had recently showed up and she asked him if she had known the Boys Mom and Gus told her no, but if she remembered the time that Gus had come in her Salon for a haircut back in the 1970's and when she had finished Gus asked her to take him home, because there was a woman waiting out by his pickup and he didn't want to see her, his Salon Friend told Gus that she did remember that, then Gus told her that the woman was the Mom of the New Son. Gus also visited a friend named Chuck that had owned a popular Bar back in the 1970's and 1980's and he had been Gus's Best Man when he had married his third wife. He and Chuck went to an old Beer Joint that had been in an out of the way area of El Campo for many years and they drank some beer and talked about the old days. Gus's five days were over and he had to drive back to Van Horn, but he had to admit that he did have a great time visiting some of his old friends and business associates. Gus got back to Van Horn and started doing chores that he hadn't finished that were left over from the winter. He had a lot of leaves to rake up and put into bags and a lot of trimming to do and then there was some chemical spraying of weeds and grass that he needed to do before they got to big. Gus also needed to go to the Ranch to see what was going on out there, but he needed to finish his work in town first then he could go out to the Ranch and spend several days out there. Gus spent a couple of weeks cleaning up things in town at his house and at his office then he went to the Ranch to spend a few days out there spraying weeds around the Camp House and cook shed. He was glad that this new Ranch had electricity, because he was getting to the age that he didn't want to be in the heat during the hottest part of the day and his Camp House had a real good air conditioner that he could cool the Camp House with and he could take a good nap then go out and either work or go looking for Indian artifacts when it was cooler. Gus loved it at the Ranch where there was peace and quiet and only the sounds of nature and no big rush to do anything. At the end of the week Gus had to hook up the 500 gallon water trailer to his pickup and take it into town to fill it with water so he could have it ready to pump into the 500 gallon water tank on the stand that supplied the Camp House with water. He took it back to the Ranch and then he drove back into town to check his computer and cell phone messages to see if there was any oil business for him to deal with. There were several business e-mails that he needed to answer and he had a cell phone message that he needed to call back, but it was to late in the day, so he would wait till the next day to do it. Gus went to his office the next day and sent his e-mails and then he made the business call. It didn't amount to much, because it was just someone wanting free advice. He got a lot of those kind of calls and tried to help the people even though it took up time and he didn't make any money on them, but who knows maybe some day someone that he helps will send him some business. Gus was looking up drilling permits on the Texas Railroad Commission's Oil & Gas website when his cell phone rang and he answered it and was pleased to hear his Hair Salon Friend Toodie's voice on the other end. She was laughing and he told her that he was glad she was laughing, because that meant that she wasn't going to tell him that another one of his friends had died. She said no that she didn't have any bad news for a change, but that she did have a message to give him from someone that he knew many years ago. She told Gus that a friend of hers that lived in England had received an e-mail joke that had his name on it along with several others and her friend told her that she had noticed Gus's name and that she had a huge crush on Gus when she was just a young girl and she wondered if Gus would remember her and want to e-mail back and forth. Gus asked his Hair Salon Friend who the girl was and she told him that it was Lorrie. Gus thought Lorrie, then LORRIE well yes he remembered her, he absolutely did remember her. Now Gus was sitting straight up in his office chair. His Friend told him that when Lorrie had e-mailed her, that Lorrie had wanted to know if Gus was her Gus and his Hair Salon Friend told Lorrie that she didn't know about Gus being Lorrie's Gus, but that she had known Gus since they had been small kids. Gus told his Hair Salon Friend Toodie to e-mail him Lorrie's e-mail and he would contact her. Gus got an e-mail from his Hair Salon Friend with Lorrie's e-mail and he sent Lorrie an e-mail with it. In a few minutes it came back to Gus, so Gus then e-mailed his Friend and told her that something was wrong with the e-mail she had given him and she sent him another e-mail with a revised e-mail for Lorrie. Gus then sent Lorrie another e-mail with the revised e-mail. After a few minutes this e-mail also came back to Gus, so Gus e-mailed his Friend again and told her that there was still something wrong, because it also came back to him. His friend then sent Gus another revised e-mail on Lorrie. Gus then sent this new revised e-mail to Lorrie and in a few minutes it also came back. By now Gus was getting very frustrated, because every e-mail that his Salon Friend sent him didn't work and he didn't know why. Here was the very girl that Gus had been thinking about from time to time all these years and he couldn't get back in touch with her. What if he wouldn't ever be able to get in touch with her and why could his Salon Friend Toodie e-mail her and he couldn't. Then all of a sudden his computer beeped and an e-mail from Lorrie in England appeared on his computer. This was September the 5th 2011, 49 years since Gus had any contact with Lorrie and he was so nervous and at the same tine excited. Gus clicked on it and it read that he and Lorrie's common Salon Friend Toodie had been forwarding all the back and forth e-mails between them and Lorrie could see that Gus was trying hard to contact her, so she decided to e-mail Gus herself. Lorrie told Gus in the e-mail that she didn't originally want to contact him herself, because of the way that they had parted 50 years before and she wasn't even sure that Gus would even remember her and if he did he might not even want to correspond with her. She told Gus that he might just be acting nice so as to not hurt her feelings and how could she know if he really remembered her. When Gus read this he just shook his head, because there was no way that she could know how often that he had thought about Lorrie. Gus e-mailed her back and told her that he had thought of her so many times over the years, but never thought that he would have the chance to talk to her again. He told her that he remembered her and her friends coming to the Service Station that he worked at in High School and flirting with him and he remembered her walking around on the street by his Mom's house when she was wearing a full body black tights and a pony tail, he told her that he remembered seeing her when the High School Band was going to Corpus Christi and she invited him to follow them and he did and then he remembered the way they kissed on the beach there in Corpus Christi and she told him that she wanted him to take her virginity, but not like that on the beach and that she would contact him, and then he told her that he remembered getting the record "In The Still Of The Night" along with a note left in his car that told him to come over to her Parents house on a certain day that they would be gone and then they would make love. He asked her how she had found out about him. Lorrie e-mailed him back and told him that she was convinced that he did really remember her and she told him about seeing his name on the list of names that were on that joke that had been passed around and that she never knew that their Hair Salon Friend knew Gus and when she saw his name that she decided that she was getting pretty old and she had always wondered what had happened that he didn't come back to her that summer when she was 16 years old and he was 19 years old. Lorrie told him that she decided that it was time to find out, if he would tell her and that she had thought of him off and on all of her life and that when he didn't come back to her and he just disappeared off the face of the earth, that he could never know what that did to her, that it had affected the way she looked at herself and her life from then on. Gus e-mailed her back and told her what had happened. He told her that he had every intention of calling her and making love to her and taking her virginity. Gus told her that after a couple of days how he had wrestled with himself with the decision of whether to call her or not and that he started thinking of her in a different way and he had never thought of any girl like he was thinking of her and he couldn't explain it to himself. All of a sudden having sex with a beautiful young virgin wasn't as important as it had been with other girls and he had experienced his share of sex with young girls. He had started thinking of other considerations about having sex with her. Things like she had two more years of High School left and that was a real consideration, because he knew that if he made love to her that he want to be with her more and more and that it would be a sure thing that she would get pregnant before she graduated from High School then there would be a big fight with her Dad and her friends wouldn't be allowed to be around her and she would be a young Mom with no education and an outcast and her and Gus would be starting out life with a huge handicap to overcome. Gus knew for sure that this would happen, because he knew himself and the way that Lorrie had molded her body to his and kissed him on the beach and then when she was almost naked in her room that day she looked so beautiful that he knew that somehow that he had to stay away from her or he would end up ruining her life, so he fought with himself everyday for a while till he made himself stay from anyplace that he thought he might run into her. Gus told Lorrie in the e-mail that he knew that something was different in the way that he was thinking about her, but he didn't know why he was acting differently toward her then he would normally act in the same situation with another young girl. Normally he wouldn't have even thought twice about making love to a young girl, he would have just done it and been happy about making another conquest. Lorrie e-mailed him back and told him that she didn't know about that excuse that it was pretty hard for her to believe, but that she would think about it. She told him that she was going to have to go and cook dinner now for her Husband and Stepson and that there in England she was six hours ahead of him in Texas, so it was 5:00 pm in England and 11:00 am in Texas. She told Gus that she would like to keep e-mailing if he wanted too and she wanted to find out more about his life and when he got back to his office after his lunch would he please e-mail her and to remember that there was six hours difference and she would be going to bed at around 10:00 pm England time, so that would be 4:00 pm Texas time. Gus e-mailed her back and told her that he would and he just signed off as Gus. It was 11:00 am and Gus would be leaving the office to get the mail and go home for lunch at 12: pm, so he just sat there and reread all the e-mails from Lorrie. He had to slap himself on the cheek to make sure that he wasn't dreaming. This was really real and he was back in touch with Lorrie after almost 50 years. Why was he so excited and so nervous about this anyway when he should be just happy to hear from an old friend, except she had never been just a friend, she had been something else that was entirely different then a friend and they didn't really know each other except from the brief encounters that they had during their young years. There was really something very strange here and there had always been something strange about the way that he had felt about Lorrie, so what was it exactly that made him so giddy about being back in touch with her and why had he wanted to sign off on that last e-mail as Love, Gus. No, he couldn't do that, but that is what he felt like doing. He was wondering how far he was ready to go with this. Gus knew right from the start that he was not going to turn his back on Lorrie this time and walk away from her if she wanted him. This was just too much and too impossible, but it was happening and now Gus had to admit to himself that he had always been in love with Lorrie and that's why he could never forget her, but for now he had to keep this from her till he found out more. Gus thought that when he was young he knew what sex was, but he didn't know the difference between lust and love and now he realized why he had felt differently about Lorrie and had left her alone so as to not mess up her life, it was because he had been in love with her, but didn't realize it, how could he have known then. If he could have known then he would have taken that chance with her and their lives would have been different. Gus turned off his computer and got the mail and went home for his lunch. He decided that he wasn't going to take a nap today, because he wanted to e-mail Lorrie some more. Gus got back to his office and turned on his computer about 2:00 pm and right away there was a new e-mail from Lorrie. She told Gus that he could ask her any questions about her life that he wanted to and she would answer them honestly, but he might not like what she would tell him. She told Gus that she wanted to ask him a lot of questions also, because she wanted to know everything about his life for 50 years. Lorrie told Gus that this was so unbelievable that they could be back in touch after so many years and that it felt so good and so natural to her. Lorrie told him that she was so afraid that he wouldn't want be in touch with her or that he may not even remember her at all. Lorrie told Gus that she was going to put this day September 5th, 2011 down in her diary as a special day, because from now on it would be the Gus and Lorrie get Back Together Anniversary that she would remember and celebrate each month for the rest of her life. Gus e-mailed her back and agreed with her about the 5th of September being their Back Together Anniversary, then he asked her how she ended up Marrying someone in England. She told him her story of being stationed there in the Navy and wanting to stay in England when her enlistment was over so she had married her Husband and he was a very good Tailor and he had a Son that lived with them and that she had been married three times including him. She wanted to know if Gus was married and if he had any children. Gus e-mailed her back that he was married and that he had been married four times and that he had four boys and one stepson that was just like his own because he had raised him from when he was only two years old. They went back and forth about their married lives with Lorrie's different Husbands and Gus's different Wives and the children that were involved until they had exhausted that subject and both of them had a good idea of how and why each of them had chosen their Spouses at the time. They both were amazed that they both used such flimsy, shallow reasoning to marry and that each had done it for their own reasons and not for love. Lorrie e-mailed Gus and told him that it was time for her to sign off for the night, but that she hoped that he would e-mail her tomorrow and she signed off —Always, Lorrie. Gus e-mailed her back and told her that he would look forward to e-mailing her and he signed off—Your, Gus. For some reason Gus was feeling like a much younger man then he had felt like in a long time and being back in touch with Lorrie seemed as natural as it could be. Except for asking so many questions of each other their conversation just flowed without a hitch and it seemed that now, for some reason, that they were taking up right where they left off and that it hadn't been 50 years that they were apart after all, now how could that be anyway, it was crazy. Gus went home for dinner and then sat down to read like he always did, but he had a hard time trying to concentrate on his book, because he kept thinking about Lorrie and other questions that he wanted to ask her about her life. He knew that they had just barely touched the surface of finding about each others lives. Gus could hardly wait to get to his office the next morning to e-mail Lorrie. She had put a whole new perspective to his life and it felt so good, so fresh and so natural and easy that he had no choice now but to follow where ever it took him. Gus got to his office at 9:00 am and turned on his computer and went to e-mail and it pinged three times, because Lorrie had already sent him three separate e-mails with questions. She wanted to know when his birthday was, what his favorite color was, the things that he liked to eat, how old he was, where he lived and how long that he had lived there and many other little things. He e-mailed her back with all the answers and then asked her about her birthday and she told him October the 26, 1945, about how long she had been married to this Husband and Gus wanted to know what had happened to her after he hadn't come back to her when she was sixteen years old. Lorrie told him the whole story of how she had waited and waited and finally realized that he wasn't going to come back to her and how she had felt that he hadn't liked what he had seen when she took her cloth's off, so that gave had a bad feeling about her body that she still had to this day and that she never let a man see her completely naked after that. Then she told him about living in Florida working as a Go-Go Girl Dancer and Waitress, living with the Surfer in Puerto Rico for a while, then getting pregnant by her first Husband, divorcing him and joining the Navy and then marrying the young Navy Seal, divorcing him and finally getting stationed in England and married her third Husband so she could stay in England. Lorrie asked him about what he did with his life after he decided not to come back to her. Gus told her all about how he had fought himself to stay from her and that he had been dating this girl at Wharton Junior College and decided to marry her so he would settle down and study, the they divorced and he got this young girl pregnant so he married her, big mistake and then they divorced and then he married his third wife so they could help each other take care of his one boy and her boy and girl, then they got divorced and he told her that he went to work for the State of Texas and moved to Sugarland and there had met his fourth wife and they had married because they were both getting older and they would be able to help each other through old age, then he retired from the State and moved out to Van Horn in the Mountains. They went off and on like this all day every day finding out more and more about each other. They would revisit the same part of each other's life getting more information about that particular time and they had a complete vision and understanding of each year of each others lives just like they had know about them as they had happened. This searching each other lives out and each others thoughts out was a very stimulating process and they were both very honest with each other and didn't try to make some thing that they had done sound proper when they knew that it wasn't. All of this brought more and more trust between them and then they were able to start talking more about their present lives. Lorrie e-mailed and told Gus that she had just got back to England from her three month vacation trip to El Campo that she took every year from the first of June till the end of August when she had seen that e-mail their Hair Salon Friend had forwarded to her, so she had been back in England less then a week and if that could have happened a couple of weeks before then maybe they could have been able to see each other. Gus e-mailed back to Lorrie and told her that he would love to be able to see her again and that he had thought about her many times through the years and hoped that she was alright and that she had a happy life. He asked her if she had ever thought about him through the years and she e-mailed back that every place and every country she had been in had played that song "In The Still Of The Night" and when she heard it she would be right back on the beach with Gus kissing him and wanting him and then wondering what had happened that he didn't come back to her. She told him that she had thought about him many times through the years, but what could she do when he didn't come back, except just try to live her life. She told Gus that maybe they could work it so they could see each other when she went back to El Campo on her annual vacation in June 2012. These kinds of e-mail talks went on day after day and Lorrie finally asked Gus to please leave her an e-mail right before he left his office in the evenings, so she would have something from him to read in the mornings in England, because it was so long till he got to the office at 8:30 am or 9:00 am in Van Horn to send her an e-mail that it would already be around 2:30 pm or 3:00 pm in England before she had anything from him. Gus e-mailed her back and told her that he would then he remembered her birthday and he thought that it was late in the month of September, so he wished her a Happy Birthday and she came back to him why he was wishing her a Happy Birthday a month early? This embarrassed Gus, but he had to admit to her that he thought it was in September and she told him that no, it was October the 26th. Gus thought to himself that at least it wasn't too late and he would need to be sure and not forget her birthday in October. Each day now Gus found himself looking forward to turning on his computer and going to e-mail to see what Lorrie had sent him and this had become an important part of his life. Lorrie's birthday October the 26th did finally get there and Gus was a good boy and didn't forget it. He was so proud of himself when he e-mailed her a big Happy Birthday. She e-mailed him back that this was the first time that they were back together on her birthday and that they were going to have a lot of firsts together from now on. Gus told Lorrie that he would be away from his computer for a few days after Thanksgiving, because he and his Sons would be at the ranch for their annual hunting get together. Gus told Lorrie that he had something else to tell her and that it was that he loved her. Gus then waited it seemed like a long time and just looked at his computer screen to see what she would say. Finally the screen blinked and beeped and Lorrie e-mailed back that she loved him too, that she had always loved him and that she wanted to tell him that the first time that they e-mailed, but she had to wait to see if he would tell her first. She told Gus that she would send him e-mails every day and tell him what was going on with her in England, so he could catch up on what had happened while he was at his ranch and then she told Gus that this was November the 11th, 2011 or 11-11-11 and from now on the 11th of each month she would celebrate as their I Love You Anniversary, so now they had two anniversaries to remember and they were the 5th and 11th of each month. Then she signed off— Love, Lorrie, Gus e-mailed her back that he would look forward to her e-mails while he was at the ranch and that he had also loved her all of his life and he signed off— Love, Gus. He knew now that this had opened a whole new side to their relationship and he wondered where it was going to go. They weren't just pin pals on e-mail any more things had changed with those three words of I Love You, but he couldn't help it he had to tell her. He had been holding it in ever since that first e-mail and he couldn't deny what he now knew was what had happened to him when he was 19 and Lorrie was 16 years old and that is why everything was different with her back then in the way he was thinking back then about her trying to protect her from himself and he couldn't understand why back then, but now he knew that he had been in love with her and that is why he could never forget her. Gus thought that it was probably why he could never really love another woman. He guessed that he was a man that could only really love one woman and that woman had always been Lorrie, man he thought what a revelation this was. He was finally figuring himself out after all of these years. This was why nothing else ever worked permanently in any other relationship with other women. The next day Gus got an e-mail from Lorrie and she was asking for pictures of him. Gus e-mailed her back that he didn't know if he had any, but he would look to see. When he went home that evening he looked and looked and finally found one that someone took of him at the Ranch with his hat on standing behind the bar. He also found a picture of him when he was a Senior in High School wearing his band jacket and one of him about the age that they were on the beach in Corpus Christi when he was standing by his Red Hot Rod Coupe and he sent those to her the next day. Lorrie e-mailed him back that she loved the pictures, but that the one with his hat and glasses on she couldn't see his eyes and she wanted to see his beautiful blue eyes, that she would never forget those ice blue eyes and would he get someone to take a picture of him without his hat and glasses. Gus e-mailed her that he would try to get someone, but that he didn't know when he would find someone to do it. The Thanksgiving Holidays came, and Gus and his Sons went to the Blue Quail Ranch for four days to hunt, cook on the pit, drink beer, shoot guns and listen to Country and Western Music. Gus got one of the boys to take his picture without his hat and glasses. When he got back to Van Horn and his office, he turned on his computer and clicked on e-mail and found that Lorrie was true to her word. She had sent Gus at least four e-mails for every day that he was out of the office and in them she told him what she was doing each day and also long messages telling him how much that she loved him and that now she never wanted to be without him in her life again and that she knew that they were getting older and that they were in an impossible situation of both being married to other spouses, but she just wanted to have what-ever she could get of him and that she wanted for them to make a promise that no one was going to be hurt because of their relationship, meaning their spouses. Gus e-mailed her the picture of him without his hat and glasses and told her that he agreed to keep that promise of not hurting their spouses. He told her everything that they had done at the Ranch and that he had missed their talking on e-mail so much, but he really appreciated the e-mails that she sent him. Lorrie e-mailed him back and she told him that she could see those blue eyes of his now and it was the first time in 50 years and yes it was really Gus she was looking at and she could see gray hair and a bit of a beer belly and how wonderful it was to really see him. Lorrie next told him that she wanted him to send her his cell phone number, because she wanted to hear his voice. She wanted to be able to call him maybe once a month and listen to his voice that she hadn't heard in so many years and she wanted to be able to wish him a Merry Christmas when it came time, so please send her the phone number. Gus sent her his phone number and it was time for him to go home for the day so he signed off—Love Gus. It was getting close to Christmas now and Gus e-mailed Lorrie and asked her if he could send her a Christmas card. She came back to him that no, because his name was never mentioned at her house and it would just lead to questions if her Husband or her Stepson happened to see it. She told Gus that she was sending him something for Christmas though and she would tell him when she mailed it, so he could kind of judge when it might be delivered. Lorrie also told him that she told her friend Jill that she was in love when she met her for lunch the day before and Lorrie said that she cried and Jill cried and then she showed Jill the pictures that Gus had sent her. She said that she couldn't hold her happiness in any longer and just had to tell somebody how happy she was, so she told Jill, because of all her friends she knew that Jill would keep it to herself. Lorrie said that she thought that her Husband wondered what was wrong with her, because she would catch herself singing old songs while she was working or cleaning and he would just look at her with a strange look, because she had never done that before. They talked on e-mail off and on all day then Lorrie had to sign off — Love Lorrie, because it was getting late at night there and then Gus wrote her something that she could read the next morning and signed off —Love Gus, as was their routine now. The next morning when Gus turned on his computer and went to e-mail he got a message from Lorrie telling him to e-mail her back as soon as he got this e-mail, because she wanted to call him and she wanted to be sure that he was in the office with his phone turned on. Gus e-mailed her back right away and in a few minutes his phone rang, and it was Lorries voice on the other end and the first words out of her mouth were Gus I love you and Gus answered back Lorrie I love you too. They both tried to talk at the same time and then Lorrie told him that she might have to hang up quick if she saw her Husband coming to the house from his work shop in their back yard. They talked and talked, and the conversation just flowed so natural and sweet. Lorrie told him that she would call him again and wish him Merry Christmas and that she would also call him and wish him a Happy New Year. She told him that she would probably only call him once a month unless there was some special occasion. After they hung up Gus was so thrilled to still hear the sound of her words in his mind and he wanted to remember that sound always. Her voice sounded lower then he had remembered it, but it was lovely and she had the cutest hitch in her voice when she started to laugh, it was sort of like a hiccup to start the laugh and it would immediately make you want to laugh also. He had never known any woman with such of a unique sweet laugh. Gus thought my goodness the first time I have heard her voice in 50 years and he thanked God for that blessing. Lorrie did call him at Christmas and she called him three more times between Christmas and New Years and Gus asked why she was changing her plan to only call him once a month and she told him that since she had heard his voice that she couldn't help it, that e-mail just wasn't enough anymore. Lorrie told Gus that if his phone was off that she would leave him a voice message and for him not to call her ever, that she would always call him. This New Years was so different for Gus, because now when he was listening to the old songs and sipping his Dad's whiskey he knew that he didn't have to just depend on a memory of Lorrie anymore that he was actually going to be able to talk to her and wish her a Happy New Year. When Lorrie's Husband went to bed on New Years Eve 2012 she called Gus and it was a little after 6:00 pm in Van Horn and she kissed him over the phone Happy New Year 2012 and they talked for a little while before she told him that she loved him and that it was the best New Years she had had in 50 years. That night Gus was listening to "In The Still Of The Night" when the fireworks and gun shots went off in Van Horn and Gus could still hear Lorrie's kisses over the phone and he wished that he could call her now, but she said not to, so he didn't all he could do was to raise his glass and give a Happy New Year 2012 Salute to Lorrie.

Lorrie—2011 came in quietly for Lorrie and she was getting ready for their annual New Years Day lunch with their friends. Lorrie always looked forward to this quiet time with her friends and the pleasant conversation that went along with a good lunch. Her Husband was in a good mood for a change and she was going to watch what she said so it wouldn't upset him, because if she did then she would pay for it when they got home. Lorrie was looking forward to getting with her tutor and really working on the verbal part of her Spanish classes. She had been told that she could do some of it over the phone, but she would have to meet with her tutor for some face to face conversations in Spanish and Lorrie was a little nervous about that. She had never even learned any Tex-Mex words when she lived in Texas much less the formal Spanish. Her Spanish speaking classes started and Lorrie had her first class with a face to face with her Tutor so the Tutor could instruct her in how the Spanish words sounded when the Spanish accents were put on the words. Lorrie took a small tape recorder with her to capture those sounds so she could practice them, because she knew that she was going to be given a speaking assignment of a simple Spanish phrase and the assignments would get more complicated as the class progressed. Lorrie's Husband went on his two week ski vacation and that left Lorrie by herself much of that time, so she studied very hard to try to learn as much as she could before their Easter Holiday that she knew that they were going to be invited on again. She was determined to learn enough Spanish by the Easter Holiday to be able to converse on at least a marginal basis with the villagers that she was hoping to some day soon be living with. Lorrie's Husband was still making a very good living in his Tailor Business. She didn't know how he maintained his ability to keep a steady hand to do such nice straight stitching when he consumed so much beer every day. When they went to the Super Market for groceries he always pushed his own cart and he filled it stacked to the top with beer and he did this twice a week and this had been going on for their entire married life of 27 years. Their Easter Holidays finally arrived and after their short flight and drive to their Friends Condo in the mountains they relaxed with drinks and discussed where they were going for the evening. Lorrie and her Friend had a special nice Club that they always liked to go to on their first evening there. The men agreed with their choice, so that is where they went. The next morning after their breakfast the women mapped out the villages that they wanted to visit that day, so they all drove up into the mountains passing herds of sheep and groves of olive trees and small fields. The beauty of the landscape always pleased Lorrie in this mountain semi-desert area and she still thought that in some ways it reminded her of Albuquerque, New Mexico the place that she had always said that it was the place in the United States that she enjoyed living the best, because she learned to love the rugged beauty of the mountain desert region and the higher, dryer climate. They went to the village Seat of Government and to the small school and Lorrie talked slowly in Spanish with officials there and they were pleased that Lorrie was trying to communicate with them in Spanish and they all complimented her on her Spanish when she told them that she had only been Speaking Spanish for three months and that she was still learning. They understood and were very patient with her when she was searching for the right word to communicate with. The next evening the men chose their Cafe and Club and Lorrie didn't think that the entertainment was as good at that Club, but the worst was that when they got back to the Condo she couldn't avoid her Husband as he made her pull her night gown up so he could have sex with her. It was always painful for her because she had passed the point of being aroused by him 20 years ago and this time he couldn't keep himself erect, so she was saved a lot of degrading by what she felt was nothing more than rape. Their next two days there were interesting for Lorrie, because she became more comfortable with her Spanish, although she knew that she was still very limited in what she could discuss in Spanish. She was able to learn a lot though about the small villages by being able to talk directly to the local citizens. When they returned to their house in Bromley they found out that her Stepson had again drank every drop of liquor in the house no matter what it was and her Husband was furious with him, because he didn't have a single beer to drink, so he had to go to the store to restock. Lorrie thought that there was going to be a big knock-down-drag-out fight between her Husband and his Son, but there was just yelling and thank goodness there was no physical confrontation, but all the cursing and yelling was so upsetting that Lorrie couldn't even eat her dinner that evening she had to resort to her thin cream of wheat that she always depended on when there were big upheavals and fights, because she just couldn't seem to swallow any solid food when she got that upset and she had to eat something, because of her Diabetes. Lorrie thought, well welcome to their normal home life where physical and verbal abuse could happen any time without a warning. Lorrie became busy with her Spanish classes trying to get all of her assignments complete before the summer break and also she was planning her annual three month vacation trip back to El Campo, Texas. This was a happy time for Lorrie when she was planning her Texas vacation, because she knew that she would be away from her abusive marriage that she felt trapped in. She would be around friends and family that were kind thoughtful toward her for three whole months and she would be able to see familiar things that were from her childhood and she could actually drive around and see the places that she had been in contact with the love of her life Gus. Lorrie was glad that her memories of Gus were no longer bitter-sweet they had evolved into a sort of fantasy sweet dream with a what happened question to them and she knew that she would never get that answer, but just the sweet memory of that young Gus kissing her was enough now to distract her from what her real life was. She would drift into that happy dream ever now and then when things would seem to be closing in on her, so she could take her next breath and renew her strength to go on another day. Her only hope now was her plan to disappear in one of those small villages in Spain out of the reach of her Husband. She thought that her Spanish classes would be over at the first of the year 2012 and then she could secretly apply for the Teachers Positions there, so maybe she would be able to flee to Spain in one more year. Lorrie left England on her flight to

Houston Texas and her Sister picked her up as usual at the airport there. Her Sister and her Husband were talking about selling their house in Houston and moving to where their only Daughter lived, so they could be around their Grandchildren and Lorrie was wondering how this would affect her plans when flying back to Texas from England in the future. Lorrie had always been a planner and she was already thinking about this. She spent a few days with her sister like she usually did, and they did some shopping mostly just enjoying being together. Her Sister then drove Lorrie to El Campo to their Mom's house where her Mom, Brother and his Girlfriend were waiting for them. This was always a happy time when everybody was full of questions and Lorrie could lay her eyes on all the familiar things in her Mom's house that she had grown up with since she had been about 10 years old. There were a lot of memories there, some happy, some sad and then of course there was the memory of Gus there also. Lorrie's family knew the routine that Lorrie liked when she first got to El Campo and that was to go to the local Mexican Cafe and get her Tex-Mex food fix. They all went to the Cafe and ate their favorite Mexican food and drank beer with it. Lorrie was so glad to see her Brothers Girlfriend and they started to make plans immediately on the things that they were going to do together when she was off of work. She worked for the city of El Campo and had all of the weekends off plus the holidays, so there would be some nice time to be able to get together and enjoy things together. Lorrie's Brother and his Girlfriend were into B-B-Q cook-offs that were held for different events and they were part of a team with another couple. They had a B-B-Q trailer with a pit and it had all the things that they would need to cook and compete with other cook-off teams for prizes. Lorrie loved going to the cook-offs with them, because it was so Texan and they would have Texas flags displayed and country and western music playing with all the good wood smoke with the delicious smell of cooking meat mixed with it and also pinto beans cooking, that Lorrie couldn't buy in England, and chili, WOW Lorrie thought what fun and no-where but Texas could she enjoy something like this. Lorrie's Mom was going to be 89 this year and she was still in good health for her age. She didn't take any medication and she still ate anything that she wanted. Her only limitations seemed to be that her balance was not good, her eyesight was getting bad and that her hands shook a lot making it hard for her to write legibly and to open bottles and tightly wrapped products. She still drove her car and did some of her own shopping and took herself to her weekly hair appointments at Lorrie's Friends Hair Salon. Lorrie was really enjoying her El Campo vacation. She was going to garage sales with her Brother's Girlfriend looking for bargains on things to decorate with and for antique objects and furniture that they could restore and also all the B-B-Q cook-offs. Going to the cook-offs had an added benefit in that sometime Lorrie would get to see old friends that she had gone to school with that she wouldn't otherwise not had the opportunity to visit with. Lorrie was doing the bills and the checkbook for her Mom while she was in El Campo, so she was getting an idea of what the utilities were costing there now and she was surprised at how much they had increased through the years. Lorrie was glad that her Dad had left her Mom a good retirement from his years with the United States Postal Service that along with Social Security let her Mom live comfortable without having to worry about money. Lorrie and her Mom would go to Lorrie's Hair Salon Friend every Thursday for her Mom's appointment, but Lorrie only had her hair cut there every two weeks and her color done once a month and as usual the color would turn out different then Lorrie thought it would. Lorrie's time in El Campo went by fast as usual and before she knew it, it was time for her to wind up her stay there. She did her Texas food shopping to take back to England as usual and then she did her Gus drive around to look at all the places that she had seen Gus, then she went back to her Mom's house to pack all of that up to take back to England with her. Her last day in El Campo she went to her Dad's grave to talk to him again. She would always sit on the ground by his grave with her hand resting on his grave Marker and talk to him like she could never do when he was alive. She had always enjoyed the time her and her Dad had spent together when she would come back to El Campo to visit, but there were always things that she kept to her self that she had always wished that she could tell him, but she could never bring herself to do it, because she was afraid that it would make him disappointed in her and also that he would tell her that she should have listened to him and she couldn't do that because it would make her feel like a failure in her parents eyes. She was always afraid of being a failure in their eyes, so she couldn't ever admit to them that she had made bad decisions for her life against their wishes. Lorrie could talk to her Dad now and it made her feel better for it, so she would unload all her problems on him now. She even told him about her plans to leave her Husband by getting a job as a English teacher with the Spanish School System and disappearing in a small mountain village. She apologized to him for not being able to die in Texas, but told him that she had made arrangements for ashes to be sent back to El

Campo and for her Brother to spread them on the beach at Matagorda, where they, as a family, always had so much fun together. Lorrie kissed her hand and placed it on her Dad's grave Marker and whispered good by to him, then she drove back to her Mom's house to finish packing. The next morning August 30th, 2011, her Brother took her to the Houston Airport for her long flight back to England. Lorrie's flight back to England was very tiring as usual and the next day she finished unpacking and started to go through the mail her Husband always left on her desk for her to take care of. She also turned on her computer and started deleting almost everything that was on there, because anybody that knew her knew that she would be gone on her annual Texas vacation. She did have some e-mails from her Open University Spanish Class notifying her of the starting date of her classes, so she answered them then she e-mailed all her friends in England as well as in Texas to let them know that she was back home in Bromley safe and sound. Lorrie was very busy, as usual, when she got back to England from her three month vacation in Texas trying to straighten out all the loose ends of her Husbands Tailoring Business and along with this she was back into her Spanish speaking classes with her Tutor. Lorrie got up extra early on the morning of September 5th, 2011 and turned on her computer because she wanted to see what kind of grades her Tutor had given her on a telephone Spanish conversation she had with him the day before. Then she went into her kitchen to put on a pot of tea. When it was ready she took a mug and went into her little office to see if her Tutor had posted her grades yet and she had several e-mails, but the one that caught her eye first was one from her Friend Toodie that owned the Hair Salon in El Campo, Texas, so she opened it first and it was a joke of some sort, but what Lorrie really saw startled her and she froze for a minute and started breathing hard as she was grabbing her mouth with her hand to keep from crying out the name GUS. That name was in a line with several other names on top of the e-mail, but it seemed huge in comparison to the rest of them and she just sat there and looked at the name of Gus. She wondered how her Hair Salon Friend Toodie knew Gus and if so, was this really Lorrie's Gus. All of a sudden Lorrie realized that now was the time for her to act and find out if this Gus was her Gus and the only way to do that was to e-mail her Hair Salon Friend Toodie right away to find out if this was true. Lorrie thought to herself and what would she do if he was her Gus, well she would think about that when she found out, but secretly she knew that it had to be her Gus, she just felt it in her heart. She typed out an e-mail to her Hair Salon

Friend Toodie, with shaking fingers taking deep breaths as she did it, asking her if that name on the e-mail joke was Lorrie's Gus. By now she had forgotten all about why she had been up so early in the first place, because she was so absorbed with finding out if that name was her Gus. Lorrie finally looked at the rest of her e-mails while she was waiting for a response from her Hair Salon Friend Toodie and it seemed like hours. She saw that her Tutor had given her just barely passing grades on her Spanish language and suggested that she needed to have more face to face meetings to work on her accent which still had too much American sound in it. This would usually upset Lorrie, but now it barely registered, because something much more important was now on Lorrie's mind. While she was waiting for the response Lorrie had decided that if this Gus on the e-mail was her Gus that she was going to see if he wanted to contact her, because if he did then the 50 year old mystery of him not coming back to her when she was 16 might finally be solved, because she would certainly ask him about it. There was so much that she would like to ask him, but this was the first thing and she just had to know because it had haunted her for the last 50 years. Finally her computer dinged and a new e-mail came on her screen from her Hair Salon Friend Toodie and it said that she had known Gus all his life, but that she didn't know if he was Lorrie's Gus and then she went on and on about him, telling Lorrie about being raised in the same Church and going to school together, playing in the High School Band together and about Gus's Red Hot Rod. She also told Lorrie that he was crazy. This startled Lorrie, because now she knew that it was really her Gus, but if he was crazy and in an Institution she would never find out what had happened and oh my, if they had been together and he went crazy then what would have happened to them. Lorrie e-mailed her back and asked her if Gus was really crazy and in an Institution. Her Friend Toodie e-mailed back telling Lorrie no, you know just crazy liking to have a good time. Lorrie took a deep breath and thanked God and then she e-mailed her Friend Toodie back and asked her to e-mail Gus and tell him who she was and see if he wanted to contact her and if he did to please give Gus her e-mail address. She told her Friend that when she was in High School that she had a huge crush on Gus and she wanted to see how his life had been. Her Friend Toodie e-mailed her back and told her that she would do it right away before it slipped her mind and that she would forward any response from Gus along to Lorrie. Lorrie thanked her and then was on pins and needles waiting to see what might happen. Lorrie worked on some of the bills that needed to be paid and then typed up invoices for work her Husband had done and needed to get paid for and got them ready to be mailed. Lorrie kept changing her screens back and forth to e-mail and it seemed like forever, but finally at 4:00 pm that afternoon Lorrie got an e-mail forwarded from her Hair Salon Friend Toodie that showed Gus trying to contact her, then she got another one and then another one and they all showed that Gus was still trying to get in touch with her. Lorrie finally decided to take over and e-mail Gus herself, because she could see that her Friend Toodie kept sending Gus the wrong e-mail for her. She hadn't wanted to contact Gus directly, but she could see that this was going to be the only way for them to make contact with each other. Lorrie had to think now it was 4:00 pm in England so it must be around 10:00 am in Texas. Lorrie typed in Gus's e-mail address and sent him her first e-mail which told him that she had seen that he had been trying to contact her, because their common Hair Salon Friend Toodie had been forwarding his e-mails to her. She told him that she hadn't originally wanted to contact him herself, because of the way that they had parted fifty years ago and that she didn't even know if he would remember her and even if he had that maybe he wouldn't even want to e-mail her. She told Gus that he might just be acting nice saying that he remembered her, so he didn't hurt her feelings, when he was really trying to remember who this girl really was, because she could remember how nice he had always been when she had been around him. She signed it, Lorrie and sent it. In a few minutes she got an e-mail back from Gus and she started smiling as she was reading it, because he was telling her of all the things he remembered about her that left her no doubt that he did know who he was e-mailing and he also said that he had thought about her so many times through the years and thought that he would never get the chance to talk to her again. He asked her how she had found out about him. This made her choke up and she almost broke down and started crying. Lorrie e-mailed him back and she told him that she was convinced that he really did remember who she was and that he had remembered more then she thought he would. She told Gus that she had seen his name along with a list of names on a joke that had been sent to her by their common Hair Salon Friend Toodie and she had never known that they both had her for a Friend. She told Gus that she was getting pretty old and she had always wondered what had happened to him that he hadn't come back to her that summer when she was 16 years old and he was 19 years old when everything had been going so good between them and she had wanted him to take her virginity. She told Gus that she thought that it was time to find out what had happened, if he would be so kind as to tell her and that she had thought of him off and on all of her life, that he had just disappeared off of the face of the earth and that he would never know what that did to her and how that affected the way that she looked at herself and her life from then on. Signed Lorrie and sent. Lorrie waited and she got a long e-mail from Gus back answering her question about why he didn't come back to her. When she got through reading it she didn't know whether to believe it or not, but surely he couldn't dream up something like this so fast if it wasn't true. She was inclined to believe him and if it was true and it probably was, then it meant that she had come to the wrong conclusion when she was 16 years old and she had punished herself her whole life for nothing and she could see now that if she had only persisted and gone after Gus one more time then they probably would have been together for all of their lives. Lorrie thought that what a mess she had made of things when she was 16. Lorrie e-mailed him back and told that she wasn't sure if she believed that excuse or not that she would have to think about it. She told Gus that she was going to go cook dinner for her Husband and Stepson and that in England she was six hours ahead of him in Texas, so it was 5:00 pm in England and 11:00 am in Texas. She told Gus that she would like to keep e-mailing if he wanted too and she wanted to find out more about his life and when he got back to his office after his lunch would he please e-mail her and to remember that there was six hours difference and she was going to bed at around 10:00 pm England time, so that would be 4:00 pm Texas time. Signed Lorrie and sent. She got an e-mail back and he told her that he would. Signed Gus. Lorrie knew that Gus had gone home for his lunch, but she e-mailed him anyway. She told Gus that he could ask her anything that he wanted to about her life and she would answer them honestly, but he might not like what she would tell him. She told him that she wanted to ask him a lot of questions also, because she wanted to know everything that she could about his life for the last 50 years. She told Gus that it was so unbelievable to her that they could be back in touch after so many years and it felt so good and natural that it was hard for her to believe that she thought that he wouldn't remember her or that he wouldn't want to be in touch with her. She told him that she had decided to put the day of September 5th, 2011 down in her Diary as a special day and would call it their Back Together Anniversary and that she was going to remember it and celebrate it each month for the rest of her life. Signed Lorrie and sent. Lorrie cooked their dinner and cleaned up her kitchen all the time going back and forth to her little office to see if she had any e-mail from Gus, knowing in her mind that she probably didn't, but she just couldn't seem to help herself. Lorrie's computer dinged about 8:00 pm and it was an e-mail from Gus. She read it and was glad that he agreed that September 5th, 2011 would be celebrated by them as their Back Together Anniversary each month. He wanted to know how she happened to marry someone in England. Signed Gus. Lorrie e-mailed him back and she told him her story of being in the Navy and being stationed in England and wanting to stay there when her enlistment was over, so she married her Husband to stay in England and he was a very good Tailor and he had a Son that lived with them and that she had been married three times including him. Lorrie asked Gus if he was married and if he had any children. She was secretly hoping that he would e-mail back that he wasn't married. She wasn't sure why she felt this way other then she had always felt that Gus was hers and only hers. Signed Lorrie and sent. She received his e-mail back and she read that he was married and that he had been married four times and that he had four boys and one stepson. Signed Gus. Lorrie was disappointed that Gus was married, and she also felt jealous that some other woman had him. All of a sudden, she became so confused at herself with all of these feelings that she had never before experienced with her husbands or for that matter even boyfriends that this was all very strange. They sent a flurry of e-mails back and forth about their married lives, Lorries Husbands and Gus's Wives and Children until they had a good idea of how and why they each had chosen their Spouses at the time and they were amazed that they both had used such shallow reasoning to choose mates to marry by using just their own reasons and not love. Finally, Lorrie e-mailed Gus and told him that it was time for her to sign off for the night, but she hoped that he would e-mail her tomorrow. Signed Always, Lorrie and sent. She got an e-mail quickly back from Gus that said that he would look forward to e-mailing her tomorrow. Signed Your, Gus. Lorrie read it and when she saw he had signed it Your Gus, she chuckled to herself and thought, you crazy thing don't you know that you have always been my Gus. Lorrie went to bed in the best mood that she had been in for years and she really had something to look forward to everyday now. She was so excited that she had a hard time going to sleep, because she kept remembering the times she had seen and interacted with him when she was young and some of those times were brought back to her mind because of what Gus had remembered that she had forgotten. He remembered so much and he was so easy to talk to and he did give her an unusual reason for not coming back to her when she was 16, but she thought he was telling the truth and she buried her head in her pillow and cried for joy, because her happiness was just overwhelming. Lorrie got up the next morning and turned on her computer to see if by chance Gus had sent her any e-mail over night, but nothing came on. She then sent him an e-mail with some questions. Signed Always Lorrie and sent. A little she sent him another e-mail with some more questions. Signed Always Lorrie and sent. Then a little later in the day she sent him another e-mail with some more questions. Signed Always Lorrie and sent. About 3:00 pm Lorrie's computer pinged and she got two e-mail's from Gus. Gus had e-mailed her back with the answers to all her questions. It was signed, Your Gus. The next e-mail from him was asking her some questions, like when her birthday was, how long that she had been married to her Husband, and what had happened to her when he didn't come back to her when she was 16 years old? Signed Your Gus. Lorrie wrote him a real long e-mail describing everything from when she was waiting for him and then realizing that he wasn't coming back to her, the rest of her High School years, to her Junior College big argument with her parents and them sending her to Florida and her short time working at NASA and then meeting the older man surfer 35 years old and living with him a short time and losing her virginity to him in Puerto Rico when she was 20 years old, then her being a Go-Go Dancer and Waitress at a Club in Florida and getting pregnant and marring her first Husband, divorcing him, then joining the Navy, then marring the young Navy Seal, divorcing him then getting Stationed in England and married her third Husband so she would be able to stay in England after her Discharge from the Navy. Signed, Always, Lorrie and sent. Lorrie then sent Gus another e-mail asking him what he did with his life after he decided not to come back to her. Signed Always Lorrie and sent. It took a while, but Lorrie's computer finally pinged and sure enough it was an e-mail from Gus. Gus told her how hard it was for him to stay away from her and how he had married a girl he was dating at Junior College, then they divorced, then how he got this young girl pregnant and had to marry her which was a big mistake, then they divorced and he kept the baby boy, then he married his third wife and she had a small boy and girl, so they got married to help each other raise their kids, then they divorced and he went to the State Of Texas in Sugarland and he met a d married his fourth wife, because they were both getting older and they could help each other through old age, then he retired from the State and they moved out to Van Horn. Signed Your Gus.

Lorrie read all that Gus wrote her very carefully and the more she learned the more she wanted to know, so she would send him more e-mails with questions and he would answer them and then ask his own questions and kept doing this all day everyday finding out more and more about each other, then they would revisit the same part of each-others life asking more questions getting all the details until they both had an understanding and vision of each-others-lives just as if they had known about them as they had happened. Lorrie could tell that all of this searching of each-others-lives and thoughts was just as stimulating for Gus as it was for her and they were very honest with each other by not trying to make things sound better than they were. She became more and more trusting of Gus and it seemed to Lorrie that Gus was just as trusting of her. Lorrie sent Gus an e-mail and decided to tell him that she had just got back to England from her three month annual vacation from the first of June till the end of August to El Campo when she saw the e-mail joke, with his name on it, that their Hair Salon Friend had sent her and she had been back less then a week and that if that could have happened a couple of weeks earlier then maybe they could have seen each other in El Campo. Signed Always Lorrie and mailed. Lorrie got an e-mail back from Gus telling her that he would love to see her again and that he had thought about her so many times through the years and he had hoped that she was alright and had a happy life. Then he asked if she had ever thought about him through the years. Signed Your Gus. When Lorrie read his e-mail it made her so happy to know that he had thought of her and that he wanted to see her again. She had to smile at his question about if she had thought of him when the question should have been how many times had she thought of Gus. Lorrie e-mailed him back that every country that she had ever been in she had heard the song "In The Still Of The Night" played and then she would be right back on that beach kissing him, wanting him then wondering what had happened that he hadn't come back to her and that she had thought about him many times through the years, but what could she do when he didn't come back except just try to live her life the best that she could. She also told Gus that maybe they could work things out so they could see each other when she came back to El Campo on her annual vacation in June 2012. Signed Always Lorrie, then sent. There were a lot of these kinds of e-mail talks that went on day after day The mornings were so long for Lorrie without any e-mails from Gus, with that six hour difference in time, that she decided to ask him to send her an e-mail each evening before he left his office, because she wasn't getting one until 2:30

or 3:00 pm in the afternoons and that way she would have something from him to read in the morning when she got up. So she sent that e-mail to him. Signed Always Lorrie. Lorrie knew that the love that she had always had for him was now growing stronger and the thought of not being in communication with him for that period of time was becoming unbearable. Her computer pinged and the e-mail was from Gus. He said that he would send her a message each day before he left the office and then he wished her a Happy Birthday. Signed Your Gus. Lorrie looked at this e-mail and she was glad that he was going to send e-mails before he left the office each day, but why in the world was he wishing her a Happy Birthday a month early she didn't know. Lorrie e-mailed Gus back and asked why he was wishing her a Happy Birthday a month early that it was October the 26th . Signed Always Lorrie, and sent. Lorrie got an e-mail back from Gus that told her that he was sorry that he had thought that it was in September. Your Gus. Lorrie was so happy when she turned on her computer the next morning and had a nice sweet e-mail from Gus. She thought that this was a wonderful way to start her morning with a message from the only man she had ever loved. She would go back to her computer every chance she got and re-read the message again and again until she a new one from him at the usual time. Lorrie was still busy doing her normal things and also her Spanish Language lessons, but now she was becoming more and more confused about what she was going to do about disappearing in Spain. Now there was Gus back in her life and she wanted to see him really bad and not only that she wanted to finish what she she had wanted to do back when she was 16 years old and that was to finally make love to Gus. She couldn't offer him her Virginity any more, but if he would just allow her to love on him, he didn't have to love on her, but if he would allow her to love on him it would be more then she could ever have hoped for. Lorrie was going to be 66 years old in just a few days and she considered herself fat and she had all kinds of dark skin spots all over her arms and back from getting old and also from little skin cancers being burned off that left spots and scars, now she had a new scar on her forehead from the skin cancer they had to cut off there, her breasts were sagging, then there was the big scar that went all across her, now, big stomach from the exploratory surgery that the English Doctors had done when she was still in the Navy and they had been looking for the extreme pain she was experiencing. They had originally thought that it might be cancer, but it turned out to be a terribly infected ovary that they had to remove. About the only part of her body that she thought looked nice was maybe her long legs. She didn't like to use a lot of make-up so what was she going to do to tempt Gus to let her make love to him. She knew that she wasn't a glamor queen and thought that if she ever got Gus close to a bed that when he saw her naked that he would probably run as fast as he could back to his Mountains, this is why she thought that if he would only let her love on him that she had so much love to give him. She had really never been able to give her love to any man and now here was the man she had always loved and she just couldn't let that go by, for she knew that life was getting short and this would be her last chance to be with the only man in the world that she loved. Lorrie's Birthday morning of October 26th came around and she went down to get what she thought would be a message from Gus that he had sent the night before and she was hoping to get a Happy Birthday message later in the afternoon. She turned on her computer and clicked on e-mail then went to the kitchen to put on a pot of tea and then she went back into her little office and saw she had an e-mail from Gus and she clicked on it and instead of just a regular message that he had written the evening before it was a beautiful HAPPY BIRTHDAY message that he sent the evening before for her to read on her Birthday Morning and he told her that he hoped that she had the happiest birthday that she ever had in her life and that he wanted to be able to wish her a Happy Birthday for many years to come. Signed Your Paul. Lorrie e-mailed him back that this was already the best Birthday that she had ever had in her life, because they were back together on her Birthday and that they were going to have a lot of first's from now on. They continued their schedule of e-mail messages back and forth and the time really went by fast for Lorrie, then on November the 11th, 2011 Gus sent her an e-mail that told her that he would be away from his computer for 4 or 5 days after Thanksgiving, because his Sons were coming down and he and them would be out at the Ranch for their annual hunting get together. He told her that he had something else to tell her and it was that he loved her. Signed Your Gus. When Lorrie read this, she was stunned. She couldn't understand how he could tell her that he loved her when he hadn't even seen what she looked like now. She thought that he would be so disappointed that he would take that I love you right back. Then she thought could he be telling me this thinking that it would make me want to go to bed with him. She whispered to herself that she wanted to do that anyway, so he certainly didn't have to tell her that he loved her. She finally answered his e-mail and she told him that she loved him too, and that she wanted to tell him that the first time that they e-mailed, but that she had to wait to see if he would tell her first. She also told Gus that she would e-mail him every day and tell him what was going on with her in England, so when he got back to his computer he would be able to catch on what happened while he was at his Ranch and then she told him that this was November the 11th, 2011 or 11-11-11and from now on, the 11th of each month she would celebrate as their I Love You Anniversary, so now they had two anniversaries to remember and celebrate and they were the 5th and the 11th of each month. Signed Love Lorrie and sent. After Lorrie sent this e-mail to Gus she started crying in happiness and couldn't stop, because this was something that she never thought in a million years would happen that Gus would love her, old Lorrie that looked like an old fat, spotted-up cow. She thought that she must have fallen asleep and dreamed this, but she looked down and read his e-mail again and yes, he had told her that he loved her. Lorrie was thinking that now her priorities were changing. She knew that she had to see Gus and kiss him and make love to him to see if he was going to run from her or if he would be true to his word that he really did love her. She was going to continue to study and finish her Spanish Language classes, but she was going to have to put her plan of moving to Spain on hold to see what Gus's attitude toward her was when they finally met face to face. If things with Gus were what she hoped they would be then she would cancel her Spain plans and instead she would flee to El Campo, Texas, so they would have more of a chance of being together. Lorrie knew that if this was real then she couldn't pass up the chance to be with Gus. She didn't know what capacity she would be able to play in his life, but she would take what she could get. Lorrie's computer pinged and disturbed her thoughts and it was from Gus. He e-mailed that he looked forward to her e-mails while he was at the Ranch and that he had also loved her all of his life. Signed Love, Gus. The next day Lorrie decided that she would ask Gus to send her some pictures of himself, because she just couldn't stand it, she had to know what he looked like, but the only thing is that with her request that he might want a picture of her too. She decided that if he did that she would send him some of her pictures from the time that she was 12 years old when she had first discovered him to in the Navy and her and her young Son and one when she was a Nurse and maybe one of her in her Graduation Gown when she Graduated from the Open University with her Art History Degree and this would fill in some of the lost 50 years for him. She decided that she wasn't satisfied with any of her more recent pictures and that if he asked for one then she might have to get someone to take a picture, but she wanted to look better on that one. Lorrie sent Gus the e-mail about sending her a picture of him and that she was so glad that he loved her. Signed Love Lorrie and sent. In a few minutes her computer pinged, and it was from Gus and he told her that he would have to look for a picture, that he wasn't sure that he had any. Signed Love Gus. Lorrie's computer pinged at 3:00 pm the next day and it was from Gus and it had an attachment to it. She opened it and there were pictures in it. One was when he was in High School in his band jacket, one standing by his Red Hot Rod Coupe and these were how she remembered him and then one in his cowboy hat with tinted glasses on standing behind some bar. Signed Love Gus. Lorrie e-mailed him back that she loved the pictures, except that the one of him with his hat and glasses on she couldn't see his eyes and she wanted to see his beautiful blue eyes that she would never forget those ice blue eyes and would he please get someone to take a picture of him with his hat and glasses. Signed Love Lorrie and sent. Lorrie then turned on her copy machine and she made copies of the pictures and put them in her special Gus file, so she could look at them when ever she wanted to. Gus e-mailed her back that he would try to get someone, but that he didn't know when he would find someone to do it. Signed Love Gus. Gus had told Lorrie when he would be at the Ranch so she wasn't surprised that she wasn't getting any e-mails back from Gus. She kept sending him e-mails everyday all day long about what she was doing and about how much she loved and missed him. Lorrie e-mailed Gus and told him that she never wanted to be without him again in her life and that she knew that they were getting older and in an impossible situation by both of than being married to two other spouses, but she just wanted to have what-ever she could have of him and that she wanted for them to make a promise that no one was going to be hurt because of their relationship, meaning their spouses. Signed Love Lorrie and sent. Five days later Lorries computer pinged and she was excited to see an e-mill from Gus there. She opened it quickly, because she was hungry to have communication with him. The e-mail had an attachment with it and she waited to open it, because she wanted to see what he had to say. Gus told her that he e-mailed the new picture of him with his hat and glasses and that he agreed with her to keep the promise of not hurting their spouses and he told her everything that they had done at the ranch and that he had missed their talking on e-mail so much, but that he really enjoyed and appreciated all the e-mails that she had sent him. Singed Love Gus. Lorrie then opened the attachment and saw the picture of her Gus as he was now. He was standing up without his hat and glasses and he was holding a big black gun, wearing Army style camo shirt and pants. She could see that he had a bit of a pot beer belly, white hair that was receding a lot from his forehead and two bright ice blue eyes that looked like two small bright blue lights shining. She thought that yes this was her Gus, oh my goodness she was actually looking at her Gus. To Lorrie he still looked handsome and sexy and all of a sudden she felt something that she hadn't felt in years, probably 20 years or more and that was that she was beginning to become sexually aroused, because she could feel the heat rising in her body and she was starting to perspire. She was amazed that she could get those long lost feelings of a sensual woman at her age of 66 and she guessed that it was like that when a woman really loved the man she was supposed to be with. This she had never experienced from just looking at a lover or husband before even when she was young. The last time that she could remember having these feelings where when she and Gus were together. Well here it was again, just as it should have been all along, how nice. Lorrie e-mailed him back and told him how much that she enjoyed his message and the picture and that she could see his blue eyes and that yes he was her Gus without mistake. She told him that she wanted his cell phone number because she wanted to hear his voice and that she wanted to be able to call him maybe once a month and listen to his voice that she hadn't heard in so many years and she wanted to be able to wish him Marry Christmas when it came time, so please send her his cell phone number. Signed Love Lorrie and sent. Her computer pinged in a few minutes and Gus had sent her his cell phone number and he told her that it was time for him to go home, but before he did he was going to get her an e-mail message ready for her to read in the morning and he knew that it was 12:00 am now in England, so she needed to cut off her computer, so the message he was going to send didn't get there to early. Signed Love, Gus. Lorrie quickly wrote his phone number down and put it in her special Gus file, then she cut off her computer and she was supremely happy with herself. She sat there for a while even thought it was late and it felt really damp and cold, because the heat in the house had been programmed to go off at 10:00 pm each night, so she had been sitting in her little office with her nightgown and her heavy robe on and she was still very cold, but she had heard from the love of her life and now she had his phone number and she could get out his picture and she could call him and look at his face and hear his voice. She was smiling and very happy as she made her way up the stairs quietly to her room. Lorrie and Gus kept in very close contact by e-mail every-day and Lorrie was fighting off the urge to call Gus to hear his voice. She got an e-mail from Gus asking if he could send her a Christmas card. Signed Love Gus. Lorrie answered him back no, because his name had never been mentioned at her house and it would just lead to questions if her Husband or Stepson would see it. Then she told Gus that she was sending him something for Christmas and that she would tell him when she was going to mail it so he could judge when it might be delivered. Lorrie told him that she had a lunch meeting with her good friend Jill, and she told her that she was in love and then she cried and Jill cried also, then she showed Jill the pictures that he had sent her. She told Gus that she just couldn't hold her happiness in any longer that she had to tell somebody how happy she was, so she told Jill, because of all of her friends she knew that Jill would keep the secret to herself. She told Gus that she thought that her Husband wondered what was wrong with her, because she would catch herself singing old songs while she was working or cleaning and he would look at her with a sort of strange look, because she had never done that before. Signed Love Lorrie and sent. They talked on e-mail off and on all day and Lorrie finally had to sign off and go to bed, because it was getting late. The next morning Lorrie turned on her computer and read the message that Gus had left for her then she e-mailed Gus and told him to e-mail her as soon as he got this e-mail, because she was going to call him and she wanted to be sure that he was going to be in his office with his phone turned on. Love Lorrie signed and sent. That afternoon Lorrie's computer pinged, and it was from Gus and he told her he was in the office with his phone on. Lorrie then picked up her home phone and her hands were shaking so bad that she had a hard time punching in his phone number and she waited listening to all the noises on the phone making all the connections and it seemed like eternity until she heard his phone ringing and then she heard the voice of the love of her life for the first time in 50 years say "this is Gus" and Lorries voice was quivering when she said "Gus I love you" and she heard him say I love you too. They both tried to speak at the same time and then Lorrie told him that she might have to hang up quick if she saw her Husband coming to the house from his workshop in their back yard. They talked and talked, and Lorrie couldn't believe how natural it was to talk to Gus and how wonderful his voice sounded. She told him that she would call him again and wish him Merry Christmas when the time came and also a Happy New Year. Lorrie told him that she would probably only call him once a month unless there was some special reason then she would let him know. She told him that she loved him and she heard him tell her that he loved her too then she hung up reluctantly, but she was to afraid to talk to him too long on her home phone, because her Husband had an extension in his workshop and he could pick up the phone and listen to their conversation. Lorrie thought that he would certainly give her a good beating then. She could not believe that she had called on her home phone. She was going to have to keep her cell phone minutes all paid up so that from now on she could use it to call Gus, because it was to dangerous calling on her house phone. Lorrie bought Gus several real nice leather book marks, a British Calendar with English pictures on each month with the explanations about them, and she also bought him a special Zippo cigarette lighter and had it engraved with "GUS and LORRIE FOREVER" on the front of it. She mailed it then she e-mailed him and told him that she had inquired at the Post Office as to how long it would take to get to Texas and was told somewhere in or around five or six days. Signed Love Lorrie and sent. Lorrie received the e-mail back from Gus that he would be looking for it. Signed Love Gus. They were e-mailing back and forth as usual, but Lorrie was having a very hard time trying to keep from calling him. She did manage to last till Christmas before she called him again and they talked for an hour and it was so hard for her to tell him good-by. She knew that she wouldn't be able to wait till New Years to call him. She was going to have to talk to him more often than once a month, she was wondering how she had ever come up with that crazy idea that she was only going to call him once a month. All the time that Lorrie had this romantic love affair going on, she didn't neglect her responsibilities to her house work or her work with her Husband's Tailoring Business or her Spanish Language Lessons, she even managed to do all the planning, shopping and decorating for the Holiday Season. It was different this year though, because Lorrie was doing it feeling happy and full of energy. When she was decorating, she was listening to her old Rock-N-Roll records and she had even bought a record of "In The Still Of The Night" by The Five Satins and she made sure that it played more than any of the others. Her Husband would look at her funny and he finally asked her why she was playing that old music, to which she just shrugged and told him that she was just in the mood for it she guessed. She got an e-mail from Gus telling her that he had received her gifts and how wonderful it was to get something from her and that he wished that he could give her a Christmas gift, but he understood why she didn't want him to send one. Lorrie couldn't stand it any longer, so when her Husband went on his ski vacation, she called Gus three times between Christmas and New Year. When they were talking Gus asked Lorrie why she was changing her plan to only call him once a month and Lorrie told him that since she had heard his voice that she couldn't help it, because e-mail just wasn't enough anymore. She told Gus that if his phone was off that she would leave him a voice message and for him never to call her that she would always call him. Lorrie's New Year's Eve small get together went of nice and quiet and she waited for her Husband to get drunk enough to go up to his room to bed. She had been helping him get drunk for a change by mixing him whiskey and getting him to chase it with beer. After she helped him up to his bed, she went down stairs and waited for a little while and sipped on her brandy then she punched in Gus's phone number. It was a little after 6:00 pm in Van Horn, Texas when she heard Gus answer his phone with a this is Gus and Lorrie told him Happy New Year and then gave him kisses over the phone and told him that she loved him then they talked for a little while and then she told him that this was the best New Year's Eve she had in 50 years, then she told him that she loved him again and she heard him tell her Happy New Year and his kisses and I love you too, then they said good night, but she sat there for a while savoring the sound of Gus's voice wishing her a Happy New Year and his kisses over her phone and she thought that this is another first for us Gus and I want to experience your real kisses again and not just hear them.

2012 GUS AND LORRIE

Gus & Lorrie—2012 started perfectly for Gus and Lorrie. They told each other Happy New Year for the first time in their lives and Lorrie was 66 years old and Gus was 69 years old, but they both were full of expectations that were as new as the New Year. This year of 2012 was going to be the first year that they were together since 1962 which meant that no longer would they start a year without each other, because from now on it was going to be Gus and Lorrie Forever just like the engraving on the Zippo lighter Lorrie had sent Gus for Christmas. Lorrie's Husband went on his two-week ski vacation and she called Gus every day that her Husband was gone. She told him that her Stepson had quit his job again and that she wasn't surprised, but he had got everyone all upset when he had contacted one of his friends and told him that he was going to commit suicide. She told Gus that she had given up on him ever amounting to anything, she just didn't want him to hurt himself. Lorrie told Gus about her Spanish Language Lessons and that she had finished and passed them. She then told him why she had decided to take them, to leave her Husband and to disappear to a small village in Spain and this shocked Gus, because she had never before let on that there was trouble between her and her Husband. Gus didn't want to press her for information on that, but as the days went on and they talked more and more on the phone she would divulge more information. Finally Gus asked her why she didn't tell him that her Husband was so brutal to her before and Lorrie told him that she wasn't proud of it and that the Police had been called to their house many times because he was beating her and making so much noise that the neighbors would call them. Gus asked her why she hadn't divorced him and she told Gus that the Divorce Laws in England were on the side of the man and also she would have to move to a Woman's Shelter and she was afraid that he would find her and really beat her to death. Gus then asked her why she hadn't just stayed in El Campo on one of her vacation trips there, that her family would have helped her start over and Lorrie told him that she was to embarrassed and ashamed to do that, because her Dad didn't want her to marry her Husband in the first place and had warned her not to marry a foreigner, but she had not listened to him, because she had wanted to stay in England after her Discharge from the Navy. This was why she could never let her family know what was going on in her marriage and that she always made out like she was real happy with her Husband, when actually she was afraid of him and she was miserable living with him and her worthless Stepson. Lorrie told Gus that she was having to go into town more often now to buy more minutes on her phone because of all the calls she was making to him. Gus didn't tell her that his phone bill had gone sky high also, because they were talking more and he was using a lot more minutes than his contract called for, so on the minutes he was paying the highest rate. He didn't want to discourage her from calling him, because he loved the sound of her voice and also it was much easier to share information then on e-mail. Gus asked her if she had found any more recent pictures of herself and she told him no that she hadn't, and she was going to have to have someone take a picture of her and she would send it to him. He told her that if she was afraid that he wouldn't like her picture that she shouldn't worry about it, because there could never be anything that would change his total love for her. He told Lorrie that he had always loved her and that once he had discovered that he knew that there was nothing that could destroy that kind of love. Lorrie told Gus that she had never dreamed that she would live long enough to hear him say those kinds of words to her. Lorrie told Gus that she had thought that she would probably die in England, so she had planned on being cremated and her ashes were to be sent to her Brother and she had instructed him to scatter them on the beach at Matagorda where she had so much fun when she was a kid and they went there as a family and then later when she was in High School and her and some friends would go down there and swim and sun bath to get a good tan. When Gus heard this another idea came to his mind. He told Lorrie that he had a family burial plot in El Campo that would hold 10 people and right now there were 5 people buried there, his Grand Pa and Grand Ma, his Dad and Mom and his young Son, so that left 5 empty places and he had already put his Grave stone in the place under his Son and he would love to have her buried beside him to rest there forever if she so desired. He told her that he didn't want to change the plans that she had made that this was just a suggestion and she could think about it and let him know. Lorrie got real quiet and then she told Gus that he had made a very big offer to her and that maybe he should thank about it also, because it could have consequences for him and that they would talk about it another time. Lorrie told Gus that she and her Husband would be going to Spain to have a Holiday with friends at their condo like they have been doing now for several years, but she would still be able to stay in touch with him with her cell phone. Gus told Lorrie that Skeeter, his friend in El Campo keeps asking him to come down and look over some land that he had bought at Port Alto, with the idea of developing an RV Park and he was wanting Gus to invest in it and he also was wanting some advice about it, so Gus told him that he would come down when the weather got better. She asked Gus when he planned on going and he told her that he was thinking about April or May. Lorrie told him that she normally went to El Campo and stayed for three months and she went at the first of June, so if he could go at the same time they could be able to see each other. Gus told her that he thought that he would be able to come to El Campo during that time and that he would like to come the first week in June, so he would be able to see her as soon as he could, after all it had been fifty years. Lorrie laughed with that hiccup catch in her voice that started her laughs, that Gus loved to hear. Gus called his friend Skeeter and told him that he was going to come down to El Campo in June to look over the property at Port Alto and Skeeter told Gus that he could stay at his house while he was in El Campo. After the phone conversation Lorrie had with Gus and he had offered her a burial place next to him in his Families Grave Plot, she was overwhelmed with emotion, because she thought that if she had ever had a doubt of how sincere Gus was about their relationship that this proved his seriousness and commitment. Lorrie knew now that there was only going to be one more test to see how they were together and that was going to be when they were actually together on their first meeting. If that was good, then she knew that she would have to completely change her plans of living in Spain to going back to El Campo, Texas, so she would be able to start her life again there, so she would have more of a chance of seeing Gus and being able to spend time with him. The Easter Holiday time came around and she called Gus and told him when she would be leaving for Spain and she told him that she would be able to sneak off and call him from time to time, but that she would miss his e-mail messages that she wouldn't be able to read each morning, but she asked him to continue to send them, so when she got back home she would be able to read them. Gus told her that he would and that he would be waiting for to call him. When Gus turned his phone on the next day, he got a voice mail message from Lorrie telling him that they were in the Air Port waiting to board the airplane for the short flight to Spain and she was in the Ladies Restroom calling him. She told him that when they got to Spain that she would find a place as soon as she could to call him. Later in the afternoon Gus got another call from Lorrie and she was whispering telling him that she was on a patio porch outside their upstairs room and her Husband was in the restroom, so she had a minute to call and hear Gus's voice and to tell him that she loved him and Gus told her that he loved her too and to please be careful, because it wasn't going to be too long before they would have the chance to see each other. She said that she would and that the next day that they were going to rent a car and drive to a couple of the mountain villages and that she would find a way to call him then. They said good-by for then. Gus thought that it was something that he could talk to her all they to Spain and her voice was just as clear as when she called him from England. Checking her time Lorrie did call Gus the next day from a Public Restroom in one of the little mountain villages and she told him that so far she had visited this one a couple of times and that she liked it the best and she was using her Spanish and seemed to be able to communicate with the local citizens pretty good and that she was pleasantly pleased at the improvement she had made. She told him that she just had a moment to talk, but just had to hear his voice and that she needed to go, but to never doubt that she loved him. She told him that she would call him the next chance she would get. Lorrie called Gus from the public restroom in nice Cafe that they were eating their dinner in, then they were going to go shopping, so she would call him the next day. She also told him that they had acquired reservations at one of the best Restaurants that was known for their wonderful Floor Shows in the city and she was excited about going there, because she had so many great reviews on it. The next day Lorrie called Gus two times and was able only to talk for a short time and she told him the time that she would be at the Famous Restaurant and she didn't know if she would be able to call him or not, but not to worry if he didn't hear from her she would call him the last day they would be there. Gus was getting ready to shut off his computer and his phone and go home when his phone rang and it was Lorrie and she was crying and he was having trouble understanding her, but she finally got herself under control and told him that she was in the Ladies Restroom in that Restaurant and that her Husband had just had a big fight with her in the Restaurant. She apologized for being so upset when Gus answered and she wanted to know if he could hear her alright, because the hand driers were making so much noise and she said that there were a lot of women in there right now. Gus told her that not to worry that he could hear her just fine and to please tell him again what happened. Lorrie said that her Husband had tried to knock her out of her chair there at their table and that he had showed his ass real good. Gus asked her if she was hurt and she told him that she might have some black marks, but she didn't know yet, because this just happened. Gus asked her to start from the beginning and Lorrie told him that her Husbands cell phone rang, so he answered it and was talking to his Son about something and then he handed his phone to her and her Stepson was in all upset and she was listening to him and trying to make sense of what he was saying and then trying to calm him down when her Husband jumped up on his feet and almost turned their table over and grabbed his phone out of her hand and was shouting at the top of his voice and then he knocked at her trying to turn her chair over and there were four old women at the table behind them they got up and they were screaming at him and all the while her Husband was still shouting at her telling her that he was going to beat her up and the friends they were with tried to calm him down, but her Husband wouldn't listed to him and then the Security Guards came and they took her Husband into custody and took him up in the Balcony away from her and they told her Husband that he could go with them to the Balcony or they would hold him and call for the Police to take to Jail. She told Gus that she had food and drinks from the table on her cloths and she was going to clean it as best as she could before she went back out to their Friends and that their Friends had never seen her Husband like this and he had really showed his ass real good and she was glad that someone had finally witnessed his anger and abusiveness, because none of his business associates or friends had ever seen him in a blind rage before. Gus ask Lorrie what had set her Husband off and Lorrie told him that she didn't have the slightest idea and that he was shouting so loud at her that it upset her so much that she couldn't understand what he was shouting about. Lorrie told Gus that she would have to call him the next day, because she needed to go back to their Friends to see what was happening. After they hung up Gus thought what a mess and Lorrie had told him that she would never know what might set her Husband off in a rage, so she tried to think about what she talked about before she would say anything to prevent any fights, but he was very unpredictable. Gus could understand more know at what Lorrie must have been going through for years. He just couldn't understand how her Husband could treat her so badly when Gus was sure that Lorrie was a woman with a mild disposition and she had told him before that she didn't like any form of confrontation. He was just going to have to wait for her call the next day, but he was wondering what was going on right now in Spain. The next day Gus was having a hard time waiting for Lorrie to call him. He was continually checking the time and is seemed to be moving much slower then usual. Finally his phone rang and it was Lorrie. He asked her if she was alright and she told him that she was a little sore and has some black spots, but that was all. Gus then ask her to update him and Lorrie told him that when she got out of the Ladies Restroom and went back to the table that their friends were ready to go back to their condo and her Husband was still being held in the Balcony by Security waiting for her to tell them what she wanted to do with her Husband. They went to talk to the Security and asked them to release her Husband that they were ready to leave the Restaurant the Security Guards brought her Husband down and they escorted them out to where their car was brought around to make sure that her Husband didn't cause any more trouble then her Husbands Friend told him to get his butt in the front with him and the women were going to sit in the back seat. As her Husbands Friend was driving back to their Condo he was giving her Husband hell all the way and all her Husband did was hang his head. When they got to the Condo she had to go to the same room as he was going to be in and as she was preparing herself to go to bed she saw him pour himself a big glass of straight whiskey from the bottle on their table. She wondered what the rest of the night was going to be like, because she would have thought that he would not want any more trouble after what had just happened, but there he was going to get even drunker. She told Gus that it took her some time to finally drop off to sleep and the next morning she found her Husband asleep in the chair. She showered and got dressed and went down to have coffee and their friend told her that he had canceled the rest of their stay and he had booked a Flight back to England in three hours, so he was going up to their room and get her Husband up and tell him to get his butt ready or they were going to leave him in Spain and if so, then good riddance. She told Gus that she would call him the next day after they got back to England because she was also going to have to find out what had been wrong with her Stepson. Lorrie finally found out what had transpired with her Stepson. He had put out computer message to some of his Friends that he was going to kill himself and they over reacted and they called the Police and Emergency Services that came to their house and almost broke down the front door before he unlocked it and then they questioned him and had the Paramedics examine him to make sure that all was good. He had called his Dad's phone all drunk and upset that is why she was having a hard time trying to figure out what was happening with him. She called Gus and told him all of this and he told Lorrie that her Stepson wasn't ever going to kill himself, that when he announced it like he was just looking for attention and sympathy. As the days went on Lorrie would either by e-mail or phone question Gus on everything including the kinds of vegetables he liked or did he like spicy foods, what kinds of soups, fried food or baked food, sweets, what kinds of music, clothing and Gus would answer her and ask her questions right back. Lorrie finally sent Gus a new picture of herself and she had it taken on the patio of the Condo in Spain. She was wearing a beautiful print creamy silk pull over loose fitting blouse and she was standing next to a stucco support column for the porch with the desert, mountain view behind her and for the first time he was seeing a recent picture of his beautiful, sweet Lorrie. Her hair was more of an ash brown color unlike the dark brown that he remembered, her lips were thinner, not nearly as full, but still the beautiful shape that demanded kissing and she told him the truth that she had gained a lot of weight, because he could see it in her face, neck and the way that her silk blouse was fitting. He couldn't quite see what color her eyes were in the picture, but the truth was that he couldn't remember what color they were when they had been together when she was 16 years old, but this was definitely his Lorrie and he loved her, all of her. Lorrie told Gus had been thinking over making her usual vacation trip back to El Campo, Texas the first of June 2012 and she was about to decide to wait till December of 2012 when she would leave her Husband and England for good and move back to El Campo and help take care of her aging Mom. She told him that this last episode her Husband had pulled made her start to seriously think about moving back to El Campo in stead of disappearing to some mountain village in Spain. She told Gus that she didn't want him to think she was going to move back to El Campo, Texas, because she was leaving her Husband for him and she didn't want her Family or anyone else to think that either. She told Gus that it was true that she wanted to see him and to be with him if that was possible, but, what had really changed things was that she knew now that he would help her navigate all the intricate things that she would have to do and relearn to be able to start over and live in the United States and Texas, because it had actually been 31 years since she had lived in the United States and Texas and she didn't know the first thing that she needed to do to get started again. Lorrie knew that everything everyone there took for granted would be completely new to her, because she had spent ½ of her life in England and she was sure that everything that she had been used to had changed. She hated to admit it, but she didn't even know the simplest things any more, not even how to do something like put gas in a car from the gas pump, much less to know what to do about all the legal stuff that she would need to know. She told Gus that she had a nice amount of money in savings in England and that she would like it if he would go to a Bank in El Campo after she got there to help her set up a Bank Account so she could get her savings transferred. Things like that she needed guidance in. She told Gus that she would need that much time so she could get a lot of things boxed up and mailed back to her Mom's house before she left, because she didn't want to have to just leave everything behind, and that was going to take a lot of time to sort through things and get them mailed without her Husband finding out what was going on, because that might be deadly for her. Gus understood, but he was very disappointed, because he was hoping to be able to see her in June when he went down there to visit his friend Skeeter and go look at the land he wanted to develop into a RV Park. Gus didn't want to say anything that would influence her decisions, so he just agreed with her, but that would mean that he wouldn't be able to see her for an additional 7 months. Gus had already made arrangements to go to El Campo and stay with Skeeter while he was there trying to figure how he could help him and he had thought that it would correspond nicely with Lorries vacation visit so he could see her in the same trip, but now it looked like he would have to make another trip to El Campo in December to be able to see her and he really didn't want to leave Van Horn in the winter, because the winter storms could get unexpectedly severe there in the winter. That would mean that if he went at all in December then he wouldn't be able to stay there more then a couple of days. If he wasn't able to go then, he wouldn't be able to see her for maybe another year from now. That possibility seemed utterly unacceptable to Gus. He hadn't seen her for fifty years and now it seemed that being able to see her had been only two months from now, but things were going to depend on the decision she would make and he hoped that she would keep her first plan of doing her Texas vacation just as she had done for a lot of years now, so he crossed his fingers and just hoped that is what she would do. They e-mailed and talked on the phone everyday and the weeks were slipping by. Lorrie was asking Gus questions about what she should do first in the way of legal stuff to start out getting her self established enough to be able to start living in El Campo as a regular citizen there. Gus told her that there were three main first steps and they were for her to get a Social Society Number, a Texas Drivers License and a Bank account and to get the Bank Account she would need to get the Social Number and the Drivers License and then she could start out the Bank Account with $500.00 dollars and then she could apply for her Social Security payments and they would be deposited electronically. He told her that she also needed to find her Discharge Papers from the Navy and her Graduation Certificates from the Open University, because both of them might become really important Documents for her. Gus was still doing his Oil and Gas Business and he would would make small Oil and Gas Deals that payed a little money, but nothing that he would call impressive. It was April now, so Gus was going out to his Ranch to turn on all the water to the Camp House, because he would turn it off after his Sons left from there after Thanksgiving and it stayed off till April when Gus was fairly sure that it wouldn't freeze hard enough to burst the water pipes. He never stayed at the ranch over a day in the winter, because he didn't want to turn on the water to the Camp House and have to go to all the work of having to drain it again for short stays there. The winters in the Van Horn area could be really severe sometimes with the winter storms coming through the mountains and they would in fast, this was why he didn't ever leave the area during the winter. He had three places to take care of and protect from high winds and freezing temperatures, his Home, his Office and his Camp House. Turning the water on out there for the first time after winter was always a little bit of an experience, because you never knew what to expect. Something might have frozen and broken, or if not that there might be air bubbles that would block the water flow in the lines and he would have to purge the system of air to get everything properly. Everything seemed to work good this time though, so his task was over quickly and he was on his way driving back to town when he got to the area that he had cell phone service again turned his phone on and it started pinging and pinging and pinging. He looked at it and it was voice messages from Lorrie. Her first message was for him to e-mail her as soon as he got to the office, so she knew that he was safe, because she worried about him when she knew he was out at his Ranch by himself. Her second message was just to tall him how much she loved him and wanted to see him again. Her third message was that she had decided to go ahead and take her annual vacation to El

Campo in June as usual, because she could see that by what Gus had told her that she would have to get a lot of things done before she could even open a Bank Account at an El Campo Bank other wise she wouldn't be able to transfer her money from her Bank in England to El Campo and she needed to do that before she left England for good. This was very good news for Gus and he was on a real high trying to get back to his office so he could e-mail her and tell her how much he liked her change of plans for her return to El Campo. Lorrie had to stay up a little later to get Gus's e-mail, because he didn't get back to his office till 4:30 pm which made it 10:30 pm in England before she got the e-mail and she called him immediately and told him that she had missed communicating with him all day and that she was so glad that he was back safe and sound, so what did Gus think of her decision to go back to El Campo in June as usual. Gus told her that he thought that it was wonderful, because she was right about all that she would have to accomplish in El Campo before she could leave England for good and also he was having a very hard time thinking about having to wait several months more when he could see her in just a few weeks if she came in June. She told Gus that he was right that she didn't know what she had been thinking until she read his e-mail and then she came to realize that she could not leave her Husband and England until she laid the right ground work in El Campo so the transition would be relative easy and also she realized that she didn't want to wait any longer then she had to see him. Gus told Lorrie that when she had told him that she was going to wait and come back to El Campo for good in December of 2012 that his heart just sunk, because he was so anxious to see her and she was putting it off for so long that he didn't know how he could stand it, but that he didn't say anything to her, because he didn't want to influence her decisions one way or the other. He wanted her decisions to be hers completely. Lorrie told him that was such a sweet way of looking at it, but that she needed his input, because she had never had to flee from an abusive Husband in another Country and that it was going to be complicated and maybe even dangerous. She told him that if she was finally going to accomplish this, that he was the one she needed to advise her, and that this was one of the main things that stopped her from leaving her Husband before and moving back to El Campo, Texas was that she had never had the support of someone who she knew who would and could give her the right information that she needed and she wouldn't have to go to her family, her being embarrassed to ask questions and then be reminded that she had been told years ago not to marry that foreigner. Gus told Lorrie that he would help her all that he could and that her decision to go back to El Campo was a good one and that he would see her there and help her get started laying the ground work for her eventual move to El Campo from England. They said goodby till the next day and Lorrie reminded Gus to send her a e-mail for her to read the next morning when she got up and went to her computer. Gus's friend Skeeter in El Campo was calling Gus at least once a week to make sure that he was going to come to El Campo when they had planned. Gus assured him that he was coming the first of June and now Gus was also thinking that since Lorrie was definitely going to be there at the same time that he needed to talk to her face to face about being buried in his family burial Plot and if so that she needed to pick out a Head Stone and decide what she wanted engraved on it so it could be placed on her grave spot and she and Gus could see it before he left to go back to Van Horn, because he wasn't going to be in El Campo more then two weeks. Lorrie called Gus and told him that she had paid for her round trip airplane ticket to Texas and that she was packing things to get ready. She told him that she was really getting excited now, because it was getting really close to the time that she would be able to lay her eyes on him for the first time in 50 years and she could actually gaze into his blue eyes again. Gus told her that he had a surprise that he was planning for her. He wanted to buy her a ring that he should have given her 50 years ago and that when they would first meet again he was going to slip it on her finger as a physical promise that he was finally claiming her for his own as he should have done 50 years ago. He wanted to know what size she wore and Lorrie told him that she wasn't sure, but he could try a size 6, then she told him that she absolutely didn't want a diamond, ruby or anything like that. She told him that when she had lived in Albuquerque she had fallen in love with turquoise and if he wanted to get her a ring with a stone she wanted silver and turquoise and please don't get a big one and something that was small and smooth, so it wouldn't catch on clothing. Gus thanked Lorrie for the help in describing what she wanted. He told her was slow, but he was sure. Lorrie told him that she would be proud to wear his ring and that she would never take it off. He asked her if her Husband would wonder where she got it and she told him that her Husband never paid any attention to her and that if he even saw it he would just think it was something that she bought somewhere. The day before Lorrie was to fly out of England for Texas she called Gus and told him that she would spend several days with her Sister in Houston before they would drive to El Campo, so she would call him after she got to her Mom's house and she was settled in there. Gus told her that it was fine and he would then drive down to El Campo after she called him. He asked her if she had a Texas map at her Mom's and she told him that she was sure that her Brother would have one. Gus wanted to know if she Gus told her that she could follow his progress driving if she wanted to, bu looking at the map when he called her while he was driving and telling her what Town he was driving through. Lorrie told him that she thought that a great idea and also that it would make the excitement build and build for her as he got closer and closer. She told Gus that she would call him from the airport in England before she got on the plane and then when she landed and went through Customs in Houston, she would call him again, so he would know that everything was good and she would also have the opportunity to tell him that she loved him each time. That evening before Lorrie went to bed her Husband surprised her when he ask her if she was going to come back to England and she looked at him wondering if he somehow knew something of her plans to leave him, then she told him that she had purchased a round trip ticket. He just looked at her a little funny and she went on to bed, because she had to be at the Airport at 5:00 am to get her luggage all checked in and get her assigned seat and make sure that all her documents were stamped before boarding her flight to Houston, Texas at 6:00 am. Lorrie called Gus right before she was stepping on the plane and told him that she knew that he was just waking-up in Van Horn, Texas and she wanted to tell him that she loved him and would call him when she arrived at the Houston Airport. When Gus got to his office at 9:00 am he turned on his phone and got Lorrie's message. He was so excited and thought that this was really going to happen and he thanked God for this opportunity to see Lorrie again that he knew must have been finally arranged by him, because there was no way that this could have been just freak accident. It had to have been all arranged by God. Later that afternoon Gus's phone rang and it was his sweet Lorrie's voice on the other end and the first thing she said was that she was safely on the ground in Texas and that she loved him. Gus told her that he loved her also and he told her that he was so excited to know how close she was to him instead of being in England that it almost seemed to be right next door compared to that even though he knew that they were still 600 miles apart, but he could drive that 600 miles, but that he couldn't drive to England. Lorrie just laughed and she told him that she was going to stay two days with her sister then they were going to drive to El Campo to her Mom,s house then he could make plans to drive to El Campo the next day. She told him that she had to prepare her Mom that she had a friend coming a long ways to visit her and also she had to get her Brother and his Fiance updated on him, by telling them the whole story about how she had loved him all her life and how she had found him again and bring them up to date that he was coming down to see her and she wanted to introduce Gus to them. Gus told her that all of that was fine and to just let him know how everything was going as soon as she could, because he was really looking forward to the first second that he could lay eyes on her. She told him not to worry, because she felt the same way and she was going to be calling him several times a day anyway to make sure that he still wanted to drive so far to see her. Gus laughed at her and then she told him that she had to go now, because she saw her Sister and that she would call him later. Gus called his friend Skeeter and told him that it looked like he would be driving down in about three days and then they could go look over the land for the development of his RV Park. Skeeter told Gus that he would be ready and that he would have a room at his house ready for him. Lorrie was true to her word and she called Gus at least three times a day to tell him what she was doing and she told him that she had told her Sister all about him and a short version of their history when they were young and she was just fine with it, so one of the family hurdles was over. Lorrie called Gus when she got to her Mom's house and she told him that everything looked good., so he could definitely keep his plans to come the next day, that is if he still wanted to see her. She told him that she had bought her a cell phone at Wal-Mart that she was only going to use in Texas and that she needed to have one anyway when she moved to Texas for good, so she gave Gus her number and told him that as long as she was in Texas he could call her on the 332-2637 number. Gus fussed at her for even thinking of such a thing that he didn't want to see her and he told her that he would be leaving Van Horn at 6:00 am the next morning and he would call her when he got on the road, so she better get that Texas map if she wanted to follow his progress. She told Gus that she was glad that he had reminded her about the map and she said something that he didn't understand and he asked her what she had said and she told him that she just asked her Brother about the map and he told her that he had one, so she was all ready for him to make his trip and she hoped that she would be able to sleep, because she was so excited, that she felt like a little girl. Gus called his friend Skeeter and told him that he would be leaving Van Horn at 6:00 am in the morning and would get to El Campo about 2:30

or 3:00 pm, but before he came to his house he had someone to see and he wasn't sure how long he would be there. Skeeter told Gus that it didn't matter that his room was ready for him anytime he got there. He next morning Gus left Van Horn on time at 6:00 am and a few miles out of town he called Lorrie's phone number 332-2637 for the very first time and she answered it immediately. He told her that he was just a few miles out of town and headed her way for their first meeting in 50 years and did she still want him to call her when he went through each town on the way so she could track him on the Texas map and when she answered yes, it was the first indication he had that she was crying. He asked her what was wrong and Lorrie told him that nothing was wrong, it was just that she was so happy to know that she was finally going to be able to see him again that all she could do was cry and she was so sorry to be blubbering like such a baby. Lorrie told him that she had slept very little, because she kept thinking that he was going to call her and tell her that he had decided not to come to see her, so she had been scared of that happening and it kept her awake. She told him that she hoped that she didn't have dark rings around her eyes from no sleep or he might just get back in his car and drive back to Van Horn. Gus told her not to worry that he would love her no matter what she looked like that it was Lorrie he loved period. Gus called her when he went through every town and she would answer and tell him to be very careful and at each town she would tell him that the closer he got to her the harder it was for her to breath, because she was so afraid that he wouldn't like her since she had changed so much. He tried to console her and told her not to worry. When he got Columbus he called her and told her where he was and she asked him how far from El Campo that was and he told her that it was about 38 miles and then she asked him how long it would it take him to get from there to El Campo and he told her probably around 45 minutes, then she screamed and told him that she was next door at her Brothers house and she needed to go and take a shower and put on some decent cloths, because all she had on were some old shorts and a ragged pull over. Gus laughed and told her that he didn't care what she was wearing. Because all he wanted to do was to see her and gibe her a great bid kiss and hug. Lorrie told him to call her when he got into El Campo. Gus was temped to drive 0ver the speed limit now, but held himself back thinking that he was much to close to take a chance of getting a speeding ticket or have an accident, so he held himself to the speed limit and when he got in to El Campo he called her and told her that he would be at her Mom's house in about 10 minutes and she asked him if he remembered what it looked like and he told her that he thought he did, then she told him that there was an old blue-gray Buick parked in the driveway. Gus remembered her Mom's street and the side of the street her house was on, but it had been many, many years since he had been down that street and when he turned down it he discovered that it looked different, because there were houses now where there had once been vacant lots and that the trees had grown huge, so it all looked a lot different and he drove down it until he realized that he had gone too far, so he turned around and went back and was looking all the time. but couldn't pick out her Mom's house and he was so excited that he had forgotten about the car in the driveway, so Gus passed it up three times until he noticed a woman coming out of the door of a house and walking in the yard and waving at him. He felt so stupid, but all of a sudden it didn't matter any more. Gus couldn't believe it, that right there was his Lorrie waving at him with that same pretty smile on her face and her eyes were flashing like they always did, so he pulled over and parked and got out of his old pick-up and she came to him and at the same time he was walking toward her and when they came together they clasp each others hands and just looked at each other in their eyes and then they hugged each other real tight and Gus told Lorrie just a second then he reached into his pocket and he pulled the ring out and asked her if she still wanted it and she told him that she had been wanting a ring from for 50 years, so he took her hand and slipped it on her ring finger and then he kissed it and turned her to him, then told her that he came to claim her for his own and kissed her. She cut the kiss short and whispered to Gus that her Mom might be looking out the window and that they would have plenty of time for kissing in just a little while. She looked at the ring and then she kissed it and told Gus that it was perfect and she never thought that she would see the day that she would be wearing his ring and that she had always been his and all he ever had to do was just what he had done which was to slip a ring on her finger to prove that he wanted her and she would have been with him forever, just like she had engraved, Gus & Lorrie Forever, on the Zippo lighter she had sent him from England. He told Lorrie that their lips fit so natural together just like he had remembered they had when they were on the beach in Corpus Christi 50 years ago and she told him that she noticed that right away and couldn't wait to continue that wonderful feeling of their lips together. Lorrie then lead him into her Mom's house and introduced him to her Mom. They stayed there talking with Lorrie's Mom for a while and her Mom told Gus that Lorrie's friends were always welcome at her house. Gus told her that he had met her once before when Lorrie had been High School. He told her that he had been driving by and say her and Lorrie in the front yard, so he just stopped for a couple of minutes and told them hello, but Lorrie's Mom didn't remember that. Lorrie got up and told her Mom that she was going to take Gus over her Brothers and introduce him to her Brother and his Wife, who had just been married not long before. Lorrie led Gus through the kitchen and Gus stopped her and told her that he remembered the kitchen well, because that is where he first saw her Sister and her Brother when they were little kids and he was coming out of her bedroom. Lorrie smiled and told Gus that she had planned their romantic adventure in 1962 very badly. They went out the back door across the patio and through a gate to her Brother's back yard and on to his patio where her Brother and his Wife were waiting for them. They were introduced and Lorrie's Brother offered them a beer which was accepted with pleasure. Lorrie told her Brother and his Wife that this was the man that she had told them about. They asked Gus some questions and wanted to know about the story of what had happened in 1962. Gus laughed and Lorrie told Gus not to embarrass her, so he just told her Brother that when he was little in 1962 he and Lorrie's Sister interrupted them in a rather delicate situation and if that hadn't happened then he and Lorrie would have been married, so what that amounted to was that he and his Sister were responsible for Gus and Lorrie not being together for all of those 50 years. Her Brother told Gus to please don't put that on him, because he was only four years old at the time and his Sister and him had a big fight and she made him come back home early from playing with kids down the street and he was very mad at her at the time and he told Gus that, heck fire, he didn't even remember it. Gus told her Brother not to worry, because he held no bad feelings and that that happened a long time ago, and the main thing now was that he and Lorrie were back together for good. When Gus told them this everyone held out their beer for the Texas salute, clicking of beer bottles then a drink which meant that everything was good. After the Texas salute Gus kissed Lorrie and then he kissed her again and all of a sudden they were so engulfed with each other kissing, that they lost all reality of anything else. It was just them again on the beach in Corpus Christi and they were 16 and 19 years old again. They had no recollection of how much time that they stood there kissing, but when they took a break Gus told Lorrie that her kisses were exactly the same as they were in 1962 at Corpus and Lorrie told Gus that it was him not her, because she was just kissing him back and that yes, it was the same as Corpus Christi and it took her breath away and it did the same thing to her that it had done 50 years ago and she told Gus that she never thought that he would be kissing her ever again. Then they looked around and they were standing there all by themselves, because her Brother and his Wife had gone into their house. Lorrie looked at Gus and laughed and told him that they must have embarrassed her Brother and his Wife, and then she added that this is the most wonderful experience. She told Gus that it was like they had never been apart for 50 years, because he came back to the same house that he had left her at 50 years ago and met her in the yard and gave her a kiss and the kisses were just like they had been with their lips matching perfectly and their conversation flowing like nothing had happened. Lorrie told Gus that it all almost seemed like a beautiful dream. They went into her Brother's house and sat and talked to them and drank a couple of more beers each then Gus told them that he really needed to go over to Skeeters and unload his luggage and visit with them for a while. He asked Lorrie if she would go with him some place for dinner and she said that she would love to go with him to the Dairy Queen like they would have done if they had been together when she was in High School. She told him that she wanted to do all the things that they didn't do 50 years ago, so she could have those experiences with him. Gus left her and went to Skeeters house and got everything arranged in the room they had given him to stay. He sat with them and talked about the land that Skeeter wanted to development into a RV Park and Gus was getting the idea that Skeeters wife didn't want him to spend the money it was going to take to do the development. Gus had known both of them for a long time, so he could tell the tension between them on that subject, but he said nothing and just went along with the conversation. Skeeter wanted them to go to Port Alto the next morning and spend the day down there looking things over, but Gus told him that it would be fine, but he wanted to go and visit someone that he hadn't seen in 50 years, so he wanted to be back in El Campo by around 3 pm. Gus picked up Lorrie from her Mom's house at 6:00 pm and they went to the Dairy Queen. Gus opened her door and Lorrie told him that she wanted them to hold hands like they would have done in High School, so the walked in and they both ordered a foot long chili-cheese dog with onions and small drink, then Gus asked Lorrie where she would like to sit and she told him to please pick it out, because she was so tired if making all the decisions in her life, that her Husband couldn't even make a decision on where to sit at a Pub or Cafe. Gus told her that this was an easy decision and he moved her toward a booth by the window that had both salt and pepper shakers on it which some were missing one or both and it was also clean. When they sat down Lorrie told Gus that this was the first time they had been together in the same vehicle together since Corpus Christi. She told him that she was so happy and that she hadn't been this happy since that evening on the beach kissing him and she meant it. Lorrie told Gus that she hoped that this time things would work out better and that he would come back to her. Gus told her not to worry that he had no ideas of disappearing this time, that he had learned his lesson the hard way. They made plans to be together the next day after Gus got back from Port Alto and to spend the night together. Lorrie was going to tell her Mom that they were going to go to Port Alto and stay with Skeeter and his Wife at their bay house. She told Gus that it was time for them to complete what she had planned for them in 1962, but she couldn't offer him her virginity any more, but if he didn't want to love on her that she would understand, but if he would just let her love on him that it would be all she would ask, because she had saved all of this love for him for 50 years and it was the love she had always wanted to give him, so please let her finally do it. Gus told Lorrie that loving on her and having her love on him wasn't a problem, because it was something that he had wanted to do for all those 50 years. Gus took Lorry back to her Mom's house, then went to Skeeters for the night. He told Skeeter of his plans with Lorrie and Skeeter gave him the combination of the lock on the front door of his bay house and told him that everything that he would need should be there. Gus picked up Lorrie the next morning and they did a little shopping for some beer and snack food along with coffee, because Gus knew that Skeeter and his Wife didn't drink coffee and Lorrie said that she loved it in the mornings. They drove to Palacious and had lunch there at a small Seafood Cafe and Lorrie got shrimp, because she said that in England they were hard to find. They then drove to Port Alto where they opened the bay house and went in to see what needed to be done. There were cleans sheets for the bed and the ice box had all sorts of food in it including some good red wine. There was a nice stereo with a good selection of country and western discs, so Lorrie chose some and Gus opened a Lone Star long neck beer for Lorrie which was her beer when she was in Texas and a dark Mexican beer for himself and they sat beside each other on a small couch with some snacks that Lorrie had fixed and sipped their beer, snacked, kissed and talked and talked and talked. They were not in any hurry, because this was a very important time. This was a time that they would never forget because it was the lead up to what they should have done 50 years ago and they both knew that as older people things like this required a lot of sweetness and understanding, if everything was to be successful. They got up and danced to some of Lorrie's favorite songs and Lorrie reminded Gus that this was the first time that they had danced together and they moved together so perfectly that it was just a natural feeling experience, like they had been dancing together for their whole lives. The evening seemed to be going by fast, because between Gus and Lorrie their conversation just flowed and suddenly both of them realized that they thought so much alike about so many subjects that they could finish sentences for each other. This was such of a wonderful feeling for both of them and they both admitted that they had never had that experience with anyone else. They both needed this time together, just the two of them concentrating on each other, telling each other their worries about not being able to do the right thing and hoping that when they had finished this long anticipated experience for the first time that it would be something so wonderful that they wouldn't have words to describe it to each other. The evening finally slipped by and they suddenly realized that the time to get ready to go to bed was upon them and all of a sudden they were showing signs of being embarrassed to go to bed together, so they decided that all of the lights had to be cut off except just a slight crack in the bathroom door so the light in there would give a little glow to see enough by to go to the bathroom during the night. This they did and once they snuggled together under the bed covers, facing each other, nature and the love they had for each other took the lead and they both responded with the passion and energy that neither had ever dreamed that they possessed. This went on for hours and hours and finally both of them being exhausted and almost unable to move any more settled down and just whispered to each other between nibble kisses. Lorrie finally mustered enough strength to try to go to the bathroom she looked at the clock she was shocked to see the time and she told Gus that they had been making love for seven hours. She came back and then he went and they snuggled back together to sleep, because it was almost sunrise. The next morning they got up late and Gus put on the coffee while Lorrie showered then he showered and when he went from the bathroom to the bedroom to dress he discovered that Lorrie had brought coffee, orange juice, toast with butter and jelly to the bedroom and she was smiling at him wearing his T-shirt and her panties and she told him to put on his undershorts and come to the little table and enjoy a light breakfast and some coffee. Gus laughed and did as she suggested then kissed her and drank his orange juice before starting on the toast and coffee. Lorrie was looking at Gus as they were sipping their coffee and she was shaking her head. Gus asked her if something was wrong and Lorrie told him that nothing was wrong and that was what she was shaking her head over. She told him that she didn't want him to get the big head, but she had to tell him that she had never had an experience like what they did in the bed, nothing to even come close, ever, in her whole life, not even when she was young and somehow when she had been 16 she had known that it would be like this with him. Lorrie told him that for 25 years when her Husband would want sex with her, her body would not cooperate like a woman's body should and she thought that maybe she had gone through the change of life early and she even talked to her Doctor about it and her Doctor told her that she wasn't going through the change of life early that it was that her body just wasn't interested with sex anymore. Lorrie told Gus that she had brought some things along that would help in case that happened, but he could see that she had no problem and that it had thrilled her when her body had responded to him like she was a young woman again, she thought that it was a miracle. Gus told Lorrie that it pleased him and that he had to tell her that he was not at all confident that he could perform like a man should, because it had been years since he had. He told Lorrie that she had rejuvenated his body and taken thirty years away from it and that he had surprised himself. They looked at each other and Gus told Lorrie that when they finished their breakfast and coffee that he wanted a replay of last night and Lorrie laughed loud with that hiccup catch in her laugh that he loved so much and she told him that was wonderful and he must be trying to kill her, but she couldn't think of a more wonderful way to die. Their day together at Port Alto together seemed to end much to fast. When they were driving back to El Campo, Lorrie slid over on the seat close to Gus and she laid her head on his shoulder. She told him that she knew now that all her instincts hadn't betrayed her when she was only 16 years old. She had been right all along and somehow she knew that he was the man for her when she was so young, even before she was 16 years old. Lorrie told Gus that she had never been so compatible and satisfied in every way with any of her husbands or her lovers. Gus and Lorrie spent several more nights together during his two weeks in El Campo and Gus also visited several old friends Like Chuck and his flying friend Norve. He spent a lot of time with Skeeter studying the land he bought to develop and running through different ways to position things to make them work to the best advantage for the least expense. Skeeter asked Gus again if he would become a Partner in the RV Park and Gus told him that he would come down and work for him at what ever wage that Skeeter thought appropriate, because he was an old man now and he worked slow and some things he wouldn't be able to do, so Skeeter might think that he wasn't worth anything. Gus told him that he would do that, but that he didn't want to invest in the RV Park, he had to keep what cash he had to use in his Oil & Gas Business. During this two weeks Gus had Lorrie get her Social Security Card, study and take her tests for her Texas Drivers License and go to a Bank that he knew and she opened a Bank Account there with her Social Security Card and her Texas Drivers License. They also talked about Lorrie being buried in Gus's family burial plot and Lorrie told Gus that something like that was a huge thing to offer her and that she was going to wait for him to bring it up, because she wanted him to have a back door to back out on it. He told her that he had been serious and suggested that they go to the local Memorial Graver Marker business and she could pick out her head stone and tell the owner what she wanted engraved on it, so he could have it ready and set in place before Gus left so he could see what it looked like. He took Lorrie out to the Burial Plot late that evening and showed her where it was and showed her his that was already there and where hers would rest. She walked around and read the head stones of hie Grand Parents, his Dad and Mom and his Son with his picture on the Stone. She told Gus that she knew his Mom and remembered seeing his Dad and she wished that she could have known his Son, but she had never thought that she would be buried next to them ans yes she liked the idea and she also wanted to be there where Gus was going to be buried. The next morning they went to the Memorial business and Lorrie picked out a small stone and she went into the owners office while Gus waked around outside and she told the owner what she wanted on her Head Stone and he told her that he would have it done and in place in a couple of days, so we both could see in in place then he made her a coup of what it would look like. She walked out and showed it to Gus and he smiled and told her that it was just fine. Sure enough the Head Stone was put in place at Gus's family Grave Plot and he and Lorrie went out to see it. They both thought that it looked real nice there among all of the others and Lorrie smiled and told Gus that all of this was a dream come true for her, but that she hoped that that the death date wouldn't put there for many, many years. Gus and

Lorrie even went to one of her Brother and his Wife's B-B-Q Cook-offs before he had to leave and they had the best time together socializing with people there and some of them were people that they had both known when they were young in school, even though they were four years apart in class. Lorrie told Gus that that was just another thing that made being with him so natural and was that they had a background that was similar with even some of the same friends, which none of her other Husband's or lovers had in common with her. Lorrie hugged him and told him that these two weeks were the most wonderful and happiest times of her whole life and that she didn't know how she was going to be able to stand it when he left and she didn't have him close by to be with at short notice. She told him that the promise that they made to each other about not hurting anyone, specifically their spouses was she could tell, going to be hard to keep after being with him, but she was determined to keep it even though it would mean that she would be at a disadvantage. She told Gus that she would bide her time know and depend on God to solve their problem. Lorrie told Gus that after all it was God that had originally put them together. She told him that she was convinced that God had sent Angles down to Earth to get us together and when they had finally accomplished it, from what they could see of us at Corpus Christi they patted each other on the back for a job well done and then they went to work on the other things that God had lined up for them to do and they forgot about us. Then one day when they had a little of a break from their responsibilities one of them told the other one that they needed to go and see how that young couple that they had out together 50m years ago was doing and how many children they had, so they came back down to Earth to check on us and they were astonished that we weren't together like we should have been, so they decided to step in, even though they could see that we had wasted our lives being married to people that we shouldn't have been. They thought that we had a few years left and it was time for us to know what we missed and also for us to know what the true feeling of real love was when were together, so that is when they decided that I should get that e-mail joke from Toodie that had all of those names on it and they made it possible for your name to stick out so I couldn't miss it. They wanted to see if I would act on it and when I decided to act by calling Toodie and then when they saw that you wanted to contact me they pushed us along for a while until they were sure this time that we were going to be dedicated and united in love with each other and then they left us to discover how wonderful it was to be together in every way and here we are. Gus Looked at her and kissed her on top of her head and told her that she had done a lot of thinking on it. Lorrie told Gus that what else could it be, because not in a million years would she have noticed his name among all of those others. Gus told Lorrie told her that he certainly believe that, because he had loved her all of his life and she had loved him all her life, so what else could keep that kind of love so strong for 50 years without even knowing anything about each other, that it had to be God's work and he would treat it as such, so she would be able to depend on him and that he would never tell her a lie and he would always keep the promises he gave her. Lorrie cried and told him that she was so afraid that when he went back to his mountains that he wouldn't come back and then she would never see him again. Gus put his finger under her chin and gently lifted it and kissed her trembling, tear wet lips, then kissed her tear stained cheeks and told her that she need not be afraid that he wouldn't come back. He told her that there wasn't anything that could hold him from coming back. He had found her again after 50 years and she gave him those Corpus kisses that he never thought that he would have again and he know knew the difference between lust and true love. Gus told her that he was going to try and come back to see her before she had to go back to England and he didn't know when it would be, but he would try to give her plenty of notice before he drove back to El Campo. He told her that he didn't think that Skeeter was going to start on developing the RV Park till sometime in 2013, and then he would probably be there a lot working with him. He told her that if she kept her schedule of coming back to El Campo for good by Christmas 2012 and taking care of her Mom then she would be there permanent in 2013, so all of that was also working out to what might be God's plan and he was going to find a small RV that he could afford so he could stay in it, when they had a chance, when he was working for Skeeter. Lorrie told Gus that she thought that it was a great idea. She told Gus that she had been mailing some boxes of things from England to her Mom's house, but she had a lot more things to go through and she needed to be careful or her Husband might suspect something and then things for her could get dangerous. Gus told her that he understood and that she probably needed that much time, but that he was real concerned for her safety after she went back to England. Lorrie told him that there was no other way that there was just to much to do to get ready. The last evening that Gus and Lorrie were together before he was to leave the next morning she invited him over to her Mom's house for dinner that she was fixing and her Brother and his Wife would also be there. She asked him what he wanted and he told her that he knew that it was a lot of work, but how about fried chicken and either rice or potatoes and gravy. Lorrie laughed with that hiccup catch in her voice that started all of her good laughs and told Gus that it wouldn't be a problem and to come over at 5:00 pm so he and her Brother could sit and drink a beer before dinner was ready. Gus was on time at 5:00 pm and Lorrie met him at the front door and gave him a small, quick kiss, because she still didn't want her Mom to know what was going on between her and Gus. He went in and visited with her Mom who was sitting in her favorite chair in their living room and Lorrie brought him a beer and it wasn't just a beer it was his favorite brand. Her Brother and his Wife came in and she went into the kitchen to see how she could help Lorrie while Lorrie's Brother, Gus and her Mom visited in the living room. The dinner was delicious and Gus thanked Lorrie and her Brothers Wife for all the hard work that they did in cooking such a delicious meal and then cleaning up the kitchen while Gus and Lorrie's Brother just sat around visiting. The time came for Gus to leave, because he had to get up early to drive back to Van Horn, so Lorrie walked him to his pick-up and there she kissed him with one of those Corpus kisses. After Lorrie gave him her Corpus kiss that Gus had yearned for for fifty years, he ask her if she wanted him to stop by in the morning on his was out of town so they could say goodby and she looked up at him with sad eyes and surprised him when she told him no that she wouldn't be able to stand it. Gus asked her if she was sure and she told him no that she wasn't sure about anything, except that she had finally been with the love of her life after 50 years and she was so afraid of loosing him again. She told Gus that she might break down in the morning in front of him and that she didn't want him to have something like that on his mind with such a long trip to make. They kissed one more time then Gus got in his pick-up, started it and pulled away slowly waving and blowing her a kiss and he saw her do just like she had done when she was maybe 14 or 15 years old when she was walking around his Mom's house on the street and kissing her hand, then blowing him a kiss and waving by-by with her fingers. She hadn't changed a thing. Gus was hoping to be able to go by her Mom's house at 6:00 am and see her for the last time, but unless she would change her mind and call him, he would honor her wishes and not stop, but he had made up his mind that he was going to drive by there and honk his horn one time as a signal that he was gone. Gus went back to Skeeters house and went to bed early, at 9:00 pm, so he could get a good nights sleep before his long trip back to Van Horn, but he had a hard time going to sleep. He really didn't want to leave Lorrie, but he had no choice. His home, business and property was there in Van Horn and West Texas and he no longer owned anything in El Campo or the surrounding area except mineral rights and Notes on some of the Real Estate Lots that he had sold on time payments and the Note on his Ranch House that he also sold on time payments. His Base for everything now was Van Horn and the Counties that surrounded it and not El Campo, Danevang and the surrounding Counties. The only things that he had that were important to him in the El Campo area were his old Friends and old Business Associates, his Sons, his Family Burial Plot and Lorrie. Gus tossed and turned until he finally went to sleep. Lorrie was torturing herself by what she had said to Gus about not wanting to see him the next morning. She did want to see him, but it was true that she was afraid that she would just become a big screaming, crying mess right in front of him and she didn't want to be like that. Her Mom had questioned her about why she was sitting there so quiet with a long face. She told Lorrie that she really liked her friend Gus and she asked Lorrie if he was going to come back sometime. She told Lorrie that she had a very good time talking to him about people from the old days that he also knew and also about some of the WWII things that he remembered. She told Lorrie that he had a remarkable memory of people, places and the War years and she loved talking to him, so she hoped that he would come back to see her sometime. Lorrie told her Mom that Gus said that he was going to come back before she had to go back to England, then she told her Mom that she was tired and going to bed. Her Mom looked at her had told her that it was only 8:00 pm, but Lorrie went to bed anyway. When she got in her room she closed the door and went to her chest-of-drawers and got out a plastic bag that had a T-shirt in it. It was Gus's T-shirt that he had given her to wear that time they had made love for the first time and she had stored it in a plastic bag to preserve his smell that it still had in it. She would open the plastic bag and smell it for just a few seconds before closing it tight, when she was lonesome for Gus, but now she was going to wear it and sleep in it, so she could feel close to him. She lay in bed with her head in her pillow crying then napping, waking up looking at the clock crying then napping and this went on and off all night. Finally at 5:00 am she sat up in bed watching the clock knowing that he would be leaving her behind at 6:00 am and driving miles and miles and miles away from her, and how on earth could she stand being that far from him.

Lorrie thought that she had to get this all figured out, because she could still call him and at the end of August she was going back to England and that was even farther away, but she could still call and e-mail him, so she had better get this all worked out or she was going to be one big mess. All of a sudden she heard a horn honk and she looked at the clock and it was on 6:00 am and she knew it had to be Gus, so she threw the covers back on the bed and opened up the front door as fast as she could and ran out bare footed, in her panties and Gus's T-shirt to the end of her Mom's driveway only to see him turn the corner and his tail lights disappear while she was crying Gus I'm so sorry please forgive me. Then she sat down on the ground in the dew and put her face in her hands and sobbed and sobbed. Lorrie finally heard some cars coming down the street and decided that she had better get back into the house, because of how scantly dressed she was. When she went back in she found that she was wet on her legs and panties, because of the dew and she had grass stuck to her, so she took off Gus's T-shirt and put it back in the plastic bag then she took a shower and stayed up waiting for him to call her later. Gus was driving out of El Campo, but he was leaving a big part of his heart behind. He had reasoned with himself that although he was going to be a long ways from Lorrie they could still communicate like they had been doing for almost a year by e-mail and cell phone. True, that wasn't like being together, but their situation was very difficult. He was married and as far as he knew was going to stay married and Lorrie was married and Gus was sure that her Husband wasn't going to give her a divorce, so what options were left for them to have, not many. Well Gus thought at least they knew that each was alive and in good health for their ages and that their love was strong for each other, so anything is possible in life and they would just have to take things as they came then deal with them. He knew that Lorrie was still going to have to do a lot in England to get herself ready leave there and relocate back in El Campo, but what he was afraid of was that her abusive Husband would beat her so bad that he might disable her so bad that she would never be able to leave England. After Lorrie cleaned herself up from sitting in the grass early that morning she thought how stupid she had been for not having Gus stop on his way out of town. She could have got that last Corpus kiss from him and felt his strong warm body against hers one more time and who knows something could happen to him as far as he had to drive and then when he would come back he would be again at risk. Lorrie told herself that she would never, ever do that again. She needed all she could get of Gus and to deny herself of that was stupid, stupid, stupid. Gus pulled into the Service Station in Junction, Texas at 11:00 am, which was about ½ way to Van Horn, to fill up with gas and go to the restroom. After he had finished he opened the lunch that Skeeters Wife had made for him and he picked up his cell phone and punched in Lorrie's number 332-2637. Lorrie answered immediately and Gus told her where he was and that he wouldn't call her again till he reached Van Horn. He told her that he had driven by her Mom's house and honked his horn and he hoped that he hadn't woke her up, but he just has to do it. Lorrie told him that she had been awake and that she heard him honk, then she told him that she was so sorry that she told him not to stop on his way out of town and that she would never do that again. Lorrie told Gus that from now on he should always stop in the mornings before he left town and she would also have his lunch fixed for him to travel with. He told her he would and not to worry about what had happened that morning, but that he needed to get back on the road, because he was still a long way from Van Horn. Lorrie told him that she knew it, and she would pray for his safety and for him to call her as soon as he got to Van Horn, so she knew that he had made it safe and sound. Gus promised her that he would and they shares kisses over the phone and he drove out of Junction west toward Van Horn and the High Mountain Chihuahua Desert region of Far West Texas. Gus got back to Van Horn about 2:30 pm and he was very tired. He punched in Lorrie's number 332-2637 before he even got out of his pick-up and she answered after a few rings. Gus told her that he had made it just fine and was sitting by his office, except that he was very tired. Lorrie told Gus that she understood and that he needed to get home and rest and she knew that his Wife would be glad that he was safe back at home. She told Gus to call her the next day when he was able to and that she loved him and always would, so he should never worry about that, she just wanted him to get some rest and they could talk in the morning, but she might leave him a message on his phone during the night. She told him that she would sleep better knowing that he had made it safe and they shared kisses and hung up. Lorrie did sleep better after she talked to Gus and was sure that he was safe in Van Horn. She got up in the middle of the night to go to the bathroom, which had become a regular routine since she had gotten older, and she called Gus's number and left him a sweet message for him to listen to when he turned on his phone. The next day Gut turned on his phone when he got to his office expecting to call Lorrie and found himself listening to her sweet voice on a phone message telling him that he had finally made all of her dreams of romance and true love come true and that she would always belong to him and love him. Gus punched in her number 332-2637 and Lorrie answered then Gus told her that he enjoyed hearing her sweet voice the first thing when he turned on his phone and told her about his trip back and what he was going to be doing. They talked for a long time, because their conversations always just flowed and they always lost track of time. After they hung-up Lorrie felt so much better, because when it came to Gus she just couldn't get enough of him and when she wasn't with him, or having some contact to him she felt like her energy level was running down and she would start to become an old woman again, but when she had contact with Gus it was like a hot charge to her battery and all of a sudden she would shed 40 years of age. She knew that this was silly, but she couldn't help it, that is how Gus affected her. Lorrie wouldn't be able to e-mail Gus until she got back to England, because she didn't have a computer at her Mom's house, but she could call him and talk to him, leave him a voice mail, or text message him. They stayed in contact everyday off and on through the day and Lorrie would almost always leave Gus a message at night so he could listen to it in the morning. Gus finally had an idea of when he might be able to go back to El Campo and he punched in Lorrie's number 336-2637 to up-date her on his plans. She answered and told him that she was with her Mom at their Friends Hair Salon for her Mom's standing appointment and that she was also going to get her cut and colored while she was there. Lorrie asked Gus if he would like her to have a different hair style or hair color and Gus laughed told her that he would like to see her in a pony tail again and that black stretch body suit that she used to wear when she would walk around on the street by his Mom's house when she was in her dancing school and she told him if she put on one of those now he would think that two of her was in it. Gus laughed again and then ask her if she had time to talk and she told him that she did for just a minute and he told her that his friend Skeeter called him and wanted him to come back and help him choose the place to start the clearing of the brush to get started on the main part of the development for the RV Park, because he had secured a loan for the money. Gus told Lorrie that he wanted to make sure that when he came that the timing would be right for them to be together during that time before he told Skeeter when it would be. He told Lorrie that he would come back the middle of August for a week and that is about all the time that he would be able to spare, because there was an Oil Company that he was going to do some business with that would be taking up his time after that and also they could celebrate his birthday together while he was there. Lorrie was excited about that and told him that as far as she knew that it would be a good time and that it would be another first for them to celebrate his birthday together and that she couldn't wait to be with him again. It was just a few weeks before she was to end her Texas vacation and have to go back to England and she had hoped that he would be able to make it to El Campo before she had to leave. Gus told her that it would be only another week and a half till he saw her again and that he was going to call Skeeter to tell him when he was coming to El Campo. The way that Gus had learned about this Oil Company was that he had received a call from one of his Clients that had been sent a letter by this Oil Company wanting to Lease his mineral rights in a certain property South of Van Horn, Texas and Gus's Client wanted Gus to handle the negotiations with the Oil Company. When Gus looked up his Clients mineral interest, Gus found that it was on a piece of property that was way out of the area that any Oil Company should be interested in at that time, so he had his Client send him that letter and when he received it he called the Representative of the Oil Company to find out why they were interested in this Wild Cat Prospect so far out of the area that was considered to be the Delaware Basin, which was what most of the Oil Companies that were working in West Texas were interested in. The Representative told Gus that he was involved with an Oil Company out of Longview, Texas and they were interested in Leasing a lot of the property known as the Lobo Valley and that it was a pure Wild Cat venture. Gus told him that he was also in the Oil and Gas Business and that he was a local in Van Horn and the only Oil & Gas man in Culberson County and could he be of help to them in getting this Wild Cat venture put together. The Oil Company Representative thought about that for a minute and told Gus that it might be a good idea after all if they could come up with compensation plan that wasn't too expensive and the Representative suggested that they meet in Van Horn for a meeting to try to work things out and Gus agreed. Now that Gus had checked with Lorrie about the time he wanted to come back to El Campo and found that it was a good time he called Skeeter and told him when he would come then he called the Oil Company and told him when he would be gone to El Campo and the Oil Company Representative suggested that they meet before Gus went to El Campo, so they would know what to expect when he came back and the Representative could get his end organized while Gus was away. Gus and the Representative had their meeting and they seemed to get along fine. Gus outlined what he would do for his part and they talked about Gus's compensation and agreed on so much money paid for each acre that Gus would Lease plus a small percentage of the production across the whole Prospect which the Representative predicted would be 20,000 to 25,000 acres. When Gus went back down to El Campo he knew that he could only stay one week, because the Oil Company expected him to go to work the Monday after he got back on the Saturday before. Gus left Van Horn on Saturday morning at 6:00 am and expected to be in El Campo about 2:00 or 2:30 pm and he punched in Lorrie's number 332-2637 when he left Van Horn and he told her that he wouldn't call her until he got to Junction to fill up with gas. She told Gus that she was awake waiting for his call and couldn't wait to see him and that she had a big Corpus kiss waiting for him. Gus told her that it was just what he needed to fix all that might be wrong with him. She asked him about the Oil Company deal and he told her that he would tell her all about it when he got there. Gus asked her if she was going to stay up and drink coffee ans she told him no, because her Mom was still sleeping and if she went into the kitchen it would wake her up and that her Mom slept so badly that she didn't want to wake her before 7:30 am. Lorrie told Gus that she did have something that she needed to tell him when he got there though, but for him not to worry about, because it wouldn't really affect them. Gus drove into El Campo about the time that he had calculated to be there and he called Skeeter to tell him that he had arrived in town, but was going over to see the same Friend that he had visited the first time he had come down. Skeeter told Gus that he and his Wife were going to take him out to dinner and that he could ask his Friend to join them. Gus told Skeeter that he would mention it to her and see if she had other plans. He pulled up in front of Lorrie's Mom"s house and Lorrie came out to meet him and they walked into the house together. They visited with her Mom for a while then Lorrie ask Gus if he would like a beer and he accepted, so they walked out to the patio so they could talk in private and Lorrie gave him that Corpus kiss she had promised him. Gus told Lorrie about working with the Oil Company and the Representative was named Rush and there would also be a Land Man named Bill that would be in Van Horn doing the research at the County Clerks Office in the Court House. Lorrie told Gus that she thought that was wonderful and that what she had to tell him wasn't so wonderful, but that it wouldn't change a thing as far as they were concerned. She told him that her Husband had called her Mom's house and he told Lorrie that he had bought a plane ticket to arrive in Houston on the exactly the same day that Gus was to leave to go back to Van Horn and he was going to stay the other two weeks that she had left to be in El Campo, so he was going to fly back with her. Lorrie told Gus that she had no idea why he wanted to do this, because he hadn't been to El Campo in years and there wasn't any reason for him to do it. Gus just smiled and he told Lorrie that the reason that he was doing it was to make sure that she was going to go back to England. He told Lorrie to remember that her Husband had questioned her if she was going to come back to England and she had told him that she had bought a round trip ticket, but she didn't come right out and tell him that she was coming back. Gus also told Lorrie that maybe she had been showing herself to be too happy, unlike the way she normally acted around the house with all her singing and playing of her music. He told her that her Husband must suspect something and that she needed to be very careful around him, because he might get drunk and have one of his rages that would be brutal and maybe even kill her. Lorrie told Gus that he might be right about her Husband suspecting that she would stay in El Campo, but that she was sure that he had no idea about their relationship. Gus then ask her about going with him to meet Skeeter and his Wife and going to dinner with them. Lorrie told Gus that she would see if her Mom would be alright with what she could fix her for her dinner, which would be around 6:00 pm, because that is when she always had her dinner each day and if so then Gus could come and pick her up about 6:30 pm and she would love to finally meet Skeeter and his wife. Lorrie and Gus went into the house to talk to her Mom and she told Lorrie that would be just fine and to go ahead and have a good time. So it was all set up for Gus to pick Lorrie up at 6:30 pm and Gus told her that he would call her before he came, then he left to go to Skeeter's house. Gus took Skeeter aside and told him about Lorrie and that he had invited her to have dinner with them. Skeeter told Gus that it was fine and he would tell his Wife so she wouldn't be surprised. Gus picked Lorrie up at 6:30 pm and they met Skeeter and his Wide for dinner at a local Cafe. They all had a great time and Skeeter and his Wife enjoyed meeting Lorrie and asking her all sorts of questions about England and Europe in general, so the evening went fast and Gus took Lorrie back to her Mom's house where they sat in his pick-up like High School kids and kissed and talked for about an hour till he took her to the door and kissed her goodnight. Gus spent the next day with Lorrie then he went with Skeeter to Port Alto for the next several days where they were making plans on how best to develop the property into a RV Park and Lorrie would call Gus several times a day to see how he was doing and mainly just to tell him that she missed him and loved him and to see what time he might back to El Campo. When they got back into El Campo Gus would punch in Lorrie's number 332-2637 to see if it was a good time to come over to her Mom's house and several times Lorrie would cook dinner there for Gus and her Mom. The week went real fast and it was the last evening that Gus would be there, so Lorrie cooked them chicken fried steaks with mashed potatoes, gravy and fresh green beans and peach cobbler for desert. She told Gus that when her Husband arrived in Houston Airport that she was going to cut off her Texas cell phone and not use it until she had a chance to call him. She told Gus that he shouldn't try to call her, that she would call him and then her and her Husband would be on the same flight back to England, so everything would be back to the way it was before and she would be working everyday to get everything done, so she could leave her Husband and England for good by Christmas. Lorrie told Gus to please come by her Mom's house in the morning on his way out of El Campo and she would have him a lunch ready for his trip back to Van Horn. She told Gus that her Brother and his Wife were driving her to the Houston Airport to get her Husband and they were going to have to leave El Campo later in the morning, so she would have time to call him several times before she cut off her Texas phone. She also told him to call her phone and leave a voice message when he got back to Van Horn, so she would know that he got their safe and she would listen to it when she could find privacy to do it. Gus left her ant drove to Skeeters for the night and visited with them then went to bed and fell to sleep rather easily, but said a prayed first that Lorrie would be able to handle the emotional strain of having her Husband there with her in El Campo for the next two weeks. The next morning Gus got up on time and he told Skeeter goodby then drove over to Lorrie's Mom's house where he found Lorrie waiting for him and as he pulled up she came out in her night gown and robe. They hugged and kissed and she handed him his lunch. He put in in his pick-up and then they talked and kissed for a few minutes and she told Gus not to worry, that she would be fine and that she planned on watching herself so that she wouldn't anger her Husband on purpose,then she started crying softly and told him to be very careful, because she wanted to be with him after she left England and that this was just the beginning of their new life. Lorrie told Gus not to forget their two anniversaries of 9-5-2011 and 11-11-2011 because they needed to tell each other Happy Anniversary each month just like they were doing now and that nothing was ever going to change now that she had found and been with him again. Lorrie told Gus thyat she had always loved him and she would always love him no matter what happened that nothing could change that or take that away from her. Lorrie told him that she would stay in contact and they kisses on of those special Corpus kissed and then Gus got into his pick-up and slowly pulled away from the curb with Lorrie kissing her hand and blowing those kisses and waving her fingers goodby just like she had done as a teenager. Gus saw her watching his pick-up turn the corner as he drove out of sight. Lorrie just hung her head and walked back into her Mom's house knowing that she wasn't going to be able to go back to sleep. She was very upset, because she had just said goodby to the man she truly had always loved and that same morning she was going to have to go to Houston Airport to pick up the Husband that she was going to leave in England in just a few months when she finished completing all of her plans for a successful return to El Campo, to be re-established in her home town as a citizen and resident. Gus had helped her set up all the basic foundations for again living in El Campo, which consisted of getting a Texas Drivers License, applying for her Social Security Card and Medicare Card, her Navy Discharge Papers, her University Transcripts in England and opening her Bank Account, so she was as ready as she could be in Texas for the eventual transfer of all her money that she had in Savings in her Bank in England. He had advised her and had helped her do all of these things and now it was totally up to her to complete what she had to do in England in a timely fashion to make it all come together without arousing any suspicion with her Husband. She was wondering what the real reason for him coming to Texas for her final two weeks in El Campo were and maybe Gus was right when he told Lorrie that her Husband wanted to make sure that she was going to return to England. He had ask her if she was going to come back to England right before she left, so maybe that was the reason. Well now there was today to deal with and she wasn't sure how that was going to go when she would see him at the Airport. Some how she was going to have to hold herself together, but she was already starting to feel sick at the stomach just thinking about it. It was for sure that her Husband was ruining her last two weeks of her El Campo vacation that had been so wonderful till this day. Lorrie was dragging her feet getting ready to go to Houston, because she hated seeing her Husband on her last two weeks in El Campo. Her Brother, his Wife and Lorrie finally set off driving to Houston with the idea of getting a bite to eat for lunch at a drive through fast food Restaurant. As they were traveling her Husband's Wife could see that Lorrie sitting in the back seat was quiet and brooding, so she decided to ask her questions about her life that she had wondered about and this would also serve the purpose of getting Lorrie talking and have her mind off her present trouble. She asked Lorrie if she would tell them about her life after High School and her time living in Florida, before she married her first Husband, if it wasn't to invasive a subject. Lorrie had never told any of her family about that period in her life, but she trusted her Brother and his Wife now, since he had gotten older. She just didn't want her Mom to ever know about whole parts of her life. She told them that she would tell them if they promised not to say anything to their Mom and they agreed. Lorrie began by telling them about the big argument with them over being caught with that boy when she was going to Wharton County Junior College and then they shipped her to Florida on a Continental Bus Line Bus to Florida to live with her Dad's Sister, her Aunt and Uncle and h had got her a job at NASA, but she got in with a group of surfers and beach bums and quit her job and went to Porto Rico with them and stayed there for a couple of months living with the older surfer between his small apartment and a Volks Wagon Hippie Bus surfing, working in a bar in San Juan, then finally getting tired of him and that life style she came back to Florida to share an apartment with two of the other girls that had been in Porto Rico with them. They had jobs at a bar that was on the main Strip and one was a waitress and the other girl was a GoGo Dancer and she told Lorrie that the Owner of the Bar was looking for another GoGo Dancer and Lorrie loved the idea, because she had always loved dancing and had been told that she was good at it, so she tried out for the job and got it. Then she had to figure what king of a dancing costume she was going to wear, and it needed to be a little sexy, so she put together a pink stretch body suit with rows of white tassels on it and some boots that had a tassel on each. She told them that she did that for a few months then the Bar went to being Topless and she didn't have the body for that, so she started to being a waitress there and then boy that she had been trouble about in Junior College had been Stationed in the Air Force in Florida and he looked her up and they started going together and got married in Florida. Lorrie decided to skip some of the more sexy parts of the story. Her Brother and his Wife were thrilled at these story's about her life that they had never known and had never suspected. They were getting close to the Houston Airport and Lorrie just couldn't stand it any longer and she lost control of herself and started crying and telling them that she didn't want to pick up her Husband and that the only thing that she wanted was to be with Gus and why did it have to be so complicated. She had tears streaming down her face messing up her make-up and her Brothers wife told him that when they got to the Airport that her and Lorrie were going to have to go to the Ladies Restroom and fix the damage settle down. They finally saw Lorrie's Husband coming out of Customs and after they retrieved his luggage and were walking to the car her Husband tried to hold her hand and she pulled away from and asked him what he was doing. He just frowned at her. Then on the way driving back to El Campo her Husband tried to kiss her and she turned her head to deflect his kiss. Then she looked out the window for most of the way back to El Campo. Lorrie never got the chance to call Gus that evening, but the next day her Brothers Wife got her out of the house with the excuse that she wanted Lorrie to help her do some shopping for a special dinner that she wanted to prepare and that is when Lorrie listened to Gus's voice message on her Texas phone and then she called him and had a nice visit with him telling him all that had happened. Gus told her to be very careful not to anger her Husband too much or he might wait till he had her back in England to take out his wrath on her. Lorrie told Gus that one good thing was that they were sleeping in the bed room that had two single beds, so at least she didn't have to sleep with him. Lorrie told him that she loved him and that she would call him when she had a chance and for him not to worry, then they shared kisses over the phone and hung up. Lorrie cut off her phone and thanked her Brothers Wife for getting her out of the house and told her that she might have to depend on her again, so she could call Gus. The next two weeks in El Campo were miserable for Lorrie, but she survived it and her and her Husband arrived back in England to find that their house was a disaster, because her Stepson had been there all by himself doing what ever he pleased and had left messes everywhere and had drunk up every drop of liquor of every kind, no matter what it was. All the mail had been just thrown on her desk in a haphazard fashion with much of it on the floor. They looked at each other and she could see that her Husband was reading her mind, but she kept her thoughts to herself, so as not to start trouble as soon as the stepped through the door of their house. Lorrie sighed and figured that she would straighten it all lot in time. Her Stepson didn't even come down from his room to greet them and Lorrie presumed that he was still sleeping even though it was the middle of the afternoon. They both drug their luggage up to their rooms and unpacked and Lorrie could hear her Husband talking to her Stepson in his room, but didn't make any attempt to ask what they were discussing. She wanted to stay out of any conflict that might stem from their discussion. Lorrie knew that from now on she would have to watch her behavior, so it wouldn't call attention to anything that might cause her Husband to become suspicious of her or to cause him to get physically brutal. Lorrie and her Husband rested for the remainder of the afternoon and Lorrie fixed sandwiches and chips for a light dinner and they went to their rooms for the night. The next morning Lorrie got up first and went directly to her office and sent Gus an e-mail telling him that she had made the flight just fine and that she would call him as soon as she had a chance and that she loved him. Lorrie fixed herself a big mug of hot tea and some toast for her breakfast and started to sort through all the mail that piled up while she was gone. Lorrie made a fast lunch and went right back to her task. She sorted it in stacks of its category and each stack it order of it's importance. She finally got an e-mail back from Gus in the middle of the afternoon and he told her that he couldn't wait to her hyer voice on the phone and that he loved her too. While she was doing this her Husband finally left the house and went into their back yard to go to his workshop and this is when Lorrie turned on her English cell phone and called Gus. Gus's phone rang and he answered it immediately hoping that it was Lorrie and sure enough it was. He was so happy to hear her voice and told her so and that he wqas already missing her so much and that he was so afraid for her safety in England. Lorrie tried to reassure him that she was being careful not to make her Husband angry. She told him about her flight and what they had found when they went into the house. She told him that after she got all of the mail and paper work taken care of that she was going to get back on sorting through things and packing the things that she wanted to mail back to El Campo and mailed off. She told him that she had several boxes in her room that were about half full that she hadn't finished before she had left for her three month vacation and it wouldn't take her to long to finish them, then she would start on some more. Gus asked her if she wasn't afraid that her husband would come into her room and find out what she was doing and Lorrie told Gus that he never came in there and for some strange reason that if he did she would just tell him that she thought it was time for her to go through her clothes and get rid of the things that she couldn't wear anymore. Lorrie thanked him for the e-mail he had sent her back and she told him that while she was still in England that they could keep corresponding on e-mail like they had always done and she would call him when she had a chance as she had done before, so they said goodby and traded kisses over the phone. September 5th, 2012 arrived and when he got into his office and turned on his computer he had an e-mail from Lorrie with HAPPY BACK TOGETHER ANNIVERSARY and I Love You on it. Then he turned on his phone and had a voice message from her that said Happy Back Together Anniversary and I love you so much. He had to smile real big, because this was the kind of romance that he loved and never had it in his life until now and he knew that Lorrie was going to spoil him with it. He sent her the same messages back and told her that she had beat him to it, but that he hadn't forgotten their Back Together Anniversary. He told Lorrie that he was beginning to get readjusted to their old way of staying in touch, but it had been hard at first because they had so much freedom when he had been down In El Campo with her. Lorrie agreed with him and told him that it wouldn't be too much longer and she would be back in El Campo for good and then they would be able to plan and have more freedom to communicate like they wanted. They talked and e-mailed everyday even when Gus was at his Ranch, because Lorrie would leave voice messages on his phone for him to listen to when he turned on and she also left him e-mails, so basically they stayed in touch off and on all day. Gus was also doing a lot of work now with that Oil Company and would soon be receiving payments for the Leases that he was buying for them and that would help offset the costs that he was planning on spending driving to El Campo to see her when she came back there from England. The weeks were going by and everything seemed to be going as planned for Lorrie in England. She was sending Gus updates on her progress mailing things back to her Mom's house in El Campo and she was asking his advice on what kind of winter clothing that she should send back there, because it had been so long since she had spent the winter on the Gulf Coast of Texas that she wasn't real sure what she would need and he told her what she might pack and send to her Mom's for her winter wardrobe. She told Gus that before she came back to El Campo she was going to have to go to her Doctor for a check-up so she would be able to get her three month supply of medicine, because she could get it so cheap in England, so there were other things to think about besides just what she was going to bring with her and then there was the thing about transferring her money from her Bank in England to her El Campo Bank and that had to be done right before she was going to leave England so her Husband wouldn't find out about it. She was going to have to go by her Bank in England to find out their procedure for that, so she didn't waist any time when she needed to get it done. They continued to stay in close contact and they made the best of things with their communication even though they were so far apart, Lorrie in England and Gus in Texas. In October Lorrie sent Gus a Happy Back Together message on the 5th, a Happy I Love You Anniversary message on the 11th and a Happy Halloween e-mail he responded back to these and he sent her a Happy Birthday message on October26th and he thought that he had never known a woman that was so attentive to the details of romance. He loved it and was thriving on it. November 5th was the same thing with her Back Together Anniversary message on her message she told Gus that her Husband was beginning to be really verbally abusive again and staying real drunk a lot for some reason, so she was being extra careful trying not to be aggravating him. Lorrie was playing her Country Music CD's and she noticed that her Husband had been drinking heavily again since he had come in from his work shop. She told him that she had made some spaghetti or dinner and she would fix him a plate for him, because she wanted to get some food in him before he got to drunk. She went into the kitchen and made him a plate and set it on the counter and he went into the kitchen and got himself another beer out of the refrigerator, then he picked up the plate of spaghetti that she had made for him and he threw it against the wall and came back into the living room and sat down next to her and started cussing her and telling her that he could make it so she would never be able to leave England to go to see her precious family again and he grabbed her arm and started squeezing it hard and she screamed and jerked free from him then started for the phone to call the Police and he doubled up his fist and told her that she would never make it to the phone. She sat down crying and he finished drinking his beer then he went up to his room and slammed the door. Lorrie stayed where she was for a while, because she was shaking so bad that she didn't want to try to get up. She finally got up and went into the kitchen and cleaned up the mess that her Husband had made and wondered how much more of this that she could take. The next morning Lorrie got up and turned on her computer and put on a pot of water to boil to make tea and then she went back into her office and read the sweet e-mail message that Gus had left her the day before when he left his office. She read it twice and was so glad for it, because she was so miserable at this moment and her arm was hurting from the night before. She then put a load of clothes in the washer drank her mug of tea and went up to her room and got dressed then came down to finish the laundry. She put the clothes into the dryer and poured herself another mug of tea. Her Husband finally came down later then usual and when he saw her he bared his teeth like a dog and growled at her with a mean look on his face then he poured himself a mug of tea and went out to his workshop. Lorrie knew that she had enough and she wasn't going to take the chance of taking another beating from him. She knew that she didn't have everything ready to leave, but she thought that she had enough, so she called her friend Jill, who had just moved into her new Studio Apartment one month earlier and it had a new phone number and Lorrie's Husband didn't know about this, so it would make a good place for her to hide until she could fly out of England for good. She told Jill what had happened and ask her to call the Landlord and tell her that Lorrie was going to rent the Guest Suite and she was going to throw things together and get over to Jill's apartment as fast as she could. She next called her next neighbor and told her what she was doing and asked her if she could take her to Jill's in Bromley and she told Lorrie that she would be more then glad to do it and that she would have her car out front waiting for her. Lorrie left the clothes dryer going and her hot mug of tea one the kitchen counter and ran up to her room and threw a few more things into two pieces of luggage that she had been slowly packing and ram back out the front door hoping to be gone before her Husband would come in the house and discover her there trying to leave, because she knew that if he caught her that she would get the beating of her life, so she had to escape immediately. Her neighbor had the car out in her driveway with the trunk open for Lorrie to put her luggage in and the motor running and Lorrie jumped in then she remembered that she hadn't taken her lap-top computer or grabbed the bag that she had always had ready that contained her extra medicine, a few bathroom items and some underwear, so she told her Neighbor to please wait a minute and she ran back in the house, so afraid that she might be caught and up the stairs to her room for the bag and on the way she picked up her lap-top computer and two very good Recipe Cookbooks that she knew that her neighbor had liked, to give to her for going Lorrie this wonderful favor. She made it out of the house and into her Neighbor's car and they took off to drive to Jill's Apartment and Lorrie then gave her Neighbor the books and she was very happy to get them. When they reached Jills she was waiting for them and Lorrie told her Neighbor how much she appreciated her doing that for her and her and her Neighbor told Lorrie that she was happy to do it and that she didn't know how she stayed with her Husband so long that she would have left him years ago and to go and never look back. Lorrie hugged her and told her that she might never see her again, but she would never forget her kindness. Jill took her to the Guest Suite and got her settled on there then Lorrie told Jill that she had a lot to do that same day real fast, because she wanted to fly out of England the next day before her Husband could locate where she was hiding. Lorrie looked at her watch and subtracted six hours from it and thought that she might be able to get Gus on the phone and tell him what was going on and also she needed him to contact her family, because she wouldn't have the time to do all of that calling, because she was going to be on a big rush to get everything done to be able to leave England the next day. She pulled her England cell phone out of her purse and punched in Gus's number and it rang several times and thank goodness Gus answered. Lorrie told him that she was on the run and she didn't have the time to explain right then and would tell him later, but she wanted him to call her family for her and keep them updated on what she was doing and she asked him if he had something to write on that she wanted to give him some phone numbers for him to call. Gus told Lorrie that he was ready and Lorrie gave him her Mom's home number, her Brother's cell phone number, her Brother's Wife's cell phone number and her Sister's cell phone number. Lorrie ask him to call each of them except her Mom and tell them what was happening and that she would call him from time to time and update him so he could call them and tell them what was happening. She told Gus that she was going to the Bank to transfer her money to the El Campo Bank and then she was going to have to buy herself a one way Air Plane ticket to Houston and when she got it she would call him and tell him when she was going to arrive in Houston, so he could call her Sister and Brother to see if one of them could pick her up. She told Gus that she would call him later after that to see which of them could be at the Houston Airport. Lorrie told Gus that she had to go and get busy and that she loved him and she would call him later. She told Gus that she had to get all of this done before her Husband caught her and that she was scared to death that he might see her in Bromley, but she couldn't help it that is where she had to go to get it all done. Gus told her that he understood and that he would pray for her safety then they shared kisses over the phone and hung up. Gus was shocked at this sudden development, but was glad that it had finally come to a head and that Lorrie had been able to run from the house with getting caught and beaten-up. He immediately started calling her family and he got each one on their phones and told them how he had their phone numbers and what Lorrie wanted him to tell them and he told them that she was going to call him from time to time and he would call them to tell them what she was doing. They seemed to be grateful and at the same time surprised at what was happening. Gus was on pin's and needle's waiting for his phone to ring to find out if Lorrie was OK. Lorrie asked Jill if she would go with her to Bromley so she could go to the Bank, to the Travel Agent to buy an Airplane Ticket and do a little shopping and they would get something to eat. Lorrie then picked up her Laptop Computer and handed it to Jill and asked her if she would have her Son take a hammer and break it up real good and then throw it into the trash, because it had a lot of information on the hard drive that she didn't want anybody including her Husband to be able to get their hands on . Jill told her that she would and they went to do all the things that Lorrie needed to do. Lorrie and Jill first went to the Bank and Lorrie was hoping that she could draw out some cash to buy the Airplane Ticket and travel money, then Wire Transfer the rest to her El Campo, Texas Bank Account and close her Bank Account there in Bromley pretty quickly and get out of the Bank before her Husband had a chance to catch her there. She went to the Service Counter there and the Service Clerk what she wanted to do and the Clerk motioned her to a desk where a Bank Vice President could help her with her business. Lorrie went there and sat down and told the lady Vice President what she wanted to do and the lady told her that she could do that for her, but Lorrie would have to fill out quite a few pages of forms to get it all going and Lorrie kept looking around her in fear, because the desk was right out in the open for all who entered the Bank to see. The lady Vice President came back with all the forms and she noticed that Lorrie was nervous and asked if something was wrong and that is when Lorrie told her that she was running away from her abusive Husband and she was terribly afraid that he might catch her at the Bank. The woman looked at Lorrie for a minute and then told Lorrie that she understood perfectly and then she told Lorrie to follow her to a private office so she could feel safer while she was filling out all the forms and also that it would take a little while to do the Wire Transfer and get the confirmation back that it had been completed, so Lorrie could have that documentation with her when she went to the Bank in Texas. This made Lorrie feel a lot more secure and she filled out the forms, the lady Vice Present brought her the cash in an envelope and a little while later she handed Lorrie the documentation that the Wire Transfer had been successful and then she took Lorrie's hand and told her to be careful, that she wished her the best of luck for the rest of her life. Lorrie gave Jill the envelope with all the cash in it, just in case her Husband caught her that he wouldn't find the money, then they went to but Lorrie's Airplane ticket to Houston, Texas. The only flight Lorrie could get was for very early the next morning, so she bought that ticket, then she found a Taxi and made an agreement with them to pick her up at Jill's Apartment at 4:00 am the next morning November the 8th. Then she paid them in advance and got her receipt, then her and Jill went shopping for just a few items for that she knew she would need for her overnight stay in the Guest Suite and the trip to freedom, safety, Gus and yes, wonderful Texas, then they had a small late dinner. After Lorrie got back to Jill's and settled some in her Guest Suite she called Gus to tell him all that she had done. Gus told Lorrie that he was so relieved to hear from her and he wrote down her arrival time, so he could call all of her family and tell them the latest news of her and to tell them the arrival time at the Houston Airport. Lorrie told Gus that she would call him back in about an hour for him to tell her to expect at the Houston Airport. Gus called Lorrie's Brother and Sister and her Sister told Gus to tell Lorrie that she would get her from the Houston Airport and not to worry. Lorrie called Gus back right on time and Gus told her that her Sister was going to be at the Airport to get her. Lorrie was so relieved, but she told Gus that she wouldn't be able to start relaxing until the airplane got over half way to the United States, because if it was less than half way and it had trouble then it would turn around and go back to England, but if over half way it would continue to the United States. Gus knew that it was getting late in England and that Lorrie had a very early time to get up which wouldn't give her much rest even if she went to sleep right away, so they told each other good-by and shared kisses and hung-up. Lorrie just dozed a little and never really went to sleep, because she was stressed out from what had happened with her Husband the night before and then in the morning again with him and the whole day had been just one stressful minute after the other trying to get everything done in a hurry and being afraid of being discovered. She thought, thank goodness for Gus to take the extra load off of her about calling her family and keeping them updated and giving her the information she needed back. She thought that she would call his cell phone and leave him a message just before she boarded her Airplane to let him know that she was safe and on her way back to Texas. She got dressed the next morning at 3:00 am and Jill helped her take her luggage down to the sidewalk in front of her Apartment to wait for the Taxi Cab and Lorrie was hoping that he would be on time, because it was real cold standing there waiting. He pulled up on time and Lorrie and Jill looked at each other and they hugged each other real tight and Lorrie thanked Jill for everything and also for being such a perfect friend for so long, then she got into the Taxi Cab and Jill waved good-by to Lorrie wondering if she would ever see her friend again. Lorrie arrived at the Airport, checked her luggage and went through the Customs Desks and confirmed her ticket then she sat in the Boarding Lounge and waited to be called to board. She was starting to feel a little weak from all the hurry, stress and very little sleep, so she pulled a couple of her cereal bars, that she always had with her for emergencies, because of her diabetes, and a bottle of water and she started munching on them. All she had before this was a mug of tea and some juice and toast at Jills. She was finally called to board and this made her feel a little better. She got settled on the Airplane and waited for it to take off, with the fear that her Husband had found out and would have the Airplane stopped and she would be drug off crying, but then she heard the Flight Attendant give the instructions and then to fasten their safety belts and she could feel the Airplane moving down the runway, then she could hear the landing gear being retracted and she could feel it climbing and climbing then turning and leveling off then the sign to remove the seat belts came on and she was on her way back to Texas and her Gus. Now all she had to do was to look for the half way sign and she would be sure that she would make it, then Lorrie put her seat back a little, closed her eyes and fell to sleep at last. Lorrie woke up later having to go to the bathroom and found that a Flight Attendant had covered her with a blanket. She went to the restroom and then came back to her seat and asked if the were half way to the United States yet and was told no that they were about an hour away from that mark. She got a pillow, inclined her seat a little more, pulled up the blanket and went back to sleep. When she awoke again they were serving a lunch and after she ate they went past the half way marker she really started to relax, so she went to the Bar and ordered her a Whiskey and water to celebrate her successful escape out of England from her abusive Husband. She almost felt like one of the feminine spies that she read so much about in the World War Two accounts of espionage behind the enemy lines and their harrowing close call escapes back into friendly lines. The Airplane landed at the Houston Airport and her Sister was waiting for her. They got her luggage and drone to her Sisters house and her Sister was wanting to hear all about what had happened.

Lorrie told her that she wanted to call Gus first and thank him for all the relay of messages that he had done. She used her Texas phone and punched in his number and he answered immediately. Gus was so relieved to hear from her and he thanked her for leaving him that message that she was boarding the Airplane. Lorrie then told Gus that she loved him and that the wanted to thank him for all that he did to keep everyone informed and that she loved him and always would love him. She told Gus that she was going to stay at her Sisters for a couple of days before they drove to El Campo and that she would call him from now on with her Texas phone and he could call her anytime he wanted to. Gus was very relieved and decided that he would let her have time with her Sister, because he knew that her Sister must have dozens of questions for Lorrie. They told each other goodby and shared kisses. Gus punched Lorrie's number 332-2637 the next morning when he got into his office. Lorrie answered her phone with a good morning my sweet Gus and Gus told her that she sounded better already and that he was glad that he could finally call her again. She told Gus that she had the best night sleep that she had in many nights and that she felt real good. She also told him that she was still carrying her England cell phone and luckily she had just paid up her account on it before she had fled England, because she expected her Husband to call her on it and try to convince her to come back to him like he had always done every time she had left him before. She told Gus that she wanted to see how long it would take him to figure out that she wasn't in England. Gus chuckled and told Lorrie that she was a mean woman and he hoped that she never got mad at him. Lorrie laughed loud, with that cute hiccup start to her laugh that Gus loved to hear from her, and told him that she just wanted to play with her Husband tell him just what she thought of the way he had treated her for so many years, because now, for once, she could really bare down on his terrible behavior for so many years, without the fear of him being able to get his hands on her to beat her and she was going to take advantage of it to rub it in on him. She told Gus that her Husband deserved it and Gus agreed with her. Gus asked her what plans that her and her Sister had made and Lorrie told him that they hadn't made any for the day, but they thought that they would drive to El Campo the next day. Gus told Lorrie that he was so glad that they were on the same time zone now and each could call the other without having to figure the time. Lorrie told Gus that she was going to have to get her another computer when she got settled in El Campo, so they could also communicate by e-mail again. She asked if it might be possible for him to come to El Campo again to see her, because she was missing him o bad and Gus told her that he was waiting for her to ask him that question, but he couldn't tell her for sure, because the winters out in Van Horn could be really hard and he never left there in the winter for fear of a bad winter storm hitting and freezing the water pipes and breaking them causing a lot of damage. She told him she understood, but if he could see his way clear that she would be waiting for him. They talked off and on all that day each one enjoying the freedom to call the other when ever they wanted. Gus was still working with the Oil Company buying Leases for them and his friend Skeeter was after him to hurry up and come back to help him with the development of his new RV Park. Gus told Skeeter that he wouldn't be able to come help him until March of 2013, because of two things. First he wanted to wait till most of the bad winter weather was about over, but still Van Horn could get severe winter weather in March, but it was unusual, and second he wanted to figure out how he was going to stay there for any length of time. Skeeter told Gus that he could stay with him and Gus told him that that was fine, but he planned on staying a month at a time and then going back to Van Horn to take of his property and business there for a month and then coming back to El Campo for another month until the winter months came then he would have to stay in Van Horn till the next March. He told Skeeter that in other words, from March till about October Gus would be able to come to El Campo to help him for every other month starting the first of March. Gus told Skeeter that he appreciated his invitation to stay at his house, but he really wanted to have his own place and he had been thinking about trying to find a small used Travel Trailer and finding place to park it in El Campo. Skeeter told Gus that he would be looking for one for him and he had a place for him to park it when Gus bought one. Gus told him that was good and they finally had a plan going. Skeeter told Gus that he had a Bulldozer pushing out brush and putting it into piles that could be burned when it all dried. Gus told Skeeter that it would really help to have all of that done before he got there in March of 2013, so they could get started right away staking everything off for the RV Park, then they hung up and Gus went back to contacting Land Owners that the Oil Company was interested in Leasing their land. Lorrie and her Sister drove to El Campo and Lorrie began trying to organize herself in a spare bedroom that had two single beds. Her Sister went back to Houston after a couple of days and Lorrie began contacting some of her old friends to tell them that she was living back in El Campo at her Mom's house and that she was going to help take care of her Mom. She called her friend Toodie, that owned the Hair Salon and told her that she would be meeting all of them for their Monday lunches from now on. She had been gone from England now for four days and her English cell phone finally rang and it was her Husband. He thought that she was in England, so it rang at an odd time there in El Campo, actually 6:00 am in the morning which made it 12:00 noon in England, so it woke her up. And she tried not to sound groggy from sleep. He was real courteous on the phone and tried to make small talk with her, but Lorrie resisted and instead she asked him what he wanted. He told her that he had been worried about her and was wondering when she was going to come back home. Lorrie told him that it was commendable that he all of a sudden was worried about her when he was about to beat her badly before she left. He told her that he didn't mean it that he had just been acting silly. Lorrie told him that he had been acting silly most of their married life then and it was so silly that she had been beaten, had a broken nose twice and had stitches from his silly behavior and that she didn't have to put up with his threatening screaming and violence any longer. He told her that they needed to meet somewhere for a lunch and talk it over. Lorrie told him that she could talk it over real nicely over the phone and she could do it without being beaten up. Her Husband asked her where she was staying and Lorrie told him that it was somewhere that was safe from him then she hung up on him. Proud of herself she decided to go ahead and get up and put on the coffee. Lorrie and Gus had been keeping up with their every month Anniversaries on the 5th and the 11th and they both enjoyed wishing each other Happy Anniversary on those dates, because they were very happy memories for them and just as Lorrie said they were the first of many happy memories that they were going to have. Lorrie's Husband was calling her twice a week now trying to get her to meet him some place to talk about their situation and Lorrie was having fun keeping the ruse going of him thinking that she was still in England. Every time he would call she would bring up another situation when he abused her either physically or verbally and she would usually tell him that she didn't have time to talk to him and maybe he should just give her a Divorce, because she didn't think she was going to come back to him. He tried crying, he tried offering to buy her new furniture, he told her that he would get her another little dog like Mitzi, that she loved so much and she always told him no and then Thanksgiving was there and it was the first Thanksgiving that Lorrie had spent back in El Campo with her family in years. Her Brothers Wife and

Lorrie were planning all sorts of great food for Thanksgiving and now Lorrie could really get in the Holiday Season mood, because she didn't have to put up with her Husband and her Stepson and she could talk to the man she had always been in love with anytime she wanted to. Lorrie called Gus and told him that her Brothers Wife told her that they were going to make a music DVD of the songs that each person that came to their Thanksgiving celebration chose and that everyone would get a copy of the DVD. Lorrie asked Gus what song would he think that he and her should choose for the DVD and Gus suggested "In The Still Of The Night". Lorrie laughed, with that hiccup beginning that Gus loved to hear so much and she told him that she knew that it would be the one that he would choose, but even though Gus and Lorrie were apart for the Holidays they stayed in constant contact with e-mails and her 332-2637 phone number. Gus was working through the Holidays on Leasing Oil & Gas acreage in the Lobo Valley and trying to figure out how he was going to help his friend Skeeter develop his new RV Park. When his Son's came out to the Ranch for hunting after Thanksgiving, Gus found out that his youngest Son was working on a small 20 foot Travel Trailer getting it ready to sell and Gus told him not to sell it to anyone until he looked at it, because it might be just the thing that he needed to stay in while he was working for Skeeter. Gus's Sons stayed their usual four days at the Ranch hunting, but they didn't see any Buck Deer to shoot, only Doe's, but they had a great time anyway and it was one of the few times that Gus got to see them. Christmas arrived and Gus sent Lorrie a book that she had wanted to read for her present, along with a sweet Christmas card and Lorrie sent him a sweet Christmas card that she wrote a long letter in telling him how much that he meant to her and how much that she appreciated everything that he had helped her with in getting settled back into being a resident of El Campo again. The sweetness of what Lorrie wrote brought tears to Gus's eyes. He had never experienced a woman writing him anything so meaningful and so loving before and it made him yearn to be with her.

New Years Eve arrived and Lorrie was going to spend it at her Brother's house. He always had a poker party for New Years Eve and Lorrie was going to be able to participate in it this year. She was also going to help her Brother's Wife prepare the dips and sandwiches for the party. Lorrie was loving the new feeling of not having to worry about her Husband getting drunk and ruining everything by threatening her or actually beating her, because she never knew what he might do, and now that threat was over and she could relax and enjoy herself. The only thing that she would like to have for New Years Eve would be to have Gus with her, so she could start the New Year of 2013 out right by giving him one of the Corpus Kisses that they both enjoyed, well maybe one day she thought. Gus told Lorrie that he would make it a point to go out with a couple of the young Oil Land men that were doing research at the Court House for another Oil & Gas Company, because they had already invited him and then he could call her on her 332-2637 number and they could exchange kisses over the phone. They both thought that this was an improvement over what they had to do before, because they were on the same time zone now even though they were 600 miles apart. It wouldn't be as good as swopping spit with Corpus Kisses, but it was an improvement. Lorrie thought that her life had certainly improved on the stress factor since she left her Husband in England and returned to El Campo, Texas, but she knew that sooner or later she was going to have to do something about finding a job to pay her expenses, because the money that she had transferred from England to her El Campo Bank wouldn't last for ever. Gus did what he told her that he was going to do and at the stroke of 12:01 he punched in 332-2637 and they wished each other a Happy New Year and traded kisses after kisses.

Gus & Lorrie—2013 New Years Day felt like a new beginning for both Gus and Lorrie. Here was a brand new year and they were together in Texas to start the year out and they could now start to make plans together for the first time in their lives. Lorrie did miss the annual New Years Day lunch that she always had with Jill and her other friends. She wondered if her Husband was going to continue to go to those New Years Day lunches. Gus's friend Skeeter called him to wish him a Happy New Year and also ask Gus when he was coming to El Campo to help him start working on developing the RV Park. Gus told him that he was planning on coming around the first of March if the winter weather let up enough and also that he was going to look at a little 20 foot Travel Trailer that he had for sale and that if it looked good then Gus would buy it from his Son and pull it to El Campo to live in while he was working for Skeeter, but he was going to have to find a place to park it that wasn't very expensive. Skeeter told Gus not to worry about that, because he would have him a place to park it for free. Gus was also still working for the Oil & Gas Company acquiring Leases in the Lobo Valley south of Van Horn. He had already told the Representative from the Oil & Gas Company that he would back and forth from El Campo to Van Horn starting in March, but that he would take his computer and a portable printer with him along with any active Lease Files that he might have to work on while he was there. The Representative told him that it would be OK to work like that. Lorrie was getting more settled in to her Mom's house in January 2013. She was rearranging the things that she had mailed from England, because she had simply not had the time to put the thought into how she wanted them arranged when she first arrived in El Campo right when the Holiday Season was about to get started. Now she could take her time to sort through through things and figure where she wanted them to be in her room. She had taken a few pictures of Gus and she was going to get them developed and buy several frames so she could have them to look at when she was in her room. There would have to be a cute one by her bed, so she could kiss it before she went to sleep and so she could kiss it when she woke up in the morning. Lorrie's Husband was still calling her at her Mom's house about three times a week and sometimes she would tell him that she was much to busy to talk to him and hang up the phone and sometimes she would berate him with more of the times that he had abused her. She always told Gus when he called her and what the conversation was about. Gus and Lorrie held no secrets from each other. Their lives were totally open to each other and for the first time for both of them they were enjoying the kind of loving, trusting relationship that both had yearned for all of their lives. They didn't feel that they had to hide things to protect themselves from the other person, in fact it was just the opposite. They felt that the more that they both knew about the other one the more secure their relationship was. This feeling was a total 180 degree turn from what their prior lives had been. How refreshing it was to be able to love each other like this and it made them feel like young people again. Lorrie was spending her time helping her Mom. She was taking her to her Doctor's appointments, doing her bills, taking her shopping, doing the laundry, exchanging the books that she had read for new ones at the Library, taking her to get her hair done at Toodie's Hair Salon and on Mondays enjoying the lunches with the Girls, one of which was Toodie. Toodie always asked about Gus now since she knew that Lorrie and Gus were a couple and she also knew that Lorrie's Mom was aware of it also. Lorrie's Mom would tell Toodie that when Gus was down that when you saw Gus you would see Lorrie beside him like they were joined at the hip. The weeks went by and the first of March arrived. Gus decided that the weather had improved enough for him to drive to his Son's house and look over the Travel Trailer and then he would go from there to El Campo for a month to help Skeeter. Lorrie and Skeeter were both impatient for him to arrive, but for different reasons. Gus liked the Travel Trailer and even though it was small it was well arranged. His Son had done a lot of renovation work on it, so it looked good on the inside and he had even repainted it on the outside. It still needed to have new faucets installed in the bathroom and the kitchen sink, but Gus told his Son that he would do that when he got it to El Campo. Gus paid him for it and they hooked it to the hitch on Gus's pick-up truck and Gus hauled it to El Campo where Skeeter met him and led him to a place that he had fixed up behind one of his Rent Houses that has access to water, sewer and electricity. Gus called his other Son that lived in Ganado and he came over to help set it up and hook up all the utilities then to help replace the old faucets with the new ones. Gus had punched in 332-2637 in his cell phone when he drone into El Campo and told Lorrie where he was going with the Travel Trailer and she drove her Mom's car over there at almost the same time that he got to where he was going to unhook from the Trailer. She was so excited that she was almost jumping up and down like a young kid. She just couldn't wait to see on the inside, because she wanted to measure the windows so she could make curtains for them and to see how much room they would have in there. She kissed Gus as soon as she saw him then she looked around and blushed when she discovered that Skeeter, his House Renters and Gus's Son were all looking at her while she had plastered that Corpus Kiss on Gus. They all started teasing her and Lorrie just smiled and told them that it wouldn't be the last kiss that they would witness if they continued to hang around. Gus helped Lorrie inside and she was thrilled to see that it had much more room inside then she thought it would have. She told Gus that she thought that when she would be at the cook stove or the sink that he wouldn't be able to get by her, but now she saw that there was plenty of room and there was even a couch against that wall that would sit three people. Lorrie had brought a tape measure, pencil and note pad with her and she had Gus help her measure the windows. She told him that she would leave him alone now so he could get his work done, because she now had her work to do also. Gus watched her go to her Mom's car and she moved like a young girl with a kind of skip in her step. As she was getting in the car she blew Gus a kiss and waved with her fingers with a big smile just like she had done more then 50 years ago. It took Gus and his Son two days to get everything done so he could move in. He had to stay with

Skeeter until all was ready. In the mean time Lorrie had made and put up the curtains, done some cleaning and her Brothers Wife and her had gone to the Resale Store and bought dishes, flat-ware, glasses, then to Wal-Mart for bedding. Lorrie was setting up house keeping at a fast rate. Gus was glad, because he had been busy with his Son on the other things and Lorrie had been working on the other things. Skeeter was also impatient and wanted Gus to hurry and get set up so he could go to Port Alto and look over what Skeeter had already had done there. Gus and Lorrie went to Wal-Mart and bought a set of cheap cook ware, along with a good cast iron skillet, a small electric coffee pot and a small crock pot, bath towels, wash cloths, bath soap and shampoo. They then went to the grocery section and bought enough groceries and spices to get things started. They went back to the Trailer and put everything up and then they sat down to drink a beer and be sweet to each other in their own little home. Lorrie told Gus that she never thought in her wildest dreams that she would be setting up house keeping with him. She told Gus that she had set up house keeping with three different Husbands and one Lover and it had never ever been so exciting. She told him that this seemed so right to her and all the other times she always held her reservations, but she felt none of that now. She kissed him and snuggled her head on his shoulder. It became time for her to go and they went out to get a hamburger for dinner, then she went to her Mom's house, because she wouldn't be able to stay in the Trailer until the weekend which was a couple of days away. She was already composing an excuse to tell her Mom why she wasn't going to be at her house for the weekend. Lorrie didn't want her Mom to know just yet that she was spending nights at Gus's Trailer. Lorrie thought to herself that she was still keeping things from her Mom like she did when she was just a young girl and wondered when she was going to be able to overcome that. Gus went to work with Skeeter and saw that he was getting ahead of himself on some of the dirt work that he was doing. Gus cautioned him about this and told him that the road he was building, that would be the main road not only to access the RV Park, but that would be the oval road for the RV's to park in their spaces, needed to be packed down tight before any hard surface material was applied to the surface and also that there would have to be trenches dug through it to install the sewer, water and electrical for the RV's, before the hard surface was applied or it would tear it up when the trenching was done. Skeeter told Gus that he had already ordered the hard surfacing to be delivered the next day and Gus told him to cancel it, until they got the road base packed down and ready. Gus punched in 332-2637 and talked to Lorrie when he was taking his lunch break and she asked him if he was going to have to work on the weekend and he told her that he already had the understanding with Skeeter that he wasn't going to work on weekends. Lorrie told him that she had plans to spend the whole weekend at the Trailer with him and she had already picked out some recipes that she wanted to cook for them, plus she had bought a small CD player and she was going to bring her music so they could listen to it. Gus thought that it was so sweet the way that Lorrie was constantly planning for them to be together in ways that they could be comfortable and content just the two of them. March was going by pretty fast for Lorrie and Gus now. When he first got to El Campo it seemed like he would be there for a long time, but the time was going by much to fast. They were both very busy with Gus working with Skeeter developing the RV Park and Lorrie taking care of her Mom, they only had the weekends to spend together and they both wanted more time together, because they got along perfectly. They each thought of the other one as an extension of themselves. The last full weekend that Gus was there Lorrie told him that she needed to go to a Dermatologist, but she wasn't going to go until he left the next weekend, because there was a place on her left cheek that felt like the one she had on her forehead when she was in England and it had been cancerous and the Doctor there removed it and she had to have Radiation on it and she didn't want to have this done while he was in El Campo. She told Gus that she could feel a small bump there and that it itched off and on just like the other one. Gus looked at it, but couldn't see anything. Lorrie told Gus that she would go after he left to go back to Van Horn, so it wouldn't disrupt their time together in case the Doctor had to cut it out. Gus had been telling Lorrie that she needed her own car and that they would go around town and look at the used car lots to see what they had and what the prices might be. He noticed that Skeeter had a used small pick truck-up parked under a tree at his house and he asked him if he wanted to sell it. Skeeter told Gus that it had been his Dad's truck and he hadn't thought about selling it, but he didn't need it. Gus told him that Lorrie needed her own transportation and maybe she would like a small pick-up truck. Skeeter didn't seem to know what he would sell truck for and Gus told him that he was going to bring Lorrie over to look at it just to see if she might like it. Gus got Lorrie over there to look at the truck and she fell in love with it and she told Gus that she never thought that she might own her very own pick-up truck like a real Texas girl should. The truck had a real big crack in the windshield, but Gus told her that it wouldn't cost much to have a new one installed. Lorrie asked him how much that Skeeter wanted for it and Gus told her that he still needed to talk to Skeeter about that. The next day when Gus and Skeeter were working at Port Alto Gus asked Skeeter what he wanted to seel the pick-up for and he couldn't make up his mind, so Gus told Skeeter that he didn't know what Skeeter was going to pay him, but he would be willing to swap the pay for the pick-up if Skeeter was willing. Skeeter smiled and agreed to do that, so when they got back to El Campo that evening Skeeter signed over the Title to the pick-up to Lorrie and the next day Gus took Lorrie to the County Tax Office to pay the tax on it and to have the Title filed in her name and Lorrie became the proud owner of her first ever pick-up truck and she told Gus that she was going to celebrate by taking him to lunch in her pick-up to the Dairy Queen for a foot long chili-cheese-dog with onions and she was going to pay for it. Lorrie's eyes were flashing and she had that big smile that Gus loved so much, so away they went to the Dairy Queen for lunch. The end of the week came and Lorrie invited Gus to come to her Mom's house for a real nice dinner that she wanted to cook for him before he left for Van Horn the next morning. She had fried chicken, mashed potatoes with good cream gravy, green beans, a garden salad, peach cobbler for dessert and Gus's favorite beer. She told him that she was going to make his travel lunch for him and that she would give it to him when he came by early in the morning to give her kiss goodby. Gus slept fitfully that night hating to leave Lorrie for a full month before he would be able to see her again, but he knew that he would be able to stay in touch with her by simply punching in 332-2637 to her phone and he would be able to hear her sweet voice. He drove over to her Mom's house while it was still dark early the next morning and Lorrie was waiting outside for him in her slippers and nightgown. They talked and had their Corpus kisses and then Lorrie handed him his lunch and put her hands on his face and looked him in his eyes and told him that he was the only man that she had ever loved and to please take care of himself and come back to her as quick as he could. Then her voice broke and he could see the rears streaming down her cheeks and Gus kissed her tear stained cheeks, then her lips and told her not to worry that he would be back to her and that she also was the only woman that he had ever loved and would ever love. They parted with a last touch of their fingers and as Gus was pulling away from her Mom's house he saw Lorrie kiss her hand and blow him a kiss and wave goodby with her fingers just like she did when she was just a young girl. The drive back to Van Horn was a hard one for Gus, because each mile was a struggle to get away from the love of his life. He punched 332-2637 three separate times to talk to Lorrie on the way back to Van Horn and then when he arrived there he punched in 332-2637 to tell her that he had arrived safely and she told Gus that he was so very far away from her and Gus told her that he was, but that he held her in his heart and would till he could hold her in his embrace again. They exchanged kisses over the phone and Gus went home and prepared himself to resume his responsibilities and take care of his properties and his business interests. The next day Gus went through his mail and payed bills, then went to his office to let the Oil Company know he was back in Van Horn, so they could direct him in what direction he needed to go first. A few days later he finally had the time to go to his Blue Quail Ranch and see what he had to do out there. While Gus was doing this Lorrie went to the Dermatologist and had the lump removed from her cheek. It left a nasty hole in her cheek that was in her left upper cheek between her nose and her eye. Lorrie looked at it in the mirror and cried, wondering what Gus was going to think about it. She called Gus and told him and Gus told her that she was worrying about the wrong thing, because nothing could ever change his total love for her and that if she had to worry about something then it should be if the lump had been cancerous. A few days later Lorrie got the results and the lump was indeed cancerous and on top of that the Dermatologist had told her to come back in, because they were going to have to remove some more of her cheek, because they hadn't taken out enough good flesh to be sure that the were able to get all of the cancer tumor. Lorrie was is in shock and was unable to call Gus because of her depression, then like he knew that something was wrong, her phone rang and it was Gus. She immediately broke out into a crying jag while trying to tell him that they were going to have to cut out more of her cheek. He finally calmed her down and told her that he knew that she didn't want that to happen, but she needed to do what they wanted, because he was stupid when it came to cancer treatment and they were the ones that were supposed to know what to do. He calmed her fears that he wouldn't love her and admonished her for not having more faith in the strength of his love for her. He told her to call him immediately after they did their surgery, so he could reassure her and she promised him that she would. The next day she called him and she was very soft spoken as she was explaining how she looked. She told him that it looked terrible and that it was going to leave a scar and a sunken place in her cheek right where he could see it all the time and she was going to look so ugly for him. Gus asked her if she would still love him and she told him that she would always love him. Then he told her that nothing else mattered, because he would always love her too and it would only be three more weeks before he would be wanting those Corpus Kisses from her again, so she had better shape up and concentrate on healing up, so he wouldn't heart her when he kissed her. This made her laugh with that wonderful hiccup sound when she started that Gus loved so much and then he knew that she would be just fine. Gus bought several more Oil & Gas Leases during that three weeks and did some maintenance at his Ranch and at the house in town. The first of May Gus was on his way back to Lorrie in El Campo and he punched in 332-2637 on his phone as soon as he got on the road at 6:00am and she answered it on the first ring. He told her that she answered it fast and she told Gus that she was sleeping with her phone on her pillow next to her ear. Gus told her that he was going to all her when he stopped in Junction for gas, because it was the half way point and that she had be ready to give him some Corpus kisses at around 2:30pm. She told him that she was ready to give him much more then kisses and they both laughed. Lorrie told Gus that she was going to do the grocery shopping right after lunch and put it all away in the Trailer before he got there and she would have something planned for their dinner and some cold beer in the icebox. Gus told her that he wanted something hot first and something cold second and they laughed together again. When Gus arrived in El Campo at the Trailer Lorrie's little pickup was right beside the Trailer and she heard him drive up and she burst out of the door and threw herself into his arms and kissed him all over his face before finally settling on his lips with one of her famous Corpus Kisses. She then helped him unload and they went into the Trailer where she opened a cold beer for him and proceeded to unpack his clothes and hang them up in the little closet and put his under cloths away in their place then she put on some good country music and opened herself a beer and sat beside him and threw her leg over his like she always did, she always told him so he wouldn't run away from her. Then she asked him what he thought of her new scar and Gus told her that he really hadn't noticed it, then he brought her closer and he kissed her new scar and her lips and told her that he considered it a new beauty mark. Later when they finished their dinner and Lorrie had cleaned up their little kitchen area they sat down with another beer and she told him how happy she had been with her little pickup. She told him that the only time that she got into her Mom's car now was to take her

Mom someplace, because her Mom couldn't get into the pickup, because of her bad hip and she did all the shopping in it because it was so easy to park and to see out of all around her. They drank a couple of more beers and then got up and danced in the very small space in the Trailer, which was mostly just moving in the same spot, but is was vary nice anyway and they both enjoyed it. Sunday morning they made coffee and sat on the side of the bed and drank it together with Lorrie's leg draped over Gus's and Lorrie called her Mom to make sure that she was alright. Then Lorrie tuned in their little radio to a Country Music Station and they listened to Christian Country Music for a while before Lorrie cooked them some breakfast. They talked constantly about every subject and every-once-in-a-while something new would come up about each ones past life that they hadn't talked about before and they would discuss it and in this way each time they were together the huge gap of 50 years was beginning to be filled in, so they were closing in all the holes in their past life quickly and bringing it up to the present, almost as if they had been together all of those 50 years, it was simply wonderful. The only thing that could have been better if if they actually had been together through those 50 years. Gus worked for Skeeter at the RV Park and the development of it was coming along fine except that there was an old lady at Port Alto that didn't like him and she was causing him trouble with the County Commissioners, so Skeeter sent Gus to their meeting and Gus straightened out everything so Skeeter could resume the development without any more trouble from her. Lorrie had forgotten all about the scar on her cheek and it had healed up nicely except for a small sunk in place and a discolored spot that Gus seemed never to notice. They went to two of her Brothers B-B-Q-cook-offs and out to eat a couple of times with friends in May, but May was over to quick for both of them and it was time for Gus to drive back to Van Horn. They had now established a pattern to how they were doing everything, so Gus and Lorrie followed the same way on his leaving as they had done in March. Leaving this time was just as hard as it was in March, but he had to go back to Van Horn. Gus just had too much there to be gone too long at time and of coarse he also had a Wife there that he was legally married to and she was a very sweet woman that did everything as she was supposed to as a wife and they got along fine without any fighting, so there was no reason for him not doing his part as a Husband should do in taking care of her and Lorrie was well aware of this. Gus had never said one thing against his wife to her and she understood exactly how everything was in this threesome. Lorrie never pressured Gus to leave his wife. All she would ever say was that she wished that they could be together all the time permanently. Gus would tell Lorrie that if they had done what God had planned for them when they were young then they would have always been together, but now only time would tell what was going to happen. Lorrie told Gus that now she would take what she could get of him and be thankful for that, but he knew that she would love to have it all. They understood each other and there was never any fighting about it, because they both knew that they had messed up back when they were 19 and 16 years old, so now this was what they had left to them and they felt that God was showing them just a sample of what they could have had all of their lives. June was a busy month for Gus with the Oil & Gas Business. His Wife flew out to Tennessee to visit her Son and Grandchildren for a couple of weeks. Lorrie and Gus stayed in close contact with their cell phones and their e-mails. Lorrie e-mailed Gus that she had been searching the Classified Section of the El Campo News Paper to see what jobs might be available. She told Gus that she needed to find some kind of employment that would give her some flexibility, so she could have the time to do things for Mom and the only thing that she had seen in the News Paper so far was job openings with a Home Health Company for Private Duty Nurses. She told Gus that she had done this type of work before when she had lived in Albuquerque, New Mexico. Gus questioned her about what would be required of her in that position and she explained what she did before, when she lived in New Mexico. Gus told Lorrie that he could see two things that might not make working for them the best choice. He told her that she had been a lot younger then and she might get put with a Patient that would need to be lifted for different reasons and did she think that she would have the strength for that and also she might have to be on duty with that Patient when her Mom needed her to drive her someplace. Lorrie told Gus that she had thought of all of those things, but she just didn't see anything else available for her to do and she needed to get some income coming into her Bank Account. Gus told Lorrie that she should maybe contact that Company to really see what they had available and in the mean time he would think about other alternatives that might be possible for her to look into. Gus hadn't thought much about Lorrie getting a job until now. He was struggling with different ideas on what might be most suited to Lorrie's situation. He knew the things that she was expected to do for her Mom and he also knew that Lorrie would have even more responsibility as time went on and her Mom got older and less able to do things for herself. Finally an idea dawned on him. He knew a few women that lived in Van Horn that were working for the Public School System in Van Horn as Substitute Teachers and they seemed to be busy most of the time teaching classes. They would never know what classes they would be teaching until they were called, but they got payed pretty good money for just taking over the class and not having to do lesson plans and all of the other things that are the responsibilities of the regular Teacher, plus she would have the option of turning down jobs on the days that she had other things to do for her Mom and all weekends would be free along with holidays and the summer vacation time. Gus knew that Lorrie had brought her Degrees from the Open University in England and that would give her a larger pay scale, because he knew that in Van Horn they got paid extra for their educational achievements and Degrees. Gus punched 332-2637 to talk to Lorrie about it, so they would be able to discuss it without the delay of e-mail and he wanted to her her sweet, sexy voice anyway. She answered after a few rings and he started out the conversation telling her how much he loved and missed her and then she was giving him kisses on the phone. She told him that she was doing laundry and that is why it took her longer then usual to answer his call. Gus asked her if she had time to talk, because he had an idea for her to think about for a job and Lorrie told him that she did have time. Gus told her his idea about Substitute Teaching and then described what he knew about the job from the women in Van Horn that were doing it there and that he was sure that it would give her the flexibility that she would need to help her Mom. Lorrie told Gus that she had never thought being a teacher, but it did sound like it might have possibilities and that she would go to the El Campo High School Administration Business Office and see what she could find out. Lorrie called Gus the next day and told him that she had signed up for the Substitute Teachers Program and she had been accepted. She told Gus that her Degrees from the Open University in England did help her some on the pay scale, that she was in the middle of the pay scale. Lorrie told Gus that she was going to have to go to an Orientation Class before she would be called to substitute teach, but that it was just a two hour class. She was going to see how things went for the first few classes that she would have to teach before she would be able to know if she could handle it. Gus told her that he thought that she was taking the right approach and that he was proud of her and was excited to find out how she was liking it. Gus's Wife got back to Van Horn from her visit in Tennessee and then their normal routine of everyday living resumed as usual. Gus made a couple of trips out to his ranch to check on things and it was time to get everything ready for his trip back down to El Campo. Skeeter called him and told him that he was going to have to move the Trailer to a different location and Gus told Skeeter that he would call Lorrie and ask her if she would go to the Trailer and fix things inside so nothing would fall and break, before Skeeter moved it. Gus punched in 332-2637 and left her a voice mail, because he knew that she was Teaching School that day and she would get back to him as soon as she could. She called him on her bathroom break and he told her what was happening and for her to call Skeeter to find out the particulars. She was upset about it, but she understood the situation and Gus left her and Skeeter to get it all sorted out, because he could do nothing from Van Horn. Lorrie called Gus and told him that all was ready with the Trailer in it's new location and she judged that it would be just in time for him to return. A couple of days later Gus was on his way driving back to El Campo and Lorrie at the first of July. When he arrived Lorrie as usual had everything ready for him and they followed their same routine which had worked wonderfully easy before. They were so comfortable around each other like they had been together for years. Skeeter had told Gus that they weren't going to work at Port Alto on Monday, so Lorrie could spend an extra night at the Trailer and then they would be able to eat lunch with the Girls at their Monday Lunch together before Lorrie had to go to her Mom's house to do things for her Mom. Lorrie told him that she really liked her Substitute Teaching job and that he had been right that it did give her the flexibility she needed and that the extra money was working out real good, because it was paying all of her personal expenses with some left over. Gus told Lorrie that he wanted to take her to Goliad to the old Spanish Missions there and that since she was very interested in Texas History that he thought that she would enjoy visiting the Fannin Battle Field and the Mission La Bahia, where Fannin and his men had been massacred during the Texas Revolution from Mexico, plus there was another real nice old Spanish Mission named Esprito de Santo close by that had some picnic tables under some trees that would make a nice place for them to have a picnic lunch before they toured that Mission. Lorrie was thrilled at the idea and wanted to do it the next weekend. This pleased Gus a lot, because he had something more also planned for the Esprito de Santo Mission that he wanted to surprise Lorrie with. The rest of the week went by quickly and Friday afternoon when Gus got to the Trailer Lorrie was already there getting things together for their evening meal and for their picnic lunch the next day. She had bought a roasted chicken and some potato salad from a grocery store in El Campo and she was cutting up the chicken so they could have some of it for their dinner and the rest for their picnic lunch the next day that she was going to make into chicken salad sandwiches and have pickles, chips, pork-n-beans, deviled eggs, bottles of cold water and a nice bottle of cold wine. She seemed so excited and she kissed Gus as hye came in and he asked her what he could do to help her and she opened him a cold beer and told him to just sit there and rest while she was finishing up and then she would join him. As she worked she told Gus that she had planned to have everything done before he got to the Trailer, but she was held at the School for a while because of a late fire drill. She finally finished and Gus told her to sit down, because he was going to get her a beer. They sat side by side and Lorrie threw her leg over Gus's as usual and they kissed and sipped their beer and talked about their day, then Lorrie asked Gus what time he wanted to leave in the morning to go to Goliad and he told her that it wasn't that far to go, so they could leave about 9:00am and have plenty of time to see everything that they wanted to see. They next morning they loaded everything in a cooler with ice, because it was going to be a very hot day and they left for their day trip to experience some of Texas history. Lorrie loved the displays at the Fannin Battle Ground and then they drove on to Goliad and the Spanish Mission La Bahia where they toured it and Lorrie bought some replica Texas Revolution Flags and then they visited the mass grave of the Texas Revolution Soldiers that were massacred. From there they went to the Spanish Mission Esprito de Santo and it was time for their picnic lunch, so Gus drove to the picnic tables under some big pecan trees and they laid out their picnic lunch banquet. By this time they were both very hungry and it was nice that they had the whole site to themselves, so they could concentrate on each other without any distractions. They devoured their meal and Gus opened the wine for them to sip on and just relax and talk about what they had seen so far and Lorrie was so excited by what she had seen, because it brought back the things that she had learned about the Texas Revolution. After they finished the wine they gathered the trash and put it in the waste cans that were at the picnic grounds then they drove to the entrance of the Mission and Gus paid the admission fee and they started their tour of the grounds, before going into the Mission Sanctuary itself. Lorrie found the restroom and Gus spotted a young couple and asked them a favor. He told them what he wanted to do and ask them if they would enter the Mission

Sanctuary about 5 minutes after he and Lorrie went in and they told him that they would be thrilled to be a part of his plan. They wandered off for a minute and Lorrie came out of the restroom and she and Gus entered the Mission Sanctuary and went down to the Alter and were observing the beautiful Religious Murals when Lorrie noticed a young couple entering the Mission Sanctuary and they were walking slowly toward Lorrie and Gus and Gus took Lorrie's hand and just before the young couple reached them he asked Lorrie if he could see the Turquoise Ring that he had given her and Lorrie had a funny question look on her face as he slipped the ring from her finger and then he looked at the young couple and asked them to step closer and would they witness what he was going to say and they told Gus that they would. Lorrie was totally confused at what was going on and Gus just proceeded by saying the Wedding Vows and then slipping the ring back on Lorrie's hand and when he looked at her there were tears running down her cheeks as she said her Wedding Vows to him, then Gus took her into his arms and kissed her soundly and the younger couple hugged both of them and Gus and Lorrie thanked them and the couple then strolled out of the Mission Sanctuary. Gus then held Lorrie, looked into her eyes, wiped the tears from her cheeks and he told her that he had planned this, because this was a House Of God and now they were Married in Gods Eyes, because they had pledged themselves to each other in front of God and the witnesses. Gus told Lorrie that the witnesses came as an accident when he saw them as Lorrie went to the restroom and it happened so easily that Gus thought that God must have provided them. They held hands and walked out of the Mission with an added strength and commitment to their union. Lorrie told Gus, as they were leaving the Spanish Mission grounds that to Marry him was the dream that she had ever since she had been a young girl and that she knew that they couldn't file any official paper work on their Marriage and that didn't bother her, because being Married in God's eyes was much more important then being Married in the Governments files. She told Gus that she had been Married three times, but this was the first time that she ever really felt Married and that this was the most beautiful Wedding that she could have ever had. They drove back to El Campo and when they got back to the Trailer Gus told her that he wished that he could carry her over the threshold into the Trailer, but the door was too small. Lorrie told him that she was too fat and it would hurt his back anyway, so they just kissed before the went in the Trailer. That evening Gus's Son and his Wife, from Ganado, came over to the Trailer to0 visit them and they drank a few beers and talked. Gus and Lorrie telling them about their visit to the Spanish Missions in Goliad and their little Wedding Ceremony, then they all went out to eat Mexican food and Gus's SoOn told Gus that he and his Wife had been talking and they wanted to invite Gus to move the Trailer to their place south of Ganado. Gus's Son told him that he had plenty of room there and he had a good place for the Trailer to hook up all the utilities and there was a laundry room right there, so he wouldn't have to keep washing his cloths at the public laundry-mat. Gus told his Son that it would be a lot of trouble to set up the Trailer and he didn't want to put him to that much trouble, but he appreciated the offer. Monday Gus and Lorrie went about their separate responsibilities, with Lorrie taking care of her Mom and Teaching School and Gus working for Skeeter. Gus,s Grandson in Ganado was raising turkeys for his 4-H project that would be auctioned off at the County Youth fair and Gus wanted to bid on them at the auction. It wouldn't be held till the first week in October and Gus didn't like this, because it would put him a little late going back to Van Horn. It made a big difference to Gus because he had so much to do in October getting all of his properties ready for the winter cold weather, that it took him a lot of time to get it all done. Gus knew that he needed to support his Grandson though, so he would just have to do the best he could when he got back to Van Horn. He told Lorrie that if he got to buy his Grandson's turkey that it would be too big for him to take back to Van Horn, so he wanted to give it to her Family for their Thanksgiving, because they always had a very big Thanksgiving dinner with a lot of Family there. Lorrie told Gus that when he came back in September that they were going to have a wedding to go to, because it looked like her Niece was getting married in September. Gus told Lorrie that September was going to be his last trip to El Campo for the year and it looked like it was going to be a busy trip. Lorrie looked at him and she had tears in her eyes as she told him that she just couldn't believe that he could leave her for so long, that it would be almost 6 months before they saw each other again. Gus could see the pain in her eyes and he knew that no matter what he would tell her that it couldn't take the place of him being with her for all of that time. The rest of July went by too quickly and Gus was once again preparing to drive back to Van Horn, so Lorrie told him to come to dinner on the Friday evening at her Mom's house, before he was to leave on Saturday morning and she would cook him a special dinner. Lorrie prepared chicken fried steak and ll the trimmings for their dinner and then they sat on her Mom's patio for a while before Gus had to leave and Lorrie told him that when he came by early the next morning she would have his travel lunch ready for him. Gus drove to her Mom's house the next morning and Lorrie was waiting outside for him and they embraced passionately knowing that it would be the last time for a month and Lorrie handed Gus his lunch and told him to be very careful traveling, then Gus went to his pickup and when he looked back Lorrie was blowing him a kiss and waving goodby in her special way using her fingers like she had always had done even as a young girl. This always gave Gus a lump in his throat and an ache in his heart, when he was leaving, but he knew that he had responsibilities back in Van Horn and they had to be taken care of also. Driving back to Van Horn Gus punched in 332-2637 several times to talk to Lorrie and when he got to Van Horn he punched in 332-2637 to tell her that he had arrived safely. She always wanted him to call her to make sure that he had arrived in Van Horn safely. During Gus's absence in August Lorrie stayed busy with her School Teaching and taking care of her Mom. She also had the added job of helping her Brother and his Wife prepare things for the wedding of her Niece, which was going to be a big celebration including a huge dinner and dance. They were making all the decorations and planning everything down to the details. Lorrie kept Gus informed with phone calls and e-mails. Gus was doing his Oil & Gas Business and contacting the property owners making the deals with them, filling out the lease forms, making sure that they were getting payed by the Oil Company and sending all the paper work to the Oil Company. He was also doing all of his usual maintenance around his properties that included the chemical spraying of weeds and grass that came up when they would get a little rain. He got a call from Skeeter that was troublesome. Skeeter tolf Gus that he needed to move the Trailer again and that he wanted to move it to Port Alto, since they were working there anyway. Gus told him that he didn't want to move it Port Alto, because the salt air down there would be hard on it and there was also the chance that a Hurricane would destroy it and also it would make it too hard for Lorrie to drive that far. Gus told Skeeter not to move it till Gus called him back. Gus then punched in 332-2637 and told Lorrie what was going on and that he had decided to call his Son in Ganado to see if his offer to move the Trailer there to his place was still open. Lorrie told Gus that it was better then going all the way to Port Alto, because it would be only 20 miles. Gus then called his Son and told him what was happening and his Son told him that he and his Wife would prepare a place for it that week and they would move it on the weekend. Gus told him that he was going to mail him some money to take care of all the expenses and if it wasn't enough that he would send him more. Gus then called Skeeter back to let him know what he had lined up, so Skeeter wouldn't try to move it. Next Gus punshed in 332-2637 and told Lorrie what he and his Son had decided and Lorrie told Gus that she would go over and prepare the Trailer for moving like she had done before. Gus told Lorrie that he was so sorry to have to put her through this again. Lorrie told him that it wasn't his fault and that maybe this would be the last time since it would be at his Son's place. When Gus drove back down there on the first of September he went to Ganado to his Son's house and there was the Trailer with Lorrie's little pickup parked beside it and she and his Son and his Wife were sitting under a tin shed roof around Gus's little lawn table sipping beer with a B-B-Q pit smoking and Country Music playing. They were smiling and Lorrie got up and helped Gus unload and put up all of his things then she opened up a cold beer for him and they went out to join his Son and his Wife at the table. Gus really liked this set-up and he looked around and saw that it was much more private with everything that he and Lorrie would need. The laundry room was right there handy and this shed roof was excellent to gather under for little parties with the music going. Lorrie said that she loved it even though it was a 20 mile drive for her. After the weekend Lorrie went back to her Mom's to take care of her and to do her School Teaching. Lorrie's Husband in England was still calling her, but not as often and most of the time he was drunk, so Lorrie would hang up on him. She kept asking him for a Divorce and he would tell her no that he wasn't going to Divorce her. Gus went back to work for Skeeter at Port Alto and they stayed in contact during the week with their phones. The middle of September they attended Lorrie's Niece's wedding and Gus got to meet the rest of Lorrie's Family, then the first week in October Gus and Lorrie attended the Youth Fair Auction and Gus bought hid Grandson's big turkey and gave it to Lorrie's Brother so he would have it for the big Thanksgiving dinner he always cooked. The auction was the very first auction that Lorrie had ever gone to and she was very attentive to all that went on there. They strolled around the livestock barn to look at all of the different animals from huge beef show steers to the rabbits. All of the animals were youth projects that were going to be sold. They also ate at the buyers B-B-Q lunch and drank a few of the free keg beer. This broke Gus's normal schedule and instead of leaving on a Saturday morning he had to leave on a Monday morning, but Lorrie had his travel lunch ready for him, but this time she and he knew that it would be almost 6 months before they would be able to see each other again. This time their parting was very, very hard and Gus stayed with Lorrie standing in front of her Mom's house much longer then usual and finally some cars were driving by with people going to work and Lorrie decided that she should go in, because she only had her slippers and robe on. She told Gus that this was much too hard for her and that it was going to take her a lot of time to understand how they could be apart so long since they had found out how wonderful it was to be together. She told him that a month was a long time to her, but she had reasoned with herself that it would pass quickly, but almost 6 months was something else and she had no idea how she was going to be able to cope with him being so far away from her for so long. Gus told Lorrie that he understood, but they both knew all along that there were going to have to be times like this even though that didn't make them any easier. They kissed for the last time and Gus walked slowly to his pickup and started it to drive away and he looked back and he saw Lorrie kiss her hand and blow him her kiss and wave with her fingers just like she always had done ever since she had been a young girl, then he drove away. On his way back to Van Horn us punched in 332-2637 several times to talk to Lorrie. When he arrived back in Van Horn he punched in 332-2637 again to let her know that he had made it safely back and to reassure her that nothing would change while he was away from her, that they would stay in touch with their e-mail and their cell phones. Gus now busied himself with getting everything on his properties ready for the cold winter months and also he still was doing his Oil & Gas Leasing. On Thanksgiving Gus punched in 332-2637 and Lorrie answered telling him that everyone was missing him for their Thanksgiving dinner and that her Mom told her to tell him that he should have been there because he had furnished their turkey and they included Gus in their prayed at the Thanksgiving dinner. Gus's Sons came out the next day for their four day deer hunt at the Ranch. When they had all left and Gus went back to Van Horn he turned on his phone to find that he had 6 voice messages from Lorrie and all of them were telling him how much she loved him and missed him and that she hoped that he was safe and that she hoped that he was having a great time with his Sons at the Ranch. He punched in 332-2637 and it only rang one time and Lorrie answered with kisses smacking over his phone. She wanted to hear all about the deer hunt time at the Ranch with his Sons and then she told him how lonely she was without him being with her. They talked for a long time catching up on things that had happened since they had talked four days before. They both stayed busy and before they knew it Christmas was upon them and Gus sent Lorrie a book that he knew that she wanted along with a Christmas card and some money to help her buy presents for her Family. Lorrie sent him lovely Christmas card designed to send to a loved one and she wrote a long sweet message in it that told him how much he meant to her and that he had saved her from the despair and thoughts of suicide that she had while she had lived in England with her Husband and that she would always love him no matter what happened in their lives and that she was sure that God had sent the Angles to reunite them after 50 long years. Gus read the card over and over and he ran his fingers over the writing so to feel the strokes that Lorrie had written with her own hands. He kissed the writing and put the card away so he could read it again sometime. New Years Eve came and Lorrie was going to her Brothers again for his New Years Eve poker party. Gus had looked up the young Lii & Gas Land-men and found a couple of them were going to be staying Van Horn for the Holidays, so he made arrangements to go with them to celebrate New Years Eve and this would give him the chance to call Lorrie several times during the evening. Gus punched in 332-2637 and told Lorrie what he was going to do and she was so glad to be able to stay in touch with him during New Years Eve. As the evening went along Lorrie would call Gus when she would take a break from the poker games and then at 12:01am on 2014 Gus punched in 332-2637 and they wished each other Happy New Year and then shared kisses over the phone.

Gus & Lorrie—2014 January was very cold in West Texas with snow and ice storms coming through the mountains and engulfing Van Horn and Gus's Ranch in a blanket of white. It was everything Gus could do to keep his water pipes from freezing and bursting through this time. The electric power went off several times and at his Ranch the electric power was off for all of January and February. The Electric Company finally got it back on just before he left to go back down to see Lorrie and work for Skeeter the first of March. It had been a hard winter and when he arrived at the Trailer in Ganado, the first of March he reminded Lorrie that this was why he had to always go back in time to get ready for winter and that he couldn't afford to leave there during the winter for fear that storms like that might happen. She told him that she understood, but that it didn't make all of that time away from him any easier. That March two of Gus's Sons and a Grandson had birthdays, so they were celebrated there by the Trailer under the tin roof of the shed with the B-B-Q pit going along with Country and Western Music playing and everyone enjoying drinking a few beers together. Lorrie had wanted to buy herself a gun, so Gus had located one that a man in Alpine, Texas had for sale and he went there and bought it for her. She was so surprised and they set up some empty beer cans for her to shoot at and of coarse all of Gus's Sons had to shoot it too. Lorrie hit the cans with almost every shot, because she hadn't forgot how to shoot from her training when she had been the Navy. Gus was so proud of her and Lorrie announced that she was truly a Texas girl now, because she had a pickup truck, boots, cowboy hat and a good pistol. Everyone agreed and this gave a little extra fun to the birthday party. Everyone now came to accept that Gus and Lorrie were a couple and they were glad to know her and be around her, because she fit in with them perfectly. The next morning when they were drinking their coffee together and talking, Lorrie told Gus that she had been thinking that they need to write a book together about their lives and how they had been together at their ages of 16 and 19 and how that should have worked, but didn't and all that they went through in their lives for 50 years till they got back together again and it was just like it should have always been. She told Gus that the book wouldn't be primarily a story of their lives, but really a story of how people can miss being with the one that is meant for them by making small mistakes and then their lives go in different directions never to come together again, so they live their lives without a real direction trying to find love from the wrong people that is never fulfilling and then they just give up or become hopeless in a sea of despair like she had been. Lorrie told Gus that the book should be written with the idea of targeting young people 15 to 22 years old and older adults and giving them some idea of what true love is, so they might use it as a guide to make decisions by. Lorrie told Gus that her idea was that if, by reading the book of her and Gus's lives and the mistakes and bad decisions they made right from the beginning, when they were searching for that special person to spend their lives with, the reader might be able to make some comparisons with what was going on in their own lives, then it might help them to know whether to follow their heart when they were young and take the chance on getting hurt and not second guessing their feelings like Gus had done, but to stick with it. Lorrie told Gus that is where they both had made their big mistake when they were 16 and 19 years old. She told Gus that he started second guessing their relationship and was thinking of all the bad things that might happen and then backed off and her mistake was that she finally gave up on him after a small amount of time, when he didn't come back to her, when she should have gone ahead and contacted him again to find out what had happened. Lorrie told Gus that when she was 12 years old, in her young heart, she had known that there was something very special about how she felt about him and that she somehow knew that he has the man for her. Lorrie then told Gus that the second group of people that can relate to the book would be the older people like us, in the age group of 50's on up that realize finally that they missed that special person that they should have been with all of their lives, for what ever reason and they know who that person is and have thought about them all of their lives and just like what happened to us, maybe it is time that they try to find that person to see if they are still alive and maybe that special person would also like to get back in touch and reignite that wonderful romance. Lorrie told Gus that they were some of the very lucky people in the world, because they had finally found the special person to love and be with for the rest of their lives and that was what everybody was looking for, but few found. Lorrie told Gus that she was convinced that if they could right a good book about their lives that it could be a source of information that people could use to compare what was going on in their own lives with what had happened in Gus and Lorries lives. She told Gus that if she had a book like that to read when she was young then he never would have gotten away from her, because she would have held onto him with both hands and defied anyone or anything to separate them. They both laughed at that statement, then Gus told Lorrie that he really believes that she would have done that and Lorrie told Gus that she damn well would have. Gus told Lorrie that she was the one that should decide what form the book should take so people would be able to easily follow the story line and not get confused when reading it and that he had no idea how to even begin something like that. Lorrie told Gus nonsense, that she had read things that he had written before and that she thought that they were real good. Gus told her that what he meant was how would you even start writing without a plan of how the separate years of their lives would fit together and flow along the story line and make any sense to the reader. Lorrie told Gus that she now understood what he was talking about, because each of their life stories could be a separate book, so how do you blend those two life stories into one book for the reader to follow. She told Gus that they would talk about that and she was sure that they could do it, because that she now believed that if they had been together when they were young they could have done anything together even building empires. Gus and Lorrie continued with their own busy lives while Gus was in the El Campo area. Gus was still working for Skeeter helping him develop his RV Park and it was making a lot of progress. Soon Skeeter would be able to start to except RV's into his Park, but there was still a lot of work to be done, because there was a total of 40 acres around the RV Park and a lot of it needed to be cleared of brush, dirt leveling done, cleaned up and mowed to make the total area more appealing. Skeeter also had the idea of making two craw-fish ponds to harvest his own craw-fish to have craw-fish boils on Holiday weekends for his RV customers and guests. Skeeter was depending on Gus for information on how to do a lot of this because had a lot of experience with dirt work and also rice growing that was needed for the craw-fish to eat. They would eat the growing rice plant and not the grain, so there was still a lot of work for Gus to do. Lorrie was still very involved with taking care of her Mom and each year her Mom needed a little more help to keep her quality of life stable. Lorrie was also Teaching School as often as she could, because she really needed the income, so she wasn't using up the savings that she had transferred from England to her El Campo Bank. She was saving that money for emergencies. Her life was a happy one now except she wished that her and Gus had more time together and also when her Husband in England would call her it would end upsetting her, because he always brought back a lot of bad memories that she would rather forget. She had a new life now and this year she was gong to be 69 years old and she was feeling better then she had felt in years. Her Doctor had already taken her off of her blood pressure medicine, because it had gone down to acceptable limits and had been stable for several months and her cholesterol level was also dropping so her Doctor was expecting her to not need that medication for very much longer. If she could get off of that then the only medication she would be taking would be her Diabetes medication. Her Doctor told Lorrie that stress was the reason for a lot of health problems in humans and her improvement could be because she had left a lot of her stress behind when she left England. The next weekend when Gus and Lorrie were in the Trailer Lorrie pulled a letter out of her purse and showed it to Gus. It was a notice that her High School Class of 1964 was going to have their 50th Class Reunion in September of 2014 and Lorrie wanted to know if Gus would go with her. Gus told her that he would be there in September, so it would work out good. Lorrie told him that she wanted to show him off to the girls that she went to school with, because some of them would probably be there that would remember when she got into trouble on the High School Band trip to Corpus Christi for staying out so late with him and she wanted them to know that it wasn't in vane that it had payed off in the end, although it took 50 years. They enjoyed their usual weekend that was mostly private and they could concentrate on each enjoying each other and talking. They were always talking, because they liked conversation with each other and also there was always something in each others past life that they needed to talk about. Gus had brought a lot of pictures with him of the Ranch and the terrain out there to show Lorrie. Lorrie loved them and she told Gus that they reminded her so much of when she lived in Albuquerque. She tolg Gus that she would like to go to his Ranch some time to watch him in his element. He asked her if she would like to come out there in the summer of 2014 and she told him that it would be a dream come true for her to stay at his Ranch with him and go hiking around looking for Indian artifacts and pretty rocks. Gus told her good, that they would plan a trip for her out there and if she liked it she could have that trip every year. Gus kept his same schedule of going down to the El Campo area for a month and working with Skeeter then back to Van Horn for a month and taking care of everything there. Summer arrived and Gus and Lorrie had planned her trip to West Texas for a stay of a couple of weeks. When Lorrie arrived they bought groceries and ice and drove out to the Ranch for a few days. After Lorrie saw the Camp House she was impressed how comfortable and accommodating a 40 foot shipping container could be when converted into a Camp House. She liked the fact of how strong it was. There was everything in it that she needed to live there and she asked Gus that if she moved out there could she live in the Camp House. He told her that she sure could and she was going to get a better idea about it after a few days. Gus showed her how everything worked, so she became familiar with the layout quickly. Gus started a fire, so they could B-B-Q some pork ribs and Lorrie was cooking some rice to make rice salad for a side dish along with pick;es, ranch style beans and stuffed jalapino peppers. Before the fire had burned down enough to cook the ribs Lorrie brought out to Gus's Cook Shed two cold beers and some stuffed jalapinos for them to snack on. They sat there looking at the fire and the mountains sipping on their cold beer and nibbling on the spicy stuffed jalapinos when Gus told Lorrie that it didn't get any better then this and Lorrie answered that he was right especially since she was with the man of her dreams in a place in the beautiful mountains that had peace. She told Gus that she had always wanted a place of peace and now she had found it, then she leaned over to him and gave him a big Corpus kiss and told him thank you for bringing her to this wonderful rugged, beautiful, mountain place with peace. Their dinner turned oug very good and then they cleaned up their dishes and sat out by the camp fire. Gus went into the Camp House to get both of them another beer and he noticed the stars were out in force, so he went over to Lorrie and told her to come with him and she told him that she didn't want to leave the camp fire. Gus told her that he wanted to show her something that would only take a minute and then she could return to her camp fore. He held her by the hand and told her to look down so she wouldn't trip because they were going in the darkness, but he had another reason for telling her that, then he lead her out away from the light and stopped and told her to look up. She did and then she gasped and told Gus that she had never seen anything like it. She felt like she was in a sea of stars and it looked like she could just keep walking out in them and become a part of them. She told Gus that she know knew how the Angles must feel when they are living in such of a beautiful place that out God had made for us. She told Gus that to just think how it would be to be able to be a Spirit and be able to sore up there with all of those beautiful stars. She looked at Gus and told him that maybe some day they could do that together after they died and their Spirits would be together there in that beautiful place with Jesus, then she told him to kiss her and kiss her real good. Gus woke up the next morning and was surprised to see some light through the window, because he seldom woke up late enough for that. He made an attempt to get up and Lorrie grabbed his arm and he told her that it was getting late, she told Gus that it was only moon light coming through the window, so he turned over and snuggled next to her. After a few minutes he opened his eyes and knew that he was facing the opposite direction that he had been before and that window was under the big car port, so he knew that there wouldn't be that kind of moon light under there and he kissed Lorrie and told her that she had fooled him and then she laughed with that hiccup sound in the beginning and she told him that she hoped that he wasn't mad at her, but it was so wonderful sleeping by him in that bed in the Camp House that she just wanted it to last a little longer before they got up. Gus told Lorrie not to worry, because he would never be able to be mad at her, because no matter what she did he knew that it was for them one way or another. Gus got up and made coffee while Lorrie was propped up in bed smiling and watching him. When it was ready she got up and they went out on the front porch and settled down in some lawn chairs to watch the birds and see what animals showed them in the cool of the morning. Lorrie spotted a couple of cotton tail rabbits and a huge jack rabbit, then with their second cup of coffee a covey of blue quail came out from the brush and were pecking around busy as could be and Gus told her that they were the inspiration for the name for his. Blue Quail Ranch. She studied them carefully, so she would be able to identify them. They weren't in any hurry, because all he really had planned for the day was to drive her around on the Ranch roads to get her familiar with the terrain and some of the Desert plants there that she wasn't acquainted with and maybe see some more wild animals. While Gus was taking Lorrie on their driving tour he pointed out some plants that that could be used in cooking and also some that could be used as medicine. He got to a large yucca that was blooming with big white flowers on it and he picked some of the waxy flower pedals and told her that they were delicious and they ate several of them. They went on the south side of the Ranch and there Lorrie saw her first prong horn antelope and she thought that it was beautiful the way it was colored and how it moved as it ran away from them. The next day Gus planned a hike to some Indian camp grounds so Lorrie could learn how to look for Indian artifacts. She learned to spot flint chips that had been flaked from rock by the Indian craftsmen to make their arrowheads and flint tools. She also found an arrowhead, but it was broken up real bad. She collected some of the chips also and then she went to looking for interesting rocks that suited her fancy. Gus was having so much fun watching Lorrie just take off with her walking stick and wander around with perfect contentment doing what she wanted to do and asking questions about things that she wasn't familiar with. She was hooping and hollering and Gus at first thought that she had seen a snake, because she was afraid of snakes, but she had found a horny toad and she hadn't seen one since she was a child and had played with them. She was so happy to know that there were still some in Texas. Lorrie told Gus that evening as they were sitting in front of the camp fire sipping on their beer that the Ranch was truly a magical place for her to be and she didn't care if she never left it. The next day Gus took Lorrie on a day trip to Fort Davis and Alpine and they visited the old Fort Davis, named after Jefferson Davis, who at the time it was built was the U.S. Secretary of War, that was built to protect the settlers in the area and the mail stages that went from San Antonio to El Paso in the 1840's, from Indian attack. In Alpine he showed her Sul Ross University and then on the way back to Van Horn they stopped by a local vineyard to sample some of their wine and to introduce her to the Owners. They spent the next couple of days in Van Horn and visited the local Museum, which Lorrie loved and they went to the old El Capitan Hotel that was built in the Spanish Colonial style and sat on their beautiful patio with the fountain splashing and the soft feel of the evening drinking cold beer and Gus introducing Lorrie to people he knew. Some of them sat for a while with them and even a couple of the young Oil & Gas Landmen that he drank beer with stopped to talk for a minute. Gus went to his office the next day to catch up on what he needed to do on his Leasing and Lorrie went with him. Lorrie looked at all the old pictures that Gus was displaying on the walls of his office, asking questions, then she watched what he was doing carefully, when he was typing Oil & Gas Lease documents. Lorrie listened to his conversations with Land Owners as he made appointments with them to meet him at a local Notary to sign the Leases, then she went with him to the Lease signing and they went to lunch afterward to eat some of the local Mexican food. During lunch Lorrie told Gus that she thought that what he was doing was very interesting and asked him if he thought that she could learn it and Gus told her that he was sure that she could and what he was really missing in his business was someone to do the research at the County Clerk's office at the Court House, because he had got to the point that he didn't like to do it anymore. Lorrie told Gus that she had done a lot of research when she was studying for her Degrees in England and that she liked it. He told her that in that case they would make a good team and he could train her to do that work. They picked up a few things at the Grocery Store for a couple of days at the ranch before Lorrie had to return to El Campo. After Lorrie left Gus spent the rest of his time in Van Horn getting everything arranged so he could go back to the El Campo area to work for Skeeter at Port Alto in July. When Gus returned to the El Campo area and went back to work for Skeeter he and Lorrie resumed their usual schedule of spending time together on the weekends and sometimes enjoying a Monday lunch together with the girl when Gus was off of work and Lorrie wasn't Teaching School. Gus left again in August to take care of his responsibilities in Van Horn and they kept in close touch with their e-mails and cell phones. September came around and Gus drove back to Ganado to stay in the Trailer while working for Skeeter and as usual Lorrie was waiting there for him with everything ready for their first weekend together again. That weekend they discussed the book that they wanted to write and talked about what should be included in it. They both knew that there were many embarrassing things about both of their lives that would be hard to make public in something like a book, but after much discussion they both came to the conclusion that if the book was to be an accurate account of their poor decisions and bad relationships then it would have to include all of the things that they would rather no one else should know, in other words it should include the good, the bad and the ugly of their lives. Lorrie told Gus that she had been trying to hide most of her life from her family for ever, because she knew that her Parents especially wouldn't have approved of how she had lived it and now she was going to expose who she really was to the whole world. She told Gus that she guessed that the old saying was true that everything catches up with you sooner or later. Gus told Lorrie that she knew that he had much to hide also, but what the hell, if the book was to portray how important it was to be with the right person, then it had to show what would happen when you were with the wrong person and also it had to show what would happen when you missed that chance and after that how everything you did went wrong. Lorrie agreed, but made a face like Oh-My-Goodness. The evening before Lorrie's Class Reunion they went by to visit one of her old Class Mate friends that was also married to an old friend of Gus. Her friend was the one that had been the Daughter of the Owner of the Service Station that Gus had worked at when he was in High School and they would come in and flirt with him. Her Husband had been fighting Cancer for several years and he didn't look very good, but he sat out on their porch and visited with Gus and Lorrie until they had to leave for the Reunion. They went to Lorrie's 50th High School Reunion and Gus found that he knew quite a few of her old Classmates and one of them was a brother to his old friend Chuck, that he always visited when he was in El Campo. Lorrie had several old girl friends stop by her table and when they realized who Gus was they talked about the trouble that Lorrie got in on the Band trip to Corpus Christi and they all told her that they were glad that she finally got him after so many years. There was a Disc Jockey playing old music from the 1950's and 1960's and no one was dancing, so Gus told Lorrie that maybe if they got up and danced that it would start other people to dance, so Lorrie went up to the Disc Jockey and asked him to play "In The Still Of The Night". When it started playing Gus asked Lorrie to dance and they were the only people on the dance floor for dancing very close when her Class Mates started clapping for them and then a few people joined them for the next song. After the Reunion they went back to the Trailer in Ganado and Lorrie told Gus that she was so proud to be with him at her 50th Class Reunion and she thanked him for going with her. Gus stayed untill the first week in October, because his Grandson was again showing a Turkey that was going to be auctioned off and Gus wanted to buy it. While they were getting dressed to go to the Youth Livestock Sale Gus noticed a bright red spot about as big as a dime and as red as a ripe strawberry in Lorrie's groin area and he called her attention to it. She was in the process of putting on her pants and told Gus that she couldn't see it. Lorrie and Gus had grown some pretty big stomach's in their old age and that made it hard to easily see things in that area, so Gus got her a mirror and she told Gus that she hadn't noticed it and that it didn't itch or hurt. He told her that she needed to go to the Doctor and find out what it was and she told him that she would go after he left to go back to Van Horn. They didn't think anything else about it and went to the Auction and again Gus bought the Turkey and gave it to Lorrie's Family for their Thanksgiving. When Gus had to,leave their parting was hard again, because they both knew that they wouldn't see each other until March of 2015. While driving back to Van Horn Gus kept in touch with Lorrie as he always did, by punching in 223-2637. Gus got busy getting his properties ready for winter and at the same time catching up on his Oil & Gas Business work in his office. Thanksgiving arrived and Lorrie called him and gave hin a description of her families Thanksgiving dinner and several of them talked to Gus on her phone and thanked him for furnishing their turkey. The next day Gus's Sons came down to the Ranch for their annual four day deer hunt. They saw a lot of does, but no bucks, but they always had a great time together anyway. When Gus was driving back into Van Horn after everyone had left, hr got to the area where he had cell phone service again and he turned on his phone and got eight voice messages from Lorrie, two for each day. He pulled over to listen to them and then he called her back. In one of her messages she told him that she had got the results from her Doctors visit and the Lab Tests. He asked what was going on and she told Gus that the red spot was a cancer tumor and that her Doctor had scheduled her for surgery in two more days. Gus asked Lorrie what the Doctor had told her and Lorrie didn't seem too worried about it and the Doctor just told Lorrie that she was going to remove the tumor and see if she had removed it all. Gus questioned Lorrie some more about it, then they went on to other subjects. Christmas was coming up real soon and Gus was already planning what he was going to send Lorrie for Christmas. He had picked out a Turquoise necklace and earrings that would match the Turquoise in the

Turquoise Ring that he had given her the first time that they had seen each other that summer in 2012, and he had it already to mail. Along with that he had selected a beautiful Romantic Christmas Card that was for a special loved one. The day came for Lorrie's surgery and Gus had not planned anything for that day, because he wanted to be available when either Lorrie or her Sister-in-law called him after the surgery was over. He had talked to Lorrie early that morning before she went in to prepared for the surgery and she sounded up beat, but a little afraid. Lorrie's Sister-in-law called Gus after Lorrie got out of the recovery room and then handed the phone to Lorrie. Lorrie told Gus that the Doctor thought that everything went well and that Lorrie was going to stay at the Hospital for a few hours to be under observation and if all was good then she could go home to her Mom's house, but she needed to return to the Doctors office the next day for a check-up. The next morning Gus punched in 332-2637 and Lorrie answered quickly and told Gus that she had a pretty good night and she had been given some good pain medicine and some antibiotics. She was getting ready to go to her Doctor's appointment and she was feeling good enough to drive herself in her little pickup. Gus was surprised that she would be able to do that and he told her to be sure to call him and let him know what the Doctor told her. Later that morning Lorrie called and told Gus that the Doctor told her that everything looked good so far and that it would take a couple of days to get the Lab. Test Results back and the Doctor would call her and have her come in for a follow-up exam and to review the results. Lorrie and Gus talked several times a day during that time waiting for the Doctor to call her and Lorrie had resumed doing almost everything that she had done before the surgery. Gus couldn't believe that Lorrie was doing so good so fast. Lorrie called Gus and told him that she had her Doctors checkup and the Doctor told her that she had got all of the cancer tumor and everything was fine so not to worry, that she could go back to doing anything she wanted to do. This was a great relief for Gus to hear and Lorrie expressed her relief also. There wasn't anymore said about the surgery and their conversation switched to Christmas and New Years. They talked on Christmas Eve and Lorrie told Gus to call her when he was able to on Christmas. Christmas Day in the afternoon Gus punched in 332-2637 and Lorrie answered thanking him so much for her lovely earrings and necklace. She told Gus that she had read his Christmas card over and over again and she thought that it was so romantic and very beautiful. They talked about the weather and what each had been doing and also about New

Years Eve. Lorrie told Gus that she was going to her Brothers again for his annual New Years Eve poker party, so they would be talking on New Years Eve. Gus told Lorrie that when it got to New Years he felt that he was on the down hill side of being away from her, because he just had January and February to go and they would see each other again on the first of March. Lorrie told Gus that it was still too long as far as she was concerned. They stayed in contact everyday until New Years Eve so both of them knew what each had planned. Lorrie had helped her Sister-in law prepare the dips and snacks for the poker party and Gus was once again going to go out with his young Landman friends. They talked a couple of times during the night and when Gus's watch showed 12:01am 2015 he punched in 332-2637 and Lorrie had been waiting for his call and she told him Happy New Year darling and they shared kisses over the phone and talked for a few minutes before telling each other goodby and promising to call later in the day.

Gus and Lorrie—New Year Day 2015 Gus punched in 332-2637 that afternoon and again wished Lorrie a Happy New Year and he asked her how she came out at the poker party. She told Gus that as usual she lost a little money, but it never amounted to much, because she never took more then $20.00 to it. He told Lorrie that he was going out to the Ranch the next day and she told him that she wished that she could go with him and that she had been thinking that she would like to experience a winter out there. They talked about the weather and then Gus told her that there would be three special things that he wanted them to do in 2015 and they were to go to some old Grave Yards where his relatives were buried, go to his High School Class 55 year Class Reunion and go to Youth Livestock Auction to buy his Grandsons project which was going to be big Roaster Roosters this year instead of Turkeys. January and February went by and Gus was on the road again driving to the El Campo area punching in 332-2637 and telling Lorrie his progress and listening to her excitement. When he arrived at the Trailer Lorrie had everything ready for him as usual and Gus told her that she had him very spoiled. Lorrie laughed with that hiccup to the start of the laugh that Gus liked so much and she told him that it was her goal in life to spoil him so no other woman would steel him from her. Gus's Son, his Wife and Gus's Grandson were also waiting there for him under the tin shed roof with the B-B-Q pit going and the Country Music playing and they were sipping on a cold beer. Everyone got up and gave Gus a big hug. Lorrie helped Gus unpack and put his cloths up and then she got him one of his favorite beers and they joined them under the tin shed roof to have a lively conversation and to tease Gus about using the cold winter weather as an excuse to stay away from them, they even conspired to play a new Country Song named "Colder Weather", that they made him listen to, to rub in their playful teasing. His Son and Daughter-in-law had planned a B-B-Q dinner for them and some of their friends were invited along with Skeeter and his Wife, so it turned to a very lively gathering that lasted longer then Gus was prepared to endure after his 8 hour drive, so by 9:00pm Lorrie suggested that they bow out and go into the Trailer for some private time together and for him to wind down before going to bed. She also wanted to talk to him about her coming back out to Van Horn again in the summer of 2015 for a vacation and also some of her ideas on the book that they were planning to write together. As they relaxed in the Trailer they could hear the Country Music playing outside, but they were by themselves and were able to totally concentrate on just each other. Gus told Lorrie that there was no reason why she couldn't come out to Van Horn in the summer for her vacation. She asked him if he could take her to Big Bend National Park and Gus told her that wouldn't be a problem and if they were going to do that then he wanted to show her other interesting that were in that area. Lorrie told Gus that she had been thinking about how to blend in each of their lives into one book so it would flow and make since to the reader and she told him that somehow their separate stories needed to be told in parallel, so the reader could make the connection to how each of them was living their life at the same exact time, but she just hadn't come to the way of doing it and maybe he could think on it to come up with a solution. Gus then changed the conversation to her health issues and asked her about exactly what her Doctor had told her and if she gave her any instructions on what was was causing the tumors. Lorrie told him that all her Doctor told her was that she had removed all of the tumor and to go ahead and live her normal life and that is all that she knew about it. Then Lorrie told Gus that there was some more good news and that her other Doctor told her that he was taking her off of her Cholesterol Medication, because her last three tests showed her within the normal limits. Her Doctor also told Lorrie that he was watching her Diabetes carefully, because it was becoming apparent that her Diabetes Tests had been showing signs of being normal, so he was giving her the lowest level of Medication to see if there was going to be any increase in her risk and if not after several good test, then he was going to terminate her Diabetes

Medication, but that would be about a year away. He told Lorrie that it looked like her health had been slowly improving since she had returned from England and it could be due to not having to deal with a very high level of stress. Gus hugged Lorrie and told her that all of that was the best news he could hear. The next week Gus went back to work for Skeeter at Port Alto and Lorrie went back to Teaching School and taking care of her Mom. Skeeters RV Park was staying full most of the time and he was seriously thing about doing an expansion. He and Gus discussed it and they selected a spot that would hole another 12 RV spaces that would be easy to add to all the established utilities that were needed for the spaces. Skeeter had Gus basically moving and leveling dirt piles and keeping everything mowed down. There was a lot of this to do, because Skeeter had been in a hurry to start taking in RV's and had ignored all of the other work that needed to be done so it would be easier to maintain the RV Park after it was fully developed. When it rained and Gus couldn't do the dirt work Skeeter had him helping with repairs on his rental property in El Campo, so Gus had work to do all the time. Gus convinced his girl Cousin to go with him and Lorrie one weekend to La Grange and Blackjack Springs, Texas to research some old family history and to locate the old Grave Yard at Balckjack Springs that had some of their old ancestors buried there. Lorrie took care of all the copying of the family history that they obtained at a Museum in La Grange and then they went to look for the Grave Yard at Blackjack Springs. The community of Blackjack Springs wasn't there anymore, but they found the Grave Yard and they tramped all over it looking for the old family graves and they finally discovered eight and Lorrie had found four of them herself. They took pictures of everything and enjoyed their day together. March soon came to an end and Gus had to go back to Van Horn to take care of his responsibilities there. He and Lorrie followed the same schedule they had used every time that he had to leave, so each knew what to expect, but that didn't make parting any easier. Gus would contact Lorrie several times driving back by punching in 332-2637 and they would discuss his progress. Lorrie was always in distress after Gus left, for a few days. It wasn't because she saw him during the week, because she rarely did, they usually only saw each other on the weekends, it was because she didn't like him being so far away from her. Lorrie thought, to herself, that it was hard to explain, but there was just something about Gus being so far out of reach, that Lorrie would have a hard time adjusting to every time he left. Gus was very busy the instant that he got back to Van Horn, with bills stacked up to pay and his Oil & Gas Business to catch up on then, there was always some maintenance to do from spraying weeds and grass when it rained to more involved repair work to do. After all he did have three different properties to take care of, so there was always something to do. He returned to the El Campo area in May and he and Lorrie continued with their regular weekend times together and some times eating lunch with the girls on Mondays, then each doing their separate jobs as usual, but keeping in touch by phone off and on all day each day that they were apart. Lorrie came out to Van Horn in the summer of 2015 for her two week vacation and Gus had everything ready for her. They spent the first few days at the Ranch where Lorrie where Lorrie absorbed the Desert sunshine and breathed the high, clean Desert Mountain air with the wonderful morning fragrance of Desert wild herbs. They left the Ranch early one morning for the Big Bend National Park trip that Lorrie wanted to do and Lorrie had made them a lunch to take with them, because Gus told her that he knew of a great place that overlooked the Rio Grand River where they could enjoy it. Gus took Lorrie on a beautiful drive that went to the old silver mining town of Shafter, then to Presidio where they visited old Fort Leaton that had been renovated by the State of Texas, then on to the Warnock Center for Desert Plants and on from there to Lahitas that had been just a dusty old Desert Town that had been turned into a Tourist Vacation spot. They stopped after that for their lunch at the Rio Grand River overlook that Gus had told her about and ate their lunch under the shade of one of the Tee Pee simulated shelters that were built by the State of Texas for this purpose and Lorrie just loved it. She took numerous pictures and kept commenting how lovely the surrounding area was and that she couldn't believe that Mexico was just across the river. From there they went to Terlingua and got a room for the night, then went to the Curio Shop for Lorrie to buy some small gifts for her friends and family and things to remember her trip with. She got all inspired by the variety of beautiful rock fragments on display and then she discovered some small replicas of Desert animals that she became interested in and she told Gus that she had an idea that would take the Desert to El Campo, so she could enjoy a small portion of it everyday when she was away from it till she could get back to the real thing. She had Gus help her pick out some of the rock and a few of the Desert animals she wanted to buy along with some small woven baskets to give away, and then before she checked out she found a bumper sticker that read VIVA TERLINGUA and she just had to have it to put on her pickup truck ahen she got back to El

Campo. They deposited all of her new loot in their room and Gus took her to an old Garve Yard there that was from the days that Terlingua was a quick silver miming town and the Graves were mostly of Mexican miners that had died there and the Graves were in the style of old Spain and Mexico with the carved Crosses and the little Christian Grottoes that held candles. The Grave Yard was mostly overgrown with cacti, tumble weeds and Desert lizards just like Gus had seen it in 1962 the same summer he had left Lorrie and he had brought his Mom on the trip to Big Bend National Park which was 53 years now. Lorrie loved it and she told him that it reminded her of old Spain in a lot of ways. She took more pictures and then Gus took her to the Starlite Theatre for an evening of fun. The Starlite Theatre had been built in the early 1900's by the owner of the mine to put on small productions for the miners benefit and enjoyment. Now it as a nice Cafe and Bar that served very good food and drinks and it was full of interesting Desert patrons that were hiding out from everything you might think of. The first time Gus had been to the Starlite Theatre was in 1982 when he had brought his then Wife and his Children out to Big Bend to show them the Desert Country that he had fallen love with in 1962. His then Wife wasn't impressed, because she was scared to death the whole time they were out there, but Lorrie thrived on it. Gus was having the time of his life watching Lorrie make the High Mountain Chihuahua Desert her own element to be in. They drank cold beer and watched the sun go down and throw different beautiful colored shades on the Mountains to the east, then they went inside and ordered themselves a nice dinner listening to a local band playing Country Music. They walked back to their room in the late evening holding hands ans Lorrie telling Gus how wonderful it was to be with him in his element and Gus told her that he had been watching her and she had also made it her element and Lorrie told Gus that she had fallen in love with it when she had been out to his Ranch the first time in 2014 and her love for the Chihuahua Desert had done nothing but grown and now it was a part of her just like it was a part of him. The next morning Gus and Lorrie got up and dressed to go find some breakfast. They found a small little stacked rock hut that had been once one of the miners shacks and a couple of enterprising women had opened a small Cafe there to serve a Mexican style breakfast and you had to sit outside at picnic tables, because there was no place inside. The food was delicious and there was a local dog that came around begging for scraps that Lorrie got a kick out of. They then took off to go to Big Bend National Park through the small town of Studdy Butte named from an old prospector that once lived there. They drove high up in the Mountains then twisted down into the Park Basin, that had once been an extinct volcano. There they visited the Park Headquarters building that had a nice display of the flora and fauna that you could expect to see there in the Park. They had a huge stuffed male Mountain Lion and Lorrie was shocked to see how big it really was. They hiked a little around the easier part of the Basin then they went to the nice Cafe there for lunch. Lorrie again took a lot of pictures and then they left the Park and went out a different way so Lorrie could see some different country. Gus drove them to Marathon where they ate their dinner at the famous Gage Hotel, but Gus took Lorrie to some small old Tourist Cabins that had been renovated, for the night and he told her that these were he and his Mom had stayed in 1962 when he first came out to the Big Bend. The next morning they went into Marathon for breakfast and then drove to Alpine and on to Van Horn. They ate lunch in Van Horn and Gus checked his e-mails to see if anything was important there then they went to the grocery store to get food supplies and ice then drove to the Blue Quail Ranch for the rest of Lorrie's vacation. They did almost all of their cooking in the Cook Shed on the B-B-Q grill and the Dutch Oven cooking pit. Lorrie made cornbread with the Dutch Ovens and Gus grilled steaks, pork chops and they even did a beer grilled chicken. They backed Irish potatoes and sweet potatoes in the coals of the grill and sat and drank cold beer watching the flames flicker and make shadows in the dark of the night while the coyote's were making their Desert music of yipping and howling like they did in the primitive times when the Indians made their home there. The year of 2015 was turning out to be a wonderful year for Gus and Lorrie. Her health problems seemed to be over and her Doctor told her that she only needed two more good Diabetes tests and he was going to take her off of her Diabetes Medication, which would mean that she wouldn't be taking any Medication of any kind for the first time in many years. Her Husband in England had quit calling her and everything in El Campo with her Mom, her job and her family was as good as could be expected and they had nothing but wonderful times to look forward to. Things were now sweet for Lorrie and Gus and all they wanted was more time together. The next day they went riding around in the old Jeep again to see what animals they might find. They drove to the south side of the Ranch first this time and saw a gray fox then a golden eagle soaring overhead. Lorrie made Gus stop so she could watch it for a while. Suddenly the eagle swooped down low, close to them, as if to grab some prey, then it came back up and over them and Lorrie got a real good look at it and she told Gus that she didn't realize that it was so big. They were driving back to survey the north side of the Ranch and they saw a large covey of blue quail crossing the road in front of them. Gus and Lorrie were enjoying the sweet smells of the Desert plants in the early morning coolness when they saw two mule deer does stand not more then 30 yards away and the deer just stood as still as statues as Gus stopped the Jeep so Lorrie could watch them and then, after a few minutes. the deer slowly walked into the brush as if they had seen enough of Gus and Lorrie. They drove down the Ranch road going through two brushy draws and then it happened so fast that it shocked both Gus and Lorrie. Not more then twenty feet in front of them a big animal leaped from one side of the road out of the brush and it bounded across the road in front of them and after three more long bounds it disappeared into the brush on the other side of the road. Gus had stopped the Jeep and they both at the same time were stretching their necks to try to follow the path of the big animal and Lorrie told Gus that it must have been a big coyote, but it had such a long tail and small ears. Gus laughed and told Lorrie that she had just seen her first real live mountain lion in it's element. Gus told her that she was really lucky to have witnessed that, because he had only seen two the whole time he had been coming to the Mountain's of the Chihuahua Desert and that there were many people that had lived out there their whole lives that had never seen one. They were so secretive in their movements that they usually saw people first and they hid themselves. Lorrie told Gus that she thought that the tail looked funny, because she thought that coyotes had bushy tails and pointed ears like a dog. They drove back to the Camp House and Lorrie decided that she wanted hot-dogs for lunch, so Gus started a camp fire and Lorrie went in to prepare some sides to go with the hot-dogs. They ate their hot-dog lunch under the Cook Shed and Lorrie decided that since this would be her last day at the Ranch before she went back to El Campo that she would make the best of it. She told Gus that she would like for them to listen to some Country Music and sip some cold beer out side, so Gus went to his Shop Building and got an electric extension cord and hooked up to the Camp House and Lorrie bought out the little CD Player and the CD's, then she went in and brought two cold beers for them and they sat in the Cook Shed in the shade listening to music and sipping beer. They would get up and dance right there on the dirt floor when an especially good song would play and of coarse Lorrie would play "In The Still Of The Night" then they would dance extra close together as if they were one person. The next morning after their coffee and a small breakfast they packed up and shut down the Camp House. Before Lorrie got in Gus's pickup truck to leave she told Gus to wait for just a minute and he watched as she walked around the whole Camp slowly looking at everything. She then got in the pickup and told Gus that she wanted to make sure that her mind took a picture of everything, because it would be a whole year before she would be able to see it again and she wanted to be able to close her eyes when she was lonesome for the Ranch and be able to see it as if she was here again, then she leaned over and kissed Gus and as they were driving away Lorrie kissed her hand and blew the Ranch a kiss and waved goodby with her fingers. Thy pulled out on the blacktop main road and Lorrie looked back one more time then she looked at Gus and smiled. That evening was Lorrie's last one in Van Horn, so they went to the El Capitan Hotel and sat on their beautiful patio and ate a light dinner and sipped a couple of beers there before gong to bed. Lorrie left the next morning to return to El Campo and Gus stayed in Van Horn to do some more Oil & Gas Leasing. Gus and Lorrie finished their summer months out with Gus's visits and the last visit in September was upon them. They would always try to make the very m0st of the September visit, because they knew that it would be months before they would see each other again and their only contact would be their e-mails and 332-2637 her phone. Gus told Skeeter that he was only going to work four days a week now, so he could eat lunch with the girls every Monday and then he and Lorrie could spend more time together at the Trailer and eat together for Monday lunch before she had to go back to Teaching School and taking care of her Mom for the rest of the week. Skeeter told Gus that it would be fine, because there really wasn't enough work right then to keep him busy until he made another expansion at the RV Park. The last weekend in September Gus tool Lorrie and his Son and Daughter-in Law from Ganado to his 55th High School Class Reunion in El Campo and introduced them to his Class. Lorrie got to see her first real boyfriend there and they had a good visit together. They had a real good time except Lorrie told Gus that the rest of his Class seemed like they had lost their zest for life, but he had retained his. Gus just smiled and told Lorrie that she was the reason for his zest for life, that she had given him a new reason to look forward to every minute of each day and she had pumped new blood into his veins. Lorrie looked into his eyes and kissed him then told him that she felt the same way and that she had never realized\, until they got back together how true love took over your life completely and that your every thought and action revolved around the one you loved and that your life no longer was yours alone, because you had become one life molded together forever. Gus stayed over till the first week in October so he could go to the Youth Livestock Auction and bid on his Grandsons Roaster Roosters. Lorrie went with him again and they had a good time and again Gus bought his Grandson's Project. He got two of the big birds and he gave them to Lorrie for her Brother to cook for their family Thanksgiving. Parting was very hard again when Gus left for Van Horn, because it was the last time they would see each other until March of 2016. Gus was now 73 years old and Lorrie was going to be 70 years old the 26th of October. They had been back together now for over four years and neither Gus or Lorrie had any idea how the rest of their lives were going to play out, but they did know that what ever it would be that it would be with them together, because not even death could completely separate them now, because they were one forever, just like the Zippo Lighter Lorrie had sent Gus for that first Christmas from England, before she had even moved back to El Campo, she had engraved on it "Gus And Lorrie Forever" and forever it would certainly be, there was no doubt about that. As Gus was driving back to Van Horn he punched in 332-2637 several times to tell Lorrie of his progress and to satisfy her that he was alright, because she always worried about him on the long trip. After Gus's return to Van Horn there was the usual catch up time with his bills and paper work, then his Oil & Gas Business had to be resumed at a fast pace, before he could even get the time to go to the Ranch to check out things there. Coming back in October always made it hard for Gus to get everything he needed to do before winter completed His first time out at at the Ranch he drove the roads that Lorrie and he had driven on her last day there and he remembered all the animals that she had been able to see and he was so glad that she was given the chance to have that experience. He was going to have to get everything ready for the winter and for his Sons to come out for the annual deer hunting season the day after Thanksgiving. He and Lorrie were keeping in close contact through their e-mails and their cell phones as usual, so they were well aware of each others activities each day. Thanksgiving arrived and Lorrie called Gus and told him that again her family appreciated his gift of the meat for their family Thanksgiving dinner and they had prayed for him and his safety through the winter and a safe return to El Campo in March. They talked about his Sons arriving the next day for their hunting time at the Ranch and how Lorrie was hating to be out of contact with Gus for the four days that he would be at the Ranch. She told him that she would leave him voice messages just like she always did and he had better call her the minute he had the chance. Gus and his Sons had a good time for the four days and once again no one saw a buck deer that they could shoot although they saw quite a few does. They left and Gus shut everything down and drained all the water lines to get the Ranch ready for the hard winter weather that was sure to come. He went to his office before going home so he could listen to all of Lorrie's voice messages and so he could call her and they could visit for a long time. Listening to Lorries voice messages she always told him that she was so lonesome to just hear his sweet voice. Then in one of her voice messages she told him that she had saved some of his voice messages that he had left her in the past and that she would re-listen to them before she would go to sleep at night, just so she could hear his voice. Gus called her and she was so glad that she sounded like she was almost in tears. Lorrie told Gus that the loneliness that she always felt when he was so far away from her for so long was compounded by not being able to be in close contact with him everyday. Now she told Gus that she thought she might be able to struggle through until he came back in March. They talked about Christmas coming up real soon and her families plans for it. Between Thanksgiving and Christmas the Oil Company that he had been working with Leasing in the Lobo Valley called him and told him to stop Leasing, that they had around 20,000 acres Leased and they was all that they wanted, so Gus's job with them was finished. He punched in 332-2637 and told Lorrie that his job with the Oil Company was finished and she told Gus that she had better news then he did. Lorrie told Gus that she had her Diabetes test and it had come back good, so her Doctor told her that she only needed one more good test and he was going to take her off of her Diabetes Medication. Gus was so happy about that and he told Lorrie that he wasn't really surprised, because her health had been improving ever since she had returned from England. Lorrie replied that she hadn't realized that staying in England with her Husband under that terrible stress for so long was causing that kind of damage to her health. She told Gus that maybe that was why she had contemplated suicide several times while she was there with him. Gus told her that those days were over with and she had only good things to look forward to in the future. Christmas came and Gus had sent Lorrie a book that she had been wanting along with a romantic Christmas Card and some money to help her buy Christmas gifts for her family. Gus received a very romantic Christmas Card from Lorrie with a sweet message written by her inside telling him how much he meant to her and that all her dreams of him, when she was just a young girl, had come true, because somehow she had known that he was the man for her and the time that they had been together had proved that her feelings of so long ago had been right and that no one but God could have brought them together at the ages of 16 and 19 and then brought them back together at the ages of 65 and 69 and given them these wonderful 4 years and 4 months together, to show both of them what they would have had, had they sealed their bond when they were young like they should have. This brought tears to Gus's eyes, because he knew that Lorrie was right about all of it. New Years Eve arrived and there were still some of the young Oil & Gas Landmen in Van Horn, for Gus to meet for some drinks for New Years Eve and Lorrie was going to her Brothers New Years Eve poker party. Lorrie would call Gus during the evening when she would take a break from the party and they would tell each other what had been happening. 12:01am 2016 finally arrived and Gus punched in 332-2637 and Lorrie answered her phone after only one ring and told Gus what kept you I have been wanting to kiss you Happy New Year for 30 seconds. They both laughed and then traded kisses over the phone. Lorrie told Gus that she was going to her Mom's now to bed to dream of them being back together in March and Gus told Lorrie that he to was going home to bed, so they told each other goodby till New Years Day when they would talk again.

Gus and Lorrie—New Years Day 2016 Gus punched in 332-2637 and Lorrie answered telling him to wait for a minute, because she had to put some corn bread in the oven to bake. They talked about what plans they had for the day and Lorrie told Gus that she hoped that some New Years they could celebrate it together and have some real contact Corpus kisses. Gus told Lorrie that he was sure that someday that New Years would come to pass. He told her that they were just two months from being together again and that he was already trying to arrange things to fall in place, so he would be able to leave Van Horn without any problems. He told her that it would be easier now that he wasn't doing any work for the Oil Company anymore, but he never knew what might turn up that he would have to deal with. As the weeks went by they both became more excited as the time got closer for Gus's return. Lorrie was going through the recipes that she cut out of magazines to see which ones that she wanted to try out on Gus and Gus was having repairs done on his old pickup that could cause him problems on such a long trip along with taking care of last minute paperwork and going to the Ranch to make sure everything was alright there and putting out rat poison and starting the motors on all his equipment there to charge the batteries while he was gone for a month. This would be the first year that they had been back together that there weren't any big events that they were to go to together. His Grandson had decided that he didn't want to raise any more animal project for Youth Fair Auction, so they wouldn't be going to that and as far as both knew there wasn't going to be any weddings or reunions to go to, so they would be able to spend more time together one on one. Gus told Lorrie that he wouldn't be working for Skeeter but four days a week now so that would give them more time together also. Lorrie was so pleased with the prospects of having more private time with Gus. Gus's long drive back down to El Campnd of January 2017. Gus punched in 332-2637 and told Lorrie what had happened and that he was going to go to El Paso on the 2nd of January for the Colonoscopy. Lorrie's voice seemed sort of raspy to him and she told him to do what ever the Doctor told him to do and that she was giving him an order on that. Gus told her that he would, then Lorrie told Gus that she was sleepy so they traded good-by kisses and hung up. Gus punched in 332-2637 on New Years Eve, but Lorrie didn't answer her phone.

Gus and Lorrie—2017 Gus punched in 332-2637 again on New Years Day 2017 and Lorrie's Sister-in-law answered her phone. Gus asked her how Lorrie was doing, and she went out in the hall to talk to Gus, because a Nurse came in to do something for Lorrie. She told Gus that Lorrie was slowly shutting down and she could only open one eye now and they suspected that the Cancer had migrated to her brain. She told Gus that Lorrie didn't even have an interest in watching TV and that she slept most of the time now. Gus told her that he would be off of the phone for a couple of days because of the Colonoscopy and then he would try to talk to Lorrie again. She went back into Lorrie's room and gave the phone to Lorrie and he told Lorrie that he had to go to El Past the next day for the Colonoscopy and he would call her to give her the results as soon as he could. Lorrie didn't say much, but she understood what he told her then they traded kisses and hung up. Gus was now afraid that Lorrie would die before he got back down to El Campo in March and he felt so helpless, but there was nothing he or anyone could do. Gus had his Colonoscopy on the 2nd of January 2017 and the Doctor told him that the results were very good, that there weren't any tumors or anything that would cause him any trouble and he had np idea what had caused the severe pain that Gus experienced. He told Gus that everything looked good and that he didn't have to have another Colonoscopy for 10 years. Gus rested the rest of the day and also the next day then he finally felt strong enough on January the 4th, so he punched in 332-2637 and Lorri's phone rang a few times before she answered and her voice sounded real hoarse, but she did talk to him for a few minutes and he told her the results and she told Gus that she was glad that nothing was wrong and that she thought that he might have a long life. The next day was the 5th, their back together Anniversary, so Gus punched in 332-2637 and a Nurse answered Lorrie's phone then handed it to Lorrie and Gus told her Happy back together Anniversary, as they had done on the 5th of every month since September 5th, 2011. Lorrie barely whispered Happy Anniversary back to him and then she told Gus that she was tired, so Gus gave her kisses, but she didn't return them and her phone went dead. Gus punched in 332-2637 every day for the next two days, but Lorrie didn't answer her phone. Finally on the third day Lorrie's Sister-in-law answered Lorrie's phone and Gus told her that he had been trying to contact Lorrie for two days without success and she told Gus that she thought that Lorrie had quite answering her phone. That was on the 8th and Gus asked her what she thought about Lorrie's condition. Her Sister-in-law told Gus that it was hard to tell, because Lorrie was sleeping most of the time and she wasn't eating anything, but she would sip a little water and the Doctor that came in to examine Lorrie told them that Lorrie could last a long time, so no-one really knew how long Lorrie had left. Gus called his Daughter-in-law as soon as he hung up from talking to Lorrie's Sister-in-law and told her what has going on with Lorrie and asked her if she could go to see Lorrie. She told Gus that she could go, but it would be a couple of days, because she had a Doctors appointment the next day then she would go on Tuesday the 10th. The next day Gus punched in 332-2637 several times during the day, but no-one answered Lorrie's phone. Gus was very impatient to learn how Lorrie was, but he had no way of finding out, so he just had to wait till his Daughter-in-law got off work the next day the 10th of January before he would find out. On the 10th Gus couldn't stand it, he just had to try to see if anyone would answer Lorrie's phone, so he punched in 332-2637 off and on during the day, with no results. His Daughter-in-law called him and told him that she was driving over to the Nursing Home then from her work out of town and she would be there about

6:30pm. His Daughter-in-law called him when she got in Lorrie's room and told him that Lorrie was sleeping and Gus told her to see if she could get Lorrie to respond to her. His Daughter-in-law talked to Lorrie and patted her hand, but Lorrie didn't respond, so then she got a cool damp wash cloth and she gently wiped Lorrie's face and hands with it, but Lorrie still didn't respond and Gus asked her if she could tell if Lorrie was moving her eyes inside of her closed eye lids and she told him that Lorrie wasn't moving her eyes at all. Gus then told his Daughter-in-law to put her phone up to Lorrie's ear so he could talk to Lorrie and she did that. Gus started talking to Lorrie and he told her that the next day was going to be their I Love You Anniversary on the 11th and they had told each other I Love You every month since November the 11th of 2011, which was the first time that they had told each other I Love You and that he had always loved her and would always love her. Then his Daughter-in law took the phone and she told Gus that Lorrie was grappling at her throat with one hand like she was trying to say something and Gus told her to put the phone back to Lorrie's ear and Gus kept telling Lorrie that he loved her over and over until Lorrie blurted out in a gruff, loud voice "I Love You Too" and that is all that Lorrie said. Gus told Lorrie over and over how he loved hearing her say those words and that he knew that she had struggled just to tell him that and how much he appreciated it and that he would always love her. His Daughter-in-law then took the phone and told Gus that Lorrie put her hand back on the bed and there was no more movement from her hands or lips and that she wasn't responding to her touch on Lorrie's hands. That happened at 6:30pm on January the 10th and then his Daughter-in-law left and went home. When Gus hung up he started to cry, because he could only imagine how much determination it took Lorrie to say those four words to him. The next day January the 11th 2017 Gus punched in 332-2637 just to see if anyone would answer Lorrie's phone, but no-one did. Gus's phone rang at 3:30pm and it was Lorrie's Sister-in-law and she told Gus that Lorrie had died at 1:30pm that day and Gus told her that it was their I Love You Anniversary and that he had talked to Lorrie the evening before and Lorrie had told Gus I Love You Too then and he guessed that those words were probably the last words that she had spoken. Her Sister-in-law agreed with him and then she hung up. Gus sent Lorrie's family a Sympathy Card, but didn't want to but in on all that must be going on there, so he didn't try to interfere while they were dealing with their grief and all the other arrangements they had to do. Gus found out that one of the girls he and Lorrie ate lunch with on Mondays had gone to see Lorrie and was with her when she died, so Lorrie wasn't by herself when she died and that girlfriend talked to Lorrie as she was dying telling her not to worry that she wasn't alone. Gus was very glad to hear this. Gus knew that he had two promises to keep for Lorrie. He had to see to it that her remains were buried by her grave stone with all the keepsakes along with the kind of grave side service she wanted, then there was the Love Story Book that Gus promised Lorrie that he would write. He hadn't ever broken a promise to Lorrie and he wasn't going to do it now. The middle of February Gus e-mailed Lorrie's Sister-in law to see how things were going with Lorrie's Mom and them, but he got no reply and that bothered Gus. He was wondering what was wrong there. Maybe there was something bad wrong with Lorrie's Mom, because she was 95 years old now and anything could happen to her. The last week in February Gus e-mailed Lorrie's Sister-in-law again telling her that he was going to make his regular trip to El Campo and Ganado on the first in March, but he still got no reply from her. Gus thought that this was really strange, so he called her cell phone and she didn't answer, so he left her a message. She never called Gus back, so all sorts of things started to go through Gus's mind. He started thinking that maybe Lorrie's family didn't want to have anything to do with him anymore since Lorrie died. If this was true, then how was he going to be able to bury Lorrie's ashes by her grave stone like he had promised Lorrie that he would. Now this really started to worry Gus. After he was at Ganado for a few days he tried to call Lorrie's Sister-in Law again and the same thing happened, he left her a message, but he didn't receive a call back from her. Gus started planning Lorrie's burial by first deciding on a receptacle suitable to preserving all of Lorrie's remains, plus all of the keepsakes that were to be placed in it and it had to be water proof and resistant to becoming destroyed by the elements in the ground over time. He settled on using 4 inch heavy wall PVC pipe with caps on each end. The caps would be sealed on the pipe with glue and then sealed again with silicone and this would leave the inside completely dry and the PVC wouldn't rust, corrode or rot, and it was very strong, so everything inside would stay safe for longer then he could imagine. Gus thought that this would be the perfect Burial Tube for Lorrie's ashes and all of the keepsakes that would be included in it. Gus started thinking of all the things that he might put in Lorrie's Burial Tube fi he was never able to get her ashes to put in it and he remembered that he had a lock of her hair and a recording of her voice from that long voice message she had sent him that night. If he didn't get her ashes those things could represent her physical being and then he would include all of the other keepsakes with them to be buried in her Burial Tube for eternity. He would just have to have patience to see how all of this was to play out. He didn't hear from Lorrie's family in March and the only information he got was from the girls that he and Lorrie always ate lunch with on Mondays and that wasn't much. During this time and ever since Lorrie died Gus had called her number in his mind 332-2637 and talked to her about what was happening every-day. She had written him a note onetime telling him that if she died before him that he could whisper 332-2637 and she would come to him just like she always had, so that was how he was still keeping in touch with Lorrie. Before Gus left to drive back to Van Horn at the first of April he called Lorrie's Sister-in-law again and left her a message that he was going back, but would be back to El Campo in May on his regular schedule and he received no answer to that call. Gus was really beginning to believe that Lorrie's family had abandoned him and it really saddened Gus, because they all had been close and he had no idea why they were treating him like this. He thought that maybe they hadn't really liked him all along, but was nice to him only because of Lorrie. All sorts of things were going through Gus's mind and he had to talk to Lorrie about it to keep from getting paranoid. April in Van Horn was good and Gus did all his cleanup and spraying in Van Horn and at the Ranch, then he e-mailed Lorrie's Sister-in-law and told her that he would be coming to El Campo the first week in May, but again he received no reply to his message. Gus drove back to Ganado the first week in May and got himself back in his and Lorrie's Trailer. He gathered all of the keepsakes that he was going to include in her Burial Tube along with the voice recording and the lock of her hair and he put them in a plastic bag to see how they fit in her Burial Tube and found that he had planned well, because there would be plenty of room left in it for her ashes if he ever got them. He was planning on going ahead with her Burial Service in May, because it had been 4 months since Lorrie had died and he thought that he had been patient enough with her family and he had heard nothing, so it was time to go ahead with things like they were, because he couldn't do anything about Lorrie's family. Gus had Lorrie's order of service all written out just like what Lorrie had instructed and he had a list of everything that was going to be included in her Burial Tube, so all that he needed to do now was to pick the date that he was going to have her Burial Service, leave her family a notice of it, so they could come if they wanted, notify some of Lorrie's friends and let them tell others and let his Sons know so they could be there. Then Gus's phone rang and it was Lorrie's Brother inviting Gus to dinner, so they could plan Lorrie's Burial Service. Gus was so relieved and overjoyed by this invitation. Gus went to Lorrie's Brother's house and Lorrie's Brother, his wife and Lorrie's Mom all greeted him warmly. They apologized for not responding to Gus's attempts to contact them, because they had been overwhelmed with all that was happening at one time. Lorrie's death plus they had been in the middle of remodeling their home so they could move Lorrie's Mom in with them, so she wouldn't have to live by herself. Gus understood and they had a nice visit then they ate a nice dinner there before getting started with talking about Lorrie's Burial Service. They liked all that Gus had planned according with Lorrie's instructions and the only point that needed to be decided was the date Lorrie's Burial Service was to take place. They all finally agreed on the 29th of July and it was agreed that they would have a before Burial Service gathering at their house then go to the grave yard for the Service then those that wanted to join them could come back to their house for food, drinks and a time to visit. It was decided that Gus would contact his family and friends that wanted to attend and Lorrie's family would contact those on that end. They now had the main part of the plans made, then Gus asked to see Lorrie's ashes and her Sister-in law got them out of a cabinet and Gus got to hold them for a long time before he left to go back to the Trailer. Gus was now assured that everything would go as Lorrie had wanted and really even better because of the things that Lorrie's family wanted to do in the way of opening their house for the gatherings that would make Lorrie's Burial Service and the gathering after it a success. Gus notified his Sons, his girl Cousin, that liked Lorrie so much and his friends that knew and liked Lorrie of the date for her Burial Service and he could do no more for now, so after doing all of his visiting Gus drove back to Van Horn with a much better feeling then he had, had for months. July went by quickly, because Gus had been busy taking care of everything in Van Horn and at the Ranch, so there wouldn't be anything that would keep him from driving back to El Campo and Ganado in July. Gus drove back to El Campo and Ganado the first week in July and set himself back up in the Trailer as usual. He had several visits and dinners with Lorrie's family discussing Lorrie's upcoming Burial Service and just having a nice time together like Lorrie would have wanted them to have. They gave Gus Lorrie's Ashes to place in her Burial Tube and he took them back to the Trailer with him. He whispered 332-2637 and told Lorrie that these few days would be the last time that her physical presence would be in the Trailer, but her memory would be there forever. He also kept up the tradition of eating lunch with the girls on Monday and visiting old friends that were still alive. The weather had been hot and dry for a long time in El Campo and Gus knew that the black ground there was going to be very hard. He had made plans to dig Lorrie's Grave for her Burial Tube himself, so he gathered up everything he would need to do the job. He went to the Grave Yard two days before the Burial Service and he watered the dirt where he was going to dig her Grave, then the next morning he went to the Grave Yard again to water it one last time, because that evening he and one of his Sons were to dig Lorrie's Grave. This they did and then all was ready for Lorrie's Burial Service the next day. That night Gus prepared everything that was to go in Lorrie's Burial Tube and he took two small samples of her Ashes and put them in separate containers to be spread at two different locations, then he gently lowered her Ashes into her Burial Tube and next he placed the lock of her hair, the recording of her voice with a transcript of that message, the Zippo lighter Lorrie had sent him from England engraved with "GUS AND LORRIE FOREVER", a copy of her Obituary, a pack of Lorrie's cigarettes, a pack of Gus's cigarettes, the turquoise Wedding Ring that Gus had slipped on her finger that first day they saw each other after 50 tears, bottle caps from Lorrie's Lone Star beer and bottle caps from Gus's beer, a note sent to Lorrie from her best friend Jill from England and a note from Gus's Daughter-in-law to Lorrie. All of these things were included by Lorrie's instructions. Gus left one cap on the Burial Tube open just in case someone else wanted to include a note or other memento at the last minute. Everything was ready now for the next day. The Burial Service time was set for 5:00pm, but there was a get together meeting planned at Lorrie's Brothers house at 4:00pm so family and friends could get together and visit then go to the Grave Yard for the Burial Service at the same time. This worked out real good and Gus had three of his Sons there, a Daughter-in-law, two Grandsons and his girl Cousin came, so Gus's family was well represented. There were a nice gathering of Gus's and Lorrie's friends that also were in attendance. Gus and his Sons left the gathering a little early to get everything ready at the grave yard. Gus and his Sons had everything ready when everyone else arrived at the grave side and about 40 friends and family assembled around Lorrie's Grave to be a part of making a last tribute to Lorrie. Gus took charge of the Burial Service and called for quiet. Gus told the attendees that this would be a different Service then they had attended in the past, but it would be all by Lorrie's instructions, then he talked about Lorrie. He told them that Lorrie wanted things in her Burial Tube from when she was alive an she named what she wanted in there with her Ashes. Lorrie told Gus that if some Archaeologist dug up her remains 1,000 or 2,000 years from now that she wanted them to know what kind of woman she was when she was alive. Gus then told them that Lorrie was a Christian and that she believed in God, Jesus, the Virgin Birth, Forgiveness of Sin, God's Grace to Mankind and Eternal Life in heaven, which are the bedrock and foundation of the Christian Faith of all the Denominations. Gus then called on Lorrie's Brother to pray and he led the attendees in the "Lords Prayer". Her Brothers church Pastor's Wife sang a Christian song, the Pastor had a few words to say then Gus told the attendees that Lorrie wanted her and his favorite song played and then his Son started the song playing and it was "In The Still Of The Night" by the Five Satins, which was the record that Lorrie had put in Gus's car in 1962. After that Gus announced that Lorrie had asked that everyone please make a last toast to her with her Lone Star Beer that she had bought herself for this very occasion of her Burial Service, so Gus and his Sons served small portions to all of the attendees and they held their glasses high as Gus told Lorrie that they all saluted her and they drank down and that concluded Lorrie's Burial Service, then Gus and his Sons stayed at the Grave Yard to finish the Burial while everyone went back to her Brother's house for food, drinks and visiting. Gus sealed Lorrie's Burial Tube and he lowered it into her Grave with his own hands and then he started filling the Grave with dirt and each of his Sons then helped fill the Grave, tamp it firm and replace the grass turf and then water it so it would grow again. Then they all drank a beer before going to Lorrie's Brother's house to join the other guests. This concluded the long struggle that Lorrie had gone through from the second week in May 2016 and she was now safely in her grave resting place next to where Gus was going to be buried someday, so Gus had completed that promise to Lorrie and now he had one more and that was to write the Love Story Book, but he had no idea how to do it. Before Gus left El Campo and Ganado to drive back to Van Horn on the first of August 2017 he took one of the small containers containing a small portion of Lorrie's Ashes and he spread them on the floor under the tin shed roof where they spent so much time together B-B-Qing, sipping beer, listening to Country Music and talking. Lorrie loved her time spent there, so now no matter what happens to that place a small part of Lorrie's physical self will always be a part of it. He had plans for the other small container of Lorrie's Ashes also. Gus had a feel of relief as he drove away from El Campo, because he was leaving this time after completing the Burial of Lorrie and that was a major promise that he had completed for her and it would bring closure for her family and her friends, but nor for Gus. Gus would never have closure, all that he would ever have was the feeling that he had completed all of his promises to Lorrie and that wouldn't be done until he wrote their book. Gus whispered 332-2637 off and on while he was driving back to Van Horn and talked to Lorrie as he had always done when she was alive and he discovered that it gave him a since of comfort, just like she told him it would. He spent August in Van Horn and he whispered 332-2637 to talk to her every-day and also to wish her Happy Anniversary on their special days on the 5th and 11th of the month. Gus kept his regular schedule and returned to El Campo the first week in September although there was no reason now to be returning on a specific time schedule anymore, but he thought that he would finish the year of 2017 out like he had always done and maybe he would change things in 2018. He drove into El Campo and arrived at 2:30pm and pulled into the Grave Yard to visit Lorrie's Grave. The grass had grown back nice and green and it looked like she had been buried there for years and not just a month. They had done a very good job on her Grave. Then Gus drove on to Ganado and the Trailer where his Son was waiting for him. Gus unloaded and then he went to the grocery store for his food supplies, so he would be all set up, before he started visiting and sipping beer with his Son, Daughter-in-law and his two Grandchildren there. This was a nice greeting for Gus, and he enjoyed it They sat out under the tin roof like they always had done when Lorrie was there with them when he first drove up and as usual his Son was B-B-Qing and had a cold beer ready for him with the Country music going and the Grandkids playing around asking Gus questions. They talked about the Burial Service and his Daughter-in-law told Gus that several people that had been in attendance related to her that it was an unusual one, but that Gus had done an excellent job of taking charge and gave Lorrie a sweet Christian Service that was to the point and it also portrayed the person that Lorrie was to those in attendance. Gus then told them that he has spread a small portion of Lorrie's Ashes on the floor right where they were now sitting, because she had always loved being right there and his Son and Daughter-in-law were pleased that Gus had done that, so they would have a small piece of Lorrie right there with them. Gus had lunch with the girls every Monday while he was there and he was invited to Lorrie's

Brothers house for dinner twice, so he got to see them and Lorrie's Mom, who was going to be 96 years old in November. Gus left to drive back to Van Horn the first week in October as he always had, and he drove by Lorrie's Grave to look at it and whisper 332-2637 to tell her that he was on his way back to Van Horn and he wouldn't have the chance to see her Grave for at least five months. He whispered 332-2637 several times as he was driving back to Van Horn to tell Lorrie about his trip and also when he arrived safely, because she always wanted him to call her so she would know he was home safe and sound. Gus worked at getting everything ready for the cold winter months that were soon to hit Van Horn and all the time he wondered how he was going to be able to write their Book. Thanksgiving and Christmas came and went and Gus whispered 332-2637 and talked to Lorrie at length on those Holidays. It was now New Years Eve and Gus stayed up to have one drink at 12:01am so he could whisper 332-2637 and talk to Lorrie and give her a New Year 2018 salute.

Gus—2018 New Years Day was the first New Year since 2011 that Gus had started without Lorrie. Everything seemed so strange now without Lorrie. He still had 332-2637 as his contact with her though and he used it all the time. Gus made a trip to his Ranch and he took the other small container of Lorrie's Ashes with him and he spread them on the floor under the Cook Shed, where she loved to sit, sip on a cold beer, watch the camp fire and look at the mountains. Here part of her physical body would always be now forever. The winter in Van Horn was cold, so Gus limited himself to staying most of the time in his Oil & Gas Office. He did some research and caught up on weather and news on his computer, but the time hung heavy on him and he found himself whispering 332-2637 and talking to Lorrie more and more. In February 2018 after whispering 332-2637 and talking to Lorrie, Gus decided that he needed to start writing on the Book. Gus pondered the problem of how to even start such a project, because it seemed so enormous to him. He finally decided to make a simple outline, for the Book that represented the different topics comprising each of their lives in chronological order. He would, using Lorrie's suggestion, be able to write about each life in a year by year comparison showing what each was doing in a side-by-side relationship to each other and this is how he started. He decided that his main goal was just to write the story and not to pay any real attention to spelling, grammar, paragraphs, etc., but to just tell the story of Gus and Lorrie. Gus wrote off and on, sometimes going several days without writing even a word for one reason or another, but he was determined to keep his last promise to Lorrie. When spring came Gus made his trip down to El Campo and Ganado, but he decided that he no longer needed to keep his old schedule of going every-other month till October and that he was going to start cutting his visits short. He still wanted to visit his old friends and his family, eat with the girls on Monday, keep his loving relationship with Lorrie's family and visit Lorrie's Grave to replace the flowers on it and to be there and whisper 332-2637 and talk to her at her Grave side. This is what Gus did all through 2018 until October when he stayed in Van Horn for the winter. Gus wrote on the Book all of this time and sometime telling this story of Gus and Lorrie was hard for him because he was actually having to relive her life and his life in tandem which brought about moments of extreme distress, that would be hard to overcome. He would regain his composure and start his momentum writing again. Gus discovered all sorts of emotions while writing the Book, that probably were all the emotions, that a human body contained. The year 2018 ended and May 2019 was where Gus came to the end of the Gus and Lorrie story, because it wasn't Gus and Lorrie any longer. Now it was just Gus with the sweet memory of Lorrie and his only contact with her was to whisper 332-2637 to talk to her. He had finished the Gus and Lorrie Book and now he would have to find out how to get it edited and submitted for printing. Gus had no idea how to do this either, but maybe he could whisper 332-2637 and talk to Lorrie and she would give him some idea of how to proceed. Yes, 332-2637 was the answer to finishing his last promise to Lorrie.

EPILOGUE

Gus still lives in Van Horn, Texas. He goes to his Oil & Gas office, to see if any business might walk through his door. He still frequents his Ranch in the Mountains and look's for Indian artifacts and enjoys the Desert and its flora and fauna. Gus still makes the almost 600 mile trips to El Campo and Ganado, but they are starting to be hard on him at his age, so he has no schedule anymore and his stays are shorter than in the past. While he is there, he visits with his old friends that are left and his Son's and Grandsons and Daughter-in laws. He still eats Monday lunches with the Girls and has dinners with Lorrie's family. Gus still keeps in close touch with Lorrie's best friend in England, via e-mail. Gus also spends time visiting Lorrie's Grave and puts fresh flowers there, and he faithfully keeps up the tradition of celebrating three very important days for him and Lorrie that were their Back Together Anniversary on September 5th, their I Love You Anniversary November 11th, and Lorrie's Birthday October 26th. Gus also talks to Lorrie everyday by whispering 332-2637.